Dr Gerhart von Westerman, who died early in
1963, was a prominent figure in German
musical life, and particularly connected with
Berlin and the Berlin Festival. His *Opera Guide*,
edited and brought up to date by Harold
Rosenthal, well-known as a critic and writer
on opera and as editor of *Opera* magazine,
begins with the study of the birth of opera in
the early seventeenth century, and traces the
history of the art through the centuries, right
up to the present day and contemporary
composers, such as Stravinsky, Britten and
Tippett.

The *Guide* gives a detailed historical and
musical analysis of the evolution of operatic
form, of both the major and minor schools and
composers, the librettists and singers, and,
besides the synopses of all the most interesting
and important works, includes the early and
lesser-known operas of the great composers. As
in the companion volume, the *Concert Guide*,
the text is supplemented by musical examples
of the main themes of many of the works
described.

Throughout the book reference is constantly
made to recent revivals, arrangements and
productions. The result is a stimulating,
reliable, and above all, comprehensive
reference book for all opera lovers, as well
as an instructive critical history for anyone
embarking on a study of this absorbing subject.

*Also by Gerhart von Westerman
and available in Sphere Books*

CONCERT GUIDE

COVER:

Acknowledgement is made to: The Courtauld
Institute Galleries, London for the use of
the picture of *La Loge* by Renoir.

Opera Guide

GERHART VON WESTERMAN

Edited, with an Introduction, by
HAROLD ROSENTHAL

Translated by
ANNE ROSS

SPHERE BOOKS LIMITED
30/32 Gray's Inn Road, London, W.C.1

First published in Great Britain in 1964
by Thames and Hudson

© Thames and Hudson 1964

Adapted from *Knaurs Operaführer*
© Droemersche Verlagsanstalt, 1952

First Sphere Books edition, 1968
Reprinted May, 1970

TRADE
MARK

Printed in Great Britain by
Hazell Watson & Viney Ltd.
Aylesbury, Bucks

CONTENTS

ACKNOWLEDGEMENTS

The Editor expresses his thanks to Mrs Judy Underhill and Mrs Hilary Ostine for typing, to Mr and Mrs Ostine for their help in checking music examples; to Mr Richard Temple-Savage, Music Librarian of the Royal Opera House, Covent Garden, and to Mr Tom Hammond of the music staff at Sadler's Wells, for making available certain scores; and especially to Anne Ross, who not only undertook the mammoth task of translating the German text, but who also gave considerable help in the actual editing of the book.

INTRODUCTION

Dr Johnson's dictum that opera is 'An exotic and irrational entertainment' dies hard, and only an English writer could have penned such a phrase, for in Italy or Germany, such an attitude to this art form is unthinkable.

Even in England, before the time of Dr Johnson, opera was highly regarded as an art form; it was only as opera in the vernacular gave way to opera in Italian that it came to be regarded as 'exotic and irrational'. In London the beginnings of operatic entertainment began in Elizabethan days with the incidental music to revels and plays, and the court masques which generally took place in connection with royal festivities. During the first half of the seventeenth century, large sums of money were spent by the four Inns of Court producing extravagant masques. Ben Jonson and Inigo Jones were two of the most famous names connected with these entertainments; but there was a third person, one William Davenant.

Davenant was the son of the owners of the Crown Inn in Oxford; his mother was a very beautiful woman, and according to rumour, Shakespeare who was a frequent visitor to the inn, was more than a Godfather to the boy! Davenant became a playwright, and in 1638 was appointed poet laureate. In 1639 he was granted a royal patent by Charles I which permitted him to build a playhouse 'behind the Three Kings Ordinary in Fleet Street, wherein plays, musical entertainments, scenes and other like presentments may be presented'. It also permitted plays to be acted 'in such a house so to be by him or them erected and to exercise music and musical presentments, scenes, dancing and the like'. The importance of Davenant's patent cannot be over-estimated for this was the document that came into the possession of the famous actor-manager Charles Rich nearly a century later, and allowed him to build the first Covent Garden Theatre.

Davenant planned to give performances of dramatic masques with the scenery, costumes and mechanical appendages imported from Italy. Indeed, if he had his way, England would have been the first country other than Italy to have seen a public performance of an opera. But in October 1639, his plans received a sudden check. The Puritans began to attack the King's entertainments and the business interests in the city and the artistic interests of the nobility were both affected.

During the civil war Davenant escaped to France where he saw a great deal of Italian opera. He then tried to make his way from France to America, but was captured by Cromwell's men and only saved from execution by the personal intervention of Milton. Almost immediately afterwards, he was appointed Master of the Revels under Cromwell's government and, in 1656, began activities at Rutland House where *The Siege of Rhodes* was performed with music by John Locke. This is generally regarded as the first operatic performance in London, for the characters were all played by singers, actors having been banned by the Puritans. More masques and musical entertainments followed, but it was not until 1685 that the next real opera was performed—John Blow's *Venus and Adonis*. Although described as a masque, it is in effect a Lully-type opera in miniature. The original Venus, Moll Davies, besides being an actress and dancer, was one of King Charles's mistresses, and her daughter by the King, Lady Mary Tudor, played the original Cupid.

Venus and Adonis undoubtedly served as a model for Purcell's *Dido and Aeneas* which was first produced in 1689 or 1690. Other than a few performances in 1700 and 1704 as an interlude to *Measure for Measure* at Lincoln's Inn Theatre, it was not heard again until 1895 when it was performed in London at the Lyceum Theatre by students of the Royal College of Music under Stanford's direction as part of the Purcell bicentenary celebrations. As is known, Purcell's death at the age of thirty-six in 1695 spelt an end to British opera until the advent of Benjamin Britten in our own day. Society had begun to encourage foreign artists with the result that by the turn of the century fashionable London was ready for Italian opera.

Handel arrived in London in 1710 ,but he had been preceded two years earlier by the celebrated castrato Nicolini, who made his début in an adaptation of Scarlatti's *Pyrrhus and Demetrius*. His success was enormous and castrati became the rage; not only Handel, but every composer of the time strove to provide these freak singers with impossibly difficult music. The story of Handel's struggles in London, of the rival opera companies, of the prima donnas Cuzzoni and Faustina who allowed themselves to be egged on by their partisans and indulge in a free fight on the stage, have unfortunately no place in this introduction. But already those elements were present which were soon to turn the art of opera into Dr Johnson's exotic and irrational entertainment. The Countess of Burlington, Lady Delaware, and most of the men led by Walpole were for Faustina, while Lady Pembroke and Lady Walpole headed the rival camp. Not only the singers, but also the composers, had their influential supporters. The King and the Tories favoured Handel, while the Prince of Wales and the Whigs supported Buononcini.

This kind of behaviour, plus the absurdity and conventions of Italian opera, led to two reactions against it. The first came from leaders of thought such as Steele and Addison in *The Spectator*, and the second from the general public who flocked to *The Beggar's Opera*. Addison's famous criticism of Handel's *Rinaldo* followed its first performance in 1711, but he had already written the following passage the previous year:

'One would have thought it very difficult to have carried on dialogues after this manner [i.e. one character singing in English and the other in Italian] without an interpreter between the persons that conversed together, but this was the state of affairs on the English opera stage for about three years. At length the audience got tired of understanding half the opera and therefore to ease themselves entirely of the fatigue of thinking, have so ordered it that the whole opera is performed in an unknown tongue. We no longer understand the language of our own stage . . . I cannot forbear thinking how naturally a historian who writes two or three hundred years hence, and does not know the taste of his wise forefathers, will make the following reflection: In the beginning of the eighteenth century the Italian tongue was so well understood in England that operas were acted on the public stage in that language.'

Things have changed little in the last 250 years though, at least, we do not now have polyglot performances. It was not so very long ago, however, that there was a performance of *Aida* at Covent Garden in which the Radames sang in German, the Aida in Italian, and the rest of the cast in English; and I remember a Covent Garden *Tosca* in the 1950's in which the Tosca sang in Italian and German, and the Scarpia in English when he addressed Cavaradossi and Italian when he conversed with Tosca! But performances sung in Italian or German are now the accepted practice. At Glyndebourne, Richard Strauss's 'conversation piece', *Capriccio*, the opera that discusses in a most intelligent way whether words or music are the most important element in opera, is sung in German to an audience that plainly for the most part is unable to understand it. This is the main difference between the attitudes of the English and American public on the one hand, and the European on the other. In Germany, for instance, where an operatic tradition has developed over the centuries and where opera is regarded as part of its natural cultural life, foreign works are almost invariably sung in the vernacular and even in specially edited versions.

In the immediate post-war period in England and to a lesser extent in the United States, there was much talk of the new operatic public—a public that had grown up in the war largely made up of young people who had come to know opera in Italy and later in Germany during the allied occupation. What has happened to that public, where is it now? Those who live in London or New York, Chicago or San Francisco, certainly have regular opera seasons, but those who live in the provinces can count themselves lucky if they hear live opera for more than a week each year; though the United States, with its many fine opera workshops, generally attached to universities, is certainly better off than England in this respect.

Yet, on the whole, the pattern of large-scale opera in the United States is very similar to that of Great Britain. This is hardly surprising, as neither country has an indigenous operatic tradition and, unlike most European countries, neither has been able to rely on their aristocracy or governments to subsidise opera (though since the war, Great Britain has accepted the idea of state subsidy). So, opera in America has relied, until relatively recently, on Europe for its artists and repertory.

In New York, during the first half of the eighteenth century, ballad operas were performed, and there were some early native American operas. But it was not until the famous Manuel Garcia came to New York in November 1825 with his company that included his daughter Malibran, that Italian opera really established itself in New York. In this Garcia season, Lorenzo da Ponte, Mozart's librettist was a leading figure. He had gone to America in 1805 and had set his heart on introducing Italian opera to New York, but it was not firmly established for another twenty years. And it has been Italian opera, more than any other genre, that has been the prime favourite in San Francisco and Chicago. True, the latter city had an expensive flirtation with French opera in the 1920's when Mary Garden was a leading operatic figure, not only as a singer, but also for a short time as director of the Chicago Company.

New York with its cosmopolitan public, has also favoured German opera, and the Metropolitan has probably heard, in its eighty-odd years of existence, as fine performances of Wagner and, to a lesser extent, of Strauss, as many central European capitals. During the last twenty years, a second opera company has established itself in New York based on the City Center. There, especially since 1957 under the direction of Julius Rudel, a progressive policy has been pursued. Many contemporary works have been produced and native American composers have not been neglected.

Chicago and San Francisco both give annual autumn seasons with star-studded international casts. Philadelphia gives a series, mostly of popular Italian opera, during the winter season; and many other cities have short seasons. New Orleans, where French opera flourished last century and where the American premières of many operas took place, had no opera between 1919 and 1943, and today only mananges a short annual season. While Boston, once the home of the Boston Opera Company which was housed in a splendid opera house, now only manages perhaps three productions a year given by the enterprising Boston Opera Group of which Sarah Caldwell is the artistic director.

It is the universities with their opera workshops that are the scenes of the vital and enterprising operatic life in the United States. Young singers cut their teeth in these centres and many

American composers have written works especially for them. It is possible that a new generation of opera-goers is growing up in America, who regard this exciting art form as something living and vital.

In England, the acceptance of a national subsidy for opera by the central government has not yet produced sufficient money to establish one provincial opera house; and local government authorities, with the honourable exception of the London County Council, have been very loathe to finance the arts from the rates. All this, coupled with the lack of a native operatic tradition, has resulted in opera in Great Britain being centred on London.

The British operatic audience is, therefore, limited geographically and also in scope. The natural curiosity of the German opera-goer is hardly reflected. While sadly we have come to expect poor audience response for the operas of Janáček, Tippett and other younger composers, it is even more depressing that *Elektra, Khovanshchina, The Rake's Progress, Eugene Onegin* and even *Andrea Chénier* fail to draw full houses. Why should this be? There are excellent recordings of these works in the gramophone catalogues and we know that many opera-goers are keen record collectors. Nor is there any lack of broadcast performances of unfamiliar operatic music, and certainly the specialist musical press and, to a lesser extent, the national press, do a great deal to tell the potential opera-goer about the unfamiliar. Is the answer to this problem that we, the opera-specialists, the enthusiasts, the critics, have over-estimated the existing demand for opera? Yet, let one of our opera houses announce an unenterprising repertory and letters pour in to the administration, the press and even to members of parliament, protesting about the lack of enterprise. Maybe it is a lack of confidence in the institutions—yet announce *Bohème, Aida, Tosca, Butterfly* and the house is filled. So we must come to the sad conclusion that this lack of interest in contemporary opera and even in unfamiliar opera of the past—unless it is a *bel canto* work with a Sutherland or Callas—is a failure of communication between the composer and the public.

This is, of course, no new problem. The young Verdi had to fight hard for recognition, at least among the critics and singers; Wagner with his 'music of the future' caused near riots in the last century. We now accept Verdi and Wagner. Indeed, we also accept Berg's *Wozzeck* far more easily today than in 1952, the date of its first British stage performance. But this is only because it has become familiar through rehearing. It is true that everything unfamiliar is something of an acquired taste, and understandable that the trained musician or informed amateur is more likely to persevere with a new work than the novice. But if the failure results from having tried to appreciate *Elektra, Jenůfa, Peter Grimes, Katarina Ismailova* or *Elegy for Young Lovers,* and found it impossible, then this is a much more serious matter; for it indicates a complete lack of contact between the creative artist and the public.

In that opera is an amalgam of all the art forms, it should be the easiest of these forms to put across to the public. For opera to survive as an art form, however, the opera house must not become a museum but remain a living theatre and, therefore, it is essential that new ideas in music, in drama, in scenic design should be admitted, otherwise it will become a stuffy, fossilised, musty repository of out-of-date ideas. Of course only the best will survive. It is rather a sobering thought that from the 42,000 operas so far supposedly composed, fewer than 100 furnish the repertory of the present-day opera houses. In the post-war period alone more than 600 new operas have been staged in the opera houses of the world.

Rolf Liebermann, the composer and enlightened Intendant of the Hamburg State Opera where *Lulu* and *Wozzeck* and the works of Henze and Britten are regularly sold out, has success-fully built up an opera company based on ensemble, not stars. In an article in 'Opera' in January 1961, he wrote:

'All that really matters [in an opera production] is artistic truth. To this end the performers can no longer be allowed to interpret a role by superficial means, but must be taught to identify themselves with the character they represent. The public will be fully convinced of the validity of unfamiliar musical language only when the singers learn to feel the role deeply and completely, and can integrate themselves into the music and the action.

'One of the serious problems of opera is that to a great extent it has lost the allegiance of the younger generation.

The blame for this is put on football, jazz, television and other diversions, but I believe that the fault lies elsewhere. In my opinion the younger generation, with its unsentimental integrity, reacts against hollowness and the spiritual vacuum of stereotyped conventional opera productions . . . They are not antagonistic to music as such whether new or old . . . the stage spoils their musical enjoyment. Carrying this situation to a logical conclusion, one cannot help admitting that the principles governing drama productions must eventually also obtain on the opera stage. It has already been proved that this is possible. The most important prerequisite for achieving this goal is naturally to turn away from the star tradition, which owes its glamour to world-famous singers who sing the same roles in all the principal European opera houses. The most important task of a theatre is, therefore, the creation of an ensemble.'

This is, of course, an ideal, and in all but a handful of theatres, an impossibility. Indeed even Hamburg, with its wonderful ensemble and artistic integrity, produces its own stars within its ensemble—signers like Helga Pilarczyk, Toni Blankenheim, Melitta Muszely—and it naturally follows that other European houses want their services for certain operas. Yet this is not a bad thing, for now the Hamburg audience has reached such a stage in its development that even the visit to Hamburg of great international guest stars for series of performances of Strauss and Verdi operas, at greatly increased prices, do not produce capacity houses. Moreover at such performances many strange faces are seen in the auditorium. This is the reverse of the coin, for it is at the unfamiliar operas in London that one sees the strange faces!

Perhaps the picture is not quite so pessimistic as I have painted it. Indeed more and more people now do their 'homework' before going to an opera—something especially necessary in England where operas are generally sung in a foreign language. They listen to records or broadcast performances, following them with scores or libretti; they read the specialist articles in the musical press; they read books about composers and about opera; and so one hopes that this English version of Gerhart von Westerman's book will help them to a better understanding, not only of individual operas in the repertory but of the place of those works in the overall development of opera and of opera as an art form. Westerman traces the growth of opera from its birth at the end of the sixteenth century down to our own times. Because of the recent interest in the works of the so-called *bel canto* school and in the whole of Verdi's output, I have added synopses of a number of operas by Handel, Rossini and Bellini, and have expanded some of the Verdi section. Further, I have added details of certain non-German works and composers often met with in English-speaking countries.

I can do no better than to conclude with the closing paragraph from Mr von Westerman's own introduction to the German edition:

'But to those who believe that they must reject opera as an art form, I would like to say something more: Beethoven fought for years to mould his *Fidelio*, and the secret love of others and a continual quest for great creative work have equally served the art of opera. And is not this very passion for and against this art form the best proof that opera lives and will live? Its most recent development seems to be a marvellous indication that no other art form can give, as opera does, such a synthesis of the discordance of our own times.'

HAROLD ROSENTHAL
London, 1964

THE ORIGINS AND FIRST
TEN YEARS OF OPERA

Around the year 1600 a group of young artists and scholars imbued with the spirit of the Renaissance gathered together in Florence to revive classical drama. They could not have known that their first timid attempts would lay the decisive foundations of a new art-form which would very soon start its triumphal progress through the Western cultural world under the name 'opera'.

The performance of Peri's *dramma per musica*, *Dafne* (Florence, 1597) marks the actual birth of opera, although suggestions of musical drama, which could be regarded as the first stirrings of opera, can be detected even earlier, for instance in the song-plays of the Middle Ages. The oldest example of these, the charming *Le Jeu de Robin et de Marion* by Adam de la Halle (1285, or 1275), of which several copies have survived, contained short singing dances to enliven idyllic, innocent dialogue. [The incorrect date 1594, given for this work in many reference books, is founded in an ambiguous passage in the preface to Peri's score of *Euridice* (1600). See the first entry in Loewenberg's *Annals of Opera*.] Interludes or *intermezzi*, introducing a light, or occasionally more serious, allegorical subject between the acts of a tragedy, may be regarded as preparatory studies for opera. They were performed at the courts on the occasions of masquerades or solemn processions, and they were rich both in the magnificence of their presentation and in their music. The insertion of dances, especially the *moresca*, a Moorish ballet, was much in favour. The music was limited to these isolated dances, or to instrumental and choral pieces which accompanied the stage action, while the dialogue, if any, was spoken. The music of the dying Middle Ages was exclusively polyphonic, and in fact solos are rarely found in the elaborate music of the *intermezzi*, though they occur in popular musical plays and songs.

The fine, complex mesh of polyphony is just as characteristic of the late Middle Ages as the bold intermingling of buttresses and arches in lofty Gothic cathedrals. Masses and motets, the forms of church vocal music, dominated serious art, but alongside them developed the madrigal, in which secular texts were set to music with all the devices of counterpoint. Here the artistic imagination could soar, unimpeded by the limitations imposed by the *cantus firmus*, or Gregorian choral chant, which was the essential basis of all religious composition. The madrigals exuded a joyful vigour which led to a stronger, more personal musical expression than had ever been known before. This new vitality was expressed in a characteristic naturalism which included the imitation of bird-calls, hunting horns, shouts, quarrels and battle noises.

In the madrigal serious music approached, and even blended with, the domain of popular song, because the composers of madrigals would adopt a crude popular melody as their *cantus firmus*, and turn it into a dignified composition through the addition of ingenious polyphonic counterpoint.

Madrigal choirs always performed the sung parts in the interludes or short dramatic *entr'actes* mentioned already, and when on the stage the heroine expressed her agony in mime, the burden of her despair was sung by an off-stage chorus and not by a soloist, as would seem natural to us nowadays. The solo would have been reminiscent of the artless popular song and was inconceivable in a setting which was so strongly governed by formal artistic discipline. Only very rarely was an attempt made to alter the form, by having one voice-part sung and the others played on instruments. This shows that the urge for development already existed at a time when serious composition was rigidly bound by the rules of counterpoint, but only towards the end of the sixteenth century did a change in fact come about with the introduction of the solo, and especially of recitative or sung narrative. It was a bold stylistic revolution which prepared the way for the first formulation and development of opera.

The group of artists and scholars who met at the house of the art-loving Count Giovanni Bardi in Florence at the end of the sixteenth century with the object of reviving Greek drama included Vincenzo Galilei (1529–91), father of Galileo, the composers Giulio Caccini (*c.* 1545-1618) and Jacopo Peri (1561-1633) and the poet Ottavio Rinuccini (1562-1621). The first attempts were made by Vincenzo Galilei, who set to music the Ugolino episode from Dante's *Inferno*, and later the *Lamentations of Jeremiah* for solo voice with a concert of viols as accompaniment. Caccini arranged a series of songs and sonnets for solo voice and theorbo accompaniment and later published them under the title *Nuove Musiche*. Eventually, in 1597, the memorable performance of *Dafne* took place in the house of Jacopo Corsi, a Florentine aristocrat who had succeeded Bardi as the Maecenas of this active group of artists, in the presence of 'Don Giovanni Medici and other leading citizens' of Florence. Ottavio Rinuccini was the author of the text, a pastoral poem in the fashionable style of the time, while Peri and Caccini composed the music. The piece was performed several times with great success but unfortunately no trace of the music survives.

The new style, the *stile rappresentativo*, was used here for the first time throughout a complete drama, the crucial innovation being the sung narrative, or recitative, the basis of dramatic musical dialogue. This new style had almost nothing in common with the sung narrative of the mystery plays, as has often been suggested. Recitative bears no relation to the old liturgical chant and the monotone settings of the psalms, which do not follow the dramatic content of the words recited.

On 6 October 1600, *Euridice*, the second opera by the trio Peri–Caccini–Rinuccini, was performed in Florence in the presence of a splendid gathering, to celebrate the marriage of Maria de Medici to King Henry IV of France. Its success was unprecedented and it put all the other wedding festivities in the shade. The music was composed by Peri with the exception of a few passages by Caccini; later, however, the latter reset the whole opera and the new version was performed at the Pitti Palace on 5 December 1602. Both compositions have survived and are very similar in project and execution, but the place of honour must go to Peri; he is certainly bolder and more ingenious both in the details and in the richness of his harmonies.

In his preface to *Euridice* Peri speaks of the properties peculiar to the new style. He tells how he had studied people's way of speaking, so as to be able to reproduce it exactly and how, at the beginning of each speech, the speaker would leave the harmony, to return to it at the end, after many variations which followed according to the meaning of the words. The tempo would quicken in moments of passion and slow down for sorrow. This treatment originated in a belief that the ancient Greeks and Romans had sung throughout their dramas and had used solos, not choruses. Opera is therefore a true child of the Renaissance. The expressive recitative of *Euridice* had instrumental chord accompaniments (Peri prescribed a cembalo, a lyre and two lutes). The printed score does not reveal how these instruments were used. Presumably the accompaniment by the individual instruments was made to fit the various situations, and the harmonies must therefore have been very powerful. At one point a flute trio was also introduced, and all these instruments were concealed from the audience behind the scenery. The declamation of the recitatives was distinctive and expressive; the harmonization of the accompaniment was always bold and occasionally even contained discords. The impressive structural development of this music cannot relieve its monotony for the modern listener, although this is occasionally pleasantly interrupted, as for instance by the chorus 'Al canto al ballo all'ombr'al prato adorno' ('Let us sing and dance'), and by the flute episodes.

EURIDICE is a treatment of the well-known legend. After a short prologue in which Tragedy appears as an allegorical character, a chorus of nymphs and shepherds appears to announce the marriage of Orpheus and Eurydice and to sing their praises, which clearly refer to the illustrious couple in whose honour the first performance was given: 'Non vede un simil par d'amanti il sole' ('the sun never saw such a loving pair'). In the second scene Eurydice enters and gaily summons her companions to dance and play. After a scene in which Orpheus ecstatically apostrophizes nature, and a brief appearance of his friends with a pretty little flute interlude, drama breaks in. Daphne appears as a messenger to announce Eurydice's sudden death. Orpheus falls into desperate lamentation (the *lamento* was to become an extremely common type of solo in the development of Italian opera). The chorus enters to console him, and one of his friends then tells of his subsequent misfortunes. Venus allows the despairing Orpheus to descend into the Underworld and ask Pluto himself for the return of his beloved. Orpheus addresses Pluto with long supplications and a renewed lament. The final scene shows the lovers happily reunited. [Rinuccini does not mention the command, which makes this reunion so poignant, that Orpheus should not look back as he returns from the Underworld.] The work ends with joyful dances and choruses.

In the first performance Orpheus was sung by Peri himself, and Eurydice by Vittoria Archilei, who was famous far beyond Florence, both as a singer and a lutanist.

Contemporary engravings representing court festivals illustrate clearly the kind of stage setting used for operas at that time. The stage was raised, and framed by a sumptuous, pillared proscenium arch, while wide steps forming a kind of terrace led down from the proscenium to the auditorium. The scenery for these first operatic performances must have been much more primitive than people were accustomed to in the single interludes, which had often involved incredibly complicated technical apparatus. The drama was enacted at the front of the stage, since a scenic effect of depth was still unknown in the theatre, and the several scene changes in *Euridice* took place without any pause; the descent into the Underworld, for instance, is not even indicated by a brief *ritornello*. The sudden change of scene can therefore only have been explained by letting down a painted perspective design or a suitable cloth hanging. The classical landscapes on these perspective designs, as well as the costumes of the actors, represented, of course, a baroque artist's conception of the ancient world: the idyllic landscape was furnished with baroque architecture, and togas and tunics became sumptuous baroque draperies.

The baroque stage, this distinctive, wayward mingling of ancient and contemporary feeling, holds great charm for the modern observer, and has a much more immediate appeal than the poetry or music of the period. Positive sensibility and joyful optimism appear in this mixture of the idyllic and the sumptuous, of arcadian landscape and baroque architecture, shepherds' garments and helmets with waving plumes.

The success of *Euridice* established opera as an art-form. In the forty years which followed the first performance of Peri's *Dafne*, more than forty operas were produced in various large Italian towns, especially Florence. Besides pastoral operas derived from the poetry of Rinuccini, another individual form developed: the allegorical opera. This was especially popular in Rome, the first example being Emilio de Cavalieri's (*c.* 1550–1602) *La rappresentazione di Anima e di Corpo*, first performed in Rome in 1600, to words by Agostino Manni. The characters personify ideas, such as Body, Soul, Intelligence, or Pleasure, and the story is given a moralizing slant, like those of the medieval mystery plays.

The so-called magic operas formed a third group which may be regarded as a further development of the little sixteenth-century interludes with their emphasis on visual effect. These were now transformed into full-scale operas by the building up of the plot and the insertion of recitative dialogue. At the Italian courts great importance had always been attached to stage machinery, and even artists of the stature of Leonardo da Vinci were not too proud to build complicated machines for the stage. Special scenic effects such as sudden transformations, flying machines, and gods hovering in the clouds, were all devised to increase interest in opera. It was inevitable that this kind of opera entirely concerned with externals should become musically trivial. The importance of décor also permeated the pastoral and allegorical opera, and in fact was to become and remain an integral part of opera through all the phases of its development.

This first phase of opera is generally known as Florentine opera, or choral opera, since the chorus was much more important then than in later periods. The most significant work of this time is undoubtedly Monteverdi's *Orfeo*. Claudio Monteverdi was born in Cremona in 1567, and died in Venice in 1643. From 1604 to 1613 he lived in Mantua, as court musician to the Dukes of Gonzaga. Monteverdi was the first composer of genius to write music for opera. The libretto for his *Orfeo* was written by Alessandro Striggio (*c.* 1535–95). Unlike Rinuccini, Striggio uses the entire classical legend; Orpheus disobeys Pluto's command that he should not look back at Eurydice on his way out of Hades, and so loses his beloved once more. (In recent years the Orpheus legend has been used several times in modern stage works and Malipiero, Křenek and Casella have set it to music.)

LA FAVOLA D'ORFEO (The Fable of Orpheus). Opera in a prologue and five acts by Claudio Monteverdi. Text by Alessandro Striggio. First performance: Mantua, 1607. (Arrangements and editions include those by Vincent d'Indy (1904), Giacomo Orefece (1909), Carl Orff (1925), Malipiero (1923 and 1930), Ottorino Respighi (1935) and Vito Frazzi (1939).)

Characters: Orfeo (Orpheus)—tenor or baritone; Euridice (Eurydice)—soprano; the Messenger—contralto; Charon—bass; Apollo—bass;

Pluto—bass; La Musica—soprano; Proserpina—soprano. Shepherds, nymphs, shades.

Prologue. La Musica appears before the audience and praises the merits of the listeners as well as those of herself, and then tells the tale of the fable (la favola).

Act I. An Arcadian landscape. Nymphs and shepherds praise the spring and rejoice at the marriage of Orpheus and Eurydice. The happy couple declare their love for one another in lively recitatives, and the songs and dances are repeated in honour of the newly-wedded pair.

Act II. An airy wood. Orpheus's song is heard from afar, and returning to the place of his youth he begins to express his feelings and to address nature. The delicate closing refrain of his aria already foreshadows the violent dramatic events that are to follow. The Messenger now enters, and in a long and dramatic narrative tells Orpheus of Eurydice's sudden death. Orpheus abandons himself to his sorrow; life has no more meaning for him. He breaks his tragic silence and declares his intention of following his wife into the Underworld.

Act III. Orpheus has descended into the Underworld and is confronted by Hope who seeks to comfort him. Charon the infernal ferryman arrives, but is deaf to Orpheus's pleadings. Orpheus wins him over with his sweet song, and when Charon is asleep he is able to cross the river Styx into Hell.

Act IV. Proserpina and Pluto discuss Orpheus's plight. Proserpina prevails upon her husband to agree to the release of Eurydice, on the condition that Orpheus will not turn and look at her on their journey back to earth. Orpheus, however, uncertain that Eurydice is with him, looks back and she is snatched away to the Underworld. The spirits lament her short-lived freedom.

Act V. The Plains of Thrace. Orpheus, now back on earth, laments his loss, and invokes nature as the only consolation in his troubles. Apollo, Orpheus's father, descends from heaven, admonishes his son, and consoles him by telling him that he will find both immortality and Eurydice in the heavenly spheres. As the chorus sings a final hymn of exultation and joy, father and son ascend to heaven.

H. D. R.

Monteverdi's music has a singular charm, and its strong, direct effect is principally created by the choruses and the short instrumental passages. The choruses are most artistically devised with fugal sequences to enliven their design. The harmonic pattern is characteristically austere, and yet varied. Some choruses, like the outburst 'Ahi, caso acerbo' ('Ah, bitter destiny') which follows the Messenger's news, are really magnificent. The recitatives throb with dramatic power and new melodic variations appear continually, especially in the pastoral episode at the beginning of the second act. The Messenger's narrative is a masterpiece of bold harmonic progressions. The climax of the opera is Orpheus's great scene in the Underworld, in which he pleads with Charon to let him pass. After a long drawn-out and richly varied section (which gives the singer the opportunity to exhibit his virtuosity), Orpheus's strong emotion breaks through, and he resumes his pleading in a simple but deeply-felt recitative which finally overcomes Charon's resistance. Solemn *ritornelli*, supported by sonorous wind chords, frame this great aria.

The basic form of *La Favola d'Orfeo* is the same as that of Peri's and Caccini's first operas, but Monteverdi's work is full of dramatic vitality. He avoids the ponderous recitatives of his predecessors; his melodic line is more fluid, his rhythms livelier and his expressive gifts stronger. Beginnings of vocal *cantilena* are noticeable throughout. Monteverdi is also the inventor of the *tremolo*, an effect which undoubtedly originated in his dramatic feeling for heightening excitement. He was also probably the first composer to use *pizzicato* as an element of orchestral colouring.

The score of *La Favola d'Orfeo* is rich in instrumental phrases, short and long, in which the mood of individual scenes is either announced beforehand, or taken up and developed in an interlude. The overture, an innovation of Monteverdi's, consists of two parts: a solemn fanfare preceding an elegiac *ritornello*, which effectively suggests the character of the opera.

The orchestra is remarkably rich: twelve violins (including two solos), five violas da gamba and two basses; a piccolo, three muted trumpets, a clarinet, trombones, two small organs, two harpsichords, harps, etc. It is not very easy to guess how Monteverdi arranged this ensemble. He undoubtedly valued the tone colour of his instruments both as solos and in groups, as a means of expression. His highly personal style is characterized by rich harmonization, by frequent use of dissonance, syncopation, passing notes and even freely introduced sevenths, as well as by the casually modulated sequences. It is small wonder that *Orfeo* is still highly effective in our day.

In 1608 Monteverdi wrote the opera *Arianna* as well as the short festival piece *Il Ballo dell'ingrate*, both settings of poems by Rinuccini, and both composed for the town of Mantua. *Arianna* was later performed in other towns as well, and in 1640 it must have dominated the repertory of the Teatro di San Moisè in Venice, where it was played every night for months. (It was actually revived in the autumn of 1639 for the inauguration of this theatre, which was Venice's third opera house.) Unfortunately the music for this exceptionally successful opera has been lost; we only have the elegiac song, the famous *Lamento d'Arianna* ('Lasciatemi morire'), which must have enjoyed unprecedented popularity; it is said to have been sung or played in every music-loving Italian household.

ARIANNA (the Greek Ariadne), abandoned by Theseus, tries in desperation to drown herself in the sea. Fishermen carry the unhappy woman back to land, but she has no words of thanks for her rescuers. She continually raises the cry 'Lasciatemi morire' ('Let me die'). Nothing can console her, and the expressive melody of the lament inexorably returns.

In *Il Ballo dell'ingrate* Monteverdi goes back to the style of the interlude. Half ballet, half courtly moral fable, this short opera has a special grace and charm. There is also a modern setting by Carl Orff entitled *Tanz der Spröden*, and one by Raymond Leppard, which was heard at the 1958 Aldeburgh Festival.

THE VENETIAN OPERA

The Florentine opera was a purely aristocratic affair; princely courts and palaces of cardinals and nobles provided its splendid setting. It was enjoyed by only a small, select group of people, which makes it all the more surprising that opera established itself so quickly and became so widely popular among the middle and lower classes that the first opera house was opened in Venice in 1637.

Command performances of operas in wealthy patrician houses had already prepared the ground, and Benedetto Ferrari (1597–1681), a playwright and composer, who founded the Teatro San Cassiano, had not misjudged public taste. First nobles and townspeople, later more humble folk, filled his theatre, and the financial success of the venture was so remarkable that more opera houses were built in quick succession. At the end of the century fourteen theatres could be counted in Venice, of which more than half, and in fact the largest and most splendid, were devoted exclusively to opera.

The Venetian opera stage was surrounded almost entirely by boxes. The original amphitheatre type of auditorium, usual at the Renaissance courts, gave way to three or four superimposed tiers of boxes; and while hitherto the seats for princes and their most distinguished guests had been set immediately in front of the proscenium, the stalls were now left to the common people. The price of a seat in the pit was probably quite low, so for financial reasons the rent of a box must have been correspondingly high. The upper classes of society made a point of maintaining a box at the theatre, which was passed on from generation to generation. For these patrons the opera was a fashionable as well as an artistic occasion. The passion for music was carried so far that the Grimani family built the beautiful Teatro San Giovanni Crisostomo and for several decades most generously subsidized its performances entirely out of their own pockets. Within two generations opera had become the pastime of virtually the whole population of Italy!

At first performances were only given during the three-month carnival period, from Christmas until the end of March. Later, however, a two or three month *Stagione di Ascensione*, an Ascensiontide season, was added; and finally an autumn season of about the same length. During each of these seasons the same opera was performed every night, so the whole audience, whether in boxes or in the pit, listened to the same work time and time again—a habit peculiar to the Italian opera-going public. The Italian opera-lover has always displayed the greatest interest in the way operas are performed. He wants to learn every detail, penetrate every nuance (especially of individual performances), and, seemingly indefatigable, savour the sensations offered by the work again and again, until he knows it inside out. This predilection is the only possible explanation for the monotony of the repertory. On the other hand, the modern repertory system, with successful works reappearing in an alternating series, did not exist. Usually an opera was dropped completely after only one season, and only very rarely was a particularly successful work revived the following year. When an opera was repeated in another town, often only the libretto was the same; the music was written by the local *maestro*, who took into consideration the abilities of his own singers.

In contrast to the Florentine choral opera, the Venetian operas concentrated purely on the soloists. Virtuoso solos were so immensely popular that the participation of the chorus seemed, in fact, to be a drawback. Perhaps economic considerations played a part in this development, for the cost of maintaining a chorus was considerable. Whatever the reason, in Venetian opera the role of the chorus dwindled more and more, until it disappeared almost completely. The leading singers were extravagantly praised, and after the prima donna it was the *primo uomo*, a soprano or alto castrato, who was most highly paid, while only minor parts were assigned to the other male voices. The use of castrati in opera resulted at first from the shortage of suitable trained female voices and the repeated bans on women taking part in operatic performances, so that castrati from church choirs had to be called on to sing the female roles. This makeshift arrangement soon became a custom, and eventually an important point of fashion.

While high fees went to the leading singers, who received up to a thousand ducats for the season, the composer was paid only a paltry hundred ducats for his music—though he might also receive a small extra sum as first harpsichordist. The author of the libretto, however, received no payment at all, and had to be content with the honour of having his work performed. When it became the custom for libretti to be printed, however, he did receive the proceeds from the sales. For this reason the printing of opera scores ceased in Venice, though not in Florence, and this explains why from the rich output of Venetian operas relatively few works have survived. In the sixty years during which Venetian opera predominated, more than three hundred operas were produced in Venice, and about the same number in the other towns of Italy, in France and in Germany; it therefore seems probable that at least six hundred works were written and produced in the Venetian operatic style.

The Venetian opera houses, the Teatro San Cassiano, the Teatro San Apollinare and others (the theatres were named after the parish in which they were built) were regarded as belonging to the wonders of the world. They were covered-in, and performances took place in the evenings by artificial light. These were fantastic innovations, since previously performances had always been given in the open air and, of course, only in daylight. The lighting was very poor and consisted only of a few torches on the stage and oil lamps on either side of the proscenium. The audience lit candles in their boxes so that they could follow the text, and as clear evidence of this custom there are patches of wax and burn marks in surviving copies of libretti.

A Venetian opera house, where the boxes glittered with the wealthy and the pit swarmed with the humble—divided and yet united in a common musical experience—faithfully reflected the lively spirit of this city of the lagoons. Seventeenth-century Venice no longer enjoyed its former power and grandeur, but it was still a city of international standing, and its great families still vied with one another to display their wealth in brilliant festivities. The pulse of life seemed to beat faster in this city, where excitements and adventures followed one another in rapid succession. Love and jealousy still provided fresh motives for bloodshed and affairs of honour, and events in the palaces found their parallels in the alleys and on the canals of the poorer quarters. Hired assassins were ready for any deed or misdeed, and unrestrained individuality and lust for pleasure gave substance and shape to life. People flocked to Venice from all parts of the world: nowhere were festivities more splendid; nowhere was the carnival so abandoned in its extravagance and gaiety. Venice led the fashion in manners and clothes: gigantic puffed sleeves, enormously full skirts, and low-cut necklines spread triumphantly throughout Europe. She had astounded the cultural world of the sixteenth century with her paintings; now she amazed that of the seventeenth century with her opera, which faithfully expressed the spirit of the age.

Whereas the Florentine opera had been known as *dramma per musica*, in the Venetian period the word 'opera' came into general use. Florence had emphasized the dramatic element and tried to deepen dramatic expression, but the predominance of the recitative seemed a handicap to the Venetians, who consciously developed in its place the purely melodic element, *cantilena* and *fioritura*. In less than forty years people had come to regard recitative, the essence of the monodic tradition, as tedious, and had broken its dominance over the form of opera. The first significant step was the introduction of *recitativo accompagnato*, recitative accompanied by the whole orchestra, in contrast to the customary *recitativo secco* with a choral accompaniment on one instrument. From Venetian opera to Mozart, the harpsichord undertook these harmonic accompaniments which only supported the *parlando* passages. The *accompagnato* led easily to a more natural treatment of the vocal part which in turn prepared the way for *canzoni*—shorter, or sometimes more comprehensive, lyrical parts, which ultimately became the grandly conceived virtuoso aria.

The greatest name in Venetian opera was Claudio Monteverdi who, from 1613 until his death in 1643, was director of music at St Mark's Cathedral in Venice. He wrote a series of operas for the city, but unfortunately only the last of these works—*L'Incoronazione di Poppea*—has survived. [This is not strictly true if we include *Il Ritorno d'Ulisse in Patria* (Venice, 1641), the music of which is now generally accepted as having been written by Monteverdi.] The recent numerous revivals of the important *L'Incoronazione di Poppea* have again shown how fresh and vital is Monteverdi's music.

L'INCORONAZIONE DI POPPEA. Opera in a prologue and three acts by Claudio Monteverdi. Text by Giovanni Francesco Busenello. First performance: Venice, 1642. (As with *La Favola d'Orfeo*, there have been several versions of *Poppea* during the last fifty years or so, including those by Vincent d'Indy (1905), Benvenuti (1937), Křenek (1937), Malipiero (1937), Ghedini (1953), Hans Redlich (1953), Walter Goehr (1959) and Raymond Leppard (1962).)

Characters: Nerone (Nero)—tenor; Octavia (Ottavia)—mezzo-soprano; Poppea—soprano; Ottone—baritone; Seneca—bass; Drusilla—soprano; Arnalta—alto. Courtiers, soldiers, populace, allegorical characters.

Place: Rome. *Time:* first century AD.

The Emperor Nero has fallen passionately in love with the beautiful Poppea, and therefore wants to divorce Ottavia in order to make Poppea his lawful wife. Poppea suspects the old philosopher Seneca, the teacher and adviser of the Emperor, of being involved in a plot against herself inspired by the Empress, and the Emperor orders Seneca to take his own life, which the old man does. Meanwhile Ottavia has persuaded the young Ottone to murder Poppea, his former mistress. Ottone borrows a cloak from his lover Drusilla, so as to pass unrecognized, and creeps up to the sleeping Poppea, but he is captured before he can fulfil his purpose. He confesses, but to save him Drusilla admits to having intended to murder

Poppea herself, and both betray the Empress's instigation to murder
Poppea. Ottone and Drusilla are banished, Nero proclaims his divorce
from Ottavia, and the same day Poppea is solemnly crowned Empress.

The theme of this opera is unattractive—it presents a coarse
picture of the customs of Nero's Rome—but it represents an
exceptional development in music, for in it the melodic element,
interspersed between long drawn-out recitatives, is highly expressive, lively and well characterized. The essential novelty of
this opera is the adoption of the polyphonic technique of church
music; canon and fugue passages are frequently used and the
bass is freely handled, so that it loses its rigid inflexibility. The
basso ostinato, a variation on a *basso continuo*, is a favourite
musical device here. The greatest charm of the work lies, however, in the melodic episodes, as for instance the simple and
most effective love-duet which brings the opera to a close.

Although he was by nature progressive, and open to new
ideas, Monteverdi remained faithful to tradition, and in particular to the strong preponderance of the dramatic recitative.
He did make certain concessions in the text, for Busenello was
the most conservative of all the Venetian librettists. The subject
matter and style of operatic libretti had changed considerably
by then, and though the old themes were still used the classic
pastoral setting had disappeared long before. New characters
and events from the more recent past, ambitious *condottieri* of
the Renaissance, burning passion and jealousy in women now
dominated the scene, all disguised in classical costume. Treachery, abduction, murder, conspiracy and ambush, in fact the most
exaggerated adventures, unfolded one after another, without
any question of a moral or even a moralizing attitude. Life was
cheap in these operas, but startling effects and often highly
dramatic situations abounded. Typical recurring themes were
the invocation of *ombrae* (Shades of the Dead), fantastic dream
scenes of consoling spirits, desperate duets by parting lovers,
and so on. Also typical of the Venetian style of opera was the
use of comic characters in the development of the plot. These
jolly creatures, usually servants, still bore archaic names, but
their impudent, good-natured humour originated unmistakably
in the *commedia dell'arte*. The farcical element was a concession
to the taste of the pit, thereby greatly contributing to the
success of opera and preparing the way for *opera buffa*.

Leading composers of Venetian opera were Cavalli and Cesti. Francesco Cavalli (1602–76) introduced popular elements in his numerous operas. His sung melodies are mostly in a lilting $^2/_3$ measure, for instance the barcarolle, which became an integral part of Venetian opera and brought Cavalli his great popularity. Despite this popular element, his work has dignity and an overriding care for dramatic truth. Recitative was more important to him than the *canzone*, which he only introduced where it would not disturb the development of the plot. Cavalli's most important opera was *Giasone* (*Jason*), Venice 1649; but for Louis XIV's marriage to Maria Theresa of Austria in Paris on 9 July 1660 he wrote *Ercole Amante* (*Hercules in Love*), which was however not performed until 1662, and was not a great success. This was the only opera Cavalli wrote for Paris, and Lully composed the music for the accompanying ballets.

Marc Antonio Cesti (1623–69) is the principal representative of the deliberately popular trend. He and his followers placed the melodic insertions completely in the foreground and arbitrarily interrupted the action for the sake of short songs, often at most unsuitable points. The recitative was quite neglected, for fear of wearying the audience. Dramatic unity, which had been sought by earlier composers, was sacrificed to the continual alternation of popular songs, short recitatives and ornamented virtuoso passages. The result is a highly entertaining, though artistically questionable medley of styles, which was, however, perhaps justified by its success.

Cesti was an exceptionally prolific composer. Among his operas (he wrote more than 150) the most important was *La Dori* (Florence, 1661), which soon became popular all over Italy. His best-known work is *Il Pomo d'Oro* (*The Golden Apple*) which tells the story of Paris and Helen. It was written for Vienna, where it was performed either in December 1666 or early in 1667 with great splendour and such outstanding success that it was repeated for a whole year. This was another of the early operas written for a royal occasion—the wedding of the Emperor Leopold I with the Infanta Margherita of Spain.

Cesti was a splendid writer of tunes; he was at his best when expressing gentle emotions in reveries and idylls and when portraying gay scenes. In construction he looked far ahead to the development of the *da capo* aria, a prominent element in eighteenth-century opera. The absolute, unquestioned predominance of the aria, and with it the triumph of *fioritura*, was finally perfected in Neapolitan opera, which put an end to the Venetian period.

THE HEGEMONY OF NAPLES

At the end of the seventeenth century opera had become all the rage in Italy: all the large towns had opera houses filled with glittering audiences, the two main attractions being the brilliance of the décor and stage effects, and the vocal acrobatics of the singers. With the introduction of thunder-machines, shipwrecks and conflagrations, drama took second place, and the music was obscured by trills, ornamental passages and improvized cadenzas which in the end suffocated the melody.

This was the golden age of the Neapolitan school; by the turn of the century the star of Venice had set and Naples, rising both politically and socially, also took the lead in opera. With its 300,000 inhabitants, Naples was the largest town in Italy at the beginning of the eighteenth century, and particularly well qualified to develop musical culture, for all southern Italians have music in their blood, and dance and sing to the rhythm of their local folk songs. As a result all ranks of society, to an even greater degree than in Venice, took a keen interest in opera and in everything connected with it. The royal court, almost unrivalled in Italy for splendour and luxury, encouraged music and opera in every way, and with four conservatories and the most splendid opera houses everything was done to establish Naples as a leading musical centre. When Alessandro Scarlatti finally settled in Naples in 1708 as musician to the court and to one of the conservatories, he became the city's musical head. Scarlatti was not only a great composer, he was also a leader, and knew how to create a school. With him and through him Naples became the metropolis of music, and remained so for decades.

The Neapolitan opera started at first with a reaction against the worthless libretti produced by the last representatives of the

Venetian school. The typical opera at the turn of the century
was little more than a colourful rag-bag of songs, tunes and
more or less coarse jokes, which had virtually nothing in
common with the rules of dramatic craft. The reaction against
these libretti started with an attempt to bring some kind of
order into the chaotic tangle of the texts. Among the first to do
this were Silvio Stampiglia (1664–1725), Apostolo Zeno (1668–
1750) and the great Pietro Metastasio (1698–1782): three poets
at the imperial court of Vienna, who were interested in the reform of operatic texts. Their merit lay in their liberation of
operatic verse from inconsequential nonsense and their restoration of sensible plots. Noble characters and moral principles
were again presented to the audience, while the usual make-
weight of intrigues was, so far as possible, omitted. Thus the
indulgence of feelings found its way into opera; it was the age
of sentiment, the rococo period with its languor and its tender
yearnings, its luxurious confessions and touching tears. All these
attributes of an over-delicate sentimentality thrived in operatic
verse.

As a result of this emphasis on the feelings lyrical music became more prominent, and dialogue and recitative were neglected in favour of the aria, in which the poet could express his
emotions. The solo song now usually took the form of the
three-part *da capo* aria which we have already met in Venice.
The main section, repeated at the end, was contrasted in mood
with a central section, which might express doubt or trouble
where the main section spoke of confidence. In the repeat the
vocal melody was usually ornamented, and gave the singer the
opportunity to display his art and skill.

As Metastasio's arias consisted of two contrasting quatrains
the form of the *da capo* aria was dictated by him: in the eighteenth century he was the undisputed ruler of the operatic stage,
whose example everybody followed and whose authority was
unquestioned. His most celebrated and admired texts, the
Olimpiade, *Artaserse* (*Artaxerxes*), *Il Re Pastore* (*The Shepherd
King*) and *Il Sogno di Scipione* (*Scipio's Dream*) were set to music
over and over again. He was the poet laureate of his time and
the Viennese court was envied for having held him for so long.

With the aria established as the nucleus of opera, the supremacy of the singer was definitely confirmed, and rested on a

most remarkable cult of singing. In the singing schools of
Venice, Naples and Bologna, the course of study lasted from
ten to twelve years. It is hard to appreciate how much was expected of the singer of this period; on the one hand power and
expression, on the other an unimaginable fluency and supple-
ness and a vast vocal range, with absolute evenness throughout
the register. A complete education in musical theory enabled
the singer at least to improvise his cadenzas and coloratura in
the correct style; and of course, virtuoso breath control, impec-
cable sight-reading, dramatic training and dancing were all
part of such an education.

These prima donnas and castrati were extremely demanding.
They thought they could get away with anything as their
wishes were generally complied with. They decided which
arias should be sung, and which omitted or replaced by others
already tried out in earlier operas; the composer could do
nothing but bow to their whims. A story is told of Handel
standing out against the wishes of his prima donna, an unparalleled and unheard-of thing to do at that time. Francesca
Cuzzoni (*c.* 1700–70), the most famous and celebrated singer
of her day, refused to sing the aria written by Handel for her
entry in *Ottone*. On her first arrival in London in 1722 this
singer thought she would be able to indulge her fancies; she
annoyed Handel so much that he completely lost his self-control
and, shaking with rage, seized her and held her out of the
window, threatening to drop her if she would not do what she
was told. Cuzzoni also went so far as to box the ears of her rival,
the famous Faustina Bordoni (*c.* 1695), on the open stage,
whereupon a regular scuffle ensued. Theatrical managements
had no power over such outrageous behaviour by prima
donnas. The great castrato Farinelli (1705–82) enthusiastically
embraced his colleague Caffarelli (1710–83) on the stage just because he had greatly enjoyed his aria! The opera itself was
quite unimportant; only the singing and the singers mattered,
and the fees received by these idolized creatures were astro-
nomical: Farinelli, for instance, received 50,000 francs (£3,000)
a year from King Philip V of Spain to sing him four arias every
day, and Caffarelli bought himself a duchy out of his savings.

The operas were tailored to fit the singers. The virtuoso *da
capo* aria was the prescribed conventional form and consequently

appeared in every scene, and on the entry of each singer, whether or not it fitted the context. In this way operas became just collections of arias, the recitative finally perished and the composers became simply song-writers; no more than that was expected of them. This new form of opera dominated by the aria was typical of the Neapolitan school, and in this guise opera made its triumphal progress through the whole of Europe.

The father of the Neapolitan opera was Alessandro Scarlatti (1660–1725). The sensitive combination of aria and recitative in his first works showed that he was still aware of the Venetian school of opera, whereas in his later works he displayed a clear preference for the *da capo* aria. The principal landmarks of Scarlatti's style were on the one hand the dramatic content of his melodies, with a preference for large intervals and broad tempi, and on the other the use he made of popular songs and rhythms to fill his lighter arias with a delicate grace. The popular Neapolitan songs (*siciliano*, *villanella* and *frottola*) appeared constantly in opera from now on, and they contributed enormously towards its increased popularity.

Scarlatti's first opera, *Gli Equivoci nel Sembiante* (1679), was produced in Rome when he was only nineteen, and so impressed Queen Christina of Sweden that she became his patron. His finest work, *Mitradate Eupatore* (1707), is occasionally revived today, as is his only comic opera, *Il Trionfo del Onore*. In all he composed 115 operas of which some seventy are extant.

In Naples, Leonardo Vinci (1690–1730) and Giovanni Battista Pergolesi (1710–36) were, with Scarlatti, the principal representatives of the new opera, but there were also Italian *maestri* in all the musical centres of Europe who furthered the glory and splendour of Neapolitan opera. The most important of these were Niccolò Jomelli (1714–74), Tommaso Traetta (1727–79) and Giovanni B. Buononcini (1670–1755), but their fame was somewhat obscured by the success of the Germans Handel and Hasse, who must also count as important representatives of the Neapolitan school. Operas by all three of these Italian composers have been revived in Italy recently.

In spite of clear indications of the beginnings of a national opera in France, England and Germany at this time, the predominance of the Neapolitans lasted for several decades, and the Italians' supremacy was unrivalled for more than a century.

Long before the Neapolitan opera was triumphantly established in all the musical centres of Europe, more or less significant
attempts had been made in Germany, France and England to
form a national opera, and the greatest success in this direction
was attained by the French. Surprisingly enough the Florentine
choral opera had met with no response at all in Paris; this is
particularly strange because Peri's *Euridice* had been performed
at the wedding of the French royal couple in Florence, and its
librettist, Rinuccini, had followed the young Queen to Paris,
where he stayed for three years. Nearly fifty years later, in
1645, Paris saw its first Italian opera, *La Finta Pazza* by Francesco Paolo Sacrati (d. 1650), which was followed in 1647 by
Luigi Rossi's (1598–1653) *Orfeo*. [According to Loewenberg,
La Finta Pazza is the second Italian opera in Paris; an unknown
one was performed at the Palais Royal in February or March the
same year. Sacrati's opera was given at the Salle du Petit
Bourbon on 14 December 1645.] Both these works were in the
Venetian style, but they did not make any marked impression,
and only the sumptuous décor and the stage machinery aroused
any wonder. Cavalli's *Xerse* suffered a similar fate in 1660, and
his *Ercole Amante* (1662), which has already been mentioned,
was even less successful, but though these performances left no
noticeable trace they did stimulate the ambition of the French
to create the equivalent of an Italian opera.

The time was obviously ripe for building up native opera in
Paris. French classical drama in the hands of Corneille and
Racine was in its heyday and had found its comic-satirical
counterpart in Molière's comedies, so that the poetic drama of
the French was on a much higher level than the operatic libretti
of the Venetians. Musical circumstances were also very favourable at the French court: at the beginning of the seventeenth
century, court music was already provided by a string orchestra
of twenty-four, the *grande bande des violons* (the Violons du Roi),
which played for all court occasions, particularly the popular
ballet-pantomimes. Such pantomimes, similar to the Italian
interludes, were already found at the French court in the sixteenth century. They did not merely consist of a set of dances
but contained whole plots portrayed in mime. The introduction

of ballet into opera started a tradition which was to dominate the French musical theatre for several centuries.

Louis XIV was particularly fond of opera and ballet. In 1669 he granted the composer Robert Cambert (c. 1628–77) and his librettist Perrin permission to build an opera house in which public performances should be given and charges made for admission. In 1671, the Académie Royale de Musique (for so the opera house was called) was inaugurated with a performance of the opera *Pomone* by Cambert and Perrin. This work was immediately successful, and played to enthusiastic audiences for eight months. In 1672, however, the concession had been withdrawn from these two pioneers of French opera and given to Jean-Baptiste Lully (1632–87), a Florentine by birth, who had been working at the French court since he was twelve. He started his career as a scullion, then became a violinist and ballet dancer, and later director of the court orchestra, finishing with the absolute authority in the sphere of music which was bestowed with the opera monopoly.

Lully's ambition was to create a French national opera. He found a worthy partner in Philippe Quinault (1635–88), a poet of the school of Corneille, who knew how to create an operatic form in line with Lully's aspirations. Though this type of opera was consciously based on the Italian pattern, it was clearly imbued with a French spirit and tradition. The subjects were the same as in the Venetian operas—ancient legends and Renaissance epics. Heroism and love were the axes round which all the plots continually revolved, but whereas in Venetian opera the classical characters were merely masks to conceal Italian personalities of the present or very recent past, Quinault and his followers strove to revive classical spirit and ideals. This spirit endowed their libretti with such lasting validity that a century later Gluck was not ashamed to use Quinault's *Armide* again.

The fusion with traditional native ballet helped to determine the style and planning of French national opera. Lully inserted dance-scenes or large and splendid processions wherever remotely possible, thereby pandering not only to popular taste but to that of the King himself, who found them particularly enjoyable and occasionally even took part in these dances with his court. This connection with ballet also explains the number of gala-scenes, splendid processions, idyllic pastorals, colourful masques, genii, sylphs, nymphs, satyrs, and so on, which now became important elements in operatic plots. Musically the ballet brought a very important impetus to opera: ballet music, and with it the dance rhythms of popular songs, gave opera a resemblance to classical tragedy.

The somewhat cumbersome nature of French verse was a real obstacle to free development of recitative; in addition, the singers suffered from a certain awkwardness and inexperience in recitative style, while the audience invariably showed its aversion to excessively prolonged recitatives. Lully was therefore very sparing in his use of it and inserted an aria at every possible opportunity. His arias were simple but very impressive in their melodic line, and their resemblance to popular tunes lent them great lightness. An important characteristic of Lully's music was the repetition of any specially memorable tune, not just as a refrain but as a reprise in a much later scene, a forerunner, in fact, of the *leitmotiv*.

Lully's orchestral forces were much larger than those of the Venetian opera. They were based on the already complete string section, to which were added chordal instruments such as harpsichord and harp, flutes, oboes, bassoons, trumpets, horns and kettledrums. With such a rich orchestra Lully was able to produce hitherto unknown sound effects, such as massive string unisons, elegant use of wind instruments (mostly as solos) and the use of full brass to illustrate warlike scenes. The many independent instrumental passages naturally brought about a change in orchestration. Apart from the dances, such as courantes, galliardes, minuets and gavottes, it is in the introductory symphonies that Lully's instrumental style appears most clearly. These orchestral pieces, which Lully already called overtures, were in three parts: the introductory *grave*; a fast, largely fugal, middle part; and a final, slow section. The first, dignified section originally accompanied the entrance of the court while the lively *allegro* drew attention to the colourful actions on the stage. The modern overture developed out of this French form with its slow-fast-slow pattern (in contrast to the Italian overture which went fast-slow-fast), with the omission of the final section.

Of Lully's nineteen operas *Alceste* (1674), *Thésée* (1675) and *Armide* (1686) are considered his masterpieces, and they remained

in the repertory of the Paris Opéra for almost a hundred years.
The secret of Lully's extraordinary success lay in his admirable
versatility. He dedicated himself wholeheartedly to the success
of his work, and only when the text really lived up to his
idealistic requirements did he start composing the music. He
even made sure that the décor was of a high quality, down to
the very smallest detail, attended to the most minute techni-
calities and supervised the preparation of the costumes. Not
only did he personally undertake the musical preparation, but
he also acted as producer and choreographer. He worked tirelessly with singers and dancers until every detail of the work
was realized just as he had conceived it.

Contemporary engravings testify clearly to the high artistic
standard of French design in Lully's time. Besides the splendid
views of palaces and streets in the Italian style, finely painted,
beautiful landscapes were a distinguishing feature of French
stage scenery. The costumes were quite exceptionally attractive:
the typical ballet figurine with wasp-waist and almost hori-
zontal *tutu* originated here. The rapid, brilliant blossoming of
French opera is due above all to the patronage of Louis XIV.
Among other things the King ordered that all works which
were performed at the Académie should be printed at the expense of the State, and in this way all the important French
operas of this period have been preserved.

Lully's followers at first adhered slavishly to his style. The
development of instrumental music in opera, which started
among Lully's followers, was of great general importance, as
it led to the tone-painting characteristic of French music. From
the madrigal-like *Chansons* of Jannequin, who died about 1560,
with their descriptions of nature and of battles, and from the
clavecin music with its programme titles, through Chopin's
piano poetry and Berlioz's programme music to Debussy's
impressionism and Honegger's technical, naturalistic expressionism, tone-painting runs inexorably through French music.
It started with pictures of nature to accompany arias and
choruses and with independent instrumental passages; pastoral
scenes and musical idylls with flute and pipe imitations of bird-
cries were particularly popular. Lully's followers also attempted
to represent nature in movement. The composer Marin Marais
(1656–1728) is said to have travelled to the seashore for the sole

purpose of seeking inspiration for the composition of a storm at sea. Since then, scenes of storm and tempest have constantly recurred as instrumental interludes in opera, both in France and elsewhere.

Among Lully's successors, the most important representative of this trend was André Destouches (1662–1749), but much more successful was his rival André Campra (1660–1744) whose *Fêtes Vénitiennes* (1710) became one of the Académie's greatest triumphs. These were a series of five one-act plays, reminiscent of Italian interludes, in which there was more dancing than singing. The scene was laid in Venice and everything referred to the city, to the carnival, the opera and the barcarolle, so that the spirit and form of Italian music was to be found here in French opera. Italian music was becoming gradually more and more popular in Paris at this time. An Italian opera troupe which had come to Paris in 1708 on a visit succeeded in establishing itself triumphantly in the teeth of the Académie, especially as the Italians started to parody French opera. The connoisseurs, innocent dilettanti here as anywhere else, went over to the Italian camp with flags flying, so that French opera, which was also threatened with financial catastrophe, would have lost its importance, at least temporarily, if it had not found a timely helper and promoter in Jean Philippe Rameau (1683–1764).

Rameau was a contemporary of Bach and Handel, and entirely their equal in certain respects. He went down in the history of music as the founder of the modern theory of harmony, and his historic significance in this field will always remain unchallenged. His greatness and importance lay essentially in the serious dramatic field, and reached its peak in the tragic operas *Castor et Pollux* (1737) and *Zoroastre* (1749). *Castor et Pollux* has enjoyed several revivals during the last quarter of a century, while *Les Indes Galantes* (1735) was restored to the repertory of the Paris Opéra with marked success in 1952, receiving more than two hundred performances during the next ten years.

Rameau's main characteristic was the refining of musical language in every respect. His masterly touch is discernible everywhere—in the enrichment of harmony, the development of polyphony, the reinvigoration of rhythm and the intensi-

fication of melody. It was with complete musical discipline
that he loosened the stiffness of baroque music and created in
its place a new, elegant variety of musical expression. At a time
when the success of Neapolitan opera was undisputed everywhere else in Europe, the Paris Opéra, though surrounded by
enemies and continually attacked and derided, stood out for
several decades as the protagonist of a great tradition, a tradition which was becoming somewhat antiquated but to which
Gluck with his reforms was to subscribe in due course.

THE BEGINNINGS OF OPERA
IN GERMANY

As in Italy and France, the first stirrings of musical drama could
be seen in Germany long before the birth of Renaissance opera.
In the medieval mystery plays, court processions, masquerades
and popular entertainments by itinerant players, there was
always an opportunity to insert dramatic fragments which
could be illustrated in music. Although choral singing predominated, popular songs and solos were also to be found. It
is not really possible to consider these modest musical and
dramatic antecedents as the first steps towards opera, since its
discovery is and always will be a creation of the Italian Renaissance. However, these first attempts may have prepared the
taste and mood of a large circle of people for the enjoyment of
musical drama and smoothed the way for this new art.

The first German opera was the work of the two most prominent artists of their time: the head of the Silesian school of
poetry, Martin Opitz (1597–1639), and the composer Heinrich
Schütz (1585–1672), the great forerunner of Johann Sebastian
Bach. The occasion was the marriage, in April 1627, of the
Princess Sophia Eleonora of Saxony to George, Landgrave of
Hesse, which was celebrated with particular splendour in the
castle of Torgau. The climax of the festivities was the gala performance of *Der Pastoral-Tragikomödie von der Dafne*, a ceremonial
play written in German by Opitz and set to music by Schütz.
While the text, a very personal adaptation of Rinuccini's famous
poem, has survived, no trace remains of the music. Schütz, who

in his studies with Gabrieli in Venice had become familiar with
the new monodic style, was one of the first musicians to introduce it into Germany. Judging by the dramatic grandeur of the
solos in his surviving *Passions*, one can safely assume that his
recitatives in *Dafne* must also have been most powerfully expressive.

While *Dafne* clearly followed the model of the Italian
monody, *Das Geistliche Waldgedicht Seelewig* (*The sacred woodland tale of Seelewig*), by Siegmund Staden (1607–55), which
was first performed in Nuremberg in 1644, represents a much
more independent operatic attempt. The poem is by the
Nuremberg poet Harsdörffer, who had evidently learned about
dramma per musica when travelling and studying in Italy and
was now trying to instil a Germanic spirit into his adaptations
of this art-form. Harsdörffer's pastoral plot still shows traces of
the medieval mystery plays. The nymph Seelewig, the embodi-
ment of the eternal soul, is pursued by Trügewalt, a spirit of
the woods, but good shepherds and shepherdesses save her from
the demon's pursuit. A jubilant chorus of angel hosts concludes
the drama in the tradition of the Christian morality. Staden
was an organist in Nuremberg who knew virtually nothing of
free recitative, and his music is very arid and stiff, relieved only
by a few popular tunes successfully inserted into the songs and
refrains. Seelewig and the shepherdesses were sung by soprano
and altos, and the spirit of the woods was given to a bass. The
orchestration seems to have been very rich; in addition to
strings, flutes and bassoons, a theorbo is also listed for the
accompaniment, and a 'deep horn' to announce the entrance
of Trügewalt.

It should not be thought that the Torgau and Nuremberg
attempts at German opera were the only ones at that time. The
terrible conditions prevailing (the Thirty Years' War was
raging through Germany) naturally prevented this new art
becoming established. It seems almost incredible therefore that,
very shortly after peace had finally descended on Central
Europe, cultural life flourished again in all the German states,
and with it the cult of opera, the new art-form which had meanwhile won the highest esteem in Italy.

It is quite clear that, in keeping with its original courtly
character, German opera at first flourished at the great royal

courts. In 1631 the opera became a permanent institution at the imperial court of Vienna, Munich followed in 1657, Dresden in 1662 and Hanover soon after. The performances were of a splendour and luxury that easily surpassed that of Venice. In the courts of these large cities Italian opera reigned from the start, and Vienna assumed a leading role in the promotion of Venetian opera. Cesti composed his *Pomo d'Oro* for Vienna and settled temporarily in the imperial city on the Danube. His share in the development of German opera was negligible, however, being confined to inserting into his works occasional German songs and arias, mostly written by the Emperor Leopold I. The texts of the operas were always in Italian, and a German translation was usually given out to help the audience understand them.

It was left to small courts, such as Brunswick, Weissenfels and Altenburg, to promote the cause of German opera, and it was in these centres—as well as in Leipzig, Nuremberg and especially Hamburg—that German operatic performances started. In Brunswick they date back to 1639, while in 1690 a public opera house was opened, with five tiers of boxes in the Venetian style. Anybody could enter and pay for a seat. At festival time the Duke, who wanted to see the opera economically stable, is said to have attended at his own expense. The performances were sung in German. Among the German composers Johann Philip Krieger (1651–1735), Reinhard Keiser (1674–1739), whose career began at Brunswick, and more especially Georg Caspar Schürmann (c. 1672–1751) should be mentioned, but Italian composers were always at hand and the German talent could not challenge Italian supremacy in the long run. There was plenty of textual material on which to build a national opera; subjects from German history and life were frequently used, but musically these operas always relied upon the Venetian pattern of siciliano and barcarolle, as well as the *da capo* aria which was very soon to eclipse all else. Italian operas gradually occupied more and more of the programmes, and in the end they completely supplanted German works.

All over Germany the situation was similar to that in Brunswick, where the opera was dissolved in 1755. The only major exception was Hamburg where a German opera house held its own successfully for more than fifty years. The operas performed in Hamburg and the artists who gathered there during these decades were so outstanding that in slightly more favourable circumstances a German national opera might have developed from these beginnings. The opening of a public opera house, built in the Gänsemarkt in 1678 on the initiative of a rich city councillor, Gerhard Schott, greatly influenced the prosperity of opera in Hamburg. At first biblical stories were performed, in which from the very beginning great importance was attached to the realistic introduction of ordinary people and their songs. Soon after, mythological subjects were added on the Italian and French models, and finally, an historical event from the recent past, the siege of Vienna by the Turks, was staged in 1686 in the opera *Cara Mustafa* by J. W. Franck. Unfortunately the Hamburg opera was not so fortunate in its poets, most of whom were no more than able writers of verse who showed little feeling for a reasonably constructed plot, not to mention taste and dignity.

Keiser's opera *Störtebecker und Joedge Michaels* (1701) is generally cited as a model of this kind of poetry. The subject of the opera was the life and love-story of a robber chief of the recent past. The production was very naturalistic: blood flowed in torrents—real calf's blood from pig-bladders which the singers tied under their clothes. The execution of Störtebecker, which was the climax of the opera, was also carried out in this realistic way.

A most important element in these texts was the frequent use of coarse peasant humour. Popular characters, like farmers, servants, market-women, serving-maids and domestics of all sorts, became as familiar at the Hamburg opera as they had been in Venice. These popular types were an enlivening element (they also spoke and sang by preference in Low German) not only in works with a contemporary German setting but even in the heroic-mythological operas, where they appeared as jesters and comic characters. They were true predecessors of the *buffo* characters in the later *Singspiel*.

Some of the composers who worked here were extremely talented. The first among them was Reinhard Keiser, in whose time the Hamburg opera reached its heyday. Keiser was a real adventurer, a gentleman of the age of gallantry, who loved to play the great lord. His life and art were equally confused, and his facility in composition led him to superficiality. Opera after opera flowed tirelessly from his pen without much critical study of texts or music and he dissipated his considerable abilities without achieving a truly personal style. Of his 120 operas—among which are *Störtebecker* and *Croesus* (1711)—none stands out through any particular qualities. The prevalent style of the time dominated and crushed his brilliant melodic gifts, on which all his contemporaries were agreed. Many years later, when Keiser's glory had already been long eclipsed, Hasse still counted him among the great musicians of the world.

The young Handel also worked for three years (1703–06) under Keiser's direction at the Hamburg Opera, and of the three operas he wrote for Hamburg, *Almira*, his first opera, produced in 1705, was the most successful. It contained forty-one German and fifteen Italian arias. In comparison with his later operas this early work is only of historical interest, for at that time the composer was absorbing more than he gave out.

The most important composer of the Hamburg Opera after Keiser was the great baroque musician Georg Philipp Telemann (1681–1767), whose cantatas, suites and trio sonatas are still very highly praised today. His numerous German operas, which were stylistically nearer to the French, were very popular in his time, but none of them has since established itself, in spite of occasional attempts at revivals, particularly of *Don Quichote*.

In spite of the most favourable theatrical circumstances, often quite brilliant décor and every endeavour to please popular taste, in spite of Keiser and of Telemann, German opera, even in Hamburg, was eventually forced to give way to the invading Neapolitans. Foreign influences pressed in from every side to suffocate the native element. This soon became obvious from the mixture of languages, as arias with Italian texts followed German recitatives and German songs jostled with scenes in French. With their respective tongues came the form and spirit of the various foreign operatic traditions, which combined in penetrating what had started as a completely independent venture. When in 1738 Mingotti's famous Italian travelling company came to Hamburg, it was enthusiastically received and the German opera had to be closed. The old and once famous opera house on the Gänsemarkt could not be saved. After the collapse of the German enterprise it was sold and pulled down.

All over Germany Italian opera was enjoying enormous success. The Viennese court attached to itself all the leading musicians of the Neapolitan school, from Scarlatti to Traetta, by commissioning operas from them, and Dresden kept Johann Adolf Hasse (1699–1783) for a long time. Hasse was a German by birth, whom the Italians rightly honoured as a great member of the Neapolitan school and fondly called their *caro Sassone*, their dear Saxon. He only composed to Italian texts and his mode of musical expression is pure Italian rococo; under him Dresden was for many years the most brilliant champion of Neapolitan opera. In Munich and in Stuttgart, where the great Jomelli worked at the splendour-loving court of Karl Eugen, the situation was no different.

In 1740 Berlin at last got its opera house, built by Frederick the Great in the Unter den Linden. It is true that German composers such as Karl Heinrich Graun (1704–59) and Georg Benda (Jíři Antonín Benda, one of three brothers of Bohemian birth), and famous German singers like Madame Schmeling (better known to English readers as Elisabeth Mara (1749–1833)) worked there, but Italian fashion completely ruled language and music from the very beginning. The same happened in all other musical towns and at the smaller courts, as for instance Bayreuth, where in 1747 the charming small state theatre was built which has been preserved to this day in its original form. Everywhere the influence of the Neapolitan opera was felt, with its brilliance, its superficiality and its concentration on external effects.

Attempts at a German opera, which also flared up here and there in South Germany (for instance at Durlach in Baden, where even Keiser tried to establish himself) were suffocated at birth. With the collapse of the Hamburg venture, the fortunes of German opera were temporarily eclipsed, and almost a century was to pass before a really important German opera could emerge again.

HANDEL AND ENGLISH OPERA

It is surprising that in England, where in the sixteenth century polyphonic style had reached its peak and where one would therefore have expected to find a conservative attachment to this rich tradition, the new monodic style was introduced almost as soon as in Italy and gained in popularity very quickly. Copies of Caccini's fundamental treatise, *Nuove Musiche*, could be found in England even before it was printed in 1602, and before the turn of the century the new style was having a stimulating effect. At first there was no thought of composing complete operas, but from solo songs and anthems with recitatives and choruses developed monodic musical accompaniments for short masques, which are definitely to be regarded as the first stages in a more elaborate form of opera. About the middle of the century several important opera performances took place in London, including one entitled *Britannia's Marriage to the Ocean*, but unfortunately nothing is left of the music of these first examples of English opera.

At about the same time a Venetian opera troupe visited England and gave some performances at the English court, which renewed interest in this art-form. French influences also made their mark and Cambert, who was ousted from Paris by Lully, went to work in London in 1672, remaining there until his death five years later.

Henry Purcell (*c*. 1659–95), acknowledged as the first important English composer, led the rapid rise of opera in England. His opera *Dido and Aeneas* (1689) relies a great deal on the chorus, stylistically following the Florentines, in contrast to the then prevalent fashion for Venetian opera. Purcell's choruses are very powerful and distinctive, and their dramatic effect often influences the development of the plot.

DIDO AND AENEAS. Opera in three acts by Henry Purcell. Text by Nahum Tate after Virgil. First performance: London, 1689.
   Characters: Dido, Queen of Carthage—soprano; Belinda, her lady-in-waiting—soprano; Aeneas, a Trojan prince—tenor (or high baritone); a Sorceress—mezzo-soprano. Witches, spirits, sailors.
   Place: Carthage. *Time*: Classical.
   The Prologue which appears in the original libretto was either never set by Purcell, or, if it was, the music was lost.
   Act I. Dido's Palace. Belinda is trying to cheer the Queen, whose

unhappiness has been caused by the presence at court of Aeneas, with whom the Queen has fallen in love. Belinda urges her mistress to marry the prince and so unite the thrones of Carthage and Troy. Aeneas enters and asks the Queen to take pity on her lover. His pleas are supported by Belinda and the court.

Act II, scene i. A cave. The Sorceress invokes her companions to join with her in bringing about the destruction of Dido and Carthage. One of their number disguised as Mercury, will appear to Aeneas and charge him to sail away with his fleet. To assure the royal party's return to court they will conjure up a storm which will spoil the royal hunt.

Scene ii. A grove. Dido and Aeneas, with Belinda and attendants, pause during the hunt for refreshments and entertainment. Aeneas displays the head of the wild boar he has killed. The approaching storm is heard, and as it breaks overhead they return to town. Aeneas however remains and is approached by Mercury (the Sorceress's trusty elf) who bids him set sail that night at Jove's command.

Act III. The harbour. The Trojan fleet prepares to sail. 'Come away, fellow sailors' sings the chorus, observed by the Sorceress and her witches who remark 'Our plot has took, the Queen forsook'. Witches and sailors both dance. Dido and Belinda, followed by Aeneas, arrive, the latter confirms Dido's fears. When the Queen rounds on him, he tells her he will stay despite the god's command. Dido will have none of her lover, and bids him go. She then prepares herself for death in the lament 'When I am laid in earth'.

Following the French example, an important place was also given to the ballet. Purcell was a wholehearted dramatist: his arias and his great recitatives, for instance the Sorceress's invocation of the witches, have an amazing dramatic power and vigour. A splendid example of his expressive power is Dido's final aria 'When I am laid in earth', a lament of Monteverdian

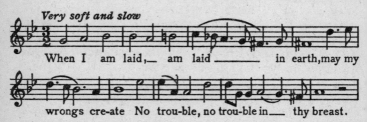

greatness. Purcell was not ashamed to use popular English songs and dance-tunes in the development of his melodies; the very lively choruses and dances of the sailors at the end of the opera clearly show this inclination towards popular song.

Dido and Aeneas was unfortunately Purcell's only original opera, though this prolific composer wrote more than forty musical works for the stage, some of which were so extensive that they can almost be called operas with spoken dialogue. Probably the most important of these were *King Arthur* (1691), written by John Dryden, and *The Fairy Queen* (1692), taken from Shakespeare's *Midsummer Night's Dream*.

Purcell's early death put an end to these important developments. He was a unique personality who could find no successor and who founded no school; with his death the growth of an English national opera was temporarily halted.

When fifteen years later George Frideric Handel (1685–1759) arrived on the London musical scene, aspirations towards an English national opera were already forgotten and here, as everywhere else, Neapolitan opera reigned supreme. It was typical of the time that the most passionate battles over Italian opera should be waged in essentially patriotic London round the person of the German composer, Handel.

Handel came to London in 1710, and apart from some very short absences remained there until his death. His incredible creative power was always concerned with opera, and in spite of his Hamburg training and the mantle of Purcell which he could have assumed in London, Handel remained faithful to the Neapolitan tradition—indeed, with his genius, he was its most important exponent. Handel was not a reformer; he was content to develop and perfect existing forms of expression, and in his many operas (he wrote nearly forty in all) we find all the characteristics of the Neapolitans: texts by Metastasio and his imitators, typical overtures, bravura *da capo* arias, passionate *accompagnati* and lilting *siciliani*. But the structure which had gradually become rigid in the hands of other Neapolitan composers, received such animation and renewed vigour from Handel that the monotony of these operas, which were in fact still a mere string of arias, was completely forgotten. Revivals of individual Handelian operas, the texts of which at least to some extent conform with modern dramatic requirements, have proved well worthwhile. The voluptuous splendour and baroque magnificence which belong to Handel's personality as much as to his art, lend his operas that heroic element which is a characteristic of his greatness. When expressing real passion and strong emotions, he wrote sublime melodies of thrilling and convincing nobility. Particularly famous are his arias of noble pathos, and such broadly sweeping *largos* as, for instance, the still popular 'Lascia ch'io pianga' ('O let me weep') from *Rinaldo*, his first London opera, or the even more famous aria 'Ombra mai fu', better known as Handel's *Largo*, from the opera *Serse*, which from its very first performance has always sent the public into ecstasies of enthusiasm.

Handel was just as successful in giving musical expression to the charming scenes of nature in his operas. This aspect of his art aroused the unreserved admiration of his contemporaries and is still impressive today. The only obstacles to successful modern revivals of Handel's operas are the often stupid and illogical libretti (no worse, however, than those of some Verdi operas) and the rigid monotony of the overall form. If one wants to enjoy the wonderful music to the full, one must approach it in an historical frame of mind and remember that its composer superbly developed the artistic style of his day.

It was due to Oskar Hagen, the Göttingen Handel expert, more than to anyone else that the Handel revival in Germany in the inter-war years was due. Hagen brought out a new arrangement of the opera *Rodelinda* for the Handel celebrations held at Göttingen in 1920. He confined himself to rewriting the text, which inevitably for dramatic reasons involved moving arias, inserting refrains and so on, but left the music unaltered. As a consequence of this Göttingen renaissance (nine operas between 1921 and 1938) as well as productions of ten other works elsewhere in Germany, Handel's operas are now frequently performed. English revivals began in 1955, when the Handel Opera Society produced *Deidamia*, and since then they have staged nearly a dozen of his operas.

RODELINDA. Opera in three acts by George Frideric Handel. Text by Salvi, altered by Nicola Haym. First performance: London, 1725.

Characters: Rodelinda, Queen of Lombardy—soprano; King Bertarido, her husband, deposed by Grimoaldo—mezzo-soprano (originally castrato); Grimoaldo, tyrant of Lombardy—tenor; Edwige, Bertarido's sister—contralto; Garibaldo, Count of Turin, Grimoaldo's friend—bass; Unolfo, a young nobleman, Bertarido's friend—contralto (originally castrato).

Place: Milan. *Time:* fifteenth century AD.

Act I, scene i. Rodelinda's apartments. The tyrant Grimoaldo asks for the hand of Rodelinda, the widow of King Bertarido whom he has deposed. Rodelinda proudly refuses him, since she is firmly resolved to remain faithful to her dead husband. Before Grimoaldo succeeded to the throne, he had wooed Edwige, Bertarido's sister; now he coldly spurns her when she reminds him of his vows. Garibaldo, Grimoaldo's friend, a cold schemer, who is plotting to overthrow the weak Grimoaldo, also despises Edwige.

Scene ii. A cypress grove, burial place of the Lombard kings. Bertarido, whom everybody believes to be dead, is in hiding here. Bitterly he reads the inscription on his own tomb and his thoughts go out to his beloved Rodelinda in the aria 'Dove sei, amato bene?' ('Art thou troubled?'). Unolfo arrives and tells the King of Rodelinda and her fidelity to him. Both hide as Rodelinda comes to pray at the tomb with her small son Flavio. Garibaldo has followed her and, seizing her child, demands her decision—she must either accept Grimoaldo's suit or the child must die. To save her child, she accepts Grimoaldo. Bertarido, who overhears this exchange, breaks down in despair.

Act II, scene i. The throne room in the royal palace. Edwige resolves to avenge herself on Grimoaldo.

Scene ii. A garden near the palace. Unolfo and Edwige explain to Bertarido that Rodelinda has only *appeared* to accept Grimoaldo's proposition.

Scene iii. Rodelinda's apartments. Grimoaldo cannot yet believe his good fortune that Rodelinda is to be his. Proudly Rodelinda approaches him. He must fulfil a condition before she will marry him. He must kill the child Flavio before her eyes, since she cannot be both mother of the true ruler and the wife of a usurper. Irresolute and perplexed, Grimoaldo leaves her. Rodelinda learns from Unolfo that her husband is still alive, and immediately Bertarido appears. The two fall into one another's arms in joy, but Grimoaldo returns and surprises them. He will grant them a few moments together, and then Bertarido must die. The act closes with a great love-duet, 'Io t'abbraccio' ('Ah my beloved!').

Act III, scene i. Edwige gives Unolfo the key to the dungeon where Bertarido lies imprisoned, and they plan to rescue him.

Scene ii. The prison. Bertarido laments his fate in a moving aria, 'Chi di voi fù più infedele' ('What in life brings more affliction'). A sword is thrown into the prison through a hole in the wall, and then as the door opens, Bertarido throws himself on the intruder and wounds him. It is Unolfo, who has come to rescue him. So that he should not be recognized in his flight, Bertarido leaves his cloak behind, and they hurry away together. Edwige and Rodelinda arrive with torches. When Rodelinda sees the blood-stained cloak, she thinks her husband has been killed.

Scene iii. The castle gardens. It is dawn. Grimoaldo is trying to find peace and quiet in nature. He lies down on the grass and falls asleep. Garibaldo discovers him sleeping and is about to fall on him, when Bertarido and Unolfo throw themselves between them. Garibaldo tries to flee, but Bertarido slays the traitor. Rodelinda and Edwige enter.

Rodelinda joyfully recognizes her husband and the people gathering there pay homage to him. Grimoaldo also recognizes him as the rightful King.

Following the pattern of Neapolitan opera, arias follow one another in close succession in *Rodelinda*; the only exception is the great love-duet at the end of the second act, an important climax in the work both dramatically and musically. The linking recitatives are often of great dramatic power. The prison scene, in which a strict tempo is maintained, is an example of the impressive construction of Handel's *accompagnati*. The most popular melody was Bertarido's 'Dove sei, amato bene?' (Art thou troubled? Music shall calm thee) which aroused violent excitement when originally sung by the castrato Senesino.

GIULIO CESARE IN EGITTO (Julius Caesar in Egypt). Opera in three acts by George Frideric Handel. Text by Nicola Haym. First performance: London, 1724.

Characters: Giulio Cesare (Julius Caesar)—mezzo-soprano or baritone (originally castrato); Curio (Curius), his captain—tenor; Cornelia, wife of Pompey—contralto; Sesto (Sextus), her son—soprano or tenor (originally castrato); Cleopatra—soprano; Tolomeo (Ptolemy), King of Egypt, her brother—bass; Achilla (Achillas), an Egyptian general—baritone; Nireno (Nirenus), Cleopatra's confidant—bass. Soldiers, attendants on Cleopatra, masquers.

Place: Egypt. *Time:* 48 BC.

Act I, scene i. On the banks of the Nile. Caesar is received by the Egyptians as their conqueror, and is begged by Cornelia and Sextus to make peace with Pompey, his defeated rival. Achillas appears to invite Caesar to Ptolemy's palace, and brings a present from his master, which turns out to be the head of Pompey, whose murder however fills Caesar with horror. Cornelia is overcome with grief, and Sextus swears to avenge his father's murder.

Scene ii. Cleopatra's apartments. Cleopatra believes she should be sole ruler of Egypt, and when she hears of Ptolemy's murder of Pompey she resolves to approach Caesar in disguise and try to win his support. Ptolemy enters and he and his sister quarrel. After she has gone out he and

Achillas plot to murder Caesar, and he promises the beautiful Cornelia to Achillas as a reward for his help.

Scene iii. Outside Caesar's camp. Caesar meditates on the transitory nature of earthly power, thinking of the dead Pompey, when Cleopatra comes in, disguised as one of her own women, Lydia, to ask for Caesar's help in recovering the property Ptolemy has taken from her. Struck by her beauty, he promises help, and Cleopatra sings of her confidence in the future in the aria 'Tu la mia stella sei'. Cornelia enters and takes a dagger to kill Ptolemy, but Sextus claims the right to avenge his father.

Scene iv. A courtyard of the palace. Caesar is greeted by Ptolemy on his arrival, both men concealing their true feelings. Cornelia and Sextus enter full of defiance, but are arrested, and Cornelia is assigned a menial task in a place where Achillas can have access to her.

Act II, scene i. Cleopatra's garden. She has arranged an entertainment to enrapture Caesar and disguised as a goddess sings to him 'V'adoro pupille'. He begs Nirenus to lead him to his Lydia.

Scene ii. The garden of the harem, where Cornelia is confined. Achillas tells her of his love but she turns away from him in utter despair. Sextus enters and reassures her.

Scene iii. Cleopatra's boudoir, where she is preparing to receive Caesar. Left alone, she pretends to sleep, and when Caesar enters and broods aloud on her beauty, she arises and expresses her own feelings for him. Shouts are heard, and Curius rushes in to warn Caesar that a mob is searching the palace for him to kill him. Cleopatra reveals her identity and implores him to flee, crying on the gods for mercy.

Act III, scene i. Cleopatra has been defeated by Ptolemy in battle, and is brought in as his prisoner. She still defies him, but left alone confesses that her plight is hopeless without Caesar's aid.

Scene ii. The banks of the Nile, where Caesar has escaped death by swimming the river, and realizes that his situation, too, is desperate. He hides as Achillas, mortally wounded in the battle, enters and meets Sextus, who is searching for Ptolemy. With his dying breath Achillas confesses his treachery and gives Sextus a seal, telling him where a hundred warriors are concealed who will lead him secretly into the palace. Caesar seizes the seal from Sextus and rushes off to rescue Cleopatra.

Scene iii. A prison, where Cleopatra is awaiting death. Caesar enters with his soldiers, and routs the Egyptian guards. They embrace in exultation.

Scene iv. At the gates of Alexandria. A crowd waits to greet Caesar, who enters with Cleopatra in a triumphal procession, to be met by Cornelia and Sextus, carrying Ptolemy's crown, for the King of Egypt has been killed in revenge for Pompey's death. Caesar acclaims Sextus as his friend and crowns Cleopatra Queen of Egypt. The opera ends as they affirm their love for each other and all join in rejoicing.

There is almost an excess of action in *Giulio Cesare* and the continual changing of fortunes in the story is confusing. The richness of dramatic events is emphasized by recitatives of particularly expressive power, and the various scenes are very impressively constructed. The most beautiful arias are those for Cleopatra, particularly the aria 'Tu la mia stella sei' in ⁶/₈ time, which overflows with excitement, and the beautiful 'V'adoro, pupille', an idyll of infinite magic.

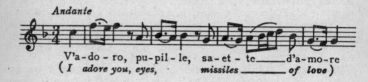

Two years after *Giulio Cesare* Handel became an English citizen and during the next decade opera followed opera, including *Admeto* (1727), *Siroe* (1728), *Partenope* (1730), *Ezio* (1732), *Orlando* (1733), *Ariodante* and *Alcina* (both in 1735).

In *Alcina* Handel's dramatic power is at its greatest. The arias are particularly powerful and the stock figure of *opera seria* become real flesh and blood beings. Any production which ignores these facts and tries to turn *Alcina* into a precious entertainment as did Zeffirelli in his London production in 1962, admittedly designed originally for a modern Italian audience, does not really understand Handel and is doing him a disservice.

ALCINA. Opera in three acts by George Frideric Handel. Text by Antonio Marchi. First performance: London, 1735.

Characters: Bradamante—contralto; Melisso, Bradamante's guardian—bass; Morgana, Alcina's sister—soprano; Alcina—soprano; Ruggiero, betrothed to Bradamante—contralto (originally castrato); Oronte, Alcina's general—tenor.

Place: Alcina's magic island. *Time:* fairy-tale.

Act I. Bradamante, disguised as her own brother, Ricciardo, has come with her guardian Melisso to Alcina's island in search of her beloved, Ruggiero, and has been shipwrecked. They are discovered by Morgana and taken to Alcina. Ruggiero has been put under a spell by Alcina, with whom he believes himself in love, and has quite forgotten Bradamante. Thinking her to be Ricciardo, he tells her of his love for Alcina. Morgana falls in love with the supposed youth, and for him rejects Oronte, her former lover, who tells Ruggiero that Alcina is in love with 'Ricciardo'. Disbelieving Bradamante's assurances of her identity, Ruggiero swears to have her banished, while Morgana begs her to flee rather than be forced to leave the island. Alcina brings the act to a close, singing joyfully of her love for Ruggiero.

Act II, scene i. Melisso, disguised as Ruggiero's former tutor Atlante, rebukes him for his behaviour and gives him a ring to break Alcina's spell, but when Bradamante appears the young man thinks this is just another trick of the sorceress's, thereby making Bradamante very angry. He pretends to Alcina that he still loves her and makes an excuse for leaving her, in the hope of escaping. Oronte betrays Ruggiero to Alcina, who conjures up her evil spirits to help her avenge herself on him.

Scene ii. Morgana and Oronte quarrel, and then Ruggiero and Bradamante plan escape, the former not without a tinge of regret for the easy life he will be leaving. When Alcina enters and calls on her spirits they do not respond to her summons, and she finds her power broken.

Act III. Melisso, Ruggiero and Bradamante prepare to escape, after restoring the beasts, rocks and trees to their rightful shapes as knights bewitched by Alcina. Ruggiero summons his army to fight the monsters barring their path and sings a warlike aria. Having won the battle he destroys Alcina's power and she and her sister vanish.

Thanks to Handel, London moved into the centre of European musical life for several decades. As a result of his presence, it was there that the most violent and indeed decisive battles for supremacy between the serious Italian grand opera, the *opera seria*, and the comic opera—*opera buffa*—were fought. Handel became famous not only as an operatic composer but also as a conductor, and eventually as an independent opera impresario as well.

In 1719 the Royal Academy of Music [not the educational institution, but the name given to an operatic enterprise which lasted from 1720–28] was founded in London and its permanence guaranteed by subscriptions and covenants from the King and members of the aristocracy. The artistic direction was given to Handel, who went to Dresden and Düsseldorf to engage a suitable ensemble of Italian singers for the coming season. In contrast to the Paris Académie, with its strong national aspirations, such aims were not to be found in its London counterpart. Handel wanted to show Londoners Italian opera in all its perfection, and to this end concentrated on highly polished musical performances. Nowhere was such seriousness and such a deep feeling of artistic responsibility evinced as in London under Handel. So far as spectacle was concerned, the Vienna court opera was still unrivalled in its quest for splendour, although London achieved wonders in this direction, too.

Musically, however, Handel's enterprise was incomparable, and included ensembles of the most prominent European singers Cuzzoni, Bordoni and the castrati Senesino and Farinelli. As his principal composer Handel engaged Giovanni Buononcini, who was especially popular in Italy, and whose operas were as successful as Handel's own. But in spite of these unquestioned glories and vast public success, the most dangerous enemy of the *opera seria* arose in London itself.

There had already been much public criticism of Neapolitan opera and it was only too easy to deride the ridiculous excesses of what was clearly a fashionable craze. But while polemical writings, like the famous satire *Teatro alla Moda* (*The Fashionable Theatre*), written in 1720 by Benedetto Marcello, added more to the popularity than to the disfavour of the opera they ridiculed, *opera seria* never completely recovered from the blow dealt it by *The Beggar's Opera*.

The Beggar's Opera (1728) was an inspired caricature of the baroque opera, and owed its effectiveness to its use of the same devices, stage settings, music and singing, with a simultaneous sharp parody of contemporary political events. The author of *The Beggar's Opera* was the poet John Gay (1685–1732), who had already written several libretti for Gluck. His composer (or rather 'arranger') was the extremely clever German Johann Christian Pepusch (1667–1752), who had settled in London in 1700. John Gay named his work *The Beggar's Opera*, pretending that it had been written by a beggar to celebrate the marriage of two street singers, James Chaunter and Moll Lay. In this way Gay pilloried the state occasion or royal marriage, for which operas were so often written, and the whole action of the work keeps to this theme. Instead of princes and princesses the characters are thieves and ladies of the town. The hero Macheath is the leader of a band of highwaymen, and also a police informer, and he carries on with six women at once. At the end Macheath is to be hanged, and is led to the place of execution accompanied by his women. But as is usual in an opera, the hero is pardoned, and the parody ends with the singing and dancing.

As everything in the text is a caricature, partly of opera and partly of contemporary conditions, the music is also conceived as a parody, with popular songs, dance-tunes and street cries to take the place of arias. [In the original there were sixty-nine numbers, of which twenty-eight were old English songs, fifteen old Irish, five old Scottish and three old French. The rest of the songs are attributed to individual composers.] Political satire and musical parody form a most effective unity, and the success of *The Beggar's Opera* was quite incredible: everyone rushed to see it, it was always sold out and the Italian opera had to close down.

But Handel was a long way from accepting defeat; quite the contrary, for after the Royal Academy of Music had collapsed financially he decided in 1729 to found an operatic enterprise of his own and to finance it out of his own savings. Once again he gathered together a brilliant ensemble of singers, and once again had great success. Some of the nobility, more from whim than malice, decided to start a rival venture with Buononcini as principal composer. It was obviously impossible for two such costly undertakings to last for long. In 1737, after years of struggle and alternating fortunes, both operas had to close.

Handel emerged completely exhausted, both physically and financially, from this struggle; his pleasure and his faith in opera, for which he had so devotedly worked for many years, were broken. And yet, on his return from a successful rest-cure in Aix-la-Chapelle, he wrote a further series of operas, among them one of his masterpieces, *Serse*. This he did only to placate his admirers, for he had now lost his pleasure in writing operas, or rather his enthusiasm for the stage. He therefore turned to another intermediate form with which he had already been successful some years earlier: this was the dramatic oratorio, which could not be performed on the English stage because of its biblical subject, and was only allowed in concert form.

The transition from opera to oratorio did not represent too drastic a change for Handel. The problems were mostly those of form and text, and involved certain important changes, particularly the use of English and the necessity for choosing biblical subjects. From the purely musical standpoint the oratorio brought certain very welcome innovations, for the *da capo* aria lost its predominance, the recitative was greatly reduced in size and choruses correspondingly enlarged. These biblical oratorios mostly have great dramatic intensity so that attempts to stage some of them are often made. In 1959 to celebrate the 200th anniversary of Handel's death, a new edition of *Belshazzar* was mounted with great success at Stuttgart. In England Covent Garden staged *Samson*, and there have also been stage productions of *Jephtha* and several secular vocal works, including *Hercules* and *Semele*.

Handel had already written the oratorio *Esther* in 1720, when he was music director at Cannons, the country seat of the Duke of Chandos at Edgware, Middlesex. It was originally only intended for concert performances, but its form clearly showed traces of opera. In the same year, also for concert performance, Handel wrote the pastoral *Acis and Galatea* to a secular text by John Gay—a charming little piece, which was also produced on the London stage in 1732. It still survives as a stage work, without needing any special editing.

ACIS AND GALATEA. Pastoral by George Frideric Handel. Text by John Gay.

Characters: Galatea—soprano; Acis—tenor; Polyphemus—bass.

Act I. An Arcadian landscape. Nymphs and shepherds praise the spring-time. Galatea alone does not share in the general delight, because her lover, the shepherd Acis, is not there. His return restores her happiness.

Act II. The chorus announces the approach of the savage giant Polyphemus, whose steps make the earth quake. Polyphemus is passionately in love with Galatea, who naturally will have nothing to do with him. Beside himself with rage and jealousy Polyphemus kills the unfortunate Acis with a rock. The nymphs and shepherds seek to console Galatea. At their suggestion she transforms her lover into a spring, to carry her love song 'whispering' into the valley.

The music for this idyll has all the charm of its period and a stylistically correct performance on a baroque stage can greatly increase its effect. The music is superbly illustrative: in the overture the chuckling of the nymphs is heard in the oboes, and in Galatea's first aria the trills of the flute and the sobbing of the violins imitate the chirruping of birds. In the famous aria 'As when the dove', the cooing lament of the dove is charmingly expressed in Galatea's little *glissandi*. Polyphemus is most forcefully characterized in the music. His unrestrained brutishness and clumsy lasciviousness are wonderfully expressed in vocal jumps, runs and trills, and his aria 'O ruddier than the cherry' is an outstanding example of Handelian characterization. The closing chorus with its imitation of the whispering of the spring is one of the most charming in this pastoral.

THE VICTORIOUS ADVANCE OF
COMIC OPERA

In the search for a humanistic ideal *opera seria* had arisen as a purely cultural product of the Renaissance, and its further development continued to be a privilege of the cultured classes. *Opera buffa* on the other hand sprang quite obviously from popular inspiration, in fact from the old Italian impromptu entertainment, the *commedia dell'arte*, which was transformed by the addition of music, without losing any of its simple originality and spontaneity.

The Italians have always taken a delight in parody and caricature and found ample scope for these pleasures in extempore entertainment. The sixteenth-century court interludes often tended in this direction and the popular *intermezzi* between the acts of the Venetian grand opera were based entirely on such gay parody. As music took an increasing part in these interludes, they were correspondingly forced to abandon their extempore character because the action, and therefore the text, had to follow the music. The standard characters and typical situations of the *commedia dell'arte* remained unchanged when set to music and so developed the full-length comedy with music, or *opera buffa*.

The grandiose world of *opera seria* with its kings and queens, its generals and princesses now found a counterpart in the world of the *petite bourgeoisie* typified by the old merchant Pantalone, the stutterer Tartaglia, and the impudent servants Arlecchino and Brighella. Their comic scenes are snatches from the daily life of the port, the tavern and back-street, the public square and the market-place, where the people live, love and laugh, where one joke follows another and where broad, quick humour reigns. The characters speak like ordinary people in deliberate contrast to the frequently stilted verses of *opera seria*. The circle of characters gradually widened during the period of Neapolitan opera to include the much travelled captain, the flamboyant soldier, the guileless doctor who shows off with Latin quotations, the attractive, sly serving-maid, the wise old nurse and the foreigner whose strange language alone is an inexhaustible source of ridiculous misunderstandings and mistaken identities.

Musically *opera buffa* has always been based on full and dexterous use of popular music. The natural lightness of popular songs and dances with their most diverse variations contrasted strikingly with the ponderous emotional style of the grand arias, and the public, tired of a certain monotony in these arias and long-winded recitatives, turned only too willingly to the simple language of *buffo* songs. With the success of *opera buffa* the composers of *opera seria* themselves started writing comic interludes and eventually full-length comic operas. When the great Scarlatti, and even Hasse, turned to this lighter art, the ban was lifted, and their example followed by almost all the composers of Neapolitan *opera seria*—Leo, Pergolesi, Paisiello, Traetta and Jomelli.

In the use of musical forms the comic opera is much freer and therefore richer than its serious counterpart. In contrast to the almost sterile form of *opera seria*, devoted to the virtuoso development of the *da capo* aria, light opera primarily introduced the *canzone*, based on a popular song, and then the rhyming song and dance-songs of all kinds, like the *siciliani* in light rocking $^6/_8$ time, which were always specially popular. The two- or three-part aria was by no means neglected, and coloratura was often used, though mostly in parody. The comic aria with its imitations of the typical extravagances of the serious aria, comic repetitions of words and so on was developed in great detail. From this fast, busy patter the so-called *parlando* style emerged—a light, running recitative derived from the rapid speech of Southern Italians, which became a basic characteristic of the *buffo* style.

One very important step was the reappearance of large ensembles and choral passages, which eventually developed into the so-called *finale*. Ensembles, artistically constructed songs for three, four or more voices, (trios, quartets, quintets, sextets and so on) had fallen into complete oblivion in the Neapolitan opera, and even duets had become a rarity. The *opera buffa* returned to the old forms which rendered its characters more effectively distinguishable from one another than the heroes and heroines of *opera seria*, who were tied to a standard pattern. The introduction of the *finale* in opera was an even more decisive, though very gradual, step. It developed from the simple song which brought the act to a close into a large ensemble, in which the most important musical moments of the act were repeated to form a striking climax. In its reappearance, however, as a continuous piece of music in Mozart's works, and later in nineteenth-century operas, it was based on recapitulation of the text. The wealth of *opera buffa* re-endowed *opera seria* and from then on any significant development of either form depended on inspiration from the other.

With Pergolesi's *intermezzo*, *La Serva Padrona*, the comic opera achieved its first real triumph. The first performance in 1733 in Naples passed unnoticed (it was performed between the acts of Pergolesi's serious opera, *Il Prigionier Superbo*). It was then produced in Graz in 1739, before reaching Paris in 1746, was given again there by an Italian troupe in 1752 and provoked such a tumult of enthusiasm that it can be said to have caused a revolution in French opera.

LA SERVA PADRONA. *Intermezzo* by Giovanni Battista Pergolesi. Text by Gennaro Antonio Federico. First performance: Naples, 1733.

Characters: Uberto, an old bachelor—bass; Serpina, his maid—soprano; Vespone, servant—mute part.

Place: Italy. *Time:* beginning of the eighteenth century.

Part I. Uberto is waiting impatiently for his breakfast which Serpina should be preparing for him. He sends Vespone to fetch her. Uberto knows only too well that it is his own fault if Serpina serves him so badly: he has spoiled her too much. She in turn knows that the old man depends on her and continually makes this clear, but when she really goes too far Uberto declares that he will marry. Serpina immediately asserts that she is the only suitable wife for him.

Part II. Serpina disguises Vespone as a soldier and presents him to Uberto as her fiancé. He wants, explains Serpina, 4,000 *scudi* from Uberto as a dowry, otherwise he will reject Serpina and then Uberto will have to marry her. Threats and tears finally compel Uberto to give way and he makes Serpina, the maid, his lady and wife.

The music which accompanies this comic plot flows easily, is full of most attractive ideas and sparkles with wit. The comic atmosphere is charmingly maintained in the arias, recitatives and the two duets which close each part; in addition *opera seria* is caricatured here and there. The two characters are most strikingly differentiated in their music—Uberto's short, tentative phrases contrast with the decisive flow of Serpina's music.

In order to build up one-act *intermezzi* into self-contained operas the range of characters in these stories had to be continually widened. The pair of lovers and the difficulties they encounter became the nucleus of the plot: supposed infidelity, jealousy and despair, or forcible separation and daring abduction. Under the influence of sentimental rococo poetry *opera buffa* acquired a new tenderness, but of course the usual amusing misunderstandings and disguises and the grotesque scenes of beatings and drunkenness still had to be included. The similarity between the two types of opera now applied to the subject-matter as well, except that in *opera seria* classical and medieval settings were the rule, while in *opera buffa* events, settings and costumes were always contemporary and as lifelike as possible. After all the rococo costumes in which these *buffo* operas are performed today were the everyday clothing of a mid-eighteenth-century audience, and the sensibility of Richardson's heroes and heroines was to the spectators a perfectly natural emotion.

The most admired work of the time was *La Buona Figliuola* (*The good daughter*) (also known as *La Cecchina*), written in 1760 by Niccolò Piccinni (1728–1800). Based on Richardson's *Pamela*, the work was first produced in Rome; it has recently been successfully revived in Italy. Piccinni most skilfully blended the gay and the touching so as to arouse not merely ridicule, but compassion as well. His delicate individual characterizations point directly to Mozart, but the greatest significance of Piccinni's work lies in his witty vocal and instrumental elaboration of themes related to the individual characters.

Coarser, and therefore nearer to popular taste than Piccinni, was Giovanni Paisiello (1740–1816), who further developed the *buffo* idiom in melody and rhythmic grace, and who was in every way, but especially in his artistic orchestration, a direct forerunner of Mozart and Rossini. Paisiello's *Il Barbiere di Siviglia* (*The Barber of Seville*) is still popular in Italy, but elsewhere it has been completely displaced by Rossini's masterpiece of the same name.

Of the innumerable Italian comic operas of the eighteenth century, which show a positive superabundance of charming musical ideas, only *Il Matrimonio Segreto* (*The Secret Marriage*) by Domenico Cimarosa (1749–1801) is well-known outside Italy. This delightful work with its graceful, pure rococo music has been enthusiastically received ever since its first performance in 1792 in Vienna when, according to reports, it was repeated the same night at the request of Emperor Leopold II.

IL MATRIMONIO SEGRETO (The Secret Marriage). Comic opera in two acts by Domenico Cimarosa. Text by G. Bartati after the play *The Clandestine Marriage* by Colman and Garrick. First performance: Vienna, 1792.

Characters: Geronimo, a merchant—baritone; Elisetta and Carolina, his daughters—sopranos; Fidalma, his sister—mezzo-soprano; Paolino, clerk to Geronimo—tenor; Count Robinson—bass.

Place: Bologna. *Time:* Late eighteenth century.

The rich merchant Geronimo has only one wish: to find aristocratic husbands for his daughters, Elisetta and Carolina, but the latter has already given her heart to Paolino, her father's industrious clerk. So as to make a good impression on his employer, Paolino introduces the impecunious Count Robinson, who writes to ask for Elisetta's hand. This causes great joy, and the Count is received most ceremoniously by everyone, but unfortunately he likes Carolina much better at first sight than his affianced Elisetta. Elisetta is furious, and accuses Carolina of causing her misery. She finds an ally in her aunt Fidalma who herself has her eye on Paolino and regards Carolina as her rival. Both of them complain bitterly to Geronimo who orders Carolina to be confined in a convent as punishment for her supposed coquetry. Paolino comes stealthily by night to elope with his beloved. A noise makes the lovers hide in Carolina's room where Elisetta overhears a hurried whisper and gives the alarm. Father, aunt and Count come in. Carolina and Paolino now confess that they have already been secretly married for eight weeks. Geronimo, who has to acknowledge his clerk's cleverness, gives them both his blessing. The Count turns to Elisetta, and the aunt submits to the inevitable.

The Italian troupe which performed Pergolesi's *La Serva Padrona* in Paris in 1752 was by no means outstandingly good, but when they aroused a real storm of enthusiasm and played incessantly to full houses for almost three years, with *La Serva Padrona* and a few other unimportant short operas, it was a clear sign that baroque opera was nearing its end. Just as in Italy *opera seria* was losing its hold, so it was in France with *tragédie lyrique*. The leaders of the *Aufklärung* (the name [literally: enlightenment] usually given to the rationalist movement in thought and letters which spread through Europe in the eighteenth century), Diderot, d'Alembert, Friedrich Melchior Grimm and especially Jean-Jacques Rousseau were passionate partisans of *opera buffa* and successfully fought out the pros and cons in a literary war which excited a great deal of notice. This battle between the *bouffonistes*, who championed the comic opera, and the *anti-bouffonistes*, who clung to the French tradition, was more than a fight over mere operatic ideal; it was obviously a precursor of the Revolution. It was a welcome opportunity to inveigh against the French tradition, against an old culture in which the stiff pathos inherited from Rameau's operas made a perfect target for attack. The new doctrine of free expression of feeling, and the sovereignty of nature over court, society and tradition could well found its ideal on *opera buffa*, which was in fact ready to break with any tradition. It had already thrown grandiose format overboard, condemned elaborate décor and stage machinery as unnecessary encumbrances, and sought its vindication in simplicity.

Rousseau, an enthusiastic and successful amateur composer, was the first to write a French opera to challenge *La Serva Padrona*, and thereby proved that the French language was suitable for singing. In 1752, shortly after attending the famous performances of *La Serva Padrona* in Paris, he wrote the verses and music for a short opera entitled *Le Devin du Village* (*The Village Soothsayer*). In the same year this first *opéra comique* was performed at Fontainebleau before the King and his court. It was so enthusiastically received that in March 1753 further performances were given at the Académie, where it had an unprecedented success.

The plot of *Le Devin du Village*, which has only three characters, is more than primitive; the little arias and duets are simple and artless resembling French folk songs, but its simplicity was delightfully novel to the audience who applauded loudly.

This is a grotesque situation: Louis XV, the last great representative of absolute monarchy, mounts in his private theatre a new work written by the principal exponent of the approaching Revolution; opposite the royal box sits Rousseau himself, unshaven and refusing an audience with the King, who is delighted with his opera.

The unquestioned success of *Le Devin du Village* in no way resolved the conflict. On the contrary, the struggle went on bitterly, with Rousseau still shouting the loudest that French opera should align itself completely with Italian taste, and denying that French vocal music had any rights. This anti-nationalist behaviour of his was strongly criticized by his antagonists and finally even resulted in the Italian troupe having to leave Paris after two years of enormous success. Such a purely superficial victory could not however prevent the acknowledgement of the fact that the *tragédie lyrique* had lost its importance and was considered retrograde.

Opéra comique, the French comic opera, the lucky winner in this great struggle, grew quickly. A true child of its time, it dealt with the latest occurrences, reflected the overall contemporary scene and depicted life and activities on all social levels. It was much nearer to truth and more realistic than the Italian *opera buffa*, which never freed itself from a strict formula.

True to Rousseau's cry of 'Back to nature', country life was now the deliberate first choice as a setting for French comic operas, followed by the dreary middle-class milieu; sentimentality had become the fashion in France.

The most important external characteristic of the *opéra comique* was the spoken dialogue, a residue of the old French *vaudeville*, and this unstylish feature, which never secured a foothold in Italian opera, has survived to our day. The term *opéra comique* implies therefore a mixture of singing and spoken dialogue even where there is no question of comedy and the subject is weighty and serious. From the French point of view even Beethoven's *Fidelio* falls within this category.

While the *recitativo secco* was completely neglected, the dramatic *accompagnato* still kept its importance as an introduction to the great arias. The most important form in these works was a short song, called an *arietta* or *romance*, which was generally a love song and only occasionally retained traces of the ballad. Other features included small ensemble sections, especially duets, choruses of, for instance, fishermen, hunters or soldiers, and almost always a ballet.

The real founder of the *opéra comique* was Egidio Romoaldo Duni (1709–75). Italian by birth like Lully, and possessed of an extraordinary gift for orchestration, he seized on and increased the French love of great tone-paintings in opera. Such descriptive pieces as his storm interludes, hunting scenes or village merry-making have since Duni's time been accepted as integral parts of a comic opera.

The most important early representative of *opéra comique* was the Belgian André Ernest Modeste Grétry (1741–1813), the immediate forerunner of the great names in later *opéra comique*, Boieldieu, Adam and Auber. In Grétry's works the *opéra comique* reached complete perfection in every way. All kinds of romantic ideas governed his emotional world and widened the range of musical expression. Of his numerous operas the best was *Richard Cœur-de-Lion* (1784), but none of them have survived. [Sir Thomas Beecham revived *Zémire et Azor* at the 1955 Bath Festival.]

The German equivalent of *opera buffa* and *opéra comique*, the *Singspiel*, also sprang from the reaction against the now super-seded heroic opera, but this movement originated in England. In 1743 the burlesque *The Devil is among us or The Exchanged Wives* was enthusiastically received in Berlin. It was a transla-tion from the English, an adaptation of a coarse musical farce in the manner of Gay's and Pepusch's famous *Beggar's Opera*. The great success of this piece induced the Leipzig poet Christoph Felix Weisse (1726–1804) to write a new version in 1752, for which Johann Georg Standfuss (d. 1756) wrote the music. So the first *Singspiel*, produced in Leipzig under the title of *Der Teufel ist Los*, with original German tunes, was born with its form and character already well shaped.

The English example was soon forgotten, and instead French influence was for a long time so decisive that the German *Singspiel* followed the French *opéra comique* through all stages of its development, from the rural comedy through the senti-mental middle-class story to the romantic fairy-tale opera, the *féerie*. The fashionable disease of the time, sentimentality, found a fruitful breeding-ground in Germany, the *Singspiel* being a particularly suitable vehicle, except that here sentimentality mostly deteriorated into pathos and the middle-class cosiness of the French models often turned into real bourgeois loutishness.

Weisse, who after Standfuss's death worked with Johann Adam Hiller (1728–1804), was extremely successful with his *Singspiele* modelled on the French pattern, in which Hiller with his considerable original talent played a decisive part. His strength lay in his songs and ariettas with gentle, touching, popular melodies.

Hiller's most successful *Singspiele* were *Lottchen am Hofe* (*Lottie at the Court*) (1767), *Der Erntekrantz* (*The Harvest Garland*) (1771) and *Die Jagd* (*The Hunt*) (1770), which contained the song 'Als ich auf meiner Bleiche' ('When on my pallor') which was then sung by all young girls. Besides such popular songs, however, Hiller's *Singspiele* also included grand arias in the style of the *opera seria* with the intriguing difference that these arias were only sung by the upper classes, whereas the songs were left to the peasants and servants. Goethe himself was so captivated by these *Singspiele* that he wrote a series of texts which greatly enriched their rather narrow realm of thought. Some of these texts, however, such as *Claudine von Villabella, Jery und Bätely* or *Lila*, were too refined and stylish to compete with Weisse's agreeable rustic pieces.

Georg Benda (1722–95) was perhaps even more varied than Hiller in the form and expression of his music. His numerous *Singspiele*, for instance *Der Dorfjahrmarkt* (*The Village Fair*) (1775), were widely known. In certain stylistic details, such as songs with variations and descriptive orchestration, Hiller and Benda are forerunners of Mozart. The atmosphere and feeling of the time is nowhere so effectively captured as in the *Singspiele*: they are pure German rococo.

Once the Emperor Josef II had expressly commanded that musical performances should be sung to German words, these *Singspiele* began to appear in Vienna, thereby obtaining official imperial recognition and support. The first work performed there was *Die Bergknappen* (*The Mountaineers*) (1778) by Ignaz Umlauff (1746–96), who was followed by Karl Ditters von Dittersdorf (1739–99), the man responsible for establishing the genre of the German *Singspiel* in Vienna. His best work *Doktor und Apotheker* (*The Doctor and the Chemist*) (1786) can still be seen in Germany, but unfortunately his numerous other works (which include a *Die Lustigen Weiber von Windsor* and a *Die Hochzeit des Figaro*) have fallen into complete oblivion together with the musically important *Singspiele* of Hiller and Benda, not to mention countless pieces by their many colleagues. This is because their texts are unbearably naïve and simple for our taste. The success of the *Singspiel* depended on the popular nature of the tunes with their lilting rhythms and light-hearted spirit. The music is hardly ever dramatic in spite of the grandly conceived *finale*, and individual characterization, as we find it later in Mozart's works, was only suggested. But songs like this one from *Doktor und Apotheker* were understandably successful.

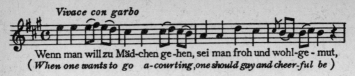

Wenn man will zu Mäd-chen ge-hen, sei man froh und wohl-ge-mut,
(*When one wants to go   a-courting, one should gay and cheer-ful be*)

It is just becoming generally known again that Joseph Haydn (1732–1809), the great master of the symphony, also wrote a series of long and short stage works. He composed for the Esterházy castle theatre, subsequently also for the imperial court at Vienna, and sometimes even for the puppet theatre, which was very popular in Vienna at the time. Most of these operas were written to Italian texts in the style of the Neapolitan *opera seria* or *opera buffa*, and only a few of them had German libretti. Haydn was not very fortunate with his operas, which rarely attained popularity outside the place where they were first performed. Only *Lo Speziale* (*The Chemist*) (1768), a charming little comic opera, became more widely known. Even though the text is by Goldoni it was already conceived in the spirit and style of the German *Singspiel*. The music is continuous and flowing. The recitatives are accompanied by strings, to which woodwind and horns are added for the arias and ensembles, and triangles and drums as well for the *finale* so as to give oriental colour to the entrance of the pseudo-Turks. This very witty closing section is the climax of an innocuous but very charming opera.

In recent years another full-length opera by Haydn has been frequently performed—*Il Mondo della Luna*, also to a text by Goldoni. The libretto is witty and the music light and rhythmical, so that the work has met with much success.

IL MONDO DELLA LUNA (The World on the Moon). Comic opera in three acts by Joseph Haydn. Text based on a play by Carlo Goldoni. First performance: Esterházy, 1777.

Characters: Ecclitico, a pseudo-astrologer—tenor; Buonafede, a rich merchant—baritone; Ernesto, a nobleman—tenor; Cecco, his valet—tenor; Flaminia and Clarice, Buonafede's daughters—sopranos; Lisetta, his housekeeper—mezzo-soprano. Pupils of Ecclitico and dancers.

Place: Italy. *Time:* eighteenth century.

Act I, scene i. Ecclitico's house. With the help of his pupils, Ecclitico sets up his spurious telescope, revelling in his role as impostor. He takes in Buonafede, who presents himself as an amateur of astrology, with stories of being able to see all the goings-on on the moon through his telescope, and by trickery shows him scenes which so titillate the mean old man's lascivious appetite that he even offers Ecclitico money, and departs, delighted. Ecclitico, Ernesto and Cecco bewail the fact that Buonafede stands between them and their loves, but Ecclitico is confident of victory through money (to be provided by Ernesto) and commonsense, which the latter lacks.

Scene ii. Buonafede's house, where Clarice and Flaminia are also bewailing Buonafede's tyranny over their lives. When he enters, Clarice is ready to rebel and her father threatens to send her to the moon to teach her a lesson, but for quite another reason he will also take Lisetta, who however protests her virtue and honesty. Ecclitico enters to announce that he has been summoned to the presence of the Lunar Emperor, who sprays an elixir on him through a telescope to make the journey possible. When Buonafede demands and is given some of the elixir he faints, believing he is on his way to the moon. While Flaminia and Clarice rush out to fetch help, Ecclitico has the unconscious Buonafede removed, and on their return shows the girls a will by which their father will leave them large sums of money provided they marry.

Act II. Ecclitico's garden, disguised as a moonscape. Buonafede is regaled with 'lunatic' tricks which completely deceive him, including apparently magical music played off-stage. Dressed in a special garment, he is presented to the Emperor (Cecco) attended by Hesperus (Ernesto), who reads him a lecture on treating women with occasional severity. When Buonafede woos Lisetta, however, she is removed by Cecco to be his Empress. Buonafede sends for his daughters, and when Cecco appoints Hesperus and Ecclitico to attend them he dare not object as ill-humour is forbidden on the moon. Lisetta is crowned Empress in an idiotic ceremonial. Buonafede cheerfully parts with the keys to his coffers when told he must provide dowries, for, he says, his money is of no use to him on the moon. Now their wishes are realized, the conspirators drop all the pretence and Buonafede sees how he has been duped.

Act III. Having at first protested, Buonafede is persuaded to pardon everyone and his keys are returned to him. The opera ends with general rejoicing and satisfaction with the lessons learned and rewards received as a result of the visit to the world of the moon.

The Vienna National Singspiel lasted only about ten years, in spite of some outstanding successes, among them Mozart's *Die Entführung aus dem Serail*, but although it then lost its official position, the *Singspiel* by no means died out in Vienna. It had already become so popular that two theatres took it in, and in both an honest attempt was made to maintain the artistic level by good musical performances, careful presentation and expensive scenery. Fantastic fairy-tale and magical pieces, for which complicated décor and machinery were needed, became

very popular. Soon however there crept in a tendency to pander
to the cruder taste of lesser folk, and this manner was encouraged
by the introduction of the *Kasperl*, and with him the Viennese
suburban slang. (Kasperl is a Punch-like character, native to
Vienna, descended from the old Viennese Hans Wurst, who is
the centre of various broadly comic episodes in plays of strictly
local and mainly topical significance.)

The various tendencies of the Viennese *Singspiel* were united
in the person of one versatile theatrical personality—Emanuel
Schikaneder (1751–1812). A successful impresario—he managed
the Theater auf der Wieden, one of the two rival *Singspiel*
theatres—he was also a popular actor, an inspired producer and
a most talented librettist. His exceptional versatility is clear
from his text for Mozart's *Die Zauberflöte* in which he strove to
unify the heterogeneous elements. His love for grand opera is
as obvious in this work as his love for fairy-tales and simple
farce, and so *Die Zauberflöte* (1791) forms a focal point in the
development of the Viennese *Singspiel*. The works of the most
famous *Singspiel* composers, such as Ferdinand Kauer's *Donau-
weibchen* (*The Girl of the Danube*) (1798), Joseph Weigl's
Schweizerfamilie (*The Swiss family*) (1809), or Peter von
Winter's *Das Unterbrochene Opferfest* (*The interrupted sacrifice*)
(1796), were foils to *Die Zauberflöte*, which overshadowed them
all.

The principal Viennese *Singspiele* mentioned above all incline
towards serious opera, but Johann Schenk's *Dorfbarbier* (*The
Village Barber*) (1796), followed the lighter, popular tendency.
It was an enchanting work with most penetrating humour.
The simple plot is enlivened by witty exchanges, comic situations and lively, bubbling music, which is throughout merry or
mocking without falling into the sentimental tone which was
so popular at the time.

Among the Viennese *Singspiel* composers, Wenzel Müller
(1767–1835) was by far the most successful; his crude and primitive works, which sometimes drifted into real musical farce,
always found enthusiastic audiences. With their robust humour
and striking tunes they helped to prepare the way for the
Viennese operetta. The original Viennese *Singspiel* with its
varied forms played an important part as the forerunner of
several other genres of art.

CHRISTOPH WILLIBALD GLUCK

Opera buffa established itself extraordinarily quickly in public favour, and the previously unchallenged dominance of *opera seria* was now seriously threatened. Neapolitan opera had never lacked adequate musical talent and *opera seria's* loss of popularity was due not to the music, but to the texts and the stereotyped forms in which the Neapolitan opera had become fettered. From Vienna the great Metastasio exercised an absolute dictatorship over opera, and nobody dared resist him. To Gluck must go the credit for taking the bold, decisive step which broke his rule.

Christoph Willibald Gluck (1714–87) was not only a great musician, he was first and foremost a great personality. The rich and varied experiences of his life had moulded his character. For twenty years he travelled all over Europe, and wrote countless operas strongly influenced by Handel, Rameau and Hasse. *Orfeo* (1762) was the first work in which Gluck made a determined and deliberate attempt to reform the whole essence of opera. His collaborator was the poet Ranieri da Calzabigi (1714–95), who, like him, was convinced of the need for reform, and the two artists were ideally complementary. Their first aim was to free operatic plots from the wilderness of subsidiary action and to concentrate on one grand and noble dramatic subject. The over-elaborate rococo verses of the school of the omnipotent Metastasio were to be replaced by clear, graceful, classical language, and the vocal line was to be cleared of all ornament, trills, unnecessary runs and coloratura. Following the French operatic custom, chorus and ballet were to be frequently introduced, but only when relevant to the context. The most important result of these drastic changes was the relaxing of existing rigid forms. The *da capo* aria gave way to short passages closely connected with the dramatic action and the *recitativo secco* was completely eliminated in favour of a continuous, unified musical line.

ORFEO ED EURIDICE. Opera in three acts by Christoph Willibald Gluck. Text by Ranieri da Calzabigi. First performance: Vienna, 1762.
    Characters: Orfeo (Orpheus)—contralto (originally written for the male contralto, Guadagni. When given for the first time in Paris in 1774,

the tenor Legros sang the role. It was first sung by a female contralto in 1859, when Berlioz revised the score and Pauline Viardot-Garcia sang Orpheus.); Euridice (Eurydice), his wife—soprano; Amor (Eros)—soprano.

Place and time: Ancient Greece.

Act I. A wood with Eurydice's tomb. Orpheus is mourning his dead wife and his lament mingles with that of his companions, who in chorus entreat her to return. When they have left him, Orpheus cries aloud to Eros, the god of love, to restore his beloved to him or to let him die, so that he can rejoin her. Eros appears, sent by Zeus himself. The gods have decreed that Orpheus may journey to the Underworld to fetch Eurydice back, but on one condition: he must not look back at his beloved until he reaches the surface of the earth again, or her life will be forfeit and he will lose her for ever.

Act II. The entrance to Hades. The spirits of the Underworld refuse Orpheus admittance with a cruelly unyielding repeated 'No', but the beauty of his voice melts even the Furies, the iron doors of the Underworld open, and the Elysian Fields shine with eternal light and splendour. The blessed spirits lead Orpheus to his beloved.

Act III. A rocky cavern. Orpheus and Eurydice are on their way to the upper world. He walks in front without turning to face her and she follows him reluctantly because she cannot understand his reserve. She doubts his love and implores the gods to send her back to Hades. This is too much for Orpheus. Her lament breaks his heart, he turns to her and immediately she falls lifeless at his feet. When Orpheus tries to kill himself in his despair, Eros seizes his arm. To reward such faithful love, Eros calls Eurydice back to life and the lovers joyfully embrace.

Concentration on the main action is complete; there are only three characters in *Orfeo*, an unheard-of innovation at the time, but the chorus and ballet take an important part in the plot throughout. Gluck's music is almost statuesque in its grandeur and nobility. In the first act the mime of the mourners, a moving short passage in E-flat major, and the soft choral lament of Orpheus's friends make a deep impression. The musical climax comes in the second act, in the famous scene

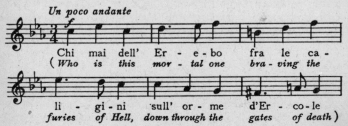

with the Furies and their harsh 'No' to Orpheus's moving love lament, and in the wonderful transition from the night of Hades into the light of Elysium. Here we are greeted by the enchanting song of the Blessed Spirits and Orpheus's great

monologue 'Che puro ciel' ('What pure light'), in which he wonders at the joys of Elysium, the radiant sky, the whispering streams, the rustling breezes and the singing winds, where Eurydice's tender and lovely aria is heard. The most famous passage in the work is the third act aria 'Che farò senz'Euridice' ('What is life to me without thee'), which some may think does not quite meet the situation. One expects here a desperate outburst rather than a quietly resigned lament.

The second work in which Gluck continued his reform was *Alceste* (1766). Here too the main subject is that of conjugal love and again Calzabigi has co-operated in all Gluck's wishes.

In the famous foreword to this opera, Gluck expressed himself very clearly. 'My intention was to purify music from all the abuses which have crept into Italian opera through the vanity of the singers and the excessive compliance of the composers and have made the most splendid and beautiful of all arts the most ridiculous and boring. I tried therefore to bring musicians back to their real task of serving the poetry, by intensifying the expression of emotion and the appeal of every situation, without interrupting the plot or weakening it by unnecessary ornamentation.'

In *Orfeo* Gluck had already completely abolished overelaboration of the vocal line, but the title role was still sung by a castrato, whereas in *Alceste* Gluck broke with this barbarous habit as well.

ALCESTE. Opera in three acts by Christoph Willibald Gluck. Text by Ranieri da Calzabigi. First performance: Vienna, 1767.

Characters: Roi Admète (Admetus)—tenor; Alceste (Alcestis), his wife—soprano; Hercule (Hercules)—baritone; Apollon (Apollo)—baritone; High Priest—baritone; Thanatos—baritone; Evandre (Evander)—tenor.

Place: Thessaly. *Time:* mythical antiquity.

Act I. King Admetus is dead, deeply mourned by his wife Alcestis and by all his people. The oracle of Apollo reveals that his life could be restored if another would give up life willingly for him. Alcestis is ready to make this sacrifice.

Act II. Restored to life, Admetus is greeted and praised by his people. Evander tells him about the condition imposed by the oracle, but does not reveal the name of the victim. Alcestis, unable to conceal her grief, tells him that she is the victim. Admetus refuses to accept the sacrifice. The Queen, left alone with the people, shares their grief.

Act III. Admetus has followed Alcestis into the Underworld, for he cannot and will not accept her sacrifice. When he confronts Thanatos, the god of death, he dares to defy him. Alcestis is torn from his arms, but by the intervention of Hercules the loving pair is finally reunited.

Gluck wrote music of great nobility for *Alceste*, starting with a magnificent overture. In his foreword he stipulated that 'The overture should prepare the spectator for the plot and so to speak present its contents'. The most important piece of music

in the opera is Alceste's great aria 'Divinités du Styx' ('Hear me, ye Stygian Gods') which closes the first act.

The dramatic recitative scenes of the oracle, and of Alceste's declaration that she had dedicated herself to death, are exceptionally impressive, and in both scenes the chorus plays an important part. The dramatic tension of the opera relaxes greatly towards the end—understandably, since the climax of the plot comes in the first act. The intervention of Hercules as *deus ex machina* is neither dramatically nor musically satisfactory.

The next of Gluck's 'reform' operas, *Paride e Elena* (*Paris and Helen*) written in 1770, is virtually devoid of physical action. Here Calzabigi and Gluck have gone too far in their conscious avoidance of by-play, and concentrated everything on the psychological juxtaposition of the characters of Paris and Helen, so that an inner conflict develops through the five acts of the opera, without any external happenings. Gluck was very angry at this criticism (which was also to be levelled at Wagner's *Tristan und Isolde*). The music of this work is perhaps his most valuable legacy to posterity, but nevertheless it was received very coolly by the Viennese public, who found it too strange in character.

The fact that his reforming operas were so little understood in Vienna made Gluck decide to move to Paris, especially when an attaché at the French Embassy in Vienna, F. L. G. Lebland du Roullet, gave him a skilful libretto adapted from Racine's *Iphigénie* and held out the prospect of staging the opera in the French capital, where he had good connections. Even so not all the opposition was easily overcome and the influence of Marie Antoinette, Gluck's former pupil, had to be invoked before *Iphigénie en Aulide* was performed at the Paris Opéra. The most brilliant part of the score is the overture, which conforms perfectly to Gluck's requirements.

No less a person than Wagner, a sincere admirer of Gluck's genius, re-edited this work in 1846, changing the orchestration, rewriting some of the recitatives and introducing a new character (Artemis) in Act III. In accordance with the taste prevailing in Gluck's day, *Iphigénie* originally ended with the gods, suddenly placated, sending a favourable wind, while the happy lovers Achilles and Iphigenia were fêted with dancing and singing. Wagner replaced this finale, which deviated from the whole feeling of the opera, with the abduction of Iphigenia as told by Euripides, which leads directly to Gluck's *Iphigénie en Tauride*.

The memorable première of Gluck's first *Iphigénie* opera in Paris in 1774 was greeted with wild enthusiasm, and the performance was interrupted several times by thunderous applause. When Achilles sang his warrior's song, all the officers present leapt spontaneously to their feet and drew their swords with military enthusiasm. When Clytemnestra and Iphigenia were greeted with the chorus 'Que d'attraits, que de majesté' the audience paid homage to the Queen as patron of the performance. The French public appreciated Gluck's style more readily than could ever have been the case in Vienna. In Paris, where the Rameau tradition was still very much alive, Gluck's ideas on the unity of poetry, music and décor fell on well-prepared ground; vigorous declamation and the prominence of the chorus were also to Parisian taste.

As a consequence of Gluck's success, which was enormously enhanced by performances of *Orfeo* and *Alceste* in French, disciples of Italian opera summoned to Paris as their champion Niccolò Piccinni, whose *Buona Figliuola* had made him popular there. The strife between *bouffonistes* and *antibouffonistes*, which twenty years previously had roused so much temper, broke out anew in a struggle between Gluckists and Piccinnists. Piccinni himself was drawn into this struggle against his will, for he admired Gluck too much to want to oppose him, but when in 1778 he tried to withdraw his opera *Roland*, which should have been performed in competition with Gluck's *Armide*, and to leave Paris in secret, destiny decided for him. *Armide* was a failure, while *Roland* was triumphantly successful, and rightly so, since it was a masterpiece of subtle characterization. Besides, in this work as in all his later serious operas, Piccinni had really observed Gluck's principles. The music is not divided into numbers but into scenes which follow the ideas of the text, and recitatives and *arioso* melodies exist within a spacious musical framework.

Piccinni's acceptance of Gluck's reforms made any further struggle between them superfluous, but it still continued between the two opposing groups of opera enthusiasts. Gluck wisely kept himself apart and let nothing distract him or deflect

him from his clearly acknowledged path. This is evident from
Iphigénie en Tauride (1779), in which Gluck again collaborated
with Calzabigi, whose text was simply translated into French.
The importance of this work was acknowledged at once and
without reservation. This was for Gluck the realization of the
ideal which had always hovered before him.

IPHIGÉNIE EN TAURIDE. Opera in four acts by Christoph Willibald
Gluck. Text by François Guillard after Euripides's play. First performance: Paris 1779.

Characters: Iphigénie (Iphigenia), High Priestess of Diana—soprano;
Oreste (Orestes), her brother—baritone; Pylade (Pylades), his friend—
tenor; Thoas, King of Scythia—bass; Diane (Diana)—soprano.

Place: Tauris. *Time:* after the end of the Trojan War.

Act I. Before the Temple of Diana. Iphigenia relates to the priestesses
and Greek maidens a dream she has had in which she beheld once again
her native land beset by misfortune. She implores the goddess to end
her life and reunite her with her father and brother. Thoas, King of
Scythia, who compels Iphigenia to sacrifice all strangers on the altar of
Diana, now enters. He demands a further sacrifice to ward off fresh
dangers of which he has been warned. A Scythian announces that two
young Greeks (Orestes and his friend Pylades), who have been forced by
a storm to land on the shores of Tauris, have been taken prisoner. Orestes
tells of a crime he has committed and of his pursuit by Furies, from
whom he seeks relief in death. Iphigenia protests at the cruel rites she
constantly has to fulfil and enters the temple with her priestesses. Thoas
exhorts the people to show their pleasure to the gods for having sent
new victims. Orestes and Pylades are led in and Thoas orders the guards
to take them to the temple of Diana.

Act II. The Temple of Diana. Orestes and Pylades are in chains. The
former laments his fate and the latter sings of their undying friendship.
Pylades is led away by the guards, and Orestes left alone thinks that the
end of sufferings is now at hand, and feels his peace of mind returning.
He falls asleep and the Furies rise up and accuse him of his mother's death.
Iphigenia enters and the Furies vanish. She begins to question Orestes
and learns that he is a Greek. She asks about Agamemnon and the fate
of the Greeks. Orestes does not reveal his identity but tells Iphigenia
that Agamemnon (their father) has been murdered by his wife, Clytemnestra, whose son, Orestes, has killed her in revenge and is himself
dead. Of the family only Electra remains. Orestes is led away, and
Iphigenia asks the priestesses to join with her in mourning her brother.

Act III. Iphigenia's apartment in the Temple. Iphigenia is struck by
the resemblance of the prisoner to her brother and resolves to save him
from the sacrifice. The two prisoners are now brought in and Iphigenia
reveals to them that she also is of Grecian birth. She can only save one of
their lives, and therefore asks Orestes to deliver a message to Electra.
The two friends are left alone while Iphigenia goes to write her message.

Orestes, who has no desire to live, declines to leave Pylades to his fate, and only when he says that he will kill himself rather than accept freedom and leave his friend to die, does Pylades agree to take the letter to Electra in his place. Iphigenia returns and, learning what has been decided, gives Pylades the letter to take to Electra. Pylades thanks the goddess for her favours and promises to save Orestes or die himself.

Act IV. The Temple of Diana. Everything is ready for the sacrifice. Iphigenia implores Diana to harden her heart so that she can perform the terrible deed. Orestes is now led in and prepared for the sacrifice by the priestesses. As Iphigenia raises the knife to slay Orestes, he utters the words 'Ainsi tu péris en Aulide, Iphigénie ma soeur!' ('Thus you perished in Aulis, Iphigenia, my sister'). Iphigenia reveals her identity and brother and sister embrace. Iphigenia acknowledges him as King. Thoas and his soldiers rush in, accusing Iphigenia of betrayal, and demanding the sacrifice. Iphigenia defies Thoas, saying that Orestes is her brother and Agamemnon's heir. She dares him to approach and exhorts the priestesses to defend their King. Pylades and a troop of Grecian soldiers rush in; a fight ensues in which Thoas is killed. The goddess Diana descends from the clouds. She forgives Orestes and Iphigenia, and bids the Greeks return to Mycenae with her statue which the Scythians had stolen. The opera ends with a joyful chorus.

H. D. R.

Through the powerful construction of individual scenes Gluck achieved amazing musical effect in this his last work. The recitative at the beginning of the first act in which Iphigenia relates her dream is fantastically impressive because of its extremely sparse orchestration, and the *arioso* outburst which follows with its mournful accompaniment from the chorus of women is among Gluck's most inspired music. The noblest scene of the opera is that in which Iphigenia and the priestesses join in mourning the supposedly dead Orestes. After Iphigenia's moving aria 'Malheureuse Iphigénie', the sacrificial vessels are

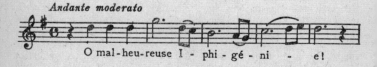

Andante moderato

O mal-heu-reuse I - phi-gé-ni - e!

lit with song and dance and all join together in prayer. This charming short phrase already appeared as the chorus of greet-

ing in *Iphigénie en Aulide*. With its sorrowful modulation to the minor this expressive melody is much more suitable here in the memorial for Orestes's death. Gluck frequently introduces melodies from earlier works in accordance with the practice of most of his contemporaries.

Iphigénie en Tauride was Gluck's last work. In 1780 he returned to Vienna, his robust health seriously impaired. He left his pupil, Antonio Salieri (1750–1825), to write *Les Danaïdes*, which he was to have composed in 1784 for Paris, and the opera was performed under their joint names. Only after the work was fully established did Salieri reveal that he was the sole author.

Gluck's attempts at reform were of course most effective in France. His ideas survived in the work of Salieri, and more particularly in that of Antonio Maria Gasparo Sacchini (1730–86). Sacchini's *Oedipe à Colone* (1786) with its demonic accentuation and dramatic outbursts apparently far outstripped Gluck; it was received with tremendous applause and lasted for at least ten years on the French stage.

Among Gluck's French successors, Étienne Nicolas Méhul (1763–1817) is the most important. His main work, *Joseph* (1807), represented textually a great exception in the history of opera, because of the absence of female characters and therefore of any love interest (the only other instances being Pfitzner's *Palestrina* and Britten's *Billy Budd*). Weber acknowledged the great dramatic truth of Méhul's music, which achieves its tremendous effects with the simplest means. This peculiar work kept its place in the German theatre until the beginning of this century.

In Italy Gluck's style was spread by Simon Mayr (1763–1845) and his pupils. German by birth, Mayr lived and worked in Bergamo for many years and from there decisively influenced the development of Italian opera. He reintroduced the chorus, made the orchestra independent and wrote larger ensembles. He also most skilfully composed crowd-scenes with self-contained stage bands and similar effects. His works, and those of his pupil Saverio Mercadante (1795–1870), dominated the Italian operatic scene for a long time, but were then completely forgotten, though his manner was preserved in the works of his pupil Donizetti. From among Gluck's later successors, two strong, self-willed personalities emerged—Cherubini and Spontini. Through these two important artists may be traced the lineal descent of essential nineteenth-century opera development. Gasparo Spontini (1774–1851) enjoyed his greatest operatic triumph with *La Vestale* (*The Vestal Virgin*), a work which impressed the young Richard Wagner so much that he quite openly used it as a model for *Rienzi*. *La Vestale* (1807) (revived at the Metropolitan, New York, in 1925 for Rosa Ponselle, and at La Scala, Milan, in 1955 for Maria Callas) is full of pure dramatic passion; Gluck's forms are here suffused with glowing fire, and bold harmonic progressions and original orchestral colours enliven the score. This is a palette full of utterly novel sounds. The tendency to put outward effect before everything else led Spontini in his later operas to seek such effects for their own sake. In 1820 Spontini left Paris for Berlin, where for more than twenty years he enjoyed absolute power as *Generalmusikdirektor* of the Royal Opera. Here (in 1821) he produced in tremendous splendour his *Olimpie*, which had greatly disappointed Paris audiences two years earlier. E. T. A. Hoffmann himself undertook the preparation of the German text and Schinkel designed the sets, while no less than thirty-eight trumpeters took part in the great processions, which even included elephants. It was a display of luxury such as Berlin had never seen before, but all too soon disillusion succeeded the first great enthusiasm. The high pathos of *La Vestale* was here degraded into mere empty display. Spontini's later works prepared the way for so-called grand opera, which culminated in Meyerbeer's Paris compositions.

Luigi Cherubini (1760–1842) at first wrote in the Italian manner, but after he got to know Gluck's works in Paris (where he lived from 1788), he openly followed Gluck's style, though he was gifted enough not to become just one of his emulators. Cherubini's most important work is *Médée* (1797), in which he revived classical style.

MÉDÉE. Opera in three acts by Luigi Cherubini. Text by François Benoit Hoffmann. First performance: Paris, 1797.

Characters: Medée (Medea)—soprano; Jason, leader of the Argonauts— tenor; Creon, King of Corinth—bass; Glauce, his daughter—soprano; Neris, Medea's servant—mezzo-soprano. Servants, guards, populace.

Place: Greece. *Time:* mythical antiquity.

Medea, through whose magical powers Jason had won the Golden Fleece in Colchis, has followed her beloved to Greece, but he now finds her a burden, and woos Glauce, daughter of the King of Corinth. Medea is banished from Corinth, but her two small sons are brought up there at the court. Medea appears at the marriage of Jason and Glauce and inter- rupts the ceremony. She tries to win Jason back, but he spurns her and the King banishes her once more. She may bid farewell to her children, but by the next morning she must have left the city. In revenge Medea sends Glauce a present of a poisoned nightgown, and Jason's despairing cries tell her of his bride's death. His sorrow spurs Medea on to further deeds of vengeance, and she kills her two sons, whom Jason loves so dearly. Surrounded by three Furies, she tells him of her terrible deed, and as the temple, to which she has set light, bursts into flames, the people flee in horror.

The music for *Médée* is in Gluck's 'pathetic' style. The title role is characterized with tragic grandeur and Medea's passionate outbursts, particularly in the last act, are full of dramatic power. Richard Wagner described *Médée* as a grandiose work of art. In our time, Maria Callas has brought the opera back to favour.

Cherubini's greatest operatic success, however, was *Les Deux Journées*, a charming work which still enjoyed great popularity at the beginning of the twentieth century, due mainly to its romantic character, but is rarely performed today. It is not a 'grand opera', because Cherubini introduced into it spoken dialogue in place of *recitativo secco*, and used the melo- drama form, and shorter songs and romances in place of great arias, thus coming nearer to the German *Singspiel* and the romantic opera which grew from it. The story of *Les Deux Journées* belongs to the so-called horror-operas, which took their themes from the confusion of revolution. Fear of death and horror on the one hand, sacrifice and heroism on the other were essential to these texts, in which echoes of the French Revolution long continued to resound.

Mozart (1756–91) occupies a central position in the history of opera. The abundant heritage of the first two centuries of opera reached its climax and fulfilment in Mozart's work, which was simultaneously the starting point for further operatic development. Despite all their reforms the Neapolitans (and even Gluck) presented a strictly limited range of plot and characters, which led to an excessive formality of style and substance. Mozart's dramatic genius was entirely directed towards the human and the personal, which inevitably led to delicate individual characterization. This laid the foundation for future development of opera towards romantic feeling, which governed the whole magical realm of the nineteenth-century musical drama.

In purely external matters also Mozart represented the start of the new type of opera. Notwithstanding the successes of Handel and Gluck, Mozart was the first composer whose operas became the solid, lasting fare of every opera house. Masterpieces such as *Le Nozze di Figaro* and *Don Giovanni* started the conception of a repertory opera which reappeared in the programme year after year—a conception wholly foreign to the Neapolitan opera.

By comparison with Alessandro Scarlatti's 115 operas (an average output for a composer of his time), Mozart's fifteen works seem almost insignificant, but one must of course remember that Mozart also wrote a wealth of other music—symphonies, chamber music, songs and piano music of lasting value.

Mozart's first opera, *La Finta Semplice*, was composed in 1767 at the age of eleven at the request of the Emperor Joseph II, but its production was frustrated by ugly intrigues. (It was eventually produced at Salzburg in May, 1769.) The boy's obvious feeling for the style of *opera buffa* was as amazing in this first work as his technical ability, but one can hardly speak of his personal style in this or in his next stage work, the *Singspiel*, *Bastien und Bastienne*, which was performed in the private theatre of the rich (and later famous) hypnotist Franz Mesmer in 1768 and greatly applauded. The text was based on Favart's parody of Rousseau's *Le Devin du Village*, and Mozart may also have been influenced by French music which he probably re-membered from his recent stay in Paris.

BASTIEN UND BASTIENNE. *Singspiel* in one act by Wolfgang Amadeus Mozart. Text after the French by Friedrich Willhelm Weis-kern. First performance: Vienna, 1768.

Characters: Bastienne, a shepherdess—soprano; Bastien, her lover—tenor; Colas, a supposed magician—bass.

Place: a village. *Time:* eighteenth century.

Bastienne believes herself forsaken by her lover, Bastien, and Colas is to help her win back his love. He advises her to be reserved and revive Bastien's love by pretended indifference. Bastien wishes to return to his Bastienne, but Colas tells him that in the meantime Bastienne has grown cold towards him and that he would find it difficult to try to conquer her afresh. Bastienne enters and acts on Colas's advice; Bastien in despair tries to leave her, but in the end she calls him back. Their reconciliation is charmingly celebrated with Colas gaily taking part.

The sixteen musical numbers are all simple songs in two parts, often with a change of time to produce delightful contrasts. The atmosphere of the *Singspiel* is excellently captured, and some of the short ariettas are reminiscent of Hiller and Neefe in their simple grace, a clear indication of the French influences common to them all.

Mozart's operas written between 1770 and 1777 (including *Ascanio in Alba* and *Il Re Pastore* (*The Shepherd King*), belong to the tradition of Italian *opera seria*. Mozart's father hoped to prepare the way to fame and wealth for his son as quickly as possible by launching his operas successfully in Italy, and to this end the young composer obviously had to follow unreservedly the trend of fashion. The words and music of these operas belong to the style of the new Neapolitan school, and few traces of the later Mozart can be detected in them.

Decisive stages in Mozart's development towards fame were marked by *La Finta Giardiniera* (1775) and *Idomeneo* (1781), which were commissioned by the Electors of Bavaria, Maxi-milian III and Karl Theodor, for the Munich opera house. *La Finta Giardiniera* (The Pretended Garden-girl), already fore-tells in many little details the later Mozart's great gift for characterization. Several attempts to revive this delightful work have failed because of the text, which is too sentimental and implausible. *Idomeneo* suffered the same fate until recently, in spite of the skilful adaptation made by Richard Strauss (1931). Gluck's influence is unmistakable in the scenario of this work, in which the chorus plays an important part. The choral scenes towards the end of the second act during the exciting storm music are magnificent and powerfully impressive.

IDOMENEO. Heroic opera in three acts by Wolfgang Amadeus Mozart. Text by Giambattista Varesco. First performance: Munich, 1781.

Characters: Idomeneo, King of Crete—tenor; Idamante, his son—high tenor; Electra, Agamemnon's daughter—soprano; Ilia, daughter of Priam—soprano; Arbace, Idomeneo's friend—baritone; the High Priest —tenor; Voice of Neptune—bass.

Place: Crete. *Time:* after the Trojan War.

While his father Idomeneo is fighting in Troy, Idamante has grown up and fallen in love with Ilia, King Priam's daughter, who is living as a prisoner on Crete; Ilia loves him but out of pride she will not reveal her love. On the return voyage to Crete Idomeneo's fleet is ravaged by a terrible storm. To appease Neptune, Idomeneo vows to sacrifice to him the first creature he meets on his native shore. The first to meet him is Idamante. To escape the terrible duty of killing his own son, he decides to send him to Argos with Agamemnon's daughter, Electra, who is also living in Crete. Electra, who loves Idamante, is transported with happiness, but when they are about to embark a terrible storm arises and to the horror of all a monster comes out of the sea. The King realizes that the god is demanding his sacrifice. Idamante, who seeks death in his fight with the monster, succeeds in killing it. Idomeneo wants to sacrifice himself, and Ilia offers herself also. Placated by such love and readiness for sacrifice, the god renounces his victim.

The first of Mozart's real master-works was *Die Entführung aus dem Serail*, which he wrote for the German National Singspiel Theatre in Vienna in 1782. This was the first libretto that fired his genius. Mozart had hardly dared to suggest any changes to the librettist of *Idomeneo*; (only through his father had he been able to approach Varesco who, as court chaplain to the archbishop, was socially far above the young musician), but he took an active part in constructing the libretto of *Die Entführung* by continually submitting his ideas to the librettist Stephanie the Younger. These ideas show very clearly how concerned he was with the musical and dramatic construction of the text and how precisely he knew which dialogue scenes could be built up into vocal ensembles. He laid great stress on clear and consistent delineation of character so that he could intensify it in his music.

DIE ENTFÜHRUNG AUS DEM SERAIL (The Abduction from the Harem). Comic opera in three acts by Wolfgang Amadeus Mozart. Text after Christoph Friedrich Bretzner by Gottlieb Stephanie the Younger. First performance: Vienna, 1782.

Characters: Pasha Selim—speaking role; Constanze—soprano; Blonde, her personal maid—soprano; Belmonte—tenor; Pedrillo, his servant, overseer of the Pasha's garden—tenor; Osmin, steward of the Pasha's house—bass.

Place: Asia Minor. *Time:* sixteenth century.

Act I. In front of Pasha Selim's palace on the seashore. Constanze has fallen into the Pasha's power and is being held prisoner by him. Belmonte is seeking an opportunity to rescue his beloved. First he wants to contact his former servant Pedrillo, who has found a post in the Pasha's palace. He meets Osmin, the steward of the harem, who roughly sends him away. Osmin hates Christians, and vents his rage on Pedrillo, who joins him in the aria 'Solche hergelaufnen Laffen' ('These young men like tomcats howling'). At last Belmonte and Pedrillo meet, and Pedrillo tells his former master that Constanze, her maid Blonde and he himself had fallen into the hands of pirates, been purchased by the Pasha and brought to his country house. He also tells Belmonte that the Pasha is trying to win Constanze's favours, without forcing her to love him, and that Osmin, who is the Pasha's favourite, is chasing his (Pedrillo's) Blonde. Belmonte has a well-equipped ship waiting in the harbour to help them escape. The Pasha approaches with Constanze and a large retinue; he pleads for Constanze's love, and sadly she tells him of the love which still fills her whole heart—'Ach ich liebte, war so glücklich' ('How enchanting, how enraptured'). When Constanze goes back into the palace, Pedrillo introduces Belmonte to the Pasha as an architect, and the Pasha takes him into his service.

Act II. The palace garden. The amorous Osmin tries to impress Blonde with such utterances as 'Ich der Herr, du meine Sklavin' ('I'm your master, you're my slave') but he cannot intimidate her, for she is protected by her mistress, to whom the Pasha can deny nothing. The Pasha however is no longer prepared to woo Constanze in vain and gives her until the morning to make up her mind to love him; otherwise he will have her killed. Constanze passionately declares that nothing can frighten her in the aria 'Martern aller Arten' ('Torture me and flay me'). Pedrillo brings Blonde good news: the escape is planned for that very night, but first they must meet in the garden to make the final arrangements. Blonde, full of high spirits, hurries away to tell her mistress the news. 'Welche Wonne, welche Lust' ('How delightful it will be'). Meanwhile Pedrillo succeeds in making Osmin drunk—'Vivat Bachus, Bachus lebe' ('Viva Bacchus, here's to Bacchus'). Now that the coast is clear, Constanze and Blonde hurry in; Belmonte enters and the lovers fall into each other's arms. The quartet which closes the act comprises, first, ecstasies of joy at their reunion, followed by a quarrel, estrangement and finally reconciliation. The quarrels between the two loving couples are vastly different: to Belmonte's anxious enquiry whether Constanze does not in fact love the Pasha, she replies with silence and tears, while Pedrillo's impertinent suggestion that Osmin may well have exercised his rights as lord and master is met with a resounding box on the ears from Blonde.

Act III, scene i. A square in front of the palace. It is midnight, and with the serenade 'Im Mohrenland gefangen war' ('Once on Arabia's golden shore') Pedrillo gives the signal for their escape, but they are discovered. Osmin calls out the guard and has the fugitives brought back, indulging in happy thoughts of revenge—'Oh, wie will ich triumphieren' ('Now for righteous retribution').

Scene ii. A hall in the palace. Pasha Selim recognizes Belmonte as the son of his mortal enemy. Constanze and Belmonte know that their last hour has come, and take leave of life in a moving duet. The Pasha however pardons them and allows all four to return to their own country; this enrages the disappointed Osmin. Soloists and chorus praise the Pasha's humanity and magnanimity.

The very first notes of the mysterious hurrying overture transport the hearer into fairyland, while the percussion suggests an oriental setting. The tender longing of the central section represents the noble lovers. (Belmonte introduces himself in his first aria with the same simple melody and its spiritual and lightly sentimental tone characterizes all his songs.) Constanze is not characterized consistently in the music, because Mozart wrote this role for a coloratura soprano, Katherina Cavalieri, and had to give her an opportunity for as great a display of *bravura* as possible. The wonderfully intense *adagio* of her first aria 'Ach, ich liebte, war so glücklich' strongly contrasts with the trills and runs which strangely enough are supposed to express her sorrow and tears. Mozart was conscious of this necessary concession to contemporary taste, but could not avoid it. What superb music he could write in this vein is demonstrated by Constanze's famous 'Martern aller Arten' which is a show piece for every great coloratura soprano.

The lighter characters in the opera are much more lively and realistic: Blonde, impertinent, sharp and passionate; Pedrillo, the faithful fellow whose worries always seem rather ludicrous. By far the most successful character is the fat, lascivious and cruel Osmin, a splendid Mozartian creation. His very first short aria 'Wer ein Liebchen hat gefunden' ('You may think you've found a woman') shows his sullen, mistrustful nature, and countless other traits of vanity, ostentation, shrewdness and brutality appear in the various arias and ensembles in which this violent man of honour pushes himself to the fore with rude simplicity. He is wonderfully characterized in the ebullient

'Vivat Bachus', called by Mozart 'Saufduett' ('Drunkards' duet'), with its attractive song in praise of women. The Turkish

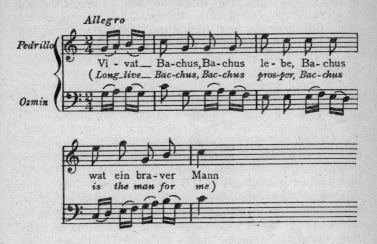

setting is emphasized by the use of piccolo and triangle, as in the lively chorus of the janissaries. The end of the opera preserves the true spirit of the *Singspiel*; each soloist expresses his gratitude in a verse in which the chorus joins, pointing the

moral of the story. The only dissentient voice is that of Osmin, who airs his fury over such appalling injustice. A gay, rhythmic choral passage in the style of the overture and of the first march of the janissaries ends the opera.

The composition and the first performance of *Die Entführung* coincided with Mozart's betrothal and marriage to Constanze Weber, and he deliberately chose her name for the heroine of his opera. In spite of its brilliant success, *Die Entführung* earned very little money for the young couple. (At that time only the theatre commissioning a work paid the composer, while performances in other places brought him honour but no further income.) Apart from the 'occasional' piece, *Der Schauspieldirektor* (*The Impresario*)—the text for which was also written by Stephanie the Younger—Mozart was not engaged again by the Vienna National Singspiel Theatre. In 1788 this theatre, which had been so important in the development of German opera, closed down, and *opera buffa* had won again, with open support from official circles. However willing Mozart would have been to write again for the German Singspiel, it was obvious that he must turn to Italian texts for his next operas. He took as his collaborator the Abbé Lorenzo da Ponte (1749–1838), an adventurer whose merits as Mozart's librettist should not however be underestimated. Mozart drew da Ponte's attention to Beaumarchais's comedy *Le mariage de Figaro*. The Emperor had banned this revolutionary play as being too dangerous for Vienna, but very soon da Ponte had the piece ready to overcome the Emperor's scruples and to secure the Viennese première.

LE NOZZE DI FIGARO (The Marriage of Figaro). Opera in four acts by Wolfgang Amadeus Mozart. Text by Lorenzo da Ponte after Beaumarchais. First performance: Vienna, 1786.

Characters: Count Almaviva—baritone; the Countess, his wife—soprano; Cherubino, page to the Count—soprano; Figaro, valet to the Count—baritone; Susanna, his betrothed—soprano; Marcellina, housekeeper at the castle—soprano (the original Marcellina was sung by Madame Mandini, a soprano, but in the course of time this has become traditionally a mezzo role); Bartolo, doctor—bass; Basilio, music master—tenor; Don Curzio, notary—tenor; Antonio, gardener at the castle—bass; Barbarina, his daughter—soprano. Peasants and servants.

Place: Count Almaviva's castle of Aguas Frescas, near Seville. *Time:* eighteenth century.

Act I. A room in the castle. Susanna is trying on her bridal headdress while Figaro, who is to marry her, measures the room assigned to them by the Count in order to arrange the furniture. Susanna tells Figaro that the Count has given them this particular room because he has designs on her. Figaro expresses his feelings about this in the aria 'Se vuol ballare, signor Contino' ('If you are after a little amusement'). Bartolo and

Marcellina enter. Figaro had once promised to marry Marcellina to settle
a debt of money, and Bartolo, who had previously been on intimate
terms with her, is ready to support her in her claims on Figaro. Cherubino,
the young page, whose ardour is easily aroused by any woman, comes
to ask Susanna for help, for the Count is going to dismiss him—'Non so
più cosa son, cosa faccio' ('Is it pain, is it pleasure that fills me'). The
Count enters and Cherubino only just has time to hide behind a chair.
When Basilio joins them, the Count also tries to hide behind the same
chair while Cherubino jumps into it and Susanna hastily throws a covering over him. When Basilio jokes about the page's flirtations with
Susanna and the Countess, the Count reveals himself, and relates how
he has surprised Cherubino with the gardener's daughter Barbarina.
To demonstrate how he found him hidden under a blanket he whisks
the cloth from the chair and uncovers the page. Susanna and Figaro, who
has come in with a chorus of peasants, intercede for Cherubino, but the
Count is not to be moved from his decision that Cherubino must leave
the castle. He will however make him an officer in his regiment, and
Figaro gives him some good advice for his new career—'Non più
andrai' ('Say goodbye now to pastime and play, lad').

Act II. The Countess's room. The Countess expresses her unhappiness
at her husband's infidelities in the aria 'Porgi amor' ('God of love'). She
learns from Figaro that the Count, apparently for selfish reasons, will not
give his consent to his marriage with Susanna. He tells the Countess that
he has slipped a letter into the Count's hand which refers to a fictitious
rendezvous with the Countess. Meanwhile Susanna is to promise to meet
the Count at the same time, but Cherubino disguised as a girl will appear
in her place. The page now enters and sings for the Countess his amorous
canzone, 'Voi che sapete' ('Tell me, fair ladies'). The Countess and
Susanna make him try on his disguise. The Count knocks at the door,
and Cherubino is bundled into the next room. The Count demands that
the door behind which he thinks the page is hiding should be opened,
but the Countess says that Susanna is in there. Since the Countess refuses
to open the door, the Count makes her go with him to fetch tools to
force the door. Susanna, who has managed to conceal herself behind a
curtain, quickly summons Cherubino from the adjacent room, and the
page jumps from the window into the garden. Susanna then shuts herself
in the room in Cherubino's place, so that the Count does in fact find her
and not Cherubino. The gardener Antonio informs the Count that somebody has jumped from the window and dropped a letter, (the page's
commission); Figaro says that it was he who jumped from the window
and that the page had given him his commission because it had not been
sealed. Marcellina enters, with Basilio and Bartolo, to plead her suit
against Figaro, and as a result the latter's marriage is again postponed.

Act III. The ballroom. Susanna offers the Count a rendezvous in the
garden, 'Crudel! Perchè finora' ('Oh, why are you so cruel'). Figaro,
entering, whispers to Susanna that they can at last get married. The
Count remains behind and gives vent to his anger in the aria, 'Vedrò
mentr'io sospiro, felice un servo mio' ('Must I forgo my pleasure while
serf of mine rejoices'). In the 'legal hearing' which follows, it is found

that Bartolo and Marcellina are Figaro's parents, so that Marcellina's
claims on him are no longer valid, and the Count cannot withhold his
consent to the marriage any longer. The Countess sings of her former
happiness in the aria 'Dove sono' ('I remember days long departed') and
then she dictates to Susanna a love-letter, 'Che soave zefiretto' ('How
delightful 'tis to wander, by the breath of evening fann'd'), which the
latter will deliver to the Count. As a sign that he will keep the rendezvous,
the Count is to return the pin which fastens the letter. A chorus of young
girls (among them Cherubino in disguise) come to pay homage to the
Countess. Then everyone assembles for the wedding festivities, during
which Susanna furtively gives Almaviva the letter.

Act IV. The garden. It is evening. Barbarina has lost the pin which she
was to give Susanna on behalf of the Count as a sign of his consent.
Figaro and Marcellina arrive and overhear her lament. Figaro now believes he is being deceived and rages against all women in the aria:
'Aprite un po' quegli occhi' ('Yes, fools you are and will be, fools till
your eyes are opened'). The Countess and Susanna enter and exchange
cloaks. The Count mistakes the Countess for Susanna and makes her a
passionate declaration of love. Susanna, in the aria 'Deh vieni non tardar'
('Then come, my heart's delight'), dreams of her own love. Figaro enters
and recognizes her through her disguise. To tease her, he behaves as
though he believes she really is the Countess, and declares his ardent love
for her. Susanna angrily boxes his ears. When they have forgiven each
other the Count enters, and thinking he has discovered the Countess in
an assignation with Figaro summons everyone else. He realizes that he
was mistaken and that he has been found out. Once more he asks the
Countess for her forgiveness, which she gives him only too willingly.

Mozart's music makes this lighthearted comedy one of the
most outstanding operas of its kind. The irresistible music captures all rococo charm and lightness, and is suffused with an
inner radiance. From the scintillating vitality of the overture to
the magic of the southern summer night when all is resolved,
the whole work pulsates with infectious, vivid delight.
Light, fluid recitatives connect the arias and ensembles. The
most popular musical numbers are Figaro's martial song,

Allegro vivace

Non più an-drai far-fal-lo - ne a-mo - ro - so,
(Say good-bye now to pas-time and play, lad,

not-te e gior - no d'in-tor - no gi-ran - do
say good-bye to your airs and your gra - ces)

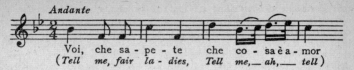

Cherubino's *canzone* 'Voi, che sapete' ('Tell me, fair ladies'), Susanna's aria 'Deh vieni non tardar' ('Then come my heart's delight'), the letter duet, and the duet between Susanna and the Count, in which the rendezvous is arranged. How magically Mozart contrasted Susanna's roguishness with the Count's ardent wooing, and one of the most beautiful melodies in the whole opera unfolds in the passionate words of the seducer.

Mozart's ability to penetrate to the very heart of character is evident in the various arias which characterize each personality. For instance, Barbarina is most charmingly described in her short *cavatina*: she betrays her nature with childish naïvety and yet in spite of the minor key and her heavy sighs her sorrow cannot be taken seriously.

Mozart's *buffo* style occasionally touches on parody, but never resorts to caricature; musical jokes, as in Figaro's last-act aria, where the horns indiscreetly obtrude through the orchestra at the words about deceived husbands, are very rare. A typical Mozartian device is to repeat a tune to new words, so that a

chain of ideas is involuntarily set up through the recollection of
the original words set to the same tune, usually shortly before.
An example of this occurs in the fine trio in the first act, when
the Count, to the same tune as that which accompanies Basilio's
piously hypocritical 'Ah, del paggio, quel ch'ho detto, era solo
un mio sospetto' ('If I mentioned Cherubino, All I said, sir, was
mere conjecture') tells how he found Cherubino with Barbarina.

Another association of ideas occurs later in the same trio, when,
finding Cherubino in the chair, the Count mockingly uses the
same vigorous melody for the words 'Onestissima Signora'
('Oh you paragon of virtue') as he had used to reject Susanna's
intercession on the page's behalf. These repetitions also give
strong internal cohesion to the various ensembles. The form
and construction of the great *concertante* passages is always
masterly, and never more so than in the second act *finale* which
increases steadily in intensity as each character joins in, until
what started as a duet becomes, with the entry of the trio of
petitioners (Marcellina, Basilio and Bartolo), a septet. At this
point the orchestral *crescendo* becomes a *tutti* and the musical
climax is reached.

In spite of its enormous success (every single number was
applauded enthusiastically and most of them had to be repeated)
the Emperor ordered *Figaro* to be taken out of the programme
after only a few performances. All the more striking therefore
was its success in Prague, which brought Mozart a commission
for a new opera; after all his disappointments in Vienna, it was
a double pleasure for him to present his new work in Prague,
where the public idolized him. Da Ponte suggested using the
story of Don Juan and in two months delivered his completed
text to Mozart.

DON GIOVANNI. Opera in two acts by Wolfgang Amadeus Mozart. Text by Lorenzo da Ponte. First performance: Prague, 1787.

Characters: Don Giovanni—baritone; the Commendatore—bass; Donna Anna, his daughter—soprano; Don Ottavio, her betrothed—tenor; Donna Elvira, abandoned by Don Giovanni—soprano; Leporello, Don Giovanni's servant—bass; Masetto, a peasant—bass; Zerlina, his bride—soprano.

Place: Spain. *Time:* early seventeenth century.

Act I, scene i. Street in front of the Commendatore's palace. It is night. Leporello is waiting impatiently for his master who is pursuing a new love affair. He hears steps and hides while Don Giovanni rushes out of the Commendatore's house, closely pursued by Donna Anna. He tries to cover his face to avoid recognition, but Donna Anna grasps his arm and calls for help. The Commendatore enters and calls on his daughter's seducer to fight. In the duel which follows the Commendatore is mortally wounded, and Don Giovanni and Leporello flee. Donna Anna has meanwhile called on her betrothed, Don Ottavio, for help. At the sight of her dead father she faints, and then recovering, passionately urges Ottavio to revenge his death.

Scene ii. A street. Don Giovanni and Leporello are discussing new adventures. When Donna Elvira enters in travelling attire, they at first withdraw. Elvira has come to Seville to find Don Giovanni, who had abandoned her after a brief love affair. Don Giovanni approaches her, hoping for a new amorous adventure, and is amazed to recognize his recently abandoned mistress. Elvira overwhelms him with reproaches and Don Giovanni slips away, leaving Leporello to tell the unfortunate woman something of his master's way of life. He has ties of love in every country, every town, in fact everywhere, says Leporello in the famous 'catalogue' aria 'Madamina', with its refrain 'Ma in Ispagna son già mille tre' ('But in Spain a thousand and three').

Scene iii. In the country. Zerlina and Masetto are to be married, and join with some peasants in a gay dance. Don Giovanni enters and invites the whole gathering to his castle. Leporello is to lure everyone else away, while he seduces the enchanting Zerlina. Leporello manages to remove Masetto, who at first resists him. Left alone with Zerlina, Don Giovanni has little difficulty in winning the innocent creature: 'Là ci darem la mano' ('You'll lay your hand in mine, dear'). Donna Elvira enters and tears Zerlina away from her seducer. Don Giovanni is left alone and disappointed. Donna Anna and Don Ottavio join him, not knowing that he is the assassin of Donna Anna's father, and ask for his help in finding the murderer. Donna Elvira returns and warns them not to trust him, but Don Giovanni tells them that she is mad and takes his leave with great relief. Donna Anna, however, has recognized his voice and in the aria 'Or sai chi l'onore' ('You know now for certain') she passionately urges Ottavio to take revenge.

Scene iv. The gardens of Don Giovanni's country house. Leporello tells his master how he took the peasants into the castle and easily befuddled them with wine. Don Giovanni gives him instructions for the party in the aria 'Fin ch'han dal vino' ('Song, wine and women'). Dance music is heard from the castle. Donna Anna, Donna Elvira and Don Ottavio enter, masked, and Don Giovanni, seeing them, bids Leporello invite them to the party.

Scene v. A crowd of guests, among them the peasants with Zerlina and Masetto, parade gaily in the lighted ballroom. The three masked figures enter and are greeted by Don Giovanni, who then gives the signal for the dancing to begin and leads off with Zerlina. Leporello tries to get Masetto to dance too, but when he sees his master drawing Zerlina towards an adjacent room he disappears, anticipating unpleasant consequences. In a few moments Zerlina is heard calling for help, but once again Don Giovanni gets out of a difficult situation; he accuses Leporello of having molested Zerlina and threatens him with severe punishment. The peasants and musicians run away in fear, but Donna Elvira, Donna Anna and Don Ottavio reveal themselves; they round on Don Giovanni, who draws his sword, boldly fights his way through his opponents and escapes unharmed.

Act II, scene i. A street in front of Donna Elvira's house. Don Giovanni manages to pacify the angry Leporello with money and kind words, but he must now help in the new adventure—the seduction of Donna Elvira's charming and attractive maid; for this purpose he and Leporello exchange cloaks and hats. First of all Donna Elvira must be removed. When she appears on the balcony Don Giovanni pays her court; the unfortunate woman falls under the spell of his voice and is ready to take him back at once as her lover. When she hurries down into the street it is the disguised Leporello who leads her away. Don Giovanni is left alone and can now serenade the maid—'Deh, vieni alla finestra' ('Look down from out your window'). Just as he believes his goal is almost in sight, Masetto appears with several other peasants, all armed in various ways, to avenge themselves on him. The supposed Leporello yields to their threats and tells them where they can find the Don. Left alone with Masetto, he first disarms him, and then violently thrashes him. Fortunately Zerlina is not far away; she hurries in in time to console her unfortunate lover—'Vedrai carino, se sei buonino' ('If you will promise not to mistrust me').

Scene ii. The courtyard of Donna Anna's house. Donna Elvira and Leporello have lost their way in the dark and wandered in here. Leporello has had enough of his adventure and of Donna Elvira's affectionate demonstrations, and he tries in vain to find the way out. Donna Anna and Don Ottavio enter with torch-bearers, without at first noticing Donna Elvira and Leporello. Only when Zerlina and Masetto arrive in their search for Don Giovanni is the couple discovered, and everyone believes they have found the culprit. Elvira defends her beloved, but Leporello prefers to shed his disguise, plead for mercy and escape. Ottavio tries to console the angry women in the aria 'Il mio tesoro intanto' ('Speak for me to my lady').

Scene iii. A cemetery with the monument and statue of the Commendatore. It is moonlight and Don Giovanni is retailing to Leporello his latest adventure. A sombre, menacing voice is heard, Don Giovanni tries to dismiss it with a laugh but the eerie, ghostly tones sound again. Turn-

ing round, he recognizes the statue of the Commendatore. Boisterously
he tells Leporello to invite the statue to dinner, Leporello, trembling with
fear, believes he sees the statue nodding its assent. When Don Giovanni
repeats the challenge and the statue replies with a distinct 'yes', Don
Giovanni and Leporello escape over the wall.

Scene iv. A room in Donna Anna's home. Don Ottavio presses Donna
Anna to marry him at last. She assures him that she loves him, but asks
him to wait a little longer—'Non mi dir' ('Say no more').

Scene v. The ballroom in Don Giovanni's palace. Don Giovanni is
enjoying his supper, while his musicians play such well-known tunes as
'Non più andrai' from Le Nozze di Figaro, at which Leporello comments:
'Questa poi la conosco pur troppo' ('Well, I can't say I think much of
this tune'). Donna Elvira enters and begs the man she still passionately
loves to lead a virtuous life, but he will have none of it, and laughingly
calls to her 'Viva le femmine, viva il buon vino' ('Here's to the women
all! Here's to the wine-cup!'). As she leaves the room Donna Elvira
utters a cry. Leporello goes after her, and at the door sees the marble
statue seeking admittance. Knocking can already be heard. Leporello
refuses to open the door, so Don Giovanni opens it himself, and the lamp
falls from his hand. Everything is plunged in darkness and only around
the statue, which now enters the room, there shines an unearthly light.
While Leporello shivers with fear, Don Giovanni welcomes his ghostly
guest. 'Pentiti' ('Repent'), cries the Commendatore, but Don Giovanni
knows neither remorse nor repentance and proudly he repeats his 'no'.
With the words 'Ah! tempo più non v'è' ('Your hour of grace is past')
the Commendatore disappears. A storm breaks, flames shoot up on every
side, an invisible chorus is heard, and Don Giovanni is devoured by fire.
Once this terrible nightmare is over, Donna Anna, Donna Elvira, Zerlina,
Don Ottavio and Masetto enter, looking for Don Giovanni in order to
wreak their final revenge. Still shaking with terror, Leporello tells of the
horrible punishment which has overtaken his master. Everybody is relieved and delighted. Don Ottavio implores Donna Anna to accept him
at last, but she still asks for another year's delay; Donna Elvira decides to
enter a convent, Masetto and Zerlina can only think of a cheerful meal,
and Leporello plans to look round for a better master. Highly satisfied
with themselves, they all join in pointing the moral 'Questo è il fin di chi
fa mal' ('Sinner pause and ponder well').

In the nineteenth century it became the general practice to end
the opera with Don Giovanni's descent into Hell, and simply
omit the closing sextet, but this attempt to highlight a tragic
side of the opera showed a misunderstanding of the style of
Don Giovanni. Da Ponte had marked his libretto a dramma
giocoso (a gay drama), and when he lets his hero sink finally into
hell-fire this conclusion is only tragic in the sense of a puppet-
show. Some of the situations seem to be taken directly from the

puppet-show tradition, as when Don Giovanni leads the silly
Masetto astray and then beats him, or when Donna Elvira is
deceived by the crude|trick of the disguises and taken in by
Leporello's exaggerated caresses. Da Ponte conceived and portrayed Leporello as the direct descendant of the harlequin of the
commedia dell'arte, but just as Mozart gives this character an
individuality which raises him far above Da Ponte's ideas so he
raises the *dramma giocoso*, which in Da Ponte's text is neither
tragedy nor comedy, into the undefinable realm of his art in
which laughter is mingled with tears, and serious-mindedness
underlies all the boisterous exuberance. It is therefore essential
to retain the final moralizing sextet by the remaining characters
after Don Giovanni's descent into hell, as it removes the last
sting from the hero's grotesque fate.

Don Giovanni is admirably portrayed by Mozart in his passionate love of life and ebullient vitality. All the themes which
characterize him, from the *allegro* subject in the overture to his
bold retorts in the dialogue with his marble guest—exude forceful vitality, a demonic urge mounting steadily towards the
final catastrophe which not even annihilation can alarm.

The other characters of the play are grouped around this
central figure; they all move in Don Giovanni's aura and depend
on him in spite of their strongly marked personalities. Only the
figure of the Commendatore stands apart—an iron mass, em-
bodying both law and destiny—in a musical sphere of its own,
a voice from the other world against the worldly ways and
trappings of all the other characters.

To conclude, one more brief reference to the most famous
passages of this opera, which have rightly become popular:
first, the minuet, played at the ball in Don Giovanni's castle.
Three orchestras play simultaneously on stage at this moment,
the solemn minuet, a fast waltz and a gentle quadrille. The three
dances in three different times, $^3/_4$, $^3/_8$ and $^2/_4$, are most skilfully
blended into a harmonic whole. Equally well known is the
tune of the duet 'Là ci darem la mano'; chivalrous and gallant

Andante

Là ci da-rem la ma-no,   là mi di-rai di   sì
(*You'll lay your hand in mine, dear,   soft-ly you'll whisper   yes*)

in mood, yet simple in melody, its many little variations and surprising movements are most delicately designed. Extremely charming and effective is Don Giovanni's serenade with its delightful mandolin accompaniment; in its intimate mood it is

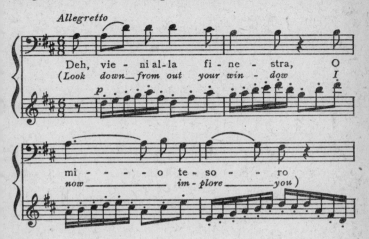

finely contrasted with the bubbling, irrepressible champagne aria or Leporello's frivolous catalogue aria.

The third text da Ponte wrote for Mozart was less fortunate. The libretto of *Così fan tutte* was harshly criticized at its first performance as being silly and frivolous, and to this day the arguments for and against the story are still under discussion.

COSÌ FAN TUTTE (Women are all alike). Comic opera in two acts by Wolfgang Amadeus Mozart. Text by Lorenzo da Ponte. First performance: Vienna, 1790.

Characters: Fiordiligi—soprano; Dorabella—soprano; Ferrando—tenor; Guglielmo—baritone; Don Alfonso—bass; Despina, servant girl—soprano. Gentlemen and ladies, soldiers, servants.

Place: Naples. *Time:* eighteenth century.

Act I. Ferrando and Guglielmo, two officers, convinced of the unswerving faithfulness of their future brides, the sisters Dorabella and Fiordiligi, quarrel with the sophisticated Don Alfonso, who does not believe in the existence of feminine fidelity, and draw their swords to defend their ladies' honour. Don Alfonso however proposes a bet to these two young men: they are to disguise themselves to test the faithfulness of the two sisters, but on condition that they follow his instructions.

Alfonso wins over Despina, the sisters' maid, to his side, and with clever, subtle talk she succeeds in undermining the girls' strict principles. In order to carry out the wager, the two lovers announce that they must leave at once for the war, and this leads to a touchingly comic scene of farewell. Disguised as Albanians the officers return and court the deserted girls, each of them wooing the other's affianced. The first offensive fails, but they make a deeper impression when they pretend to poison themselves in front of the girls. Despina, disguised as a doctor, brings the two lovers back to life.

Act II. Dorabella is the first to succumb to the test but Fiordiligi stands firm and wants to follow her beloved to the war. But when the disguised Ferrando tries to kill himself at her feet, her heart also is moved. The marriages are arranged, and preparations made for the double wedding. Despina, disguised as a notary, presents the marriage contracts for their signatures. Suddenly a roll of drums is heard: the regiment has returned. The lovers disappear to return in a moment as their real selves. Their future wives have to admit their infidelity, and Don Alfonso triumphs—'Così fan tutte'.

Così fan tutte suffered the same fate as so many operas, which in spite of all their beauty enjoyed no lasting success because of their poor texts. It is solely because of the text that this enchanting work of Mozart's has always lagged far behind his other mature dramatic works in popularity. [This is purely the personal view of the author and one not shared by either the English editor or translator. This work's English popularity dates from the splendid Busch–Ebert productions at Glyndebourne, 1934–39]. In fact for a time it was completely forgotten. Several attempts to rewrite the text were only moderately successful because the music lost some of its character and charm through being rearranged and given different significance. Ernst von Possart, the first Intendant of the Prinzregenten-theater in Munich, has earned undying merit for remounting this work in its original form and for stressing its buffo character by a lively production, which transformed the frivolous plot while leaving the music to exercise its true, rare magic.

However superficial the text and unreal the action, one must not forget that this is a farce in which everything is fun and laughter, without any deeper significance, though perhaps with a slight tinge of irony. Musically Così fan tutte is a masterly opera buffa. Thanks to Mozart's genius all the characteristics and stylistic rules of this form of opera here achieve their final and most perfect fulfilment. If one just listens attentively to the music in conjunction with the relevant words and situations, one automatically experiences Mozart's delicate art of musical characterization. Take for instance the gay, charming maid (a typical *opera buffa* character), first giving her opinions of men

Di pas - ta si - mi - le son tut - ti quan - ti
(*Man's not com - poun - ded of su - gar and spi - ces*)

and of the true art of love and then, disguised as a doctor, indulging in comic hocus-pocus. Both in that scene and in the scene when the lovers pretend to be dead, one recognizes unmistakable signs of parody—in fact, parody of serious opera, in the age-old tradition of the *opera buffa*. Other instances of pure comedy are the heart-beats heard in the music during the duet between Guglielmo and Dorabella, and the laughing trio of the three men at the end of the first act. The rare and immediate charm of most scenes is due to Mozart's skill in handling these old comic tricks. Beside the humour there are the most wonderful and pure love melodies of exquisite beauty which belong among Mozart's most glorious inspirations; for instance, Fiordiligi's splendid E major aria in the second act, and Ferrando's passionate first act aria.

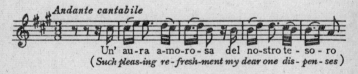

Un' au - ra a - mo - ro - sa del no - stro te - so - ro
(*Such pleas-ing re - fresh-ment my dear one dis - pen - ses*)

The ensemble passages are full of vitality, especially the great finales which crown both acts in splendid *crescendo*. The overture contains an effervescent *presto* passage, which in many ways recalls the overture to *Figaro*. The slow introduction starts with a *cantabile* love-tune, which leads into the motif, 'Così fan tutte', (taken from Alfonso's very short aria) which ends the overture and also recurs in the finale of the second act as the concluding moral of the story.

Co - sì   fan   tut - - - - te
(*That's   what   they   all ————— do*)

In the middle of August 1791, when Mozart was already working hard on *Die Zauberflöte*, he received from Prague the great honour of a commission to write the opera which was to celebrate the coronation of Leopold II as King of Bohemia. Metastasio's *La Clemenza di Tito* had been chosen as the text and Mozart had only a few weeks in which to compose the music. The score was ready in eighteen days but the *recitativo secco* passages were probably written by Mozart's pupil Süssmayer. In spite of a strong cast and magnificent décor the gala première was not very successful. Mozart, who had high expectations for this propitious occasion, returned to Vienna very disappointed, and plunged again into the final work on *Die Zauberflöte*.

La Clemenza di Tito has never since made a very strong impression. The fact that one hears it occasionally today (more often in concert form or on the radio than on the stage), is due to the interest which any work by Mozart will arouse.

LA CLEMENZA DI TITO (The Clemency of Titus). *Opera seria* in two acts by Wolfgang Amadeus Mozart. Text after Metastasio by Caterino Mazzolà. First performance: Prague, 1791.

Characters: Titus, Roman Emperor—tenor; Sextus, Roman nobleman —alto; Annius, his friend—alto; Servilia, Sextus's sister—soprano; Vitellia, daughter of the Emperor Vitellius—soprano; Publius, commander of the bodyguard—bass.

Place: Rome. *Time:* 79 AD.

Act I. Vitellia, daughter of the Emperor Vitellius who has been overthrown by Titus, persuades her lover Sextus to start a conspiracy against Titus. Servilia, Sextus's sister, who is in love with his friend Annius, is being courted by Titus, and Vitellia therefore presses Sextus to move against Titus at once. Titus meanwhile has granted Servilia's plea to be allowed to remain faithful to Annius, and renouncing her has turned his attentions to Vitellia. She repents too late, having brought about his downfall, for the rebellion is already in full spate, the Capitol is burning,

and when Sextus announces that the Emperor has been assassinated everyone is struck dumb with horror.

Act II. Titus has escaped the attempt on his life, and the conspirators
have been arrested. Sextus is condemned to death by the Senate, but
Titus is prepared to spare his life on condition that he reveals the name of
the person who incited him to this conspiracy. Sextus heroically keeps
silent. When he is about to be executed, Vitellia resolves to confess her
guilt to Titus, who pardons everyone. The opera closes with a hymn of
jubilation in praise of the Emperor's nobility and magnanimity.

It is quite understandable that Mozart, who had probed the
minutest subtleties of the human spirit in *Don Giovanni*, was
not inspired by this libretto. The textual form of the completely
obsolete *opera seria* left him indifferent; the empty words of the
arias meant nothing to him, and even he could not breathe life
into the conventional characters of this opera, but in spite of all
this, the finale of the first act and Vitellia's great second act aria
were moments of strongly expressive dramatic power. The
fact that the roles of both Sextus and Annius were written for
women's voices is explained by the fact that the Prague singers
who were to take these parts in the gala performance were both
women.

In spite of Mozart's masterly treatment, the characters in *La
Clemenza di Tito* seem like lifeless statues in comparison with
the complexity and vitality of those in *Die Zauberflöte*, which
he wrote at the same time. Mozart was fascinated by the novelty
and variety of the fairy-tale atmosphere of this text and after
some initial reserve he allowed himself to be completely carried
away by it. The libretto of *Die Zauberflöte* has been harshly
criticized, but also acclaimed as being absolutely ideal for an
opera. The fact that this work was appreciated immediately,
and that in a very short time its characters became household
words, speaks only too clearly in favour of the libretto, and
Goethe himself was so fascinated by it that he decided to write
the text for a sequel.

The librettist, Emanuel Schikaneder, was a most experienced
man of the theatre. He was already an old friend of Mozart's
when in 1791 he asked the composer to write him a 'magic'
opera, since he urgently needed a successful work to save his
theatre from collapse, and Mozart readily agreed to help him.
So began a collaboration in which composer and librettist
complemented one another with mutual encouragement and

inspiration, and which resulted in Mozart's magnificent last opera, *Die Zauberflöte*.

DIE ZAUBERFLÖTE (The Magic Flute). Opera in two acts by Wolfgang Amadeus Mozart. Text by Emanuel Schikaneder. First performance: Vienna, 1791.

Characters: Sarastro—bass; Tamino—tenor; the Queen of Night—soprano; Pamina, her daughter—soprano; Papageno—baritone; Papagena—soprano; Monostatos, a Moor—tenor; the Speaker—bass; three Ladies-in-waiting to the Queen of Night—two sopranos, one alto; three Boys—two sopranos, one alto. Priests and people.

Place: an eastern country. *Time:* legendary.

Act I, scene i. A wild, rocky place. While hunting, Tamino is attacked by a giant serpent and rescued from mortal danger by the three ladies of the Queen of Night, who kill the monster with their spears. The beauty of the young man captivates the women, who all want to watch over him as he regains consciousness, but duty calls them to their Queen. Papageno enters with the song 'Der Vogelfänger bin ich ja' ('Now tell me, did you ever see'). He speaks with Tamino, and makes him believe that he is his rescuer. Papageno leads a very strange life. He catches coloured birds and takes them to the palace of the 'sternflammende Königin der Nacht' ('radiant Queen of Night') where he receives bread and wine as a reward. But his strongest, and so far unfulfilled, desire is to find himself a wife. The three Ladies come back and put a padlock on Papageno's mouth as a punishment for his lie. The Ladies then give Tamino a picture of Pamina, the Queen's daughter, with which he instantly falls in love—'Dies Bildnis ist bezaubernd schön' ('Oh loveliness beyond compare'). The Ladies tell Tamino that Pamina has been kidnapped by the wicked magician Sarastro. Thunder announces the approach of the Queen, to whom Tamino promises that he will bring back her daughter. After the Queen has disappeared, the three women give Tamino a magic flute which will protect him from danger. Papageno is to accompany Tamino to Sarastro's fortress and, after being freed from the padlock, he also receives a present from the Queen: a peal of magic bells. They are told of the three Boys who will guide them to their destination and whom they are to trust implicitly.

Scene ii. A room in Sarastro's palace. Pamina, who wants to escape, is brought back by the Moor Monostatos, and he tries to make love to her. Papageno enters and Moor and bird-catcher frighten each other to death, each believing the other to be the devil. They both run away, but Papageno soon returns, reveals himself to Pamina as her mother's messenger and tells her of the prince Tamino. They decide to go at once in search of him, but first Pamina consoles Papageno, who complains that he has no sweetheart—'Bei Männern, welche Liebe fühlen' ('The kindly voice of mother nature').

Scene iii. A grove in front of the temple of Wisdom. The three Boys accompany Tamino into the precincts of the temple and leave him with the warning, 'Sei standhaft, duldsam und verschwiegen' ('Be silent, patient, persevering'). Tamino tries to enter the temple, but from all sides thunders a threatening 'Zurück' ('stand back'). The Speaker comes out of the temple of Wisdom to tell him that Sarastro is no magician or tyrant, and that he has only taken Pamina from her mother in order to save her. Tamino, too, will soon see how noble and wise Sarastro is. The Speaker withdraws and Tamino plays on his flute, attracting wild animals which lie down at his feet. By his song, Tamino hopes to attract Pamina, and when he finally hears Papageno's voice he hastens happily towards him. Papageno and Pamina enter from another direction, but Monostatos is already there with his fellow-slaves to capture them both. Papageno plays his bells, and fascinated by the music Monostatos and the slaves begin to dance. Jubilant sounds announce Sarastro's arrival. Pamina tells him how she tried to escape because the Moor importuned her with love and violence. Sarastro pardons her, but will not yet release her. Monostatos now drags Tamino in; the lovers recognize one another and joyfully embrace. Furious, the Moor separates them, but instead of praising him for his vigilance Sarastro sentences him to a beating. Tamino and Papageno are to be taken into the temple where they must undergo certain trials.

Act II, scene i. A palm-wood. Sarastro is in council with the priests, and tells them to summon Tamino to the temple to be prepared for his high destiny; he also tells them that Pamina has been chosen by the gods as his companion—'O Isis und Osiris'.

Scene ii. A forecourt of the temple. It is night. Tamino and Papageno are brought in and commanded to observe absolute silence. The three Ladies appear and try to make them talk. Papageno is on the verge of breaking his vow, and Tamino with difficulty succeeds in stopping his chatter.

Scene iii. A garden by night. Pamina lies asleep on a couch, and the love-sick Monostatos gloats over her and the opportunity of kissing her —'Alles fühlt der Liebe Freuden' ('All with passion's fever tingles'). The Queen appears and frightens off Monostatos; she then gives her daughter a dagger and commands her to kill Sarastro—only in this way, she says, can Pamina be freed to enjoy Tamino's love once more—'Der Hölle Rache kocht in meinem Herzen' ('I'll have revenge, no longer can I bear it'). The Queen vanishes and Monostatos, who has heard the conversation, once again demands Pamina's love. The arrival of Sarastro foils him and he flees. Pamino begs for mercy for herself and her mother, and Sarastro assures her that vengeance is not in his mind—'In diesen heil'gen Hallen' ('We know no thought of vengeance').

Scene iv. A forecourt of the temple. Tamino and Papageno are still to keep silence but Papageno is induced to chatter by an old woman, without his realizing that under her disguise is hidden his longed-for Papagena. The three Boys appear bringing the flute and the bells which had been taken away from the two men during their trial. Papageno delightedly conjures up a table covered with exquisite dishes. Pamina enters, but as Tamino persists in his silence towards her she believes that he loves her no longer—'Ach, ich fühl's, es ist verschwunden' ('Ah,' tis gone, 'tis gone for ever').

Scene v. The Temple precinct. Tamino is told that as a reward for his endurance he will now be admitted into the sanctuary. Pamina enters and again believes that Tamino's coldness means he has no love for her. Papageno, on the contrary, has no wish to be initiated into the temple mysteries, he would prefer a glass of wine, andfost of all 'Ein Mädchen oder Weibchen' ('A girl, or a little wife'). The magic bells must help him. Again the old woman appears, but this time reveals herself as Papagena. As Papageno is about to embrace her, there is a clap of thunder and she vanishes.

Scene vi. A garden at dawn. The three Boys enter and catch sight of Pamina who, almost beside herself with grief for the loss of her love, wants to kill herself. The Boys prevent her and promise to lead her to Tamino.

Scene vii. The temple of the final ordeal. On one side is a waterfall, on the other blazes a huge sea of fire. Two Armoured Men show Tamino the gates he must enter to pass through the fire and water. Pamina arrives and the lovers greet one another joyfully. She is allowed to accompany her beloved, and the magic flute will protect them on their way.

Scene viii. A garden. Papageno, in despair at the loss of Papagena, wants to kill himself, but the three Boys tell him to set the magic bells ringing, and by playing them he conjures up his beloved Papagena.

Scene ix. A vault beneath the earth. Led by Monostatos, the Queen of Night and her three Ladies have penetrated into Sarastro's palace. The Queen promises the Moor Pamina's hand in marriage as soon as she has taken her revenge on Sarastro. Suddenly a storm arises and the powers of darkness are dispersed amidst thunder and lightning.

Scene x. Sarastro's Temple of the Sun. Radiant light surrounds him and his priests in the sanctuary which now Pamina and Tamino also enter. A chorus of rejoicing closes the opera.

In writing the text of *Die Zauberflöte*, Schikaneder drew on the most diverse sources, apparently caring more for theatrical effect than psychological accuracy in the development of the plot. This is the only possible explanation for the astonishing *volte-face* in the characterization of the two opposing spheres. The Queen and her Ladies, who at first command all our sympathy, suddenly become the representatives of evil, while the magician Sarastro appears in the noble guise of a prince of wisdom who had simply been slandered by the Queen. Mozart was genuinely fascinated by this fairy-tale, which offered him a mass of charming contrasts, the combination of cordiality and humour, and above everything a noble fundamental idea expressed in the masonic symbolism to which Mozart, who belonged to the same Viennese Lodge as Schikaneder, was immediately attracted.

The most extraordinary aspect of the composition of *Die Zauberflöte* is the certainty with which Mozart's delicately graduated characterization draws together the figures in this opera into a unified whole. His musical material, ranging from simple popular song to figured *chorale*, is always at the service of the drama, and is fused into an artistic whole with such clarity that the diverse spheres of *Singspiel*, *opera buffa*, *opera seria* and musical drama here achieve a splendid unity born of genius. Papageno, in his coloured feather costume, (a successor to Harlequin, or a sort of Viennese Kasperl) belongs musically to the world of the popular song and the *Singspiel*; his arias 'Der Vogelfänger bin ich ja' and 'Ein Mädchen oder Weibchen' have become widely popular, and in the charming Pamina-Papageno duets, 'Bei Männern, welche Liebe fühlen' and 'Könnte jeder brave Mann' are reproductions of genuine folk tunes.

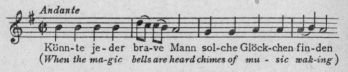

Könn-te je-der bra-ve Mann sol-che Glöck-chen fin-den
(*When the ma-gic bells are heard chimes of mu-sic wak-ing*)

The world of the supernatural fairy-tale—a typical *Singspiel* subject—is reflected in the numbers for the three Boys, whose trios all contain infinitely delicate and charming tunes. The character of the Moor, Monostatos, is enriched with comic elements; an example of this is his lecherous, excited patter song:

Al — les fühlt der Lie-be Freuden, schnä-belt
(*All with pas-sions fe-ver tin-gles, snatch a*
tän-delt, herzt und küsst
kiss and give it back)

The Queen's magnificent arias belong to the field of *opera seria*, and this has often been criticized—quite unjustly—as stylistically wrong. In fact, the demonic character of the Queen *could* only be defined in the forceful style of the *opera seria* and the brilliant fireworks of her coloratura are not mere ornamentation, but the expression of a passionate agitation. Elements of musical drama are found in Pamina's aria, a moving and touching lament which hovers between aria and recitative. The juxtaposition of the various styles appears most clearly in the finales where they mingle without transitional passages of dialogue. The great scene in front of the temple at the end of the first act starts with the altercation between Tamino and the Speaker, a sublime musical drama as Gluck conceived it and Wagner later developed it. Tamino's flute aria, the playing of the bells and the slaves' dance are taken from the lovable traditions of the *Singspiel*. There are also independent comic elements within the general framework, as for instance Monostatos's appearance. The second finale is even more varied. Here the musical climax is reached in the noble *chorale* of the Armoured Men, accompanied by a deliberate fugue in the orchestra.

The success of *Die Zauberflöte* was unsurpassed and filled Schikaneder's pockets for many years, but Mozart was left empty-handed. Nine weeks after the first performance he died and found his final resting-place in a pauper's grave. Richard Wagner wrote of *Die Zauberflöte*: 'Germany can never pay enough tribute to this work. Before it German opera hardly existed: this was its moment of creation.'

THE GERMAN NATIONAL OPERA AND 'FIDELIO'

After the rapid growth of the German *Singspiel*, it was only a short step to the creation of serious German opera. The original prejudice against German as a language for singing (an objection which Rousseau had also raised against French) had been refuted by the astonishing success of the *Singspiel*. Eminent German men of letters were interested in and indeed enthusiastic about opera. Lessing upheld it vigorously in the *Laokoön*, saying that music and poetry should be ideally united in opera—'each yielding to the other as much as possible'. In opera (he wrote) there are two relationships between poetry and music, 'in the aria, where poetry is the auxiliary art, and in the recitative, where music plays the secondary part'. Herder (the Prussian pastor and philosopher) compared opera to the unreality of a dream. He wrote a libretto entitled *Brutus* (1774) which was set to music by Johann Christian Friedrich Bach.

The most successful poet in the field of opera was C. M. Wieland (1733–1813). He wrote an *Alceste* which was set to music by Anton Schweitzer (1735–87), the music director of Abel Seyler's drama company. This *Alceste* was performed in Weimar in 1773 and attracted attention as the first step towards a German national opera. Wieland was wildly enthusiastic; he placed Schweitzer's music far above Gluck's *Alceste*, and even compared his own libretto with Euripides' poetry, which earned him many lampoons, culminating in Goethe's satire *Götter, Helden und Wieland* (*Gods, heroes and Wieland*). Even though Wieland's judgment, especially of music, should not be taken too seriously, the general effect of this first attempt at German opera was still enormous. In 1775 *Alceste* was revived, this time in Mannheim, which under the patronage of the luxury-loving Elector Karl Theodor was becoming the focal point of national artistic strivings. Here French drama had in 1770 given way to German *Singspiel* companies, and in 1776 the building of the Nationaltheater was started, in which Schiller's epoch-making *Die Räuber* had its première in 1782. Mannheim was the right place for building up a national opera.

In 1777 *Alceste* was followed by *Günther von Schwarzburg*, a work with a text inferior to Wieland's, but with music (by the Mannheim conductor and composer Ignaz Holzbauer, 1711–83) which was an improvement on Schweitzer's. The Mannheim writer Anton Klein, who wrote the libretto, adapted for it an episode from German history—the first time such a subject had been used in opera. The production was mounted with great splendour with designs created by Quaglio, but it was still less successful than *Alceste*. Mozart, who was present at performances of both operas in Mannheim, was very critical of Schweitzer's music, but impressed by Holzbauer's ability. He spoke very enthusiastically of the melodramas of the *Singspiel* composer Georg Benda, which he also saw in Mannheim, and which consisted of spoken solo scenes with orchestral accompaniment. In particular his *Ariadne auf Naxos* (1775), the first

of this new genre, was generally admired. Benda also ventured
on serious opera subjects, as for instance in his one-act opera
Walder (1776). Christian Gottlob Neefe (1748–98), who was
Beethoven's first teacher in Bonn, also wrote successful *Singspiele*, but tried in *Adelheit von Veltheim* (1780) to enlarge the
framework of the genre by introducing a more lofty content
and a more grandiose form. His use of an oriental milieu and
choice of subject made Neefe's opera seem like the stepping-
stone to Mozart's *Die Entführung aus dem Serail*.

Wieland and Schweitzer wrote another opera, *Rosamund*,
which was performed four times in Mannheim in 1780. In the
meantime Karl Theodor had become Elector of Bavaria, and
transferred his residence to Munich, where artistic life was still
so completely dominated by Italian influence that there was no
room for national aspirations. These first attempts to create
German grand opera were therefore abandoned.

Although the libretto of Mozart's *Die Zauberflöte* consciously
belonged to the German *Singspiel* tradition, its music contains
many traces of the Mannheim innovations, especially Holzbauer's *Günther von Schwarzburg*. The bass role of Rudolf,
Count Palatine, can be regarded in some respects as a predecessor
of Sarastro; the form of the overture to *Die Zauberflöte*, with
its *maestoso* passages, is reminiscent of Holzbauer and one can
even find melodic references to him in Mozart's opera, all of
which establishes Mozart's indirect connection with German
opera seria. This struggle towards a national opera had not been
in vain, even though the first genuine representatives of this art-
form are *Die Zauberflöte*, and soon after, Beethoven's *Fidelio*.

Ludwig van Beethoven (1770–1827) often had plans for
operas in mind. He continually pondered on dramatic themes,
and to the end of his life he was obsessed with the idea of setting
Goethe's *Faust* to music. The various texts submitted to him
did not meet with his approval, and even Grillparzer's suggestion for an opera based on the legend of a water-nymph did
not please him. Only the text of *Fidelio* aroused any response in
him, for its revolutionary theme and high ethical values corresponded to his own ideals.

Bouilly, the librettist of Cherubini's *Les Deux Journées,* was
the author of the original text, which was performed to music
by Pierre Gaveaux in Paris in 1798 under the title *Léonore ou*

l'Amour Conjugal. The text also became known in an Italian version with music by Ferdinand Paer (1804), and it was the German translation by Joseph Sonnleithner, the secretary of the Vienna Theatre, which impressed Beethoven so strongly.

Beethoven composed *Fidelio* in a period of great creative activity. The Eroica Symphony had been completed in 1804, and in 1806 there followed the violin concerto and the Fourth Symphony. The opera was ready in the autumn of 1805; rehearsals started at once and the first performance of *Fidelio* took place on 20 November 1805 at the Theater an der Wien in Vienna. The timing of this first performance was unfortunate, being a week after the French had entered Vienna, and hardly any of Beethoven's friends and supporters had remained in the town. There was therefore not the slightest response and, after only three coolly received performances, Beethoven withdrew his work. In the following year it was altered, and reduced to two acts by S. von Breuning, while Beethoven deleted several musical numbers, rewrote both finales, and changed the overture several times. In this revised form it received two performances only in 1806, but was revived on 23 May 1814 at the Kärtnertor Theatre, this time with great success, and performed twenty-two times that same year. In spite of this, a long period elapsed before *Fidelio* established itself in the German theatre.

FIDELIO. Opera in two acts by Ludwig van Beethoven. Text after Jean Nicholas Bouilly by Joseph Sonnleithner and Georg Friedrich Treitschke. First performance: Vienna, 1805.

Characters: Don Fernando, Minister of State—baritone; Don Pizarro, Governor of the state prison—baritone; Florestan—tenor; Leonore, his wife, alias Fidelio—soprano; Rocco, chief goaler—bass; Marzelline, his daughter—soprano; Jacquino, janitor—tenor. Prisoners, townspeople.

Place: near Seville. *Time:* end of eighteenth century.

Florestan, Leonore's husband, has been imprisoned in an underground cell by his enemy, the prison governor Pizarro, and Leonore is resolved to free him. Disguised as a man under the name of Fidelio, she obtains employment with Rocco, whose daughter Marzelline falls in love with the supposed youth.

Act I, scene i. A room in Rocco's house. The janitor Jacquino, who has long been in love with Marzelline, tries to persuade her to accept his hand, but her heart belongs only to Fidelio. Jacquino's impetuous wooing is interrupted by a knocking at the door. He goes to open it; Rocco and then Fidelio enter. Rocco likes his young helper and is quite willing to accept him as a son-in-law. Leonore asks Rocco to trust her completely, since she wants to help him in looking after all the prisoners. Rocco agrees, but tells her there is one prisoner that he cannot let her see; in any case, this one will not live much longer, since on the governor's orders he is given hardly any food. Leonore guesses that this unfortunate man is her husband Florestan.

Scene ii. The prison courtyard. Pizarro is warned by a letter that the Minister is coming, unannounced, to inspect the prison, and decides to have Florestan killed, to prevent his being found. Since Rocco refuses to murder Florestan, Pizarro resolves to kill his hated enemy himself. Rocco is to dig a grave in Florestan's dungeon, so that the body can be buried there. Leonore senses that something terrible is about to happen. At her request, Rocco has the doors of the prison opened and lets the prisoners into the courtyard. To her deep disappointment Leonore fails to find Florestan among them, but Rocco promises to take her with him to the unfortunate man who is to die that day. Pizarro returns in a fury because Rocco has let the prisoners out into the courtyard.

Act II, scene i. An underground dungeon. Florestan is in chains; in a delirium he sees Leonore beside him, leading him to freedom; he then sinks back, unconscious. Rocco and Leonore descend into the dungeon and start to dig the grave. Florestan recovers consciousness and asks for bread and water. Now Leonore recognizes him, but controls herself with a great effort, for she must not yet disclose her identity. Rocco allows her to give the unfortunate man some bread and wine. Pizarro now enters; before raising his dagger to strike, he reveals his identity to Florestan. Leonore throws herself between them, and Pizarro tries to tear away the young man. With the cry 'Töt 'erst sein Weib!' ('First kill his wife!') she holds back Pizarro. Leonore firmly draws a pistol, but at that moment a trumpet call rings out and Jaquino announces the Minister's arrival. Pizarro hurries out to meet him, and, left alone, Leonore and Florestan render thanks for their great good fortune—their 'namenlose Freude' ('joy beyond all telling')—on being finally reunited.

Scene ii. The square in front of the prison. The Minister grants the prisoners their freedom in the king's name, and is deeply moved to recognize in Florestan the friend he had long thought dead. He hears from Rocco of Leonore's heroic action, and declares that she alone must release her husband from his chains. Pizarro is led away by the guards. Deeply affected and exalted by what has passed, all join in a chorus of rejoicing: 'Wer ein holdes Weib errungen' ('He whom such a wife has cherished').

Both the form and content of the libretto of *Fidelio* are clearly derived from French opera, of which the most important exponent at the turn of the century was Cherubini, whom Beethoven himself greatly admired. The individual musical numbers in *Fidelio* are connected not by recitative but by spoken dialogue, as was customary in *opéra comique* as opposed to French grand opera. The layout of the text resembles that of the German *Singspiel*, which Beethoven developed in the direction of grand opera with the result that *Fidelio* emerges as an *opera semi-seria.* Short, light songs alternate with the great sung monologues, but the tragic aspects in words and music far outweigh the comic, so that scraps of the *Singspiel*—Marzelline's aria and especially her first duet with Jacquino at the beginning of the opera—seem almost extraneous. Even the original overture in E major belongs to this rather homely atmosphere, but with the entry of Leonore and the beginning of the great quartet we enter the actual drama. This quartet in delicately

elaborated canon form is one of the most beautiful inspirations in the score. The very introductory notes with their restrained melody in the cellos and violas, supported by *pizzicato* on the basses, command our close attention—they are pure Beethoven. As the voices join in, the mood becomes more and more homely and the vocal texture is intensified as each voice takes up the tune of the canon. The return to bourgeois *Singspiel* tone in Rocco's aria 'Hat man nicht auch Gold beineben' ('Love will not suffice for marriage') is almost an embarrassment, and sometimes this aria is omitted.

The musical climax of the first act is Leonore's great aria, 'Abscheulicher'. The wonderful phrase in the recitative 'So leuchtet mir ein Farbenbogen' ('I see afar a rainbow shining') leads into the *adagio* section which can be profoundly moving

if well sung. The first Prisoners' Chorus marks the dramatic climax of this act, and in it the changes of mood between child-like joy and a dull fear produce a fantastic effect of human anguish.

The musical and dramatic construction of the second act is wonderfully concise. Beethoven's motto 'Durch Nacht zum Licht' ('Through darkness to the light') finds renewed and perfect expression here. The all-embracing, sweeping *crescendo* mounts from the dark desolation of despair to the radiant hymn of rejoicing after the prisoners have been freed. Florestan's aria, the eerie stirrings of the drama at the entrance of Rocco and Fidelio and the trio through which shines the first glimmer of hope lead to the passionate climax of 'Töt' erst sein Weib!' ('First kill his wife!'), to the trumpet-call of freedom and the overwhelming joy of reunion in the duet; breaking finally into

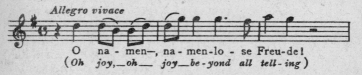

the chorus of freedom and joy of the grand finale, which anticipates the hymn of joy in the same composer's Ninth Symphony.

It is customary today to play the third *Leonore* overture before the last scene and the desire to include this splendid piece of music is quite understandable. It does however disturb the close-knit form of the second act by recalling the earlier, sombre atmosphere which was utterly dissolved by the duet 'O namen-lose Freude'. This overture cannot be played at any other point of the opera. At the beginning the shorter overture in E major (the *Fidelio* overture) is much better suited as an introduction to the first *Singspiel* scenes; played before the second act, the jubilant finale of the grand *Leonore* overture would prevent our return in mood to the darkness of the Florestan scene. Therefore inserting it in the usual place is the best solution so that during the performance of the opera one can experience this orchestral poem which in an ideal, concise form recaptures symphonically the drama of the human spirit.

It is generally thought today that the custom of playing the *Leonore No. 3* overture at this point was started by Mahler, but this is not so. When *Fidelio* was revived at Her Majesty's Theatre, London, in 1851, Benedict conducted the overture before the final scene; the same year at Covent Garden, Costa conducted it before the *beginning* of the act. The fact that the critics of the day commented on this at length, but not on the playing of it between the two scenes of the second act does seem to indicate that the playing of the *Leonore No. 3* overture at this point was a habit known to the London opera-goer.

It is also interesting to note that when Mahler conducted the opera in London in 1892 he played the overture, *not* between the two scenes as he did in Vienna and elsewhere, but before the dungeon scene.

H. D. R.

ROSSINI—DONIZETTI—BELLINI

Italian opera has always been strongly rooted in tradition, and even such shattering events as the French Revolution and the Napoleonic Wars scarcely influenced the development of opera in Italy, which did not undergo any crises such as shook the Paris or Vienna Operas. The pre-eminence of the human voice was always unquestioned even though in the course of time solos were greatly enriched by the introduction of larger ensembles, chorus and ballet. Despite this tendency towards French forms Italian opera remained faithful to its vocal tradition—and this explains its extraordinary popularity among the Italian people. In Italy everyone thinks he knows something about singing, and opera is the most easily understood and cherished form of art, and therefore of interest to the whole nation. The success or failure of a work is not proclaimed from the elegant boxes but from pit and gallery, and the popularity of an opera can be measured by the extent to which its tunes become part of everyday life and are sung and whistled in the street.

As in Venice in the seventeenth century, so an operatic industry now reappeared in the most important centres of Italian musical life, to sponsor and promote opera on a truly magnificent scale. Domenico Barbaja (1775–1841) was the most striking personality in this field. He started as a waiter, became a circus impresario, bought the San Carlo theatre in Naples, and finished by directing La Scala in Milan and two theatres in Vienna as well. Barbaja not only engaged the singers, orchestra and chorus, but even composers on a salaried basis, for which they provided him with one or two new operas each year. The most successful opera-provider was Gioacchino Rossini (1792–1868), whose name is associated with what was perhaps the most splendid period of Italian opera.

Rossini's first five operas passed almost unnoticed, but *Tancredi* (Venice, 1813) brought the young composer enormous success and a fame which spread beyond Italy to every place where Italian opera was known. After that each new Rossini opera was an event to be celebrated with equal enthusiasm everywhere. His unprecedented triumph rested mainly on his extraordinarily singable and catchy tunes. Many of them may seem banal, but they are all graceful and vivacious. The wars in Europe gave a military touch to music at this time and the march made its triumphant entry into opera. These strong elements gave Rossini's music its impetus, and helped its triumphal progress through Europe, which lay in the grip of a Rossini-fever and greeted each new work with storms of enthusiasm. Rossini was a master of effect, and the finales of his overtures and arias evoked immediate applause.

Soon after the success of *Tancredi*, Rossini was engaged as composer by the Teatro Argentina in Rome. He undertook to compose two operas a year, at 400 *scudi* apiece, without having much say in the character of his texts. *Il Barbiere di Siviglia* (*The Barber of Seville*) was composed in this way. Rossini was very unhappy about this choice of subject, since it meant composing music for a text which was already very well known in Paisiello's setting (first performed in St Petersburg in 1782), but once he had overcome his reservations and started work, the enchanting libretto quite captivated him. Because of various delays he had only thirteen days to compose the music before the première. The sheets of music were literally torn from his hands, quickly copied, and passed on to the singers to learn their roles. Such feverish pace forced Rossini to make use of music from his earlier works for certain parts of the opera and the overture had in fact served two other operas of his already—

Aureliano in Palmira (1814) and *Elisabetta, Regina d'Inghilterra* (1815). The audience took this very badly and there was in fact a real scandal at the première, not, as has been suggested, on account of under-rehearsal, but of an organized demonstration on the part of Rossini's enemies, coupled with the fact that a number of things went wrong on-stage, which amused the audience. Mme Giorgi-Righetti, the first Rosina, has left a personal account of this famous first night and wrote of the 'hot-headed enemies assembled at their posts as soon as the theatre opened'. She also reported that at the insistence of the tenor Manuel Garcia, who sang Almaviva, Rossini permitted him to substitute a Spanish air for the melody that Almaviva sings as his Serenade to Rosina in the opening scene. On this occasion no one had thought of tuning the guitar on which Garcia was to accompany himself, and he had to do so himself on the stage, whereupon one of the strings broke. When Sgr Zamboni, the Figaro, entered to sing his 'Largo al factotum', the fact that he was carrying another guitar convulsed the audience. In the second scene, the Don Basilio fell through a trap-door that had been inadvertently left open, and during the first-act finale a cat wandered across the stage. When Rossini rose from his place in the orchestra to applaud his singers, the audience considered his behaviour insulting and took their revenge during the second act, of which hardly a note was heard. As Castil-Blaze recorded, 'All the whistlers in Italy seem to have given themselves a rendezvous for this performance'.

The composer refused to conduct the second performance and instead stayed at home and retired to bed. But this time it was an enormous success. The sparkling vitality of the music overwhelmed the audience, who shouted wildly for Rossini. When he did not appear, the public rose from their seats and went to his house, where they gave him an enthusiastic ovation. This masterpiece is still invariably successful today.

IL BARBIERE DI SIVIGLIA (The Barber of Seville). Comic opera in two acts by Gioacchino Rossini. Text after Beaumarchais by Cesare Sterbini. First performance: Rome, 1816.

Characters: Count Almaviva—tenor; Doctor Bartolo—bass; Rosina, his ward—mezzo-soprano (or soprano); Basilio, music-master—bass; Bertha, Bartolo's housekeeper—mezzo-soprano; Figaro, barber—baritone; Fiorello, the count's servant—bass.

Place: Seville. *Time:* middle of eighteenth century.

Act I, scene i. A street in Seville in front of Bartolo's house. Count Almaviva has fallen in love with Rosina, Doctor Bartolo's charming ward, but she is strictly watched by her elderly guardian, who wants to marry her himself. Almaviva serenades Rosina, but unfortunately she does not appear on the balcony. Figaro, the barber, appears, and introduces himself in the aria 'Largo al factotum della città' ('Room for the city's factotum'). Almaviva bribes Figaro to help him. After Bartolo has left the house, Rosina finally appears on the balcony. Almaviva gives himself the simple name of Lindoro, for he wants her to love him for himself, irrespective of his rank or wealth. Their short conversation is interrupted, and Rosina has to retire. The Count is furious, but Figaro suggests he should introduce himself into the house disguised as a soldier.

Scene ii. A room in Dr Bartolo's house. Rosina has just written a letter to Lindoro, and reads it over in the aria: 'Una voce poco fa' ('A little voice I heard just now'). Basilio, Rosina's music-master, tells Bartolo that Count Almaviva, who they both know loves Rosina, is back in Seville. Basilio suggests that Bartolo should get rid of Almaviva by slandering him—'La calunnia'. Figaro has meanwhile told Rosina that Lindoro is coming to see her that very day, and in her happy excitement she is twice as pert as usual towards her guardian. Bartolo gets very angry, and puts her in her place in the aria: 'A un dottor della mia sorte queste scuse, signorina' ('To a man of my importance dare you offer such excuses'). The Count, disguised as a soldier, noisily enters the house, pretending to be drunk and swearing and shouting. Eventually he succeeds in speaking to Rosina. The din brings the watch to the house, and they arrest Almaviva; they soon release him, however, when he tells them who he really is—much to the surprise of Dr Bartolo—'Fredda ed immobile' ('Awe-struck and immovable').

Act II. A room in Dr Bartolo's house. Almaviva, this time disguised as a music-master, appears to give Rosina her music lesson on behalf of Basilio, who he says is ill. During the music lesson Bartolo is being shaved by Figaro in the same room, so as not to let Rosina out of his sight for one moment. Basilio, unaware of what is going on, quite unexpectedly appears to give Rosina her music lesson, but a purse of money slipped to him by the Count quickly persuades him to keep quiet. Figaro makes him believe that he has yellow fever and in the quintet they all urge him to go home to bed as quickly as possible: 'Buona sera, mio Signore' ('Fare you well then, good Signore'). The Count becomes more and more daring, and when Bartolo surprises the couple embracing, he throws both the Count and Figaro out of the house. There is no time to lose. He sends for a notary to draw up the marriage contract at once, and meanwhile tries to persuade Rosina of Lindoro's treachery by telling her that he is only trying to win her for Count Almaviva. Rosina, infuriated, discloses to her guardian that Lindoro and Figaro intend to kidnap her that very night, and Bartolo hurries out to alert the watch. Storm music introduces the final scene. Almaviva and Figaro climb in over the balcony and quickly explain to Rosina that Almaviva and Lindoro are one and the same person. The notary and Basilio appear, and the Count and Rosina sign the marriage contract. Bartolo, arriving at last with the watch, has to acknowledge that he has been outwitted.

The story of *Il Barbiere di Siviglia* with its brilliantly drawn characters and amusing situations was a source of the happiest inspiration to a consummate musician like Rossini. The score overflows with musical gems, and every aria is enchantingly melodious, delicately characterized and subtly humorous. The music is in fact imbued with the true spirit of comedy. The arias reveal most perspicacious musical portraits of all the characters. Whether describing the cunning, crafty Figaro:

or the conceited Bartolo:

these studies and those of Rosina, the Count, Basilio, and even of the busy, ingenuous housekeeper Bertha, are wonderfully pointed. The various ensembles are equally delicious, as for instance the agitated finale to the first act and the comic entrance of the Count as the music-master:

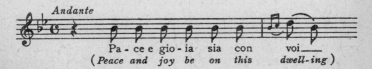

and above all the great quintet in the second act, in which the
supposedly ailing Basilio is bowed out of the house:

Il Barbiere embraces the full range of expression of the comic
opera, from the rapid chatter of *parlando* through the sighs of
love to robust derivatory jokes. This happy marriage of a
delightful libretto to the music of a genius produced a masterpiece which can even stand the obvious comparison with
Mozart's *Le Nozze di Figaro*.

After the success of *Il Barbiere*, Rossini took employment
with Barbaja, who paid him a high salary for writing two
operas every year. Barbaja presented Rossini's works at his
various theatres, thus ensuring their success. In our day there
have been most successful revivals of *La Cenerentola*, *L'Italiana
in Algeri*, *Il Turco in Italia*, *La Pietra del Paragone* and *Le Comte
Ory*—not only in Italy, but in England and Germany too.

L'ITALIANA IN ALGERI (The Italian Girl in Algiers). Comic opera in
two acts by Gioacchino Rossini. Text by Angelo Anelli (originally
written for L. Mosca and performed at La Scala, Milan in 1808). First
performance: Venice, 1813.
    Characters: Elvira, chief wife of Mustafà—soprano; Zulma, a slave,
confidante of Elvira—mezzo-soprano; Mustafà, Bey of Algiers—bass;
Haly, Captain of the Bey's Pirates—baritone; Lindoro, a young Italian
and Mustafà's favourite slave—tenor; Isabella, an Italian lady—mezzo-
soprano; Taddeo, Isabella's admirer—bass.
    Place: Algiers.
    Act I, scene i. A room in the Bey's palace. Elvira bemoans her un-
requited love and her behaviour annoys the Bey, who confides to Haly
that he wants to marry her off to his favourite slave Lindoro. Lindoro on
the other hand is miserable in his captivity and thinks longingly of his
sweetheart, Isabella.

Scene ii. The seashore. A ship has been captured by the Bey's pirates, and is being unloaded. One of the captives is the beautiful Italian Isabella, who was on her way to Africa in search of her sweetheart Lindoro. She is accompanied by her elderly admirer Taddeo.

Scene iii. The court of the Bey's palace. The Bey, who has offered Lindoro his freedom if he marries Elvira, is told by Haly of the beautiful Italian girl who has been captured. She is brought in and the sight of Mustafà amuses her. She then comes face to face with Lindoro and Elvira, and on discovering that Elvira is the Bey's wife she upbraids him for his cruel treatment of women. She orders him to take Elvira back and demands the slave Lindoro for herself.

Act II, scene i. A room in the Bey's palace. Mustafà sends a message to the Italian girl, asking her to come and take coffee with him. But first he enlists the help of Taddeo by appointing him Grand Kaimaikan of Algiers.

Scene ii. An apartment in the palace. Isabella pretends to comply with Mustafà's wishes, but at the same time she tells Elvira how to handle a husband.

Scene iii. The palace gardens. Haly, who has also fallen under the Italian girl's spell, sings the praises of Italian women. Taddeo and Lindoro now join together to plan Isabella's escape. They decide they will make Mustafà a member of the mythical order of 'Pappataci', and explain to him that he must obey the roles of the order: the duties of the model husband being to eat and sleep soundly, no more, no less.

Scene iv. Another part of the gardens. Isabella prepares her companions for their escape.

Scene v. A terrace near the seashore. Mustafà is initiated into the Society of Pappataci by Lindoro, Taddeo and the captured Italian sailors in disguise. While Mustafà is eating the ceremonial meal, Isabella and her companions prepare to escape, but Haly and Elvira give them away. It is too late however, and Mustafà realizes that his love for the Italian girl was no more than a passing fancy, and sees Elvira in a new and attractive light.

There is much charm and sparkle in this, Rossini's tenth opera. Isabella's music, which requires a formidable coloratura technique, includes the mock-heroic 'Pensa alla patria' in the second

act, and a series of delightfully comic duets, notably 'Ai capricci della sorte' with Taddeo in Act I, scene iii.

LA CENERENTOLA (Cinderella). Opera in two acts by Gioacchino Rossini. Text by Jacopo Ferretti, after Etienne's French libretto. First performance: Rome, 1817.

Characters: Don Ramiro, Prince of Salerno—tenor; Dandini, his valet —bass; Don Magnifico, Baron of Mountflagon—bass; Clorinda and Tisbe, his daughters—soprano and mezzo-soprano; Angelina, known as Cinderella, his stepdaughter—contralto; Alidoro, a philosopher—bass.

Act I, scene i. Tisbe and Clorinda are admiring themselves in a mirror and trying on dresses while their stepsister, Cinderella, is preparing their coffee. There is a knock at the door, and Alidoro, the philosopher and Prince Ramiro's tutor, appears in the guise of a beggar and asks for charity. The two sisters refuse to help him, but Cinderella gives him some bread and coffee. The Prince's retainers now arrive with the news that the Prince himself will shortly appear to invite Don Magnifico and his daughters to a ball at which he will choose his bride.

Don Magnifico relates a dream he has recently had, which he interprets as meaning that one of his daughters will soon marry well in the social scale. The Prince now appears, but disguised as his own valet, and his valet, Dandini, follows a few minutes later in the guise of the Prince. Don Magnifico and the two daughters set out to the ball, and are deaf to Cinderella's appeals that she be allowed to accompany them. No sooner have they gone than Alidoro returns to tell Cinderella that she too can go to the ball and provides her with a beautiful dress, jewels and a fairy coach.

Scene ii. Ramiro's palace. Dandini, still dressed as the Prince, appoints Don Magnifico chief butler. Tisbe and Clorinda pursue the 'prince', who suggests that as he can only marry one of them, the other should marry his valet. They are both indignant at such a suggestion. Alidoro announces the arrival of an unknown lady, wearing a mask. When she is persuaded to show her face, the sisters are struck by her resemblance to Cinderella.

Act II, scene i. The wine cellars in the Prince's palace. Don Magnifico celebrates his appointment as chief butler by sampling the Prince's wines.

Scene ii. A room in the palace. Ramiro, who has fallen in love with the mysterious lady, suspects that Dandini entertains similar feelings for the beautiful stranger. When Dandini does in fact make advances to her, she tells him she loves another, his valet. Ramiro (still disguised as his valet) reveals himself to her, but she tells him that before she agrees to marry him, he must discover her identity. She gives him one of the pair of bracelets she is wearing, so that he may eventually recognize her when he finds her. Dandini now tells the Baron that he is not really the Prince, but his valet. The Baron and the sisters leave in indignation.

Scene iii. Don Magnifico's castle. Cinderella is again by the fire. Her father and stepsisters return, in ill-humour. A storm breaks out (conjured up by Alidoro, who also arranges for the Prince's coach to break down near the castle). Dandini and Ramiro arrive and the latter, recognizing the bracelet on Cinderella's arm, claims her as his bride.

Scene iv. The Prince's palace. Cinderella, now the bride of Don Ramiro, forgives her stepsisters and father, and all ends happily amidst general rejoicing.

Among the musical items in this charming and scintillating score, attention should be drawn to the charming duet for Cinderella and Ramiro early in the first act, the great sextet of

DANDINI

Questo è un nodo av - vi - lup -
(Here's a mess there's no de -

pa - to, questo è un gruppo rin - trec - cia - to
ny - ing; here's a knot that needs un - ty - ing)

stupefaction after the Prince and Dandini have taken shelter in Don Magnifico's castle in the second act, and of course Cinderella's brilliant rondo finale 'Nacqui all' affanno e al pianto' ('Born to a life that was lonely').

In 1824 Rossini went to Paris to continue his series of triumphs there. He of course had to adapt himself to the Parisian taste which was not content with pure 'musician's' operas such as his previous works, but demanded historical grand opera. Although this was not really his métier, he became more successful in Paris year by year, until his career there reached its climax in 1829 with *Guillaume Tell*.

GUILLAUME TELL (William Tell). Grand romantic opera in four acts by Gioacchino Rossini. Text after Schiller by Hippolyte Louis Florent Bis and Victor Joseph Etienne de Jouy. First performance: Paris, 1829.

Characters: Governor Gessler—bass; Mathilde von Hapsburg—soprano; Rudolf—tenor; William Tell—baritone; Walter Fürst—bass; Melchthal—bass; Arnold, his son—tenor; Leuthold—baritone; Hedwig, Tell's wife—mezzo-soprano; Gemmy, Tell's son—soprano; a fisherman—tenor. Peasants, soldiers.

Place: Switzerland. *Time:* beginning of the fourteenth century.

Act I. Tell's house on the lake. Tell is burning to liberate Switzerland, which had once been a free country, from the yoke of its Austrian governor. The young Arnold Melchthal, however, is torn between patriotism and his love for the Princess Mathilde von Hapsburg. While the peasants are gaily celebrating a wedding with dancing and singing, a severe storm spreads over the lake. Leuthold stumbles in, a fugitive from the law, because he has killed with an axe one of the governor's mercenaries who tried to dishonour his daughter. Nobody dares ferry him across the lake to safety because of the storm, but when his pursuers are heard approaching William Tell decides to act. Furious that their prey has escaped the guards seize old Melchthal and drag him away.

Act II. Mathilde and Arnold meet in a woodland clearing. She tries to persuade him to swear loyalty to Austria, and promises him a great future at her side. Tell and Walter Fürst enter, and Mathilde withdraws. When Arnold's friends break the news to him that his old father has been murdered by the militia without any cause, Arnold's patriotism revives. The scene changes to the summit of the Rütli. The conspirators from the three original cantons meet secretly by night. Tell calls the peasants to arms and they all swear to take resolute, concerted action.

Act III. A market place. In the centre is a pole on which hangs the governor's hat. Gessler enters with his retinue to attend festival celebrations. This is the excuse for the full-scale ballet. Tell, who did not salute the hat in passing (as ordered), is seized and taken before Gessler, who commands him to shoot an apple from his son's head with an arrow, or prepare to die. Tell decides to obey this appalling demand, and his arrow pierces the apple. When Gessler asks Tell what he intended to do with the second arrow he had drawn, he replies, after the tyrant has assured him that his life is no longer in danger, that the arrow was for Gessler himself, if the first one had missed. He is seized by the soldiers and dragged away.

Act IV. Melchthal's house. Arnold decides to try and save Tell, and leaves home. The scene changes to a rocky part of the lake shore. A storm is raging. Mathilde brings Gemmy, Tell's son, back home. She too has decided to try to save Tell, and intends to remain with the peasants as a hostage. The boat carrying Gessler, his retinue and Tell approaches across the stormy lake. Tell has been freed from his chains so that he can steer the boat. He brings it towards the shore, with a great leap lands on a flat rock and pushes the boat back into the mountainous waves. Tell's house can be seen burning in the distance; Gemmy himself has set fire to it as a sign that the rebellion is to start. Gessler, who has escaped from the lake, appears with his soldiers, but Tell seizes his bow and shoots him. The Swiss enter from all sides, having defeated the mercenaries everywhere. The storm has abated and the glaciers gleam in the evening sun.

Any study of the music of *Guillaume Tell* must begin with the overture, which is rightly popular. The first passages—the lyrical *andante* with the divided cellos, the tremendous storm and the idyllic pastoral with cor anglais and flute which follows—exude mountain air. After this the brisk march seems very conventional, but its rhythm and sparkle are always effective. This juxtaposition of dazzling inspiration and slight, trivial routine is also found elsewhere in this opera.

With the tremendous success of *Guillaume Tell*, the thirty-six-year-old composer reached the height of his fame and was wise enough to retire from the theatre. He still intended to write a few sacred works in his free time. He had in any case become extremely wealthy, the first composer to draw an ample income from the success of his operas. Greatly honoured and admired, Rossini lived another thirty-eight years, a cheerful lover of good living, a well-known gourmet, and a most lovable character.

Donizetti and Bellini were contemporaries of Rossini, and in their operas too Italian melody reached a peak. Like Rossini, Gaetano Donizetti (1797-1848) was greatly honoured during his lifetime. Until the recent revival, only two of Rossini's operas, *Il Barbiere di Siviglia* and *Guillaume Tell*, had survived into this century, while until recently Donizetti was represented by five operas in regular repertory. He also enjoyed great success in Paris, where in 1840 his opera *La Favorite* was first performed. *La Fille du Régiment* (*The Daughter of the Regiment*), the music of which is Gallic in its elegance, was also composed for Paris in the same year. Both these works are now almost forgotten, though his Italian comic operas *L'Elisir d'Amore* (1832) and *Don Pasquale* (1843) are often seen on the modern stage. The latter, with its elegant charm and pointed wit, is undoubtedly Donizetti's masterpiece, and can well compare with *Il Barbiere di Siviglia*.

DON PASQUALE. Comic opera in three acts by Gaetano Donizetti. Text by the composer and Giovanni Ruffini. First performance: Paris, 1843.

Characters: Don Pasquale, an old bachelor—bass; Doctor Malatesta, his friend—baritone; Ernesto, Don Pasquale's nephew—tenor; Norina, a young widow—soprano; a notary—baritone.

Place: Rome. *Time*: eighteenth century.

Act I. Room in Don Pasquale's house. Don Pasquale, a miserly old bachelor, has decided to get married; he would be only too glad to disinherit his impecunious nephew Ernesto, who wants to marry a young widow, Norina, entirely against his uncle's wishes. Doctor Malatesta, Pasquale's physician and confidant, is in league with Ernesto and exerts himself to help his friend. He suggests to Pasquale that he should marry his 'sister' Sofronia, a gentle creature newly emerged from her convent school. Don Pasquale delightedly agrees to this proposal. The scene changes to a room in Norina's house. Norina receives a letter from Ernesto, telling her that Don Pasquale is betrothed to the sister of the treacherous Doctor Malatesta, and has turned him out of the house. He must therefore renounce his Norina. Malatesta soon calms Norina by explaining his plot to pass her off as his sister Sofronia and pretend to marry her to Pasquale, so as to give that conceited old man a salutory lesson.

Act II. A room in Don Pasquale's house. Malatesta presents the heavily veiled Norina to Pasquale as his sister Sofronia. Don Pasquale is delighted with the gentleness and modesty of this charming attractive girl and wants to marry her at once. A supposed notary enters immediately, and Malatesta and Ernesto (who has been quickly initiated into the plot) act as witnesses. As soon as the contract is signed the old man tries to embrace his modest wife, but the little dove suddenly turns into a naughty cat with unsheathed claws who mocks her husband and contemptuously takes Ernesto as her gallant. She then proceeds to give such ridiculous instructions for alterations and innovations in the house that Pasquale is beside himself at her impudence and effrontery.

Act III, scene i. Don Pasquale's house. Norina has managed to turn the whole house upside down, so that Don Pasquale's only wish is to be rid of her. When he finds a note about a rendezvous which Norina has dropped on purpose, Don Pasquale in desperation sends for Doctor Malatesta. The servants gather together and whisper about the foolish things going on in the house, the real cause of which can already be perceived. Malatesta arrives, and in a comic duet with Pasquale decides what is best to be done.

Scene ii. In the garden. Ernesto serenades Norina. When she arrives, Don Pasquale and Malatesta surprise her, and the latter suggests to Don Pasquale that he should now agree to the marriage of Ernesto and Norina. Pasquale agrees to everything, and even when he realizes how he has been fooled he still takes it all in good part.

The old *opera buffa* theme, already known from *La Serva Padrona*, here takes on a new and charming variation. The eighteenth century breathes through the music, which has a rare lightness and grace, even if the individual characterization is a little conventional. The capricious Norina is the best piece of musical portraiture and provides a real display role for a coloratura soubrette. Donizetti's greatest quality is his humour, which is always elegant, even in farce, such as the quarrel between Norina and Pasquale. The servants' chorus in the third act—'Che interminabile andir e vieni' ('What perpetual coming and going')—is unique of its kind.

L'Elisir d'amore is as attractive as *Don Pasquale*, although this early work has not the mature musical balance of the later one.

L'ELISIR D'AMORE (The Elixir of Love). Comic opera in two acts by Gaetano Donizetti. Text by Felice Romani. First performance: Milan, 1832.

Characters: Adina, a wealthy farm-owner—soprano; Giannetta, her friend—soprano; Nemorino, a young peasant—tenor; Belcore, a sergeant—baritone; Dulcamara, a quack doctor—bass. Peasants, soldiers.

Place: an Italian village. *Time:* eighteenth century.

Nemorino is desperately in love with the coquettish Adina, but she does not show much interest in him. She prefers reading books and tells her village neighbours about them. She recounts to them the story of Tristan and Isolde and of the love-potion which had such miraculous effects on them both. A troop of soldiers arrives in the village, and the sergeant, Belcore, makes advances to Adina, who receives them most favourably, while Nemorino is consumed with jealousy. Doctor Dulcamara arrives, extolling his magical remedies, and the whole village greets him enthusiastically. Nemorino asks him secretly for a love-potion and the astute Dulcamara sells him a 'magic liquid' (in reality a strong Bordeaux) which will not take effect for twenty-four hours, but when it does will make all the girls of the village fall in love with him. Nemorino drinks the strong wine, to which he is not accustomed, and is convinced that he will soon win even Adina. His behaviour towards his beloved is so changed that she now at last becomes conscious of her love for him, but she is so piqued by his new self-assured manner that to vex him she encourages Belcore's suit. This drives Nemorino to despair and he believes that only another potion can save him. To earn some money, he is even prepared to enlist as a recruit under Belcore, his rival. Meanwhile the news has spread round the village that Nemorino's uncle has died and left him a rich legacy. Now all the girls run after Nemorino, flatter him and pretend to be in love with him, but Nemorino thinks this is the effect of the potion. In the end Adina also declares her love for him, and when the news of the rich inheritance is confirmed Nemorino's happiness is complete. Dulcamara explains to him that all is due to his love-potion.

Pure comedy music accompanies this simple story. Musically, of course, Doctor Dulcamara is readily recognized from his chattering *parlando*, but the swaggering Belcore is also a well-known comic type. There is grand opera in Adina's coloratura and Nemorino's sighs. Nemorino's *romanza* 'Una furtiva lagrima' ('A furtive tear') has become one of the most famous

U—na fur-ti—va la-gri-ma___
(*Who can de-ceive a lov-ing heart,___*)

negl' oc-chi suoi___ spun-tò
love is not blind___ but wise)

of Italian arias. But comedy triumphs over all sentimentality and one gay melody follows another, for example the charming barcarolle, which is originally sung by Adina and Dulcamara, and which recurs at the end of the opera.

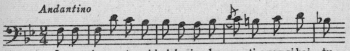

Io son ric-co,e tu sei bel-la, io du - ca - ti,e vez-zi hai   tu
(*I am rich and you are love-ly, I have gold and you have charms*)

Donizetti's tragic grand opera *Lucia di Lammermoor* used to be considered unquestionably his best work.

LUCIA DI LAMMERMOOR. Tragic opera in three acts by Gaetano Donizetti. Text by Salvatore Cammarano after Walter Scott. First performance: Naples, 1835.

Characters: Enrico (Henry Ashton)—baritone; Lucia (Lucy), his sister —soprano; Edgardo (Edgar, Master of Ravenswood)—tenor; Arturo (Arthur Bucklaw)—tenor; Raimondo (Bide-the-Bent), Lucy's confidant— bass; Alisa (Alice), Lucy's companion—soprano; Normanno (Norman), follower of Henry—tenor. Nobles and servants.

Place: Scotland. *Time*: about 1700.

Henry Ashton wrongfully holds the estates of Edgar, between whose family and his own there has long been a deadly feud. In addition Ashton's political activity against the King has placed him in a perilous situation, and he has resolved to re-establish his family's position by marrying his sister Lucy to Arthur Bucklaw.

Act I, scene i. A wood near Ravenswood Castle. Norman tells Lord Henry that he believes Lucy has been secretly meeting Edgar in the castle garden, and he has dispatched his huntsmen to discover whether this is so. Henry swears that he will prevent the union between the two lovers, even if it means that their lives will be forfeit. The huntsmen return and reveal that the nightly visitor is in fact Edgar.

Scene ii. In the castle garden. Lucy, accompanied by Alice, awaits Edgar at the fountain. She sings of a young woman murdered long ago by one of the Ravenswoods whose ghost she believes she has seen. Her thoughts turn to Edgar however, and she sings of her love for him. He now enters and informs Lucy that he has to leave for France. He suggests he should tell Henry of his love for Lucy, and propose a reconciliation. Lucy tells him such an interview would be useless and begs him to keep their secret. They vow eternal love, exchange rings and bid each other a passionate farewell.

Act II, scene i. Henry's room in the castle. Lord Henry tells Norman that although Lucy has so far refused to marry Lord Arthur, he is certain that he can now persuade her to change her mind by showing her a forged letter from Edgar which will make her believe that he is in love with someone else. In the duet that follows between Lucy and her brother, Henry reveals that only Arthur can save him from death for conspiring against the crown; this and the forged letter force Lucy to agree to the marriage. First however she seeks advice from Raymond, who adds his persuasions to those of her brother.

Scene ii. The great hall of the castle. The guests have assembled for the signing of the wedding contract, and sing of the happy bridal day. When Lucy enters looking pale and distraught, Henry tells Arthur that she is still mourning for their mother, who died recently. No sooner has Lucy signed the contract than Edgar rushes into the hall. In the great sextet which follows Edgar asks why he is restraining himself from vengeance; Henry expresses sorrow for his sister's plight; Lucy sings of her despair at her brother's treachery; Raymond invokes the aid of Heaven; and Alice and Arthur pray that there will be no bloodshed. Swords are drawn, but Raymond orders all to sheath their weapons. Edgar gives Lucy back her ring; she returns his, which he hurls to the ground and stamps underfoot. Cursing the Lammermoor family, he rushes out.

Act III, scene i. (The scene in which Henry challenges Edgar to a duel while a storm rages is generally omitted.) The great hall of the castle. The celebrations in honour of the wedding continue. The guests' rejoicings are rudely interrupted by the entrance of Raymond, with the news that Lucy has lost her reason and killed her husband. Lucy herself now appears, and in the most famous 'mad scene' in all opera goes through an imaginary wedding ceremony with Edgar. She begs that no tears be shed when she dies, but that flowers be placed on her grave.

Scene ii. The tomb of the Ravenswoods. Edgar, unaware of Lucy's fate, wanders amidst the tombs of his ancestors, anxious to join them as now he has nothing to live for. A group of people sadly make their way from the castle. From them Edgar learns that Lucy has lost her reason and is dying. He determines to try and see her once more, but is restrained by Raymond. The tolling of a bell informs them that Lucy is dead. Edgar mourns her passing and, promising her spirit that nothing can part them, stabs himself.

The famous sextet at the end of the second act and Lucy's great mad scene are outstanding pieces of dramatic composition and

jewels of early operatic literature, but in spite of them the opera, once so enthusiastically acclaimed, is now neglected—in Germany, at any rate—possibly because of its exaggeratedly romantic story. In Italy, England, America and France, however, such great singers as Callas and Sutherland have made this work popular once more.

In contrast to his great contemporaries Rossini and Donizetti, almost all the operas of Vincenzo Bellini (1801–35) were tragedies. He managed to express strong passions in great rhythmical melodies while containing dramatic outbursts in a musical balance, which makes him a direct precursor of Verdi. Bellini had a remarkable talent for writing tunes and his vocal line is always attractive and very characteristic. He had the good fortune to find a most cultured collaborator in Felice Romani, whose libretti corresponded to Bellini's ideas in every way.

La Sonnambula and *Norma* both date from 1831, and in them Bellini's lyric gifts reach their maturity. *La Sonnambula* was the fourth of seven operas by Bellini for which Felice Romani furnished a libretto, and the tender rustic idyll certainly inspired the composer to write some of his most beautiful melodies. Amina's 'Ah! non credea' in the last scene has in it the essence of Bellini's art, and the first notes of the aria are inscribed on the composer's tomb in his native Catania. The success of *La Sonnambula* was phenomenal: created by Pasta and Rubini in Milan in March 1831, by 1850 it had been produced in forty-five different cities in twelve different countries.

LA SONNAMBULA (The Sleepwalker). Opera in two acts by Vincenzo Bellini. Text by Felice Romani. First performance: Milan, 1831.

Characters: Count Rodolfo, lord of the castle—bass; Teresa, proprietress of the mill—soprano; Amina, her foster-daughter—soprano; Lisa, proprietress of the village inn—soprano; Elvino, a young farmer—tenor; Alessio—a villager.

Place: a village in Switzerland. *Time:* early nineteenth century.

Act I, scene i. The village green. The villagers assemble to celebrate the betrothal of Amina, foster-daughter of Teresa, owner of the village mill, and Elvino, a rich young farmer. Lisa, the proprietress of the local inn, expresses her jealousy at the coming wedding, for she is herself in love with Elvino. Amina enters and expresses her joy in the aria 'Come per me sereno' ('How, for me brightly shining'). The notary and Elvino now arrive, and as the contract is signed Elvino places a ring on Amina's finger. The noise of a horse and carriage is heard, and a handsome stranger appears on the scene; it is Count Rodolfo, lord of the castle, who is returning home after many years' absence. He looks around and recalls the scenes of his childhood, then turns his attention to the beautiful young Amina, much to Elvino's annoyance. Lisa invites the stranger to spend the night at her inn and Teresa urges everyone to retire for, she says, the village is haunted by a phantom in white. As the villagers disperse, Amina and Elvino again pledge their love.

Scene ii. A room in the inn. Count Rodolfo muses on the rival attractions of Amina and Lisa. The latter enters, and behaves in a coquettish manner, also informing Rodolfo that his identity has been discovered, and that later that evening the villagers are coming to welcome him home. A sound outside the window causes Lisa to hurry from the room quickly, and in her flight she drops her kerchief, which Rodolfo picks up and puts on the bed. The window opens, and Amina enters. She is sleepwalking, dressed in white—in other words, she is the 'phantom' of whom the superstitious villagers are afraid. In her sleep she talks of Elvino and his jealousy, and of their marriage the next day. The Count is moved by her innocence and, extinguishing the candles, steps out on to the balcony, leaving Amina alone asleep on his bed. The villagers now arrive to greet Rodolfo. They are somewhat amused to see the sleeping figure of a girl on the bed, and are about to withdraw discreetly, when Lisa returns with a light. She has overheard Amina's voice and, thinking the worst, brings in Elvino and shows him the sleeping girl. The noise awakens Amina, who is at a loss to explain her presence in the Count's bedroom. Elvino accuses her of betraying his love. All share his suspicions, except Teresa, who tries to comfort her. She picks up Lisa's kerchief and drapes it around Amina's shoulders. As Elvino turns away from Amina, she faints in her foster-mother's arms.

Act II, scene i. A wood near the village. The villagers are on their way to the castle to ask Rodolfo to intercede with Elvino on Amina's behalf. Elvino enters and meets Amina and Teresa. Still believing her false to him, he snatches the ring from her finger; in spite of this gesture, he cannot bring himself to hate her.

Scene ii. The village near Teresa's mill. Lisa has seized the opportunity offered by the situation, and induced Elvino to promise to marry her. Preparations for the wedding are being made; Count Rodolfo enters, and tries to dissuade Elvino from this marriage, explaining that Amina is innocent and that she is a sleepwalker. Elvino, ignorant of such a phenomenon, still refuses to believe him. Teresa now enters and begs the villagers to be quiet as Amina is sleeping in the nearby mill. When she learns that Elvino intends to marry Lisa, she produces the kerchief that she had picked up in the Count's bedroom. Elvino feels that he has been betrayed a second time. Once again Rodolfo protests that Amina is innocent. 'Who can prove it?' asks Elvino. 'She herself,' replies the Count, and points. Amina, walking in her sleep, comes up to the assembled villagers. She kneels and prays for Elvino, and speaks of the ring that he had snatched from her finger and the flowers he had given her the day before—'Ah! non credea mirarti' ('Scarcely could I believe it!'). Elvino, now convinced of the truth, replaces the ring on her finger,

and as the villagers cry 'Viva Amina' she awakens. Her sorrow turns to
joy, which is expressed in the brilliant final rondo 'Ah! non giunge!'

Besides *La Sonnambula* (*The Sleepwalker*), it was *Norma* which
really made Bellini world-famous; a work of austere grandeur
which is still very impressive today.

NORMA. Tragic opera in two acts by Vincenzo Bellini. Text by Felice
Romani. First performance: Milan, 1831.
  Characters: Pollio, Roman pro-consul in Gaul—tenor; Flavius, his
confidant—tenor; Oroveso, arch-Druid—bass; Norma, his daughter,
high-priestess—soprano; Clotilda, Norma's friend—soprano; Adalgisa, a
virgin of the temple—soprano.
  Place: Gaul. *Time:* first century AD.
  Act I, scene i. The sacred grove of the Druids. The Druids and warriors
of Ancient Gaul, who are on their way to watch the rising of the moon,
pause at the altar of the God Irminsul where, led by the high-priest
Oroveso, they beg the gods to rouse the people to war against the
invading Romans. They retire from the scene and Pollio, the Roman
pro-consul, appears, accompanied by his friend Flavius. He tells Flavius
that he no longer loves Norma, daughter of Oroveso and high-priestess
of the Druids, who has borne him two children. He has seen Adalgisa, a
priestess of the temple, and fallen in love with her. The sacred shield is
struck, summoning the priests and priestesses to the altar, and the two
Romans retire. Norma, who has broken her vows of chastity, and whose
relationship with the Roman pro-consul is unsuspected, rebukes the
Druids for demanding war against Rome without divine sanction. She
then prays for peace, singing the famous 'Casta Diva' ('Chaste goddess').
The Druids and Norma now leave the grove. Adalgisa enters and prays
for strength to resist her love for Pollione, who begs her to flee with him
to Rome, where they can live together in safety and happiness.
  Scene ii. Norma's dwelling. Norma confides in Clotilda her fears that
Pollio is going to desert her. Someone is heard approaching, and Norma
bids Clotilda conceal the two children. Adalgisa enters. She has come to
confess to the high-priestess that she is in love. Norma, thinking of her
own similar plight, releases Adalgisa from her sacred vows, and asks who
is the man. As Pollio enters, Adalgisa reveals that it is he. Norma
accuses her lover of treachery, and Adalgisa declares that she would die
rather than flee with the betrayer of the high-priestess whom she loves
so well. The sacred shield is again heard, summoning Norma to the
temple.
  Act II, scene i. Norma's dwelling. Norma, dagger in hand, tries to
bring herself to kill her sleeping children, but cannot. She sends for
Adalgisa and asks her to take the children to Pollio in the Roman camp,
marry him and look after the children for her. Adalgisa again refuses to
leave Norma, and in the duet 'Mira, O Norma' ('See, oh Norma') says

Mi-ra, O Nor-ma, a' tuoi gi-noc-chi ques-ti
(*See, oh Nor-ma, they kneel be-fore thee, thy be-*)

ca-ri__ tuoi par-go let-ti.
(*lov-ed__ and guile-less chil-dren*)

she will never leave the temple, but will go to Pollio and try to persuade him to return to Norma.

Scene ii. The temple of Irminsul. The Gallic warriors and Oroveso
once more assemble. They learn from the high-priest that Pollio is
being replaced by an even crueller commander. He advises them to bide
their time and then to revolt. Norma is awaiting the return of Adalgisa,
with, she hopes, the penitent Pollio. Instead of listening to Adalgisa,
however, Pollio has tried to carry her off. This is reported to Norma
by Clotilda. Norma now strikes the sacred shield three times and summons all the Druids, priestesses and warriors. She announces that the gods
have decreed war against Rome, and that the sacrificial victim must be
offered to the war-god. At that moment a tumult is heard outside and
Pollio, who has tried to break into the temple to abduct Adalgisa, is
brought in. Norma cannot bring herself to strike the fatal blow against
him. She pleads with him for the last time, and says that she will spare
his life if he gives up Adalgisa. He refuses. She then threatens to kill his
children and he offers himself as the victim. Norma summons the
assembly for the last time and bids them prepare the sacrificial pyre. She
declares that the victim for the sacrifice is to be a priestess who has broken
her vows of chastity. They ask who it is, and Norma replies that it is
herself. She confesses everything and asks her father to care for her children. Turning to Pollio she says that despite his treachery she loves him
even to death. His love is now rekindled and he asks to be allowed to
share her fate. Slowly they go to their death together.

I Puritani, Bellini's eleventh and last opera, was immediately
preceded by *Beatrice di Tenda*, which had been produced at the
Teatro La Fenice, Venice, in March 1833. The following month
Bellini went to London, where he heard for the first time the
famous Malibran in *La Sonnambula*; he broke his journey in
Paris, where he was approached by the director of the Opéra to
write an opera in French; this he agreed to do after his journey
to England. But when he returned to Paris in August that

year, he found that although the Opéra still wanted a new work
from him, the terms were far less generous than those he had
been offered a few months earlier. Bellini, who wanted to settle
in Paris, hoped that the Théâtre-Italien, where his *La Sonnambula, Il Pirata, La Straniera* and *I Capuleti ed i Montecchi* had all
been performed with great success, would now invite him to
write an opera. Negotiations were protracted, and it was not
until the following January that he was able to sign a contract
to complete an opera for the 1834–35 season. He was promised
four of the leading singers of the day for the cast: Giulia Grisi,
Rubini, Tamburini and Lablache.

Bellini had meanwhile taken an apartment in the Boulevard
des Italiens and began to look around for a suitable librettist.
His choice fell on Count Carlo Pepoli, whom he had met in the
salon of Princess Cristina of Belgiojoso, whose admirers included Heine and Chopin. Like the Princess, Count Pepoli was
a refugee from the Austrian occupation of Italy and was a minor
literary figure. After a month's research he offered a number
of possible subjects to Bellini, of which the composer was most
attracted by *Les Têtes Rondes et Les Cavaliers*, a vaudeville by
François Ancelot and Xavier-Boniface Saintine dating from the
previous year. Perhaps Bellini's stay in London attracted him
to this subject, which was set in Plymouth at the time of the
Civil War. In any case the correct title *I Puritani di Scozia* is still
something of a mystery geographically, for whoever heard of a
Plymouth in Scotland?

Count Pepoli was inexperienced in writing for the theatre,
and Bellini had indeed been spoilt by his previous librettist
Felice Romani, whose simple natural verses allowed him to
write the kind of music for which he had become famous.
Pepoli, on the other hand, insisted on correct poetry; and as
Rossini had suggested that Bellini should devote special attention
to the cultivation of dramatic effect in this opera, as well as to
his orchestration, the composition of *I Puritani* was not an easy
task. Bellini began work in mid-April 1834, but soon left Paris
for Puteaux, where he stayed in the house of an English friend,
one Mr Lewis.

Bellini spent the whole summer at Puteaux, accepting some
of Pepoli's verses, rejecting others. Towards the end of October
he returned to Paris, the score virtually complete. He then

sought Rossini's advice and together they went through the score page by page, the older composer making valuable suggestions to the younger. Rehearsals began at the Théâtre-Italien at the end of December, and the first night took place three weeks later.

I PURITANI (The Puritans). Opera in three acts by Vincenzo Bellini. Text by Count Carlo Pepoli. First performance: Paris 1835.

Characters: Sir Bruno Robertson, a Puritan, Captain of the Guard—tenor; Sir Riccardo Forth (Sir Richard), Puritan Colonel—baritone; Sir Giorgio Walton (Sir George), a Puritan—bass; Elvira, daughter of Lord Walton—soprano; Lord Gualtiero Walton (Lord Walter Walton) Puritan governor-general—bass; Lord Arturo Talbot (Arthur Talbot), cavalier—tenor; Enrichetta di Francia (Queen Henrietta of France), widow of Charles I—mezzo-soprano.

Place: The vicinity of Plymouth, England. *Time*: Period of the Civil War.

Act I, scene i. The fortress. As dawn breaks, the fortress slowly comes to life and the soldiers, expressing their determination to defeat the Stuarts, prepare for the day's duties. From inside the fortress, voices are heard singing a hymn of praise to the Creator. Soon the whole fortress is bustling with activity as preparations are made for the wedding that day of Elvira, daughter of Lord Walter Walton, to Sir Richard Forth, a Puritan general.

Sir Richard enters in a despondent mood and tells Sir Bruno Robertson, captain of the guard, that Lord Walton has refused him Elvia's hand as she is in love with Lord Arthur Talbot, a Stuart sympathizer. Sir Bruno tries to comfort Richard by urging him not to think of Elvira, but of the brilliant military career that is sure to be his.

Scene ii. Elvira's apartment. Elvira, ignorant of the fact that her father has told Sir Richard that he cannot marry her, is sad and filled with misgivings. Her uncle, Sir George Walton, enters to tell her she is to be married that very day; she replies that if she has to marry a man she does not love her heart will break. Then, greatly to her surprise, Sir George tells her that he has been able to intercede with her father on her behalf, and that her bridegroom is to be Lord Arthur Talbot. A horn is heard heralding his arrival.

Scene iii. The main hall of the fortress. Lord Arthur, attended by his squires and pages, is welcomed to the fortress. He tenderly greets Elvira in the aria 'A te, o cara, amor talora' ('To thee my beloved, love lead me'). Lord Walton then tells the couple that the wedding ceremony will have to proceed without him, for he has to conduct an important prisoner to London. Further, no one may leave the fortress in his absence on pain of death; however, he gives Lord Arthur a safe-conduct which will permit him and Elvira to make their way to the church.

The prisoner, Queen Henrietta, is now led in. Lord Arthur asks Sir George, 'Is she not a friend to the Stuarts?' and the latter replies, 'She has been a prisoner many months and was supposed to be a friend and emissary of the Stuarts under a false name'. Then in a brief conversation with the prisoner, Lord Arthur tells her that as his own father was killed for supporting the Stuart cause, he is prepared to save her, whoever she may be. She reveals her true identity to him and Lord Arthur is determined to put his loyalty to the throne even above his love for Elvira.

Elvira enters in her wedding dress carrying a magnificent veil; she expresses her happiness in the polonaise 'Son vergin vezzosa'. Elvira approaches Queen Henrietta and asks her to show her how to arrange the veil; in a playful moment she places the veil on the Queen's head. The Queen is thankful that the veil can conceal her grief but Arthur is suddenly struck with the idea that if he could persuade the Queen to disguise herself as Elvira he could help her escape.

Elvira is led away by her uncle and Lord Arthur bids the Queen keep on the veil, so that, using the safe-conduct, he can lead her out of the fortress and so to safety. At this moment Sir Richard, distraught at the thought of losing Elvira, rushes in with drawn sword and challenges Arthur to a duel. The Queen throws herself between the two men and in so doing the veil falls from her face to disclose to Sir Richard's great surprise, not Elvira but the female prisoner. Seizing this situation as an opportunity of ridding himself of his rival and at the same time discrediting him, he allows the pair to escape, just a few moments before the wedding procession enters the hall.

Elvira asks, 'Where is Arthur?' 'He has just left,' replies Sir Richard. 'And where is the traitress?' asks Elvira; 'She's fled with the false one,' replies Sir George. The alarm is sounded and orders given for the couple to be pursued. Elvira, believing she has been betrayed, loses her reason and imagining she sees Arthur, begs him to accompany her to the altar. As her thoughts appear to wander even more wildly, all present invoke a curse on the two traitors.

Act II. The people within the fortress are in despair at Elvira's madness. Sir George enters and all ask him for news of Elvira. He describes how she wandered through the fortress, a crown of roses on her dishevelled head, acting out the marriage ceremony. Sir Richard enters with an order from Cromwell demanding the capture and death of Lord Arthur.

Elvira, her mind still deranged, enters and, recalling the sound of the voice of her beloved, pleads for his return or for her own death. After Elvira has left, Sir George, believing that the mere sight of Arthur will restore her senses, begs Richard to spare his life. Moved by Sir George's entreaties, Richard agrees, provided that Arthur is captured unarmed. If, however, he is taken while fighting with the Stuart army, he must perish. The two men swear to defend their country and to fight for liberty.

Act III. A grove near Elvira's house. A storm is raging and Arthur, who has wandered abroad, has returned to his own country. He is glad that he has evaded his pursuers and has come to seek Elvira. He hears her voice singing his love-song. He replies to it by singing of his exile. The sound of his voice brings Elvira into the garden; at first she thinks the sound is an hallucination but when she finds it really is Arthur, her joy knows no bounds and the lovers throw themselves into each other's arms. Arthur

explains that the lady he helped escape was the Queen and that he has
never loved anyone but Elvira, who now begins to recover her reason.
At that moment the soldiers searching for Arthur are heard approaching.
Arthur attempts to flee with Elvira but she, believing he is again trying
to leave her, lapses once more into delirium. The soldiers enter and arrest
Lord Arthur: 'God and your country have condemned you to death!'
declares Sir Richard. At these words Elvira's reason is fully restored and
she begs to be allowed to die with her lover. The soldiers cry out for
immediate vengeance on the traitor and grow impatient at the delay of
the execution. Suddenly the sound of trumpets is heard and a messenger
hurries in with a letter from Sir George. The Stuarts have been defeated
and Cromwell has pardoned all prisoners. Amidst general rejoicing, the
lovers embrace and happily contemplate their future together.

The first night was a triumph for all concerned. The great duet,
'Suoni la tromba' brought the entire audience to its feet;

ladies waved their handkerchiefs and men their hats. Bellini was
summoned to the stage, despite a rule that the composer should
not appear until the end of the opera; but it was impossible to
proceed with the performance until Bellini had taken a call.
Rossini, writing to a friend in Milan, said, 'It is unnecessary for
me to describe the duet for the two basses; you must have heard
it where you are!' Elvira's 'Qui la voce' moved the house to

audible weeping; and the finale to the opera was the signal for
an unparalleled outburst of enthusiasm.

Originally Bellini intended to end *I Puritani* with a big scene
for the soprano. In a letter dated 30 November 1834 to Francesco Florimo, Bellini's closest friend who had been a fellow-
student with him at the conservatory of San Pietro a Majella in
Naples, the composer wrote: 'I have just heard of Mme
Malibran's brilliant success in *La Sonnambula* [in Naples] . . .
You advise me to finish up my *I Puritani* with a big scene for
the prima donna. I did intend to do so, but, in consequence of
some very proper changes in the second act, the singer's scene
comes in the middle of this act, a situation rather like that
quator of *Nina* [an opera by Paisiello], but with a different
setting, passing through phases of melancholy, gaiety, dimness,
and ending in a vigorous *agitato*. So another scene at the end,
perhaps misplaced, could only injure the whole I have
decided to close it with a little duet, graceful or passionate,
between the tenor and the prima donna, like that in the first
finale of *La Sonnambula*. It would be preceded by a *largo* concerted between the two basses, the tenor, the soprano and the
chorus, as in *Norma*. I think it will go pretty well, the situation
being interesting during the whole performance. Yes certainly I
will do a new *cavatina* for Mme Malibran . . . Lastly tell her
[Malibran] that I will arrange and adapt *I Puritani* for her voice,
and she need not fear the part, as it is as passionate as *Nina*, and
the situations spoken and acted in prose by her would by themselves be tremendously effective.'

Difficulties arose and despite efforts by Florimo and Malibran
herself, *I Puritani* was not given in Naples until after the deaths
of both Bellini and Malibran. Indeed the latter never sang the
role of Elvira. When the news of Bellini's death reached her in
Milan at the end of September 1835, she burst into tears, and
putting her hand on her forehead exclaimed, 'Sento che non
tarderò molto a seguirlo' (I feel I shall soon follow him). In
fact she died one year later to the day – 23 September 1836.

H. D. R.

GERMAN ROMANTIC OPERA

The wave of romanticism which engulfed European poetry at the beginning of the nineteenth century was the natural consequence of the shattering era of the French Revolution and the Reign of Terror through which the people had passed. Men fled into the world of unreality to forget the horror of the previous decade, and a welcome contrast was offered by the magic realm of romanticism with its fairy-tales, sagas and legends, with the glitter and mystery of the Middle Ages and the perfume and secrecy of the East. A new vision of the world arose and classical severity gave way to the romantic drive towards freedom.

Folk music—even that from foreign countries—found its way into 'artistic' music and fertilized it most beneficially. Delicate observation of nature found expression in musical sounds; the world of fairies, spirits and elves was brought to life, and strange moods and frontiers of the spirit were explored in music, while this new world of wonder and marvel found an enthusiastic echo in the hearts of the new generation. Opera was also affected by this trend, which was championed by the poet, painter and composer E. T. A. Hoffmann (1776–1822), who in 1813 wrote in his essay 'Der Dichter und der Komponist' ('Poet and composer'): 'I believe romantic opera is the only genuine opera, for music belongs in the realm of romanticism alone'.

Hoffmann started by composing several *Singspiele*, musical dramas and operas, as for instance *Aurora*, which, although written for the Bamberg theatre, where Hoffmann was conductor from 1808–11, was never produced there in his lifetime. In fact its first performance did not take place until 1933, when it was produced in a revised version by L. Böttcher. He then wrote *Undine* (Berlin 1816), the first example of romantic opera, for which the poet Friedrich de la Motte-Fouqué wrote a libretto based on his famous short story in verse. The music is continuous, thereby establishing the type of opera which Weber developed in his *Euryanthe* and Wagner was later to perfect in *Lohengrin*. Although *Undine* (particularly its libretto) is full of signs of later romantic opera, Hoffmann's music is still strongly bound to the style of his predecessors.

If Hoffmann hoped to lay the foundations of German romantic opera in *Undine*, Carl Maria von Weber (1786–1826) did in fact do so a few years later. An adventurous life had thrown him into close contact with the theatrical profession from his early youth. His first deep impressions emanated from the theatre, it was for the theatre that he wrote his first important works, and the theatre that moulded his considerable talents. Weber was not very successful with his early works *Waldmädchen* (*The forest maiden*) (1800), *Peter Schmoll* (1803) and *Abu Hassan* (1811), but with his collection of songs of freedom set to poems by Theodor Körner he suddenly became famous, and in 1817 was summoned to Dresden to found a German opera. His gifts for training an orchestra, directing an ensemble, conducting and designing sets made him a brilliant opera director, and since he was also a composer he possessed all the necessary qualifications for successfully taking up the fight against the ever-dominant Italian influence on behalf of German opera. In 1826 Munich dismissed its Italian opera troupe, in 1828 Vienna did the same, and when Dresden followed in 1832 the last Italian musical bastion on German soil had fallen. Of Weber's early operas only *Abu Hassan* is still performed on stage and on the radio.

ABU HASSAN. *Singspiel* in one act by Carl Maria von Weber. Text by Friedrich Carl Hiemer. First performance: Munich, 1811.
   Characters: The Caliph—spoken role; Zobeide, his wife—spoken role; Abu Hassan, favourite of the Caliph—tenor; Fatima, his wife—soprano; Omar, a money-changer—bass. Retinue, messengers and servants of the Caliph, and creditors.
   Place: Bagdad. *Time:* legendary times.
   Abu Hassan is up to the ears in debt. Instead of enjoying wine and fine dishes, he now has to content himself with bread and water. With his wife he sings the duet 'Liebes Weibchen, reiche Wein' ('Lovely women, sparkling wines'). His creditors press the unfortunate man in an agitated and grotesque chorus, and Omar says he will take over all the debts for the time being. Meanwhile Fatima has had the Caliph's wife informed that Abu Hassan is dead, in the hope that she will pay his debts, but Abu Hassan tells the Caliph the same about Fatima in the same hope. Omar, who loves Fatima, comes back to claim his reward for having paid off the creditors, but Fatima cannot endure the attentions of the fat old man. They sing a duet: 'Siehst du diese grosse Menge' ('Look at this great heaving monster'). Fatima makes him so frightened of Abu Hassan's jealousy that he hides in terror when the master of the house

returns. Abu Hassan pretends to be furiously jealous and Omar almost faints with fear. The Caliph and his wife send messengers to find out who actually has died. In the end they both come personally to convince themselves of the truth of this calamity, and find Abu Hassan and Fatima lying there dead. When the Caliph offers a thousand ducats to anyone who can tell him who died first, Abu Hassan jumps up declaring that he died first and asks for the money. The Caliph makes the best of it and pardons this lovable rascal.

Almost all the music of this *Singspiel* is as exuberant and gay as the charming short overture. The love scenes touch on deeper things, but the comic character of the piece is always most delightfully preserved.

On 18 June 1821 the first performance of *Der Freischütz* took place in the Berlin Schauspielhaus, and it was acclaimed with incredible enthusiasm. It is difficult to realize today the effect it had in its triumphal progress throughout Germany. *Der Freischütz* found friends and admirers among all sections of the population, and its catchy tunes were sung everywhere.

The story is based on the old folk-legend of the wild huntsman, which Friedrich Kind, who had a flair for the theatre, turned into a libretto which is both effective and a suitable vehicle for Weber's music.

DER FREISCHÜTZ (The Marksman). Romantic opera in three acts by Carl Maria von Weber. Text by Friedrich Kind. First performance: Berlin, 1821.

Characters: Prince Ottokar—baritone; Kuno, hereditary forester—bass; Agathe, his daughter—soprano; Ännchen, her friend—soprano; Kaspar and Max, young huntsmen—bass and tenor; Hermit—bass; Kilian, a peasant—tenor; Samiel, the wild huntsman—spoken role; the prince's retinue, huntsmen and peasants.

Place: Bohemia. *Time:* after the Thirty Years War.

Act I. An open space in front of a tavern in the wood. Kilian has just been named the winner of a shooting match, in which Max was unlucky and is consequently being teased by Kilian and the chorus of peasants in the aria 'Schau der Herr mich an als König' ('There's the man who thought to beat me'). Max is in great despair, since on the following day he is to compete in the final shooting trial in the presence of the Prince; if he fails, he must renounce the hand of Agathe, the daughter of Kuno, the hereditary forester, and with it the prospect of succeeding him. Kuno exhorts him to pull himself together. The huntsmen retire and the peasants start dancing to a waltz tune. Max stays behind, alone and in despair, and gives voice to his feelings in the aria: 'Durch die Wälder, durch die Auen' ('Through the forest and o'er the meadows'). Enter Kaspar, who has sold his soul to Samiel, and will forfeit it if he cannot provide the wild hunts-man with a new victim. He has decided on Max and tries to make him drunk—'Hier im ird 'schen Jammertal' ('In this earthly vale of woe'). He then makes him shoot an eagle from the darkening sky with his rifle, and explains to him that he has shot with a magic bullet which alone can help him in the shooting trial on the following day. In the end Max accepts Kaspar's proposal and agrees to come to the Wolf's Glen at mid-night to receive his magic bullets. A sinister song of triumph by Kaspar closes the act.

Act II, scene i. A room in the forester's house. Agathe is full of vague foreboding, but Ännchen tries to cheer her up—'Schelm, halt fest' ('There, that's done!'). It is late, and Max has not yet returned. Agathe anxiously waits for her beloved, and opening the window, sings of her love for Max—'Leise, leise, fromme Weise' ('Softly sighing, day is dying'). When Max finally arrives, he announces that he must leave again at once to fetch a deer he has shot near the Wolf's Glen. The girls try to stop him —'Wie, was? Entsetzen! Dort in der Schreckensschlucht' ('Where, what? Oh horror! There in the haunted glen').

Scene ii. The Wolf's Glen. Kaspar begs Samiel to prolong his life as he is about to bring him another victim. Max appears on the rocks above, and looks down with horror into the eerie ravine. The ghost of his dead mother and an apparition in whom he recognizes Agathe appear to him and warn him against his plan, but he decides to go down to Kaspar. Kaspar starts casting the magic bullets with secret incantations. Six of them will unfailingly hit their mark, but the seventh will be guided by evil powers. The devilish uproar becomes more and more macabre and horrifying till it fills the whole glen. At the casting of the sixth bullet the wild hunt rushes by, and at the seventh Samiel appears amidst thunder and lightning. Max collapses unconscious. In the distance a clock strikes one.

Act III, scene i. Agathe's room. Agathe in her bridal dress is deep in prayer—'Und ob die Wolke sie verhülle' ('And though a cloud the sun obscure'). She is oppressed by forebodings of evil from which Ännchen tries to distract her with the frivolous aria: 'Einst träumte meiner sel'gen Base' ('An aunt of mine whom you'll remember'). The bridesmaids enter and sing a round: 'Wir winden dir den Jungfernkranz' ('We give you your bridal garland'), but when Agathe opens the box she finds instead of her garland a funeral wreath. Ännchen quickly weaves a gar-land out of the white roses given to Agathe by a hermit. The bridesmaids resume their song, and the happy atmosphere seems to have been restored.

Scene ii. The wood. Prince Ottokar with Kuno and his retinue of huntsmen are in a ceremonial tent. Among those present are Max and Kaspar. The men sing of the pleasures of the hunt—'Was gleicht wohl auf Erden' ('The joy of the huntsman'). Max has already shot successfully six times, but the prince now demands the final trial shot, and points out a white dove which he is to hit. Max takes aim and fires. 'Don't shoot,' Agathe cries out, as she emerges from the group of trees where the dove was sitting. The dove flutters away, and Agathe falls senseless to the ground. Everybody rushes to her aid, and gradually she recovers consciousness. It is Kaspar who has been mortally wounded and is now writhing in his death agonies and uttering horrible maledictions. 'Stürzt das Scheusal in die Wolfsschlucht' ('Throw the monster into the Wolf's Glen') orders the Prince, and then asks Max to explain these mysterious happenings. Max confesses his sin, and the Prince banishes him from the country. Only when the Hermit intervenes on Max's behalf and implores the Prince to show mercy is the latter moved to grant Max a year's probation. If he acquits himself well he will be pardoned and given Agathe's hand in marriage.

For all its naïvety the libretto of *Der Freischütz* exactly conformed to the romantic spirit of the time, and Weber's music raises the plot to the level of a work of art, shrouds it in romantic enchantment, and thereby breathes life into the characters of Agathe, Ännchen, Max and Kaspar.

The peculiar charm of the music to *Der Freischütz* is its irresistible melodiousness which has made some minor numbers a part of German folk music, as for instance the bridesmaids' song, the huntsmen's chorus, and the simple, sincere prayer 'Leise, leise, fromme Weise' from Agathe's great aria. Tunes like

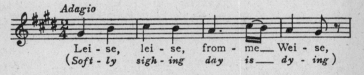

that in Max's aria to the words 'Jetzt ist wohl ihr Fenster offen'

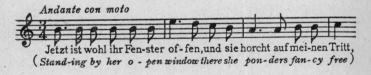

have also become popular, as well as the rude mocking chorus of the peasants or the simple waltz in front of the tavern. Then there is the affinity with nature in Weber's music. Hans Pfitzner described the German forest as the main character in *Der Freischütz*, and this is precisely so. The very first bars of the inimitably beautiful overture set the woodland atmosphere with soft strains from the horns and faint *tremolo* in the violins, and when it breaks into a weird *pizzicato* on the basses and kettle-drums this woodland atmosphere has gripped the listener; it also sounds through the great arias of Max and Agathe and through both trios and both finales.

Weber found a completely new range of orchestral colouring for his descriptions of nature. His original use of clarinet, piccolo and lower strings blended with bassoons and muted horns produced an entirely novel tonal effect which was later developed by Berlioz and Wagner. Another important stylistic innovation is the introduction of *leitmotivs*, such as Samiel's eerie theme which goes right through the opera or Agathe's

love-music at the end of the overture which also dominates the conclusion of the opera, as a symbol of the triumph of good over evil.

The unprecedented success of *Der Freischütz* brought Weber a commission for another work in the same style for the Vienna Kärntnertor Theatre. This he accepted with enthusiasm, but this time he was determined to abandon the *Singspiel* tradition entirely and to write a work with continuous music which would correspond to his romantic operatic idea. It was by chance that he stumbled on *Euryanthe* by Helmine von Chézy when choosing a text for his opera. The romanticism of this old French story attracted him so strongly that he overlooked the many defects which obscure the good central idea. The first performance in Vienna was very well received, but Weber himself foresaw only too clearly that this work could never enjoy a lasting success.

EURYANTHE. Opera in three acts by Carl Maria von Weber. Text by Helmine von Chézy. First performance: Vienna, 1823.

Characters: Louis VI of France—bass; Lysiart de Forêt—baritone; Adolar de Nevers—tenor; Euryanthe de Savoie—soprano; Eglantine de Pulset—mezzo-soprano; Berthe—soprano.

Place: France. *Time:* twelfth century.

Act I. A hall in the royal palace, where peace is being celebrated. In a romance 'Unter blühenden Mandelbäumen' ('' Neath the almond blossom waving') Adolar recalls his beloved Euryanthe, and everybody applauds him. Lysiart, filled with envy, throws doubts on all feminine integrity and particularly on Euryanthe. He declares that he could destroy her fidelity, and challenges Adolar to a wager, on which each of them stakes his entire possessions. Adolar accepts this senseless proposal.

Scene ii. The garden of the Palace of Nevers. In the background is the tomb of Emma, Adolar's sister, who committed suicide after her lover had died in battle. Adolar has made Euryanthe swear never to reveal to anyone this tragic family secret. She thinks longingly of him in the *cavatina* 'Glöcklein im Tale' ('Chimes in the valley'). Eglantine approaches her, and with false protestations of friendship extracts from Euryanthe the secret of Emma's death. Eglantine herself is in love with Adolar and hopes to be able to destroy Euryanthe, now that she knows the secret— 'Betörte, die an meine Liebe glaubt' ('Deceived one! Who in my feign'd love believed'). Lysiart enters and summons Euryanthe to the court in the name of the King.

Act II, scene i. The garden of the Palace of Nevers. Lysiart is in despair because his plans have foundered on Euryanthe's innocence. Eglantine approaches and he hides. To prove that Euryanthe has broken faith, she has stolen the ring from Emma's tomb. From her soliloquy he guesses her intentions and offers himself as her ally—'Komm denn, unser Leid zu rachen' ('Come then to revenge our sorrow').

Scene ii. The hall in the King's palace. Adolar is waiting for Euryanthe —'Wehen mir Lüfte Ruh' ('Waft me, ye Zephyrs, rest'). Euryanthe enters and the lovers fall into each other's arms—'Hin nimm die Seele mein' ('Now that our hearts entwine'). The King arrives with a great retinue and Lysiart steps forward, showing the ring and claiming that Euryanthe gave it to him as a pledge of her love. Euryanthe defends her innocence but has to confess that she has betrayed Adolar's secret. Adolar can no longer believe her faithful and renounces all his goods and possessions in favour of Lysiart.

Act III, scene i. A wild, rocky gorge. Adolar is about to slay Euryanthe when a serpent appears, and Euryanthe throws herself between it and Adolar, thereby saving his life. He kills it and, moved by her heroism, rushes out, abandoning his intention to kill the woman he had once loved so deeply. Euryanthe, who remains behind, still longs for death. The King approaches with a large hunting party, and when Euryanthe explains to him the circumstances of her supposed infidelity he promises to help her.

Scene ii. The garden at Nevers. Preparations are being made for the wedding of Lysiart and Eglantine. Adolar arrives in black armour; he is recognized and told of the bond between Lysiart and Eglantine who are shortly to be married. The wedding procession approaches. Tormented by her conscience, Eglantine confesses that she has betrayed Euryanthe. Adolar steps forward and challenges Lysiart to a duel, but the King forbids them to fight, and to punish Adolar tells him that Euryanthe has died with his name on her lips. Eglantine now triumphantly reveals the plot she hatched with Lysiart, but he stabs her. At that moment Euryanthe enters and the lovers are reunited.

Weber must be admired for writing such beautiful music to this chaotic string of scenes, and for the splendid tunes he invented for the largely insipid text. The superb overture depicting the splendour of the Age of Chivalry is an ideal introduction to a medieval setting veiled in romanticism. It is difficult to resist the magic of the passionate love theme which returns later

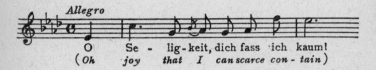

as the main theme of Adolar's great aria. The ensemble which ends the first scene, based on a powerful and noble theme from

the overture, is also unforgettably lovely. Euryanthe's *cavatina* 'Glöcklein im Tale' is intensely tender and full of pure naturalism but cannot compare in originality with Agathe's arias in *Der Freischütz*, which are cast in the same mood. There is a spirituality and noble fervour in the love duet 'Hin nimm die

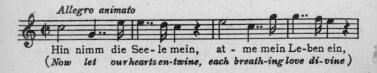

Seele mein', but the strongest impression is made by the arias
of Lysiart and Eglantine, especially the great vengeance duet in
the second act. Its demonic grandeur and formal construction

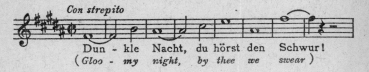

Con strepito

Dun - kle Nacht, du hörst den Schwur!
(*Gloo - my night, by thee we swear*)

make it a prototype of the Ortrud-Telramund duet in Wagner's
Lohengrin. In contrast to *Der Freischütz* with its transitional
passages of dialogue, in *Euryanthe* the musical scenes are completely continuous, including the insertion of a few, apt recitatives, which in their dramatic power are predecessors of
Wagner's *sprechgesang*. The influence *Euryanthe* had on
Wagner's early operas is surprisingly great. Both in *Tannhäuser*
and in *Lohengrin* numerous parallels can be found to illustrate this
connection. Weber's opera therefore opens up new vistas, for
it stands at the beginning of the road which led romantic opera
to its fulfilment in Wagner.

All the leading German theatres staged *Euryanthe* in the years
that followed, but it has never had a lasting success. Weber
could not overcome this set-back after the splendid success of
Der Freischütz. His declining health and financial worries destroyed his will to continue the work of reform, but when in
the summer of 1824 Charles Kemble, the actor-director of
Covent Garden Theatre at the time, invited him to write an
opera for London so far as possible in the style of *Der Freischütz*,
he accepted. The proffered subject was the story of Oberon,
which exactly suited his talents, but he had no influence on the
development of the text since it was sent to him act by act.

OBERON. Romantic opera in three acts by Carl Maria von Weber.
Text by James Robinson Planché. First performance: London, 1826.
   Characters: Oberon, King of the Fairies—tenor; Titania, his wife—
mute role; Puck—mezzo-soprano; Haroun el Raschid, Caliph of Baghdad—spoken role; Reiza, his daughter—soprano; Fatima, her confidante
—soprano; Babekan, a Persian prince; Almansor, Emir of Tunis; Roshana,
his wife; Abdullah, a pirate; The Emperor Charlemagne—spoken roles;
Sir Huon of Bordeaux—tenor; Sherasmin, his page—baritone; mermaid
—soprano.

Place: France, Baghdad and Tunis. *Time:* beginning of the ninth century.

Act I, scene i. Fairy garden in Oberon's kingdom. Oberon and Titania have quarrelled and sworn not to be reunited until they have found a pair of lovers of unshakable fidelity. Puck tells Oberon about Huon de Bordeaux, who has slain Prince Karlmann in single combat and as a punishment has been commanded by Charlemagne to go to Baghdad, where he must surprise the Caliph at a banquet, kill the Caliph's left-hand neighbour, kiss the Caliph's daughter and abduct her to France. Oberon shows the sleeping Huon a vision of Reiza, consumed with longing for him. When Huon awakes, Oberon gives him a magic horn which will protect him in all dangers. At a sign from Oberon Huon and Sherasmin are spirited away to Baghdad. Huon expresses his delight in the adventure —'Oh 'tis a glorious sight to see!'

Scene ii. The hall in the Caliph's harem. Fatima tells Reiza that the knight she has longed for (whom she also had seen in a dream) has arrived in Baghdad. The guard opens the doors of the harem, and Fatima and Reiza join in a happy duet to the strains of an oriental march.

Act II, scene i. The banqueting-hall in the palace. Babekan is sitting on the Caliph's left and Reiza is brought in dressed as a bride. Huon appears, stabs Babekan and kisses Reiza. As the guards make to fall on him, he blows his magic horn. Everyone stands motionless except Reiza, who escapes with her rescuer. With a kiss Sherasmin awakes the charming Fatima, who willingly follows him.

Scene ii. The garden of the palace. The fugitives are caught by the keepers of the garden, and in the struggle Huon loses his magic horn, but a ship of Oberon's lies in the harbour ready to bear them away.

Scene iii. A deserted shore. Puck invokes the spirits of the sea to raise a storm and throw the ship on to the shore. Huon lays the unconscious Reiza on a flat rock and hurries away to fetch help. Reiza watches the storm passing over and the evening sun shining down from the sky; she apostrophizes the sea in the famous aria 'Ocean, thou mighty monster'. In the distance she sights a boat, and hoping for rescue joyfully signals to it with her veil; but it is a pirate-ship which comes in to anchor. Huon is overcome, and Reiza taken away by force. Oberon appears to rescue the unconscious Huon. Mermaids emerge from the water singing 'Oh 'tis pleasant to float on the sea', while elves, fairies and spirits of the air raise their voices, and Neptune passes by with a great retinue.

Act III, scene i. The palace garden of the Emir of Tunis. Fatima and Sherasmin have been sold as slaves. Puck flies down bearing the sleeping Huon, who on waking learns from Fatima that Reiza is also in the Emir's palace.

Scene ii. The hall of pillars in the palace. The Emir Almansor woos Reiza, but in vain, while his wife Roshana turns her attentions to Huon, whom she has seen in the garden, and promises to make him Emir if he will kill Almansor. Huon resists the temptation of her beauty, but they are surprised by Almansor, who orders Huon to be taken away.

Scene iii. An open place in front of the palace. Slaves, among them Sherasmin, are preparing a pyre on which Huon is to be burnt alive.

When Reiza declares she is his wife, she is condemned to die with him, but meanwhile Sherasmin has found the magic horn and when he blows it everyone begins to dance and sing. Huon and Reiza are freed, and Oberon appears, reconciled with Titania, for the lovers' fidelity has freed them from their oath. With a magic word Huon and his companions are spirited back to France.

Scene iv. The Throne Room of Charlemagne who, appeased, welcomes Huon and Reiza to his kingdom.

For this colourful picture-book overflowing with its fairy-tale plot Weber wrote a profusion of beautiful music, which is unfortunately continually interrupted by lengthy dialogue. Franz Wüllner (1832–1902), who tried replacing it with recitative and musical accompaniment, is to be commended, but the success of *Oberon* largely depends on lavish sets and costumes to match its fairy-tale character.

The best-known, and also the most important, part of the work is the overture. It starts with a dreamlike horn call, evokes in a few phrases all the romantic magic of the supernatural and then unfolds the splendour of noble chivalry in a fiery *allegro*. In it we hear two motifs from the opera's greatest musical numbers: Huon's passionate aria in the first act and

Now comes— the splen-dour, a gen - tle way

Reiza's song of praise, the 'ocean' aria. This magnificent

My— hus-band, my— love, we are saved,—we are saved

aria once again displays Weber's splendid genius. The wonderful imitation of nature and the gradual transition from meditative observation through dramatic excitement to highest ecstasy are most thrillingly effective. Weber also sketched in the oriental background with a few masterly strokes, but however much foreign magic he evoked, the popular, romantic character of his music is still basically German.

Weber completed *Oberon* in feverish haste, as though he already sensed his approaching death and, gathering all his strength, he travelled to London, where he rehearsed his work with great precision and conducted the first successful performances. After a concert he was conducting in London he collapsed, and died shortly afterwards. His body was taken to Dresden in 1844, and among his mourners was Richard Wagner.

Jessonda, the most important opera by Ludwig Spohr (1784–1859), was first performed in the same year as *Euryanthe*, and remained in the repertory of German opera houses for many years. It is still heard occasionally today. In spite of its many beautiful musical passages, the somewhat weak melodic invention in all the vocal parts is tedious in the long run, particularly since no effort is made to differentiate musically between the characters. The duet 'Lass für ihn, den ich geliebet' ('Left for him, whom I did love') and 'Schönes Mädchen, wirst mich hassen' ('Lovely maiden, will you hate me') were on everyone's lips at the time. For us these once beloved tunes are too *biedermeier* and sugary. *Jessonda* was Spohr's attempt to attain the romantic ideal of opera. The music is continuous, whereas his earlier works, among which *Faust* had a certain temporary popularity, were more in the style of the *Singspiel*.

The third master of early romantic opera, Heinrich Marschner (1795–1861), combined romantic fire and popular humour without sacrificing dramatic effect. He dedicated himself exclusively to opera, and after several failures made a decisive break-through with *Der Vampyr* (1828). Wohlbrück's text, the fundamentally grisly atmosphere of which is continually interrupted by humorous episodes, greatly appealed to Marschner's temperament and he fully appreciated the potentiality of his material. The first performance was incontestably successful. Hans Pfitzner, an enthusiastic admirer of Marschner's works, re-edited *Der Vampyr* (first performance in this version—Stuttgart, 1924), and it is still performed in Germany in this new form. The music clearly reveals Marschner's strong dependence on Weber. The overture is very similar to that of *Der Freischütz* both in construction and theme, without being nearly as concise as Weber's overtures. The demoniac element is characteristically indicated by the gloomy key of D minor with passionate triplets, chromatic passages and diminished sevenths, and as in *Der Freischütz* Agathe's expressive diatonic tunes challenge the spectre world so the heroine of *Der Vampyr* in her faith and love contrast with the diabolical vampire. On the other hand *Der Vampyr* is a stepping-stone towards Wagner's *Der Fliegende Holländer* in its musical suggestion of the supernatural world.

Marschner's best work is *Hans Heiling* (1833), written to a libretto by Eduard Devrient on a mythical story treating the tragic relationship between spirits and human beings, in the tradition of E. T. A. Hoffmann's *Undine* and Wagner's *Der Fliegende Holländer*.

Only a few examples of romantic opera have survived into the twentieth century. Even Weber's and Marschner's best works paled beside Wagner's music dramas and can only just hold their ground in modern times, while innumerable operas by lesser composers are now completely forgotten. In Germany one can occasionally still see *Der Nachtlager von Granada* (*A night's camp near Granada*), Konradin Kreutzer's (1780–1849) lovely and most popular work. Kreutzer's music is fresh, original and intensely emotional. The characters are musically well differentiated, and there is plenty of rhythm and melody in the score, with imaginative use of orchestration to describe moods and great skill in building up ensembles. In spite of his use of Spanish and Moorish rhythms, Kreutzer's music, like Weber's, is essentially German, with its lively, popular romanticism centred round deeds of chivalry and the hunt.

Robert Schumann (1810–56), the leading German romantic musician, wrote one opera, *Genoveva* (1850), a child of his sorrow, on which he lavished great love and care. He himself wrote the text, based on Hebbel's drama, but it was not very good, for instead of lessening the improbability of the legendary plot or giving it deeper psychological meaning his libretto made things worse. Naturally a genius like Schumann could cover a bad text with a wealth of wonderful music, but the weaknesses are still very apparent. The musical characterization is no more than conventional, but the dramatic scenes have real power and the lyrical passages breathe the true spirit of Schumann's *lieder*.

Less ponderous than its serious sister, comic romantic opera became well established in popular favour, and the works of

Lortzing, Nicolai and Flotow are still, with undiminished success, the bread-and-butter of every German opera house.

Albert Lortzing (1801–51) was a particularly attractive personality. A true man of the theatre like Weber, he was familiar with the stage from his earliest years. He acted and sang as a child, and started very early in life to write verses and music, thereby fulfilling Hoffmann's romantic ideal of a poet who is also a composer. Besides this he also worked as a stage-producer, conductor, actor, singer and orchestral player, and in all capacities he displayed enormous talent. But all this was not sufficient to ensure him a more or less care-free life, even in his greatest successes. Widespread performances of operas did not earn the composer any regular income at that time, and Lortzing was obliged to take on lowly jobs to keep his family from poverty.

In spite of these difficulties his music exudes high spirits and real humour, thanks to his happy, balanced personality. He was always ready to help a friend, and was a touchingly devoted husband and father—in fact a real product of the German *biedermeier* tradition. The feeling of his operas is also typically German; a genial, contented bourgeois atmosphere with a romantic overlay, which explains the special attraction Lortzing holds for German audiences, and also his lack of success abroad.

Lortzing's first great operatic success was *Die beiden Schützen* (*The Two Riflemen*) (1837), a work which gives a foretaste of all the qualities in his later works, and in the same year came *Zar und Zimmermann*. The story of Peter the Great and the carpenter in Holland had already been used as a libretto for several operas, among them those of Grétry and Donizetti. Lortzing's version of this popular story was very successful, especially in his excellent characterization of the mayor van Bett which, he said, cannot go wrong and assures the success of the opera. *Zar und Zimmermann* spread through every German theatre, and was even occasionally performed abroad. In Russia it was called *Flemish Adventure*, and since no Tsar could be portrayed on the stage, the Emperor Maximilian was substituted for Peter the Great.

ZAR UND ZIMMERMANN (Tsar and Carpenter). Comic opera in three acts. Text and music by Albert Lortzing. First performance: Leipzig, 1837.

Characters: Peter I, Tsar of Russia, under the name of Peter Michailov, and disguised as a journeyman-carpenter—baritone; Peter Ivanov, a young Russian journeyman-carpenter—tenor; van Bett, burgomaster of Saardam—comic bass; Marie, his niece—soprano; Admiral Lefort, Russian ambassador—bass; Lord Syndham, English ambassador—bass; Marquis de Châteauneuf, French ambassador—tenor; the widow Brown —alto. Dutch officers, soldiers, inhabitants of Saardam, carpenters, magistrates, beadles, sailors.

Place: Saardam. *Time:* 1698.

Act I. The Tsar Peter I, under the name Michailov, has taken service as a carpenter in the shipyard of the widow Brown at Saardam. He sings a carpenter's song to Peter Ivanov, a young Russian. Ivanov loves Marie, the Burgomaster's niece, but he lives in constant fear of being discovered since he has deserted from Russia. He confides in Peter Michailov, since he suspects that the latter also has something to hide. A Frenchman makes advances to Marie and Ivanov creates a jealous scene. Marie tells him that her uncle is coming to the shipyard, having presumably discovered her attachment to Ivanov, but he suspects there is another reason; the Tsar also fears that his identity has been discovered. Admiral Lefort brings the Tsar news of unrest in Russia and he decides to leave Holland.

The Burgomaster has been instructed to inquire into the activities of a carpenter named Peter, but which Peter? Van Bett's suspicion falls on Ivanov, and in order to observe him more closely he invites himself to the wedding feast of widow Brown's son. The English ambassador promises the burgomaster £2,000 if he can find out Peter's plans regarding England. Van Bett is completely mystified but behaves as though he knows all about it. Ivanov finds fresh cause for jealousy as Marie is again seen with the Marquis. Peter Michailov enters and the Marquis (the French ambassador) penetrates the Tsar's incognito without anyone else suspecting anything.

Act II. An inn garden, gaily decorated, where the wedding feast is in progress. The Marquis, the Tsar and Lefort take their places at the same table, and near by sits Lord Syndham with Ivanov (who he thinks is the Tsar) and van Bett. The widow Brown invites everyone to dance, and Marie sings the betrothal song—'Lieblich röten sich die Wangen' ('Cheeks that blush with maiden's shyness'). Soldiers march into the garden, and any foreigner who cannot give a satisfactory account of himself is to be arrested. The 'wise' burgomaster sets about interrogating the foreigners present somewhat abruptly, but finds himself surrounded by ambassadors of foreign powers. When he finally tries to have Ivanov and Michailov arrested, the English ambassador points out Ivanov as the Tsar, and the French ambassador Michailov. The result is confusion and a general scuffle.

Act III. A room in the Town Hall. Van Bett is rehearsing a choir to welcome the Tsar 'Heil sei dem Tag, da du bei uns erschienen' ('Blest be the day when you did come among us'). He still believes that Ivanov is the Tsar. Marie is very unhappy, because in that case she could never marry him, but Michailov promises her that her happiness will be restored in an hour's time. He envies these young people who know nothing of the cares of kingship, and sings 'Einst spielt ich mit Szepter, mit Krone und Stern' ('In youth I did toy with my kingship and throne'). To Marie's amusement Ivanov seems uneasy in his new found majesty. The Tsar needs a pass if he is not to disclose his identity, and Ivanov gives him the one made out by the English ambassador, in return for which the Tsar hands him a letter which he must not open for an hour. During the great demonstrations for Ivanov, in the middle of the burgomaster's speech, an official announces that Peter Michailov is just leaving the harbour at the head of a great fleet. Ivanov now opens the mysterious letter, which explains everything and also appoints him Imperial Inspector-General and gives him permission to marry Marie.

The doors of the hall open, and a ship can be seen in the harbour, with the Tsar Peter I standing on its bridge in a splendid uniform. All those present spontaneously acclaim him.

Zar und Zimmermann represents the climax of Lortzing's creative activity. The work is completely homogeneous and its original brand of humour is unique. The light catchy tunes, especially those of the sung numbers, helped substantially towards the popularity of the opera. The overture, which contains a skilfully arranged collection of the best tunes, is followed by the Tsar's carpenter song, which is original in both rhythm and melody. The highlight of the first act is the stupid, cunning burgomaster's aria 'O Sancta justitia' with its climax of self-adulation 'Oh ich bin klug und weise' ('Oh! I am wise and cunning').

In the second act there are two particularly delightful arias, in which the chorus joins in the refrain; the Marquis's aria 'Lebe wohl, mein flandrisch' Mädchen' ('Fare thee well, my Flemish maiden') and Marie's charming bridal song. In between there comes the famous sextet 'Zum Werk, das wir beginnen' ('To work, now let's get busy') which is one of the most effective ensemble passages in operatic literature.

The most popular number in the opera has always been the Tsar's aria in the third act, 'Einst spielt ich mit Szepter, mit Krone und Stern', though this sentimental song is not one of Lortzing's best inspirations. Much lovelier is the subsequent duet between Marie and Ivanov, 'Darf ein niedre Magd es wagen' ('May a lowly maiden venture'). Lortzing gives a splendid example of a comic dramatic situation in the ensemble which opens the third act when van Bett is rehearsing the cantata in honour of the Tsar. Musically this is an exquisitely conceived and executed piece of burlesque.

Without any doubt Lortzing's masterpiece is *Der Wildschütz*, even though it has never been nearly as popular as *Zar und Zimmermann*.

DER WILDSCHÜTZ (The Poacher). Comic opera in three acts. Text and music by Albert Lortzing. First performance: Leipzig, 1842.

Characters: The Count of Eberbach—baritone; the Countess, his wife—soprano; Baron Kronthal, brother to the Countess—tenor; Baroness Freimann, a young widow, the Count's sister—soprano; Nanette, her maid—mezzo-soprano; Baculus, a schoolmaster—bass; Gretchen, his betrothed—soprano; Pankratius, the castle steward—baritone. Servants and villagers.

Place: The Count's castle and a village nearby. *Time:* 1803.

Act I. The village square. The villagers are celebrating the betrothal of the schoolmaster, but their revels are spoiled by the Count's order that the schoolmaster be dismissed from his job for poaching. Baculus has in fact killed a roebuck to be roasted for his wedding feast. Gretchen will have to intercede for her lover with the Count, who is not unsusceptible to maidenly beauty. The jealous Baculus is finding it difficult to agree to this idea when the Count's sister, Baroness Freimann and her maid appear, both disguised as students. The Baroness offers to go to the castle herself, disguised as Gretchen. The Count enters with Baron Kronthal and a retinue of huntsmen. Kronthal, the Countess's brother, is living, unrecognized by her, as a groom on his brother-in-law's estate. Both gentlemen are so taken with Gretchen (and even more with the Baroness), both of whom are in peasant's clothes, that the Count invites everyone present to a party at the castle.

Act II. The billiards room in the castle. The Countess reads passages from Sophocles to the assembled servants, who sing in chorus 'Die Frau Gräfin liest vortrefflich, unnachahmlich, wunderschön, Tränen möchte man vergiessen—schade, dass wir's nicht verstehen! Schade!' ('Our mistress reads beautifully, incomparably, wonderfully, so that we are ready to weep—a pity that we don't understand a word!') On the suggestion of the steward Pankratius, Baculus interlards his remarks with classical quotations, which makes a good impression on the Countess, but before he can plead with her to mediate on his behalf with the Count, the latter arrives and tries to throw him out. The Baroness appears disguised as Gretchen and both the Count and the Baron want to be left alone with her. The Baron succeeds in this for a few moments, and declares his love for the Baroness, but the Count comes back at once. Since neither of the two men wants to give way, they decide to play a billiards match. While playing, the Count knocks over the lamp, and both men try to seize Gretchen in the dark. The tumult brings the Countess and the servants to the scene. The Baron offers Baculus 5,000 thalers if he will give up his betrothed. The act closes with the famous aria 'Fünftausend Taler' in which Baculus expresses his bewilderment at this enormous sum.

Act III. The castle gardens. The Baron tells his brother-in-law that he plans to marry the schoolmaster's affianced bride, but when Baculus brings in Gretchen and explains that *his* Gretchen was only a student in disguise, the Baron lays hands so roughly on the disguised Baroness that she is obliged to reveal her identity. After a few amusing misunderstandings, everything is happily resolved, and Baculus is also pardoned when it is shown that he had killed not a roebuck but his own donkey.

The musical humour in *Der Wildschütz* is not as crude as in *Zar und Zimmermann*. Everything in this opera is more elegant and the large ensembles are reminiscent of Mozart in their careful construction; for instance, the delicious billiards quintet in which Baculus's powerful bass singing the choral 'Wach auf mein Herz und singe' ('Awake my heart and sing'), acts as *cantus firmus* to the sparkling vivacity of the upper parts. The same applies to the enchanting and simple children's chorus in the third act finale which, like the servants' chorus, always provokes a contented smile. The comic climax of the opera is Baculus's great aria 'Fünftausend Taler', which is perhaps even more effective than its counterpart, van Bett's aria in *Zar und Zimmermann*.

Lortzing tried his hand at grand opera when he wrote *Undine*. Although the romantic scenes of this work are too cloyingly sentimental, its strong dramatic effect helped to give it a certain and lasting success. In any case it completely eclipsed Hoffmann's *Undine*. Lortzing considered this his best work, but he was in fact mistaken, for comedy came much more naturally to him than high drama. Easily the most successful characters in *Undine* are the two comic figures he invented, the lively page Veit and the fat steward Hans, because here this master of comic opera was on familiar ground. He manages a light conversational tone with great assurance, as for instance in the famous duet at the beginning of the second act, when Veit boasts of his adventures to the gaping, wondering Hans. Delicate but intense orchestral passages accompany the fussy quaver movement which illustrates the page's talkativeness. The excellent little songs interpolated here and there, such as 'Ich war in meinen jungen Jahren' ('When I was just a callow stripling') and 'Vater, Mutter, Schwestern, Brüder' ('Father, mother, sisters, brothers') have become really popular and never fail in their effect. Lortzing is unbeatable in setting simple verses in the tradition of the old German *Singspiel*.

Lortzing's last great opera *Der Waffenschmied* is nowadays as popular in Germany as *Zar und Zimmermann*. In it he succeeded in creating realistic and lovable characters who also provide very rewarding roles for the singers.

On 20 January 1851, the first performance of Lortzing's last work, the charming one-act opera *Die vornehmen Dilettanten oder Die Opernprobe* (*The noble dilettantes or the opera rehearsal*) took place in Frankfurt. This work was full of amusing situations and showed Lortzing's gift for parody at its best. The composer, who was in Berlin at the time, fell ill on the day of the première, and died the following morning.

Friedrich von Flotow (1812–83) spent the formative years of his musical development in Paris, and the resulting decisive influence on his work is very clearly seen in his most important opera *Martha*, and indeed is probably one of the reasons for its great success abroad. After Caruso had chosen to sing the role of Lionel, *Martha* became a world-wide success, unlike any of Lortzing's works which are of incomparably greater musical value.

MARTHA ODER DER MARKT VON RICHMOND (Martha or Richmond Market). Comic romantic opera in four acts by Friedrich von Flotow. Text by Wilhelm Friedrich after the French ballet-pantomime, *Lady Henriette ou la Servante de Greenwich*. First performance: Vienna, 1847.

Characters: Lady Harriet Durham, Maid-of-Honour to the Queen—soprano; Nancy, her companion—mezzo-soprano; Sir Tristram Mickleford, her cousin—bass; Lionel—tenor; Plunkett, a rich farmer—bass; the sheriff of Richmond—bass; farmers, maids, servants. Hunters and huntresses in the Queen's retinue, pages, servants.

Place: Richmond and the surrounding district. *Time:* the reign of Queen Anne (about 1700).

Act I, scene i. Lady Harriet's boudoir. Lady Harriet is bored. Her cousin, the foppish Sir Tristram, is not very successful in his ideas for cheering her up. Off-stage are heard the merry songs of some serving-girls passing by, and this gives Lady Harriet the idea of going to Richmond Fair with Nancy, both disguised as servants. Sir Tristram is to accompany them, disguised as a farmer.

Scene ii. The market-place in Richmond. In accordance with an old custom, the Sheriff is hiring out the girls. Those who accept the wage must do one year's service. The rich farmer Plunkett and his foster-brother Lionel enter. When under sentence of banishment, Lionel's father had once been kindly sheltered by Plunkett's family, and had left his son a valuable ring, which in case of need he was to send to the

Queen, who would then come to his aid. Lady Harriet and Nancy
appear calling themselves Martha and Julia. Plunkett and Lionel engage
them, one for the house and stables, the other for the fields and garden,
and give them their wage. When the ladies tire of the game and try to
slip away, Plunkett asserts his right over them. For fear of being recognized by everyone they have to follow their masters.

Act II. Plunkett's farmhouse. Martha and Julia are very unskilled at
household work, and Plunkett even has to show them how to use a
spinning-wheel. The 'maids' laugh heartily about it, and Plunkett jumps
up menacingly and runs after the frightened Nancy. Lionel holds back
Lady Harriet, who at his request sings to him 'Die letzte Rose' ('The last
rose of summer'); mindful of her true position, she rejects Lionel's courtship. Plunkett and Nancy return. Left alone, the two women are in despair
at the consequences of their frivolity. Fortunately Sir Tristram suddenly
appears at the window and all three furtively make their escape.

Act III. A forest clearing. Plunkett is sitting in front of a small inn with
some other farmers, enjoying his beer. The Queen and her followers are
hunting near by. Nancy is one of the party and Plunkett, recognizing in
her his Julia, tries to take her away with him, but she escapes. Lady Harriet
also meets Lionel, but for fear of the Queen she pretends not to know him,
and calls on Sir Tristram for help. Lionel in despair accuses Lady Harriet
publicly of having come to his house as a servant in order to drive him
to his wits' end. Lady Harriet says that he is mad and he is arrested, but
not before he has given Plunkett his ring and asked him to present it to
the Queen.

Act IV, scene i. Plunkett's house. Lady Harriet is full of remorse. She
loves Lionel and has herself conveyed his ring to the Queen, who has
realized that he is the son of the unjustly banished Lord Derby. Filled
with love and remorse Lady Harriet offers Lionel her hand, but he no
longer trusts her. Meanwhile Nancy and Plunkett are getting on very
well.

Scene ii. An open space in front of the farmhouse. To win the man she
loves, Lady Harriet has everything arranged as on the day of the Fair.
A farmer is disguised as the Sheriff, peasant girls and farmers appear, and
everything happens as on that day. Lionel believes that it was all a dream,
and joyfully embraces his Martha.

The success of the opera was largely due to a certain mixture
of gaiety and sentimentality, which always finds an audience.
Flotow excels in merry scenes, where his music is fresh and
direct, as in the charming choruses of the maids and peasants
in the first act, and the scenes with Lord Tristram and Nancy,
which are full of charming little ideas in melody, rhythm and
instrumentation. A typically romantic feature is the insertion
of the Irish folk song 'The last rose of summer' to the words
'Die letzte Rose', to which the opera owes a great part of its

popularity. Also well known are Plunkett's drinking song—an essential in romantic comic opera—and Lionel's third act aria 'Ach, so fromm' (Like a dream') which is still a popular and sure hit for tenors today. Finally, one should not forget Lionel's famous aria 'Mag der Himmel Euch vergeben' ('Heaven alone may grant you pardon'), which already appeared as the first theme of the overture and also in the finale of the third act as a mounting ensemble to bring the apparent tragedy to its climax.

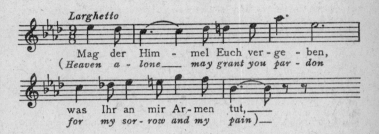

Of Flotow's many operas the only other one still remembered is *Alessandro Stradella* (1844). The text is based on a true story, the hero of the opera being the seventeenth-century composer, particularly famous for his church music, but also well known as a singer and as a writer of romantic adventure novels. Bandits, pursuing him as the abductor of a noble Venetian's affianced bride, were so moved by an oratorio of Stradella's that they gave up their murderous intentions. Later on, though, in 1681, he was murdered, but it is not certain that this was the delayed vengeance of the Venetians. Wilhelm Friedrich arranged this love-story most expertly in his libretto.

Otto Nicolai's (1810–49) best known work *Die lustigen Weiber von Windsor* stands on a much higher artistic plane. Nicolai had been strongly influenced by Italian music and also by Mozart and Weber. In *Die lustigen Weiber* he was trying to create a German opera, and he succeeded in doing so despite the Italian features in his work; his humour is essentially German and so is his tendency towards dreamy romanticism, not to mention his feeling for nature noticeable from the beginning of the charming overture, which starts with the delicate sounds of muted violins, soon joined by a mysterious song on the cellos

and basses, which anticipates the mood of the final scene of the
opera when the moon rises over the softly murmuring trees of
Windsor Forest. A whispering starts on all sides, elves and
goblins come out to dance and play, the action becomes livelier
and more vigorous, and over it soars a lovely and joyful melody.

DIE LUSTIGEN WEIBER VON WINDSOR (The Merry Wives of
Windsor). Fantasy comic opera in three acts by Otto Nicolai. Text after
Shakespeare by Hermann Salomon Mosenthal. First performance:
Berlin, 1849.

Characters: Sir John Falstaff—bass; Herr Fluth (Mr Ford)—baritone;
Herr Reich (Mr Page)—bass; Fenton—tenor; Junker Spärlich (Slender)—
tenor; Doctor Caius—bass; Frau Fluth (Mistress Ford)—soprano; Frau
Reich (Mistress Page)—mezzo-soprano; Jungfer Anna Reich (Anne
Page)—soprano. Townspeople.

Place: Windsor. *Time:* beginning of the seventeenth century.

Act I, scene i. A street in Windsor with the houses of Ford and Page
on either side. In front of her house Mistress Ford is reading a love-letter
from the fat knight Falstaff, at which she is partly amused and partly
indignant. Mistress Page, her friend, has received an exactly similar letter
from Sir John and the two women decide to punish him. After they have
gone, Page enters with the suitors for his daughter Anne's hand, the rich
Squire Slender, whom he favours, the French Doctor Caius, whom his
wife likes, and poor Fenton, who has in fact won Anne's love. Fenton,
abruptly dismissed by Page, holds to his faith in the triumph of true love.

Scene ii. A room in Ford's house. In the aria 'Nun eilt herbei, Witz,
heitere Laune' ('Come, aid me, humour, happy laughter') Mistress Ford
expresses her disgust at the wickedness of men. A slightly comic march
heralds the fat knight's arrival. Tenderly he approaches the lady who
assumes a bashful air. When he is becoming amorous, there is a knock at
the door. Falstaff hides himself behind a folding tapesty screen. Mistress
Page comes in to relate how Ford has got wind of the rendezvous and has
sworn to kill his rival. Falstaff is hidden in a large clothes-basket. The
women have in fact told Ford, to punish him for his continual jealousy,

but first of all Sir John must learn his lesson. They order two servants to empty the contents of the basket into the Thames. Ford rushes into the room with a mob of neighbours while the servants carry away the basket. Ford searches the whole house without any success, and this gives Mistress Ford the upper hand. At first she simulates sorrow, then indignation, and finally she declares that she wants an immediate divorce. Ford is deeply ashamed, since everyone takes his wife's side.

Act II, scene i. The Garter Inn. Falstaff leads a drinking song with the other customers in the inn. Ford presents himself to Sir John under the name of Master Brook (Bach in German) and brings the conversation round to the subject of Mistress Ford. A full purse helps to loosen Falstaff's tongue, and he discloses that during a rendezvous with Mistress Ford he was disturbed by her jealous husband. Today he will be more successful, since the husband is out hunting. Ford, inwardly seething with rage, pretends to be glad about Falstaff's success, saying that once Falstaff has shaken the virtue of this beautiful woman he will more easily attain his own ends with her.

Scene ii. The garden of Page's house. Slender hopes to meet 'sweet Anne' here. He anxiously hides himself when Dr Caius appears. The doctor in turn conceals himself from Fenton, whose serenade 'Horch, die Lerche singt im Hain!' ('Hark, the lark doth sing in the wood!') finally draws Anne out into the garden, where the lovers exchange vows. Slender and Dr Caius the hidden witnesses of their own defeat.

Scene iii. A room in Ford's house. Mistress Ford is trying to console Falstaff for the misfortune of the previous day. Mistress Page, this time really frightened, brings the news that Ford has interrupted his hunt and is on the way home. Falstaff must disguise himself as a fat old woman. Ford is this time quite sure of his ground and ransacks the whole house, even furiously running his sword through the clothes-basket, but he discovers nothing. At first Mistress Ford will not let her husband into her bedroom and finally the fat 'lady' waddles out, supported by Mistress Page, and painfully answers Ford's indignant questions in a high falsetto. The furious Ford throws the old woman out of the house.

Act III, scene i. A room in Page's house. The two couples are sitting happily together, for the women have told their husbands the whole story, and they all decide to summon Sir John to Windsor Park at midnight, dressed as Herne the Hunter, where, disguised as elves and spirits, they will torment him. At the same time Anne's betrothal is to be celebrated. So that Slender may find her in the confusion, Page tells her to wear a green elfin robe, but her mother tells her to wear a red dress, so that Dr Caius may be able to pick her out. Anne sends Caius the green costume, and Slender the red one, while she decides to dress herself in white and plight her troth to Fenton.

Scene ii. Windsor Forest, near the oak of Herne the Hunter. The moon rises, and a mysterious mood pervades the wood; an invisible chorus is heard, midnight strikes. Falstaff, disguised as Herne, with massive antlers on his head, enters and is received by Mistress Ford and Mistress Page. He is extremely flattered, but a confused clamour from above makes them disperse. Spirits and goblins enter and start a graceful dance. Anne

appears, dressed as Titania, queen of the fairies, and is joined by Fenton,
disguised as Oberon. The lovers run away together hand in hand. Page
appears as Herne the Hunter. When he tries to wind his horn no sound
comes: a human being is near by! Everyone rushes angrily in and all too
soon discover the fat knight, trying to hide behind the oak. They all set
on him pitilessly, and the poor old man cowers in terror on the ground.
Finally he begs for mercy. Caius and Slender arrive dressed in red and
green; they had meanwhile plighted their troth to each other and have
only just realized their mistake. Anne and Fenton are now also betrothed,
and ask Anne's parents for forgiveness, which is readily given. Sir John
is invited to the wedding, so that he can drown his sorrows.

Graceful rhythms and really lovely tunes make up the magic of
Nicolai's music. His musical range of happy emotions is delightfully varied, from subtle allusive humour to robust wit. In the
Falstaff scenes Nicolai seizes every opportunity for a joke, even
a crude one, like the gurgling horn in the orchestra which
accompanies the drinking scene, or the sounds of a grotesque
funeral march played as the empty wine cask is carried out.
Falstaff's drinking song then recurs in subtle, characteristic little

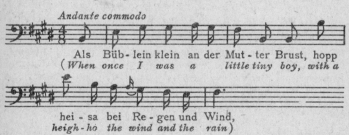

nuances and an underlying irony accompanies the duet with
Ford. Falstaff rubs his hands in anticipation of the pleasures of

his adventure, and Ford takes up the lilting tune, pleased to think that he will be able to punish this smart fellow soundly. The romantic tones of the overture recur chiefly when describing the lovers, as in the famous duet, interwoven with the delicate arabesques of the solo violin. Later in the same scene the voices of the two rivals listening from their hiding-places take part as comic counterpoint.

The success of the first performance of *Die Lustigen Weiber* has remained undiminished over the years, but Nicolai did not live to enjoy it: eight weeks after the first performance, when not yet forty years old, he died of a severe cerebral haemorrhage.

FRENCH OPERA IN THE NINETEENTH CENTURY

While in the eighteenth century Naples and Vienna, Paris and also London had played a decisive part in the development of opera, from the very beginning of the nineteenth century it was Paris which surpassed all other musical centres, and within ten years became the musical capital of Europe. The strange inter-relation of politics and opera which had created a very important eighteenth- and nineteenth-century art-form, became evident in the age of 'grand opera'. The operatic themes of the period reflect the great contemporary events which cast their shadow over the whole of Europe—the French Revolution, the rise of Napoleon and the Empire, the Restoration, the civil war, the Revolutions of 1830 and 1848 and the splendour of the Second Empire. Some operas even made history themselves, as for example *La Muette de Portici* by Auber, the first performance of which in Brussels sparked off the 1830 revolution. Inflamed by the revolutionary story the excited audience rushed out into the streets, and, firing the crowds with its enthusiasm, gave the signal for the liberation of Belgium from Dutch rule. Even Rossini's *Guillaume Tell*, a 'display' opera in the grand tradition, was revolutionary in subject and in 1829 helped to prepare the way for the coming political events.

By that time French opera had developed into two clearly defined types—*grand opéra* and *opéra comique*—which had still

often overlapped in the eighteenth century. The chief characteristics of *grand opéra* were its heroic-historical subjects and continuous music; while in contrast the subjects treated in *opéra
comique* tended to belong to the middle-class milieu, and spoken
dialogue replaced recitative as a matter of course. It was inconceivable that a single spoken word should come from the
stage in grand opera, which was produced by that stronghold
of sacred tradition the Académie, later known as the Grand
Opéra. Another unwritten law was that a spectacular ballet
should be inserted in each opera, generally in the second half.
Weber's *Freischütz* was so enormously successful at the Opéra-
Comique under the title *Robin des Bois* that the management of
the Grand Opéra wanted to secure it, too, but first the spoken
dialogue had to be replaced by recitatives, and a ballet inserted.
Berlioz, a fanatical admirer of Weber, agreed to compose the
recitatives and to orchestrate Weber's famous keyboard piece
Aufforderung zum Tanz (*Invitation to the Dance*) for the ballet.

Even Wagner had to bow to the fashion and insert a ballet
into *Tannhäuser* so that it could be performed in Paris. He refused however to introduce the ballet into the second act during
the singing contest on the Wartburg, as was suggested to him.
Instead he so enlarged the Venusberg scene that it could stand
a great ballet, and thus gave us the wonderful bacchanale composed for the Paris edition.

The century of grand opera was introduced by Gasparo
Spontini (1774–1851), whose works show the transition from
Gluck's classicism to the later heroic-historical opera. His prin-
cipal work *La Vestale* (*The Vestal Virgin*), first performed in
Paris in 1807, is in the style of Gluck, but in spite of its unity in
design and construction it already aims strongly at effect.
Napoleon expressed his liking for this opera, and also for
Spontini's next work, *Fernando Cortez* (1809), which introduced
the long series of operas in grandiose historical settings. Here
Gluck's ideals are renounced in favour of external effects, and
the text and music tend towards splendour and pathos. *Olimpie*,
first performed in Paris in 1819, concentrated entirely on external effect, and a quarter of a million francs were spent on its
décor and costumes alone.

In 1828, Daniel François Esprit Auber (1782–1871) conquered
Paris with his *La Muette de Portici*. The most successful librettist

of the first half of the century, Eugène Scribe (1791-1861), wrote
the text, which started him on his great career in grand opera,
for he had previously only written comic operas. Auber composed most impressive music for this rather confused but effective story, and the first performance in Paris was a sweeping
success. After the sensational effect of the 1830 Brussels performance, already mentioned above, this opera spread all over
Europe. Schumann referred to it rather condescendingly as the
'Opera of a musical child of fortune'; Wagner, on the other
hand, wholeheartedly acknowledged the strong original value
of the music.

LA MUETTE DE PORTICI (The Dumb Girl of Portici). Grand historical opera in five acts by Daniel Auber. Text by Eugène Scribe.
First performance: Paris, 1828.

Characters: Masaniello, a fisherman—tenor; Fenella, his sister—mute
role (usually taken by a ballet dancer); Pietro and Moreno, fishermen—
basses; Alfonso, son of the Viceroy of Naples—tenor; Elvira, a Spanish
princess—soprano; Selva, an officer—bass.

Place: Naples and Portici. *Time:* 1647.

Act I. The Viceroy's garden. The betrothal of Prince Alfonso to Elvira
is to be celebrated. Pursued by the guards, a beautiful dumb girl forces
her way to the noble bride. It is Fenella, who by means of signs explains
that she has been loved and betrayed, then put into prison and finally
has escaped. Elvira promises to protect her and goes in to the ceremony.
When the betrothal procession returns from the chapel, Fenella goes to
meet the young couple, and is horrified to recognize her lover in the
Prince. She flees before the guards can seize her.

Act II. The seashore. Fenella's brother Masaniello is the leader of the
oppressed fisherfolk. He wants to avenge his sister, without knowing the
name of her betrayer who promised to marry her, and incites the fishermen to rebel against the tyrannical ruler. When troops arrive on the
scene, the conspirators assume an air of innocence by singing a gay
barcarole.

Act III. The market in Naples. Fenella is recognized and is to be arrested
by the guards. Masaniello stabs the commander of the guard; this sparks
off the general popular unrest.

Act IV. Masaniello's hut. The people have won. Alfonso and Elvira
seek refuge from their pursuers in Masaniello's house. He gives them
protection and defends them successfully against his fellow-conspirators
who demand the Prince's life.

Act V. The Viceroy's palace. Pietro tells the fishermen that he has
poisoned the traitor Masaniello. Prince Alfonso attacks with fresh troops,
and the people demand that Masaniello shall lead them into battle, but
his mind seems clouded by the poison, he falls in the struggle and the

Prince's troops win. At the news of her brother's death Fenella throws herself into the sea.

Auber's music reveals a strong passion which reaches its climax in the march themes, and it is quite understandable that these fiery, martial tunes taken up fervently by the chorus should have had an inflammatory effect. Spontini had already introduced marches most effectively into opera and since Auber the march has been used deliberately to obtain dramatic effects; there are excellent examples of these in Meyerbeer and Verdi.

In Giacomo Meyerbeer (1791–1864) we meet the most important French exponent of grand opera in the second half of the nineteenth century. He was the son of a rich Berlin banker, and received an excellent musical education. After successes in Italy with operas in the style of Rossini he went to Paris, where he bowed to contemporary taste by following in the footsteps of Spontini, Auber and Rossini, to some extent improving on their achievements. He was very fortunate in his association with Eugène Scribe, who provided all the libretti for his Paris operas.

Meyerbeer has been much envied and much criticized. One cannot deny that he very often aimed at effect for its own sake, and preferred external impressions to deeper spirituality, but it must be admitted that he had an instinct for grandeur and an outstanding talent for effective dramatic expression, that he prepared his scores with great care and that his orchestration was invariably skilful.

In his first Paris opera, *Robert le Diable* (*Robert the Devil*), first produced in 1831, he tried to surpass his predecessors in scenic effects, large crowd scenes and impressive ensembles. He brought the organ on to the stage, and created the 'church scene', which was to become a popular standby in grand opera. The most famous scene in *Robert le Diable* was the 'resurrection of the nuns', a full-scale ballet in which the spirits of nuns who had died in carnal sin were invoked; their grey shrouds shed, they joined in a bacchanalian ballet as seductive women.

With *Les Huguenots* (1836) Meyerbeer had a greater and more prolonged success. Scribe's very dramatic text is set in a period when political intrigues were everyday affairs and its central theme is the Massacre of St Bartholomew.

LES HUGUENOTS (The Huguenots). Grand opera in five acts by
Giacomo Meyerbeer. Text by Eugène Scribe. First performance: Paris,
1836.

Characters: Marguerite de Valois—soprano; the Comte de St Bris,
leader of the Catholics—bass; Valentine, his daughter—soprano; the
Comte de Nevers, a Catholic nobleman—baritone; Raoul de Nangis, a
Huguenot nobleman—tenor; Marcel, his servant—bass; Urbain, page
to Marguerite de Valois—soprano; Bois Rosé, a Huguenot soldier—
tenor; Maurevert, a Catholic nobleman—bass. Aristocrats, soldiers,
populace.

Place: Touraine and Paris. *Time:* 1572.

Act I. The hall in the castle of the Comte de Nevers. Nevers has
invited to a banquet some of his Catholic friends and also the Huguenot
nobleman Raoul de Nangis, since on the occasion of the Queen's marriage,
peace between Catholics and Huguenots is to be finally concluded.
During the banquet each guest is asked to tell the company about his
beloved. Raoul, the first to be called upon, tells of an unknown beauty
whom he rescued from a band of unruly students, and whom he has
since been unable to banish from his thoughts. A lady is announced to
Nevers. Raoul sees her from a distance and recognizes her as his unknown
beauty. It is Valentine, Nevers' betrothed, who asks him, in private, to
release her from her vows. Since this is also the Queen's wish, Nevers
complies. The Queen's page, Urbain, appears with a letter from his
mistress to Raoul; he must follow the page with his eyes bound. Everyone envies Raoul his good fortune.

Act II. A garden in the Queen's castle. The Queen tells Valentine, the
daughter of the Catholic leader, that she wishes her to marry Raoul, to
put an end to the religious strife between Catholics and Huguenots.
Valentine, who has not forgotten Raoul since her rescue, agrees very
willingly. Raoul is brought before the Queen, who tells him it is her wish
that he should marry Valentine, and demands that all present should forget
their religious hatred. Raoul, greatly troubled, refuses Valentine's hand,
since he has seen her with Nevers and believes her to be unfaithful to him.
The Catholic nobles are deeply indignant, and only the presence of the
Queen prevents them from showing open hostility.

Act III. A square in Paris, in the background a chapel with inns on
both sides. The act opens with the square full of people, choruses of
soldiers and a gipsy ballet. Valentine and Nevers have been married, and
Valentine stays in the chapel to pray. A duel between St Bris and Raoul
is to take place at midnight in the square, when St Bris and Maurevert
plot to kill Raoul. Valentine has overheard their conversation, and to save
Raoul, whom she still loves, she confides in Marcel, who agrees to fetch
help. When the duel is about to start, soldiers pour into the square from
all sides, and Catholics and Huguenots draw their swords. The Queen
enters with her attendants. Marcel, interrogated, replies that the Catholic
conspiracy was revealed to him by the veiled woman, in whom St Bris
recognizes his daughter. Only now that she is married to Nevers does
Raoul learn why she was at his house. Nevers takes his young wife home
in the wedding procession and Raoul is left behind in despair.

Act IV. An apartment in the palace of the Comte de Nevers. Raoul comes to Valentine to implore her pardon, but she has to hide him in an adjoining room, as her father is expected for a conference with his supporters. In the name of the Queen the Catholic leaders resolve to destroy the Huguenots. Nevers alone refuses to take part in this cowardly massacre and is placed under arrest. Their swords are solemnly consecrated by a priest. Raoul, who has overheard everything, wants to warn the Huguenots as quickly as possible, but Valentine begs him not to go as this will mean certain death, and in her fear she confesses her love for him. Overwhelmed, Raoul forgets everything and remains with her. Only when the tocsin tolls as a signal for the massacre to start does he tear himself away and leaping through the window, rushes to join his friends. (In many productions the opera ends with this dramatic scene.)

Act V, scene i. A ballroom. The Huguenots are celebrating the Queen's marriage. Raoul, already wounded, bursts in and calls his friends to arms.

Scene ii. A churchyard. The wives and children of the Huguenots have fled, and take refuge in the little church. Here at last Valentine finds Raoul and implores him to embrace her faith so as to save himself. They hear from Marcel that Nevers has fallen in the fighting and Valentine decides to embrace Raoul's faith. The Catholics break into the church. Raoul declares himself a Huguenot, and a volley fells him, Marcel and Valentine. St Bris, horrified, recognizes his daughter.

With such a thrilling story, this opera does not lack great moments; even Liszt warmly defended Scribe: 'If one continually reproaches the poet for striving after dramatic situations, it would be unjust not to acknowledge how thrilling these can often be'.

The musical climax of the opera is the fourth act, with the impressive consecration of the swords and the moving melody of the great love-duet. The conception of the whole act is an

impressive musical and dramatic accomplishment. Meyerbeer's talent for enhancing effects through the music is especially evident in the construction of the crowd-scenes. He was also very successful in his characterization of individuals, even minor ones like the rough, stolid Marcel, the elegant and capricious Queen, the slightly affected page, and Nevers, somewhat flamboyant, but always honourable.

After an interval of thirteen years, Meyerbeer and Scribe combined again to produce *Le Prophète* (*The Prophet*), which was first performed in Paris in 1849. In this work the concentration on external effect is particularly apparent. The story itself, about Johanns van Leyden and the rising of the Münster Anabaptists, offered plenty of opportunities for sensation and display. Some individual musical numbers, such as the coronation march, the skaters' ballet and the two alto arias of Fidès, became extremely popular. Pauline Viardot-Garcia shone in this magnificent role, which served as a model for Verdi's Azucena.

Meyerbeer's last grand opera, and perhaps his best work, *L'Africaine*, was not performed in Paris until after his death.

L'AFRICAINE (The African Maid). Opera in five acts by Giacomo Meyerbeer. Text by Eugène Scribe. First performance: Paris, 1865.

Characters: Don Pedro, President of the Royal Council—bass; Don Diego, admiral—bass; Ines, his daughter—soprano; Vasco da Gama, a naval officer—tenor; Don Alvar, member of the Council—tenor; Nelusko, a slave—baritone; Selika, a slave girl—soprano; High Priest of Brahma—bass.

Place: Lisbon and the East African coast. *Time:* about 1500.

Act I. The Council chamber at the Admiralty in Lisbon. Don Diego wants his daughter Ines to forget her betrothed, Vasco da Gama, who has disappeared on a sea voyage, and to marry Don Pedro, but Vasco returns as the only survivor of the expedition. As evidence of the existence of an unknown land he brings back with him the negro slaves Selika and Nelusko. When he is denied support for his plans, he hurls insults at the Council and is thrown into prison.

Act II. The Prison of the Inquisition. Selika, who was a Queen in her own country, has been imprisoned with Vasco. Nelusko steals into the cell to murder Vasco, in whom he sees a rival for Selika's affections. Selika protects Vasco, whom she loves, and tells him how he can find his way to the shores of her country. Vasco is set free again, for Ines has bought his freedom by agreeing to marry Don Pedro, who has been appointed commander of a new voyage of discovery which Vasco is allowed to join.

Act III. On board Don Pedro's ship. Ines and Selika are also aboard. Nelusko steers the ship on to the rocks where the ships of the first expedition were wrecked. Vasco pleads with Don Pedro to change course, but his warning goes unheeded. The ship founders, natives storm the wreck and massacre most of the crew.

Act IV. On the African coast. Vasco has escaped death and is enchanted by the sight of this beautiful country. When the natives find him they try to kill him, but Selika comes to the defence of her beloved and tells how he once saved her life. The High Priest marries them.

Act V, scene i. The garden of Selika's palace. Ines tells Selika that she and Vasco have loved each other for a long time. Selika most generously renounces Vasco and has a ship equipped to carry him and Ines back to their country.

Scene ii. On the seashore. Selika is lying under a manzanilla tree, the flowers of which produce poisonous vapours, for she wishes to die. Nelusko finds his death beside his beloved mistress, while Vasco's ship passes out of sight on the horizon.

Meyerbeer deepened his musical style quite remarkably in this work, where external effects give way to pure lyricism without any loss of dramatic effect. The tunes are more like recitatives in style and thereby become very much loftier and less trivial. This tendency was foreshadowed in the love-duet in *Les Huguenots* and is especially evident in Vasco's famous aria in the typical gentle style of Meyerbeer.

O pa-ra-dis,— sor-ti de— l'on-de—
(*Pa-ra-dise,—   lulled by the   lisping sea*)

Jacques Fromental Halévy (1799–1862) shared Meyerbeer's ability to write rewarding roles for his singers, which explains the enduring success of *La Juive* (*The Jewess*), first performed in Paris in 1835. Scribe, the librettist, created a mass of improbabilities which were still accepted by opera-goers long after the whole concept of grand opera had been superseded by that of musical drama.

The opera, set in fifteenth-century Constance, tells of the persecution of the Jews of that city, led by Cardinal Brogni. Rachel, the supposed daughter of the Jewish goldsmith Eleazar, is in love with Prince Leopold, and she refuses to betray him to the Christian authorities. Eleazar and Rachel are condemned to death, and as Rachel goes to execution, Eleazar reveals that she is not, in fact, his real daughter, but that of Cardinal Brogni. The opera has some fine music in it, and with great singing-actors in the roles of Eleazar and Rachel has been successfully revived from time to time.

Living and working in Paris at the same time as Meyerbeer was Hector Berlioz (1803–69), a fervent admirer of Beethoven and Weber and a friend of Wagner and Liszt. His life was one continuous struggle, and even when he finally gained some acknowledgment in the field of symphonic music in spite of great hostility his operas were never really successful. While Meyerbeer was savouring triumphs, Berlioz fought desperately for each work in vain, until through the help of his friend Liszt they were finally performed in Germany. His early comic opera *Benvenuto Cellini* (1838) was, after a long struggle, performed in Paris. In 1835 Berlioz suggested a work for the Opéra-Comique inspired by *Les Mémoires de Benvenuto Cellini*, to a text prepared for him by Léon de Wailly and Auguste Barbier, but the director, afraid of letting Berlioz into his theatre, rejected the libretto, whereupon the composer turned to the new director of the Opéra, proposing *Benvenuto Cellini* as a grand opera in four acts. The director however would only accept two acts from an unknown composer. The work was at last produced in 1838, but later Berlioz changed it to a three-act work by calling the second scene Act II, and the second act Act III.

BENVENUTO CELLINI. Opera in three acts by Hector Berlioz. Text by Léon de Wailly and Auguste Barbier. First performance: Paris, 1838.
  Characters: Benvenuto Cellini, Florentine goldsmith and sculptor— tenor; Giacomo Balducci, Papal Treasurer—bass; Fieramosca, sculptor to the Pope—baritone; Cardinal Salviati—bass; Francesco and Bernardino, artisans in Cellini's workshop—tenor and bass; Pompeo, swordsman—baritone; Teresa, Balducci's daughter—soprano; Ascanio, Cellini's apprentice—mezzo-soprano. Four players, servants and neighbours of Balducci, goldsmiths, craftsmen, apprentices, masks, guards, monks, swordsmen and citizens of Rome.
  Place: Rome. *Time:* 1532.
  Act I. Balducci's apartment. It is nightfall on the Monday before Lent. Teresa plans to elope with Cellini during the Carnival but their plan is overheard by Fieramosca, who is also in love with Teresa.
  Act II. The Piazza Colonna. It is Shrove Tuesday evening and the Carnival is at its height. Cellini pays some comedians to satirize Balducci, who has opposed him both as an artist and a suitor for the hand of his daughter. Balducci is present and sees this improvised performance. The elopement is prevented by Fieramosca's arrival disguised as a white friar, exactly like Cellini, so that Teresa does not know which one is her lover. In the ensuing fight Cellini kills Pompeo and escapes as midnight strikes, the Carnival comes to its abrupt conclusion and all is plunged into darkness.
  Act III, scene i. Cellini's studio. It is Ash Wednesday. Ascanio has guided Teresa to his master, but their flight is once more forestalled.

Cardinal Salviati enters and demands the statue for which he has paid Cellini, only to find it is not yet cast. Balducci and Fieramosca appear and accuse Cellini of abduction and of killing a man in the fight the previous night. The Cardinal gives Cellini until midnight to cast the statue or be handed over to the law.

Scene ii. Cellini's foundry in the Coliseum that evening. Fieramosca tries to hinder Cellini by challenging him to a duel and by bribing his workmen to strike. The Cardinal arrives to watch the casting. Cellini, who has not enough metal for the task, throws into the crucible every piece of gold, silver or bronze within reach, all of them valuable examples of his superb work. When the metal is poured it exactly fills the mould for the statue of Perseus, the artist's best-known work. Cellini has thus earned his pardon and won his bride.

The general reaction to the first performance was of violent opposition, no doubt predetermined by Berlioz's stormy and controversial reputation, but the work was greatly admired by intellectuals and by some sections of the general public. It was withdrawn after a few performances, the last of which was well received by a full house, because of the defection of the tenor, the famous Duprez, who was piqued by the greater success of the two ladies in the cast, Dorus-Gras and Stolz. It was later given (slightly revised by the composer) in Weimar by Liszt in 1852 and by Berlioz himself at Covent Garden in 1853. This London production was a fiasco; an engineered opposition ruined the performance, despite the presence of Queen Victoria.

The music is full of verve and fire, and many passages are extremely attractive, including particularly the overture, and the brilliant Carnival music for the second act, which Berlioz later adapted for his concert overture 'Carnival Romain'. The action is however not without its absurdities and the characterization is very conventional. The heroic and comic elements in the story do not really blend and lend confusion to the general atmosphere. Berlioz however was most enthusiastic, not only about his own music but also about the libretto.

Berlioz's next important operatic work was the dramatic legend, *La Damnation de Faust*, which like his *Roméo et Juliette* falls between two stools. Its cantata form prevents it being really effective dramatically on the opera stage, though the thrilling dramatic quality of the music is undeniable. It was adapted for the operatic stage in 1893 by Raoul Gunsbourg,

then director of the Monte Carlo Opera, where he mounted
the work.

LA DAMNATION DE FAUST (The Damnation of Faust). Dramatic
legend in four parts by Hector Berlioz. Words by the composer, Gérard
and Gandonnière after Gérald de Nerval's version of Goethe's play. First
performance (concert form): Paris, 1846. First stage performance: Monte
Carlo, 1893.

Characters: Marguerite—soprano; Faust—tenor; Mephistopheles—
baritone; Brander—bass. Students, soldiers, citizens, men and women,
fairies, etc.

Place: Hungary and Germany. *Time:* sixteenth century.

Part I. Faust on the plains of Hungary sings of nature and of solitude,
when his reverie is broken by peasants, who dance and sing in chorus.
Soldiers then march by to the strains of the Rákoczy March (the national
air of Hungary).

Part II. Germany. Faust in his study sings of the joyless existence of a
man of learning, and is about to end it all by taking poison when he sees
as in a vision the kneeling congregation in a church singing the Easter
canticle. He is restored for the moment to his faith in life, when Mephistopheles appears to offer him all possible earthly joys and experiences.
They set off together and the scene changes to Auerbach's cellar in Leipzig
where students and soldiers are revelling. After Brander's 'Song of the
Rat', which is echoed by a mocking 'Requiescat' and fugal 'Amen',
Mephistopheles sings the 'Song of the Flea'. The scene changes to the
banks of the Elbe, where Faust is sleeping. Mephistopheles sings his lovely
aria 'Voici des roses' ('Here are roses') and the Sylphs dance to an
exquisitely delicate accompaniment. The scene ends with the soldiers'
chorus, mingled with a Latin song from the students.

Part III. A view into Marguerite's house. Soldiers and students are
strolling by in the street, singing. Faust sings 'Merci doux crépuscule' ('I
thank thee, gentle dusk') in his joy at being in Marguerite's room. He
hides as she enters and sings the ballad of the King of Thule. Mephistopheles then invokes the will-o'-the wisps, and sings his mocking serenade.
The love duet 'Ange adorable' is harshly broken into by Mephistopheles,
urging Faust to depart.

Part IV. Marguerite, alone, sings 'D'amour l'ardente flamme' ('Love,
devouring fire') to describe her forlorn, deserted state, in place of Goethe's
famous 'Meine Ruh' ist hin'. The chorus of soldiers and students fades,
'retreat' is sounded on drums and trumpets, and Marguerite faints at her
window, overcome with remorse. The scene changes to a mountain
gorge where Faust invokes nature in an impressive aria 'Nature, immense,
impénétrable et fière' ('Nature, vast, unfathomable and proud'). This is
followed by the tempestuous, eerie and headlong 'Ride to Hell' with its
moving panorama and accompanying pandemonium. The work ends
with the redemption of Marguerite and her welcome by angels into the
heavens.

The setting of the first part in Hungary was undoubtedly a
device to allow the interpolation of the splendid Rákoczy
March, which Berlioz had orchestrated on his tour of Austria-
Hungary in 1845. It is only one of many wonderfully evocative,
varied and vivid tunes in this work, ranging from the lyricism
of Mephistopheles's 'Voici des roses' and Faust's 'Merci doux
crépuscule' to the coarse parody of the students' 'Requiescat'
and 'Amen' and the fierce, harsh mockery of Mephistopheles's
serenade. One most touching moment is Marguerite's 'King of
Thule', for which Berlioz wrote a tune and accompaniment of

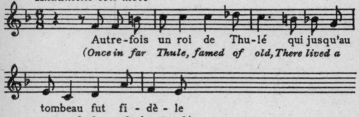

primitive simplicity, which he characterized as a 'Chanson
Gothique'. In Part II, the 'Dance of the Sylphs' is one of the
most effective illustrative passages, with a pedal-point in the
muted cellos, and a gossamer fabric of melody and harmony
woven above it.

Berlioz's next dramatic work was the opera *Béatrice et
Bénédict* (1862), based on the short version of Shakespeare's
Much Ado about Nothing which omits the sinister side of this
comic plot. The composer never succeeded in having this work
performed in Paris in his lifetime, and only in 1890 did it reach
the Opéra-Comique. Meanwhile it had been produced in
Baden-Baden in 1862, and performed through Liszt's good
offices in Weimar in 1863.

The mammoth *Les Troyens* was Berlioz's major stage-work in
every way. It was written in two parts, *La Prise de Troie* with
two acts of 52 and 22 minutes, and *Les Troyens à Carthage*, in
three acts of 40, 47 and 45 minutes respectively. It was not performed in its entirety until twenty-one years after the composer's
death, and in fact he only saw Part II, on the stage of the

Théâtre Lyrique, Paris, in 1863, when it ran for twenty-one performances. Since 1890, when the whole was given on two consecutive nights, the two parts have been performed separately and together in France, Germany, Italy, the U.S.A., Sweden and Great Britain.

LES TROYENS (The Trojans). Opera in two parts and five acts by Hector Berlioz. Text by the composer from Virgil's *Aeneid*. First performance: Karlsruhe, 1890.

Part I: *La Prise de Troie* (*The Capture of Troy*).

Characters: Cassandre (Cassandra), a Trojan prophetess, daughter of Priam—soprano; Chorèbe (Choroebus), her betrothed—baritone; Priam, King of Troy—bass; Hécube (Hecuba), his wife—mezzo-soprano; Enée (Aeneas), a Trojan hero—tenor; Ascagne (Ascanius), his son—soprano; Helenus, son of Priam—tenor; Polyxène (Polyxena), daughter of Priam —soprano; Panthée (Pantheus), a Trojan priest—bass; Ghost of Hector— bass; a Trojan soldier—baritone; a Greek captain—baritone; Andromaque (Andromache), widow of Hector—mime; Astyanax, her son— mime. Soldiers of Greece and Troy, citizens, women, children, shepherds, priestesses.

Place: In and near Troy. *Time:* more than nine years after the start of the Trojan War.

Act I, scene i. The plain outside Troy. The Greeks have withdrawn, leaving behind them the Wooden Horse. The Trojan people have come joyfully out of the city and are singing and dancing. They depart to look at the huge horse, leaving behind Cassandra, who foretells the destruction of Troy in the aria 'Malheureux roi' ('Unhappy king'). Even her lover Choroebus ignores her prophecies, believing her deranged. When he will not accede to her plea to leave the city, she resigns herself to die.

Scene ii. An open space before the Citadel. The people are celebrating their supposed deliverance with hymns and games, before Priam, Hecuba, their children, priests and generals. Andromache and her son Astyanax enter in mourning, a most unwelcome interruption of the general mood of gaiety. Cassandra also enters, prophesying terrible disaster, but no one will listen to her. Aeneas then rushes in and succeeds in striking terror into everyone with his tale of Laocoön, the priest who, deeply suspicious of the wooden horse, threw a spear at it, and was immediately devoured by two great serpents which emerged out of the sea. 'Châtiment effroyable' ('Appalling punishment') they cry. This is taken as a sign of Pallas Athene's wrath at the outrage to the horse, which was dedicated to her, and at Aeneas's suggestion the people drag the wooden horse into the city and place it in Pallas's temple, once more rejoicing and singing to the strains of the Trojan March.

Act II, scene i. Aeneas's tent. Noises of battle are heard, but Ascanius does not dare disturb his father's sleep. The Ghost of Hector, who had been Aeneas's closest friend, appears to him, telling him that Troy is being sacked and commanding him to take his son and found a new

Troy on Italian soil. Pantheus enters and tells Aeneas how the Greeks were hidden in the horse, that Priam is dead and the city is burning. Aeneas rallies the chiefs to battle.

Scene ii. The Temple of Vesta. The priestesses and women of Troy are bewailing the fate of their city. Cassandra enters to tell them of Choroebus's death and Aeneas's escape. She urges the women to kill themselves rather than fall into Greek hands and the few dissentients are driven from the temple. When Greek soldiers rush in demanding the treasure all the women, led by Cassandra, stab themselves, crying 'Italy' as they die.

Part II: *Les Troyens à Carthage* (*The Trojans at Carthage*). First performance: Paris, 1863.

Characters: Didon (Dido), Queen of Carthage—mezzo-soprano; Enée (Aeneas)—tenor; Ascagne (Ascanius)—soprano; Panthée (Pantheus) —bass; Anna, Dido's sister—contralto; Narbal, Dido's minister—bass; Iopas, a Carthaginian poet—tenor; Hylas, a young sailor—tenor; two Trojan soldiers—baritone and bass; the god Mercury—bass; Ghost of Cassandra—soprano; Ghost of Choroebus—baritone; Ghost of Hector— bass; Ghost of Priam—bass. Soldiers of Troy and Carthage, courtiers, hunters, sailors, naiads, fauns, satyrs, and wood-nymphs.

Place: In and near Carthage. *Time:* shortly after the end of the Trojan War.

Act III. The grounds of Dido's palace in Carthage. A festival is being held to celebrate the progress made in building the city. The different branches of the populace file past Dido, offering her evidence of their toil. She praises them, but reminds them of all that still remains to be done, and they in turn promise to protect her and her kingdom from their neighbour Iarbas, the Numidian, who seeks to marry her and is threatening to invade her territory. Dido, left alone with her sister Anna, resists the latter's attempts to persuade her to remarry and give Carthage a king. She cannot forget her dead husband Sichaeus, and swears to remain faithful to his memory and his ring. Iopas enters to tell of the foreign fleet which has been driven by the recent storm into their harbour and has anchored there. Its leaders wish to speak with the Queen, and she receives them (the fugitive Trojans led apparently by Pantheus) most graciously. Suddenly Narbal rushes in with the news of a Numidian invasion and the threat to Carthage itself. Aeneas, who had stood aside disguised as a sailor, throws off his cloak and revealing himself, declares that he and his troops will help to repel the invaders. The Trojans arm the young Carthaginians and depart into battle, Aeneas leaving his son tenderly in Dido's care.

Symphonic Interlude—La Chasse royale et Orage (The Royal Hunt and Storm). A virgin forest near Carthage, where naiads and satyrs disport themselves until forced to flee by the approach of a hunting party led by Aeneas, Dido dressed as Diana, and Ascanius. A storm is brewing and Dido and Aeneas take refuge in a cave while cries of 'Italy' are heard. The storm breaks, a tree is struck by lightning, and dark clouds obscure the scene. Gradually the storm dies down, and peace returns to the glade. (In modern scores this scene is sometimes moved to the end of Act IV.)

Act IV. The gardens of Dido's palace by the sea, festively decorated
to greet Aeneas's victorious return. Narbal tells Anna of his fears for
Dido and for Carthage now that Aeneas, who will be driven by the gods
to leave again for Italy, is absorbing all Dido's attention to the exclusion
of her cares for her people, but Anna can think only of Dido's love for
Aeneas and ignores the possible danger. Dido and Aeneas enter with
Ascanius, dressed symbolically as Cupid, and are entertained with a ballet,
and a song by Iopas. Dido soon tires of anything which keeps her attention from Aeneas and begs him to recount again the story of the fall of
Troy and the fate of its royal inhabitants. The tale of Andromache re-
marrying, (the son of her husband's murderer at that) adds its influence to
Dido's own wish for remarriage. 'O Pudeur,' she sings, 'Tout conspire
à vaincre mes remords' ('Oh for shame, all conspires to vanquish my
remorse'). Her hand rests on Ascanius's shoulder and he playfully removes
Sichaeus's ring from her finger, while Anna comments on his likeness to
Cupid. Aeneas joins in, and Iopas and Narbal add their voices to a beautiful ensemble in which each comments on Dido's love for Aeneas. This
is followed by a hardly less beautiful septet (Ascanius and Pantheus have
now joined in) 'Tout n'est que paix et charme' ('All is peace around us').
All leave the garden except Dido and Aeneas who now confess their love
for each other in an exquisite love-duet 'Nuit d'ivresse et d'extase infinie'
('Oh sweet night, night of ecstasy unending') which continues with the

words from Shakespeare's *Merchant of Venice* 'On such a night as this'—
'Par une telle nuit'. As they leave the gardens the figure of Mercury
appears, strikes Aeneas's shield and utters the fateful cry 'Italy'.

Act V, scene i. The harbour at night. The Trojan ships lie at anchor.

A young sailor, Hylas, sings sadly of his homeland 'Vallon sonore' ('Oh vale resounding'). The Trojan chiefs are preparing for departure, fearing that each moment's delay will incur the wrath of the gods. The cry 'Italy' is heard from disembodied voices. Two Trojan sentries speak with impatience of this talk of departure. Another long sea-voyage is a tedious prospect, and they are quite content with conditions in Carthage. Aeneas enters, torn between his overwhelming love for Dido and his sense of destiny. He *must* leave, but cannot bear the thought of farewell, and is deeply agitated when he hears and sees the ghosts of Priam, Choroebus, Cassandra and Hector who command him to follow his destiny. With a slow, sad farewell to the absent Dido, he gives orders for departure and is about to embark when Dido rushes in, reproaching, raving, pleading with him to stay. He almost gives in, but the distant sound of the Trojan March stiffens his resolve, and crying 'Italy' he embarks.

Scene ii. Dido's palace. The Queen begs her sister to intercede with Aeneas on her behalf, but Anna believes in the inevitability of Aeneas's departure, in spite of his love for Dido. This is incomprehensible to the unhappy woman who declares that her love would make her disobey Zeus himself. Iopas enters to announce that the Trojan fleet has set sail, and Dido in a rage orders her people to pursue and destroy the traitors, lamenting that she had ever treated them as honoured guests. The only course left is to burn everything connected with Aeneas on a great pyre dedicated to the gods of Hades. Left alone, her grief overflows, and she resolves to die on the pyre herself. 'Ah, je vais mourir' ('Now must I die') and perhaps Aeneas will see the flames from afar. In a moving aria she bids farewell to her life's work 'Adieu, fière cité' (Farewell, proud city').

Scene iii. A terrace overlooking the sea. A funeral pyre has been built and consecrated by the priests of Pluto. Dido mounts it, takes Aeneas's sword and, prophesying that a son of her race, Hannibal, will one day arise to avenge her injury, she plunges it into her breast. Before she dies a further vision, of Rome triumphant at the last, is granted her and the strains of the Trojan March challenge the curses hurled by the Carthaginians against their former guests, and a vision of the eternal city rises behind the pyre.

Though this opera is full of the most beautiful lyrical, stirring and dramatic music, and contains some splendid singing roles, it was not at first successful in Paris, where classical subjects had been so repeatedly used that yet another could only meet with disaster. It has met with greater success since then, though the immense complexity of the stage sets and the huge forces required, together with its enormous length, serve to make it a 'special' undertaking for any opera house. The role of Aeneas is also hard to cast, as only a dramatic tenor of great personality, range, vocal flexibility and stamina can possibly sustain it. It has however been successfully revived in the 1950s in England, Italy and France, the whole work being performed on one evening though with certain cuts. The particular highlights of the opera are perhaps the spectacle of the entry of the Wooden Horse into Troy, the exquisite love-scene in Act IV and Aeneas's wonderful *scena* in Act V. The music for 'The Royal Hunt and Storm' is very familiar from concert performances, and is sufficiently self-contained as an episode to bear its occasional removal from the position originally intended by Berlioz at the end of Act III to either the beginning or the end of Act IV.

French comic opera, or *opéra comique*, also received an extraordinary impetus in the first half of the nineteenth century. The leading exponent of these musical comedies is François Adrien Boieldieu (1775–1834), who made a splendid entry into the field of opera in 1800 with his *Le Calife de Bagdad* (*The Caliph of Baghdad*). His works *Jean de Paris* (*John of Paris*) (1812) and *La Dame Blanche* (*The White Lady*) (1825)—his finest and best remembered work—spread his name and the fame of French comic opera all over Europe.

LA DAME BLANCHE (The White Lady). Comic opera in three acts by François Adrien Boieldieu. Text by Eugène Scribe after Scott's *Guy Mannering* and *The Monastery*. First performance: Paris, 1825.

Characters: Gaveston, former steward of the Earl of Avernel—bass; Anna, his ward—soprano; Margaret, former nurse at Avernel Castle—alto; George Brown, an English officer—tenor; Dickson, a farmer—tenor; Jenny, his wife—soprano; McIrton, Justice of the Peace—bass.

Place: Scotland. *Time:* middle of the eighteenth century.

Act I. A courtyard in front of the farm. The young officer George Brown asks the Dicksons for lodgings, and they in return ask him to be their son's godfather, to which George agrees. When they question him about his origin, he has little to tell. He was brought up together with a girl, but at an early age was put on a ship where he was very badly treated. He has now been a soldier for a long time. Aria: 'Ah, quel plaisir d'etre soldat' ('Ah, what a joy to be a soldier'). Jenny, the farmer's wife, tells him about the Earl of Avernel, whose castle is going to be sold by auction on the following day, since the family, who are Jacobites, have had to flee to France. The neighbouring farmers want to combine together to purchase the castle. Jenny sings the Ballad of the White Lady. George does not believe in the white lady, but Dickson swears that he has received money and help from her himself and since then has sworn to serve her. Dickson is disturbed when he returns from the farmers' gathering. In the dark forest a dwarf had given him a letter from the white lady, commanding him to go to the door of the old castle that very night. George, thirsty for adventure, offers to go in his place, and sets off amid thunder and lightning.

Act II, scene i. A room in Avernel Castle. It is evening, and Old Margaret sits spinning. Anna enters with her guardian Gaveston; she knows the secrets of the late Countess Avernel, whom she followed into exile. There is a knock at the door and George Brown begs admittance. When Anna has promised to reveal the Countess's secret on the following day, Gaveston opens the door. Margaret—Anna having retired—thinks she sees in George a likeness to the Avernels. Gaveston derisively wishes him good luck with the white lady. George sings the *cavatina* 'Viens gentille dame' ('Come, gracious lady'), and starts to doze. While he is half-asleep, the white lady appears to him. It is Anna, who has been waiting for Dickson and now recognizes in George the young officer whom she once nursed back to health. George believes in supernatural powers and promises to follow all her commands.

Scene ii. At the auction on the following day Anna approaches George unnoticed, and instructs him to overcall every bid on behalf of the white lady. George now recognizes in Anna his beloved nurse, and purchases the castle in spite of threats that he will be put in prison if he cannot pay. He completes the purchase to the joy of the farmers.

Act III. The Baronial hall in the castle. The fortune of the Avernels is hidden in the statue of the white lady, and this is the secret of the late Countess. George, accompanied by the peasants, comes into the baronial hall. Old memories surge in upon him, especially when the peasants sing a Scottish folk song. Unnoticed by everybody, Anna, disguised as the white lady and veiled, has stationed herself on the empty pedestal, and gives George the family treasure of the Avernels. To everyone's joy George proves himself to be the forgotten son of the last earl and therefore the rightful heir. Gaveston tears the veil from the face of the white lady, everyone recognizes Anna, and George, delighted, takes her in his arms.

Boieldieu's music is both unaffected and vital, and therefore also sounds very spontaneous. The march song 'Ah, quel plaisir d'être soldat' as well as the elegant *cavatina* 'Viens gentille dame',

Andantino con moto

Viens gen-til-le da-me,   Viens gen-til - le da-me
(*Come gra-cious la-dy,   Come gra-cious la - dy*)

are really enchanting, and Boieldieu's ensembles are also extremely cleverly constructed. The Ballad of the White Lady is also beautifully composed: from the faint introductory verse rises the mysteriously whispered refrain, the repeat of which is emphasized by the chorus in anxious, staccato chords. The

septet at the auction, the finale of the second act, stands out as the supreme musical climax 'Oh ciel, oh ciel, quel est donc ce mystère?' ('Oh heav'n, oh heav'n, what deep mystery lurks here?') Above Gaveston's suppressed rage at the failure of his plan, and the continuous cries of Dickson and his wife, Margaret and the magistrate, rise in joyful and radiant *crescendo* the voices of Anna and George. Finally the chorus joins the ensemble in secret excitement.

Just as German comic opera at the beginning of the nineteenth century is represented by the names of Lortzing, Flotow and Nicolai, so too in French musical comedy there is a third name to be joined with those of Boieldieu and Auber—Charles Adolphe Adam (1803–56), whose evergreen *Le Postillon de Longjumeau* contains such delightful humour and such rewarding roles for singers that it stands out as musically the most charming comic opera of the period.

LE POSTILLON DE LONGJUMEAU (The Coachman of Longjumeau). Comic opera in three acts by Charles Adolphe Adam. Text by A. de Leuven (Adolf, Graf Ribbing) and Léon Lévy Brunswick. First performance: Paris, 1836.

Characters: Chappelou, a postillion—tenor; Bijou, a blacksmith—bass; Marquis de Corcy, director of the Paris Opéra—baritone; Madeleine, a hostess—soprano; Bourdon, a chorister—bass; and others.

Place: The village of Longjumeau and Fontainebleau. *Time:* 1766.

Act I. A square in Longjumeau. Chappelou and Madeleine are celebrating their wedding. It has been prophesied to both of them that they

could each have made a much better match. Chappelou asks the blacksmith Bijou to employ him, but Bijou, who had courted Madeleine
himself, refuses. Chappelou's hope that no more travellers will come to
the inn is not fulfilled, for the Marquis de Corcy, who has broken a wheel
of his coach, seeks Chappelou's services to help him continue his journey.
The young couple asks him to wait a little, but in vain, for the Marquis,
who is looking for a new tenor for the Paris Opéra, does not want to
waste any time. The wedding party returns and when Chappelou is
asked to sing, he obliges with the Postillion's song 'Mes amis, écoutez
l'histoire' ('My friends now listen to the story'). The Marquis is delighted
by Chappelou's wonderful tenor voice and persuades him to go to Paris
with him. Bijou, who has meanwhile put the coach to rights, is astonished
to hear of Chappelou's plans. He too considers that he has a good voice
and starts singing. The Marquis thinks he is drunk, and makes haste to
leave. Bijou is left behind alone. From the oriel window Madeleine
sweetly calls down to her young husband. Bijou tells her what has happened, as the neighbours hurry in, and the postillion's song is heard in the
distance. Everyone is angry with Chappelou for running away on his
wedding night, and poor Madeleine collapses in a faint.

Act II. A room in Mme de Latour's house. Ten years have passed.
Madeleine, who has inherited a fortune from a rich aunt, is living on her
country estate near Paris as Mme de Latour. The many letters she wrote
as Madeleine to the tenor St Phar (as Chappelou, now singing at the
Opéra, is called) have remained unanswered, whereas those of Mme de
Latour have been answered affectionately. Her most ardent admirer, the
Marquis de Corcy, has invited a group of singers, among them St Phar,
to her house, where a serenade, written by the Marquis, is to be performed. But the singers who have been invited say that they are hoarse.
Only when St Phar hears that he is in Mme Latour's house, does his
hoarseness vanish. To the delight of the Marquis he sings 'Viens, viens,
ô ma tourterelle' ('Come, come little turtle dove'). St Phar is left alone
with Alci dor, alias Bijou, who is singing in the chorus at the Opéra
but feels that he is called to higher things, and sings 'Oui des choristes
du théâtre' ('Indeed the best flower of the chorus'). St Phar declares
his love to Mme Latour, when just at the worst moment Alcindor
brings him a letter from his wife Madeleine. St Phar denies that he has
ever been married and declares that he is ready to marry at once. In an
aside he commissions Alcindor to find an opera extra to solemnize a fake
marriage. The Marquis overhears the conversation and tells Mme Latour
about it.

Act III. Mme Latour's bedroom. Alcindor (Bijou) and Bourdon, the
chorister who is to impersonate a priest, tell St Phar that the Marquis is
going to charge him with bigamy—'Pendu, pendu,' ('Hanged, hanged').
While St Phar is alone, Mme Latour appears, a lamp in her hand, disguised as a maid in the peasant dress of Madeleine. St Phar recognizes
Madeleine, and she him. She drops the lamp and in the dark plays a
double game with the bewildered man, one moment being the peasant
girl and the next Mme Latour. The Marquis arrives with the watch to
have the bigamists arrested, but Mme de Latour explains everything,

and St Phar throws himself, conscience-stricken, at the feet of his Madeleine.

The famous postillion song with the well-known refrain is without any doubt the 'hit' of this altogether delightful opera. Its top C means that only tenors with a particularly light and high range can sing it, but for them it is invariably a sure success.

The most successful comic opera melodies became what today would be called popular hits. Among these were the postillion's song, 'Ah, quel plaisir d'être soldat' from *La Dame blanche*, and the *romance* from *Fra Diavolo* 'Voyez sur cette roche' ('See upon those rocks'), which every child could sing a hundred years ago.

Fra Diavolo (1830) was Auber's greatest success in the field of comic opera, to which he turned after his triumphant promotion of grand opera. He wrote a series of charming comic operas to texts by Scribe, including *Le Philtre* (*The Love Charm*) (1831), *Le Domino noir* (*The Black Domino*) (1837), and *La Part du Diable* (*The Devil's Share*) (1843). It is difficult to understand why these works, especially the elegant and graceful *Domino noir* are now completely forgotten, while *Fra Diavolo* on the other hand is always enthusiastically received.

FRA DIAVOLO. Comic opera in three acts by Daniel Auber. Text by Eugène Scribe. First performance: Paris, 1830.

Characters: Fra Diavolo—tenor; Lord Cockburn, an English traveller—baritone; Pamela, his wife—mezzo-soprano; Lorenzo, an officer of the Roman dragoons—tenor; Matteo, an inn-keeper—bass; Zerlina, his daughter—soprano; Giacomo, a bandit—tenor; Beppo, a bandit—bass; Francesco, a farmer—bass; a miller—bass. Dragoons, servants, peasants.

Place: An inn near Rome. *Time:* 1830.

Act I. Matteo's inn, near Terracina. Matteo's penniless daughter Zerlina cannot marry her beloved Lorenzo, who is also poor, and is to be married to the rich Francesco instead. Lorenzo has been ordered with his dragoons to capture the notorious bandit chief Fra Diavolo, on whose head a high price has been set. Lord Cockburn arrives with his wife. They have just been attacked by the bandits. During their journey a certain Marchese San Marco aroused Lord Cockburn's jealousy by his behaviour towards Lady Cockburn, and he leaves the room with his wife when the Marchese appears. Zerlina, in the famous romance 'Voyez sur cette roche' ('See upon those rocks') tells the Marchese, who is none other than Fra Diavolo, about the bandit's exploits. The two bandits Giacomo and Beppo slip in to report to their chief, the Marchese, that the band has stolen the Englishman's jewellery but found no money. The Marchese quickly tells them that the money is sewn in the lady's dress. Meanwhile the dragoons have recovered the jewels from the bandits. Lorenzo returns the jewels to Lady Cockburn, but refuses the high reward offered him by her husband, whereupon she gives the money to Zerlina. The lovers can now face the future with a little more hope.

Act II. Zerlina's bedroom. While Zerlina shows the English couple to their room, the Marchese is looking over her room, in the hope of being able to rob the English people from there. He is joined by Beppo and Giacomo, who climb in through the window; all three hide and listen to the unsuspecting Zerlina, who sings 'Oui, c'est demain' ("Tis tomorrow') as she undresses for bed. Just as Beppo is about to stab the sleeping girl, Lorenzo returns with his dragoons, and the resulting turmoil brings everyone rushing in. Fra Diavolo, still playing the part of the Marchese, explains his presence by asserting that he had been summoned to a rendez-vous, thus arousing the jealousy of both Lord Cockburn and Lorenzo.

Act III. In the hills near Terracina. Fra Diavolo, now dressed as a bandit, hides a written command for his followers in a hollow tree. The wedding procession of Zerlina and Francesco approaches. Lorenzo is in despair because of Zerlina's supposed infidelity. Beppo and Giacomo find their orders and mingle with the wedding-guests, but give themselves away by talking carelessly and are arrested. The letter is found on them and they are forced to give their chief the agreed signal. Fra Diavolo appears on the rocks, the dragoons shoot, and he falls into the abyss. Horrified, Lady Cockburn finds that her Marchese and the bandit were one and the same person, but Lorenzo gets his Zerlina.

Auber's music, and particularly his rhythms, are essentially his own creation. The best-known tune in the opera is Zerlina's *romanza*. According to a sardonic remark by Wagner, no opera can do without a drinking song and a prayer. Both are to be found in *Fra Diavolo*; the drinking song in the introduction at the beginning of the first act, and the prayer in Zerlina's great second act *scena*.

In Paris at that time any opera with spoken dialogue fell into the category of comic opera, a term which has always led to misunderstandings. Originally *Fra Diavolo* did not have a tragic ending, which would have been inconceivable in the heyday of comic opera, but finished simply with the arrest of the bandit-chief. Only later did the authors decide to make a more effective version of the final scene, but since the light-hearted scenes predominate, good triumphs and evil is punished, the label of comic opera is still entirely applicable to this work.

This label seems however, totally unsuitable for a work such as *Zampa ou La Fiancée de marbre* (*Zampa or the Marble Betrothed*) by Joseph Ferdinand Hérold (1791–1833); it was his masterpiece and dominated European stages for almost a century, and in its grisly story even outdid Meyerbeer's horror-opera *Robert le Diable*. Both operas were first performed in Paris in 1831. The story of *Zampa* is, briefly, that of a corsair who forces his brother's bride to marry him by threatening to kill her father, who is languishing in his pirate prison. The marble statue of Zampa's former betrothed, whom he has disdainfully abandoned, takes an active part in the plot on several occasions and finally drags the unfaithful pirate with her into the sea.

In the second half of the nineteenth century opera was essentially dominated by Wagner. His ideas, and his conception of musical drama had a decisive influence on all operatic compositions, though this is not apparent in each individual work. A whole series of French operas written during this period won great popularity throughout the world, and the Paris Opéra only gradually began to lose its influence towards the end of the century. At the time when Meyerbeer's reign was still unchallenged, Charles Gounod (1818–93) had a tremendous success with his opera *Faust*, based on Goethe's play. It quickly became popular in Germany, where it is always known as *Margarethe* out of reverence for Goethe's masterpiece. Though the authors are often rightly reproached for distorting Goethe's characters, it is difficult not to escape the spell of Gounod's beautiful music.

FAUST. Opera in five acts by Charles Gounod. Text after Goethe by Jules Barbier and Michel Carré. First performance: Paris, 1859.

Characters: Faust—tenor; Méphistophélés—bass; Marguerite—soprano; Valentine, her brother—baritone; Marthe Schwertlein—contralto; Wagner—baritone; Siebel—soprano. Students, soldiers, people.

Place: Germany. *Time:* sixteenth century.

Act I. Faust's study. Tired of life, Faust seizes a phial of poison. The merry songs of the peasants passing by are heard. The word 'God' in these songs exasperates Faust. He abjures all faith and invokes the devil. Méphistophélés appears and offers his services. Faust wants his youth back, and Mephisto promises to fulfil this wish if Faust sells him his soul. When Faust hesitates, Mephisto conjures up a vision of Marguerite. Captivated by her youth and beauty Faust assents to the pact with the devil and drinks the elixir of youth.

Act II. Outside the city gates. Students, soldiers, citizens, girls and women are strolling about, singing. Valentine, who is going to the war, bids farewell to his friends Siebel and Wagner. He prays to God to protect his sister Marguerite. Mephisto joins the students and sings the song of the golden calf, but he only provokes dislike with his cynical prophecies. He tells Siebel that every flower will wither in his hands. When by magic he makes wine come out of the inn's signboard and proposes a toast to Marguerite, Valentine in a fury throws himself upon him, but his sword shatters in pieces. Everyone realizes that they are in the presence of an evil spirit, and, reversing their swords, make the sign of the cross with them. Faust enters and demands that Mephisto should lead him to Marguerite. The students and girls have gathered again and start to dance to the tune of the famous waltz. Marguerite enters and Faust offers himself as her escort, but she refuses him. Disconcerted, Faust is left alone.

Act III. The garden of Marguerite's house. Siebel comes to pick a bouquet, but all the flowers he touches fade. Only after he has dipped his fingers in holy water can he gather a bunch of flowers for Marguerite. Faust and Mephisto enter, but Mephisto hurries off at once to fetch a costly present for Marguerite. The simplicity and tidiness of Marguerite's home make a deep impression on Faust, and he apostrophizes it in the *cavatina:* 'Salut! demeure chaste et pure' ('All hail, thou dwelling pure and lowly'). Mephisto returns and places a jewel-box before Marguerite's door. In the great *scena* which follows Marguerite confesses that she would dearly like to know who the man was who offered her his arm. At her spinning-wheel she sings the ballad of the King of Thule, breaking off frequently as her thoughts stray to the unknown cavalier. Suddenly she sees the jewel-case. Impelled by curiosity and vanity she decks herself with earrings and a necklace and looks in the mirror; this is the famous 'Air des Bijoux' (The Jewel Song). Her neighbour, Marthe Schwertlein, enters and soon after Faust and Mephisto return. Marthe is flattered by Mephisto's bold, sardonic courtship. and in the meantime Marguerite tells Faust about her life. Dusk has fallen. Faust becomes more and more affectionate, 'Laisse-moi contempler ton visage' ('Let me gaze upon thy beauty') he sings, and Marguerite falls in love with him. She implores him to go away, and finally she herself hurries into the house. Faust tries to follow her, but Mephisto restrains him. Marguerite appears at the window, and longingly calls to her lover; Faust can no longer control himself and hurries to her. Mephisto, laughing sardonically, leaves the lovers alone.

Act IV. In the church. Marguerite prays to God for mercy, but her conscience, speaking with Mephisto's voice, weighs more and more heavily on her. Her agony of fear is not alleviated by the sacred hymn of the congregation and she faints.

Scene ii. The street in front of Marguerite's house. Soldiers, among them Valentine, enter the town to a lively military march. Faust and Mephisto arrive and Mephisto tries to draw Marguerite out of her house with a serenade, 'Vous qui faites l'endormie' ('Catarina, while you play at sleeping'). Valentine steps angrily forward and challenges Faust to a duel. After a short fight Faust stabs Valentine and flees with Mephisto. The noise of the fight attracts the neighbours, among them Marguerite, Marthe and Siebel. Valentine curses Marguerite and dies.

Act V, scene i. The Brocken, in the Harz Mountains. Mephisto brings Faust to witness the Walpurgis Night revels, and Faust meets the great courtesans of antiquity. This is the great ballet scene, a *sine qua non* at the Paris Opéra. Suddenly Marguerite appears to him, pale and disfigured, with a red streak round her neck. Faust implores Mephisto to take him to the wretched girl.

Scene ii. The prison. Marguerite is sleeping, condemned to death for having killed her child. Faust enters and, agitated, awakens her. She throws herself happily into his arms, but when Faust urges her to flee with him he is horrified to find that her senses have left her. She relives the happy days of her love; the waltz is heard, the theme of their first meeting, and the melody of the great love-duet. Mephisto enters to say that dawn is breaking and there is no time to waste. At the sight of Mephisto, Marguerite recoils, throws herself on her knees and commits her soul to God. Faust tries to drag her with him, but she tears herself from him and collapses. Mephisto shouts triumphantly 'Jugée!' ('Condemned'), but the chorus of angels cry 'Sauvée!' ('Saved'). An Easter hymn is heard, and Marguerite is borne by the angels up to heaven.

Several traits in Gounod's music, such as the characteristic construction of the recitatives and the use of *leitmotivs*, clearly show Wagner's influence. The beginning of the first act, for instance, is dominated by powerful recitatives, and the beautiful melody which rightly made the opera so popular only appears in the final duet, when Faust passionately demands the return of his

A moi_ les plai-sirs,___ les jeu - nes maî-tres-ses
(*Be mine__ the de - light__ of Beau - ty's ca - res-ses*)

youth. The climax comes with the appearance of the delicate
love theme in the orchestra to accompany the vision of Mar-

guerite. The finale of the second act is built on the famous waltz.
One lively waltz tune follows another, to emphasize the action.
The short *andantino* in which Faust first addresses Marguerite

is doubly captivating in its delicate simplicity. Equally emotional
is Faust's intense and musically inspired *cavatina* which often
returns as a *leitmotiv* symbolizing purity.

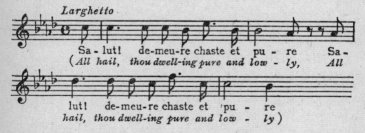

The third act is a great musical accomplishment in construction and development. The second part with the quartet, the
love-duet and the dramatic finale is particularly effective, while
one of the most popular passages of the opera has always been
Valentine's prayer, which was written by Gounod for the great
English baritone, Santley, for the production in English in 1864.

Marguerite's so-called Jewel Song, a brilliant waltz tune with trills and short coloratura passages, is both impressive and rewarding to sing. Mephisto's two songs, the rondo of the golden calf, a springy *tarantella* with really demoniac impact, and the satanically ironic serenade, are clearly the work of a genius. Gounod's *Mireille* and *Roméo et Juliette* are rarely performed outside France.

Ambroise Thomas (1811–96) had a less striking, but equally long-lived success with his *Mignon*. This story also came from Goethe and was also sentimentalized in the operatic manner.

MIGNON. Opera in three acts by Ambroise Thomas. Text after Goethe by Michel Carré and Jules Barbier. First performance: Paris, 1866.

Characters: Wilhelm Meister—tenor; Frédéric—tenor; Philine, an actress—soprano; Laertes, an actor—tenor; Lothario—bass; Mignon—mezzo-soprano; Giarno, chief of a band of gipsies—bass.

Place: Germany and Italy. *Time:* eighteenth century.

Act I. The courtyard of a German inn. The townspeople are drinking beer. The wandering singer Lothario enters, searching for his daughter, who has been stolen by gipsies; his mind is deranged. Some gipsies enter, and Mignon is told to dance for the onlookers. She refuses, and Giarno tries to hit her. The young Wilhelm Meister steps angrily between them, and out of pity buys Mignon from the gipsies. She tells him she knows very little of her origin—'Connais-tu le pays' ('Knowest thou the land'). At her wish he keeps her with him dressed as a page. Because of his interest in the actress Philine, Wilhelm Meister joins a troupe of players who have been invited to a near-by castle.

Act II, scene i. A boudoir in the castle. Philine has managed to enslave Wilhelm Meister and laughs at Mignon and her blind devotion to him. When Wilhelm sees Mignon in one of Philine's costumes, he realizes that he must part from the beautiful girl and bids her farewell. 'Adieu, Mignon, courage' ('Farewell, Mignon, have courage').

Scene ii. The castle gardens. Mignon wants to drown herself in her despair, but Lothario prevents her. Applause for Philine can be heard from the castle, and in her blind jealousy Mignon wishes that the castle would go up in flames. She hurries out, and Lothario also slips away. The party from the castle enter and Philine, as the star of the evening—they have been performing *A Midsummer Night's Dream*—sings her great polonaise-aria 'Je suis Titania' ('Behold Titania, fair and gay'). Lothario tells Mignon that he has set fire to the castle. Mignon is asked to fetch the bouquet of flowers given to Philine by Wilhelm from the theatre and she hurries to fulfil his request. Shortly afterwards flames leap up from the castle and Wilhelm, rushing after Mignon, rescues the unconscious girl. In her hands Mignon is holding the half-burned bouquet.

Act III. A room in an Italian villa. The ailing Mignon has been brought here by Wilhelm Meister. Philine's voice is carried to him across the lake, singing the polonaise-aria coquettishly, but it makes no impression on him, for he now knows he loves Mignon. Lothario has accompanied Mignon. He recognizes the villa which he abandoned when he went in search of his daughter, and thus recovers his sanity and his memory. Mignon is also disturbed, for many things here remind her of her childhood. She recognizes some jewels, a prayer-book. There is no doubt— Lothario has found Mignon, his long-lost daughter.

Thomas's strong creative power shows itself in the two most important musical features in the opera, which also dominate the overture and emphasize the extreme antipathy between the characters of Mignon and Philine. The melancholy opening of Mignon's romanza finds its contrast in the passionate fervour

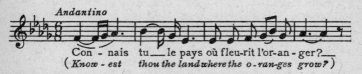

of the refrain 'C'est là, c'est là que je voudrais vivre, aimer, aimer, et mourir' ("Tis there, 'tis there the land where I long to live, to love, to love and die'). In contrast Philine's brilliant polonaise-aria is based on splendid effects, sparkling runs and coquettish coloratura. This aria forms the focal point of the

highly effective finale to the second act, which is the musical climax of the opera. Beside it the music associated with Mignon, Lothario and Wilhelm Meister seems very sentimental. Of Thomas's other operas, *Hamlet* is occasionally revived in the French provinces.

The most important French opera of this period is undoubtedly *Carmen*, by Georges Bizet (1838–75). It was a failure at its first performance; the savage passions in the story and the highly sensual music had a disagreeable effect on the audience. Only gradually was recognition give to the quality of this sensitive yet powerful music, and then, quite suddenly, *Carmen* became a world-wide success. In Germany Friedrich Nietzsche, who was extremely interested in music, gave this work his wholehearted support. After he had turned away from Wagner, he thought he recognized in *Carmen* a healthy antithesis to all the exaggerations of Wagner's music. Bizet did not live to enjoy his work's triumphant success, for he died three months after the first performance.

CARMEN. Opera in four acts by Georges Bizet. Text by Henri Meilhac and Ludovic Halévy. First performance: Paris, 1875.

Characters: Zuniga, a lieutenant—bass; Don José, a corporal—tenor; Morales, a sergeant—baritone; Escamillo, a toreador—baritone; Dancairo and Remendado, smugglers—tenor and baritone; Carmen, a gipsy—mezzo-soprano; Frasquita, a gipsy—soprano; Mercedes, a gipsy—mezzo-soprano; Micaela, a peasant girl—soprano. Soldiers, smugglers, townspeople.

Place: Spain. *Time:* nineteenth century.

Act I. A square in Seville, on the right the entrance to the tobacco factory, on the left the guardhouse. Micaela makes her way to the guardhouse, looking for Don José. The relief guard approaches to the music of their band, with them Lieutenant Zuniga and the corporal, Don José. They chat about the cigarette girls, mostly gipsies of loose reputation. During the midday break the factory girls pour out into the street, and Carmen comes last. She sings the *habañera* 'L'amour est un oiseau rebelle' ('Love is like a gipsy boy'). She scornfully rejects her many persistent admirers, and only José is favoured with her smile. Annoyed by his indifference she addresses him provocatively and throws him a flower. The girls return to work and the square empties; Micaela comes back to bring José greetings from his old mother. A turmoil is heard from the factory, where Carmen has been fighting another girl and has wounded her with a knife. On Zuniga's orders José arrests her. While Zuniga goes to the guardroom to fill in the warrant, Carmen provokes José as she sings the *seguidilla* 'Près des remparts de Seville' ('Nearby the ramparts of Seville'), saying she will meet him at Lillas Pastia's tavern if he lets her escape now. José loosens her bonds. When he starts to lead her away, she hits him, as they had previously agreed, and flees.

Act II. In Lillas Pastia's tavern. Carmen, Frasquita, Mercedes and other gipsy girls are drinking wine with some officers, including Zuniga. To the music of a wild gipsy dance Carmen sings 'Les tringles des sistres tintaient' ('Ah, when of gay guitars the sound'). She learns from Zuniga that José has been released from prison that day after serving a sentence for allowing her to escape. Escamillo, the toreador, arrives and is greeted with cheers. He sings the famous 'Couplets du Toréador' (toreador's song) with the refrain 'Toréador, en garde' ('Toreador, e'er watchful be'). Carmen receives his advances with reserve, for she is confidently expecting José's arrival that evening. When everyone else has left the inn, the smugglers Remendado and Dancairo try to persuade the three gipsy girls to engage the attention of the customs men at the frontier. Carmen refuses, but promises to bring José to join the band. José enters, heralded by the sound of his voice singing 'Halte là! Qui va là? Dragon d'Alcala! ('Halt there! Who goes there? Dragoon of Alcala'). Carmen is now alone with her lover, and sings and dances for him. The trumpet is heard sounding the retreat, but when José prepares to leave, Carmen is furious. She accuses him of not loving her; in reply he produces from his tunic the flower she had thrown him, now faded. 'La fleur que tu m'avais jetée' ends with the words 'Carmen, je t'aime' ('Carmen, I love you'). Carmen tries to persuade José to escape to a free life with her, but he is unmoved, and is about to take his leave. At that moment Zuniga returns, hoping to find Carmen alone. The two men draw their swords and begin to fight; the smugglers enter, and seize and bind Zuniga. José has no choice now but to join their band.

Act III. A wild place in the mountains. The smugglers descend and rest for a little while. Carmen, already tired of José's love, joins Frasquita and Mercedes who are passing the time laying out cards. However much Carmen shuffles the cards, they always spell death. The smugglers go off, leaving José on guard. Micaela appears looking for José. When José shoots at a man climbing down the gorge, Micaela hides behind a rock. Escamillo appears; the shot has gone through his hat and he is unhurt. He tells José casually that he has come on Carmen's account. José draws his knife, and Escamillo accepts the challenge. Carmen intervenes and throws herself between the two men. Escamillo quickly recovers his self-confidence, invites everybody to his next bull-fight in Seville and hurries away. Micaela is discovered. She begs José to follow her to his dying mother. José tells Carmen that he will soon return to her. In the distance Escamillo's voice is heard, singing of his sure success.

Act IV. A square in front of the arena in Seville. The procession of bandilleros and picadors passes through, and finally, to the sound of the toreador's march, Escamillo appears, with Carmen on his arm. Frasquita and Mercedes who have seen José, warn Carmen against him, but she has no fear and is ready to speak to him. The crowd enters the bull-ring, and Carmen is left alone. José, dishevelled, enters and implores her to return to him, but Carmen retorts that she no longer loves him. Enthusiastic applause for Escamillo is heard from the bull-ring. Carmen tries to run into the arena, but José stands in her way. Carmen, furious, throws at his feet the ring which he gave her as a token of their love. In desperation, José draws his knife and stabs her as she tries to escape into the arena entrance, then kneels beside her body. The crowds streaming out of the arena are horrified to see what has happened. José rises to his feet and confesses his crime: 'C'est moi qui l'ai tuée! ah Carmen! Ma Carmen adorée!' ('I killed the one I love. She is dead, Oh my Carmen, how I loved you!').

The extraordinary popularity won by *Carmen* all over the world is due to its well-balanced construction and its fascinating originality. The very first notes captivate the audience; the passionately animated, rather gaudy introductory music carries us at once into the world of the bull-ring; its mysterious and exciting aura is thrillingly caught. As the well-known toreador's song 'Toréador, en garde' sounds in the distance, the mysterious

fate motif leads into the first act, faintly underlined by two drum-beats.

Carmen stands at the centre of the music. Intoxicating sensuality is excitingly expressed in every passage, in the downward chromatic scale of her *habañera*, in the supple rhythm of the accompaniment, and in the opalescent fluctuation between the major and minor. By contrast, Micaela is characterized very sentimentally. As in the course of the drama she is always put in the shade by her full-blooded rival, so her rather sugary music pales beside Carmen's fiery rhythms and accents. José's slightly irresolute character is admirably captured in his music.

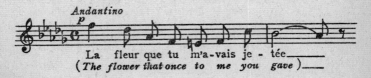

His flower-song is a wonderfully self-contained piece of music, delicate and yet powerful in emotion, with an intense melody and a thrilling natural crescendo. Especially impressive here is the restrained final phrase to the words 'Carmen, je t'aime', with strange, veiled chords in the upper woodwind. Bizet is to be admired for the way he often outlines a situation so fully with so few strokes, for instance in José's song 'Holle holla' with its hint of chromatic counterpoint, and the straightforward march tune with the cautiously mounting steps in the accompaniment, which splendidly convey the stealthy coming and going of the smugglers.

The various ensembles are superbly constructed, as for example the card trio, in which Carmen's sinister contributions stand out above the busy chatter of the two lively girls, but the most immediate impression is made by the Spanish folk tunes and rhythms scattered throughout the work, which really create the magic of the *Carmen* score. A masterly touch in this line is the interlude before the final act; a passionate melody, which finally flickers away into nothing, rises repeatedly above a fast and fiery dance rhythm.

Bizet's earlier opera *Les Pêcheurs de Perles* (*The Pearl-Fishers*) (1863) enjoys occasional revivals.

The most important work of Camille Saint-Saëns (1835–1921), *Samson et Dalila*, seems today typically French, but in its time was considered distinctly Wagnerian, and therefore some time elapsed before the Paris Opéra opened its doors to this glowing and original work. Since then *Samson et Dalila* has been a regular standby in French opera repertories, though its popularity seems to be waning elsewhere.

SAMSON ET DALILA (Samson and Delilah). Opera in three acts by Camille Saint-Saëns. Text by Ferdinand Lemaire. First performance: Weimar, 1877.

Characters: Dalila (Delilah)—mezzo-soprano; Samson—tenor; high priest of Dagon—baritone; Abimelech, Satrap of Gaza—bass; an aged Hebrew—bass; a war messenger of the Philistines—tenor. People of Israel, Philistine people, priests and maidens.

Place: Gaza, Palestine. *Time:* 1150 BC.

Act I. An open place in Gaza. The people of Israel are languishing under a foreign yoke, but Samson incites them to rise and fight. When the tyrant Abimelech dares to blaspheme against the God of Israel, Samson tears his sword from him, slays him, and drives the Philistines away. The high priest of Dagon swears terrible vengeance. Young Philistine maidens, among them Delilah, come out of the temple of Dagon to celebrate the spring. With flattering words Delilah turns to Samson, the hero of the day, and in her seductive aria 'Printemps qui commence' ('On mountain and meadow') challenges him to join her.

Act II. Delilah's house in the valley of Sorek. It is late evening. Delilah is waiting for Samson, who has recently shunned her. She knows he is in her power and is bound to return to her. She has not yet succeeded in extracting from him the secret of his supernatural strength. The high priest comes secretly to see Delilah, to strengthen her in her purpose, which is wholly consecrated to vengeance. Delilah promises to do everything in her power to win Samson's secret. At last he comes to her, and she goads his passion to such a point that he surrenders to her absolutely and tells her his secret. At a signal from Delilah, Philistine soldiers enter her house and overcome Samson.

Act III, scene i. A prison. Samson is in chains, his hair shorn, his eyes blinded. A chorus of captive Jews is heard behind the scenes. Samson prays for God's pity on his people.

Scene ii. A hall in the temple of Dagon. The Philistines are celebrating a joyful festival. The blind Samson is led in by a young boy, and is greeted derisively by Delilah and the high priest. With cold contempt Delilah tells Samson that she only pretended to love him so as to discover his secret. Samson suffers derision and mockery in silent prayer. Meanwhile he has made the boy lead him between the two marble columns on which the domed roof of the temple rests. He now embraces the columns and tries to shatter them. He beseeches God to restore to him his former strength, and indeed succeeds in bringing down the columns. The temple collapses on Samson and on his enemies amid the cries of the Philistines.

The frequent participation of the chorus gives the first and third acts an oratorio-like character. In the first act Samson's song of triumph rises in great strength and the chorus joins in

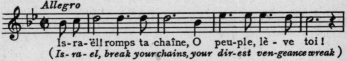

it with fervour, while the same theme crowns the powerful *crescendo* in the last act. The second act, on the other hand, unfolds a magnificent canvas of human passion. Delilah's fanaticism is most strongly depicted in the harsh line of the aria

'Amour, viens aider ma faiblesse' ('O love, lend me now dark enchantment') in which her hatred and her thirst for revenge and for power choke all other feelings. A passionate *crescendo* marks her duet with the high priest, a *scena* of shadowy grandeur. The climax comes in the love-scene; after the lyrical effusion of the famous love-song 'Mon coeur s'ouvre à ta voix' ('Now turns my heart to thee') with the languorous,

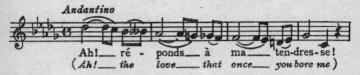

enticing refrain, the excitement increases, the dramatic accentuation intensifies and finally bursts into the breath-takingly forceful catastrophe.

Among the numerous operas by Jules Massenet (1842–1912) which are frequently performed in France, *Manon* has perhaps been most successful abroad. Massenet's operas are characterized by flowery melodies; good taste and technical skill counterbalance the tendency towards excessive sentimentality.

MANON. Opera in four acts by Jules Massenet. Text after Abbé Prévost's novel by Henri Meilhac and Philippe Gille. First performance: Paris, 1884.

Characters: Manon Lescaut—soprano; Poussette—soprano; Javotte—soprano; Rosette—contralto; the Chevalier des Grieux—tenor; the Comte des Grieux, his father—bass; Lescaut, a royal bodyguard, Manon's cousin—baritone; Guillot de Marfontaine, an old roué—bass; de Brétigny, a nobleman—baritone. Soldiers, various people.

Place: France. *Time:* Early in the eighteenth century.

Act I. The courtyard of an inn in Amiens. The wealthy old roué Guillot and the nobleman de Brétigny are eating with their women when the post-coach arrives, bringing among other strangers the sixteen-year-old Manon, who is to enter a convent-school, in spite of her vivacity and thirst for life. The men, charmed by her beauty, make her open advances, but Manon laughs at them. Her cousin Lescaut warns her to behave with prudence. The Chevalier des Grieux enters, and the young people fall in love with each other at first sight and decide to elope to Paris.

Act II. A room in des Grieux's house in Paris. Des Grieux is writing a letter to his father, asking him for his blessing on his marriage with Manon. Lescaut and Brétigny enter. Lescaut questions des Grieux about his intentions concerning Manon, but the letter to his father appeases him. Manon learns from de Brétigny that des Grieux is to be abducted by his father that day. She wants to warn her lover, but de Brétigny makes proposals to her which are altogether too attractive. She indulges her love for luxury and good living, tells her lover nothing, and allows him to fall victim to the plot.

Act III, scene i. The Cours de la Reine. Manon, who is acclaimed by everyone for her beauty, sings of her gay life. She then learns from the Comte des Grieux that his son is thinking of taking holy orders as a consequence of his deep disappointment.

Scene ii. An ante-chapel in the Seminary of St Sulpice. Manon has come to find des Grieux. She succeeds in making her lover decide to renounce the Church and to run away with her.

Act IV. The gambling room in the Hotel Transylvanie. Lescaut, Guillot, des Grieux and others are playing at the tables. Des Grieux wins continually until Guillot accuses him of cheating. The Comte des Grieux enters and allows Manon and his son to be arrested by the police whom Guillot has summoned.

Scene ii. The road to Le Havre. Des Grieux was freed immediately after his arrest, but Manon is to be deported. Des Grieux and Lescaut are waiting on the highroad for the convoy of condemned prisoners. Lescaut manages to bribe the sergeant in charge to let them take Manon, who is seriously ill. Des Grieux wants to escape with the unhappy girl, but Manon's will to live is now broken, and she ends her life in the arms of her beloved.

Other works by Massenet include *Werther* and *Thaïs*. *Thaïs* (1894) tells the story of a famous fourteenth-century Egyptian courtesan who tries to seduce the Cenobite monk, Athanaël, but who is instead converted to Christianity by him. *Werther* (1892), a setting by Blau, Millet and Hartmann of Goethe's *Die Leiden des Jungen Werther*, still enjoys success in France. In England and America, however, it has failed to establish itself in the repertory, and it is seldom performed in Germany. Yet it has some fine music, and dramatically it offers excellent opportunities to the interpreters of both Werther and Charlotte.

Claude Debussy (1862–1918) is the last independent representative of the romantic movement. His only opera, *Pelléas et Mélisande*, can be regarded as the end of the great tradition of French romantic opera. Its musical impressionism shows a parallel with impressionism in painting and poetry—the antithesis to naturalism; in the same way musical impressionism arose as a reaction against the too powerful pathos of Wagner. This impressionism also sacrifices subject-matter to atmosphere; ideas are more tangible than characters, and atmosphere is the decisive factor in shaping the music.

Obviously drama could have very little to do with such a purely lyrical field of expression. An impressionistic opera is in fact an absurdity, and Debussy's *Pelléas et Mélisande* is thus in every way an exception. The extraordinary stylistic affinity in feeling and creativity between Debussy and his librettist, Maeterlinck, made possible an absolutely unprecedented harmony between text and music, from which sprang a unique masterpiece that aroused immense admiration. Every scene is an experience in itself, but a work saturated in beauty and based on the interplay of colour, light and atmosphere, without dramatic trappings or tension, must all too easily pall.

PELLÉAS ET MÉLISANDE. Musical drama in five acts by Claude Debussy. Text by Maurice Maeterlinck. First performance: Paris, 1902.

Characters: Arkel, King of Allemonde—bass; Geneviève, mother of Golaud and Pelleas—contralto; Golaud and Peléas (King Arkel's grandsons)—baritone and tenor; Mélisande—soprano; little Yniold, Golaud's son by his first marriage—soprano; a doctor—baritone.

Place: Allemonde castle and its surroundings. *Time:* legendary.

Act I. In the depths of the forest Golaud meets Mélisande, sitting by a spring. She is young and beautiful and when questioned can only give a confused account of her origin. Golaud takes her to the castle and marries her.

Act II. In the castle gardens Mélisande plays with Pelléas, Golaud's much younger brother. While they are playing, the ring Golaud has given her falls into a spring. Golaud makes her continue the search for the ring far into the night, and Pelléas accompanies her in her fruitless task.

Act III. Mélisande is combing her long hair at the window of the castle tower as Pelléas passes by. In a moment of childish exuberance, Mélisande leans so far out of the window that Pelléas is covered by her tumbling tresses. Golaud arrives and sends his brother off, warning him to keep away from Mélisande, who is soon to become a mother.

Act IV. Pelléas tells Mélisande that at the wish of his father, who is ill, he must go away on a journey. Mélisande is unhappy. They decide to meet once more in secret, and as they say farewell they realize their mutual love. Golaud enters and murders his brother.

Act V. Golaud is suffering agonies of remorse at Mélisande's bedside. In the meantime Mélisande has borne him a little daughter, but there is nothing now to hold her to life, and without suffering she quietly dies.

Even where the too delicate verses have a dramatic impetus, as in the parting scene of Pelléas and Mélisande, when they suddenly notice that Golaud is watching them, the music is restrained and calm in its tone colour, until the final passage, where it breaks into a passionate outburst. The short example from this scene given below is characteristic of the style of the whole work. Above the faint shimmer of the orchestra, the voices move in pure speech cadences, which naturally often rise to climaxes but always in soft, restrained tones.

In connection with Debussy two other composers must be mentioned as final representatives of French romanticism, even if their work really spreads over into the twentieth century; these are Maurice Ravel, the second great master of Parisian impressionism, and the Spaniard Manuel de Falla, who as a pupil of Debussy is generally counted as belonging to the French school.

Maurice Ravel (1875–1937) wrote two operas, the charming comedy *L'Heure espagnole* and the setting of Colette's libretto *L'Enfant et les Sortilèges*. In complete contrast to Debussy, Ravel, especially in the former, writes real theatrical music, enchanting and unrestrained, to an impudently funny text, the stage effect of which is assured if the performance is aptly elegant and charming.

L'HEURE ESPAGNOLE (The Spanish Hour). Comic opera in one act by Maurice Ravel. Text by Franc-Nohain. First performance, Paris, 1911.
   Characters: Concepción, Torquemada's young wife—soprano; Gonzalve, a poet—tenor; Torquemada, a clockmaker—tenor; Ramiro, a muledriver—baritone; Don Inigo Gomez, a banker—bass.
   Place: Toledo. *Time:* nineteenth century.
   The action takes place in a clockmaker's shop. Ramiro enters the shop to have his watch repaired. Torquemada cannot attend to him at that moment, as he must go out to wind up the clocks at the town hall. Concepción, Torquemada's young wife, is waiting impatiently for this hour, which comes every week, and which she always uses for an amorous rendezvous. Before going to the town hall, Torquemada asks Ramiro to wait in the shop for his return. This is very awkward for Concepción, and to get rid of the inconvenient witness she asks him to carry the large grandfather clock from the shop to her room on the first floor. In the meantime her lover Gonzalve makes his appearance, but is so busy with witticisms that his passions do not become as inflamed as Concepción hoped. The fat banker, Don Inigo Gomez, who enters soon after, is also unable to satisfy Concepción's demands; she hides both her admirers inside the clocks, and Ramiro carries them patiently up and down the stairs. In the end Concepción has both clocks taken back into the shop with her lovers locked inside them, and hurries to her room with the sturdy Ramiro. Torquemada returns and finds the two admirers inside the clock-cases. They explain that they wanted to study the clocks more closely and are prepared to buy them. Concepción and Ramiro come back, and all the characters turn to the audience with a cheerful last word from Boccaccio.

Ravel writes in a light, springy and effervescent comic vein. The voices sustain a fluent *parlando*, with nicely differentiated characterization, Spanish dance tunes keep recurring, and the whole action is enveloped in the iridescent robe of Ravel's orchestral colours. The climax comes in the final quintet, an enchanting, sweeping *habañera*, in which elegant wit and bold irony remind us of the best period of the *opéra comique*.

We may also regard as a product of impressionism *La Vida breve* by Manuel de Falla (1876–1946), a work which is still undeservedly neglected. Its use of Spanish folk music and textual similarities make this opera an offshoot of Bizet's *Carmen*.

LA VIDA BREVE (A Short Life). Play in two acts by Manuel de Falla. Text by Carlos Fernández Shaw. First performance: Nice, 1913.

Characters: Salud—soprano; the grandmother—mezzo-soprano; Carmela—mezzo-soprano; Paco—tenor; Uncle Sarvaor—bass; Manuel—baritone; a singer—baritone.

Place: Granada. *Time:* beginning of the nineteenth century.

Act I. The courtyard of a gipsy house. Salud is waiting for Paco. She is frightened by gloomy presentiments, and her grandmother tries to reassure her. At last Paco arrives; Salud is beside herself with joy, and keeps on asking him to swear eternal love to her. Her uncle comes home and quietly tells the grandmother that Paco is betrothed to a rich girl of good family and is to marry her the following day.

Act II, scene i. A street in Granada, where the wedding between Paco and Carmela is being celebrated. Through the big open windows of a house, which look into the inner courtyard, one can see a splendid party in progress, to celebrate the marriage of Paco and Carmela. Salud enters and recognizes the bridegroom as Paco. Her grandmother and her uncle Sarvaor have followed her. Salud, torn by despair and beside herself with grief, rushes into the house.

Scene ii. The inner courtyard. Paco thinks he has heard Salud's voice through the open window and can scarcely conceal his agitation. Carmela watches him. Salud comes in with the old gipsy Sarvaor, goes over to Paco and implores him to kill her since he has abandoned her so shamefully. Paco tries to lie. This is too much for Salud; she staggers and falls dead to the ground.

This terse, impressive story is told amid a rich and lovingly developed setting. The description of the milieu takes up a great deal of the opera, starting with the gipsies' wearisome, arduous life. The end of the first act, when in the background the panorama of Granada lights up as evening draws in, is filled with distant voices, which slowly die away as darkness falls. The splendid party in the second act is a contrast to the atmosphere of this delicately descriptive scene. To a passionate guitar accompaniment a *bolero* is sung and the people join in wild dancing which becomes more and more frenzied with 'ahs' and 'olés' from the chorus, till the gay excitement turns into mad confusion and ends with a single cry. The scenes with Salud and her happy and tragic love detach themselves from the crowd scenes as strong, glowing vocal and dramatic climaxes. Both levels of the opera—drama and popular life—are enlivened with the vigour of Spanish folk music, the fascination of

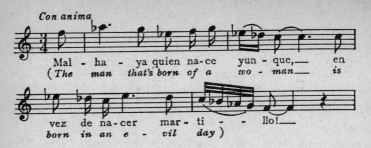

Con anima

Mal - ha - ya quien na - ce yun - que,— en
(*The man that's born of a wo - man— is*

vez de na - cer mar - ti - llo!—
born in an e - vil day)

which lies in its dance rhythms and perhaps even more in its
unique melismatism.

RICHARD WAGNER

The history of opera in the second half of the nineteenth
century is dominated by the outstanding personalities and
achievements of Wagner and Verdi, both of whom fulfil and
perfect the many and varied experiments and attempts made
since Gluck and Mozart. Verdi's work represents the crowning
of all the dreams and aspirations of the Neapolitans, of Mozart
and of Rossini, while Wagner's grandiose conception of musical
drama sets a temporary term to the development which led
from the Florentines to Gluck, to French grand opera and to
romantic opera.

No other composer has aroused such passionate controversy
in artistic circles as Richard Wagner (1813–83). He was a
controversial figure during his lifetime and he defended his
work and ideas in his polemical writings. To this day every
generation has debated afresh these problems, and the literature
about him has risen to gigantic proportions. In the conflict of
opinion the pendulum has swung widely, from the most
fervent enthusiasm and even idolization on the one hand, to the
strongest opposition on the other; but whichever way it
swings, nobody can ignore the fact of Wagner's immense
significance in the cultural and spiritual life of the nineteenth
century.

Wagner's aim was the creation of a 'Gesamtkunstwerk'—a complete work of art—in this case the musical drama, in which all the arts were to be combined in a noble unity. In his capacity as poet and composer Wagner had the task of proving the equal claims of text and music, and almost always both these main components of his works must have been simultaneously created. The conception of a 'Gesamtkunstwerk' of course also included the visual arts, and it was only in intensive co-ordination that Wagner could see the means of attaining his coveted artistic ideal. Such high intensity can only be demanded of a work which serves a noble, ethical idea, and so his music-drama had to be removed from the often profane sphere of opera to emulate the example of ancient drama. His clear realization that this extremely exacting ambition could not be fulfilled in the normal life of the theatre, led him inevitably to the idea of the festival.

The conception of a festival as a holy rite to which artistic disciples journey as to a place of pilgrimage and from which emanates a morally uplifting influence—a way of thinking which dominated Wagner's world—could only occur in Germany. Since the time of Goethe and Schiller enormous importance had been attributed to the theatre, so that the time was ripe for regarding the stage as a moral institution.

Wagner created a completely new world of opera, although this new creation was by no means a revolutionary action, for Wagner in fact continually acknowledged the claims of tradition, calmly remoulded the obsolete to suit his own purposes and so built up the colossal monument of his life's work with the assurance of a sleepwalker. An historical consideration of each of Wagner's works will best explain the elements which seem to us completely new; for instance, among the purely musical aspects, his continuous melodies, the *leitmotivs*, the symphonic construction of each act, and all the external characteristics of his originality of style.

His first attempt at music-drama was the rough draft for an opera, *Die Hochzeit* (*The Wedding*) (1832), of which he composed only the first number. His tutor Theodor Weinlig, the Cantor of the Thomasschule at Leipzig, approved of it, but his sister Rosalie found it shocking. Wagner refused to continue the composition and destroyed the text, which belonged to the genre of romantic horror-opera. A year later, at the age of twenty-one, while holding the position of choirmaster in Würzburg, he completed his first opera, *Die Feen*. The story is freely arranged from Gozzi's *La Donna Serpente*.

DIE FEEN (The Fairies). The fairy Ada loves a mortal, King Arindal. At their wedding Ada forbids her beloved to ask her or try to discover anything about her origin. Arindal breaks his pledge and loses Ada. Only after hard trials, which take him finally into the realm of the Underworld, does Arindal succeed in breaking the spell which binds Ada and winning her back.

The music of *Die Feen*, which is particularly reminiscent of Beethoven and Weber, hints at motifs which Wagner used again later. To the composer's great disappointment no theatre was interested in mounting this work and only after his death was it performed for the first time, in Munich in 1888.

During the two years Wagner spent as an opera conductor in Magdeburg where he soaked up the theatrical atmosphere, he composed his second opera *Das Liebesverbot* (*Love's denial*), writing the libretto himself from Shakespeare's *Measure for Measure*. His musical inspiration was drawn mostly from Donizetti and Auber, but also from Rossini and Bellini, while flashes of the later Wagner can be detected as well. (For instance, the grace motif from *Tannhäuser* appears at the beginning of the second scene.) In this work Wagner consciously follows the pattern of the successful operas of the time. *Das Liebesverbot* was first performed—badly under-rehearsed—in Magdeburg in 1836, and soon after the theatre went bankrupt. Wagner moved to Königsberg, where he married the actress Minna Planer, and then to Riga where he was again engaged as a theatre conductor, and worked on another new work, *Rienzi*, writing the text after Bulwer Lytton's novel of the same name. Unpleasant personal relationships at the Riga theatre made his stay there disagreeable, and he decided to go to Paris, to try his luck in the world centre of opera. During a stormy voyage from Pillau to London he drew up a plan for *Der fliegende Holländer*, and completed this and *Rienzi* during his difficult years in Paris (1839–42), where he had to arrange and write about music to keep himself from bankruptcy. In 1842 came the turning-point: the Dresden Court Opera had already accepted *Rienzi* in 1841, and the first performance proved a real triumph.

RIENZI, DER LETZTE DER TRIBUNEN (Rienzi, the Last of the
Tribunes). Tragic opera in five acts by Richard Wagner. First performance: Dresden, 1842.

Characters: Cola Rienzi, Roman Tribune and Papal Notary—tenor;
Irene, his sister—soprano; Steffano Colonna, head of the Colonna family
—bass; Adriano, his son—mezzo-soprano; Paolo Orsini, head of the
Orsini family—baritone; Raimondo, papal legate—bass; Baroncelli—
tenor; Cecco del Vecchio—bass; a messenger of peace—soprano.
Ambassadors, Roman nobles, citizens, legates, priests, soldiers and
populace.

Place: Rome. *Time:* middle of the fourteenth century.

Act I. A street in Rome. It is night and the henchmen of Paolo Orsini
are climbing into Rienzi's house to abduct his sister Irene by force.
Colonna arrives with retainers, and a fight ensues between the dependants
of the two hostile noble families. Adriano, Steffano Colonna's son, succeeds
in freeing Irene. The populace joins in the mêlée and the Papal Legate,
Raimondo, tries in vain to make peace. Only when Rienzi enters is order
restored. The people recognize him as their leader and the nobles are
forced to bow to his authority; unwillingly they retire to continue their
fight outside the city gates. Baroncelli and Cecco, representing the people,
urge Rienzi to move against the nobles and take their power himself. He
promises to act at dawn. Rienzi tells Adriano of his plan to make Rome a
free city and wins him over to his side, although Adriano recognizes the
great danger in this to his own family. Rienzi promises Irene his protection. Left alone, Irene and Adriano declare their mutual love. Dawn
breaks, heralded by a long trumpet call. The people enthusiastically
acclaim Rienzi, who appears in full armour and promises them security
against the depredations of the nobles and freedom from servility. As
their Tribune he will protect them all. The people swear loyalty to him.

Act II. A hall in the Capitol. Rienzi has beaten the nobles and freed
the territory of Rome. Even the Colonnas and Orsinis arrive with their
supporters to offer him their homage, which Rienzi accepts coldly. The
nobles therefore decide to kill him during the banquet that very day.
When Adriano finds he cannot dissuade his father from this treacherous
plot, he decides to warn Rienzi. The peace celebrations are in progress
when, towards the end of a symbolical pantomime glorifying Lucretia's
death and the expulsion of the Tarquins, Orsini creeps up to Rienzi to
stab him, but his poignard is turned by the mail jerkin which Rienzi
wears under his robe for protection. The conspirators are condemned to
death by the axe, the sentence to be carried out at once. Adriano and
Irene beseech Rienzi to pardon Colonna and the other condemned men.
While the solemn chanting of the monks can already be heard preparing
the conspirators for death, Rienzi yields to the prayers of the two lovers
and grants the traitors life and freedom. Nobody can understand his act of
mercy, but Rienzi convinces his followers of the magnanimity of this
step. Again they praise him as the hero of peace.

Act III. A square in the old Forum. The nobles have left Rome in
secret and have gathered an army with which they are now marching
against Rienzi. The people are roused to anger, saying that Rienzi's senseless

reprieve alone is responsible for this fresh misfortune. Rienzi however succeeds in inspiring the people once more with resolve for a new struggle. Adriano sees that his life will be forfeit, and implores Rienzi to renounce the fight. The call to arms is heard. Rienzi leads his army into battle on horseback. Adriano comes towards him, and offers himself as a hostage for peace, but Rienzi will no longer listen to him and the warriors march out accompanied by the priests. Only the women, among them Irene, and Adriano stay behind; they implore God to send victory, while Adriano vainly tries to tear himself away from Irene. The noise of battle gradually fades as the army of the nobles is defeated. In the procession of prisoners and wounded the corpse of Steffano Colonna is carried on to the stage. Adriano throws himself onto his father's body swearing revenge against Rienzi. Some of the people want to fall on Adriano, but Rienzi holds them back. Everyone acclaims him victor and liberator.

Act IV. The square with the Lateran church. Adriano has called Baroncelli, Cecco and their followers to a secret council to incite them to rise against Rienzi. When the latter enters to celebrate a solemn Te Deum in the church, the people call him to account for their brethren who were killed through his fault, and he has difficulty in pacifying them. When he is about to enter the church, the cardinal meets him: the church disowns him, and the Pope has excommunicated him. Everyone abandons him, except Irene who remains faithful to her brother.

Act V, scene i. A hall in the Capitol. Rienzi fervently implores God to help him—'Allmächt'ger Vater, blick herab' ('Almighty Father, strong to save'). Irene is ready to stand by her brother to the death, and not even Adriano can shake her resolve.

Scene ii. The square in front of the Capitol. The people are hurling firebrands into the palace. Rienzi and Irene stand on the balcony in each other's arms. When Adriano attempts to enter the burning Capitol, the tower collapses with the balcony on which Rienzi and Irene are standing and buries Adriano in the ruins.

The text of *Rienzi* clearly shows Wagner's adherence to the style and nature of grand opera. The historical subject with an extraneous love action, the division into five acts, the predilection for grandiose stage effects and crowd scenes, all these are characteristic of grand opera at that time. Wagner also follows contemporary musical examples, principally Spontini, with his rigid insistence on march rhythms and somewhat strident orchestration. This is obvious in the extremely effective overture, although Wagner inclines towards Weber in form and content by constructing it on the principal themes of the opera.

The slow introduction is dominated by the theme of Rienzi's prayer in Act V, a melody which hints at later Wagner in its

grand, sweeping line. After a passionate beginning the *allegro*
first introduces the prayer-theme in double time, and then passes
on to the powerful battle-song 'Santo spirito cavaliere' and

finally to the march of homage, which recurs at the climax of

the second act finale, while the wonderful battle-song, without
any doubt the most impressive passage in the *Rienzi* score,
dominates the finale of the third act, and also reappears, muted
and distorted, at the end of Act V when the Capitol collapses,
transforming Rienzi's theme of victory into tragic greatness.

Wagner's mastery in handling the gigantic apparatus required
for *Rienzi* was astonishing in a man of only twenty-five, particularly his skill with crowd scenes, as for instance in the great
finale of the third act. Warlike cries and march rhythms dominate the *Rienzi* score, and overshadow the lyrical episodes. The
entry of the messenger of peace at the beginning of the second
act and the impressive melody of his solo is charmingly idyllic.

Adriano's great *scena* 'Gerechter Gott, so ist's entschieden schon' ('Powers above! Alas, the die is cast!') is constructed in the style of the romantic 'recitative and aria', and with its most moving tragic theme represents a climax. There are also

In sei - ner Blü - te   bleicht___ mein Le - ben, da-
(*Nipped in the bud, my   life___   now fa - deth   and*

hin, da - hin ist all mein Rit - ter - tum,
gone and   gone is all   my knight-ly pride)

moments of strong emotion in Rienzi's various speeches, but one should not try to relate them to the composer's maturer works since there is no significant connection.

Rienzi, like *Das Liebesverbot*, can be considered as a pre-paratory stage in Wagner's development; as a tribute to, and a means of escape from the taste of his time. Had he continued to write in this style, he could have enjoyed triumph after triumph, but he deliberately left the easy path to success in pursuit of his ideal. *Der fliegende Holländer* is the first milestone on this road—the first work in which Wagner's true originality is clearly shown.

DER FLIEGENDE HOLLÄNDER (The Flying Dutchman). Romantic opera in three acts by Richard Wagner. First performance: Dresden, 1843.

Characters: Daland, a Norwegian sea-captain—bass; Senta, his daughter —soprano; Erik, a hunter—tenor; Mary, Senta's nurse—mezzo-soprano; Daland's steersman—tenor; the Dutchman—baritone. Members of the Norwegian and Dutch crews, girls.

Place: The Norwegian coast. *Time:* eighteenth century.

Act I. A rocky bay on the Norwegian coast. A sudden storm has over-taken Daland just as he is about to enter his home port, and he seeks shelter in the bay. Having cast anchor close to the shore where the storm has driven him, he comes on deck and bids the steersman keep the watch; Daland goes below, and the steersman soon falls asleep. As the storm rises again, a spectral ship with blood-red sails set on a black mast enters the bay and casts anchor—it is the Dutchman's ship. Pale, and dressed in black, the Dutchman comes ashore. Every seven years he is allowed on shore to seek his salvation, in the shape of a woman who will be faithful to him unto death, but until he has found her he must sail the seas without rest; he tells of this in the aria: 'Die Frist ist um' ('The term is past'). Daland is amazed at the sight of the spectral ship and hails its captain. The Dutchman asks Daland to give him hospitality, to which the latter readily agrees especially when the Dutchman shows him some of his treasure. He asks Daland whether he has a daughter and, hearing that he has, the Dutchman excitedly cries 'So ist sie mein!' ('She shall be mine!').

Act II. A room in Daland's house. On the wall over the door hangs a picture of the Flying Dutchman. Girls are spinning and singing, but Senta is sunk in dreamy contemplation of the picture. The girls tease her about her passion for the subject of the portrait, saying that her fiancé, the huntsman Erik, should be jealous of him, but they listen intently when Senta sings the ballad of the Dutchman with deep emotion and obvious sympathy. As she sings she becomes conscious of the task before her, and in great excitement she cries, 'Ich sei's, die dich durch ihre Treu' erlöse' ('It is I who will redeem you by my love'). Erik, who enters at that moment to announce Daland's arrival, hears her cry and while the others hurry out to welcome Daland he holds Senta back. He can no longer understand her or her strange behaviour, and as a warning tells her of a dream in which he has seen her and the pale seafarer embracing and fleeing together to the sea. Enraptured, Senta welcomes this as an omen and Erik, understanding that he has lost her, stumbles out. While Senta lingers dreamily before the picture, the door opens and there, framed in the aperture, stands the Dutchman, an exact replica of the painting. Senta falls in love with him at once, and in a passionate act of dedication vows to be faithful to him unto death.

Act III. Outside Daland's house. The Dutch and Norwegian ships are lying at anchor close to the land, but whereas the Norwegian ship is full of light and movement the Dutch vessel is dark and silent. Girls come out of the house with baskets of food and drink which they want to offer to the Dutchmen, but their calls remain unanswered. Suddenly a faint light is seen on the ship, and an eerie song is heard. Daland's sailors try to drown it with a cheerful chorus to dispel their own fear, but in vain. Terrified, they make the sign of the Cross and leave the deck amid mocking laughter from the other ship. Both vessels lie there as if deserted. Senta and Erik enter. He seems unable to understand that she is now be-trothed to the stranger, and begs her to think of her former love. The Dutchman, entering, overhears his words, and thinks he has been deceived and betrayed. Ignoring Senta's protestations, he gives orders for the immediate departure of his ship, then turning once more to Senta he tells her that he is leaving in order to save her from eternal damnation, the fate of all those who have been unfaithful to him. He hurries on board and at once the ship makes for the open sea. Senta tears herself desperately away from Erik and her father who try to hold her back, climbs a spur of rock and throws herself into the sea crying 'Hier sieh mich, treu dir bis zum Tod ('See, I am faithful to you unto death'); at the same moment the Dutchman's ship sinks. The Dutchman has won salvation and peace at last. Above the horizon the sky shines clear and calm.

Der fliegende Holländer is in every way the work of a genius. The libretto was written in ten days, and the music finished seven weeks later! This flow of happy creativity explains the work's easy coherence and the inspired spontaneity of its design and execution.

The nucleus of the score is the ballad, which Wagner composed first of all, and which contains the whole atmosphere of the opera—the tempest-tossed sea, the howling gale and the eerie cry of the Dutchman. This gloomy atmosphere is then

balanced by the simple and moving theme of salvation, and these two themes dominate the whole work. Even the overture, and in a way the development of the original ballad, is built

round these contrasting elements. The atmosphere of the stormy sea persists throughout the first act, emphasizing the Dutchman's aria as the important climax of the act—an aria conceived with the same grandeur as Senta's ballad, in which the wild demonic figure of the Dutchman is perfectly drawn in a few strokes. The whole construction of his monologue is wonderfully effective, with its final passionate outburst and the modulation to the major third, which is typical of the music of this

Ew - ige Ver - nich - tung, nimm___ mich auf!
(*End - less de - struc - tion on___ me fall*)

work. The echo from the chorus which ends the scene is sombre and eerie. The simple melody and emotion of the steersman's song ('Mit Gewitter und Sturm') brings a charming contrast to the dramatic entrance of the Dutchman. The 'Ho! He!' of the

Mit Ge - wit - ter und Sturm aus fer - nem Meer, mein
(*Through the thun-der and storm, from dis-tant seas, My*

Mä - del bin dir nah!
mai - den come I near)

sailors from the beginning dominates the finale and the intro-

Ho!____ He!____

duction to the second act, from which develops the gay, pleasant

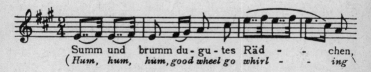

Summ und brumm du - gu - tes Räd - - chen,
(*Hum, hum, hum, good wheel go whirl - - ing*

spinning-song. The music of the duet between Senta and the
Dutchman is magnificent and glows with vitality, although in
some details it recalls older examples. Another splendid passage
is the Dutchman's wooing as it grows from shy reserve to a
proud ardour, while Senta's replies, which sound at first as
though she is in a trance, gradually change to a passionate
declaration of love.

The music of the sailors' chorus is strong, fresh and healthy,
and develops into a rough, merry dance. Wagner constructed
this scene with the masterly dramatic feeling which characterized
his later works. Ignoring all convention he presents us with a
mundane scene, which then undergoes an eerie, horrific trans-
formation. Erik's account of his dream anticipates the later
Wagner: the atmosphere is created with *tremolos* on the strings
and the call of the Dutchman in the bassoons and bass *pizzicato*,
while the narration is given the strongest dramatic tension;

otherwise Erik's character is very conventionally drawn. Daland is also rather out of place in his bourgeois simplicity; his home-spun aria, though it is actually very much in keeping with his character, seems foreign to this work—a kind of remnant of the Italian operatic convention.

The opera ends with the calm splendour of the redemption theme. The idea of redemption through love is the fundamental motif of all Wagner's subsequent operas. The poetic inter-pretation and presentation of sagas and myths, and their spiritual intensification, are both to be found in *Der fliegende Holländer* for the first time, and from then on became the most original characteristics of Wagner's operas. His versions are so com-pellingly powerful that one tends to forget the original story.

In *Tannhäuser* Wagner blended several overlapping legends in a bold synthesis. The Tannhäuser of the legend who lingered on the Venusberg, is identified by Wagner with the minnesinger Heinrich von Ofterdingen, who took part in the song contest on the Wartburg. The realm of Venus is transferred to the Hörselberg, near Eisenach, and to make the romance with Tannhäuser credible the Countess Elisabeth has become the niece of the Landgrave. Thence springs the contrast between Venus and Elisabeth, which represents for Tannhäuser the con-flict between sensual lust and spiritual love.

Tannhäuser was also first performed at Dresden, where Wagner had meanwhile been appointed court conductor. The audience which had acclaimed *Rienzi* but rejected *Der fliegende Holländer*, at first reacted to *Tannhäuser* with very limited appreciation.

The revision made for the Paris Opéra in 1860 has already been mentioned. This enlarged the first scene into a great ballet-pantomime, and necessitated the re-composition of the Venus scenes, which in their original form no longer pleased Wagner. The result is quite out of keeping with the mood of the original score. Nowadays the original Dresden score is generally pre-ferred for its unified and compact effect.

TANNHÄUSER UND DER SÄNGERKRIEG AUF DER WART-BURG (Tannhäuser and the song-contest on the Wartburg). Opera in three acts by Richard Wagner. First performance: Dresden, 1845.

Characters: Hermann, Landgrave of Thuringia—bass; Tannhäuser—tenor; Wolfram von Eschenbach—baritone; Walter von der Vogelweide

—tenor; Biterolf—baritone; Heinrich der Schreiber—tenor; Reinmar von Zweter—bass; Elisabeth, niece of the Landgrave—soprano; Venus—soprano; a young shepherd—soprano; four noble pages—sopranos and altos. Thuringian earls and nobles, pilgrims, sirens, nymphs, etc.

Place: Thuringia and the Wartburg. *Time:* beginning of the thirteenth century.

Act I, scene i. Inside the Venusberg. Tannhäuser is lying at the feet of Venus, while nymphs, naiads, sirens and satyrs dance among the grottoes. Satiated with pleasure and love, Tannhäuser remembers his former life on earth with longing and wishes to return there. When Venus tries to hold him back, he calls on the Blessed Virgin to protect him. The Venusberg collapses and Tannhäuser finds himself at the foot of the Wartburg. It is springtime, a young shepherd is singing, and the hymns of pilgrims walking through the valley are interspersed with the joyful sound of the shepherds' pipes. Tannhäuser is overcome and falls to his knees. Hunting-horns are heard and the Landgrave appears with a great hunting retinue. Astonished, the knights recognize Tannhäuser, who has long been absent, but who appears reluctant to join them. But Wolfram's magic words 'Bleib bei Elisabeth!' ('Stay for Elisabeth!') move him deeply. Wolfram tells him that during his absence Elisabeth's love for him has become quite apparent. Joyfully Tannhäuser cries 'Oh, führet mich zu ihr' ('Oh lead me unto her').

Act II. The hall in the Wartburg. Happy and excited, Elisabeth greets the hall in which she is at last to see Tannhäuser again 'Dich, teure Halle, grüss' ich wieder' ('Dear hall of song, I give thee greeting'). Without noticing that he avoids replying to her questions about his long absence, she tells him of her love, shyly at first, but gradually with mounting assurance. After Tannhäuser has left her, the Landgrave enters and guesses the reason for Elisabeth's confusion. He approves her love for Tannhäuser and tells her that the song-contest to be held that day should further her happiness.

A fanfare of trumpets sounds, and the local nobles with their wives arrive at the Wartburg for the contest. The Landgrave announces that the subject for the singing contest is to be the very essence of love; he also says that Elisabeth will give the winner as his prize whatever he is bold enough to demand. The contest begins. The medieval ideal of love as expressed by Wolfram and the other singers sharply contrasts with Tannhäuser's more outspoken ideas, which meet with general dis-approval. This lack of comprehension finally goads Tannhäuser into singing an enthusiastic hymn in praise of Venus. The women hurry out of the hall in horror, and the men furiously draw their swords. Elisabeth throws herself before Tannhäuser to shield him from the angry knights—'Zurück von ihm! Nicht Ihr seid seine Richter' ('Away from him! Not ye shall be his judges!'). In her desperation she even implores the Landgrave to pardon her beloved. Tannhäuser is filled with despair and remorse, and the Landgrave tells him that the only way to obtain forgiveness for his sins is to go to Rome with the pilgrims to seek salvation. The pilgrims' hymn can be heard in the distance, and crying 'Nach Rom' ('To Rome') Tannhäuser hurries out to join them.

Act III. Countryside as in the first act. It is now autumn, and evening
is approaching. The pilgrims are returning from their journey to Rome,
and Elisabeth looks in vain for Tannhäuser among them. She prays to
the Virgin to receive her soul. Wolfram, who has followed her unobserved, wants to accompany her, but she refuses his offer. Night has
now fallen, and Wolfram confesses his love for Elisabeth in his Song to
the Evening Star. Tannhäuser, his pilgrim's garb torn, stumbles in. When
Wolfram asks him whether he has been to Rome, he commands him
'Schweig mir von Rom' ('Speak not of Rome!'), but then goes on to tell
of his pilgrimage. He had reached Rome in penance and prayed for pardon for his sin, but the Pope had condemned him—'Wie dieser Stab in
meiner Hand nie mehr sich schmückt mit frischem Grün, kann aus der
Hölle heissem Brand Erlösung nimmer dir erblühn' ('As on this dead
staff in my hand, Never again a leaf shall grow, So from hell's all-consum-
ing brand Salvation canst thou never know!'). Now Tannhäuser is
looking for the way back to the Venusberg; out of a rosy mist the goddess
of love appears to the magic sounds of the Venusberg music. Tannhäuser
tries to go to her, but Wolfram holds him back once again reminding
him of Elisabeth. The spell is broken; Tannhäuser is left, confused; Venus
and her followers vanish. Dawn breaks, and from the Wartburg
approaches a funeral procession with the body of Elisabeth. With the
cry 'Heilige Elisabeth, bitte für mich!' ('Holy Saint Elisabeth, pray thou
for me') Tannhäuser falls dead across her bier. Dawn bathes the
scene in a rosy light, as the younger pilgrims return, carrying the Pope's
leafy staff as a token of the miraculous pardon: Tannhäuser has been
cleansed from his sin and is redeemed.

Two worlds stands face to face in *Tannhäuser*—the humility of
the Middle Ages and the urge for freedom of the Renaissance—
and both are illustrated and explained in the music. In the overture the simple folk song of the pilgrims' chorus is contrasted

with the glittering, iridescent series of melodies which depict
the happy sensuality of the magic world of the Venusberg.
These are the two basic symbols of the story of *Tannhäuser*
which recur continually throughout the opera in various forms,
and from them spring the great moments of dramatic tension.
The strongest effect in the first act lies in the abrupt change of
atmosphere when the Venusberg collapses. All the magic of
Venus's erotic, exciting music still echoes in one's ears while

the limpid spring air is already around one, and an idyllic landscape delicately unfolds to the sound of shepherds' pipes, their unaccompanied songs and the pilgrims' hymn, like a woodcut by Ludwig Richter.

The second act is completely dominated by the figure of Elisabeth, and the music is amazingly unified and highly impressive, from the jubilation of her first aria, through the shy reserve of her scene with Tannhäuser and the Landgrave, to her passionate outburst in the finale. On Elisabeth's wonderful theme is built the great ensemble in which her soprano rises

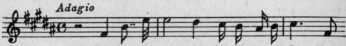

Ich fleh für ihn,   ich fle - he für sein Le - ben!
(*I plead for him,   oh spare him, I im-plore   you!*)

ever brighter and more radiant above the male voices and above Tannhäuser's pleas for mercy. Of the music in the song-contest Wolfram's second song 'Dir, hohe Liebe' and Biterolf's defiant

Dir, ho - he Lie-be, tö - ne be - gei-stert mein Ge-sang
(*Oh love most ho-ly, prai - ses flow forth to none but thee*)

challenge 'Heraus zum Kampfe mit uns Allen!' ('We call thee forth to mortal combat') are outstanding. The best known is Wolfram's opening recitative-like speech, 'Blick 'ich umher in diesem edlen Kreise' ('Gazing around on this august assembly'), which with its rather gentle melodic line is a particularly apt piece of musical characterization of Wolfram.

The *leitmotiv* technique already suggested in *Der fliegende Holländer* is used consciously in *Tannhäuser*, especially clearly and effectively in the prelude to the third act, which describes Tannhäuser's pilgrimage to Rome: Elisabeth's theme shines as a guiding star to the unhappy man, while the journey is accompanied by the pilgrims' hymns, with their tormented and

compelling motif which dominates this section. The climax
comes in the radiant outburst of the theme of pardon. But Tann-

häuser is not absolved, the motif fades away, and as consolation
Elisabeth's theme is heard once more in the delicate notes of the
woodwind. The same *leitmotiv* treatment also governs Tannhäuser's great narration of the pilgrimage to Rome, which is
clearly a forerunner of Wagner's later style, the fusion of
declamatory melodic song with a flowing symphonic orchestral
accompaniment.

Immediately after completing *Tannhäuser* Wagner turned to
new projects, and chose the story of *Lohengrin* from the mass
of operatic themes suggested to him. The text was ready by the
autumn of 1845. Once again he blended together two epic
cycles—the legend of the swan knight and the myth of the
Holy Grail. The introduction of the idea of the Grail into the
story of *Lohengrin* gives the work that mystic obscurity which
foreshadows his future achievements.

LOHENGRIN. Romantic opera in three acts by Richard Wagner. First
performance: Weimar, 1850.
  Characters: Heinrich der Vogler (Henry the Fowler), German King—
bass; Lohengrin—tenor; Elsa von Brabant—soprano; Duke Gottfried,
her brother—silent role; Friedrich von Telramund, Count of Brabant—
baritone; Ortrud, his wife—mezzo-soprano; the King's herald—bass.
Earls and nobles, pages, ladies, servants.
  Act I. On the banks of the river Scheldt. King Henry has come to
Antwerp to raise a Brabantian army to fight the Hungarians, but the
Brabantians are seething with discord; Friedrich von Telramund is
claiming the throne since he maintains that Elsa, the daughter of the late
Duke, has killed her brother in order to ascend the throne with her lover.
The King summons Elsa to appear before him, and she passionately
invokes the aid of a knight who has appeared to her in a dream as her
champion. Everyone is impressed and the King calls for a trial by combat,
but nobody dares to challenge Telramund. Twice the herald's summons

resounds and still no one comes forward. Elsa then falls on her knees in prayer and at once shouts are heard from the river-bank: a miracle has happened, for a boat drawn by a swan is seen approaching and in it stands a knight in shining armour. The boat draws in to the bank, the knight steps from it and with touching affection dismisses the swan, which floats away down the river with the boat. The knight then turns to the King, declaring that he is ready to fight for Elsa, of whose innocence he is utterly convinced. Elsa and the knight plight their troth to one another, and he makes of her only one demand—that she will never ask him his name or his origin. He urgently repeats this one request, which Elsa solemnly promises to observe. The King invokes God's judgment before the combat. Telramund is defeated, but the swan knight has mercy on him. The act closes with general rejoicing.

Act II. The castle of Antwerp. It is night, and Telramund and Ortrud are discovered in the shadow of the cathedral. Telramund, who has been banished by the King, accuses Ortrud of causing his misfortune; only under her influence had he slandered Elsa, and now he has lost his possessions, his lands and his honour, and must leave the country. Ortrud suggests that they represent the strange knight's deed as magic, in order to shake Elsa's belief in him and to induce her to ask him the fatal question. Elsa comes from her room onto the balcony and sings of her happiness. Ortrud plaintively calls her by name and by guile she finally persuades Elsa to take her into her own apartments. As Ortrud and Elsa disappear into the castle, Telramund cries 'So zieht das Unheil in dies Haus !' ('The pow'rs of darkness entered there').

In the castle courtyard the herald announces that the King has banished Telramund and given the Dukedom of Brabant to the mysterious knight. The wedding will be celebrated that day, and the Protector of Brabant requires the knights and nobles to set out with their army to Mainz on the following day. In solemn procession the ladies pass from the castle to the cathedral, and pause at the portal to give precedence to Elsa, but as she is about to enter the church, Ortrud blocks her way, claiming the right to enter first and raising doubts about the origin and nobility of the strange knight. Elsa still has the strength to reject these accusations, but when the King and her knight appear and Telramund charges the latter with sorcery, Elsa's mind is beset with serious doubts. The King, the knights and the people range themselves on the side of the Protector of Brabant, and finally Elsa also renews her vow of love. The wedding procession re-forms to enter the church, but from the highest step Elsa turns once more, and her eyes fall on Ortrud whose arm is raised threateningly against her.

Act III, scene i. The bridal chamber. Elsa and her knight are led by the King in solemn procession to the bridal chamber. Alone for the first time, they declare their love for one another, but Elsa is torn with doubt. Not only out of curiosity, but also to possess him completely and to be able to stand protectively by him, she tries to force his secret from him. Everything he says to calm her only increases her desire to know all, and she asks him the fatal question. At that moment Telramund rushes in with drawn sword, and the knight fells him with a single blow. Elsa sinks unconscious to the floor, and the knight, calling her women to look after her, goes to the King to justify himself.

Scene ii. The banks of the Scheldt. The knights and their retinues are gathering in the dawn to set out to war with the King. The King greets Elsa warmly, and is disturbed by her pale, distraught features. The knight enters. First he justifies his killing of Telramund, then accuses Elsa of having broken her pledge. He can remain there no longer, and may not even lead the Brabantians to war, but before he leaves them, he will reveal his secret: he was sent by the Grail, whose knights constantly seek to intervene where help is needed, but can only accomplish their good deeds so long as they remain unknown. His father is Parsifal, King of the Grail, and he himself is called Lohengrin. Elsa's despair is of no avail, for the swan has already come with the boat to fetch the knight. As he turns to the river-bank, Ortrud triumphantly announces that the swan is Duke Gottfried, Elsa's brother, bound by her in an irrevocable spell. Lohengrin falls to his knees and prays briefly. The white dove of the Grail swoops down over the boat, the swan sinks into the water and in its place Lohengrin draws the young Duke Gottfried from the river. The knight then enters the boat which is drawn away by the dove, and while the Brabantians acclaim their young Duke, Elsa falls to the ground, dead.

The music of *Lohengrin* is extremely unified, considering the very different spiritual spheres it portrays. Here for the first time Wagner perfects the consistent musical line already to a great extent attained in *Der fliegende Holländer* and in *Tannhäuser*. *Lohengrin* is therefore a transitional work, being the epitome of romantic opera and simultaneously the first step towards a new genre of art, the music-drama, which was to recall the musical mystery plays.

The prelude to *Lohengrin* is an expression of the mystery play in an already perfect form. The miraculous music descends as though from ethereal heights, intensifies in harmonies of increasing power, deepens, broadens, rises with the resonance of the full wind section and then fades away to the far distance in the flageolet sounds of the violins; this is the music of the mystery, further enriched with the expression of the power of love as symbolized by the Holy Grail.

The prelude is built on one theme, the Grail Motif, which in

its radiant, luminous harmonies is the hallmark of the unique and unmistakable *Lohengrin* music. It first appears in Elsa's account of her dream, and is followed by the brilliant, chivalrous Lohengrin Motif, which is closely related to it in atmo-

sphere. Both themes accompany the further development of the act, which from that point mounts in a steady crescendo. The chorus plays a very important dramatic and musical role in *Lohengrin*. On these two principal *leitmotivs* are based all the climaxes in this act: the famous swan chorus, the delicate double chorus at the approach of Lohengrin, his arrival and his farewell to the swan 'Nun sei bedankt, mein lieber Schwan!' ('I give thee thanks, my trusty swan!'), the *pianissimo* chorus which follows and the great chorus of jubilation which ends the act.

The third *leitmotiv* which is also introduced in the first act, is that of Warning, which Lohengrin urgently repeats, the second

Nie sollst du mich be - fra - gen
(*Ne - ver as thou dost love me*)

71 - 86

time a semitone higher. It recurs with particular significance in the second act, when Telramund agrees to Ortrud's diabolical plan of revenge, when Ortrud gives Elsa her deceitful warning, and when Elsa can no longer banish her own doubts. It is especially impressive in the awful grandeur of trumpets and trombones at the end of the act, when Ortrud makes her silent threat.

The dark world of Ortrud is expressed in two motifs of

creeping horror, which accompany both Telramund's and her

own entrance, but they are offset again and again by the luminous harmonies of the Grail and the Lohengrin Motifs. The
musical climax of the second act is the great scene between Elsa
and Ortrud, which starts with the delicate lyricism of Elsa's
song to the breezes, painfully and sharply interrupted by
Ortrud's accusing cry. The contrast between these two
characters is portrayed most tellingly in the music, which in
this scene skilfully blends the two opposite spiritual poles of
this opera into an intimate duet. One of the most famous musical scenes from the second act is the procession to the church,
a march-like passage taken from the realm of the Grail music.
By contrast the break of day in the castle courtyard seems very
conventional, and the sweeping introduction to the third act
and the famous bridal chorus do not appeal so much to modern
audiences. The music of the bridal chamber scene is by contrast
rich and splendid, and wonderfully constructed in a broad
melodic and psychological *crescendo*. The theme accompanying
Lohengrin's words 'Fühl ich zu dir so süss mein Herz entbren-
nen' ('When thou dost bend o'er me thy glance of splendour')
acquires the significance of a *leitmotiv* when it reappears in the

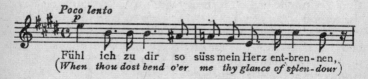

orchestra at the end as a sorrowful echo of the happiness which
has now collapsed in ruins. Lohengrin's Grail Narration forms
the climax of the final scene, and like the prelude is based
entirely on the Grail Motif. As this passage was composed before
the prelude, it is in a way the kernel of the *Lohengrin* music.
The harmonies only very gradually intensify around the theme,

and the recitative-like vocal line soars ethereally above the bewitchingly delicate orchestral accompaniment.

The political events of 1849 had forced Wagner to flee from Saxony, and as there was a warrant out against him, he escaped to Switzerland with forged papers and under an assumed name. In these circumstances Liszt's action in organizing the first performance of *Lohengrin* in Weimar in 1850 showed the true value of his friendship. If *Tannhäuser* had at first been greeted with considerable astonishment, *Lohengrin* aroused complete perplexity in the audience, while the small circle of its supporters were fired with proportionately greater enthusiasm and worked tirelessly to promote further performances elsewhere.

During his exile in Zurich Wagner first of all completed the text for *Der Ring des Nibelungen* and started work on the music for this gigantic undertaking in November 1853. When he had finished composing the first two acts of *Siegfried*, he temporarily broke off his work on the *Ring* and turned to a new sphere of thought. Two important experiences at this time influenced the composer's creative work: the philosophy of Schopenhauer, and his passionate yet self-denying love for Mathilde Wesendonck, the wife of his Zurich friend and patron. The first stirrings of this powerful emotion had released the consuming fire of the first act of *Die Walküre*; the ecstasy of fulfilled love which could face even death, as it appears in the story of *Tristan und Isolde*, represents the climax of this relationship which compelled his restraint. His final renunciation finds its poetic and musical expression in the Eva–Sachs relationship in *Die Meistersinger*.

TRISTAN UND ISOLDE (Tristan and Isolde). Opera in three acts by Richard Wagner. First performance: Munich, 1865.

Characters: Tristan—tenor; König Marke (King Mark)—bass; Isolde—soprano; Kurwenal—baritone; Melot—tenor; Brangäne—mezzo-soprano; a shepherd—tenor; a helmsman—baritone; a young sailor—tenor.

Place: Tristan's ship, Cornwall, Brittany. *Time:* The Middle Ages.

Act I. On board the ship which is bearing Tristan and Isolde to Cornwall. Isolde, who is being taken to Cornwall against her will to marry King Mark, is resolved to die; she tells her confidante Brangäne to call Tristan to speak to her, but Tristan answers this imperious summons through his trusted companion Kurwenal, who praises Tristan in a satirical song as 'Herr der Welt' ('Lord of the world'), whom no one can

command. Isolde hears this reprimand and tells Brangäne how she cured
Tristan of the wound inflicted on him in his victorious duel against her
betrothed Morold, without knowing at first the identity of the ailing
knight, who called himself Tantris. When she recognized him, she felt it
her duty to kill the sick and defenceless man, but could not bring herself
to do this when he looked her in the eyes. This same hero had then
ventured to woo her on behalf of his king, Mark. Only one thought, the
thought of vengeance and of death for Tristan and herself now possesses
her. Brangäne tries to calm her, and reminds her of the various potions
her mother had given her on her departure; but Isolde will not hear of
elixirs of love, only of the elixir of death, which she orders Brangäne to
prepare for her. Kurwenal enters the tent to announce their imminent
landing and the approach of Tristan. Isolde offers Tristan the potion of
expiation and Tristan, recognizing the elixir of death, drinks to Isolde.
She wrenches the cup from his hand and drains it herself. In the face of
certain death they confess their mutual love. This is Wagner's wonderful
new interpretation of the old saga: not a love-potion, but the thought of
death, makes them conscious of their love and breaks their silence. Overcome by emotion, the lovers fall into each other's arms. In fact it was an
elixir of love that Brangäne had offered her mistress; the lovers must live
once more, and can hardly grasp this fact. The ship has reached the shore,
and while the crew acclaim King Mark as he steps on board to greet his
bride, the curtain falls.

Act II. The garden in front of Isolde's apartment. It is a summer night;
horns can be heard in the distance as King Mark sets out hunting. Isolde
is impatiently awaiting her lover. Brangäne warns her mistress, particularly against Melot, who had persuaded the King to go hunting. Isolde
throws all caution to the winds, and extinguishes the torch burning by
the door as a signal to Tristan that he can come to her safely. Brangane
retires to the watch-tower while Isolde listens and looks for her lover.
When he enters, the lovers fall passionately into each other's arms. There
follows the famous love-duet 'O sink hernieder, Nacht der Liebe' ('O
sink upon us, night of love').

Brangäne's warning is heard from the tower. Tristan yearns for the
night of death, in which alone he can be for ever united with his Isolde.
Again Brangäne's warning voice is heard—'Habet acht! Schon weicht
dem Tag die Nacht' ('Have a care! Now night gives way to day!'). The
lovers pay no heed. Brangäne suddenly screams, as Kurwenal rushes in
crying 'Rette dich, Tristan' ('Save thyself, Tristan!'). The King, with
Melot and the huntsmen, enters, and sees what naturally appears to him
the most horrible treachery. Tristan cannot give any explanation; his
eyes are still focused only on death, and turning to Isolde, he asks her
whether she is prepared to follow him. She understands him only too
well; if he will show her the way, she will follow him. As Tristan kisses
her gently on the forehead, Melot draws his sword. Tristan throws himself
on his unfaithful friend, seeking death by his hand. Badly wounded he
collapses in Kurwenal's arms.

Act III. Tristan's castle of Kareol in Brittany. Kurwenal has brought the
wounded Tristan to his hereditary castle in Brittany and laid the un-

conscious man in the courtyard. Messengers have been sent to Isolde and Kurwenal is hourly awaiting her ship. The old shepherd has been told to sing a merry song when he sees the ship in the distance. Tristan recovers consciousness; Kurwenal joyfully tells him how he has brought him to the castle of his ancestors where his wound will heal, but Tristan does not believe in recovery and is filled only with longing for Isolde. Half dreaming, half awake, he relives all the phases of his passionate love. The shepherd's song is heard; the ship is in sight. Kurwenal hurries down to the shore to lead Isolde up to his master. In his feverish desire to reach his beloved, Tristan tears the bandage from his wound when he hears her distant call. Isolde hurries breathlessly in, and Tristan sinks slowly to the ground in her arms and dies. A second ship arrives, and King Mark, Melot and their retinue pour into the castle. Kurwenal in a rage kills Melot, but collapses, seriously wounded. Brangäne has told the King of the love-potion and Mark understands the circumstances. But nothing now can touch Isolde. Her love was the work of destiny and not the result of a magic potion. In a blissful aura of love, singing of the realms of eternal joy, she breathes her last.

In *Tristan und Isolde*, as in none of his other works, Wagner's ideal of the intermingling of music and text attained reality. This unity seems miraculous: what the words cannot express is indicated in the music. The wealth of musical expression is dominated by the chromatic scale which as it rises and falls contains the twin basic motifs of this work, longing and renunciation. These and the restless, colourful harmonies are the unmistakable characteristics of this passionate score. The *leitmotivs*, which only refer to spiritual events, are exceptionally moving and lucid.

The orchestral prelude portrays yearning and ecstasy. The principal motif in the score, the Motif of Longing, sounds like

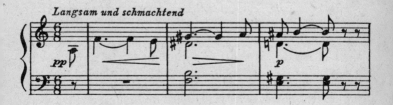

a question, to which a surging tune in the cellos gives the answer, pressing upwards to a climax throbbing with passion

and sinking back into gentle longing. These themes of longing are challenged by the stark grandeur of the Death Motif, thus

closing the circle of motifs which carries the enormous tension of the conflict between the two lovers in the first act. The overwhelming dramatic *crescendo* is attained by means of an orchestral accompaniment which conveys each spiritual emotion.

The themes of expectation and impatience dominate the introductory scene of the second act, crowned by a passionate motif, sometimes delicate and tender, sometimes urgent and

tempestuous. There is a magical effect in the transition from the sound of hunting horns to the murmur of the spring, as the sounds of the summer night are spun from the fading noises of the hunt. The construction of the great love-scene is very clear, as the lovers' duet is twice interrupted by Brangäne's song from the watch-tower, and so naturally falls into three parts. The wonderful harmonies of 'O sink hernieder, Nacht der Liebe' ('O sink upon us, night of love,') close the first part in which

Tristan summons up the night. The second section is devoted to the longing for death, and for the first time the theme of readiness for the Love-death (*Liebestod*) appears. In the third section

So stür-ben wir, um un - ge-trennt
(*So should we die, no more to part*)

the duet assumes the grandeur of a hymn and the delicate theme of the ecstasy of love is heard repeatedly in the orchestra and

then in the voices, while the lovers' oneness grows ever more compellingly, cleansed of all sensuality in its ultimate ecstasy.

The same themes later dominate Tristan's passionate and delirious monologue in the third act, and blaze up again in the glorious apotheosis of the work, Isolde's transfiguration. This closing passage, known as Isolde's Love-death, first repeats the theme of readiness for death, interwoven with the love-ecstasy figure, then mounts in a ceaseless, breathtaking *crescendo* to the theme of final rapture. Crying 'Unbewusst, höchste Lust'

('Unaware, highest bliss') Isolde expires in Brangäne's arms. The Motif of Longing from the prelude is heard, infinitely delicate, in the orchestra, like a question which must ever remain unanswered.

Wagner's banishment from Germany was rescinded in 1860, though Saxony only followed suit in 1862. He gave concerts as far afield as St Petersburg and Moscow, trying to obtain recognition for himself and for his works, but in spite of great

successes and the faithful help of his friends he did not manage
to attain any kind of financial stability for the future. He was,
in fact, in desperate straits at Stuttgart when, in 1864, Ludwig
II of Bavaria invited him to settle in Munich. The nineteen-
year-old King, who had just ascended the throne, placed at his
disposal all the necessary means for realizing his artistic plans.
The first great feat was the première of *Tristan und Isolde* with
Ludwig and Malvina Schnorr von Carolsfeld in the title roles.
The King was planning the foundation of a music academy, and
in particular the building of a Wagnerian Festival Theatre as a
worthy setting for the *Ring* tetralogy.

The young King's unbounded enthusiasm aroused among his
entourage a marked opposition to Wagner, which finally
resulted in the composer's leaving Munich for Switzerland,
where he could live and work untroubled by machinations and
intrigues. Since the King still supported him most generously,
he found that he could at last dedicate himself to his work without material worries. His wife Minna, from whom he had been
living apart for many years, was dead, and Wagner found his
ideal wife and companion in Cosima von Bülow, Liszt's
daughter. He spent the following years in Triebschen, near
Lucerne, where in 1867 he completed *Die Meistersinger von
Nürnberg*, which was first performed the following year in
Munich amid enthusiastic acclaim.

The subject of this opera is the bitter lot of the artist whose
vocation leads him boldly beyond everyday life and who has
to contend with the incomprehension and conservatism of his
contemporaries and colleagues; in fact the age-old struggle
between self-sufficient Philistinism and genius. The background
of this evocative and very dramatic plot is sixteenth-century
Nuremberg, with its flourishing middle-class, its love of art and
delight in song, as revealed in the poetic and musical life of the
mastersingers and of their foremost representative, Hans Sachs.

Wagner wrote the first draft at Marienbad in the summer of
1845, directly after completing *Tannhäuser*, intending to contrast the contest of the noble Minnesingers at the Wartburg
with a similar contest in the middle-class milieu of the Nuremberg mastersingers. A related basic theme therefore had to be
developed, but on lighter, non-tragic lines. When Wagner
finally put this plan into execution sixteen years later, his whole

conception had become richer, deeper, warmer and more mature, so that fresh humour took the place of cool irony, especially in Hans Sachs himself and his relations with Eva. Using artistic licence, Wagner transferred all the happy and sad experiences of his love for Mathilde Wesendonck into the principal characters of his drama. Just as he had shared with Mathilde all that was best and most personal of his spiritual riches and wealth of creative thought, so Hans Sachs is the great formative influence on the mind and heart of Eva, who feels bound to him in love and gratitude, yet cannot give herself to him. So this comedy also reflects as clearly in the rich, subtly evocative music as in the text itself, its author's grave struggles, which touched on bitter tragedy yet ended in personal triumph.

DIE MEISTERSINGER VON NÜRNBERG (The Mastersingers of Nuremberg). Opera in three acts by Richard Wagner. First performance: Munich, 1868.

Characters: Hans Sachs, cobbler—bass-baritone; Veit Pogner, gold-smith—bass; Kunz Vogelgesang, furrier—tenor; Konrad Nachtigal, tin-smith—bass; Sixtus Beckmesser, town-clerk—bass-baritone; Fritz Kothner, baker—bass; Balthasar Zorn, pewterer—tenor; Ulrich Eisslinger, grocer—tenor; Augustin Moser, tailor—tenor; Hermann Ortel, soap-boiler—bass; Hans Schwarz, stocking-weaver—bass; Hans Foltz, coppersmith—bass; Walther von Stolzing, a young Franconian knight—tenor; David, apprentice to Hans Sachs—tenor; Eva, Pogner's daughter—soprano; Magdalene, Eva's nurse—mezzo-soprano; night-watchman—bass.

Place: Nuremberg. *Time:* middle of the sixteenth century.

Act I. St Catherine's Church in Nuremberg. The congregation, gathered for the afternoon service on the eve of Midsummer Day, sings a chorale in praise of St John the Baptist. Eva and Magdalene are sitting in one of the back rows, and the mutual attraction of Eva and Walther von Stolzing, who is leaning against a pillar and has succeeded in attract-ing her attention, is clearly established. Stolzing had met and fallen in love with Eva the previous evening when he visited her father, the rich goldsmith Pogner. While the congregation is leaving the church, Walther approaches the two women and asks Eva whether she is already engaged to be married. Eva explains that Pogner has decided to give her in marriage only to the man who wins the prize at the singing contest on St John's day, adding that she is at liberty to decline him if she so wishes. Stolzing quickly makes up his mind to become a mastersinger in order to win his beloved. Apprentices, among them Hans Sachs's David, start preparing for the meeting of the mastersingers in their usual place in the antechapel. Magdalene promises David a treat from Pogner's kitchen if he will teach Stolzing the rules of the guild of mastersingers.

She tells Walther to remain, as Pogner is also expected, and Eva arranges to meet the Knight that evening. To his horror David realizes Stolzing's complete ignorance of the mastersingers' art, and the young knight's head is soon in a whirl as David tries to explain to him all the rules.

The mastersingers enter: first comes Pogner talking to the town-clerk Sixtus Beckmesser, who wants to compete for Eva's hand, and, angry that the final decision rests with Eva herself, asks Pogner to speak to her on his behalf. The last to come in is Nuremberg's famous poet, the shoe-maker Hans Sachs. Pogner's announcement of his decision to give his only child in marriage to the winner of the morrow's contest meets with general enthusiasm, but the stipulation that Eva must have the last word rouses resentment. Pogner explains that it must be a mastersinger chosen as winner by the masters, and that if Eva rejects him, she must remain unmarried. Hans Sachs's suggestion that the people should also be invited to judge the contest is indignantly rejected. Pogner announces that the knight Walther von Stolzing has asked to be admitted to the guild, an unprecedented event. When asked under whom he has studied, the knight names Walther von der Vogelweide as his teacher, and in the words 'Am stillen Herd in Winterszeit' ('In snowbound hall by fireside') describes how he learned to sing. Walther must now demonstrate with a 'master song' that he is worthy of admission to the guild. It is Beck-messer's duty as marker to note each fault; if more than seven are recorded, the singer is rejected. Walther takes his place in the singing chair, and taking up Beckmesser's customary invitation 'Fanget an' ('Now begin') develops from it his 'master song' on Spring, whose call finds thousands of echoes in the woods. Walther's verses are too new and too strange for the masters and only Sachs recognizes his genius. Beckmesser chalks up the mistakes, until his slate is completely covered with strokes; he inter-rupts Walther, saying his song is rejected, and the other masters agree with him, but Sachs insists that Walther finish, even through the general tumult. Everyone disperses in high excitement but Hans Sachs is deep in thought.

Act II. A street with the houses of Pogner and Sachs. It is evening, and the apprentices are closing the workshops. Pogner and Eva return from their evening walk. Eva, who has not dared to ask her father how Walther fared at the Singing Trial, hears the bad news from Magdalene. Meanwhile dusk has fallen; Sachs makes David move his work-bench and stool to the open window, but cannot settle to his work. Walther's song still rings in his ears. Eva approaches softly and wakes him out of his day-dreaming, but she cannot bring herself to ask him openly about Walther's failure. Sachs understands her feelings but cannot console her. Eva, deeply hurt by what she takes for lack of sympathy, leaves him. Magdalene tells her that Beckmesser is coming to serenade her that night and they decide that Magdalene should put on one of Eva's dresses and listen to Beck-messer's serenade from the window, while Eva goes to meet her knight. When Walther enters Eva throws herself into his arms and is ready to elope with him, but Sachs is watching them and is determined to prevent their flight. He brings his bench out into the street so that Eva and Walther cannot get past and are forced to retreat into the gardens and sit on a bench there. Beckmesser enters to sing his serenade, but when he starts to play a prelude on his lute, Sachs interrupts him with a coarse shoemaker's song. Beckmesser is beside himself at this disturbance, but Sachs will not stop. In the end Beckmesser persuades Sachs to listen to his serenade, but not until he has agreed to Sachs's condition that he will mark Beckmesser's faults by taps on the shoe on which he is working. Beckmesser's plaintive song and Sachs's noises have woken the neighbours. David recognizes the figure at the window as Magdalene, whom he is wooing, and furiously throws himself on his supposed rival to thrash him. The neighbours come into the street and the apprentices rush in. Walther and Eva try to take advantage of the tumult to escape, but Sachs separates the lovers and forcibly drags Walther into his house, while Eva runs frightened into hers. The horn of the night-watchman is heard near by, and the crowd disperses. Beckmesser with broken lute and bruised back limps wearily away from the scene of his discomfiture. The moon sails out from behind the clouds. In a slightly trembling voice the night-watchman calls eleven o'clock. His horn dies away in the distance.

Act III, scene i. Sachs's workshop. David asks Sachs's pardon for his behaviour of the night before and sings his offering for St John's Day 'Am Jordan Sankt Johannes stand' ('St John baptized in Jordan's tide'). Sachs is left alone with his thoughts, and sings 'Wahn, Wahn, überall Wahn' ('Craze, craze, everywhere craze'). Walther enters and cheerfully greets Sachs, who with tactful humour explains to him the rules and formal laws of the masters' guild. Walther now recites his prize song, which relates the dream he has just had, and Sachs writes down the words as he sings them; one verse remains to be written. The sheet of paper with the song in Sachs's handwriting falls into the hands of Beckmesser, who thinks he has discovered in Sachs a dangerous rival, but Sachs calms him and finally gives him the poem, promising that he will never tell anybody that he wrote it. Beckmesser hurries out, overjoyed. Eva enters in festive dress, on the pretext that her shoe hurts her, and her confusion only disappears when Walther comes into the room and in his surprise and joy at seeing his beloved improvizes the third verse of his song. 'Lausch, Kind ! Das ist ein Meisterlied' ('Hark, child! That is a master-song') says Sachs. Eva, grateful and happy, rests her head on his breast, and confesses that he alone would have been her choice had she not been so suddenly engulfed by her passion for Walther. Sachs replies that he knows the story of Tristram and Isolde only too well, and he has no wish to share King Mark's lot. The new master-song must have a title, and be baptized in song. David and Magdalene are summoned and join in the quintet 'Selig, wie die Sonne' ('Radiant as the dawn').

Scene ii. The Festival Meadow outside the gates of Nuremberg. The guilds march in, the apprentices dance with the girls and the townsfolk assemble. Finally the mastersingers enter in solemn procession, and Sachs is enthusiastically greeted by the people in a chorale 'Wach 'auf! es nahet gen den Tag' ('Awake! The dawn of day draws near'), the words of which are by the real Hans Sachs. Sachs is moved by this demonstration and gives thanks for the 'undeserved honour'. Beckmesser is the first competitor to be called. He is not altogether happy with the verses, which

he does not quite understand. In his excitement he loses the thread and
his pathetic stuttering and lamentable singing make him utterly ridiculous.
Beside himself with rage, he declares that Sachs is the author of his poem,
and Sachs calls to his defence the true poet of the grossly distorted song.
Walther wins unanimous approval from populace and mastersingers
alike, and Eva delightedly adorns her beloved with the victor's crown.
Pogner wants to give Walther the golden chain of the guild, in recogni-
tion of his masterly skill. The knight instinctively recoils and refuses this
honour. This causes offence, but in a splendid speech Sachs draws
Walther's attention to the importance of the masters and of German art,
'Verachtet mir die Meister nicht!' ('Disdain our masters not, my friend').
Everyone enthusiastically echoes his sentiments. Eva takes the crown from
Walther's head and places it on Sachs's while the latter hangs the masters'
chain around Walther's neck. The curtain falls amid acclamation for
Sachs.

Although the text of *Die Meistersinger* brilliantly depicts its
milieu, and most subtly characterizes the many roles, only the
music can truly fulfil the implications of Wagner's libretto.

The festive splendour and lucid construction of the prelude
make it a masterpiece in itself, and it also introduces the main
themes and ideas of the opera. The Mastersingers' Motif is

heard in a broad, weighty crescendo; into this strict circle
steps Walther with freely flowing recitative and expressive
courtship and these two contrasting themes give the essential

outline of the *Meistersinger* score. A second group of themes
contains the Spring Motif, which is first heard in Walther's
Spring song 'Fanget an' and in slightly varied form accompanies

Sachs's 'Flieder' monologue beneath the elder tree—'lenzes Gebot, die süsse Not' ('Spring's wond'rous strain its sweetest pain'). Three other, independent motifs are Beckmesser's theme,

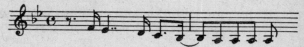

David's gay festive St John's Day Motif which emphasizes

Pogner's address and is also often used later, for instance in the 'Wahn' monologue, and the melancholy 'Wahn' Motif itself, which dominates the serious prelude to the third act. Eva is

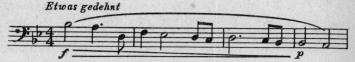

characterized by a whole series of themes of particular grace and warmth, which accord with her every mood.

Recitative-style monologue is perfected in *Die Meistersinger*. The great vocal scenes, like Sachs's 'Flieder' monologue or his closing speech, and Pogner's narration, are model examples of a specifically Wagnerian type of singing in their melodic style and polyphonic orchestral accompaniment. Then there are the important, more formal vocal numbers, such as Walther's songs 'Am stillen Herd', 'Fanget an' and the Prize Song. Slighter, but richly melodic examples of this style are Sachs's Cobbling Song, David's St John's Day Song, the tailors' chorus and the 'Wach auf' chorus.

This score is easily understood and appreciated, and its extraordinary, world-wide popularity stems essentially from the zest for life which fills every note, even the powerfully quiet resignation of Sachs himself.

The gigantic tetralogy of *Der Ring des Nibelungen*, the central work in Wagner's life, was at this time approaching completion. The necessary setting for the execution of this mighty creation had to be provided by building a Festival Theatre. Munich was virtually out of the question once the King had had to renounce his plans in view of the opposition to Wagner, so the composer decided to realize his greatest aspiration for himself, and for this purpose chose Bayreuth, a former small administrative centre, where he met with willing co-operation. He spread his ideas by the written and spoken word, and gave concerts to raise the funds for his Festival. The first stone was laid on the 22nd May 1872, his fifty-ninth birthday, and four years later the first Festival performances were given—the first complete cycle of the *Ring*. This was a tremendous occasion in which the whole cultural world took part; after twenty-five years of hoping and dreaming, Wagner had realized his bold ideal.

The first draft of the *Ring* libretto, *Siegfrieds Tod (Siegfried's Death)* was written in 1848, and its plot essentially corresponded to the later *Götterdämmerung*. It was clear from the beginning that Wagner's representation and interpretation of this saga was based more on the Nordic traditional epic, the *Edda*, than on the *Nibelungenlied*. When Wagner later returned to this first draft, he turned the story of Siegfried's youth into an introduction to the events of *Siegfrieds Tod*. The awakening of Brünnhilde in the final act called for a separate drama about Brünnhilde herself, and finally a detailed introduction was needed to establish the mythical foundations for understanding the tragedy of Siegfried and Brünnhilde. So originated the four-part composition, with *Das Rheingold* as the prelude in heaven, the two heroic tragedies *Die Walküre* and *Götterdämmerung*, and between them the lively idyll of *Siegfried*. The expansion of the Siegfried tragedy by the addition of the preliminary story led to the whole work revolving around the character of Wotan. It is not Siegfried the radiant young hero who stands at the centre of the tetralogy, but the god who conjures up his own end, and is ready to give way to 'dem ewig Jungen in Wonne'—eternal youth and wonder. To Wagner the greatness of his hero lies in the final supremacy of will over power in the Schopenhauer sense.

The language of the *Ring* is of rare charm, attributable to the conscious use of alliteration as found in the *Edda*. The alliteration in the *Ring* has been much derided, but characteristic phrases, such as 'Weibes Wonne und Wert', are uncontrovertably effective.

The use of *leitmotiv* was developed into a special system in the music of the *Ring*. Those *leitmotivs* which spring from individual thoughts and events accompany the plot appropriately, and emphasize it by evoking a complexity of associations. They explain and underline the stage action while also indicating unspoken spiritual developments, and their continuous symphonic flow, like the themes in a symphony, gives the work its musical unity. In spite of the tremendous range of emotions and concepts they have to express, the *leitmotivs* in all Wagner's later works are so closely bound together that it seems almost impossible to transplant themes from one work to another. The motifs of the *Ring* are of elemental power, and with symbolic naturalism they express in music primeval urges and forces. The gigantic structure of each act grows from the germ of the motifs in a mounting symphonic surge, as has been most convincingly demonstrated by the Wagnerian scholar Alfred Lorenz (1868–1939), an Austrian writer on music, who edited Wagner's literary works and Weber's early operas.

The natural forces of earth, air, fire and water are personified by Wagner as elemental symbols, and given human actions and feelings to free them from pallid allegory and make them more comprehensible. The natural innocence of the Rhinemaidens symbolizes the water and in contrast Loge, the god of fire, embodies the principle of evil. The fateful primary power of the earth to which all are bound is embodied in the mysterious figure of Erda, and lesser earthbound forces in the legend are the Nibelungs. The foremost representative of this lower stratum of the world is Alberich, who becomes the antithesis of Wotan, the most powerful of the gods who are striving for Valhalla, the fortress of air and light. The fundamental concept of the text, the conflict between power and love, is at first expressed in the struggle of will between these two opponents; Alberich renounces love, which is anyhow denied him, in favour of wealth and power; Wotan, possessing the supreme fullness of life, strives for power, without being able to renounce love or pleasure. The ring, the highest symbol of power, forged from the gold stolen from the Rhinemaidens, is cursed by Alberich. Anyone who comes in contact with it will be destroyed by the curse, and only by restoring the ring to the Rhinemaidens can the curse be lifted. Only the realization that love is infinitely more important than any power leads to the renunciation of power and to the voluntary return of the ring to the primeval element of water.

Every section of the orchestra has to be reinforced to sustain the more important role given to it in the *Ring*. The woodwind instruments are increased in number, tubas join the brass and have a noticeable effect on the character of the orchestral sound. Such a large wind ensemble naturally calls for a greater number of strings, but so that this powerful body of sound should not hamper the singers too much there arose the idea of covering the orchestra, which was done at Bayreuth.

DER RING DES NIBELUNGEN (The Ring of the Nibelung). A stage-festival-play for three days and a preliminary evening; words and music by Richard Wagner. First complete performance: Bayreuth, 13–17 August, 1876.

DAS RHEINGOLD (The Rhinegold). Prologue in one act to the festival drama *Der Ring des Nibelungen* by Richard Wagner. First performance: Munich, 1869.

Characters: Wotan—baritone; Donner—bass; Froh—tenor; Loge—tenor; Fricka—mezzo-soprano; Freia—soprano; Erda—contralto; Alberich—bass-bar.; Mime—tenor; Fasolt—bass; Fafner—bass; Woglinde and Wellgunde—sopranos; Flosshilde—contralto.

Time: legendary.

Scene i. At the bottom of the river Rhine. Steep rocks rise from the depths. The ceaselessly flowing water becomes lighter towards the surface, while the river-bed is wrapped in impenetrable gloom. The Rhinemaidens swim round the rocks singing and playing. Alberich comes out of a cleft in the rocks and makes advances to the Rhinemaidens. Suddenly the gleam of the Rheingold is seen on the rocks above. Alberich learns of the significance of the gold; he who will renounce love for ever and succeeds in fashioning a ring out of the Rheingold will become ruler of the world. Intoxicated with dreams of power and wealth, Alberich renounces love and, taking the gold from the rock, disappears with it into the depths. Lamenting, the Rhinemaidens try to stop him, but night has suddenly fallen and the waters slowly subside.

Scene ii. An open space on a mountain summit. Far up in the clouds can be seen Valhalla, the castle of the gods; Fricka and Wotan lie on the slope beneath. Fricka awakens and rouses her husband; they drink in this view of the fortress, built for them by the giants Fafner and Fasolt, but Fricka reminds Wotan that the goddess of eternal youth, Freia, had been promised to the giants in payment for their work. Without Freia the gods would tire and age, and she must not therefore be relinquished.

The cunning Loge must be asked for advice, for Wotan trusts and relies on him. Freia and the giants, Fafner and Fasolt, enter. Donner and Froh, Freia's brothers, hurry in to protect their sister, but the giants rightly invoke their contract. At last Loge joins them, and tells of many things, including how Alberich has stolen the Rheingold and made a ring, which gives him supreme power. The giants are greedy for the gold and would willingly exchange Freia for it. Wotan is also filled with desire to possess the ring. To obtain the gold as ransom for Freia, Wotan and Loge journey to Nibelheim.

Scene iii. Nibelheim. A subterranean cavern. Alberich has compelled his brother, the skilled smith Mime, to forge him the Tarnhelm, a magic helmet which enables its wearer to assume any form at will. Wotan and Loge enter Nibelheim, and Alberich gloats over his magic helmet. To demonstrate its powers he turns himself into a gigantic serpent, and then, on Loge's cunning suggestion, into a toad. In this shape the two gods easily capture him, bind him and drag him away.

Scene iv. An open space as in scene ii. Alberich is forced to give up the golden treasure he has had cunningly moulded from the Rheingold, so as to regain his freedom, but he is utterly ruined when Wotan wrenches the ring from him as well. Beside himself with rage Alberich curses the ring; he who possesses it will die. The giants enter with Freia, and plant two stakes in the ground on either side of her to measure the gold they demand as her ransom. The whole Nibelung hoard is piled between the stakes, and Wotan is compelled to surrender the Tarnhelm. Finally the giants also demand the ring. Although Wotan perceives that the ring will only bring him misfortune, he does not want to part with it. The mother of mankind, Erda, appears and warns the gods of impending disaster. Wotan can see no way of escape, and with sudden resolve throws the ring on to the pile. Freia is free again. In the struggle for the ring Fafner kills his brother Fasolt, and the gods in horror recognize the working of the curse. Heavy clouds conceal Valhalla, and Donner conjures up a storm. After it has passed, Valhalla lies gleaming in the evening sun before the delighted eyes of the gods, with a rainbow bridge spanning the intervening space. As the gods ascend to Valhalla, the lament of the Rhinemaidens for their lost gold is heard from the depths.

Like a true 'prelude' or 'overture', *Das Rheingold* lays the dramatic and musical foundations for the tragedy to be unfolded in the three principal works of the festival drama. The basic myth and its nature symbols are contained in this work, and also the most important *leitmotivs*, on which are built the music of the whole cycle.

The orchestral introduction to the first scene consists solely of gliding music on the chord of E-flat major. The *pianissimo* deep E-flat in the basses leads to a hollow fifth, horns and bassoons join in, and as the music gradually develops and grows the flowing sea of sound assumes an ever clearer shape: the Motif

of Nature. The violins, and finally the woodwind, enter and the
sound grows in a steady stream to its climax as the curtain rises
and the Rhine is heard flowing, murmuring along its way.

The most important *leitmotiv* introduced in the first scene is
the Ring Motif, a strangely impressive chain of thirds of extra-

ordinarily expressive power. At the beginning of the second
scene comes the theme of Valhalla in the solemn tones of the

lower brass, and this is also Wotan's *leitmotiv*. The Spear and
Treaty Motif with its powerful, measured steps is also mostly

connected with Wotan. The restless licking of the flames in the

Loge Motif, the powerful, rugged Giants' Motif and the
Forging Motif with its marked rhythm, all these are drawn

from elemental nature. The mysterious harmonies of the Tarn-helm Motif accompany Alberich's transformations in the third

scene, while the downward sliding theme of the eclipse of the

gods, an inversion of the Motif of Nature from the first scene, emphasizes Erda's gloomy prophecies in the final scene. Essential to this last scene is also the Curse Motif, first introduced by Alberich, and repeated several times, culminating with its

Wie durch Fluch er mir ge - riet,   ver-flucht sei die-ser Ring
(As by curse came it to   me,_   ac-cursed now be this Ring)

appearance after Fafner has slain his brother. The mighty climax in the final scene is reached with the recurrence of the Valhalla theme in the orchestra, while the castle of the gods stands resplendent in the sky and Wotan, deeply moved by this wonderful spectacle, greets his Valhalla. The Sword Motif,

announcing the hero on whom the gods are to depend for their salvation, is now first heard in the orchestra.

The themes mentioned here recur through every part of the tetralogy, while new motifs also appear and are blended with them. Growth and decay, fire and water, power and love: round these fundamental symbols revolves the world of the *Ring*, and to them the whole range of musical expression is bound through the *leitmotivs*.

DIE WALKÜRE (The Valkyrie). First day of the festival drama, *Der Ring des Nibelungen* by Richard Wagner. First performance: Munich, 1870.

Characters: Wotan—baritone; Hunding—bass; Siegmund—tenor; Fricka—mezzo-soprano; Sieglinde—soprano; Brünnhilde—soprano; the eight Valkyries—sopranos and contraltos.

The living-room in Hunding's hut. In the middle stands a huge ash-tree. Siegmund, completely exhausted, stumbles in and sinks to the ground. Sieglinde, Hunding's wife, gives him a drink. He is being pursued, and wants to leave again at once so as not to cause her any misfortune, but Sieglinde begs him to stay, saying that he cannot bring misfortune to the very home of misfortune. Hunding returns, and abruptly questions Siegmund about himself. Siegmund tells his name and also something of his former life with his father. When once as a boy he came home with his father, he found his mother killed and his twin sister kidnapped. Later he also lost his father, whom in his story he calls Wolfe. (Siegmund has no idea that Wotan is his father; he knew him as Wälse, and therefore calls himself Wälsung.) Siegmund further recounts how he recently tried to defend a woman, but finally had to yield to superior force, being unarmed. Hunding jumps up, he also was called to the fight, and on his return finds the enemy in his own house. For tonight Siegmund is protected by the law of hospitality, but on the following day they must fight a duel. He orders Sieglinde to prepare his evening drink and follow him to their bedchamber. As she leaves the room she points significantly to the trunk of the ash-tree. Siegmund is left alone, musing how his father promised he would find a sword in his direst need. Sieglinde steals back to the room and tells Siegmund that a stranger entered the hut while she was being betrothed to Hunding (whom she does not love), and plunged a sword into the ash-tree, saying that it would belong to the hero who was able to pull it out of the trunk. In Siegmund she sees the owner of the sword and her own rescuer. The door flies open, and the magic of a moonlit spring night floods the room. Elated, Siegmund cries out his name and drawing the sword out of the tree, he calls it Notung. Joyfully Sieglinde reveals herself to him as his sister, and Siegmund enfolds her in a passionate embrace.

Act II. A wild, rocky mountain. Wotan orders Brünnhilde to protect Siegmund in his duel against Hunding and make him victorious, but Fricka, the defender of marriage vows, demands that Wotan should severely punish Siegmund for the sins of the Wälsungs. After a long argument he gives in to his wife's wish and withdraws the order he gave Brünnhilde: Siegmund, not Hunding, must die. Siegmund could have become the deliverer of the gods, but Wotan, pursued by the curse and bound by his undertakings, must destroy his hero. Siegmund and Sieglinde are in flight from Hunding. The exertion is too much for Sieglinde,

who collapses, unconscious. Brünnhilde appears, to announce to Siegmund his imminent death. She describes to him the wonders of Valhalla
where she will lead him. He is filled with tender protective love for
Sieglinde, from whom he does not wish to be parted. Filled with compassion, Brünnhilde promises him life, and victory in the fight. A storm
rises and Sieglinde is rudely awakened. Hunding enters and Siegmund
goes to meet him. Brünnhilde intervenes to protect Siegmund, but
Wotan steps between them, interposes his spear and Hunding pierces
Siegmund. Siegmund's sword is shattered, Brünnhilde seizes the pieces
of the sword and flees with Sieglinde, to protect them both from her
father's wrath. At a contemptuous gesture from Wotan, Hunding falls
dead.

Act III. The top of a rocky mountain, The Valkyries are gathering on
their return from battle; Brünnhilde enters with Sieglinde, and gives her
new courage to live by revealing that she bears in her womb the greatest
hero in the world. She gives Sieglinde the pieces of Siegmund's sword, and
tells her to save herself for the child's sake. Sieglinde flees, and Brünnhilde
stays to face Wotan's rage. He enters and pronounces sentence on
Brünnhilde for her disobedience: she will fall into a magic slumber and,
stripped of her immortality, will fall victim to the first man who finds
her. Lamenting, the Valkyries flee from Wotan. Brünnhilde, appalled
by her punishment, humbly pleads for mitigation of the penalty, asking
that only a hero may awake her from her slumber. Wotan promises to
grant her wish, kisses her on her eyes, thus depriving her of her godhead,
and plunges her in sleep. He then invokes Loge, the god of fire, to surround
with leaping flames the rock on which Brünnhilde lies. Declaring that he
who fears *his* spear shall never pass through the fire, Wotan leaves his
beloved daughter.

With *Die Walküre*, the first tragedy of the great drama, we
are on heroic ground. The hero born of a god enters the scene,
and being a man, is freer in emotion and action than a god.
The plain, calm and concordant *Rheingold* music, representing
nature and the gods, is now joined by the music of fluctuating
human passions and emotions.

The prelude depicts a storm with elemental realism: a wildly
agitated subject rages in the cellos and basses, and lightning
flashes across the sky. When the curtain rises, the storm is
already dying away. The thematic material of the first scene is
completely new, and the Love Motif recurs repeatedly with
passionate chromatics as the compelling force of the whole

scene. The arrogant, brutal Hunding Motif dominates the
scene which follows. When Siegmund sings 'Den Vater fand
ich nicht' ('My father found I not') the Valhalla-Wotan theme
from *Das Rheingold* sounds faintly from the orchestra, the first
hint of a connection between the two dramas, revealing what
Siegmund himself does not yet know; namely that he is the
hero begotten by Wotan to be his deliverer. The Sword Motif
is similarly significant, as it also is taken from *Das Rheingold*.
Sieglinde suspects the connection and pointedly draws Siegmund's attention to the ash-tree while the Sword Motif sounds
softly in the orchestra. The radiant climax of this act is magnificently effective, when to a fortissimo 'Sword' fanfare Siegmund
pulls the sword from the tree.

In the second act an important new theme is introduced—the
Valkyries' Motif. The quarrel between Wotan and Fricka and

Wotan's great narration which follows it are interwoven with
strong recollections from *Das Rheingold*—the Nature Motif,
the Treaty Motif, the Ring Motif, the sword fanfare,
Alberich's curse and the Valhalla theme, which form a symphonic accompaniment to both scenes. The entrance of
Siegmund and Sieglinde is passionately agitated, while the
Flight Theme from the introduction to the second act is here
closely mingled with the Love Motif and greatly intensified.
Sieglinde's agitation and fear are movingly expressed in the
feverish line, and the orchestra flashes with ever more brilliant
colours until Sieglinde loses consciousness. While Siegmund in
tender concern kneels at her side, the Love Motif is heard in a
fading *pianissimo*.

The highly agitated *allegro* is followed by the calm grandeur
of the announcement of coming death which, like the allegro,
is a wonderfully concise piece of symphonic music. The important Fate Theme, a crucial and broadly impressive motif,
introduces this great scene.

The prelude and the first scene of the third act are homogeneous, the Valkyries' Motif, extended and partly altered, forming the thematic skeleton of its musical structure. The dotted rhythm of the Ride of the Valkyries dominates ensemble and orchestra. The entry of Brünnhilde and Sieglinde is accompanied by the Flight Motif, and the wild agitation of the music persists until Brünnhilde's promise to Sieglinde about the child she bears, when the Siegfried Motif is first heard. The

Sword Motif from *Das Rheingold* flares up in a fanfare, referring to the sword which the hero will one day brandish. In overflowing exaltation Sieglinde breaks into one of the most beautiful melodies of the whole tetralogy, full of passionate

ardour, the theme which later in *Götterdämmerung* brings the whole work to its splendid climax.

The final scene is musically immediate and touching in its effect. In the face of Brünnhilde's humble explanation of her conduct Wotan's rage abates; it is he who feels humbled.

Mysterious chords announce the magic sleep into which Wotan
lulls his beloved child, and a tender lullaby begins, followed by

the all-absorbing quivering chromatics of the magic fire, the
Loge Motif from *Das Rheingold*. Wotan's last words are
accompanied by the recurring Siegfried Motif, majestically
repeated in the orchestra. As Wotan disappears in the fire, the
Fate Motif is heard again, interwoven with the fading notes of
the magic fire and slumber themes.

The composition of *Siegfried* took fifteen years. It is like a
light idyll between the sombre mighty tragedies of *Die Walküre*
and *Götterdämmerung*. It is the natural spontaneous strength of
youth in his hero which inspired Wagner to compose music of
such thrilling and rhythmic impetus.

SIEGFRIED. Second day of the festival drama, *Der Ring des Nibelungen* by
Richard Wagner. First performance: Bayreuth, 1876.

Characters: Siegfried—tenor; Mime—tenor; the Wanderer—baritone;
Alberich—bass-bar; Fafner—bass; Erad—contralto; Brunnhilde—soprano; the woodbird—soprano.

Act I. In a cave opening on to the wood. Mime is striving to forge a
strong enough sword for the young Siegfried, so that he will not break
it like a toy. There is one steel which Siegfried could not break: the two
pieces of Notung, Siegmund's sword; but Mime cannot weld them
together. If he could do so, he would make Siegfried kill Fafner who, in
the form of a dragon, guards the Nibelungen hoard in the dark forest.
Siegfried enters the cave, dragging a bear after him to frighten Mime.
He then demands the new sword that Mime has forged for him, and breaks
it easily. He can scarcely conceal his hatred for the dwarf who has brought
him up, and whom he cannot believe is his father. He asks Mime who his
parents were, and hesitantly Mime tells him how Sieglinde gave birth to
him in the cave and, dying, named him Siegfried. All she left him were the
pieces of a sword. Siegfried charges Mime to forge these two pieces together, and then rushes out into the wood. Wotan, disguised as the
Wanderer, arrives. Mime grudgingly receives his uninvited guest, who
sits down by the fire. Wotan wagers his head that he can answer any
three questions Mime may ask him. To get rid of the stranger the dwarf
asks who lives under the earth, who on it, and who above it. The answers
are: under the earth live the Nibelungs, with their ruler, Alberich, who
should have won power over the world through a magic ring; the earth

is ruled by the giants: Fasolt and Fafner won the Nibelungen hoard, including the ring, and Fafner as a dragon now guards the treasure; among the clouds, in Valhalla, rule the gods. Wotan naturally answers these questions correctly. Now it is Mime's turn to answer three questions: what race did Wotan beget, and love dearly, yet punish, and which was the only sword that could kill Fafner? Mime can answer these two questions; Wotan begot the Wälsungs, the son of Siegmund and Sieglinde is Siegfried, the strongest of the Wälsungs, and Notung is the sword which Siegfried must wield in his fight with Fafner. But the third question: who can forge Notung? the dwarf cannot answer, and his head is now forfeit. Wotan then gives him the answer, saying that he who knows no fear can reforge Notung, thereby sealing the dwarf's fate. When Siegfried returns, Mime asks him whether he knows fear; so that he can learn what it is, he will take him to Fafner. Siegfried wants to forge the sword for this combat himself. While Mime prepares a draught of poison to kill Siegfried after the fight with the dragon, Siegfried sets to work at the forge. Singing the forging song he succeeds in this great feat, and with a shout of joy he swings Notung and splits the heavy anvil with one powerful blow.

Act II. In the depths of the forest. Alberich lies near the dragon's lair. Wotan appears, and warns him against Mime, who intends to use Siegfried to get the ring for himself. He then goes to the mouth of the cave to awaken Fafner and warn him also, but Fafner is not afraid and asks to be left in peace. The Wanderer disappears. As dawn breaks Mime brings Siegfried to the spot and describes to him how terrible an opponent Fafner is. Siegfried, unimpressed, lies down under a lime-tree, and dismisses Mime as he wishes to be alone in the silent wood. He drinks in the wonders of nature: the rustling of the wood around him and the song of a bird, which he tries to imitate on a reed. When this does not work very well, he blows his silver horn. Something moves behind him: it is Fafner, transformed into a monstrous dragon, who has risen from his sleep and is heaving himself out of the cave. When Fafner threateningly challenges him to fight, Siegfried faces him fearlessly and plunges his sword into the dragon's heart. As he lies dying Fafner warns his slayer against Mime. When he pulls his sword out of the dragon's body Siegfried's hand is sprinkled with the dragon's blood, which burns him so violently that he puts his hands to his mouth. When the blood touches his lips he finds he can suddenly understand the language of the birds, and the pretty voice of a woodbird reveals to him that the tarnhelm and the ring hidden in Fafner's cave could make him ruler of the world. Siegfried goes down into the cave, and Mime tries to slip in after him, but is prevented by Alberich. They are both actuated by the same idea—to obtain the ring for themselves. Siegfried returns with the tarnhelm and the ring, and the bird's voice now warns him against Mime, who at that moment appears and with hypocritical concern offers him the poisoned draught. Siegfried kills him with one blow, and Alberich's derisive laughter is heard in the distance. While Siegfried is resting, the woodbird promises to lead him to a most beautiful woman, who sleeps on a high cliff surrounded with fire. Only he who knows no fear can pass through the flames. Rejoicing, Siegfried follows the bird which flutters ahead, leading him to Brünnhilde.

Act III, scene i. A wild rocky place. Wotan, the Wanderer, summons the omniscient mother of mankind, Erda. In a veil of bluish light, she emerges from the depths of the earth and Wotan begs her to tell him what the future holds. Reluctantly she keeps silence. Wotan tells her he sees the end of the gods approaching and that he would gladly leave all his power to Siegfried. Erda disappears. Not without a struggle does Wotan accept the fate he foresees. He raises his spear as Siegfried approaches, while the gleam of the magic fire lights up the horizon. He challenges Siegfried to pass the weapon which once shattered Notung, but this time Siegfried's sword shatters Wotan's spear—the Wanderer can hold him back no longer; his power is broken; he steps back and is lost to sight in the darkness. The rock in the background is bathed in a sea of flames into which Siegfried plunges, while waves of fire flow over him, then gradually pale and die away in the first, rosy light of day.

Scene ii. The summit of the Valkyries' rock. Day is dawning and Brünnhilde, in glittering armour, is asleep beneath a fir-tree. Siegfried gently loosens her helmet and breastplate, and stands transfixed by the sight before him. For the first time he knows fear; this is the first woman he has ever seen. He kisses her long and ardently, until she opens her eyes and slowly raises herself up. First she greets the sun, then asks the fateful question: who is the hero who has awakened her. Ecstatically she recognizes her rescuer, but as she remembers the loss of her goddess's impregnability, she rejects him vehemently and implores him not to humiliate her. Siegfried however woos her more and more urgently until, carried away by his passion, she joyfully renounces the glories of Valhalla to give herself to him in love and happiness.

The *Siegfried* music is a whole world in itself, free and fresh in conception and brilliantly coloured. In contrast to the dramatic impulse which beats in each note of *Die Walküre*, the first two acts of *Siegfried* are like an idyllic fairy-tale, and only in the final act is there a return to the dramatic pathos of the *Ring* music. There are few new *leitmotivs* in *Siegfried*: the first act is mainly concerned with the Smith and Sword Motifs, which have already appeared earlier, but they are joined by Siegfried's gay horn-call. The second act is infused with the fairy-tale

magic of the forest, the wonderful woodland sounds in the divided strings and the high bird-call in the woodwind. A light,

untrammelled, happy atmosphere reigns here and even the
fight with the dragon is not horrifying, nor the murder of
the treacherous dwarf Mime. The Wanderer's entrance,
marked always by solemn chords on the lower brass, contrasts
with this light, fairy-tale world. Themes which recall connections with previous events frequently recur. A musical and
dramatic climax is reached in the meeting of the two worlds, as
represented by Wotan and Siegfried, and their clash at the foot
of Brünnhilde's rock. Here again the most important motifs
interweave and the end of the gods is foretold with melancholy
grandeur.

The music of the final scene is indescribably lovely. A great
symphonic arc of exceptional musical richness spans the distance
from the vast calm of nature to the passionate ecstasy of love.
To the long series of *leitmotivs* is added a profusion of splendid
new ideas which create the magic of this love-scene: for instance the noble grandeur of Brünnhilde's greeting to the world
'Heil dir, Sonne. Heil dir, Licht!', ('Sun I hail thee! Hail oh
light'), the wonderful melody which follows to her words
'Ewig war ich, ewig bin ich' ('Ever was I, ever am I') and
'Siegfried, Herrlicher! Hort der Welt' ('Oh Siegfried, highest
hero, wealth of the world') and finally the lively theme of
Love's Surrender, which crowns the end of the scene and recurs
as a *leitmotiv* in *Götterdämmerung*.

Wagner worked on *Götterdämmerung* for five years, finishing
it in the autumn of 1874. The following summer preparations
began for the first complete performance of the tetralogy, which
took place in August 1876 in the Festival Theatre at Bayreuth.

GÖTTERDÄMMERUNG (The Twilight of the Gods). Third day of
the festival drama, *Der Ring des Nibelungen* by Richard Wagner. First
performance: Bayreuth, 1876.

Characters: Siegfried—tenor; Brünnhilde—soprano; Waltraute—
mezzo-soprano; Gunther—baritone; Hagen—bass; Gutrune—soprano;
Alberich—bass-bar; first Norn—contralto; second Norn—mezzo-
soprano; third Norn—soprano; Woglinde—soprano; Wellgunde—
soprano; Flosshilde—contralto.

Prologue. Brünnhilde's rock, as at the end of *Siegfried*. A misty day is
dawning. The Norns are sitting on the rocks weaving the thread of fate
and telling of the destiny which binds everything together. The thread
snaps, and the Norns sink from view. Dawn breaks and Siegfried and
Brünnhilde come out of their rocky abode. Siegfried wants to set out in

search of new adventures. In pledge of his faith he gives Brünnhilde the ring and she in return gives him her war horse Grane. In happy mutual trust the lovers part.

Act I, scene i. The hall of the Gibichungs on the banks of the Rhine. Gunther, his sister Gutrune and Gunther's half-brother Hagen, Alberich's son, are gathered there. Hagen tells of Brünnhilde whom Gunther must rescue and of Siegfried, who alone can pass through the sea of fire. Gunther objects that he has no use for a woman whom he cannot win for himself. Hagen reveals his plan, and Gunther and Gutrune agree to it: a magic potion must make Siegfried forget that he has ever desired a woman, and must turn his thoughts to Gutrune. In exchange he will help Gunther to win Brünnhilde. Siegfried's horn is heard from the river, and looking out Hagen sees him sailing across the Rhine in a boat. Siegfried's appearance makes a great impression on Gutrune, and at a sign from Hagen she leaves the hall to prepare the potion. Gunther warmly welcomes the hero, who frankly tells him that he owns nothing but his mighty sword. When Hagen asks him about the Nibelungen treasure, he replies that he only took the ring and the tarnhelm, and Hagen tells him the secret of the helmet. Gutrune enters and gives Siegfried the cup of welcome; the magic potion immediately takes effect: Siegfried forgets Brünnhilde and passionately woos Gutrune. It is agreed that Gutrune shall become his wife, if he will help Gunther to win Brünnhilde. There is a terrible moment when at the mention of Brünnhilde's name Siegfried tries to think of her, but the memory of her is already gone. He says he is willing to use the tarnhelm to assume Gunther's shape, and to win Brünnhilde. Siegfried and Gunther seal their pact with the solem oath of blood brotherhood and they at once prepare to depart.

Scene ii. Brünnhilde's rock. Brünnhilde, awaiting Siegfried's return, is contemplating the ring when Waltraute, one of her sisters, comes to her. Filled with fear and foreboding, she tells Brünnhilde of the plight of the gods. Since Wotan at last returned home with his shattered spear, he has only been waiting for the end, the twilight of the gods. Waltraute heard him sigh in his sleep, remembering Brünnhilde, who alone could save the gods and the world from the curse by giving back the ring to the Rhinemaidens. Waltraute implores her sister to do this but with powerful dramatic impact comes Brünnhilde's reply; she will never abandon love, though the glories of Valhalla should dissolve in ruins. Waltraute rushes away in anger. The curse of the ring, from which even Brünnhilde cannot escape, is taking its course. Disguised as Gunther, Siegfried passes yet again through the fire and wins Brünnhilde by tearing from her the ring. Powerless and defenceless Brünnhilde must bow to her fate.

Act II. Before the hall of the Gibichungs. Hagen sits sleeping holding his spear and shield, when Alberich appears to him to remind him of the ring. In his sleep Hagen promises to obtain the ring. Day breaks and Siegfried enters gaily to announce the imminent arrival of Gunther and Brünnhilde. He tells Gutrune how he won Brünnhilde, thereby keeping faith with her and her brother. Preparations for the wedding feast begin. Hagen summons the vassals to make everything ready for the ceremony.

The boat carrying Gunther and Brünnhilde comes alongside the river-bank. Gunther proudly presents his wife, who enters with bowed head. Only at Siegfried's name does she raise her eyes and recognize her beloved. She cannot believe that he has now betrayed her and is to marry Gutrune, but when she sees on his hand the ring which Gunther took from her, she guesses at his treachery without understanding the circumstances. Indignantly she accuses Siegfried of breaking his vows, while he swears that he is innocent. There is general consternation; only Siegfried remains unmoved and cheerfully leaves the scene with Gutrune and her retinue. Brünnhilde, Hagen and Gunther are left alone. Deeply wounded and filled with passion and desire for vengeance, Brünnhilde eagerly agrees to Hagen's proposal to kill Siegfried, and tells him that Siegfried is only vulnerable in the back. Gunther is easily persuaded to join the conspiracy, for a mention of the ring stimulates his lust for power. Gutrune will be told that Siegfried has been killed by a boar while hunting. The wedding procession enters, headed by Gutrune and Siegfried who are then joined by Gunther and Brünnhilde.

Act III, scene i. A wooded landscape near the Rhine. The Rhinemaidens rise out of the waters and sing to the goddess of the sun to lead to them the hero who will restore their gold. Siegfried, who has lost his way while hunting, appears. He playfully teases the Rhinemaidens, pretending he is about to give them the ring. But when to encourage him they warn Siegfried against its curse, he withdraws it. He will not let himself be frightened by their threats, and his fearlessness is his undoing. The Rhine-maidens swim away. The horn calls, which also introduced this scene, are heard again and announce the approach of the hunt. Gunther, Hagen and Siegfried lie down to rest in the wood while their followers spread out round them. Hagen asks Siegfried to tell them about his earlier adventures, and while he is relating these, recollection slowly returns to him, for Hagen has given him a drink to destroy the effect of Gutrune's magic potion. The image of Brünnhilde comes to him, and he remembers how he awoke her and passionately embraced her. Wotan's two ravens of fate at this moment circle above Siegfried's head and as he turns to watch them with his back to Hagen, he is mortally wounded with the latter's spear. All are stricken with horror. Night falls; the men lay Siegfried's body on a shield and carry it solemnly over the rocky heights which are once again bathed in moonlight.

Scene ii. The hall of the Gibichungs. It is night and Gutrune is rest-lessly awaiting the return of the hunters. Her anxious question is answered by Hagen who points derisively to Siegfried's body which lies on a bier outside the hall. Beside herself with sorrow, Gutrune accuses Gunther of the murder; but Gunther tries to throw all the blame on Hagen, who acknowledges the deed and demands the ring as a reward. When Gunther opposes him, Hagen draws his sword and kills him. Then Hagen goes to Siegfried's body to tear the ring from his finger, but the hand of the dead man rises threateningly against him. Horrified, everyone draws back. Brünnhilde enters the hall. The Rhinemaidens have told her everything, including Siegfried's and Wotan's destiny. Now she accepts his legacy and takes the ring which, purified by the fire that must immolate Siegfried

and herself, will return to the Rhinemaidens. Meanwhile at her command
a pyre has been built on the banks of the Rhine and on it Siegfried's body
is laid. Brünnhilde herself lights the fire and leaping on to her steed
Grane she rides into the flames. Ecstatically she cries out her final greeting
to Siegfried, then joins him in annihilation. The fire spreads to the hall,
which collapses in smoking ruins. The Rhine overflows its banks, envelop-
ing everything around and bearing the Rhinemaidens with it; with a
cry, Hagen plunges into the waters and is dragged down by the Rhinemaidens, who triumphantly raise the ring on high. A rosy glow in the
sky tells that the fire on earth has enveloped Valhalla also, and that the
twilight of the gods has come.

As the culmination of the whole *Ring*, *Götterdämmerung* is built
up on a complex mesh of connections with the other three
dramas, but it has an immediate effect of its own due to its
mighty dramatic impact. The interplay of the *leitmotivs* is so
dense that one can hardly unravel single themes from the great
symphonic flow of the orchestra; they are indissolubly interwoven and integrated with the symphonic development.

The prelude opens with the mysterious chords of Brünnhilde's salute to the world from the final act of *Siegfried*, subtly
supported by the Motif of Nature from *Das Rheingold* and that
of the fated question from *Die Walküre*. The scene with the
Norns is completely built on motifs from *Das Rheingold*, for
the message of the Norns is that all events are indissolubly
bound to fate. With the appropriate *leitmotivs* to accompany
them, they tell of Wotan (Valhalla theme), of his spear which
protects the contracts, of the Rhinegold, of the ring and of the
sword. But the thread breaks at Siegfried's horn-call. The curse
theme resounds menacingly, the Norns disappear and the theme
of the fated question dies faintly away.

The second scene of the prelude introduces two new themes:
first, Siegfried's strong, proud Hero Motif which, accompanied

by the ebullient horn-call, indicates his masculine maturity.
The second theme is the fervent and feminine Brünnhilde

Motif. Hagen, Gunther and Gutrune also have their own *leitmotivs*, but these make no important contribution to the progress or significance of the action.

The music of the second act exudes unprecedented dramatic power; the symphonic moulding of the consistent *leitmotiv* construction here attains a unique concision, and splendid details, such as the daybreak, the scene of recognition or the weighty oath, are lost in the floodtide of gigantic *crescendo* on which the whole act is based.

The Rhinemaidens' scene is one of the most charming musical episodes in the whole tetralogy, full of wonderful new melodies which blend with the well-known *leitmotivs* in effortless grace, framed by the hunt music. The following scene is in violent contrast to this poetic idyll. Siegfried falls wounded to a distorted version of his motive, and a sinister, throbbing string figure is heard for the first time, characterizing his end. This intensely gripping theme dominates the orchestral interlude which leads into the final scene. This is the mourning music for Siegfried's death, and in it all the motifs that have characterized and accompanied his life appear and merge into a powerful piece of tone-painting.

Brünnhilde's great final outburst reunites the most important themes of the tetralogy in a symphonic apotheosis of overwhelming polyphonic power, in which none of the individual themes lose their clarity. Towards the end of this great vocal passage the principal themes (the Valhalla, Siegfried and Valkyrie Motifs) are combatting the ever increasing urgency of the surging Motif of All-Powerful Love. After Valhalla and Siegfried have disappeared in the blaze of the Götterdämmerung Motif, there echoes once again this wonderful melody from *Die Walküre*, as both hymn of love and a symbol of the central concept of the drama.

Parsifal marks the completion of Richard Wagner's life's work, not in the sense of a final climax, but as the further development and consolidation of his ideals for life and creative work which were already present in embryo in his earliest works. Though they had come to fruition at the height of his creative power, in *Parsifal* they were given a final depth and symbolic significance. Paths lead from all Wagner's operas to *Parsifal* and parallels can be found in them all. Through *Parsifal* the unity of Wagner's artistic work is most tellingly conveyed. Wagner prepared the first draft for the text in 1857, but his mind had been occupied with related subjects since 1845; thus the concept of *Parsifal* slowly matured in close relationship with his other works, until the text was completed in 1877. Several epic cycles have been fused together to create a work of independent stamp, and the principal ideas which govern the purpose and content of this mystery play are entirely Wagner's own, unique spiritual creation.

PARSIFAL. Dedication festival drama by Richard Wagner. First performance: Bayreuth, 1882.

Characters: Amfortas—baritone; Titurel—bass; Parsifal—tenor; Gurnemanz—bass; Klingsor—bass; Kundry—soprano. Knights of the Grail, pages, Klingsor's Flower Maidens.

Place: Spain, in the region of and in the castle of the Holy Grail.
Time: The Middle Ages.

The nucleus of the story is the concept of the Grail, the cup in which the blood from the crucified Saviour's side was caught and which is revered as the holiest relic by the knights of the Grail. Each year a white dove descends from heaven to fill the Grail with renewed miraculous powers and to stimulate the knights to feats of bravery in the cause of salvation. In the Castle of the Grail, which has been consecrated as a temple, the band of knights preserve a second sacred object, the spear with which Our Lord was wounded. They have a bitter enemy, Klingsor, who was judged unworthy of the community and driven out by them, and who in his thirst for revenge has built a magic castle to corrupt the knights of the Grail, where beautiful women tempt them to forbidden pleasures, and any who succumb fall into Klingsor's power. Also in Klingsor's power is Kundry, the woman who laughed at Christ on the road to Calvary and ever since has wandered despairingly on earth, seeking release from her sin. Until she finds her rescuer Kundry must remain an enchantress in Klingsor's power, but in another guise she tries to expiate her guilt by serving the Grail.

Act I, scene i. The domain of the Grail. In a shady wood outside the castle, Gurnemanz and two pages are saying their morning prayers. The ailing King, Amfortas, is to be brought to bathe in the holy lake in the woods to refresh him; nothing can relieve his pain, not even the balm which Kundry zealously prepares. Gurnemanz tells the pages of the events which led to Amfortas's wound; the King, armed with the Holy Spear, went out to fight Klingsor, but fell victim to the seductions of an enchantingly beautiful woman, and Klingsor was able to seize the spear and inflict on him this terrible wound. The lost spear must be recovered, for it alone can heal the wound. The King has been told in a dream that only one man can help him—a guileless fool, made wise by pity. As the pages are softly repeating the oracle's words a loud scream is heard from the lake. Parsifal is brought in; he has killed a swan in the sacred domain of the Grail. Gurnemanz rebukes the young man for his misdeed, and asks his name and where he comes from. To every question Parsifal has only one reply—I do not know. Gurnemanz believes that he has found in Parsifal the promised saviour, and takes him with him to the castle of the Grail.

Scene ii. A high, domed hall in the castle of the Grail. The knights are celebrating Holy Communion. Parsifal watches in astonishment, and though Amfortas's despairing cry of anguish touches him with its pain he asks nothing more; no pity has made him wise, and Gurnemanz angrily drives him away.

Act II. Klingsor's realm. From a high watch-tower Klingsor sees Parsifal approaching. He tells Kundry, who once seduced Amfortas, to entice Parsifal as well. Against her will Kundry must obey the sorcerer. The scene quickly changes into a magic garden; Flower Maidens, creatures of Klingsor's, try to entice Parsifal who has come into the garden, but he laughingly waves them aside and passes on, until he hears Kundry's voice, calling him by name. Bewildered, Parsifal stands still and looks in amazement at the beautiful woman approaching him. Kundry tries to win Parsifal by moving allusions to his mother and her death, but when she presses 'love's first kiss' on his lips he awakes to the realization that Amfortas must have experienced the same fate, that sensuality can rule one's destiny and that even the noblest man can incur torment. He thinks that by overcoming sensuality he can save Amfortas. Kundry approaches him again: she believes he is *her* rescuer and in desperation she confesses her sin and implores him to take her to himself, to free her from her curse. Parsifal feels that they would both be damned if he followed her; he therefore rejects her advances and demands to be shown the way to Amfortas. Kundry curses him; never shall he find the castle of the Grail again. Klingsor appears and throws the Holy Spear at Parsifal, but it remains suspended in the air above the guileless fool. Parsifal seizes it and makes with it the sign of the Cross. The enchanted garden collapses and Parsifal finds himself once more in a deserted wilderness; he hurries away to find the castle of the Grail.

Act III, scene i. A beautiful spring landscape near Gurnemanz's hut. Years have passed, and distress and misery have entered the castle of the Grail; since the day when Parsifal attended the Communion service Amfortas has refused to unveil the Grail which only brings him renewed suffering. The strength of the knights has waned, and in deep despair they await their deliverer. Gurnemanz, now an old man, lives as a hermit in a hut at the wooded limit of the Grail domain. Gurnemanz hears a cry and finds Kundry in the undergrowth, lifeless and numbed. He succeeds in restoring her to life and in thanks she only has one word for him: to serve. Gurnemanz gazes after her, astonished by her altered manner, and hopes that deliverance may come to her today: it is Good Friday. Parsifal enters. After long wanderings and battles he has at last reached the realm of the Grail. When Gurnemanz recognizes the Holy Spear in his hand, he is transported with joy; at last the hour of deliverance is come. Parsifal is consecrated King of the Grail by Gurnemanz; Kundry washes his feet and receives from him the baptism of absolution.

Scene ii. The castle of the Grail, as in the first act. The knights, gathered in the temple, implore and urge Amfortas to unveil the Grail so that new life may flow into them; in despair, he refuses their demand and in deepest anguish asks them to kill him. Parsifal appears, declares that his sin is pardoned and heals his wound. On Parsifal's order the Grail is unveiled: the holy vessel glows and a white dove hovers in the bright light which streams from the dome. Parsifal lifts up the Grail and blesses the knights.

The music of *Parsifal* is crystal-clear. Two groups of self-sufficient themes oppose one another, as in *Tannhäuser* and *Lohengrin*—the world of the Grail and the world of Klingsor. While the Grail themes are based on triads and built on a pure diatonic scale, Klingsor's music shimmers in restless chromatics. There are very few *leitmotivs* compared with the thematic complexity of the *Ring*.

The prelude introduces three of the most important themes in clear succession; first the Communion Motif, which emerges

mistily in the strings and woodwind and is repeated by oboe and trumpet with a delicate string accompaniment. Trumpets and trombones bring in the Grail theme, which fades away in an

echo on the woodwind. This is followed by the powerful
strains of the Motif of Belief. These themes, which are then

joined by the theme of the Guileless Fool in Gurnemanz's story

Durch Mit - leid   wis-send,   der rei - ne   Tor
(*Made wise through pi - ty,   the blame - less   fool*)

and later by the Bell Motif, define the scenes in the Grail

domain. Three themes from the Klingsor music take a repeated
and vital part in the story—the two Kundry themes:

and the eerie, shimmering Klingsor Motif. The two groups of

themes intermingle and contrast, and around them the music
flows with continuous melodic richness. The themes of Parsifal

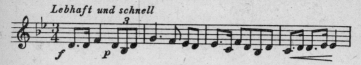

and Amfortas are also used as *leitmotivs*. The best-known pas-

sages in the opera are the march-like interlude music, the
Flower Maidens' scene, full of sensuous, bewitching melody,
Kundry's long second-act narration and the fervent music of
Good Friday, which is closely related to the Grail music. All
the scenes with the ailing Amfortas are deeply impressive,
musically and dramatically, especially his great lament in the
first Grail scene. The sacred final scene, in which the three Grail
Motifs blaze up once more in solemn grandeur and then fade
into nothing, is incomparably moving.

   Parsifal is a 'mystery' of faith, just as one could call *Tristan*
a 'mystery' of love and the *Ring* a 'mystery' of power. Wagner
called this work a 'Bühnenweihfestspiel'—a sacred festival
drama—and so, to protect its solemn, religious character from
the dangers of repertory performances in lesser theatres, he
gave orders that *Parsifal* should only be performed at the Bayreuth Festival. There were several performances however which
'broke' the copyright, among them those at the Metropolitan,
New York, in 1903, Boston (in English) in 1904, and Amsterdam in 1905. On 1 January 1914 the copyright expired, and
Parsifal became the common property of all opera houses.
Performances during Holy Week, which have become customary in large theatres, are wholly appropriate to the solemn
dignity of this 'mystery'. The heated arguments originally
engendered by the pros and cons of presenting the Last Supper
and a celebration of the Mass on stage have long since died
down. In fact, the problems surrounding Wagner's philosophy
of life as it appears in his work are no longer a matter of general

interest. Nowadays Wagner is appraised exclusively as a musician, though as a poet he is also accorded some recognition.

Wagner has had an immense influence on the whole theatrical world. His far-reaching innovations and incisive reforms in all branches of the theatre, which were so revolutionary in his day, are now taken as a matter of course. Extinguishing the houselights before the overture, refusal of admission even to the boxes once the curtain has risen, intense quiet during performances, restriction of applause to the ends of the acts, all these apparent trivialities, which nevertheless result from greater regard for the work of art, are due to Wagner. Wagner also made extraordinarily varied innovations in theatrical technique with novel lighting and scenic effects, use of gauzes, cloud effects which plunge the stage in heavy mist, transformations and so on. The whole concept of opera production took on a new meaning, and even if the Wagnerian style of presentation has become as obsolete as Wagnerian scenery, one must not overlook the fact that only since Wagner have gesture and deportment on stage been related to the music as a matter of course. Wagner's most important legacy, however, to the presentation of his works is the unconditional participation of everyone concerned in the service of the work. This spirit of ensemble, which spread from Bayreuth to other theatres to the benefit of all other operatic works, derived from unswerving attention to the work itself, to which everything else must be subjected.

WAGNER'S SUCCESSORS

After a hard struggle Wagner's stage works eventually became established and with them German opera not only reached its undisputed peak but also for the first time attained world-wide recognition. Obviously German operatic works were governed by the influence of the music-drama for some time thereafter. Among the few exceptions was Karl Goldmark (1830–1915), whose most famous work *Die Königin von Saba* (*The Queen of Sheba*) (1875), continued the tradition of French grand opera.

Everything bowed to the spirit of Bayreuth and opera composers took the conception of the music-drama and the
'Gesamtkunstwerk' as their pattern and even followed the
great example in their choice of subject. The historical opera,
which is still often found in the middle of the century—as for
instance *Catarina Cornaro* (1841) by Franz Lachner (1803–90)—
was completely played out and German epic cycles came decisively into the foreground. Musical eclecticism reigned
everywhere: the influence of romantic opera mingled with
ideas drawn from the French, while *arioso* passages rubbed
shoulders with strict 'Sprechgesang' and its continuous melody.
The many operas called *Gudrun* and *Wieland der Schmied* which
sprang up in those years bore only a formal and superficial
resemblance to their Bayreuth models and were quickly forgotten, as were even the more remarkable works such as Cyril
Kistler's *Kunihild* (1884), or the tetralogy *Homerische Welt* (*The
World of Homer*) (1896–1903), by August Bungert, which at
first was greatly respected. Gradually Wagner's musical idiom
also became common property, and Wagnerian tonalities or
melodic phrases crept imperceptibly into the scores of his
imitators, so that by the turn of the century Wagnerian musical
expression had become so overpowering and had so permeated
all operatic composition that no opera composer could entirely
escape its influence. Even outstanding musicians paid tribute to
Bayreuth in their early works—Richard Strauss in *Guntram*
(1894), Max von Schillings in *Ingwelde* (1894), and Hans
Pfitzner in his musical drama *Der arme Heinrich* (*Poor Henry*)
(1895).

It is understandable that such a towering, exceptional personality as Wagner never established a school, that no further
development was possible along his exact lines, and that not
even a new style of singing grew up, for his highly complex
work depended too much on its creator. Those among his
disciples who tried to adopt his ideas and style fell into mere
imitation. Wagner's most important successors, Bruckner and
Wolf, who did succeed in developing his musical language in a
wholly personal way, did so outside the field of opera; Bruckner
in the symphony, and Hugo Wolf in *lieder*.

In the field of opera the only composers at this time who
managed to escape the overpowering influence of Wagner

were those who renounced pathos and solemnity and struck
out on their own for musical comedy, folk-opera or fairy-tale
opera. Their independence from Wagner is most marked in
their comedies; the three most outstanding during the second
half of the nineteenth century were Cornelius's *Der Barbier von
Bagdad*, Goetz's *Der Widerspänstigen Zähmung* and Wolf's *Der
Corregidor*, although admittedly Wolf's language always betrays a convinced Wagnerian, and the other two works contain
occasional Wagnerian passages, especially *Der Barbier von
Bagdad* in Felix Mottl's later version. On the whole these scores
are outstandingly original, but their undoubted musical value
was not sufficient to counterbalance their texts which, despite
some charming details, lacked dramatic impetus, much like
Weber's *Euryanthe* and Schumann's *Genoveva*, and this prevented any lasting success on the German stage.

Like Hugo Wolf, Peter Cornelius (1824–74) was a lyric composer and it is the purely lyric elements, the original humour
and emotional sincerity which give his opera its value.
Cornelius was firmly convinced of his dramatic vocation, and
since he was also his own very fine librettist it seemed that he
might become an author of music-dramas, but unfortunately
he lacked strong dramatic impulse both as poet and as musician.
Especially his two serious music-dramas, *Der Cid* (1865) and
Gunlöd (1891) suffer from this shortcoming, and in both these
later works, which reflect Wagner's influence more markedly
than *Der Barbier von Bagdad* (1858), the most impressive passages
are the lyrical ones.

Der Barbier von Bagdad, Cornelius's best work, was a complete
fiasco when it was first performed in Weimar in 1858 under
Liszt's direction. On the first night the opera house became a
battleground between the followers of Liszt, the theatre's
musical director, and Dinglestedt, the manager. As a result
Liszt resigned as court conductor at Weimar, and the opera
was not performed again while Cornelius was alive. Even when
it was produced at Hanover in 1877 it was again a failure.
Felix Mottl then took it up in 1884 and mounted a highly
successful new version at Karlsruhe. He completely failed,
however, to grasp the great intrinsic value of the delightful
music, and by entirely reorchestrating it he covered it in a
highly inappropriate Wagnerian mantle. Nevertheless Mottl

did break the ice, and his version—with further alterations by Hermann Levi—was given in Munich the following year, and was soon heard all over Germany. Finally, in 1904, the work was revived by Max Hasse in Weimar in its original form, which was thereafter accepted as the standard version. Cornelius's libretto is unmistakably the work of a poet, and features elegant verses with amusingly elaborate rhymes. It does lack plot and dramatic development, but this is largely compensated for by the enchanting music, which is by turns highly poetic and gaily rhythmic.

DER BARBIER VON BAGDAD (The Barber of Baghdad). Comic opera in two acts by Peter Cornelius. First performance: Weimar, 1858.

Characters: The Caliph—baritone; Baba Mustapha, a Cadi—tenor; Margiana, his daughter—soprano; Bostana, a servant of the Cadi's—mezzo-soprano; Nureddin—tenor; Abul Hassan Ali Ebn Bekar, a barber —bass. Nureddin's servants, friends of the Cadi, people of Baghdad, wailing women and the Caliph's entourage.

Place: Baghdad. Time: legendary.

Act I. A room in Nureddin's house. Nureddin is sick with love and longing for Margiana, the daughter of the Cadi Baba Mustapha. Since he does nothing all day but lie groaning and sighing on his bed, his numerous servants believe he is about to die. Bostana, the confidante of the beautiful Margiana, brings Nureddin a message from his beloved, asking him to visit her that very day, when the Cadi goes to the mosque for his midday prayers. The news cures him at once, and he hastens to prepare himself for the rendezvous. Bostana recommends the barber Abul Hassan Ali Ebn Bekar, who is the epitome of all barbers, old, fat, loquacious, and a veritable fount of learning. He gives Nureddin his horoscope straight away; this is a good day for him to shave, but he must not go out. He talks so much that he does not get down to his job, and in the end Nureddin calls his servants to throw the old chatterbox out, but Abul Hassan defends himself by opening his mighty razor and throwing himself on the frightened men. To prevent a murder, Nureddin dismisses his servants from the room. Abul Hassan finally gets to work, while Nureddin sings of his Margiana. In order to learn more about her, Abul Hassan improvises a love-song, and Nureddin gaily joins in the refrain. The barber is so carried away by the song that he stops shaving again. In desperation Nureddin begs him to finish the job, and explains why he is in such a hurry. In this way the barber learns that Margiana is the daughter of the Cadi, an enemy of his, because he shaves himself. He implores Nureddin to let him accompany him to the rendezvous, since any excursion might be dangerous for the young man today. This however is too much for Nureddin, who calls his servants together and orders them to put the barber to bed. The servants take great delight in holding down the angry old man while Nureddin makes his escape.

Act II. A hall in the Cadi's house. Margiana and Bostana are singing 'Er kommt, er kommt, o Wonne meiner Brust' ('He comes, he comes, beloved of my heart'), their thoughts on Nureddin. The Cadi joins in their song, but he is thinking of the arrival of his friend Selim from Damascus, who will bring rich treasure and ask for Margiana's hand in marriage. A chest full of rich presents does in fact arrive, and Margiana dutifully echoes her father's exclamations of delight. The Muezzin's call summons the people to prayer. At last the Cadi goes out, and Bostana hurries off to inform Nureddin, who enters at once and declares his love to Margiana. The barber, who has escaped from Nureddin's servants and wants to keep an eye on his young friend, starts singing his love-song from below, which distracts Nureddin and Margiana in their love-making. Suddenly there is a great clamour outside; the Cadi has returned and is punishing a slave for his clumsiness by beating him. Nureddin cannot escape, and the women hide him in the treasure-chest which they quickly empty. The slave's cries bring in the barber, who believes that Nureddin is being beaten, and enters with some of Nureddin's servants to rescue him. Although Bostana explains that Nureddin is lying hidden in the chest, Abul Hassan is convinced that his corpse has been concealed there, but just as the servants are carrying out the chest the Cadi returns and accuses the barber of robbery. The barber retaliates with accusations of murder, and people come in from the street, together with mourning women and friends of the Cadi, all of which adds to the general confusion. When the tumult is at its peak the Caliph enters with his bodyguard. Ignoring the accusations now addressed to him, he orders Margiana to open the chest and display her 'Schatz' (which can mean 'treasure', or 'darling'). There is universal consternation when the chest is opened to reveal Nureddin's senseless body. Abul Hassan revives him with his song and the smell of a rose given by Margiana. The Caliph pronounces judgment: the Cadi himself has said that the chest contained Margiana's 'treasure', and this is Nureddin. The Caliph invites the barber to go with him, and Abul starts a song of praise to the Caliph 'Heil diesem Hause' ('Blessed be this house') and all join in the refrain 'Salem aleikum'.

The text is dramatically unambitious but spiced with lovely verses, while the music is artistically constructed and of great charm. A tender fervour fills the love theme, an inspired

romantic melody closely related to Schumann's idiom. How different is the barber's improvised love-song, which exactly

catches the old braggart's boastful tone. Characterization in a few strokes is Cornelius's special skill and the best example is Abul Hassan's theme as the vocal line first introduces it.

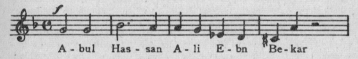

Equally impressive is the Muezzin's call, on which is built the

prelude to the second act, and which then recurs frequently in the course of the action. Finally a word about the many catchy tunes which keep the fun moving; for instance, the duet between Nureddin and Bostana with its lively rhythm, which

breaks up the melancholy mood of the first scene, introduces
the comic spirit which is maintained to the end of the opera.

Der Widerspänstigen Zähmung, by Hermann Goetz (1840–76)
is also an outstanding work.

DER WIDERSPÄNSTIGEN ZÄHMUNG (The Taming of the Shrew).
Comic opera in four acts by Hermann Goetz. Text after William
Shakespeare by Joseph Viktor Widmann. First performance: Mannheim,
1874.

Characters: Baptista, a rich Paduan nobleman—bass; Katharina and
Bianca, his daughters—sopranos; Hortensio and Lucentio, Bianca's
suitors—baritone and tenor; Petruchio, a nobleman from Verona—
baritone; Grumio, his servant—bass; a tailor—tenor; a steward—tenor;
a housekeeper—contralto. Wedding guests, and servants to Petruchio
and Baptista.

Place: Padua. Time: seventeenth century.

Act I. A street in Padua outside Baptista's house. It is late evening.
Lucentio tries to serenade his beloved Bianca, but is interrupted by the
noise coming from Baptista's house. The servants run out excitedly into
the street, unable to stand life any longer in the house, which is ruled by
the unbearably headstrong and bad-tempered Katharina, and they all
give notice. Baptista finally manages to calm his servants with offers of
money, wine and kind words, although Katharina shouts indignant
protests to him from the balcony. When everyone has gone back into the
house, Lucentio resumes his serenade. Bianca comes on to the balcony
and joyfully accepts his adoration, but just then old Hortensio enters with
a group of musicians, driving Bianca back into the house. Hortensio is
also courting Bianca, to the fury of Lucentio who does not like his serenade at all. Attracted by the noise, Baptista comes out and declares that
Bianca as the younger daughter cannot think of marrying until Katharina
is happily married. Hortensio and Lucentio are left disconsolate, but both
of them have the happy inspiration of getting into Baptista's house as a
teacher. Lucentio goes out, and Hortensio is joined by the rich, wild
young Petruchio, one of his old acquaintances. When he hears about the
wilful Katharina he decides to court her himself.

Act II. Baptista's house. Katharina has no sympathy for her love-sick
sister: 'Ich will mich keinem geben' ('I'll give myself to no one') she
proudly sings. Baptista is delighted to receive a visit from the rich
Petruchio who asks for Katharina's hand. Petruchio now introduces
Hortensio under the name of Cembaloni as a music-master, while
Lucentio introduces himself as a teacher of languages. They are both to
start teaching at once and they go out to find the girls. Baptista warns
Petruchio of Katharina, but he is unmoved, even when Hortensio rushes
in, complaining that Katharina has behaved very badly to him and broken
the lute over his head. When Katharina comes in, Petruchio repeats his
offer of marriage to her, and refuses to take her emphatic 'No' seriously.
His domineering manner clearly makes an impression on Katharina, who
has never come across a man like this before. Finally Petruchio seizes her

and kisses her. When Baptista and the others return Petruchio announces bluntly that the wedding will take place the following Monday.

Act III. A room in Baptista's house. Katharina in her bridal attire is waiting in vain for her bridegroom. The wedding-guests arrive, but finally leave again, since there can be no wedding without. Only Hortensio and Lucentio stay, to give Bianca further instruction. Lucentio has brought a volume of Virgil and from it he translates a fervent declaration of love. Bianca proves an apt pupil, as her translation also resembles a declaration of love. On the other hand she treats Hortensio so badly that he decides not to concern himself with her any more. Baptista enters with the joyful news that Petruchio is on his way. Katharina also appears, justifiably indignant at the humiliation she has suffered at his hands. Petruchio comes in making a lot of noise, followed by Grumio, both of them carelessly dressed. Everyone is struck dumb with astonishment, but Petruchio declares that the marriage will be celebrated without further delay. Katharina has no choice but to follow him to church. Meanwhile the servants set the tables for the wedding-feast, but when the wedding procession returns, Petruchio announces that he and Katharina will be leaving immediately. He pays no attention to the remonstrances of her father or of the guests, nor even to Katharina's pleas. When the guests try to force him to stay a while, he draws his sword and with the help of his servant Grumio clears a way through them, dragging Katharina with him.

Act IV. Petruchio's country house. The servants complain to Grumio about the impossible situation in the house, where the young couple do nothing but quarrel and fight. Petruchio and Katharina enter to take their midday meal, but Petruchio declares that the food is inedible and finally throws it all out of the window, although Katharina is already quite exhausted with hunger. Katharina is left alone, her obstinacy broken. In her aria 'Die Kraft versagt, des Kampfes bin ich müde' ('My strength is spent, I'm weary of the struggle') she admits defeat. A tailor is shown in, and displays to her some exquisite new fashions, from which she delightedly makes several purchases, but Petruchio enters, declares that everything she has chosen is ugly and badly made, and finally tramples all the pretty dresses and lace underfoot. The tailor flees. Katharina tearfully acknowledges that her will is broken and she is nothing but his creature, yet can still be happy in that state. After all these torments Petruchio at last drops his mask and tenderly embraces his reformed and gentle wife. Baptista, with Lucentio and Bianca who have meanwhile become man and wife, and Hortensio with his newly-wed bride enter and rejoice at the astonishing change in Katharina and at the young couple's happiness.

It is incomprehensible to a musician that this opera should never have been a popular success. Admittedly German theatre directors have shown their sense of responsibility by repeated revivals of *Der Widerspänstigen Zähmung*, and it is of course quite possible that one day this opera will break through, and in a really good production become a popular attraction, for it contains all the necessary ingredients for success. The vocal writing is splendid and the characterization very marked, so that all the roles are most rewarding. Petruchio's domineering manner is clearly expressed in the theme from his aria at the end of the first act, which also describes his scheme for taming Katharina. A delicate variation on this theme however gives a

glimpse of the tender emotions which may also be hidden beneath his rough exterior. The change in Katharina is perhaps even more vividly portrayed in the music. In her aria of the last act an expressive phrase recurs in the orchestra to describe

the humble love of the tamed shrew. Goetz's main talent is as a master of musical humour, especially in the scenes with Bianca and her suitors where one delightful inspiration closely follows the last; or, for example, the lesson trio or the first act duet which maintains a tone of gay comedy. A comic theme which might have been written by Rossini introduces a charmingly

ironic undertone into the two lovers' reflections, after Baptista has interrupted the serenade in Act I.

Hugo Wolf (1860–1903), the *lieder* composer, wrote only one opera, *Der Corregidor*—a second one, *Manuel Venegas*, was never completed—and it has always been an operatic Cinderella. The text is highly original, but it aroused little interest and the many fascinating details in the music could not compensate for its lack of dramatic strength. The basic quality of the opera, as one would expect from Wolf, is the lyrical vocal music, which predominates throughout the opera in the form of solos, duets or larger ensembles. The vocal passages connecting these *lieder* are models of declamatory style in Wagner's manner, yet always translated into Wolf's very personal emotional realm. Exquisite subtleties of idea and execution distinguish the various preludes and interludes, which are also on a small scale.

DER CORREGIDOR (The Magistrate). Opera in four acts by Hugo Wolf. Text after a story by D'Alarcón by Rosa Mayreder-Obermeyer. First performance: Mannheim, 1896.

Characters: Don Eugenio de Zuniga, the Corregidor (magistrate)—tenor; Juan Lopez, the alcalde (mayor)—bass; Pedro, his secretary—tenor; Tonuelo, a court messenger—bass; Repela, servant to the Corregidor—bass; Tio Lucas, a miller—baritone; a neighbour—tenor; Doña Mercedes, the Corregidor's wife—soprano; Frasquita, the miller's wife—mezzo-soprano; Manuela, maid to the alcalde—mezzo-soprano.

Place: Andalusia. *Time:* beginning of the nineteenth century.

Act I. In front of the mill. Tio Lucas is not pleased at the frequent visits the old Corregidor pays to the mill, but Frasquita laughs him out of his jealousy and suggests he should eavesdrop when next she entertains the Corregidor. When the old man enters, Lucas conceals himself and overhears a fervent declaration of love. In reply Frasquita asks the Corregidor to give her nephew a job as secretary at the court, and he agrees, eager to do anything to obtain her love. When he tries to embrace her she runs away laughing, so that he falls over and the miller has to help him to his feet.

Act II, scene i. The mill kitchen. Tio Lucas is summoned to town by the drunken official messenger, Tonuelo, to wait on the alcalde. Frasquita suspects something unpleasant. She hears cries for help and the Corregidor enters with his clothes saturated. He has fallen into the mill-stream. He again assails Frasquita with expressions of love and shows her the nomination of her nephew as secretary. Since all is of no avail, he draws his pistol, and Frasquita seizes the miller's musket. The Corregidor faints, and Frasquita hurries out to find her husband. The Corregidor recovers consciousness, takes off his wet clothes and lies down in a bed in the adjoining room.

Scene ii. A room in the alcalde's house. The Mayor and his secretary are drinking wine. When Tio Lucas is announced, they are at a loss to know why he has been summoned and invite him to have a drink. The miller realizes that it was all a trick of the Corregidor's. He pretends to be drunk and when they leave him alone he jumps out of the window and hurries away.

Act III, scene i. A wood, at night. Tio Lucas is on his way back to the mill, and Frasquita on her way to town, and they pass each other in the darkness.

Scene ii. Inside the mill. Tio Lucas finds the house unlocked, the Corregidor's clothes in the kitchen and their owner in bed. At first he thinks of killing him, but on reflection decides to pay him out in his own coin. He dresses himself in the Corregidor's clothes and leaves the mill. The Corregidor wakes and since he cannot find his own clothes puts on the miller's instead. The alcalde enters with his officers and Frasquita, whom he has met on the way, to arrest Tio Lucas. They mistake the Corregidor for the miller and thrash him. When the Corregidor manages to make himself known, they all hurry back to the town.

Act IV. A street outside the Corregidor's house. It is early morning. The Corregidor enters and tries to enter his own house, but he is sent away by his servants who point out that the Corregidor came home an hour before and has gone to bed. Mercedes appears on the balcony and behaves as though she has taken her husband for Tio Lucas. The miller also appears, and before he can explain everything to the Corregidor's wife, he is mistaken for the murderer of the Corregidor and also soundly beaten. Day breaks, and all give each other a gay 'Good morning'.

Although *Der Freischütz* and *Der fliegende Holländer* existed as ideal examples for the development of German popular opera, and Lortzing's works existed as a complement on the comic side, this genre never really established itself in the second half of the nineteenth century. Attempts to develop romantic opera along popular lines quickly deteriorated into embarrassing sentimentality. A typical example of such excess is *Der Trompeter von Säckingen* (*The Trumpeter of Säckingen*) (1884), by Viktor Nessler (1841–90). This work was once highly praised, and the melancholy farewell song 'Behüt dich Gott, es wär so schön gewesen' ('Farewell, my love, all hope of joy goes with you') became extremely popular.

Wilhelm Kienzl (1857–1941), who in his early works still leaned heavily on Wagner, trod the path to popular opera with his *Der Evangelimann* (1895) in which he tried to develop his own style, drawing on the examples both of Wagner and of Italian *verismo*.

DER EVANGELIMANN (The Evangelist). Music drama in two acts by
Wilhelm Kienzl. First performance: Berlin, 1895.

Characters: Friedrich Engel, Administrator of the Monastery of St
Othmar—bass; Martha, his niece—soprano; Magdalena, her friend—
contralto; Johannes Freudhofer, a teacher—baritone; Matthias Freudhofer, his brother—tenor; the tailor Zitterbart—tenor; the nightwatch-
man—bass. Members of the bowling club, children.

Place: Benedictine Monastery of St Othmar in Lower Austria, and
Vienna. *Time:* 1820–50.

Act I. The monastery cloisters. Martha, the niece of the monastery
administrator, is being courted by the two brothers Freudhofer. She clearly
prefers the younger, Matthias, and rejects the pressing suit of Johannes
with the words 'Du Schurke, ich verachte dich' ('You scoundrel, I despise
you'). Johannes plots a terrible revenge, and tells Martha's uncle of the
love between his niece and the poor clerk Matthias. Engel dismisses
Matthias from his post and tells him to leave the monastery that very day.
As welcome light relief, the village people meet for their evening at
bowls, during which the tailor Zitterbart, who is constantly being made
fun of, knocks over all nine pins. Meanwhile night has fallen, and
Matthias and Martha meet to bid each other farewell and to vow eternal
fidelity. Johannes, who has been spying on them, sets fire to the threshing
floor near which they are sitting. Everyone hurries in to put out the
flames. Suspicion falls on Matthias; the labourers and farmers try to
lynch him and the administrator has him arrested.

Act II, scene i. A courtyard in Vienna. Thirty years have passed. In
spite of his protestations of innocence Matthias was condemned to twenty
years imprisonment and after serving his sentence learned that Martha,
in her despair, had drowned herself in the Danube. Having been unable
to find work anywhere, since no one would help an ex-convict, he
became an evangelist, going from house to house preaching the Bible and
receiving some small gifts in return. So he has come to the courtyard of
the house in Vienna where his brother Johannes lives with Magdalena
as his housekeeper. Matthias reads from the gospel 'Selig sind, die Ver-
folgung leiden' ('Blest are they that are persecuted'). Some children
enter, and Matthias makes them repeat the words from the Scriptures and
then sing the whole verse with him. He reveals his identity to Magdalena,
and tells her of his sufferings and of how he became an evangelist.

Scene ii. A room in Johannes Freudhofer's house. Johannes is on his
deathbed. He is consumed with remorse and the thought of his terrible
guilt will not let him die in peace. Through the open window he hears
the voice of the evangelist, and believes he recognizes it. He asks Magdalena to bring in the holy street-singer. The brothers recognize each other,
and Johannes confesses his crime. After a great inner struggle Matthias
pardons his brother. Johannes dies, while the children's singing is heard
through the window.

Kienzl's strong dramatic sense and feeling for popular humour
explain the original great success of *Der Evangelimann* in

German-speaking countries. The highly entertaining bowling scene starts with slow polka rhythms and reaches its climax in a lively waltz. In spite of the sugary love-duet this extremely dramatic first act should still be effective today, though it is questionable whether the second act with its almost embarrassing sentimentality is still tolerable. However, the evangelist's song is still very impressive.

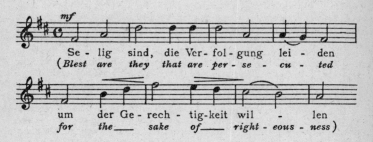

Se - lig sind, die Ver - fol - gung lei - den
(*Blest are they that are per - se - cu - ted*

um der Ge - rech - tig-keit wil - len
for the___ sake of___ right - eous - ness)

Engelbert Humperdinck (1854–1921) followed a path similar to Kienzl's in that he avoided empty imitation of Wagner and chose a popular fairy-tale for the basis of his libretto. *Hänsel und Gretel* (1893) was the most successful opera from among Wagner's immediate successors. Humperdinck goes back to the romantic woodland atmosphere of *Siegfried*, but Wagner's musical language and particularly his over rich orchestration do not always suit this childlike, naïve story. These defects cannot however destroy the pure fairy-tale atmosphere which gives the score its charm. The most enchanting passages of the opera are the various children's songs scattered through the score—a delight to young and old alike. *Hänsel und Gretel* is a classic international repertory opera.

HÄNSEL UND GRETEL. Fairy-tale in three scenes by Engelbert Humperdinck. Text by Adelheid Wette. First performance: Weimar, 1893.

Characters: Peter, a broom-maker—baritone; Gertrude, his wife—mezzo-soprano; Hänsel and Gretel, their children—mezzo-soprano and soprano; the witch—mezzo-soprano; the sandman—soprano; the dew fairy—soprano.

Act I. The broom-maker's hut. Hänsel and Gretel are passing the time while their mother is away singing and dancing instead of knitting and making brooms. Their mother, Gertrude, comes in and chases the two lazy children into the wood to look for berries. Exhausted and hungry, Gertrude falls asleep with her head on the table. The broom-maker, Peter, returns home, rather drunk. He has had a good day selling his brooms and has brought back food and drink for supper. He is horrified when his wife tells him that she has sent the children into the wood, which is inhabited by the wicked witch. The mother rushes desperately out to look for the children, and the father, seizing his bottle of liquor, goes after her.

Act II. In the wood. While Gretel is making a little garland and singing, Hänsel is gathering strawberries. A cuckoo is heard, and the children imitate his call as they fill their mouths with berries until the whole basket is empty. It has gradually become dark, and Gretel is frightened; Hänsel tries to reassure her, but he too is afraid. The children's shouts return to them as echoes. The sandman comes and sprinkles sand in their eyes. The tired children kneel down, sing their evening prayer and soon fall asleep. Fourteen guardian angels, as they had sung in their hymn, descend to stand guard over them.

Act III. Dawn is breaking. The mist rises slowly, and the dew-fairy comes to awaken the children. They greet the morning cheerfully, and then tell each other their wonderful dreams. It is now completely light, and in the sunshine glitters a little house made of cake and sugar, surrounded by a hedge of gingerbread children. Hänsel and Gretel at first stand still in amazement, then they venture nearer, and finally Hänsel can stand it no longer and breaks a piece of cake off the little house. From the house they hear the witch's voice, but the sugar-cake tastes so good that the children cannot stop their nibbling. The witch creeps out from the house and throws a rope round Hänsel's neck. With honeyed words she tells the children how she loves them. Hänsel manages to free himself from the rope and tries to run away with Gretel, but the witch casts a spell over them so that they cannot move. Hänsel is locked up in a cage to be fattened, and Gretel is to help in the kitchen. Gretel however succeeds in breaking the spell the witch has cast on Hänsel, by using the witch's magic juniper branch and repeating the magic words. The witch lights the oven and then rides round the house on her broomstick. Gretel is told to look into the oven and see how the fire is going, but she pretends to be stupid and asks the witch to show her how to put her head through the wide oven door. Gretel and Hänsel, who has crept out of his cage, push the witch into the oven and shut the door behind her. The children sing and dance for joy. The oven explodes with an enormous bang, and the gingerbread coverings fall from the children in the hedge. Their spell is broken with the magic branch and they join Hänsel and Gretel in a merry dance. The parents arrive and share in their rejoicing. Meanwhile the children have found that the witch herself has turned into gingerbread in the oven. The father seriously points out that this is the judgment of Heaven, and to the solemn notes of the evening hymn they all sing 'Wenn der Not aufs höchste steigt, Gott der Herr die Hand uns reicht' ('When past bearing is our grief, God the Lord will send relief').

The simple, chorale tune of the evening prayer is the principal
theme of the opera, with which the well-known overture starts

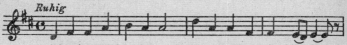

A-bends,will ich schlafen gehn,vier-zehn En-gel um mich stehn
(*When at night I   go   to sleep, Four-teen an-gels watch do keep*)

and finishes, and which recurs repeatedly in the course of the
three scenes. This melody, which embodies the idea of heaven,
is contrasted with the two themes of the witch's ride and her
sinister question, 'Knusper, Knusper, Knäuschen' ('Nibble,

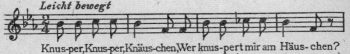

Knus-per,Knus-per,Knäus-chen,Wer knus-pert mir am Häus- chen?
(*Nib-ble, nib-ble,mouse-kin,Who's nib-bling at my house-kin?*)

nibble, mousekin'). Folk songs, dance tunes and woodland
verses on the other hand characterize the children's world.
Humperdinck's music is direct and simple and finds its way
straight to the heart of the listener, but when one studies the
score more closely one sees how skilfully it is constructed, and
how delicate is its symphonic pattern.

Humperdinck's second successful opera, *Königskinder*, unfortunately lacks the originality of *Hänsel und Gretel*, due to
the rather self-consciously intellectual text, but it is still a fairy-
tale of great charm and depth. In the love-duets, in the fiddler's
songs, and in the three admirable preludes, Humperdinck has
poured out the best of his wonderful melodies and luxurious
harmonies. Nevertheless *Königskinder* has scarcely penetrated
outside Germany despite the fact that it enjoyed an American
première. Humperdinck's four other operas are now completely
forgotten.

KÖNIGSKINDER (The Royal Children). Musical fairy-tale in three
scenes by Engelbert Humperdinck. Text by Ernst Rosmer. First performance: New York, 1910.

Characters: The Prince—tenor; the goose-girl—soprano; the witch—contralto; the fiddler—baritone; the woodcutter—bass; the innkeeper—bass; his daughter—mezzo-soprano; the stable-girl—contralto.

Place: Hellawald and Hellabrunn. *Time:* The Middle Ages.

Act I. The goose-girl lives in a lonely hut with the witch, who orders her to bake a magic loaf: whoever eats half of it will die. The goose-girl has never seen a human being and is therefore deeply impressed at the sight of the Prince, who has come into the dark wood in search of adventure. The young people fall in love with each other. He gives her his crown and wants to take her away with him, but she is bound by a spell and cannot follow him. The fiddler appears with the woodcutter and the broom-maker to ask the witch on behalf of the townspeople who will be their king. The witch replies that whoever enters the town on the following day at the sound of the midday bells, will be their king. The two workmen go away, but the fiddler stays behind to find out who the beautiful girl is who lives in the witch's hut. The goose-girl tells him about the Prince, whom she cannot follow. The fiddler has the skill to free her from the evil spell, and she joyfully hurries away.

Act II. A square outside the gates of the town of Hellabrunn. All the town is awaiting the arrival of the new king at the sound of the midday bells. The Prince, who entered the town in the middle of the night, has found accommodation in the innkeeper's pigsty. The innkeeper's daughter is much impressed by the handsome young man, but he can only think of the goose-girl, and is quite indifferent to the wealthy innkeeper's daughter. Among the crowd the woodcutter and the broom-maker arrive, the latter with his numerous children. The broom-maker's smallest daughter offers the Prince a broom; since he cannot pay, they dance together instead. Meanwhile the town councillors have entered to welcome the king, whom they all imagine wearing splendid robes and seated in a coach. When the Prince suggests that even a king might wear simple garments he is laughed at as a fool. At the sound of the midday bells the gate opens, and there stands the goose-girl, the crown on her head, surrounded by her geese, with the fiddler at her side. The Prince goes to her and greets her as his queen. At first they all laugh, then they become furious at this 'deceit' and try to throw themselves on the girl, but the Prince draws his sword and takes his stand in front of her. People crowd in on them from all sides, and the fiddler vainly tries to calm the crowd, who chase the royal children out of the gates with stones. The stage is soon empty, except for the broom-maker's little girl who is in tears. Asked by the elder councillor why she is crying, she sobs 'They were the king and queen'.

Act III. The woodland clearing as in Act I. It is midwinter. The fiddler is living in the hut now that the witch has been burnt by the inhabitants of Hellabrunn. They have also beaten the fiddler until he is crippled, but they now want him back in the town, and he is ready to go there for the children's sake. First he wants to look for the royal children once more and, accompanied by the children, he sets out. The woodcutter and the broom-maker return to the hut. Over the hillside the Prince and the goose-girl are climbing down towards the hut, half frozen and starving.

The Prince has lost the way back to his father and mother and their kingdom and is appalled at the misery to which he has brought his beloved. She dances and sings to show him that she is well, but then collapses, exhausted. The Prince gives his crown to the woodcutter in exchange for some stale bread. It is the witch's magic loaf. Suspecting nothing, the Prince and the goose-girl devour the bread, and locked in each other's arms they sink dreamily into the sleep of death. This is how the fiddler and the children find them. They make a litter of pine branches, and lay the two bodies on it. The litter is slowly carried out towards the setting sun, the children following as mourners, while their cry 'Royal children' dies away in the distance.

Another representative of German fairy-tale opera is Siegfried Wagner (1869–1930). As a pupil of Humperdinck he very soon found that this was his special talent, and scored considerable success with his first work *Der Bärenhäuter* (*The Sluggard*) (1899). Siegfried Wagner was a tragic personality: as the son of Richard Wagner, the far-reaching Wagnerian movement at Bayreuth helped his career, but on the other hand he was handicapped by living in his father's shadow. Siegfried's talent should not however be underestimated. It is best to pass over his later works, *Sternengebot* (*The Command of the Stars*) and *Schwarzschwanenreich* (*The Realm of the Black Swan*), but he created a number of graceful and engaging episodes in his gay fairy-tale operas, especially in *An allem ist Hütchen schuld* (*It is all Hütchen's doing*) (1917).

THE CLASSICAL OPERETTA

Although the origins of operetta can be traced through the development of the *Singspiel* and of *opéra comique*, a new genre only came into being in the second half of the nineteenth century; it was in fact born in 1858, the year of the first performance of *Orphée aux Enfers* by Offenbach. The satirical undertones and social criticism which Offenbach consciously introduced into *Orphée* and his later works marked out this new genre as something apart from comic opera, and thereafter these two art-forms grew increasingly away from each other.

The source from which Offenbach's operettas sprang was *The Beggars' Opera* of 1728, which contains all the elements

Offenbach was to use with the same great success one hundred
and thirty years later. *The Beggars' Opera* was also a satirical
work of bitter social criticism and operatic parody. Light songs
to rhyming texts took the place of grandiose arias, and all the
characteristics of Offenbach's epoch-making works were
already clearly incorporated here. There is also a curious parallel
in their further development, for just as the satirical vein of
The Beggars' Opera was completely lost in the *Singspiel* and the
French *opéra comique* which followed, and was replaced with a
bourgeois sentimentality, so Offenbach's mocking spirit was
swallowed up in the sentimentality of the later Viennese
operettas of the 1870's. This first great generation of operetta
is generally known as the period of classical operetta; it includes
the works of Offenbach and his circle, as well as the period of
the three great Viennese masters of operetta, Millöcker, Suppé
and Johann Strauss the Younger, together with a few attractive
minor composers such as Zeller and Genée.

Originally operetta was hardly distinguishable in form from
comic opera; indeed the first operettas are still called comic
operas, just as in the days of the *Singspiel* works by Hiller and
Neefe were occasionally called operettas. The external characteristics of the two forms are still imprecisely defined, and the
border between them is somewhat blurred.

Offenbach's satires and parodies were expressed to a great
extent in dancing, and this was also a vital part of Viennese
operetta. Thus the cancan characterizes Offenbach's work, and
the light, sentimental waltzes that of the Viennese. As operetta
developed, dances assumed a more important place in them.
The operatic arias and duets became flowing, rhythmical songs
to rhyming texts, and to these lesser elements were added
ensembles and extensive finales. Besides the cancan and the
waltz, operettas were often enlivened by the polka-mazurka,
the 'rheinländer' and the gallop; then there were the various
national dances, from the *csárdás* and the polonaise to the bolero
and the tarantella. As a matter of course all fashionable dances
soon found their way into operetta, which as a result became
increasingly a reflection of social development. This fashionable
element gradually became the most salient feature of operetta,
and the sentimental fairy-tales of happy love of the classical
operettas gave way to fantasies of good-living and sophisticated

flirtation, until the spirit of classical operetta completely disappeared.

Jacques Offenbach (1819–80) is rightly considered the father of operetta. His first successes were one-act *Singspiele* which he called 'Musiquettes', but his first full-length work, *Orphée aux Enfers*, marked the beginning of operetta. Its first performance created an unprecedented sensation. The witty text—a burlesque of gods and heroes in which Paris society recognized itself—was set to a wealth of honeyed melodies and irresistible rhythms. The audience was fascinated and completely overwhelmed under this onslaught of whirling vitality.

ORPHÉE AUX ENFERS (Orpheus in the Underworld). Burlesque operetta in two acts by Jacques Offenbach. Text by Hector Crémieux and Ludovic Halévy. First performance: Paris, 1858.

Characters: Pluto, god of the Underworld, on earth alias Aristée—tenor; Jupiter, King of the gods—baritone; Orphée, a violinist—tenor; Eurydice, his wife—soprano; John Styx, a fool—baritone; L'Opinion Publique—mezzo-soprano. Gods and goddesses, etc.

Place: Greece. *Time:* legendary.

Act I, scene i. Orpheus, violinist and director of the Music Academy at Thebes, is not happy with his wife Eurydice. He is wrapped up in his music, in which she takes very little interest. They have both fallen in love with someone else. The object of Eurydice's affections is the shepherd and bee-keeper, Aristée, who is in fact Pluto, King of the Underworld. After a quarrel with her husband, Eurydice easily falls a victim to Pluto's charms and agrees to go with him to the Underworld. This suits Orpheus well enough, but Public Opinion, an elderly, moralizing aunt, threatens him with terrible scandal if he does not try to get her back. She and Orpheus, the latter complaining bitterly, set off on their journey.

Scene ii. Mount Olympus. The gods are peacefully asleep. On waking they murmur rebelliously against Jupiter's highhanded interference in their affairs. When news comes that Pluto has abducted Eurydice, Jupiter tries to rebuke him, and all join in open defiance of their leader. When Orpheus enters to make his complaint to Jupiter, Pluto denies having had any hand in the abduction of Eurydice. Orpheus's plea for her return immediately appeals to the gods. They take up the song, Jupiter insists that Pluto should return her to her husband, and they all decide to descend to the Underworld.

Act II, scene i. Eurydice's boudoir in the Underworld. Eurydice is hopelessly bored, and her only companion is the tedious John Styx. He keeps telling her how he was once King of Boetia. Pluto hides Eurydice from the gods, but disguised as a fly Jupiter succeeds in charming her and finally admits his identity.

Scene ii. The gates of Hell. Pluto offers the gods a magnificent party where nectar flows in streams and the cancan unchains the Spirits. Jupiter is about to go off with Eurydice, whom he has changed into a bacchante, but Pluto stops them. Just then Orpheus and Public Opinion make their appearance and ask Eurydice to return with them. For better or for worse, Jupiter must give up his enchanting companion, but he makes the condition that Orpheus should not turn back to look at his wife. Orpheus agrees to this, and led by Public Opinion he starts on his way, but Jupiter throws a thunderbolt at him and Orpheus involuntarily looks round, thus losing Eurydice for ever. Happy with this solution he hastens back to Thebes and Eurydice stays on as a bacchante.

Orphée was the first of Offenbach's great successes and quickly became established in the repertories of the main European theatres. This success was principally due to the music, since the text lost a great deal in translation and was based too much on Parisian life and atmosphere to be really effective elsewhere. Offenbach's music on the contrary has a charm which is independent of the words and plot, and the vivacity of his dance-tunes is irresistible.

Offenbach's second successful operetta, *La Belle Hélène*, was also a burlesque, this time of Greek heroes instead of Olympian deities. Again Parisian high society could recognize itself in amusing and captivating caricatures. In the frenzied cancan the light-hearted Parisian quest for pleasure was convincingly expressed, and nobody was worried by the often pungent and serious satire which held up a mirror to the superficiality of the day. The Empress Eugénie herself referred to the brilliant epoch of the Third Empire as 'just one great Offenbach operetta'.

LA BELLE HÉLÈNE (The Beautiful Helen). Burlesque operetta in three acts by Jacques Offenbach. Text by Henri Meilhac and Ludovic Halévy. First performance: Paris, 1864.
    Characters: Menelaus, King of Sparta—baritone; Hélène, his wife—soprano; Paris, King Priam's son—tenor; Agamemnon, King of Greece—baritone; Calchas, Great Soothsayer to Jupiter—bass; Ajax I, Ajax II and others.

Place: Sparta. *Time:* before the Trojan war.

Act I. The forecourt of the temple of Jupiter in Sparta. The High Priest, Calchas, enters, bemoaning the fact that the people of Sparta are neglecting their worship of the gods. Venus, however, is still popular, particularly since her recent action in promising the most beautiful woman in the world (Helen, wife of Menelaus, King of Sparta) to a shepherd, who was in fact Paris, one of the sons of King Priam of Troy, in disguise. With this promise she had bribed him, in a contest with Juno and Minerva, to give her his Golden Apple. Helen enters, very excited at the rumours about the Judgment of Paris, but concerned about her reputation. When Paris, still disguised as a shepherd, comes in, she is instantly attracted to him. The kings of Greece now enter to compete in an Intelligence Test, but Paris easily defeats them all, and to Helen's delight reveals himself as the Prince of Troy and therefore the man to whom Venus promised Helen's love. Calchas then stages a thunderstorm and declares to Menelaus that it is the wish of the gods that he should go to Crete. This will enable Venus's promise to Paris to be more easily fulfilled.

Act II. Helen's bedchamber in the palace in Sparta. A banquet is to be given for the visiting kings, but because of her husband's absence Helen insists on wearing her most modest dress. Paris enters and tells her that in order to win her without compromising her he will use discretion and intrigue. The kings enter with Calchas to take part in a game of chance at Helen's invitation, and when it is over (after a great fuss over Calchas's cheating) she retires to bed, rather than go to the banquet where she is bound to meet Paris. Calchas agrees to send her a beautiful dream of the young shepherd, and when Paris shortly afterwards appears at her side, having taken the place of one of the guards, Helen pretends to herself that this is Calchas's promised dream. Menelaus unexpectedly returns, and filled with righteous indignation he calls on the other kings to see how he has been betrayed, and they drive Paris out.

Act III. The promenade at Nauplia. The Spartan court has already moved to the seaside for the summer, although it is still early in the year, because Helen hopes that at Nauplia she may be able to forget the unhappy episode with Paris, which her husband refuses to believe was only a dream. Clearly the Goddess of Love is angry with the Spartan people, because everybody's love affairs are going wrong. Agamemnon decides that Venus must be placated, and obviously the King must make the necessary sacrifice. Calchas announces that he has called on the high priest of Venus to help in this matter, and a ship arrives, bearing a stately, bearded form, who disembarks and declares that at Venus's command he must take Helen to Cythera with him. Menelaus has to agree, but once Helen and the high priest have embarked on his ship the latter reveals himself as Paris, and sails away with Helen to Troy.

Offenbach wrote more than a hundred operettas, all of which were first produced in Paris. The one-act *Singspiele*, some of which were quite charming, are now almost completely forgotten, though a few of them, such as *Le Mariage aux Lanternes*

(*The Lantern Marriage*) and *La Chanson de Fortunio* (*Fortunio's Song*) survived for a time. Among his full-length operettas *La Vie Parisienne*, a sort of satirical tourist guide to the elegant Paris of the Third Empire, and *La Grande Duchesse de Gerolstein*, a parody on life in the small German States, also deserve a mention.

Offenbach had a secret passion for opera. This celebrated master of musical satire, who could whip up real frenzy with his cancan, felt continually drawn towards it. In 1860 his three-act opera *Barkouf* was performed at the Opéra-Comique, but it was a failure because of its inadequate text, and his other attempts in this field, *Rheinixe* (*The Rhine Maidens*) and *Boule de Neige* (*The Snowball*) were equally unsuccessful. Shortly before he died, however, Offenbach wrote *Les Contes d'Hoffmann*, though the orchestration had to be completed by Ernest Guiraud after his death and he did not live to enjoy the extraordinary success of this unusual work.

Les Contes d'Hoffmann turned the well-known German romantic poet E. T. A. Hoffmann into an operatic hero, who lives through three of his famous fantasies. An opponent to Hoffmann is introduced into the libretto in the form of the scheming Councillor Lindorf, who appears as the hero's evil genius in each act in the varied guises of Coppelius, Dappertutto and Dr Miracle. The original intention was to give the three female roles to the same singer, but it is preferable to cast them separately in order to differentiate between these varied and individual characters. The French librettist, Barbier, transposed the action (i.e. the setting of the prologue and epilogue) to Nuremberg, though the name of the innkeeper Luther clearly indicates Berlin, where Hoffmann was a regular customer in the wine-cellar of Luther and Wegener.

LES CONTES D'HOFFMANN (The Tales of Hoffmann). Fantastic opera in three acts, a prologue and an epilogue by Jacques Offenbach. Text by Jules Barbier after the play by Barbier and Carré founded on E. T. A. Hoffmann. First performance: Paris, 1881.

Characters: Hoffmann—tenor; Nicklausse, his companion—mezzo-soprano; Lindorf, a councillor, Coppelius, a scientist, Dappertutto, a sorcerer, Dr Miracle, a doctor—baritone (one performer); Andrès, Cochenille and Frantz, servants, Pittichinaccio, an admirer of Giulietta—tenor (one performer); Olympia, a mechanical doll—soprano, Giulietta, a courtesan—soprano, Antonia—soprano, Stella, an opera singer—

speaking role (originally one performer); Spalanzani, an inventor—
tenor; Schlemil, Giulietta's lover—bass; Crespel, Antonia's father, a
Munich councillor—baritone; the voice of Antonia's mother—contralto;
Luther, an innkeeper—bass; the Muse of Poetry—soprano. Students,
Spalanzani's guests, Giulietta's friends.

Prologue. Luther's tavern in Nuremberg. Hoffmann is in love with
the beautiful singer Stella. During the interval after the first act of
Mozart's *Don Giovanni*, in which Stella is singing Donna Anna, Hoffmann and Nicklausse join some student friends in the adjoining tavern,
but the presence of Councillor Lindorf puts Hoffmann in a bad mood.
To Lindorf's malicious pleasure he starts to get drunk. His friends urge
Hoffmann to sing the song of the dwarf Kleinzack, and in the middle of
it he drifts into a reverie on Stella's beauty and has to be brought back
to earth by his friends. The thought of Stella reminds him of his three
earlier loves, the doll Olympia, the courtesan Giulietta and the singer
Antonia, whose different personalities all seem to be incorporated in
Stella. Hoffmann's friends press him to tell them about his adventures,
and he willingly begins 'The name of the first was Olympia'.

Act I. The drawing-room of Spalanzani's house. Spalanzani has constructed a mechanical doll, so perfect that he decides to introduce her
into society as his daughter Olympia. Hoffmann has fallen in love with
this incredibly beautiful creature without suspecting that she is lifeless.
Spalanzani had enlisted the help of a miraculous scientist Coppelius to
make the doll's eyes, but now, drawing a cheque on a bank which has
already failed, he buys from Coppelius the latter's half-share in the doll.
When Olympia is introduced to Spalanzani's assembled friends, she
immediately makes a wonderful impression. She sings a brilliant aria,
thanks to a device inside her, but has to be wound up several times.
Finally she dances a waltz with Hoffmann, but moves faster and faster so
that he falls exhausted to the floor. Olympia is taken to an adjoining room
and soon after noises and cries issue from it. Spalanzani's servant comes
in saying that Coppelius, in his fury at the worthless cheque, has broken
the doll in pieces. Hoffmann is bitterly disillusioned to learn that his love
was only a doll.

Act II. Giulietta's palazzo on the Grand Canal in Venice. The beautiful
but cold Giulietta is utterly dominated by the demoniac Dappertutto.
She has already, on Dappertutto's orders, captured the shadow of her
lover, Schlemil, and with it his soul, and her master now commands her
to do the same to Hoffmann by making him look into the magic mirror.
Hoffmann learns that Schlemil still has the key to Giulietta's house, and
beside himself with jealousy he challenges Schlemil to an immediate
duel. Schlemil is fatally wounded, but as Hoffmann seizes the key and
rushes off to Giulietta, she is seen floating down the canal in a gondola
with Pittichinaccio, her hunch-back admirer, at her side.

Act III. A room in Crespel's house. Antonia, Crespel's only child, has
a wonderful voice, but he will not allow her to sing for fear that, like her
mother who was a celebrated singer, the exertion might exhaust her and
cause her early death. He is also afraid of Hoffmann's influence on her,
and has brought her to Munich to escape his attentions. Antonia and

Hoffmann love each other and, thinking of her father's warning, Hoffmann also implores Antonia to give up her singing. The terrible Dr Miracle, who in Crespel's opinion was guilty of Antonia's mother's death, gets into the house in spite of Crespel's instructions and tries to induce Antonia to sing. He describes to her in glowing colours the life of an artist; the picture of Antonia's mother seems to come to life and a voice from it also urges her to sing. Dr Miracle seizes a violin and plays to her enticingly. Bewitched, Antonia starts to sing with exquisite skill and beauty until she falls dead. Hoffmann and Crespel rush in to find her body. Dr Miracle bursts into demoniac laughter and vanishes.

Epilogue. Luther's tavern as in the prologue. Hoffmann has finished his tales and his audience is deeply moved. The performance of *Don Giovanni* has already finished, and Stella enters to meet Hoffmann. With a contemptuous sneer Lindorf points to the poet, completely drunk at the table. Stella turns away in disgust and leaves the inn on Lindorf's arm.

The original production at the Opéra-Comique omitted the Venice scene, which in the score comes *after* the Antonia scene. When the work was revived in Paris in 1893, it was restored but in the wrong place, *before* the Antonia scene. The score was arranged by Maximilian Morris for the Berlin production in 1905, not only with this wrong order retained, but with the barcarolle sung by Giulietta and Nicklausse as a love-duet. Morris also changed the whole point of the opera by altering the Epilogue. These and other drastic changes have been done away with in some recent revivals, for example at Covent Garden in 1954, and in East Berlin (by Felsenstein) in 1958.

Offenbach lavished a wealth of caressing and lovely melodies on this opera. The doll's song, with its staccato rhythms and fluent coloraturas, and the brilliant waltz drawn from it melodically and rhythmically, makes the greatest effect. The Venice episode contains the famous barcarolle and Dappertutto's mirror aria. The final act reaches, if possible, even greater heights. Besides the delicate love-song it contains the exciting

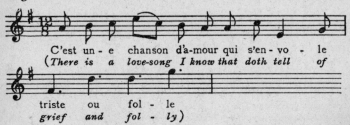

melody with which the mother's voice calls on her daughter in the great trio for Antonia, her mother's voice and Dr Miracle. This same tune recurs most effectively during the act. Offenbach's recitatives are often flat and undramatic, yet he attains strong effects by means of lyrical expression, and the success of this opera is the success of its melodies.

Besides Offenbach the period of classical Paris operetta is represented by a series of talented composers whose best works can still be heard in French theatres. Names such as Alexandre Charles Lecocq (1832–1918) with his *La Fille de Madame Angot*, Edmond Audran (1842–1901) with *La Poupette*, Robert Planquette (1848–1903) with *Les Cloches de Corneville*, and André Messager (1853–1929) with *Véronique*, were also well known outside France at the turn of the century. But Offenbach's biting satire and the fiery exaltation of his music are absent from these contemporaries, whose scores however are all most carefully constructed. The marked preference for dance rhythms is almost the only element which distinguishes these operettas from the comic operas of the time.

The first Offenbach work to reach Vienna was the one-act *Le Mariage aux Lanternes*, which was performed there with great success in 1858. Other one-acters soon followed, and in 1860 *Orphée* reached Vienna in triumph. The ground was well prepared for Offenbach's style by the Viennese *Singspiele* and farces which had always contained elements of parody. Offenbach went to Vienna in person to rehearse the first Viennese performance of each of his full-scale operettas, and his very presence aroused great enthusiasm and a commensurate rise in box-office takings.

It was natural that the exceptional financial success of Offenbach's operettas should have made Viennese theatre directors turn their thoughts to a native operetta which would compete successfully with the imported products. Johann Strauss the Younger (1825–99) was at that time already world-famous as a composer of waltzes which were played everywhere.

In 1871 Johann Strauss's first operetta *Indigo und die Vierzig Räuber* (*Indigo and the Forty Thieves*) appeared. Though the first performance was a sensational occasion, the work did not live up to expectations. The text was unsatisfactory, and compared with the Offenbach operettas which could be heard at that time in Vienna it made a poor showing. In spite of the attractive waltzes the public did not yet grasp the essentially Viennese character of this music, and so *Indigo* disappeared from the repertory. In 1906 it was revived with a completely new libretto under the title *Tausend und eine Nacht*. This new version was and still is successful. The conclusive breakthrough, however, for Viennese operetta with its recognition as an original, independent genre, came in 1874 with the first performance of *Die Fledermaus*, which was instantaneously appreciated and acclaimed. This heralded the arrival of the Viennese operetta as an art-form of international standing.

DIE FLEDERMAUS (The Bat). Operetta in three acts by Johann Strauss. Text by Karl Haffner and Richard Genée after the French comedy *Le Réveillon* by Meilhac and Halévy. First performance: Vienna, 1874.

Characters: Gabriel von Eisenstein—tenor; Rosalinda, his wife—soprano; Frank, governor of the prison—baritone; Prince Orlofsky—mezzo-soprano; Alfred, a singer—tenor; Dr Falke, a friend of Eisenstein's—baritone; Dr Blind, Eisenstein's attorney—tenor; Adele, Rosalinda's maid—soprano; Frosch, the goaler—speaking role.

Place: A watering-place near Vienna. *Time:* 1870.

Act I. A room in Eisenstein's house. Alfred can be heard off-stage serenading Rosalinda. Adele reads a letter from her sister Ida, a ballet-dancer, saying that she can take Adele (if she can borrow a dress) to a party at Prince Orlofsky's that night, to which the whole ballet has been invited. Adele is bubbling with excitement, but Rosalinda refuses to let her have the evening off. Eisenstein is about to start a five-day prison sentence and must be given a good dinner before he leaves that evening. She hears Alfred's voice and gives in to his plea for a rendezvous that evening, declaring that she is lost when she hears his top A. Eisenstein enters with Dr Blind, whom he blames for the whole affair of the prison sentence, particularly its extension to eight days. Rosalinda expresses her heart-felt grief at the prospect of this prolonged separation and Blind thinks up legal expedients. Eisenstein's friend Dr Falke enters with an amusing plan to revenge himself on Eisenstein: after a recent masked ball which Falke had attended dressed as a bat, Eisenstein had left him to walk home through the streets in broad daylight to the jeers of the citizens. Falke gives Eisenstein an invitation to Prince Orlofsky's ball, and suggests he attend it in disguise before going to prison. Eisenstein agrees and leaves merrily with Falke, not knowing that the latter intends to take Rosalinda to the party, wearing a mask. Now Rosalinda gives Adele the evening off so that she can receive Alfred without being disturbed; Rosalinda, Eisenstein and Adele sing a delicious farewell trio, in which none of them can conceal their delight at the pleasures in store. Alfred arrives, makes himself comfortable and puts on Eisenstein's dressing-gown. When Frank, the prison governor, comes in person to fetch his important prisoner, Rosalinda, not wanting to be compromised, introduces him (Alfred) as Eisenstein and, better or for worse, he has to accompany Frank to the prison.

Act II. Prince Orlofsky's palace. The Prince, a languid, blasé young man, is renowned for his wonderful parties; he insists that his guests do whatever they like. 'Chacun à son goût' ('Everyone to his taste'). Falke introduces his friend Eisenstein to the Prince under the name of the Marquis Renard; Adele is introduced by her sister as an actress, and the prison governor Frank arrives using the name Chevalier Chagrin and immediately makes friends with the supposed Marquis. Naturally the Marquis recognizes his maid, preening herself in her mistress's dress. Adele indignantly denies that she might be a domestic in the enchanting waltz song 'Mein Herr Marquis'. Finally Rosalinda enters, introduced by Falke as a Hungarian countess and, as proof, she sings a fiery csárdás. Since she is wearing a mask, her own husband does not recognize her and pays ardent court to this fascinating foreigner. While flirting with him, Rosalinda manages to gain possession of his watch. The gaiety reaches its climax, and the Prince proposes a toast to 'King Champagne', in which everyone joins with enthusiasm. Falke suggests that they found a society of brothers and sisters. The band strikes up the famous waltz which draws everyone into the dance. Suddenly a loud clock strikes six, startling Falke and Eisenstein, for the former must go to his work, the latter to prison. In a great hurry they call for their coats and rush out, without disturbing the gaiety of the other guests.

Act III. An office in the prison. The gaoler Frosch has been drinking, and holds the stage in a comic, non-singing episode. When Frank enters, no less drunk, and tries to sleep it off, Frosch insists on making his report, saying that the prisoner Eisenstein has been restless and insists on singing. In fact Alfred's voice can be heard from his cell. Adele and Ida are announced; at the ball, Frank had promised them his protection, and Adele has now come to ask him to launch her on a stage career. She feels she has natural talent and demonstrates her acting abilities. Frank has no time for the girls and has them shown into a cell. Eisenstein enters to start his prison sentence, and of course both he and Frank learn each other's identity with astonishment. Another lady is announced (it is Rosalinda, come to try to secure Alfred's release) and while Frank goes out to receive her Eisenstein borrows Blind's robe, glasses and wig, determined to find out who was arrested in his place. He interrogates Alfred and Rosalinda most sternly and finally, in his indignation at their treachery, throws off his disguise. Rosalinda however produces his watch as proof of his own infidelity. She is now more indignant than he and wants an immediate divorce. Led by Falke and Orlofsky, all the latter's guests come to the prison, and Falke explains to Eisenstein the practical joke that has been played on him. Alfred's and Rosalinda's tête-à-tête is explained as part of the game, and Eisenstein can only ask his wife's forgiveness, which she willingly grants. The Prince himself undertakes to look after Adele's artistic future. It was the champagne that caused everything, and the operetta closes with another song in its praise.

The superb, extended second act finale of *Die Fledermaus* set
the style for grand operetta finales, for it greatly excelled any of
Offenbach's finales and even the one in *Tausend und eine Nacht*.
The champagne song 'Im Feuerström der Reben' ('Good wine
to youth restores us') gives it a fiery impetus and is followed by
the elaborate canon ensemble with the refrain 'Erst ein Kuss

Brü-der- lein,＿＿ Brü-der- lein und Schwester lein,＿
(*Bro-ther dear*,＿＿ *bro-ther dear and sis-ter dear*,＿

wol - len al - le wir sein, stimmt mit mir＿ ein!
— hence-forth we must all be, I'm sure you'll a - gree)

dann ein Du' ('With a kiss I claim you'), leading into the gay
whirling waltz which carries all before it. From now on the

waltz was the driving, dominating force in operetta and only
broke into a cancan-like gallop in moments of utter abandon.
The great ensemble as the nucleus of the finale became a regular
feature of Viennese operetta and still kept its place when this
genre returned to popularity in Vienna. Despite the fact that
the final act of *Die Fledermaus* is musically somewhat weak, it
was taken as a formal precedent for subsequent operettas.
Though Frosch's rather tedious clowning is offset by two
independent musical numbers, this act becomes more and more
the comedian's province, while the music is restricted to
reminiscences from the first two acts.

  Johann Strauss had little luck with his librettos, and not even
his delightfully inventive music could disguise their weakness
and make them theatrically acceptable. As a result neither
brilliant casting nor meticulous production could ensure them
more than a brief existence in the repertory. Although *Die
Fledermaus* owed much of its success to its Viennese setting,

none of Strauss's librettists thought of adopting Vienna or Viennese atmosphere as the milieu for other operettas, which were set in Italy, France or the Balkans. Of these *Der lustige Krieg* (*The Merry War*) (1881), and *Eine Nacht in Venedig* (*A Night in Venice*) (1883) came off relatively well. *Der Zigeunerbaron* (1885), however, was performed with sensational success, which has lasted to the present day.

DER ZIGEUNERBARON (The Gipsy Baron). Operetta in three acts by Johann Strauss. Text by Ignaz Schnitzer after Maurus Jókai. First performance: Vienna, 1885.

Characters: Count Homonay—baritone; Carnero, Commissioner for Public Morals—bass; Sándor Barinkay—tenor; Kalmán Zsupán, a wealthy pig-breeder—bass; Arsena, his daughter—soprano; Mirabella, her governess—contralto; Ottokar, Mirabella's son—tenor; Czipra, a gipsy—contralto; Saffi, her daughter—soprano.

Place: Hungary and Vienna. *Time:* middle of the eighteenth century.

Act I. The young Sándor Barinkay has returned to his home which his father had had to leave twenty-five years earlier, following the last Turkish war. In the meantime the wealthy pig-breeder Kalmán Zsupán has annexed most of the Barinkay property and is reluctant to return it. Sándor Barinkay loves Zsupán's daughter Arsena, but she refuses his hand because she loves Ottokar, her governess's son. The old gipsy Czipra recognizes Sándor as the son of the former landowner, and persuades the gipsies to name him the Gipsy Baron. He falls in love with Saffi, who returns his affection.

Act II. A gipsy camp near the ruined castle of the Barinkays. Sándor looks for and finds the treasure his father had buried there. The Commissioner for Public Morals objects to Sándor and Saffi living together. In reply to his questioning, they sing a happy duet 'Wer uns getraut?' ('Who married us?') saying that a 'Dompfaff' performed the ceremony. ('Dompfaff' means either a cathedral canon or a bullfinch!). Carnero is moved by this frivolity to say some highly unflattering things about Saffi. Czipra searches among some old documents and produces a paper proving that Saffi is of noble blood, the daughter of the former Turkish Pasha. Now Sándor believes that being a commoner he must renounce Saffi, and enrols in the Spanish Army. Zsupán and Ottokar, who have fallen into the hands of a press-gang, are also forced to join the army.

Act III. Outside the Vienna Kärntnertor. The army, including Sándor, Zsupán and Ottokar, has returned victorious. Sándor has so distinguished himself in battle that he has been raised to the nobility. Nothing can now prevent him from marrying Saffi, while Arsena and Ottokar also celebrate their wedding.

Der Zigeunerbaron is Johann Strauss's second great operetta. Musically it is rich and original, its Hungarian setting lends it a very colourful flavour and the *csárdás* is used as effectively as

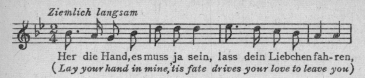

Her die Hand, es muss ja sein, lass dein Liebchen fah- ren,
(*Lay your hand in mine, 'tis fate drives your love to leave you*)

the Viennese waltz. The development of the large-scale arias, songs and ensembles is so careful and so elaborate that *Der Zigeunerbaron* has rightly been called a comic opera.

It was natural enough that Strauss, like Offenbach, should try his hand at opera, but here again he had trouble with his libretto. *Ritter Pázmán* (*The Knight Pazman*) was launched in great splendour at the Vienna State Opera in 1892, but aroused little public response. Strauss's last operettas, including *Jabuka* (1894), which is set in Yugoslavia and contains some excellent music, were equally unsuccessful. Shortly after his death, however, Adolf Müller concocted another operetta, *Wiener Blut*, from music by Strauss with a charming Viennese text by the famous librettists Viktor Léon and Leo Stein.

WIENER BLUT (Viennese Blood). Operetta in three acts by Johann Strauss, edited for the stage by Adolf Müller, junior. Text by Viktor Léon and Leo Stein. First performance: Vienna, 1899.

Characters: Prince Ypsheim-Gindelbach, prime minister of Reuss-Schleiz-Greiz—bass; Balduin, Count Zedlau, ambassador of Reuss-Schleiz-Greiz—tenor; Gabriele, his wife—soprano; Count Bitowski—speaking role; Frankiska Cagliari, a dancer—soprano; Kagler, her father —comedian; Pepi Pleininger, a mannequin—soprano; Josef, a man-servant—tenor.

Place: Vienna. *Time:* 1815.

Act I. A villa at Döbling. Count Zedlau is separated from his wife, an elegant Viennese, who could not endure life with her stiff, provincial husband. Life in Vienna, however, has turned the Count into a man of the world. He has furnished a villa at Döbling for his mistress, the dancer Franzi Cagliari, but has also fallen in love with the mannequin Pepi, to whom he is paying marked attention, without knowing that she is engaged to his manservant Josef. Zedlau's superior, Prince Ypsheim, comes unexpectedly to Döbling and mistakes the dancer Franzi for the Countess. The real Countess arrives inopportunely at her husband's villa and is mistaken by the Prince for the dancer.

Act II. At a ball given by Count Bitowski the misunderstandings become increasingly complicated. The Countess Zedlau, who has seen through her husband, is resolved to win him back, while Franzi does not want to lose him to a new mistress. Each asks him to take her to the wine-harvest at Hietzing, but the Count has to refuse them both since he has already arranged to meet Pepi there.

Act III. The casino garden at Hietzing. Zedlau takes Pepi to an arbour where he can make love to her undisturbed. Josef, who has escorted Franzi to Hietzing, tries to warn his master of her arrival, and of course finds his Pepi with the Count in the arbour. Furious indignation is followed by reconciliation. The Countess then enters the garden on the Prince's arm, and so rouses her husband's jealousy that he agrees to a reunion with her. Meanwhile Franzi and the Prince have paired off together.

Franz von Suppé (1819–95) can also be regarded as one of the founders of Viennese operetta—albeit a minor one. Suppé's music has an Italian melodiousness about it which can be attributed to his early musical education in Italy. When he came to Vienna, he easily adapted himself to true Viennese style, and a note of youthful extravagance crept into his work. Suppé's best-known operetta is *Boccaccio*; its hero is the great Renaissance poet and author of the *Decameron*; the role of Boccaccio is written for a mezzo-soprano.

BOCCACCIO. Operetta in three acts by Franz von Suppé. Text by F. Zell and Richard Genée. First performance: Vienna, 1879.

Characters: Giovanni Boccaccio—mezzo-soprano; Pietro, Prince of Palermo—tenor; Scalza, a barber—bass; Beatrice, his wife—soprano; Lotteringhi, a cooper—baritone; Isabella, his wife—soprano; Lambertuccio, a grocer—baritone; Peronella, his wife—soprano; Fiammetta, their foster-daughter—soprano; Leonetto, a student—tenor. Other students, beggars, populace.

Place: Florence. *Time:* 1331.

Act I. A square in Florence with a church and the house of the barber Scalza. The whole town is up in arms against Boccaccio, who uncovers some new scandal every day and publishes it with his biting pen. While the people are making merry in the square, Leonetto, a gallant and friend of Boccaccio's, enters stealthily to keep an appointment with Beatrice, Scalza's pretty little wife. Scalza discovers them together, and Beatrice's cries for help are the cue for a feigned duel by means of which Boccaccio helps her and Leonetto out of this scrape. Disguised as a beggar Boccaccio then approaches the beautiful Fiammetta, whom he sincerely loves. Prince Pietro of Palermo, who has come to Florence *incognito* for a little amusement, has got involved with the beautiful cooper's wife, Isabella, and by mistake attracts to himself the beating which the neighbours intended for Boccaccio. Apologies and excuses follow when the Prince is recognized, but the injured husbands cry out for a victim and burn

Boccaccio's latest stories publicly. Boccaccio, still disguised as a beggar, is called on to set fire to his own writings.

Act II. A street with the workshop of Lotteringhi the cooper and the house and garden of the grocer Lambertuccio. The three friends draw up a plan of battle: Fiammetta is assigned to Boccaccio, Isabella to Pietro, and Leonetto has to sacrifice himself and take on Fiammetta's foster-mother Peronella. Lotteringhi is made to crawl into a barrel to examine it thoroughly, while Boccaccio sends Lambertuccio up a tree from which he says one can see, by magic, pairs of lovers all around. Thus they all get their own back, but this idyll soon comes to an end when Scalza arrives with his friends to catch the poet. They beat up a stranger instead, who turns out to be a messenger from the Duke sent to fetch Fiammetta to the palace.

Act III. The duke's palace. Fiammetta turns out to be the duke's daughter, and Boccaccio declares to her his fervent love. The jealous husbands are prepared to forget their grievances and Boccaccio is made a professor amid unanimous expressions of esteem.

Despite some original situations, this very complicated story has little to offer the musician by way of inspiration; yet Suppé wrote some really sparkling music for it. He is a master both of short, simple numbers, witty, pointed couplets and the construction of grand ensembles. Of the many lovely tunes Fiammetta's aria 'Hab ich nur deine Liebe' ('If I but have your love, dear') and the vital rhythms of the third act duet, stand out in particular.

Flo-renz hat schö-ne Frau-en,— die Schön-ste bist du !
(*Flo-rence has love-ly wo-men,— the love-liest is you*)

In addition to *Boccaccio*, Suppé's operetta *Fatinitza* (1876) enjoyed a long period of popularity, but his best work is *Die schöne Galathee*, which was loudly acclaimed on its production in Vienna in 1865.

DIE SCHÖNE GALATHEE (The beautiful Galatea). Comic mythological opera in one act by Franz von Suppé. Text by Poly Henrion (pseudonym of L. Kohl von Kohlenegg). First performance: Vienna, 1865.

Characters: Pygmalion, a young sculptor—tenor; Ganymede, his servant—contralto; Mydas, an art-lover—tenor; Galatea, a statue—soprano. Women, youths, populace.

Place: Cyprus. *Time:* legendary.

Pygmalion has carved a statue of the nymph Galatea and fallen in love with this ideal portrayal of womanly beauty. To put an end to his tragic passion for a lifeless block of marble he has decided to destroy it. Pygmalion hears the voices of young boys and girls going to the temple of Venus and prays fervently to the goddess to give Galatea a soul. His prayer is heard and Galatea awakes; Pygmalion joyfully woos her and enfolds the modest, shrinking girl in his arms. All too soon she develops a very human and wayward nature, and shows an inclination to rule the household. She flirts with Mydas and accepts presents from him; she tries to seduce Ganymede and to persuade him to elope with her. This is too much for Pygmalion, who tries to destroy this faithless woman with his hammer, but she runs terrified to her pedestal and calls on the gods for help. They hear her prayer and turn her back into a statue, whereupon, greatly relieved, Pygmalion sells Mydas his statue for a very high price.

This work is strongly reminiscent of Offenbach: a parody of an episode from Greek mythology moulded into a most effective text, with music which heightens the meaning of the words and is in perfect harmony with them.

The first scenes of this operetta are really in operatic style; for example, the impressive Venus chorus which introduces the work and returns to play an important part in the plot. Pygmalion's prayer is skilfully and delicately interwoven with this chorus, and both themes are Italianate in melodic line and simple harmonies. The awakening of Galatea is magnificently portrayed from the first delicate 'Ach' to the radiant 'Ich bin erwacht' ('I am awake'), which is followed by Pygmalion's ecstatic outburst and the ensuing melodic duet. Pygmalion's servant Ganymede and the connoisseur Mydas are true operetta characters. Ganymede's slumber aria is wholly naturalistic, with a descending chromatic tune to convey his yawns and finally a real snore. Mydas's affectations are excellently portrayed and his short *arietta* is an exemplary piece of parody.

Galatea's capricious character is conveyed in coloratura and trills; she has wonderful but taxing music to sing, so that this role has always been considered a coloratura showpiece. Thanks to the apt musical characterization of the individuals all the ensemble passages are crystal-clear, and show Suppé's exceptional sureness and fine feeling for style.

The third master of the classical Viennese operetta, Karl Millöcker (1842–99) gradually found his way to operetta via

popular pieces and the incidental music for farces. Of these
three classical composers he is the most plebeian, and his
melodies are often closely related to popular songs. His first
very successful operetta *Das verwunschene Schloss* (*The Haunted
Castle*) (1878), with its very popular songs such as 'A bisserl
Lieb und a bisserl Treu' ('A little loving and a little faith') and
'O du himmelblauer See' ('Oh thou lake of purest blue')
established an agreeable style to which Millöcker adhered,
though with varied success, throughout his numerous operettas.
His masterpiece was *Der Bettelstudent*, which is full of delightful
and skilfully written tunes.

DER BETTELSTUDENT (The Beggar Student). Operetta in three acts
by Karl Millöcker. Text by F. Zell and Richard Genée. First performance:
Vienna, 1882.

Characters: Palmatica, Countess Novalska—contralto; Laura and
Bronislawa, her daughters—sopranos; Colonel Ollendorf, governor of
Cracow—bass; Jan Janicki and Symon Rymanowicz, students at Cracow
University—tenors; Enterich, the prison governor—baritone. Saxon
officers, their wives, prisoners, Polish nobles and their families.

Place: Cracow. *Time:* 1704.

Act I, scene i. The prison courtyard. Countess Laura struck the
Saxon governor of Cracow, Colonel Ollendorf, with her fan, when he
kissed her shoulder during a ball the night before. Ollendorf has thought
of a way to avenge this humiliation, for the beautiful Countess's mother
has said that only a prince would be an acceptable husband for her
daughter, and he will use this arrogance displayed by a proud but impoverished noblewoman to make her the laughing-stock of Cracow
society. Ollendorf chooses from among the prisoners two young Polish
students, Symon and Jan, who have been arrested for political reasons.
They are to be disguised as Prince Wranicki and his secretary, and are to
make love to Countess Laura and her sister. In this way they will earn
their freedom. Ollendorf provides them with suitable clothes and money.

Scene ii. An open square in Cracow. Ollendorf introduces Symon to
the Countess Palmatica and her daughters. Everything goes according to
plan: the Countess and Laura are ravished by the supposed prince, and
Bronislawa shows an interest in Jan.

Act II. The Countess's palace. Symon and Laura have really fallen in
love with each other. He would like to confess everything to her but is
bound by his word to Ollendorf. Bronislawa and Jan join in the fervent
duet 'Nur das eine bitt' ich dich, liebe mich' ('Only this I ask from you,
love me, please'). Jan is in fact Count Opalinski, who is heading a conspiracy to drive the Saxons out of Cracow. Ollendorf's moment of
revenge is come. As all Cracow society gathers for the wedding reception,
the gaoler Enterich enters with a number of ragged prisoners, who greet
Symon as the beggar student, their fellow-convict. Laura is overwhelmed

with shame and grief, and Symon is taken off to prison amid the derisive laughter of the Saxon officers.

Act III. Jan pretends to Ollendorf that Symon is the leader of the conspiracy, and he is at once condemned to death, while Jan receives a reward and his freedom. He can now organize the insurrection, which is successful. The King confers on Symon the rank of Count as a reward for his courage, and both couples are therefore happily reunited.

The best-known tune in this operetta is the caressing, swaying waltz-song, 'Ach, ich hab sie ja nur auf die Schulter geküsst' ('Oh, 'twas just on her shoulder I planted a kiss') from the first act, which returns in the finale to Act III. Also typical of Millöcker's music is the simple grace of Symon's mazurka-song in which he pays homage to Polish girls.

Of Millöcker's numerous other works his horror-operetta, *Gasparone* (1884), was one of the most successful, though it never became as popular as *Der Bettelstudent*. In 1931 Theo Mackeben made a very skilful new edition of an early Millöcker work, *Die Dubarry*, which was in excellent taste and highly dramatic.

Besides the three main stars of Viennese operetta—Johann Strauss, Suppé and Millöcker—two other very good musicians helped to spread its fame abroad: Richard Genée and Karl Zeller. Richard Genée (1823–95) was, together with F. Zell, the most sought-after operetta librettist of the classical period, and among others he wrote *Die Fledermaus*. In the operettas he composed himself Genée showed great skill and a considerable ability in inventing tunes. His most successful works were *Der Seekadett (The Naval Cadet)* (1876), and *Nanon, die Wirtin zum goldenen Lamm (Nanon, the Hostess of the Golden Lamb)* (1877), both charming works which deserve attention today.

Karl Zeller (1842–98) also became famous beyond Vienna on the strength of two works: *Der Vogelhändler* (1891) and *Der Obersteiger* (*The Master-miner*) (1895). The melodic inspiration and subtle construction of these two scores show that Zeller's talent was almost equal to that of the three great masters.

DER VOGELHÄNDLER (The Bird-seller). Operetta in three acts by Karl Zeller. Text by Moritz West and Ludwig Held. First performance: Vienna, 1891.

Characters: The Electress Marie—soprano; Baroness Adelaide, her lady-in-waiting—contralto; Baron Weps, the Electoral Steward of Forests and Game—bass; Count Stanislau, his nephew, an officer in the guards—tenor; Adam, a Tyrolean bird-seller—tenor; Christel—soprano; Schneck, a village-magistrate.

Place: Rheinpfalz. *Time:* beginning of the eighteenth century.

Act I. The market place in a Rhineland village. The Elector intends to go hunting and Baron Weps has come to the village to make the necessary preparations. Here he learns that because of poaching by the peasants there is not a single wild boar left in the whole district. The village magistrate Schneck is ready to provide a domestic sow and to indemnify the Baron for his collusion with money from communal funds. The Baron, who is continually in financial trouble because he has to pay his nephew's debts, agrees. At the last moment the Elector cancels the hunt, but so as not to lose his money Weps carries on all the same, and persuades the frivolous Stanislaus to pretend to be the Elector. The jolly bird-seller Adam comes to the village with a band of Tyrolean friends to visit his betrothed, Christel, and is welcomed by everyone. He sings the merry 'Grüss euch Gott, alle miteinander' ('Greetings, friends, good day, friends and neighbours'). Disguised as a peasant girl the Electress herself also comes to the village with her lady-in-waiting, Adelaide, so as to observe her husband, who has a taste for rustic flirtations. She enters with the song, 'Fröhlich Pfalz, Gott erhalt's' ('Sunny land, may God preserve it'). Adam quickly falls for the beautiful stranger, who calls herself Marie, and she gaily encourages his advances. Christel takes advantage of the Elector's presence in the village to present him with a written petition, asking him to appoint Adam to the post of menagerie director. She is graciously received by Stanislaus and Weps and follows the supposed Elector into the pavilion. The inhabitants of the village gather to pay homage to their prince, among them the disguised princess and Adam, who calls the Elector a seducer and tries to break into the pavilion. Only the Electress's swift action in flatteringly presenting him with her roses serves to pacify him and prevent a scandal. Joined by the chorus they sing the duet 'Schenkt man sich Rosen in Tirol' ('If one gives roses in Tyrol'). Brimming over with excitement, Christel comes out of the pavilion, having obtained Adam's nomination as director of the menagerie, but he has no further interest in her and throws the letter of appointment at her feet.

Act II. The Elector's castle. In spite of his complete ignorance, Adam passes the test for the post of menagerie director, because the Electress has indicated her wishes in the matter to the examining professors. Christel meets Stanislaus in the castle, and takes him for the Elector, so that the whole subterfuge is brought to light. Adam and his Tyrolean friends sing for the castle folk that evening, 'Wie mein Ahnderl zwanzig Jahr' ('When my grandpapa was twenty'). Since Stanislaus has wounded his honour, he must pay a penalty, and marry Christel, to make her an honest woman again.

Act III. In the castle gardens. Christel will not hear of marrying Stanislaus and persuades Adam that nothing culpable happened in the pavilion; reconciled, he takes her in his arms. Stanislaus is betrothed to the elderly, but very rich Adelaide.

Zeller's originality consists mostly in his folk-song style of music; this has resulted in such tunes as 'Grüss euch Gott' and 'Wie mein Ahnderl zwanzig Jahr' becoming popular songs in Germany. *Der Vogelhändler* has not declined in popularity over the years, and like the operettas of the three classical masters, it has long been accepted as worthy of performance in the great opera houses.

The 'seventies and 'eighties saw the heyday of the Viennese classical operetta. The exceptional success of this stylistic fashion produced a horde of librettists and composers who thought they could profit from a lucrative field, and a positive operetta industry started up, adapting and exploiting the style and form of the classical prototypes in a thousand different ways, without however propagating any new ideas. As a result operetta wasted away and lost its enthusiastic following so quickly that the whole genre died while its leading exponents were still alive. Indeed by the turn of the century little or no interest in operetta existed, and nobody seriously believed in the possibility of its renaissance. Then in 1905 the triumphant and unexpected arrival of *Die Lustige Witwe* opened a new era for operetta. It was a world-wide triumph, such as had not been seen since Offenbach and Johann Strauss. The composer, Franz Lehár (1870–1948), has become a byword in modern operetta. The first performance took place in Vienna, but it is significant that this operetta only became world famous after its tremendous success in Berlin, where its fiery spirit, which bourgeois, conservative Vienna had not rightly appreciated, was at once recognized and acclaimed.

DIE LUSTIGE WITWE (The Merry Widow). Operetta in three acts
by Franz Lehár. Text by Viktor Léon and Leo Stein. First performance:
Vienna, 1905.

Characters: Baron Mirko Zeta, Pontevedrinian ambassador to Paris—
bass; Valencienne, his wife—soprano; Count Danilo Danilovich,
secretary at the embassy—tenor; Hanna Glawari—soprano; Camille de
Rossillon—tenor; Njegus, a clerk at the embassy—comedian. Ladies and
gentlemen of Parisian and Pontevedrinian society. Grisettes, musicians,
servants.

Place: Paris. *Time:* beginning of the nineteenth century.

Act I. At a ball given by the Pontevedrinian ambassador Hanna
Glawari meets the former friend of her youth, Count Danilo. Danilo
had loved Hanna, but lost touch with her after her marriage to the rich
Glawari. Hanna has now come as a young widow and multi-millionairess
to Paris, where Danilo has been leading an idle life. Baron Zeta suggests
that Danilo should marry Hanna, to secure all those millions for their
country, Pontevedro, but Danilo rejects this proposal, because he does
not want Hanna to think that he is wooing her for her money. Zeta is so
taken up by the Glawari millions that he does not notice Camille de
Rossillon's courtship of his young wife, Valencienne. They are in love
with each other, but Valencienne decides to renounce Camille and marry
him to Hanna. Hanna is surrounded by a host of admirers, but none of
them makes any impression on her except Danilo, who persists in a
proud reserve.

Act II. Hanna uses all her resources to make Danilo declare himself,
since she is sure that he loves her. During a party she gives in the garden
of her villa, Hanna finds an opportunity to test him. Valencienne and
Camille have met secretly in the pavilion, and Hanna arrives on the
scene just as Zeta and Danilo discover the young couple, without yet
being sure who they are. Hanna slips into the pavilion through a side
entrance and comes out again with Camille. There is general astonishment, which increases even more when Hanna announces her betrothal
to Camille. This is too much for Danilo, who furiously accuses Hanna of
playing a trick on him. She now knows that Danilo loves her.

Act III. Hanna resorts to a stratagem. She tells everyone that she will
lose all her money if she ever remarries, and when at last Danilo declares
his love to her she confesses that in fact this was untrue.

The effective and amusing text is most splendidly set off by
Lehár's music. One cannot pick out individual items, for every
musical number is a little masterpiece: the great *leitmotiv* of the
love-waltz, the brisk Maxim march, Hanna's brilliant entrance
song, the sentimental, extremely melodious Vilja song, the
poetic pavilion-duet, the piquant chorus of the grisettes: one
can well understand the enthusiasm which *Die Lustige Witwe*
aroused soon after its appearance. Everyone sang and whistled
the principal tunes, danced only to the Sirens' Waltz, and, as

an American paper said, 'everywhere in the world there were Merry Widow biscuits, puddings, salads, hats, shoes, cigars and so on'. This work founded the style of the great modern operetta, which has dominated the development of this genre in many variations, until the present day.

Lehár's work is also a waltz operetta, but his waltzes are more caressing and sweeter than the classical Strauss waltz; they carry in them a foretaste of the slow waltz. Lehár's exceptional and well-deserved success rests mainly on his original, pliable but never banal, tunes. A standard example of a typical Lehár melody, which often moves around the tonic for bars on end in a fine mesh of notes, is the opening of the ravishing pavilion song.

After *Die Lustige Witwe* Lehár wrote operetta after operetta, with very varied success. *Der Graf von Luxemburg* (*The Count of Luxembourg*) (1909) and *Eva* (1911), made the greatest impressions, but he then became a 'hack' composer and settled into a routine groove, with two couples singing duets in turn, the serious pair in a langourous $^6/_6$ time, the comic pair in $^2/_4$ time, with an obligatory dance, and the second finale invariably introducing a tragic note. In fact his original creative ability fell off sharply.

In 1925 Lehár's *Paganini* launched a new type of operetta: the great singing operetta, which required singers of outstanding ability in the two leading roles. Lehár found in Richard Tauber the ideal interpreter for his dashing tenor roles, and for Tauber he wrote his next four operettas, *Der Zarewitsch* (*The Czarevich*) (1927), *Friederike* (1928), *Das Land des Lächelns* (*The Land of Smiles*) (1929), and *Schön ist die Welt* (*The World is Beautiful* (1931), which were so successful that the importance of the new style of operetta was established. In these works, which relied entirely on singing, great Lehár melodies such as we heard in the pavilion song of *Die Lustige Witwe* acquired more and more importance. It was no longer the waltz, but great melodies like 'Gern hab ich die Frau'n geküsst' ('Girls were made to love and kiss') from *Paganini* that became the dominant feature of an operetta.

Besides Lehár, Leo Fall (1873–1925) and Oscar Straus (1870–1954) were the brightest stars in the constellation of modern Viennese operetta composers. Straus's *Ein Walzertraum* (*A Waltz Dream*) (1907) and Fall's *Die Dollarprinzessin* (*The Dollar Princess* (1907) were international hits, but while Oscar Straus only had the one great success, Leo Fall went on to others that included *Die Geschiedene Frau* (*The Divorcee*) (1908) and *Madame Pompadour* (1923). Fall also had his own very original hall-mark, a lively dance-tune in $^2/_6$ time, to counter-balance the Viennese waltz, which he by no means neglected.

The Hungarian Emmerich Kálmán (1882–1953) is another highly original composer of the second period of Viennese operetta. His skilful introduction of the *csárdás* into operetta gives to his music an excitement which is particularly effective in dramatic *crescendos*. His greatest successes were *Die Csárdás-fürstin* (*The Csárdás Princess*) (1915), and *Gräfin Mariza* (*Countess Maritza*) (1924).

Lehár is the legitimate heir of the classical Viennese operetta, which owed its revival to him, and during this second period its independence from opera became increasingly clear. The lack of definition between operetta and comic opera, which existed at the time of the classical operetta, now completely disappeared, and the form, content and general atmosphere of the operetta were so clearly developed that there was no ques-tion of confusing it with the forms of comic opera, even in Lehár's great singing operettas. The operetta had in fact de-tached itself completely from opera and become a world of its own, as the further development of modern operetta has proved.

GIUSEPPE VERDI

Like Wagner, Verdi must also be assessed and admired as a leading cultural personality of the nineteenth century, but the fundamental approach of the two composers is entirely differ-ent; Wagner's world is that of egocentric conflict, and Verdi's that of conscious reserve. What each of them achieved in his own field and bequeathed to posterity was quite unique, and its effect is still felt in the development of opera today.

The comparison between these two outstanding personalities is naturally prompted by their identical age (both were born in 1813) and simultaneous creative activity. Ever since, over-popularity and total disregard has been the fate of each in turn, alternating more or less generation by generation. Only gradu-ally have people come to recognize the greatness and achieve-ment of both composers and to accept the works of both (which serve the same ends though in different ways) without perpetually comparing and contrasting the one with the other.

Giuseppe Verdi was born on 10 October 1813 in the small town of Roncole, near Busseto in the province of Parma. In spite of great poverty his father managed to buy a spinet and to pay for the first lessons for his music-hungry son. Later on Verdi attended a school in Busseto and eventually went to Milan, where he had the humiliation and disappointment of failing to gain admission to the Conservatory on the basis of his examination and of the works he presented. Verdi's begin-nings as a musician were by any standards discouraging. He met with much opposition in his first post as organist and orchestral conductor at Busseto, and his first operas, *Oberto* (1839) and *Un Giorno di Regno* (*King for a day*) (1840), were scarcely even *succès d'estime*. Added to this his happy family life was utterly destroyed at one blow when in 1840 he lost his young wife and both his little sons within a few months.

Verdi's first success, which made him immediately popular and spread his name throughout Italy, was *Nabucco*, which was first performed in 1842 at Milan. The story, which tells of the fortunes of the Jews during the Babylonian Captivity— Nabucco is Nebuchadnezzar—appealed to Verdi's patriotic feelings, for he longed for the liberation and unification of Italy, the greater part of which was then governed by Austria.

The most impressive passage in *Nabucco* was the chorus 'Va, pensiero, sull 'ali dorate', which was taken up by the people as

Va, pen - sie - ro, sull a - li do-ra - te
(*Speed your jour-ney, my thoughts and my long - ings*)

their hymn of freedom; the powerful melody and the stirring
rhythm excited spontaneous enthusiasm. *Nabucco* was an important landmark in Verdi's life in another respect also, for in
Giuseppina Strepponi (1815–97), the original Abigail, he found
new companionship and support. They began their liaison in
1849, and married in 1859.

The next two operas, *I Lombardi* (1843) and *Ernani* (1844)
also had revolutionary undertones, and in these works the
powerful unison choruses to political words again aroused intense enthusiasm, and largely contributed to the speed with
which these operas were taken up by every theatre in Italy.
Then in quick succession came *I due Foscari* (1844), *Giovanna
d'Arco* (1861), and *Alzira* (1845). They were followed by two
more political operas, *Attila* (1846) and *La Battaglia di Legnano*
(*The Battle of Legnano*) (1849), the latter glorifying the struggle
of the Milanese against the Emperor Barbarossa. On the occasion of the first performance of *La Battaglia di Legnano* in Rome
there were demonstrations and emotional scenes almost equal
to the tumult caused in its time by Auber's *La Muette de Portici*.
However much the political tempests raging throughout Italy
at that time contributed to the rapid popularity of Verdi's
works, it would be most unjust to attribute this success entirely
to political circumstances. The principal reason for the unconditional recognition won by Verdi lay in the completely new
impetus behind his music; following on Bellini's sweetness and
Rossini's elegance came Verdi's powerful, sometimes austere
virility, which corresponded so much more to the restless
spirit of the time.

The words 'Viva Verdi' which appeared everywhere were
generally assumed to replace the forbidden 'Viva l'Italia', and
later, when Victor Emmanuel, King of Sardinia, had been
offered the throne of a united Italy, people saw a symbol in
Verdi's name: V(ittorio) E(manuele) R(e) d'I(talia).

Among his later operas *Les Vêpres Siciliennes* (1855) and *Un
Ballo in maschera* (1859) were especially felt to be revolutionary
and aroused patriotic ardour in their audiences. After the Italian
victory over Austria in 1859, Verdi composed no more operas
with any political implications. At the request of Cavour,
however, he became a member of the new Italian parliament,
and during his short period of service with this body (1861–65)

he composed *La Forza del Destino*. The fervent patriot who had passionately shared in the struggle for freedom, retired completely from the political scene, bought a property, Sant'Agata, near his birthplace, and there rested in rural seclusion, hunting, and managing his estate.

Throughout his life Verdi had difficulties with his librettists and only for his last two operas, *Otello* and *Falstaff*, did he find a congenial collaborator in the composer Arrigo Boito. Verdi was always looking for effective dramatic material: he set four works by Schiller to music—*Giovanna d'Arco* (*Joan of Arc*), *I Masnadieri* (*Die Räuber*), *Luisa Miller* and *Don Carlos*; three Shakespearean works—*Macbeth*, *Otello* and *Falstaff*, and two by Victor Hugo—*Ernani* and *Rigoletto* (*Le Roi s'amuse*). To inspire him, a text had to contain great passions, distinctive characters and dramatic situations. His librettists Piave and Cammarano satisfied these requirements, but they did not attach much importance to clear dramatic construction, and had little idea of psychological development in their plots.

The first of Verdi's operas based on a Shakespearean play was *Macbeth*, which he wrote for performance in Florence in 1847. It was however not very successful, and even the revisions he made for Paris in 1865 did not ensure it immediate popularity. Subsequent revivals have, however, shown *Macbeth* to be emphatically worthy of survival.

MACBETH. Opera in four acts by Giuseppe Verdi. Text after William Shakespeare by Francesco Maria Piave. First performance: Florence, 1847. (Revised version: Paris, 1865.)

Characters: Duncan, King of Scotland—silent role; Macbeth, a general—baritone; Banquo, a general—bass; Lady Macbeth—soprano; Malcolm, Duncan's son—tenor; Macduff, a Scottish nobleman—tenor; Fleance, Banquo's son—silent role; a doctor—bass; a maid—contralto; witches—soprano and contralto.

Place: Scotland. *Time:* eleventh century.

Act I, scene i. A heath. Three groups of witches meet and sing a fantastic chorus as they await the victorious Macbeth. When the latter enters with Banquo and his son, Fleance, he is greeted by the witches not only by his title of Thane of Glamis, but as Thane of Cawdor and King of Scotland; Banquo is told that he shall not be a king, but that he shall beget kings. As the witches vanish messengers arrive from Duncan, announcing that Macbeth has been created Thane of Cawdor. Macbeth looks fearfully to the future, and Banquo comments on the effect of the news on him; they then proceed on their journey.

Scene ii. The great hall of Macbeth's castle. Lady Macbeth enters, reading a letter from her husband, telling her of his encounter with the witches. She expresses doubts as to whether he has the driving ambition to gain a throne, but she resolves to give him the necessary courage. A servant enters and announces Macbeth's imminent arrival with Duncan, who will spend the night at the castle. This news determines her immediate course of action, and she calls on the powers of evil to harden her heart to help her to further her aims. Macbeth arrives, and his wife, by insinuation, persuades him to murder Duncan that very night. The King enters, accompanied by Banquo, Malcolm and Macduff, is greeted by Macbeth and Lady Macbeth, and conducted to his apartments. Macbeth bids his servant tell his wife to strike on a bell when his evening drink is ready, which is the sign that the castle is asleep. Left alone he imagines he sees before him a bloody dagger. The bell sounds and Macbeth steals into the King's room. He soon reappears, the dagger dripping with blood in his hand. He tells Lady Macbeth that the deed is done, describing the scene in detail; he tells how he had heard one of the grooms murmuring a prayer in his sleep; how he (Macbeth) was unable to utter the word 'Amen', which stuck in his throat, and in his imagination he hears a voice saying 'Macbeth shall sleep no more'. Lady Macbeth urges her husband to return to the King's chamber to replace the dagger, and smear the grooms with blood so that it shall look as if they had murdered the King. Macbeth, quite terrified by what he has done, is unable to do so, but Lady Macbeth snatches the dagger from her husband's hand and enters the King's room herself. A loud knocking is heard, and Lady Macbeth hurries Macbeth from the scene so that they can wash the blood from their hands. Banquo and Macduff enter. The latter goes to arouse Duncan, the former broods on portents of the night. The murder is discovered, and the whole castle is awakened. Malcolm flees in terror to England.

Act II, scene i. A hall in the castle. Lady Macbeth persuades her husband (now King) that the deaths of Banquo and his son are necessary; left alone she first broods on the situation, and then exults in her new-found position as Queen.

Scene ii. A park near the castle. The murderers hired to kill Banquo and Fleance assemble to await their victims. Banquo and Fleance enter on their way to a banquet at the castle; the former gives voice to his anxieties. The murderers kill Banquo, but Fleance escapes.

Scene iii. The banqueting hall in the castle. Lady Macbeth drinks to her guests in a brilliant *brindisi*. In between the verses of the song, Macbeth learns from one of the murderers of Banquo's death, and of Fleance's escape. He complains to the assembly that Banquo's absence detracts from his pleasure; as he turns towards the vacant chair he sees Banquo's blood-stained ghost. He is overcome with terror, but Lady Macbeth tries to calm him by taking up the drinking-song once again. The ghost reappears and Macbeth, his nerve completely broken, virtually confesses his guilt. He decides to seek the witches' help. Macduff resolves to join Malcolm in England, and raise an army against the usurper.

Act III. The witches' cavern. Macbeth arrives and demands to be told his destiny. This is revealed to him in a series of apparitions. First, an

Armed Head tells him to beware of Macduff; then a Bloody Child reveals that none born of woman shall harm him; finally a Child wearing a crown and bearing a tree tells him he will not be defeated until Birnam Wood comes to Dunsinane. Macbeth asks whether any descendant of Banquo will ever inherit the throne. There then follows a procession of eight kings, all bearing a likeness to Banquo, the last of whom is Banquo himself; he holds up a mirror to Macbeth in which are reflected the images of countless other kings—Banquo's descendants. At the sight of the last apparition Macbeth faints. Lady Macbeth now arrives and learns from her husband what he has just witnessed. She tries to rouse his spirits again in a short and vigorous duet in which they vow vengeance and death to Macduff and the descendants of Banquo. Macbeth rushes out to destroy Macduff and his family, while Lady Macbeth, driven mad by anxiety, falls to the ground—ambition has 'o'er-reached itself'.

Act IV, scene i. On the borders of Scotland and England. Near Birnam Wood, a band of Scottish exiles bewail their fate and lament the sufferings of their country in a chorus very much in the mood of the famous 'Va pensiero' chorus in *Nabucco*. Macduff, receiving a letter telling him of the savage murder of his wife and children, sings a lament. Malcolm's English army arrives, and Malcolm urges the exiles to join forces with him, ordering each man to cut a branch from a tree in Birnam Wood in order to camouflage their advance on Macbeth's castle.

Scene ii. The great hall of Macbeth's castle. The haunted Lady Macbeth sleepwalks through the castle, and relives pitifully her crimes, trying to cleanse her bloodstained hands.

Scene iii. The battlements of Macbeth's castle. Macbeth, remembering the witches' prophecy that none born of woman shall harm him, still hopes to defeat Malcolm and Macduff; he laments the path of crime along which ambition has led him. News of Lady Macbeth's death is brought to him. Immediately after these tidings, he is told that Birnam Wood is moving towards him as the witches had prophesied. The English army storms the castle, scattering before them the frightened remnants of Macbeth's followers. Macduff confronts Macbeth, and telling him, in reply to the latter's cry that no man born of woman can harm him, that he was torn prematurely from his mother's womb, slays him. Malcolm and his victorious army of rebels and English soldiers enter, and as Macduff passes the crown to the new young King, all join in thanking God for the defeat and death of the tyrant and the deliverance of their country.

H.D.R.

In *Macbeth* Verdi was successful for the first time in expressing and developing character in music. Lady Macbeth is one of the finest singing-acting roles he ever wrote, and the various arias, beginning with the conventional 'Vieni t'affretta' with its *cabaletta* in the first act, through the short but exciting 'La luce lange' in Act II (this was added for the Paris version in 1865), to the Sleepwalking Scene, reveal the hand of a master.

Since *Macbeth* was written in 1847 and was quite unlike anything yet heard on the lyric stage, it must have amazed its first
listeners by its boldness of form and the expression of character
in music. In fact these characteristics, together with Verdi's
sure sense of theatre and patriotic feeling, evident in the Chorus

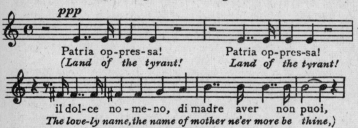

of Exiles and the Malcolm-Macduff tenor duet in the last act,
combine to make *Macbeth* an outstanding opera on any count.

While it is true that the witches' music and the jaunty little
march that accompanies the entrance of Duncan might sound
trivial, there is so much atmosphere elsewhere, especially in the
duets for Macbeth and Lady Macbeth, that one must not dismiss the opera as a weak work. Given fine interpreters in the
leading roles, and a conductor and producer who believe in it,
Macbeth will appear as the near-masterpiece it undoubtedly is.

RIGOLETTO. Opera in three acts by Giuseppe Verdi. Text after Victor
Hugo's *Le Roi s'amuse* by Francesco Maria Piave. First performance:
Venice, 1851.

Characters: Duke of Mantua—tenor; Rigoletto, his court jester—
baritone; Gilda, Rigoletto's daughter—soprano; Giovanna, Gilda's
nurse—mezzo-sporano; Count Monterone—bass; Count Ceprano—
baritone; Countess Ceprano—soprano; Marullo, a courtier—baritone;
Borsa, a courtier—tenor; Sparafucile, a bandit—bass; Maddalena, his
sister—mezzo-soprano.

Place: Mantua. *Time:* sixteenth century.

Act I, scene i. A hall in the ducal palace. A feast is taking place with a great deal of coming and going, dancing and chatter. The Duke tells his courtier Borsa that he has fallen in love with a charming girl he has often noticed in church, but while he is speaking he is looking admiringly at the young Countess Ceprano and sings a ballad, 'Questa o quella' ('This one, or that one'). When the musicians strike up a minuet, the Duke offers his arm to the Countess, jealously followed by the Count, to whom Rigoletto makes a derisive comment. Marullo has some news to announce, and to everyone's amazement tells them that Rigoletto, the hump-backed jester, has a mistress, whom he keeps concealed from everyone in a lonely house. The Duke is angry with Count Ceprano for refusing to leave his young wife's side, and Rigoletto suggests getting rid of him. Hearing this, the Count is most indignant, but the Duke laughingly defends his favourite. A loud voice is heard off-stage; Count Monterone is demanding satisfaction from the Duke who has seduced and dishonoured his daughter. Rigoletto conveys the Duke's answer to the unhappy father with cruel derision. When Monterone flares up in indignation, the Duke has him seized and, drawing himself up to his full height, Monterone curses both the Duke and his jester.

Scene ii. A street outside Rigoletto's house. A high wall separates both house and garden from the street, on the other side of which can be seen Count Ceprano's house. It is late evening and Rigoletto, wrapped in a mantle, has come secretly to see his daughter. He cann ot forget Monterone's curse. The cut-throat Sparafucile joins him, offers him his services as a hired assassin, and disappears again into the darkness. Rigoletto curses the fate which has made him court jester to the Duke whom he hates as much as the heartless courtiers who show him nothing but contempt. All this is forgotten, however, when he enters the garden and is joyfully greeted by Gilda. She knows neither her father's name nor position; she is not allowed to leave the house, except to go to church on feast days with her nurse Giovanna. Rigoletto believes he has heard a noise, and opening the garden door inadvertently allows the Duke to enter unobserved. The Duke throws a purse to Giovanna as a bribe and, concealing himself behind a tree, hears that Gilda is Rigoletto's daughter. After a fond farewell, Rigoletto goes out and Gilda tells Giovanna of her love for the unknown young man she has seen in church. From his hiding-place the Duke hears this confession and throws himself at Gilda's feet. There follows a love duet, but when the terrified Giovanna announces that she hears footsteps outside, Gilda, thinking that her father has returned, tells the Duke to leave. When Gilda asks him his name, he tells her that he is a poor student, Gualtier Maldè. The happy Gilda repeats this in the aria, 'Caro nome' ('Dearest name').

Meanwhile the courtiers have gathered in the street to abduct Rigoletto's supposed mistress. When Rigoletto enters, sensing danger, they tell him that Ceprano's wife is to be kidnapped and ask him to help, which he is quite willing to do. They tie a mask over his face, so that he can see nothing, and make him hold the ladder. They then enter the house and hurry away with the struggling Gilda, laughing derisively. Too late

Rigoletto realizes he has been deceived; he rushes into the house and, finding it empty, collapses with the words 'La maledizione' on his lips.

Act II. A hall in the Duke's palace. The Duke has been back to Rigoletto's house and discovered that his beloved has been kidnapped. He learns from the courtiers, who laughingly tell him about the abduction, that Gilda is in the palace, and hurries to her full of joy. Rigoletto enters, feigning gaiety, but obsessed by only one thought; to discover where Gilda has been taken. When he hears that she is in the palace, he at once drops his pretence of gaiety and passionately urges the despised courtiers to tell him where his daughter is, humbling himself to plead with them, then breaking out in fury with 'Cortigiani, vil razza dannata' ('Ah, ye courtiers, vile rabble accursed'). Gilda enters, and the courtiers retire. She tries to explain to her father her love for the Duke, whom she believed to be a poor student, but Rigoletto is only filled with thoughts of revenge. The Duke must die, and then he will flee from Mantua with Gilda. At this moment Monterone passes through the hall on his way to prison, and his farewell words strengthen Rigoletto's resolve for vengeance, to which he gives vent in the duet 'Si, vendetta, tremenda vendetta' ('Aye, my soul, naught but vengeance desiring').

Act III. A deserted place on the banks of the river Mincio. For a month Rigoletto has waited for an opportunity to prove to Gilda the Duke's infidelity, and then to avenge himself on his daughter's seducer. At last the moment has come. He takes Gilda to the derelict inn and through a crack in the wall they can both follow what is going on in the house. The Duke has entered the inn in the guise of an officer. Sparafucile receives him and then goes to fetch wine. The Duke sings the famous aria 'La donna è mobile' (Wayward as thistledown'). Sparafucile returns with his sister Maddalena, who has led the Duke to this solitary place, and then goes out, leaving the Duke and Maddalena alone, but observed by Gilda and Rigoletto. Rigoletto tells Gilda to go home, put on male attire and then proceed to Verona where he will join her. Rigoletto knocks on the door of the inn and instructs Sparafucile to kill the officer, saying he will come at midnight to fetch the body and throw it in the river. Sparafucile takes the payment of ten gold *scudi* and goes back into the house. Meanwhile a storm has broken out and Sparafucile shows the Duke, who does not want to leave the house in such weather, to an attic bedroom. Maddalena begs Sparafucile to spare the handsome young man and to kill Rigoletto, but he refuses. Finally he agrees to let the stranger go if a substitute appears before midnight. Gilda, who has come back disguised as a youth, overhears this conversation and, resolving to sacrifice herself for her lover, knocks at the door. Maddalena opens the door, behind which stands Sparafucile, a dagger in his hand. He stabs Gilda as she enters, while the storm reaches its height. Slowly it dies down again, and midnight strikes. Rigoletto returns and knocks at the door of the inn. Sparafucile opens to him and hands him a sack containing the body. Rigoletto triumphantly drags the sack to the edge of the river, to throw the body in. Suddenly he hears the Duke's voice, merrily singing 'La donna è mobile' as he leaves the inn. Beside himself with horror Rigoeltto opens the sack and discovers his daughter, who with her dying breath declares her love for the Duke. Rigoletto, uttering the words 'La maledizione', collapses over Gilda's body.

The first performance of *Rigoletto* took place in Venice and was greeted with wild enthusiasm. There was some distaste at the title-role hero being a hunchback dwarf, so that Verdi's achievement in winning pity and understanding for him by his moving portrayal of fatherly love is all the more remarkable. Rigoletto is a show part, and, however sharp the characterization may be, the laurels will always go to the singer with the loveliest voice. This natural blend of subtle characterization and radiant *bel canto*—a distinguishing mark of Verdi's art—is perfected in *Rigoletto*. If the rather stereotyped accompaniments make some of the tunes sound a little banal at first, this is due partly to insufficient understanding of the character of Italian operatic music, and partly—unfortunately only too often—to a ponderous interpretation.

Light, trivial march tunes give a distinctive character to the colourful scenes at the court and the Duke's arias, such as 'La donna è mobile' with its enchantingly simple rhythms, betray

La don-na è mo-bi- le   qual piuma al   ven - to
(*Way-ward as this-tle-down tossed on the sum-mer wind*)

his frivolity and love of life. This melody is no more banal than Gilda's aria 'Caro nome', in which the delicate, simple yet

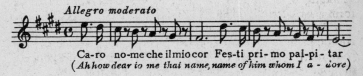

Ca-ro no-me che il mio cor Fes-ti pri- mo pal-pi- tar
(*Ah how dear to me that name, name of him whom I a - dore*)

moving sequence of notes creates a most distinctive mood while the graceful coloratura passages and trills are ethereally sweet, almost like a foreboding of the horrible events to follow, for from this moment on the sinister aspect of the plot gradually begins to predominate.

The short orchestral prelude to the opera is based on a sombre theme in the trumpets and trombones, which is then taken up menacingly by the full orchestra. This is the curse theme, which

Andante sostenuto

recurs significantly several times in the course of the action. Rigoletto is most brilliantly portrayed: his despair continually breaks through his armour of artificial gaiety and the constant humiliations he undergoes finally make him obsessed with thoughts of vengeance. The great quartet in the last act brings together the various characters and defines each of them with individual tunes appropriate to their nature, feelings and attitudes; this quartet is remarkable as evidence of Verdi's great powers of characterization. The scene revolves around the Duke and his lustful desires, and round his seductive song are grouped

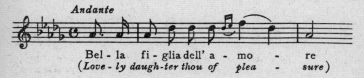

Andante

Bel - la fi - glia dell' a - mo - re
(*Love - ly daugh-ter thou of plea - sure*)

the melodies of the other characters; the cool, detached, yet enticing jests of Maddalena, Gilda's despair and Rigoletto's brooding revenge. Put together, these independent melodies form a wonderfully blended harmonic unity.

Il Trovatore was for a long time Verdi's most popular opera. Although the story is exceptionally confusing, it inspired the composer's genius, and the passionate score is so convincing that one completely forgives the textual shortcomings.

IL TROVATORE (The Troubadour). Opera in four acts by Giuseppe Verdi. Text by Salvatore Cammarano. First performance: Rome, 1853.
Characters: Count of Luna—baritone; the Duchess Leonora—soprano; Inez, her confidante—soprano; Manrico, a troubadour—tenor; Ruiz, his retainer—tenor; Azucena ,a gipsy-woman—mezzo-soprano; Ferrando, a

captain in the army—bass. Followers of the Count of Luna and of Manrico. Messenger, gaoler, soldiers, nuns, gipsies.

Place: Spain. *Time:* fifteenth century.

Act I. 'Il Duello' (The Duel). Scene i. An anteroom in the Count of Luna's castle of Aliaferia. Ferrando exhorts the servants to be watchful while their master, the Count, is absent, pacing up and down restlessly beneath the windows of his beloved, the Duchess Leonora. Jealousy keeps drawing him back to his lady, jealousy of the troubadour Manrico, whom he knows to be his favoured rival. To keep the servants awake, Ferrando tells them the story of the old Count of Luna and his two sons. While the younger was still a baby, an old gipsy bewitched him as he lay sleeping in his cradle, whereupon the Count had her seized and burned to death in punishment. In revenge the gipsy's daughter kidnapped the child and soon afterwards the burnt bones of a baby were found on the old woman's pyre, but the Count would not believe that his son was dead. Before his own death he exhorted his elder son, the present Count, to trace the gipsy, but to that day all efforts had been in vain. She must still be alive, says Ferrando, and carrying on her evil trade as a witch.

Scene ii. The palace garden. In the *cavatina* 'Tacea la notte placida' ('In silence and in calm serene'), Leonora confesses to Inez her love for Manrico, whom she saw for the first time at a tournament. Manrico serenades Leonora in the *romanza* 'Deserto sulla terra' ('Lonely and unbefriended'). The Count of Luna enters the garden, and confronts his rival. Despite Leonora's pleas, the two men fight a duel.

Act II. 'La Gitana' (The Gipsy). Scene i. A gipsy camp. Azucena invokes the memory of her mother and her death at the stake with the *canzone* 'Stride la vampa' ('Harsh roars the greedy flame'). Manrico has won the duel, but an inner voice induced him to spare his rival's life. Azucena cannot understand such magnanimity; she tells Manrico how she had wanted to avenge her mother, but in her frenzy threw her own son into the flames instead of the young Count. Immediately she withdraws these words, saying that she had only spoken them in her agitation. A messenger enters with a letter for Manrico which reports that Leonora, having been told that he was dead, intends to enter a convent. Manrico rushes to save his beloved.

Scene ii. The cloisters of the Jerusalem Convent. The Count of Luna has come to abduct Leonora; he sings of his love for her in the aria 'Il balen del suo sorriso' ('No faint star in heav'n's vault swinging'). Manrico arrives just in time to prevent his rival carrying off Leonora.

Act III. 'Il Figlio della Zingara' (The Gipsy's Son). Scene i. An army camp. Azucena has been captured by Luna's men, and Ferrando has recognized her as the gipsy who kidnapped the old Count's small son years before; when the Count learns that she is also Manrico's mother, he decides to have her executed.

Scene ii. A room in the castle of Castellor. The castle is besieged by Luna's soldiers. Manrico, who is about to marry Leonora, learns that his mother has fallen into his enemy's hands and that she is to be burnt at the stake. He resolves to rescue her in the rousing *stretta* 'Di quella pira' ('That foul flame yonder').

Act IV. 'Il Supplizio' (The Penalty). Scene i. Outside the palace of Aliaferia. The attempt to rescue Azucena has failed, and Manrico is now imprisoned with her. Leonora has hastened to rescue her lover. A *miserere* is heard off-stage, and Manrico's voice calling longingly to her from his prison. The Count enters, and Leonora implores him to spare Manrico, offering herself in exchange for her lover's liberty. The Count happily accedes to her request, but Leonora takes poison.

Scene ii. A dungeon. Manrico tries to calm Azucena, who is tormented by terrible visions, and they sing the duet 'Ai nostri monti' ('Home to our mountains'). Completely exhausted she at last falls asleep. Leonora enters, bringing Manrico the news of his release, but the poison has already taken effect, and she dies in his arms. When the Count finds her dead, he orders Manrico to be executed, only to learn too late from Azucena that in his rival he has killed his own brother.

To this story of passion and violence Verdi wrote a score of such inspired dramatic power, wealth of melody and brilliant use of radiant top Cs that it has outlived generations of operas with carefully developed plots. The soldiers' choruses in the third act glow with the revolutionary ardour of the Italian uprisings, and Manrico's famous *stretta* with its stirring rhythms

Di quel-la   pi - ra   l'or-ren-do   fo - co
(*That foul flame yon - der,   ra-ging so   cru - el*)

became the musical symbol of the liberation movement, but the climax of *Il Trovatore* is certainly the sombre, oppressive *miserere* ensemble in the fourth act.

After he had written *Rigoletto*, Verdi said that he did not believe he would ever compose anything so beautiful again, but subsequent developments disproved this opinion, and the triumphant success of *Il Trovatore* far surpassed that of *Rigoletto*.

Barely two months after the tremendous success of *Il Trovatore* in Rome, *La Traviata* had its première in Venice which, due to the most inadequate presentation, was a disastrous failure. Verdi was vindicated by the revival given the following year in the same theatre, this time with a brilliant cast, and *La Traviata* became an outstanding success.

La Traviata, based on the famous play by Alexandre Dumas the Younger, *La Dame aux Camélias*, established the new Verdi style with its accent on spiritual values and simple humanity, in contrast to the heroic pathos of his early operas.

LA TRAVIATA (The Frail One—literally: 'The Woman who has been led astray'). Opera in three acts by Giuseppe Verdi. Text after Alexandre Dumas the Younger, by Francesco Maria Piave. First performance: Venice, 1853.

Characters: Violetta Valery—soprano; Flora Bervoix, her friend—soprano; Annina, Violetta's confidante—mezzo-soprano; Alfredo Germont—tenor; Giorgio Germont, his father—baritone; Gastone de Letorières—tenor; Baron Douphol—baritone; Marchese d'Obigny—bass; Doctor Grenvil—bass; Giuseppe, Violetta's servant—tenor. Friends of Violetta and Flora, servants and dancers.

Place: In and near Paris. *Time:* about 1850.

Act I. Violetta's elegant salon. A lively company is gathered round their beautiful hostess, the celebrated courtesan Violetta Valery. Alfredo Germont has been brought to the party by his friend Gastone; he has long admired Violetta from a distance, and during her recent illness has inquired after her health every day. He praises beauty and love in a passionate drinking song, in which everyone joins. Violetta invites her guests to join in the dancing in the next room, and as they go out she is held back by a sudden severe attack of coughing. Alfredo rushes to her and declares his passionate love. Violetta warns him against losing himself in love for her, but at the same time she is deeply impressed by the strength of his emotion. She gives him a camelia, saying that as soon as it withers, perhaps the following day, he may return. After he has gone, she remains lost in thought, her heart touched for the first time; then coming back to reality, sings of her glorious and continual round of pleasure. Alfredo's voice is heard off-stage, and Violetta realizes that she truly loves him.

Act II, scene i. The garden-room of a country house near Paris. For three months Alfredo and Violetta have been living only for their love, but Alfredo now learns from Annina that Violetta has sold all her possessions to pay for their luxurious ménage. Alfredo leaves at once for Paris to raise the necessary money. Violetta has received a letter from her friend Flora, inviting her to a party, but the pleasures of Paris no longer mean anything to her. A visitor is announced; it is Alfredo's father. He tells Violetta that Alfredo's sister is to marry shortly, but his relations with Violetta are jeopardizing the proposed match. Violetta must therefore renounce Alfredo for his sister's sake. With heavy heart she promises to part from Alfredo. Deeply moved by such generosity Germont embraces the unhappy young woman as he departs. Violetta is left alone, and on a sudden impulse she writes to accept Flora's invitation. She is still writing a farewell letter to Alfredo when he returns and tells her that his father is expected at any moment. She does not mention her encounter with the elder Germont but embraces Alfredo passionately and, leaving the room, immediately slips out of the house unnoticed. A letter is brought to Alfredo soon after, to tell him that Violetta has decided to go back to Paris. Alfredo is shattered and his father, who enters at that moment, tries to console him in the aria, 'Di Provenza il mar, il suol' ('From fair Provence's sea and soil'). Alfredo, however, rushes out, resolved to go to Flora's party himself.

Scene ii. The ball-room in Flora's house. The party is in progress, and the revelry is enlivened by the songs and dances of guests dressed as gipsy girls and toreadors. Flora and her friends know that Violetta has left Alfredo and has formed a liaison with Baron Douphol. Alfredo enters and soon after Violetta comes in on the Baron's arm. The two rivals meet at the gambling-table and Alfredo wins large sums of money from the Baron. The tense game is interrupted by the announcement of supper. Violetta goes over to Alfredo and begs him to leave the party to avoid further unpleasantness. He replies that he will leave if she will go with him, but Violetta explains that she is bound by her promise to a man whose name she cannot disclose. Alfredo believes that she means the Baron, and asks her whether she loves him. Violetta sees no alternative but to answer yes. Alfredo loses his self-control and summoning the guests from the other room, insults Violetta and throws at her feet the money he has just won. Alfredo's father, who has followed his son, witnesses this scene. With moving words Violetta assures Alfredo that only her love for him has prompted her to behave like this. Alfredo is deeply ashamed, and the Baron challenges him to a duel.

Act III. Violetta's bedroom. It is early morning, and the ailing Violetta is sleeping, watched over by her faithful Annina. The doctor enters, and speaks encouraging words to Violetta, but as he leaves the room he whispers to Annina that it can only be a matter of hours. Left alone, Violetta takes out a letter from Alfredo's father, which she received some time ago and has read again and again; the Baron was slightly wounded in the duel and Alfredo, who was unharmed, then went abroad. Germont has told Alfredo of Violetta's sacrifice, and he is now on his way back to her. This was some while ago, and Violetta has been waiting in vain. Cheerful singing is heard from the street, for it is carnival-time. Annina enters with good news and Violetta guesses that Alfredo has come. He comes in and the lovers fall happily into each other's arms. When Violetta tries to dress herself, she finds her strength has left her. Germont, Annina and the doctor hurry in. Violetta bids farewell to Alfredo and gives him her portrait, asking him to give it to the woman he will one day marry. Suddenly her pains cease and Violetta feels new life in her, but she collapses; the effort has been too much for her and the doctor confirms that she is dead.

The music of *La Traviata* spreads like a veil of sorrow over the whole story, and it is the power to evoke atmosphere which gives the score its charm; the few strongly-drawn scenes, like the introductory drinking scene and the noisy party in Flora's house, pale beside the broadly developed lyrical scenes. The transmutation of spiritual happenings and emotions into music and melody is more clearly illustrated in *La Traviata* than in any of Verdi's previous works, and even if conventional devices still recur in the rhythms and the accompanying passages it is evident that Verdi was working towards new ways of adding spiritual intensity to his story. Even Violetta's brilliant coloratura in the first act is no mere florid ornamentation but an expression of her frivolous and superficial way of life; in the scenes which follow there is no more coloratura. In *La Traviata* the orchestra stays very much in the background, while the *bel canto* vocal line carries the melody throughout and alone serves to define the character and deeper content of the music. Alfredo's love song, an expression of the lovers' devotion, recurs as a *leitmotiv* throughout the opera and dies away in

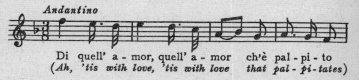

Di quell' a - mor, quell' a - mor   ch'è pal - pi - to
(*Ah, 'tis with love, 'tis with love   that pal - pi - tates*)

a sorrowful violin solo at Violetta's death. Violetta's musical portrait is clearly painted in the short prelude where in the *pianissimo* divided violins a delicate theme is heard which characterizes this woman already singled out for an early death.

The fervent tune which grows out of these ethereal sounds is taken from the second act, where it accompanies Violetta's last passionate declaration of love.

Verdi's contacts with Paris, then the metropolis of music, where the Grand Opéra of Auber and Meyerbeer was still the accepted standard, were of great importance for his creative activity. He had already been very successful there in 1847 with an adaptation of *I Lombardi* under the title *Jerusalem*, and the performances of *Luisa Miller* in 1853, and of *Il Trovatore* in 1854, had also met with the approval of Parisian audiences. It was therefore natural that he should be asked to compose an original work for the Paris Opéra. Verdi was well aware that

the road to world fame must pass through Paris, and also that
he would have to make great stylistic concessions to meet the
requirements of the Grand Opéra, but still he was uneasy with
the projected work, *Les Vêpres Siciliennes*, because the libretto
by Scribe and Duveyrier did not please him, least of all its
various ceremonial processions and arbitrarily inserted ballets.
The months of rehearsal, including continuous changes in the
libretto and stage action (and therefore of course in the music)
proved an arduous and trying period for the composer, but at
last the opera was performed with outstanding success to mark
the inauguration of the World Exhibition. Its success did not
last, but it does contain much worthwhile music and is today
occasionally revived.

LES VÊPRES SICILIENNES (I Vespri Siciliani: The Sicilian Vespers).
Opera in five acts by Giuseppe Verdi. Text by Eugène Scribe and Charles
Duveyrier. First performance: Paris, 1855.
   Characters: the Duc de Montfort, the Governor of Sicily—baritone;
Arrigo, a young Sicilian—tenor; Procida, a doctor—bass; Duchesse
Hélène—soprano. Populace, guards, etc.
   Place: Palermo. *Time:* 1282.
   Act I. The Great Square, Palermo. The French are maintaining a strict
regime in Sicily while the Sicilians, led by young Arrigo and the Duchesse
Hélène, are plotting for their freedom and revenge. De Montfort, the
Governor of Sicily, makes overtures of friendship to Arrigo; he feels
strong sympathy for the bold young man, and asks him about his family
and origins, but Arrigo refuses to associate with his country's oppressor.
   Act II. A valley outside the city. The noble Procida returns home from
exile and joins Arrigo and Hélène in preparing the uprising against the
French. Arrigo declares his love to Hélène, and she demands that he kill
the governor as an act of patriotic vengeance. Arrigo is invited to a feast
given by the governor, and when he refuses the invitation he is arrested.
   Act III, scene i. De Montfort's room. De Montfort has established that
Arrigo is his son, but the latter will not trust the enemy of his country,
and tearing himself from his father's arms he escapes.
   Scene ii. The ballroom. A ballet is performed for de Montfort's
guests. When the conspirators are about to fall on Montfort, Arrigo
prevents them, and they are all arrested, including Hélène.
   Act IV. The courtyard of the fortress. Arrigo visits Hélène in the
fortress and explains the situation to her. Procida tells his friends that a
ship is lying in the harbour with arms for them. De Montfort enters and
undertakes to pardon the conspirators if Arrigo will acknowledge him as
his father. Only when Hélène and Procida are about to be led to the
scaffold, does Arrigo throw himself at his father's feet. De Montfort
pardons them and unites Hélène to Arrigo.

Act V. The gardens of de Montfort's palace. Procida tells Hélène that when the bell rings for Vespers the conspirators will attack the French. Hélène does not dare pass on this secret to her beloved. As the bells ring, the Sicilians burst into the Governor's palace to kill him. Arrigo tries to protect his father, but he falls with de Montfort. Hélène stabs herself, but Palermo is free.

This passionate and violent action is interspersed with grand processions and ballets in the style of French opera, and the highly impressive overture, which had been originally composed for *Giovanna d'Arco*, is very conventional. However, the great Verdian *cantilena* flowers wonderfully even in this opera, for example in the beginning of Procida's famous monologue;

its combination of fervent yet powerfully dignified phrases make it without any doubt one of the most beautiful bass arias.

Verdi's next opera was *Simone Boccanegra*, which he wrote for Venice in 1857, but after the somewhat unfortunate first performance it was more or less neglected. Verdi hoped to reawaken public interest by completely revising it, and this he did with the help of Arrigo Boito, his prospective librettist for *Otello*. In 1881 the new version was produced with great splendour at La Scala, amid popular acclaim. Nevertheless this opera with its rather rough text has never enjoyed wide popularity.

SIMONE BOCCANEGRA. Opera in a prologue and three acts by Giuseppe Verdi. Text by Francesco Maria Piave after Gutierrez. Revised and added to by Arrigo Boito. First performance: Venice, 1857. (Revised version: Milan, 1881.)

Characters: Simone Boccanegra—baritone; Giacopo Fiesco, a patrician —bass; Paolo Albani, a plebeian—baritone; Pietro, a plebeian—bass;

Gabriele Adorno, a patrician—tenor; Amelia Boccanegra (in Act I, *alias* Grimaldi)—soprano; a captain—tenor. People of Genoa, patrician and plebeian councillors, guards, etc.

Place: Genoa. *Time:* fifteenth century.

The plebeian Boccanegra has won some personal glory by his exploits against the African pirates who have been harassing Genoese trade. He loves Maria (the daughter of Fiesco, the elected Doge) and she returns his love. Their child, a daughter, has disappeared without trace from her foster home at Pisa, and Maria is being kept prisoner by her father.

Prologue: A square in Genoa outside the Doge's palace. Boccanegra is nominated plebeian candidate for the Doge's office, which gives him hope of being able to overcome Fiesco's opposition to his marriage with Maria. Just then the hated Fiesco emerges from his palace, mourning the death of his daughter. In a great duet with Boccanegra, Fiesco taxes him afresh with the wrong he has done Maria; Boccanegra tells him of the disappearance of his little daughter, Fiesco's grandchild whom he has never seens and Fiesco as he leaves the square tells him that only the sight of her can heal the breach between them. Boccanegra enters the palace to find Maria dead, then emerges as the crowd surge into the square, acclaiming him as their new Doge.

Act I, scene i. The garden of the Grimaldi palace near the sea. Twenty-five years have passed and Amelia, Boccanegra's lost daughter who has been brought up in the noble house of the Grimaldis, greets the beautiful morning and recalls her childhood. Her lover, Gabriele Adorno, seren-ades her, and when he enters she confides in him her fears for his safety and that of Andrea (Fiesco in disguise) who is plotting against the Doge. Pietro enters to tell Amelia that the Doge will visit her that day, and as she and Gabriele fear that he will try to persuade her to marry his hench-man Paolo Albiani, Gabriele at once asks the blessing of Andrea (Amelia's guardian in the absence of the banished Count Grimaldi) on his suit. Andrea tells Gabriele that Amelia was only adopted by Grimaldi (he has no idea of her identity) but Gabriele only reiterates his love for her and Andrea gives him his blessing. The Doge enters and tells Amelia that Count Grimaldi is to be pardoned. Amelia confides in him that she has a lover, and also that she is an orphan, the only clue to her origin being a locket with a portrait of her mother. Boccanegra recognizes the portrait as that of Maria and ecstatically acknowledges his daughter. He then tells Paolo that he can entertain no further hope of marrying Amelia, and Paolo immediately plots with Pietro to abduct her.

Scene ii. The Council Chamber of the Doge. The Doge with his Council of plebeians and patricians receives an envoy from the King of Tartary, and then reads a message from Petrarch, advocating peace between Genoa and Venice. A rioting mob is heard outside, dragging Adorno to the palace and crying 'death to the patricians'. Immediately the Council splits into opposing factions and all draw their swords, while Boccanegra tries to calm them and the mob as well, by sending his herald to open the palace doors and invite the crowd to enter the council chamber. Adorno is dragged in, and admits to the murder of a plebeian who tried to abduct Amelia, and who has confessed that he was only the

tool of a man of great power. Adorno believes Boccanegra to be responsible · nd is about to stab him when Amelia throws herself between them,
and corroborates Adorno's story. The tumult which ensues between
patricians and plebeians only subsides after the Doge's great plea for peace
and unity. Adorno gives his sword to Boccanegra, who then turns on
Paolo, speaking with tremendous force and emphasis of his resolve to
find the man who has molested Amelia. His cry of vengeance is taken
up by the crowd who carry it to the edge of hysteria. Paolo rushes
out.

Act II. The Doge's private apartments. Paolo, alone, is fearful for his
own safety and threatens to kill the Doge by poison. Adorno and Fiesco
are brought in, and he offers the latter his freedom in return for killing
the Doge, saying that otherwise his name and those of his fellow-
conspirators among the patricians will be given to the Doge. Fiesco
refuses. Paolo then tells Adorno that Amelia is at the palace as the Doge's
mistress and Adorno believes him. Amelia enters, and her lover taxes her
with infidelity which she indignantly denies. The Doge enters and
Adorno hides himself. Amelia tells her father that Adorno is her lover.
The Doge is deeply disturbed that she should have chosen a traitor and
plotter against him and when she has left the room he drinks from a jug
of water which Paolo has poisoned, musing on his sad destiny, and falls
asleep. Adorno comes out of hiding, intending to kill the man who is
both his father's murderer and his own rival, but Amelia prevents him
and Boccanegra, awaking, discloses that she is his daughter. Adorno begs
Amelia's forgiveness and asks the Doge to kill him, but the latter nobly
pardons him. Sounds of the patrician conspirators gathering outside are
heard, but when the Doge tells Adorno to join his friends the young man
swears loyalty to his ruler and undertakes to try and stop the fighting.

Act III. A great hall in the palace, overlooking the harbour. The city is
lit with torches to celebrate the crushing of the revolt. Fiesco is given back
his sword and released, but Paolo, who has also taken part in the rebellion,
is led in on his way to execution. He exults in the thought that the Doge
will soon die of his slow, deadly poison, and Fiesco regrets that Boccanegra's death should be brought about so treacherously. Adorno's and
Amelia's wedding-hymn can be heard. A proclamation is made that the
torches should be extinguished in honour of the valiant dead. The Doge
enters, already suffering from the poison, but revives at the sight and
smell of the sea on which he had once lived so happily and freely. Fiesco
comes out of his hiding-place and reveals himself as Boccanegra's old
enemy, long thought dead. The Doge tells him they can be reconciled
now that Amelia is found. Amelia and Adorno enter, and Boccanegra
with his dying breath tells the former of her descent and appoints the
latter his successor. Fiesco announces the name of the new Doge to the
people from the balcony and tells them that Boccanegra is dead.

This opera is full of noble and moving music, particularly the
two great duets for Fiesco and Boccanegra in the Prologue and
in Act III, and Boccanegra's great plea for peace in Act I,

'Piango su voi, sul placido raggio del vostro clivo' ('Sadly I see the sweet bloom of spring on our native hillside'). There are also wonderful lyrical moments, as for instance Amelia's greeting to the dawn at the beginning of Act I, 'Come in quest'ora bruna' ('See how sky and ocean') with its shimmering, impressionist accompaniment, and Simone's lyrical reaction to the possibility of having found his daughter. The second scene of the first act, in the Council Chamber, is entirely an addition of Boito's, and certainly serves to clarify the plot. Verdi also made extensive revisions to the rest of the score and added most of the Prologue, the opening of Act III up to Boccanegra's entrance and most of the final quartet with chorus. Boccanegra is one of Verdi's finest characters, most clearly and consistently drawn in every note of his music and one of the most taxing and rewarding baritone roles he ever wrote.

Between the three successful operas of the years 1851–53 and his later masterpieces, *Un Ballo in Maschera* and *La Forza del Destino* in particular have been most lastingly effective. These transitional works display Verdi's change of style, as heralded in *La Traviata*; beautiful melody for its own sake gives way to themes of characterization and *bel canto* is increasingly made to serve emotional expression, and though the highly dramatic texts often rest on purely external effects, they are intensified, and raised to a higher level of spiritual sensibility.

The original story of Scribe, on which *Un Ballo in Maschera* is based, and which had already been used by Auber in 1833 for his opera *Gustave III ou le Bal Masqué*, concerned the assassination of King Gustavus III of Sweden, but the Austrian censorship forbade the stage presentation of a successful conspiracy against a reigning prince following an attempt on the life of Napoleon III by an Italian revolutionary, which took place while Verdi's opera was being rehearsed for its first performance at the San Carlo in Naples in 1858. The opera was withdrawn, and only passed the censorship when the scene was transferred to North America, with the Governor of Boston as the victim of a negro conspiracy. Since then it has often been performed in the Boston, and even a Neapolitan, setting, but undoubtedly the drama is most effective and the characters and motivation most convincing when it is restored to its original historical framework in late eighteenth-century Sweden. This has been done in post-war productions in Germany, England, Italy and especially at the Royal Opera, Stockholm.

UN BALLO IN MASCHERA (A Masked Ball). Opera in three acts by Giuseppe Verdi. Text after Eugène Scribe by Antonio Somma. First performance: Rome, 1859.

Characters: Riccardo, Count of Warwick (King Gustavus III of Sweden) —tenor; Renato, his secretary (Anckarstroem)—baritone; Amelia, Renato's wife—soprano; Ulrica, a fortune-teller (Mamzelle Arvidson)— contralto; Oscar, a page—soprano; Silvano, a sailor (Cristian)—baritone; Samuele (Count Ribbing) and Tomaso (Count Horn) conspirators— basses. A judge, Amelia's servant, populace, guards, courtiers.

Place: Boston or Stockholm. *Time:* end of the eighteenth century or March, 1792.

Act I. A reception hall in the governor's house. Courtiers and officers are awaiting the governor's arrival, among them a group of conspirators, who are only waiting for a suitable opportunity to kill the esteemed and beloved governor. Riccardo enters; he has little interest in affairs of state that day, and is more concerned with the list of invitations to the masked ball, which his page Oscar hands to him and which includes the name of Amelia, the wife of his secretary and friend Renato whom he secretly loves. Renato enters to warn his master against danger from the conspirators. A sentence of banishment on the fortune-teller Ulrica is laid before Riccardo for his signature. Oscar describes her doings to the governor, who decides to visit her personally, accompanied by his friends, all in disguise.

Scene ii. The fortune-teller's hut on the sea-shore. Ulrica sits in front of her magic cauldron and invokes the spirits, while women and children watch her in awed terror. Riccardo enters, disguised as a fisherman. He is soon followed by a sailor, Silvano, who asks to have his fortune told. Ulrica's prophecy that he will soon receive wealth and promotion is quickly fulfilled by Riccardo, who secretly slips some money and an officer's commission into his pocket. While everyone rejoices with him, Amelia's servant enters and speaks to Ulrica, who sends the crowd away as Amelia comes in. Riccardo conceals himself and overhears the subsequent dialogue. Amelia tells Ulrica that she has a secret love and implores her for a remedy to cure her of this tormenting passion. Ulrica knows a herb to quell forbidden love, which grows in a lonely and horrible place under the gallows outside the town and must be picked at midnight. Amelia prays to God to strengthen her in her fearful task and Riccardo resolves to accompany and protect her. Amelia goes out and the crowd returns, among them Riccardo's followers and the conspirators, all in disguise. Riccardo teasingly asks Ulrica to tell his fortune, and she prophesies that he will fall by the hand of a friend. This arouses general horror, and Riccardo also is impressed, though he hides his concern, asking her jokingly who could possibly be the murderer. Ulrica replies that it is he who will next take his hand in greeting. At that moment Renato hurries in, anxious for Riccardo's safety, and the Governor hastens to take his hand. Now he believes he can laugh away the prophecy, as it is the hand of his most faithful friend which he has just shaken. Recognized by everyone, Riccardo is joyfully acclaimed.

Act II. A lonely place at the foot of a hill. Amelia appears on the hill and slowly descends, full of the fear of death. Riccardo hastens to meet her; he asks nothing of her but an admission that she loves him. Unable to resist his pleas she confesses that she does indeed love him, but declares that she intends to remain faithful to her husband. Steps are heard approaching; it is Renato, who has come to warn his master against the conspirators who have followed him and are preparing to fall on him in this solitary place. Amelia has drawn a heavy veil over her face. Riccardo reluctantly agrees to flee, since he can see no other solution, but first he makes Renato promise to conduct the unknown lady safely to the gates of the town without attempting to follow her further or to penetrate her disguise. He exchanges cloaks with Renato and hurries out as the conspirators enter from the opposite direction. When instead of the Count they find Renato they are furious, and demand at least to see the face of the veiled beauty. Renato draws his sword when they threaten him, and to save him Amelia drops her veil. Renato is completely shattered; Sam starts a derisive song and the others join in mocking him. Renato recovers his self-possession and summons the chief conspirators to meet him the following morning at his house.

Act III, scene i. Renato's study. Amelia tries to exonerate herself but cannot persuade Renato to believe her, and resigns herself to die at his hand. Renato however believes that not she, but Riccardo, is the sole cause of this misfortune, and that he alone must die. The principal conspirators Sam and Tom come in. Renato announces that he is on their side and asks them to let him kill the Count. Sam and Tom also long for personal revenge and they therefore agree to draw lots to decide who shall kill him. Amelia enters to announce that the page Oscar is waiting outside. They make her draw out the chosen name: it is Renato. Amelia suspects what it is all about and is determined to send the Count a warning. Oscar enters and gaily conveys the Count's invitation to the masked ball.

Scene ii. Riccardo's study. Riccardo is thinking about Amelia, but he is firmly decided to renounce her; he will send Renato back to England and Amelia will accompany him. Oscar brings him a letter from an anonymous lady, warning him not to go to the masked ball, as an attempt will be made on his life. Riccardo does not want to seem cowardly, and in any case hopes to see Amelia once more at the ball.

Scene iii. The ballroom. Renato tries to make Oscar tell him how Riccardo is dressed and eventually learns that he is wearing a black domino with pink ribbons. Amelia approaches in a white domino and implores Riccardo to leave the ball. In spite of her mask and disguised voice, Riccardo recognizes her, and tells her that she is to leave for England with Renato on the following day, so that he must now bid her a final farewell. Renato, who has been watching them both, throws himself on Riccardo and stabs him with a dagger. (In the Swedish setting, the King is shot.) With his dying breath Riccardo assures Renato of

Amelia's innocence, and asks that his murderer and all the conspirators should be pardoned.

The various changes of milieu have not spoiled the opera, for the colour and the atmosphere of the music remain unmistakably Italian. Among the quantity of splendid moments of musical inspiration one can single out in particular Renato's *scena* and aria in the second act 'Eri tu' ('It was you') when he decides to take revenge on Riccardo. The passionate outburst of hatred with its hammering rhythms in the accompaniment is contrasted with the delicate love melody which recalls his devotion to Amelia; it is a display number for any lyric baritone.

Andante sostenuto

O dol - cez - ze per-du - te! O me-mo - rie d'un am-
(*Oh how sad - ly I call to re-mem-brance hopes of*

ples-so che l'es - se - re in - di - a!
love for ev - er de - par - ted)

LA FORZA DEL DESTINO (The Force of Destiny). Opera in four acts by Giuseppe Verdi. Text by Francesco Maria Piave. First performance: St Petersburg, 1862.

Characters: Marchese di Calatrava—bass; Donna Leonora di Vargas and Don Carlos di Vargas (his children)—soprano and baritone; Don Alvaro—tenor; Il Padre Guardiano—bass; Fra Melitone—baritone; Preziosilla, a gipsy—mezzo-soprano; Trabucco, a muleteer—tenor; the Alcalde of Hornachuelos—bass; a surgeon—tenor; Curra, Leonora's maid—soprano. Monks, soldiers, people.

Place: Spain and Italy. *Time:* middle of the eighteenth century.

Act I. Leonora's room in the Marchese's country house. Leonora is in love with the Peruvian Alvaro. Since her father would never agree to her marrying him, Leonora has decided to elope. With a guilty conscience, she bids her father goodnight and sadly takes leave of all the beloved objects around her. At the agreed sign—a lighted candle at the open window—Alvaro enters. Leonora begs him for a day's grace, but Alvaro assumes that her faltering determination means that she has changed her mind. His accusation decides Leonora, who throws herself into his arms, declaring that she is ready to accompany him. The Marchese and some servants who have heard sounds enter to investigate. Alvaro chivalrously stands in front of his beloved, taking all the blame and, throwing himself on the Marchese's mercy, he discards his sword and pistol. As he does so, the gun goes off and mortally wounds the Marchese who curses his daughter as the desperate Alvaro takes to flight, dragging Leonora with him.

Act II. The inn at Hornachuelos. In their flight, Alvaro and Leonora have been separated. Leonora, disguised as a youth, is on her way to seek refuge in a Franciscan Monastery where she hopes to be admitted through the intercession of the holy Father Cleto. Her brother Don Carlos, disguised as a student in black attire, is looking for her. Leonora, who has spent the night in the inn, recognizes him without his seeing her, and keeps herself hidden. Crowds throng the scene; soldiers are being recruited for a campaign in Italy, and the fortune-teller Preziosilla arrives and is greeted on all sides. Don Carlos tells his story in the form of a ballad. Leonora listens unnoticed and learns that Alvaro has fled abroad. She feels herself abandoned and betrayed.

Scene ii. The monastery of the Madonna degli Angeli. Leonora asks to be admitted and first meets the grumbling Fra Melitone. He announces her arrival to the Father Guardian, who already knows of her coming through a message from Father Cleto. She wishes to spend the rest of her life in a solitary cell near the monastery, atoning for her sin.

Act III, scene i. The camp of the Spanish and Italian troops near Velletri. Alvaro has joined the army and has been promoted to captain for his great courage in the face of the enemy. He thinks that Leonora is dead and despairingly bewails his fate. Don Carlos is set on by a gang of thieves near the camp, and Alvaro, hastening to his aid, rescues him. Without recognizing one another, they vow eternal friendship. A little later Alvaro, who has been seriously wounded in the battle, gives Don Carlos a casket of letters, asking him to burn them after his death. Don Carlos senses a mystery behind this and his suspicions are aroused because Alvaro had reacted with horror at the name Calatrava. He can hardly resist the temptation to open the casket and discover the secret, and when he throws the letters away from him a portrait falls out of the box, which he recognizes as that of his sister; he has no doubt that he has found Alvaro, his father's murderer.

Scene ii. The military camp. Preziosilla the fortune-teller, Trabucco the muleteer and even Fra Melitone as an army chaplain, have followed the troops. Each of them appears in a short scene; Fra Melitone preaches to the people an extremely witty moral sermon, which at Verdi's request Piave took from Schiller's famous Capucin sermon in his drama, *Wallensteins Lager*. A chorus of soldiers, recruits, camp-followers and the like make the background for these scenes. Meanwhile Alvaro has recovered from his wounds, thanks to Carlos, who had cared for him only in order to challenge him to a duel. Alvaro refuses to take arms against his beloved's brother. Only when Carlos tells him that Leonora is still alive and that he intends to kill her as well does Alvaro draw his sword and throw himself on the furious Don Carlos. Guards separate them and Alvaro breaks his sword in two, for he has resolved to seek peace in a monastery.

Act IV, scene i. The monastery of the Madonna degli Angeli. Fra Melitone is distributing soup to the people; they do not like his rough manners, and praise the holy Father Raffaele who had previously dispensed the soup. This Father Raffaele is Alvaro, who found refuge in this monastery several years earlier without having any idea that Leonora was living close by. Don Carlos has finally discovered Alvaro's refuge, and faced at last with his enemy he provokes Alvaro with insults until the latter seizes the sword that Don Carlos has brought for him, and they hurry out.

Scene ii. A rocky place in front of Leonora's hermitage. Leonora's life of penance has greatly weakened her body, and her soul longs for peace. Carlos and Alvaro enter fighting, and Carlos is at that moment seriously wounded. Alvaro knocks at the door of the hut and calls on the hermit for help. Leonora comes out and recognizes Alvaro; in horror he confesses that he has killed her brother; Leonora hurries to the dying Carlos, who summons up enough strength to stab his sister. The Father Guardian enters and blesses Leonora, who dies in Alvaro's arms.

The grandly designed and exceptionally effective overture is dominated by the theme of destiny. It appears at the very be-

ginning and can be heard faintly through the other themes developed in the course of the overture, which also return later in the opera. Especially remarkable is the beautiful *cantilena*

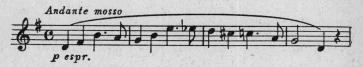

from Leonora's second act aria, which is the grandiose climax of the overture. Both textually and musically the first act is exceptionally lofty and concise. The plot opens like a misty ballad-story with the fervent love-scene as its nucleus. The music is magnificently built up to a climax, from the doom-laden *moderato* of the first scene, and the melancholy *andante* of Leonora's farewell aria to the passionate *brio* of the love-duet and the agitated *presto* of the final scene.

The second act is built on a sharp contrast between the colourful movement of the crowd scene and the religious atmosphere of the monastery. The dramatic and musical climax comes in the monastery scene when the organ is heard, and the first rosy glow of dawn appears in the sky as the noble melody from Leonora's aria rises again in the orchestra.

The third act contains not only fine arias for the two men but also their duet, in which Alvaro's wonderful rhythmic

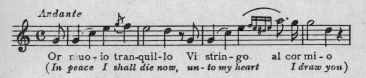

Or muo - io tran-quil-lo   Vi strin - go.   al cor mi - o
(*In peace I shall die now,   un - to my heart   I draw you*)

cantilena is joined by Carlos's more sombre and restrained melody; dark foreboding already shudders through his oath of friendship.

The final act overflows with musical wonders; in the introduction the agitated theme of destiny is heard again, and Leonora's aria imploring God for peace ('Pace, pace, mio dio') is of outstanding melodic beauty. The final trio with each voice distinguished by its characteristic music, with its dramatic strength and exquisite melodies, shows Verdi's genius at its purest.

When he wrote *Les Vêpres Siciliennes* for the Paris Opéra in 1855, Verdi had felt limited by the strict requirements of grand opera, yet he was obsessed with the fascinating task of creating a true musical tragedy even within the framework of melodramatic splendour. The decisive step in solving this problem was the composition of *Don Carlos*, which he wrote in 1867 for the Paris Opéra, and the culmination of his efforts was reached in *Aida*, composed in 1871. Before *Don Carlos*, Verdi revised *Macbeth*, for production at the Théâtre Lyrique in Paris, but in spite of extensive alterations the revival made relatively little impression.

Much more significant in Verdi's work is *Don Carlos*. Whereas much in *Les Vêpres Siciliennes* still seemed superficial, in *Don Carlos* action and music are knit together more naturally and more profoundly.

DON CARLOS. Opera in five acts by Giuseppe Verdi. Text after Friedrich von Schiller by Josephe Méry and Camille du Locle. First performance: Paris, 1867. (Revised version: Milan, 1884.)

Characters: Philippe II, King of Spain—bass; Élisabeth de Valois—soprano; Don Carlos, Philippe's son—tenor; Rodrigo, Marquis de Posa—baritone; Princesse Eboli—mezzo-soprano; Count Lerma—tenor; the Grand Inquisitor—bass; Tebaldo, a page—soprano; a monk—bass; a herald—tenor; a voice from heaven—soprano. French and Spanish courtiers, monks, priests, townspeople, guards.

Place: France and Spain. *Time:* mid-sixteenth century.

Act I. The forest of Fontainebleau. Don Carlos has come secretly to France to see Élisabeth de Valois, who has been chosen to be his wife. She enters with her page, Tebaldo, searching for her hunting companions from whom she has been separated. Carlos sings of the love which has filled him at sight of her, and on her return offers to escort her home, saying he is one of the staff of the Spanish envoy. The Princess questions him about Don Carlos, her betrothed, and the Prince, assuring her that their marriage will be one of love, shows her a portrait of himself. They confess their love for one another in the duet 'Di qual amor, di quant' ardor' ('Ah yes, 'tis love). Tebaldo returns and warns the Princess that the Spanish envoy is coming to ask for her hand in marriage to the King of Spain, not to Don Carlos. Elisabeth accedes to the prayers of the crowd who beg her to accept the offer and so put an end to the war between France and Spain. The two lovers express their anguish while the crowd acclaims the Princess.

Act II, scene i. The monastery of San Yuste in Madrid. A monk is kneeling in front of the chapel containing the grave of the Emperor Charles V, while a chorus sounds faintly from the chapel. Day is slowly dawning. Don Carlos, pale and troubled, enters and bewails the cruel fate which has deprived him of his bride. The monk, who has heard Don Carlos's outburst, tells him that only in death can salvation be found. Carlos believes he recognizes the monk's voice as that of the late emperor, his grandfather, who it is rumoured is still alive and spending his last years in the monastery. The Marquis of Posa, the Prince's friend who has just returned from Flanders where the population is longing for freedom, enters. Don Carlos tells him of his passion for his stepmother. Posa advises him to ask his father to send him to Flanders as viceroy so as to help the population and at the same time to master his passion. The King and the Queen enter on their way to prayer. Carlos and Posa fervently affirm their friendship for one another; their highest aim is the struggle for freedom.

Scene ii. A garden outside the monastery. The Queen's ladies, among them the beautiful Princess Eboli, are passing the time with singing and chatter. The Queen enters and soon after Posa is announced, craving an audience so that he may hand her a letter from Paris, from her mother the Queen of France. Together with this letter, Posa slips a note into the Queen's hand. It is from Carlos, who also craves an audience. She sends the page to call him, and Posa leads the Princess Eboli out of earshot by regaling her with gossip from Paris. Carlos enters, and asks the Queen to intercede for him with the King as he wants to leave

Madrid and go to Flanders. When after a short interview the Queen tries to dismiss Carlos, he can no longer restrain his feelings, and she also is carried away by his passion. In the end Carlos embraces his beloved and flees in despair. The King enters and is enraged to find the Queen alone. When the frightened courtiers gather quickly round, he banishes the lady-in-waiting in charge, the Countess of Aremberg, the Queen's only compatriot and true friend. After a touching farewell the Queen retires in tears. The King calls back Posa as he is about to follow the other courtiers. He respects the Marquis, who has never tried to gain favour with him. Philip is a lonely man and would like to confide in Posa, who seizes the opportunity to plead for a less rigorous regime in the unhappy land of Flanders. The King listens sympathetically, but warns Posa against the Grand Inquisitor.

Act III, scene i. The palace gardens in Madrid. Carlos has received a letter making a rendezvous in the garden for that night, and he is convinced that it was sent by the Queen. Princess Eboli enters, heavily veiled; it was she who wrote the letter; she loves Carlos, and believes that he returns her love. Carlos, believing that he is embracing the Queen, presses her tenderly to his breast, only to learn his mistake too late. The Princess finds herself repulsed and realizes that Carlos loves the Queen. Posa enters to help Carlos, and when the Princess threatens to reveal everything he draws his dagger to kill her. Carlos prevents him, and the furious Princess hurries away. Posa persuades his friend to hand over to him all his correspondence, since anything may happen now.

Scene ii. The great square in front of the cathedral. The King with his court and the populace are gathered to watch the grisly spectacle of an *auto-da-fé*. Carlos enters at the head of a Flemish delegation and asks the King to make him Viceroy of Flanders. The King declares that Carlos is out of his mind, and the latter draws his sword. Posa saves the situation by obeying the King when no one else will and quietly disarming his friend. Carlos is marched off under guard and the *auto-da-fé* continues. As the procession moves off, a heavenly voice is heard, promising peace in the next world to the sufferers.

Act IV, scene i. The King's study. It is dawn. The King is sitting at his desk, where the candles have almost burnt out. Tormenting thoughts beset him and he sings of Élisabeth, 'Ella giammai m'amo' ('She has no love for me'). He wishes he had the gift of understanding the hearts of men and is filled with a sense of bitter loneliness. Peace is not for him on earth, but only when he sets out on the last journey of death. The Grand Inquisitor is announced. Philip tells this Prince of the Church that Carlos is trying to rebel against him and the Inquisitor agrees that Carlos must die if he is threatening the authority of the church. Above all, however, he insists that the King must have the Marquis of Posa executed as well. The King demurs but finally has to yield to the power of the church. After the Inquisitor has gone, the Queen rushes into the room: someone has stolen her jewel-casket. To her horror she sees it on the King's desk; he forces it open and takes out a portrait of Carlos. Taking this as proof of the Queen's infidelity, he calls her an adulteress, whereupon she faints. The King calls for help and Princess Eboli and Posa enter. The

King deeply regrets the injustice he has done the Queen, and Eboli in despair accuses herself of slandering the innocent Queen. Alone with the Queen, she throws herself at the latter's feet and confesses her crime. Out of jealousy she stole the jewel-case and took it to the King. She tells Élisabeth that she loves Carlos, but he does not return her love, and worse still, that she has been the King's mistress. The Queen banishes her from the court, and the Princess, cursing the fatal beauty which has caused her downfall in the aria 'O don fatale' ('O fatal beauty'), resolves to retire into a convent, but first she will save Carlos.

Scene ii. A prison. Through the iron grating one can see into the courtyard where guards pace up and down. Posa comes to bid farewell to Carlos; he has taken on himself the suspicion of having incited the Flemish to revolt, and Carlos's letters serve as a proof. Carlos wants to go at once to the King to explain everything, but it is too late. A bullet from the courtyard strikes Posa, who collapses, fatally wounded. The King enters to set his son free again, but Carlos turns away from his father, the murderer of his friend. The crowd, spurred on by Eboli, presses into the prison in an uproar, calling for the Infanta. The Grand Inquisitor succeeds in calming the people and bids them kneel before their King.

Act V. The monastery of San Yuste as in Act II. It is night. The Queen comes to the tomb of Charles V to implore his spirit to give her consolation. She had promised Posa to reason with Carlos, and has summoned him here for a last meeting. Carlos enters; he must go to Flanders to complete the work of peace begun by his friend. Sorrowfully they part for ever. The King arrives with the Grand Inquisitor, and the Inquisition guards come forward to arrest Carlos, who steps back with drawn sword. The mysterious monk comes out of the chapel of Charles V and takes Carlos back with him into the darkness.

Don Carlos was conceived in the grandiose, spectacular operatic style which had been established by Meyerbeer at the Paris Opéra, but for performances elsewhere its great length was, and is, a disadvantage. In 1884 Verdi and Ghislanzoni (the librettist of *Aida*) undertook the production of a shorter version to an Italian translation of the text. This involved cutting out the ballet music and most of the first act, which is of course essential for the subsequent dramatic action. In Germany the opera is always performed in the four-act version, but in France it is generally given in full. Recent revivals in Italy and England have made a point of retaining the first act, even if cuts have to be made elsewhere.

Apart from its dramatic importance, Act I contains some beautiful music, particularly Carlos's romance and his lovely duet with Élisabeth, in which the delicate phrase sung by her to the words 'Di qual amor, di quant'ardor quest'alma è piena!'

('Ah yes 'tis love, 'tis fervent love, with which my heart is
beating') is used later in the opera as a motif, particularly in
Élisabeth's fifth act aria 'Tu che le vanità' ('God, who knowest
the hearts and the frailty of mortals') when she recalls the
happiness of her youth.

The whole opera is full of exquisite and inspired melody, as
well as impressive dramatic effect, as for example in the scene
at the Emperor's tomb in Act II, where the atmosphere is
created with a few deft strokes in the mysterious progression
from minor to major. The most strikingly drawn character is
that of the King; his great *scena* 'Ella giammai m'amo' has
immense intensity and power and shows Verdi's supreme
mastery of characterization. Another convincing portrayal of
Philip's character is his great dialogue with Posa, where the
younger man's fiery enthusiasm is contrasted with the King's
calm, balanced judgment and sombre warning. From a
recitative-like reserve spring urgent melodies which make this
scene the climax of the second act. Princess Eboli's great aria
in Act IV is a particularly effective piece of dramatic vocal music,
though somewhat in the style of the younger Verdi; in contrast,
a splendid example of later Verdi characteristics is to be found
in the Queen's aria in the fifth act. The broad sweep of the

S'an-cor si pian-ge in   cie - - lo,
(*Hear my com-plaint in   heav'n,____ I pray*)

melody, the passionate *espressivo* which is directly contrasted
with the delicate idyll, the thematic detail in the accompaniment and the freely improvised breadth of structure: everything
points to Verdi's final perfection of his style.

The promise contained in *Don Carlos* was gloriously fulfilled
in *Aida*: all the ideas which French opera could offer Verdi had
now been absorbed by him and reproduced in his own original
style. The splendid structure of grand opera served purely as
the frame for a plot of human and spiritual significance; the
gulf between recitative and *arioso* was extensively bridged; the
dramatic flow of the vocal line now surged forward without

hindrance and the orchestra was also most variedly handled in what is perhaps Verdi's greatest technical triumph.

Verdi was commissioned to write *Aida* by the Khedive of Egypt for the opening of the Italian Theatre, and not, as is often erroneously stated, for the opening of the Suez Canal. He was at first opposed to this idea, but was won round by the story suggested to him as a basis for the libretto. The composer took such an active part in the detailed preparation of the dramatic scenario that his librettist Ghislanzoni was left with just the verses to write. The result was complete harmony between text and music, and also a balance of traditional and novel ideas which has been a lasting model for the next genera-tion of Italian opera composers. Owing to the Franco-Prussian War, there was a delay in the completion of the opera, and when it was eventually produced in December 1871, the theatre had already been open for two years.

AIDA. Opera in four acts by Giuseppe Verdi. Text by Antonio Ghislan-zoni. First performance: Cairo, 1871.

Characters: the King—bass; Amneris, his daughter—mezzo-soprano; Aida, an Ethiopian slave—soprano; Radames, captain of the guard—tenor; Ramfis, the high priest—bass; Amonasro, King of Ethiopia, Aida's father—baritone; a messenger—tenor; a priestess—soprano. Priests and priestesses, populace, warriors, guards, Ethiopian prisoners.

Place: Egypt. *Time:* the epoch of the Pharaohs.

Act I, scene i. A hall in the royal palace at Memphis. The Ethiopians are threatening to invade Egypt again; who will lead the Egyptian army into battle? Ramfis tells Radames that the gods have already made known their choice, and he looks significantly at the young hero. Radames's greatest wish is to be made commander of the army and to return victorious, so that he can wed his beloved Aida, who is now living as a slave at Pharaoh's court. These thoughts he expresses in 'Celeste Aida' ('Radiant Aida'). Amneris, who loves Radames and expects her love to be returned, now enters, and when Aida appears she starts involuntarily, but masters herself and greets Aida with feigned kindness. Amneris believes she has detected a secret understanding between Aida and Radames and is full of suspicion. The King enters with his retinue, and a messenger announces that the Ethiopians have invaded Egypt and that their plundering hordes, laying waste the country, have already reached Thebes. Amonasro is their leader: 'My father,' murmurs Aida. The King announces that Isis has chosen Radames to lead the Egyptian army. The forceful war march, begun by the King, is fervently taken up by every-one else. When the crowds cry 'Ritorna vincitor' ('Victorious return'), Aida finds herself joining in the general tumult. Left alone, however, she realizes the implication of her own words: she is wishing him victory,

victory over her own people. In desperation she implores the gods to let her die, that she may be freed from her anguish.

Scene ii. The Temple of Vulcan. From within echoes the ritual song of the priestesses. Before the altar stand Ramfis and the priests. Radames is brought in that he may be given the consecrated sword, and the god is invoked in solemn supplication.

Act II, scene i. A room in Amneris's apartments. The Egyptians have won the battle and victory celebrations are being prepared for Radames's return. Slaves are adorning the Princess for the occasion, while negro slaves perform a dance. Amneris can only think of seeing Radames again, but the sight of Aida re-awakens her suspicion and she determines to discover Aida's secret. To test her, she tells her that Radames has fallen in battle, and Aida is visibly overwhelmed with grief. Then Amneris puts her to the final test. Gazing fixedly at the poor girl, she tells her she was lying: Radames is alive. Aida's cry of joy removes Amneris's last shred of doubt and she now knows that Aida is her rival. The battle-chorus is heard from without and reminds Amneris of the celebrations. Aida must accompany her to the festivities, kneeling in the dust before her as a slave. Aida is left alone, and again she implores the gods to protect and have mercy upon her.

Scene ii. An open space outside the gates of Thebes. The King and the people are awaiting the victorious warriors' return, and as they pass by they are hailed by the rejoicing populace. Dancers and dancing girls follow with the captured treasure, and finally, Radames. The King thanks him for the victory and promises to fulfil his every wish, and Amneris places the victor's crown upon his brow. The Ethiopian prisoners are led in under guard, among them Amonasro, who is concealing his identity. Aida hurries to her father's side, but he tells her not to betray him. Proudly he approaches the King and tells him of the battle in which King Amonasro has lost his life, imploring the King's clemency for himself and for his people. Radames also pleads for the prisoners, and his wish must be fulfilled. The priests oppose this act of mercy, but Ramfis reluctantly agrees on condition that Aida's father is kept as a hostage. Finally the King announces that Amneris offers her hand to the victorious general and that Radames will one day reign over Egypt. General rejoicing breaks out, and only Aida is in despair; Amonasro exhorts her to take courage.

Act III. On the banks of the Nile. It is a moonlit, starry night. The temple of Isis is half hidden among the palm-trees. Amneris comes to the temple to spend the night there in prayer before her marriage. Aida enters hesitantly; Radames has asked her to meet him here. If this is to be their final parting, death alone must be her lot. Sorrowfully Aida thinks of her native land which she will never see again. Amonasro has followed her, guessing that she is to meet Radames. The Ethiopians have again taken up arms, to deal a decisive blow to the Egyptians. Only one thing remains to be learned: by which route the Egyptian army will attack them, and Aida must discover this secret from Radames. When Aida refuses, Amonasro casts her furiously from him crying 'Non sei mia figlia—Dei Faraoni tu sei la schiava' ('You are no longer my daughter—you are the Pharaoh's slave!'). Aida humbly submits to her fate; her patriotism must come before her love for Radames. Radames enters joyously, and Amonasro quickly hides himself. Radames is full of confidence. If he is victorious in the coming battle against the Ethiopians, he will confide in the King and claim Aida as his reward. Aida points out that Amneris will never tolerate a union between them. There is only one solution: flight! Aida makes every effort to persuade her beloved to take this course. First flattering and seductive, then passionately demanding, she brings him to a firm decision: he is ready to flee with her. When Aida asks him which way they should go to avoid the Egyptian forces, Radames chooses the route which the army will take on the following day, and names it. Amonasro emerges from his hiding-place and reveals his identity to Radames. Radames is horrified to realize that he has betrayed his country. Amneris arrives with Ramfis, and Amonasro throws himself on Amneris to kill her, but Radames steps forward to protect her. Dragging Aida with him, Amonasro escapes, leaving Radames behind. With the words 'Sacerdote, io resto a te' ('Priest of Isis, I remain with you') Radames gives his sword to Ramfis.

Act IV, scene i. A room in the palace, above the underground hall of judgment. Amneris sends for Radames, whom she still loves, and when he is brought in she asks him to vindicate himself before the priests. He, however, has no wish to live any longer and welcomes the thought of death. Amneris breaks out passionately 'Ah! tu dei vivere! Sì, all'amor mio vivrai' ('Ah, you must live! Yes, for my love you shall live').

But what can life offer to Radames, if Aida is no longer alive? To give the man she still passionately loves new courage to live, Amneris decides to tell him that Amonasro has been killed in flight, but that Aida has escaped. Radames draws a deep sigh of relief; death will be easy for him now that he knows his beloved is still alive. Amneris accepts his scorn and hands him over to the priests. From the subterranean hall of judgment are heard the sombre choruses of the priests. Radames must vindicate himself, but he keeps silence in the face of all accusations. Amneris then hears the terrible sentence pronounced: Radames is to be buried alive.

Scene ii. The stage is divided in two; the upper part represents the inside of the temple of Vulcan flooded with light, while below is a crypt with arches which disappear from view in the darkness. Radames is alone in the crypt, his thoughts dwelling on Aida. A sound makes him start; it is Aida who has slipped into the dungeon secretly, to die beside him. In vain does Radames try to remove the stone from the entrance. 'O terra addio, addio valle di pianti' ('Farewell, oh earth, farewell thou vale of sorrow') sings Aida, and Radames joins her even as her voice is dying away. Above the mighty chorus of the priests invoking the omnipotent Ftah (Vulcan) in the temple is heard. Aida and Radames ecstatically abandon themselves to death, and Aida expires in Radames's arms.

The music of *Aida* is of marvellous beauty. Verdi's unique skill in finding a valid means of expression through the power of the melodic line alone here reaches its climax. Some important

themes are consciously used as *leitmotivs,* for instance the yearning Aida motif, on which the delicate, reserved prelude is

based. A proud theme always accompanies Amneris's entrance,

and a spirited motif also recurs to express her jealousy. Verdi

has lavished an exceptional wealth of melody on *Aida.* Passionate sensuality fills Amneris's 'Ah, vieni vieni, amor mio,
m'inebbria', '(Ah, come love, come love, with rapture fill me'),
while Radames's romance is fervent and intense. What joy

pervades Radames's shout of love, and what supreme ecstasy

is expressed in the wonderful melody in which Aida and Radames take leave of life! Verdi is amazingly skilful in evoking

an atmosphere with the simplest devices, for instance in the delicate whispering prelude to the third act, with its spread *pianissimo* octaves in the muted violins, the flageolet sounds of the cellos, and above them a solo flute which at first only touches on the tonic and dominant, but then hovers between the major and the minor. These are just suggestions of orchestral colouring, which evoke a landscape of compelling atmosphere. The chorus of the priestesses from within the temple, which also varies between the major and the minor, underlines the exotic charm of the introductory scene.

Verdi's predilection for march rhythms comes into its own with the series of splendid martial tunes in the final scene of Act II, in which the stirring rhythms of the people's chorus are contrasted with the sombre canon of the priests. Best known is the triumphal march which accompanies the procession of victorious Egyptian warriors past their king. At the centre of this brilliant pageantry is Amonasro's plea to the King, and on

it is built the great ensemble in which the prisoners, Aida and Amonasro, supported by the people, plead for mercy, while the priests rigidly stand out against them.

The first performance, which Verdi did not attend because he was afraid of the sea-voyage, created a world-wide sensation, intensified at the Italian première which took place six weeks later at La Scala, Milan. Before long this opera had enjoyed tremendous success all over the world.

Sixteen years passed between *Aida* and Verdi's next opera, *Otello*, a silence only broken by the composition of the *Requiem* (1874) and of some minor works, in addition to the revision of *Simone Boccanegra* for La Scala, Milan in 1881.

Boito's libretto for *Otello* is poetry in the best sense of the word, and inspired Verdi as much by its dramatic construction and delineation of the principal characters as by its beautiful language. The libretto itself tends more towards music-drama than opera and cannot be broken down into arias, duets and ensembles as that of *Aida*. During his long silence, Verdi had witnessed Wagner's struggle and victory. Bayreuth had been founded, and Wagner's conception of music-drama established. Obviously a composer as bold and sensitive as Verdi could not remain untouched by these events and changes in his own field. When Verdi finished *Otello* he was already seventy-three, but he was ready to seize on the new ideas and to interpret them in his own manner. Whereas Wagner found his way from 'Sprechgesang' to continuous melody, for Verdi the splendid vocal line of the aria was his starting point on the way to the same goal. Though *Otello* may rank as a music-drama, it is still firmly founded on the everliving tradition of Italian vocal opera.

OTELLO. Opera in four acts by Giuseppe Verdi. Text after William Shakespeare by Arrigo Boito. First performance: Milan, 1887.

Characters: Otello, a Moor, general in the Venetian army, appointed Governor of Cyprus—tenor; Cassio, his lieutenant—tenor; Iago, his ensign—baritone; Rodrigo, a Venetian noble—tenor; Lodovico, ambassador of the Venetian republic—bass; Montano, former governor of Cyprus—bass; Desdemona, Otello's wife—soprano; Emilia, Iago's wife and Desdemona's lady-in-waiting—mezzo-soprano; a herald—bass. Venetian soldiers, sailors, ladies and gentlemen, Cypriot men and women.

Place: Cyprus. *Time:* end of the fifteenth century.

Act I. A square in front of the castle with a view over the harbour and the sea. It is a stormy evening and a strong gale is blowing. An excited crowd has gathered on the shore, looking out to sea where a galley is fighting against the waves. It is the general's ship which is in danger of sinking. The crowd kneels down and prays for God's help. Among those watching the terrifying scene are Iago and Rodrigo. At last there is a cry of joy: the ship, its mast already broken, has entered the shelter of the harbour. Otello enters with his retinue and announces his victory over the Turks. The populace acclaims him as he goes into the castle. Meanwhile the storm has subsided and a bonfire is lit on the shore. Iago plays on Rodrigo, inciting him against the lieutenant Cassio, whom he hates, as he also hates Otello, because the latter has promoted Cassio to lieutenant over his head. Iago has ordered some wine and gaily drinks to Cassio, whom he gradually succeeds in making drunk. Rodrigo's laughter suddenly inflames Cassio's temper, and Montano's interference drives him into a towering rage. He draws his sword, and Montano has to defend himself. Iago incites the crowd to cry murder and the general tumult brings Otello to the scene. To Iago's secret delight Cassio is deprived of his rank. Desdemona, frightened by the noise, enters, looking for her husband, who commands everyone to be quiet. Otello and Desdemona are left alone; the moon has risen and the sea and the harbour are enveloped in infinite peace as their voices join in an exquisite love-duet.

Act II. A hall in the castle with a view over the gardens. Iago maliciously suggests to Cassio that he ask Desdemona to intercede for him with Otello. After Cassio has left him, Iago reveals his true nature in the famous 'Credo' monologue. He only believes in evil and despises all that is noble. Desdemona appears in the garden with Emilia; Cassio hurries towards her and she receives him kindly. Otello must see this scene! As Iago goes to call him he is already on his way in. With simulated naïvety, Iago arouses Otello's jealousy; Otello demands proof, but suspicion has already taken firm root in his mind. A gentle chorus is heard from sailors with their wives and children, who come to pay homage to Desdemona. This peaceful scene makes Otello forget his troubled thoughts, but they are at once revived by Desdemona herself, who in all innocence asks her husband to pardon Cassio. He roughly rejects her request, and then pleads a headache as the cause of his abruptness. She tries to bind his head with her handkerchief but he impatiently throws it to the ground. Emilia picks it up, and Iago snatches it from her unobserved. Desdemona is perplexed by her husband's aloofness, and asks him for a kind word, but he roughly dismisses her, and then abandons himself to his despair; all his former joys have vanished. Iago pretends to console him, but Otello angrily throws himself on the scoundrel, demanding proofs. Iago's cynicism knows no limits; he tells Otello that he has heard Cassio murmuring Desdemona's name in his sleep, in rapturous recollection of happiness with his beloved. He then draws Otello's attention to an embroidered handkerchief which he says he saw in Cassio's hands. Otello is beside himself with rage, for this handkerchief was his first gift to Desdemona. His oath of vengeance, in which Iago joins him, mounts in a *crescendo* of terrible grandeur.

Act III. The great hall in the castle. Iago is still pursuing his ends. He suggests to Otello that he should talk with Cassio, while Otello hides and listens. As Iago goes out he calls to Otello to remember the handkerchief. Desdemona enters and Otello greets her with cold irony. Again he complains of a headache, and again she wants to cool his forehead,

but this time she does not offer the right handkerchief, which Otello
demands from her. He shakes her roughly and tears well up in her eyes;
she has never see him like this before. Otello is left alone, torn with
mistrust. When Iago and Cassio enter together, he hides and listens to
their conversation, which Iago conducts so ingeniously that Otello just
hears broken fragments, from which he concludes that Desdemona is
betraying him with Cassio. He even sees in Cassio's hands the handkerchief which Iago has passed to him. This is too much, and when he is
alone again with Iago he asks how he should kill her. Iago suggests
suffocating her in the bed where she sinned. Out of gratitude Otello
promotes Iago to captain. The Venetian ambassador enters with a
retinue, and Desdemona and Otello's court come in to receive their
guests. The ambassador brings orders from the Doge that he is to set sail
at once for Venice, while Cassio is named as his successor. Unfortunately
Desdemona at this moment intercedes again for Cassio. This sends
Otello into an ungovernable rage and he throws her to the floor. Desdemona is overwhelmed with shame and horror. 'Yield to Otello's
anger,' shouts the general, and to Desdemona, who approaches him
imploringly, he cries 'Curses and damnation on your soul'. Everyone
leaves the hall, and only Iago stays with the raging Otello. This outburst has completely exhausted him, and he collapses unconscious.
From without is heard a joyful chorus in praise of the lion of Venice.
Pitiless and scornfully triumphant, Iago points to Otello on the floor:
'Ecco il leone!' ('There is the lion!').

  Act IV. Desdemona's bedroom. It is night. A lamp burns over the
prie-dieu and a candle stands on the table. Emilia combs Desdemona's
hair as her mistress sings the willow-song. A presentiment of death pervades this scene and enters into Desdemona also; her desperate farewell
to Emilia and her humble prayer of supplication seem filled with fear.
When Otello enters, Desdemona is asleep in her bed. He approaches,
watching her for a long time, and then awakens her with a kiss. Otello's
decision is immutable, and his voice like ice. To her plea to be allowed to
live through the night he answers sharply no, and then smothers her.
The tragedy now hastens to its end; Emilia enters, and when she cries
out that Otello has murdered Desdemona, Cassio, Lodovico and Iago
hurry in. In a few words the diabolic plot is revealed and Iago flees.
Otello's end is terrible; the sword with which he had wanted to kill Iago
drops from his nerveless hand. Utterly crushed he bends over the body
of his beloved, and before the onlookers can stop him draws a dagger
from his doublet and kills himself.

  The taut strength of the *Otello* libretto is emphasized by the
broad, sweeping lines of the music. The first act in particular
is of a masterly, unified construction. The restless fluctuations
of the choral and ensemble scenes, only briefly interrupted by
Otello's triumphant appearance, gradually raise the tension. The
introductory chorus with its evocation of the storm is followed

by the fire ensemble, in which chorus and orchestra pointedly illustrate the blazing and dying down of the flames. The drink-

ing song and the fight scene add to the mounting tension and there is something diabolical in Iago's rendering of the drinking song. After the excitement of these scenes, the infinite calm of the love-duet has a strong and lingering effect, and the music reaches a great climax with the first appearance of the splendid love theme. By the end of the first act all the main characters

have been clearly established in the course of their brief appearances: Otello, a man of forceful authority yet almost humble in love; Desdemona with her true womanliness; the slightly foolish Cassio; and finally Iago, his Mephistophelean stature immediately recognizable. His dedication to vileness and his devilish grimace come out best in his confession of faith, his 'Credo'. From an insistent triplet *appoggiatura* which dominated the preceding scenes, there develops a figure which accom-

panies Iago's all-annihilating monologue like demoniac laughter. From the same sphere of villainy springs the theme of jealousy

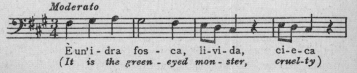

which also opens the dark, brooding prelude to the third act.
The last orchestral prelude prepares us for Desdemona's great,
fear-ridden *scena* with the infinitely melancholy tune of the

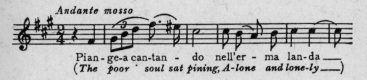

Pian-ge-a can-tan - do nell'er - ma lan-da__
(*The poor soul sat pining, A-lone and lone-ly*__)

willow-song; apart from the love-scene in the first act this is
certainly the most compelling and moving passage in the *Otello*
score. A sinister, creeping bass theme accompanies Otello's

entrance in the final scene, clearly expressing his murderous
intentions. As he kisses Desdemona once again, the love theme
from the first act is heard in the orchestra, and with this
beautiful theme, the opera comes to its sublime close.

The musical world understandably thought that Verdi's
operatic work had reached its culmination in *Otello*. It seemed
most improbable that the seventy-four-year-old master should
write another opera after this triumph, especially as it seemed
impossible to surpass *Otello*; and yet the swan song of this
highly gifted life was a comic opera, a genre which Verdi had
not attempted since his sole unlucky buffo work, *Un Giorno di
Regno* (1840). He brought maturity, considered wisdom, experience of life and real mastery of his art to the creation of *Falstaff*
—the happy smile with which the octogenarian composer
bade farewell to opera. *Falstaff*, for which Arrigo Boito wrote
the libretto after Shakespeare's *The Merry Wives of Windsor*
(but with borrowings from *Henry IV*), is a chamber opera built
round great ensembles supported by a transparently sparse
orchestra. The self-contained solo scenes and ensemble passages
are connected by flexible dramatic recitatives, which move
effortlessly from lightly flowing *parlando* to *arioso*. To ensure
that this opera had the right, almost chamber-music, flavour

Verdi demanded that it should be played in an intimate stage setting, maintaining that only in this way could the skilfully woven filigree of his score be fittingly performed.

FALSTAFF. Comic opera in three acts by Giuseppe Verdi. Text after William Shakespeare by Arrigo Boito. First performance: Milan, 1893.
  Characters: Sir John Falstaff—baritone; Ford, a wealthy burgher—baritone; Fenton, a young gentleman—tenor; Dr Caius—tenor; Bardolph (Bardolfo) and Pistol, followers of Falstaff—tenor and bass; Alice (Mistress Ford)—soprano; Anne (Nannetta), her daughter—soprano; Mistress Quickly—mezzo-soprano; Meg (Mistress Page)—mezzo-soprano. Citizens of Windsor, Ford's servants, women and children.
  Place: Windsor. *Time:* around 1400.
  Act I, scene i. The Garter Inn. Bardolph and Pistol, followers of the fat Sir John Falstaff, have made the worthy Dr Caius drunk and robbed him. Dr Caius comes to the inn where Falstaff is usually to be found, to complain. Falstaff has just finished two important letters which he has signed and sealed, and is now enjoying some wine; he is quite indifferent to Caius and his affairs and, after listening to him for a while, he has him abruptly shown the door. Falstaff studies the innkeeper's bill; he cannot pay, for his purse is always empty. Something must be done about this, for what would become of Sir John if he lost his stately figure and imposing paunch? Falstaff has had an idea. He knows two charming women, wives of wealthy citizens, who have both thrown inviting glances in his direction. They must be fleeced, and to this end he has written letters to both of them. He commands Bardolph and Pistol to deliver the letters, but they refuse, as such a duty is not consistent with their honour. This is too much for Falstaff: fancy these scoundrels, these fools, talking of honour! He gives the letters to his page to deliver at once, and then lectures Bardolph and Pistol about his idea of honour. What is the use of honour? Why get excited about it? He cannot stand the presence of the two ragamuffins any longer and in a fury throws them out.
  Scene ii. The garden of Ford's house. Meg Page and Mistress Quickly, entering, meet Alice Ford and her daughter Anne. Alice and Meg have each received an identical letter from the same person. Such impertinence must be punished. While the ladies are eagerly discussing how best this can be achieved, Ford, Caius and Fenton enter, followed by Bardolph and Pistol, who have told Ford about Falstaff's plans. Fenton, who wants to marry Anne, puts himself at once at Ford's complete disposal and declares himself ready to punish Falstaff severely. Dr Caius, also a suitor for Anne's hand and preferred by Ford, gives a warning that Bardolph and Pistol are not to be trusted. These two keep up a ceaseless flow of talk in Ford's ear, until he is so confused that he does not know what to believe. When he asks angrily what Falstaff is really trying to achieve, Pistol explains that the fat knight has designs on Ford's purse, while Bardolph mentions cuckolded husbands. Anne and Fenton, who have been making signs to one another, both leave their companions to steal a secret kiss. The ladies decide to send Mistress Quickly as a messenger to

Falstaff, to summon him to a rendezvous with Alice. On the other hand Ford charges Bardolph to present him to Falstaff under an assumed name.

Act II, scene i. The Garter Inn. With sorrowful humility Bardolph and Pistol offer Falstaff their services again. Almost immediately Mistress Quickly appears and greets Falstaff with exaggerated curtseys, repeatedly calling him 'Reverenza' ('Your worship'). She has come on Mistress Ford's behalf to arrange a rendezvous at the latter's house between two and three o'clock, when Ford will be out—'Dalle due alle tre'. Falstaff is beside himself with joy and sings rapturously of the delights in store for him, ending with a self-satisfied little march 'Va, vecchio John' ('Go then, old John'). Bardolph announces a certain Master Brook (Signor Fontana), who is of course Ford in disguise. He gives Falstaff a purse of money as an incentive, and invites him to drink a bottle of Cyprus wine. 'Brook' then divulges that he loves Mistress Ford, but cannot overcome her moral scruples. He therefore wishes to enlist the help of Falstaff, who is so experienced in love affairs. Falstaff must first win this prudish beauty so as to prepare the way for Master Brook. Falstaff patronizingly takes Ford's hand, assuring him that it will be a very easy task, and that he can confidently accept the purse since in an hour's time he will be with Alice. He just wants to change quickly, and Master Brook can then accompany him to Mistress Ford's house. Left alone, Ford already feels his scalp tingling with the growing horns, and swears vengeance. Magnificently attired and in the sunniest mood Falstaff returns, and after an overpolite argument about who shall go first, they finally leave the inn arm in arm.

Scene ii. A room in Ford's house. Mistress Quickly reports on her conversation with Sir John, who will be arriving very shortly. Alice instructs her servants to bring in a huge laundry basket. Anne, Meg and Mistress Quickly leave the room, to play their parts in the coming comedy. Alice seats herself to await Falstaff, and strums on a lute. He enters and starts to court her with great charm, but when he tries to embrace her Quickly enters to warn Alice and Falstaff that Meg is approaching. Falstaff hides behind a screen, and Meg enters breathlessly to announce that Ford is on his way home, since he suspects that his wife is entertaining a lover. Ford storms in, in a towering rage, followed by Caius, Fenton, Bardolph and Pistol, and searches for Falstaff everywhere, even in the laundry basket, scattering the washing all over the floor. He then rushes out to search the rest of the house. Overcome by fright Falstaff emerges from behind the screen and the ladies hide him in the basket. Meanwhile Anne and Fenton have slipped behind the screen where they can kiss happily and safely, undisturbed by the tumult raging around them. In a moment of quiet a kiss is clearly heard from behind the screen. Ford is convinced that he has at last found his rival, but instead discovers Fenton and Anne. He indignantly sends Fenton away, and Anne runs off in a fright. Meanwhile Alice tells the servants to empty the laundry basket out of the window into the river. She leads her husband to the window to see Falstaff bobbing about in the water, and so averts his wrath.

Act III, scene i. In front of the Garter Inn. Falstaff is in a fearful temper, brought on by his cold bath and everyone's mockery, but a tankard of mulled wine serves to revive him. Mistress Quickly enters with her

'Reverenza', and manages to overcome Falstaff's indignation and convince him that it was all a misunderstanding. She now invites the fat knight to another rendezvous with Alice, this time at midnight in Windsor Forest under Herne the Hunter's oak, disguised as the black huntsman himself. According to tradition, Herne hanged himself from this tree and the spot is now haunted. Falstaff agrees to the plan and goes into the inn with Mistress Quickly to talk over details. The ladies have listened to this conversation with satisfaction and proceed to lay their plans for Falstaff's further discomfiture. Anne is to be disguised as the fairy queen and Mistress Quickly as a witch, and together they will lead a crowd of sprites who will teach Sir John a lesson. Ford and Caius, who are also party to the plot, lay plans for Anne's betrothal to Caius, who will come to the forest disguised as a monk. Mistress Quickly however overhears this plot as she leaves the inn.

Scene ii. Windsor Forest, with a large oak in the centre of the stage. It is night. Horns are heard, moonlight bathes the forest in romantic radiance, and Fenton enters, singing a passionate love-song. Anne and the other ladies enter, all disguised, and give Fenton a monk's habit to wear. All hide as Falstaff, disguised as Herne the Hunter, is heard approaching. Midnight strikes. Alice enters and Falstaff tries to embrace her. Alice tells him that Meg is also there, but this does not trouble him. Then Meg cries out and both women flee as though in terror. The superstitious Falstaff is frightened, and tries to hide himself behind the oak. A whole host of elves and goblins, led by Anne, drag Falstaff out of his hiding-place and torment him. They are followed by the men, disguised as witches and led by Bardolph, who treat him even more roughly. Falstaff humbly begs for mercy and promises to lead a better life, when he suddenly recognizes Bardolph's red nose. The high-spirited horseplay is over, and all disguises are dropped. Falstaff takes the trick in good part and there is a general reconciliation. Ford now announces another surprise, as Caius, disguised as a monk, leads in a heavily veiled fairy queen, whom he (and Ford) supposes to be Anne, but it turns out that he is fondly embracing Bardolph. Anne enters on Fenton's arm, and in the general atmosphere of goodwill Ford is persuaded to give the loving couple his blessing. It is Falstaff who pronounces the final moral: 'Tutto nel mondo è burla.' The gay, warmhearted work closes with this brilliant fugue.

Grace and elegance, which sometimes break into whirling merriment, characterize the score of *Falstaff*. Even the fat Sir John has a certain charm, for instance in his little aria 'Quand'ero paggio del Duca di Norfolk', with which he courts Alice; and

Allegro con brio

Quand 'e - ro pag - gio del Du - ca di Nor - folk
(*When* I *was* page to the Duke of Nor-folk's grace)

the march theme which accompanies his little solo scene in the Garter Inn in Act II ('Va, vecchio John') is quite delightful. This vain philanderer is always a great charmer, a connoisseur of life, and so his bad temper after his compulsory bathe is simply depicted by petulant, slightly mocking orchestral trills. Verdi again and again conveys a situation most tellingly in a few strokes, for instance, the parodied 'amen' which Bardolph and Pistol chant after the indignant Dr Caius's retreating form, or Mistress Quickly's wonderful caricature obeisance 'Reverenza'.

The lovers' songs are set to deeply sentimental melodies, and

the delicate love refrain recurs frequently. The great ensemble passage at the end of each act makes an emphatic climax, especially the bubbling, flowing *allegro vivace* in the second scene. The merry chatter of the ladies is mostly in swinging $^6/_8$ time, while the masculine bustle is rendered in $^4/_4$, and in between is heard the sweet and languorous love-song of Fenton and Anne. At the end of the scene $^6/_8$ and $^4/_4$ join forces in a gay tussle around the sweet *cantilena* which Fenton maintains as a sort of *cantus firmus*. The high-spirited staccato theme which accompanies the second act finale is equally thrilling and continually reappears with new variations throughout the crazed confusion on the stage.

The final scene positively overflows with charming and graceful new melodic ideas. The atmosphere of the summer night, the elfin games and the haunting moonlight breathe the true romantic spirit infused with a typically Mediterranean lightness and grace. The crowning glory of the work is the wonderful fugue with which Verdi bade farewell to the musical stage. This supreme master of opera kept for his final word a genial, understanding smile as the culmination of all wisdom, which can be paraphrased as 'All the World's a Stage'.

So Verdi's whole life was rounded off like a perfected and complete work of art, a fulfilment rare in the career of a great artist.

'VERISMO' OR REALISTIC OPERA

Towards the end of the nineteenth century naturalism had established itself as an intellectual movement in literature, bringing with it an interest in social problems; Zola's novels were read all over the world and Gerhard Hauptmann's first dramas aroused great interest, all a natural reaction to romanticism. In the sphere of music, especially in opera, a school of realism arose at the same time, as a reaction against the romantic ideals so powerfully represented by Verdi and Wagner.

Cavalleria Rusticana (1890) by Pietro Mascagni (1863–1945) marks the birth of this musical naturalism. Its strongest expression and following originated in Italy, and so the term *verismo* (the Italian word for naturalism) was adopted everywhere to denote this new trend in opera.

The text for Mascagni's opera was based on a very successful one-act play of the same name by Giovanni Verga, which related a violent episode in Sicilian peasant life. It served as the inspiration for Mascagni's elemental score and rustic local

atmosphere which is painted in harsh, unsophisticated colours
with strongly contrasted and even shocking effects. *Verismo*
already existed in Bizet's *Carmen*, but there the passions and
their musical reflection seem, for all their naturalness, veiled in
romanticism. In Mascagni one is struck by the starkness of the
passions and the naked power of the music, even when it is
wrapped in voluptuous melody.

Cavalleria Rusticana won the first prize in a competition for a
one-act opera, organized by the music publisher Sonzogno.
This was not Mascagni's first opera, as he had already written
both *Guglielmo Ratcliff* and *Pinotta*, but after the unprecedented
success of the first performance of *Cavalleria Rusticana* in Rome
the young composer's name became world-famous overnight.
Mascagni subsequently wrote more than a dozen other operas,
but none of them approached the success of *Cavalleria Rusticana*
and they have all practically disappeared from the repertory.

CAVALLERIA RUSTICANA (Rustic chivalry). Opera in one act by
Pietro Mascagni. Text after Giovanni Verga by Giuseppe Targioni-
Tozzetti and Guido Menasci. First performance: Rome, 1890.
    Characters: Santuzza, a village girl—soprano; Turiddu, a young soldier
—tenor; Mamma Lucia, his mother—mezzo-soprano; Alfio, a teamster
—baritone; Lola, his wife—mezzo-soprano. Villagers, peasants, boys.
    Place: A village in Sicily. *Time:* Easter, 1890.
    The scene is the square of a Sicilian village. After a Prelude, which
includes a *siciliana* sung behind the curtain by Turiddu in the manner of
a serenade to Lola, the curtain rises. It is early on Easter morning, and the
village slowly comes to life. The church bells ring and the people wend
their way to church. Santuzza enters and asks Lucia, Turiddu's mother,
why he is not there. Lucia tries to get rid of Santuzza quickly by telling
her that Turiddu has gone to the next village to fetch some wine, but
Santuzza says that she saw him the previous evening in the village; this
is also confirmed by the village teamster Alfio, who says he met Turiddu
near his own house earlier that very morning. The people go into the
church. Santuzza holds Mamma Lucia back, to tell her of her misfortune:
before he left to become a soldier, Turiddu was betrothed to Lola, but
when on his return he found Lola married to Alfio, he turned to Santuzza.
Forgetting everything, she gave herself to him completely, but now he
has deserted her and gone back to Lola. Santuzza has come into the
village to try to win him back. Perturbed by what she has heard, Mamma
Lucia enters the church, while Santuzza waits alone outside for Turiddu.
At last he arrives, but brushes past her without a glance. When she implores him to come back to her, and out of jealousy insults Lola, Turiddu
pushes her away roughly. Lola comes into the square, singing a coquettish
little song. Turiddu steps forward to meet her, but Santuzza fiercely holds

on to him, insisting that she must speak with him. Lola enters the church alone. In an outburst of real passion Santuzza pleads with Turiddu once more, but he no longer cares for her and when she threatens him he throws her to the ground and hurries into the church. Beside herself with fury, Santuzza hurls a curse after him. Alfio enters and meets Santuzza who, deeply wounded by Turiddu's behaviour, tells Alfio of Lola's and Turiddu's guilty love. Alfio reacts with a savage vow that he will be avenged. Santuzza realizes too late what she has started. They both leave the square, and while the stage is empty, the famous *Intermezzo* is played, delicately and briefly evoking a gentle mood before the drama moves towards its inevitable climax. The people come out of church, among them Lola and Turiddu who invites everyone to drink with him. The gaiety of his drinking song, in which all join lustily, sounds somewhat forced. Alfio joins the group. When Turiddu offers him a glass, he knocks it away with a rough refusal, so that Turiddu spills the wine. This is an open insult, and the women present recoil in fear. Turiddu bites Alfio's ear which, according to Sicilian custom, signifies his assent to a fight with knives. Alfio goes out to wait for Turiddu, who bids his mother farewell and with moving words asks her to care for Santuzza, should he not return alive, then rushes out. Mamma Lucia is left bewildered. Santuzza hurries, followed by some of the villagers. A cry is heard from offstage: 'They have murdered neighbour Turiddu'. Santuzza collapses.

From the first note to the last the score of *Cavalleria Rusticana* is an improvisation of genius. The prelude is built up on a series of the opera's most impressive melodies, starting with the prevailing impression of the peaceful atmosphere of Easter morning, but then leading to the centre of the drama in a powerful *crescendo*. Santuzza's love-song rises from the orchestra

like a delicate lament, but at once her pride reveals itself in a theme of defiance, which reaches a passionate climax as the orchestra breaks off and the *siciliana* is heard from the unseen stage: the unfaithful Turiddu is serenading his beloved Lola. As soon as his song has died away, the orchestra bursts out again in a wild fury with the theme of the passionate conflict between Santuzza and Turiddu. The melody breaks off

fortissimo, Santuzza's lament is heard again and the prelude ends as it began, with the solemn Easter theme. Santuzza's principal theme is first heard in the orchestra when she appears on the

stage. This is a humble, submissive theme, yet always ready to break out in defiance. In a few strokes of genius the music paints the full portrait of the proud peasant girl who, though she knows she has lost her honour by taking Turiddu as her lover, will fight for her love to the end. The fluctuations of her feelings are heard in the restless melodic line and the uncertain hovering between minor and major which prevails in all her music. The dramatic climax is the clash between Santuzza and Turiddu. Here again we find savage passion (which appeared as a theme in the overture) changing to a humble plea for love, which in turn gives way to the curse, accompanied in the orchestra by a grandiose version of Santuzza's theme. Alfio's song in praise of the teamster's life and Turiddu's drinking-song have been thrown in with a lighter touch. Mascagni achieves astonishing effects by these contrasting moods in the music. The introductory crowd-scenes are also very colourful; the women sing in a flowing waltz-rhythm, while the men's song has a strong march-like character, until the two finally join together and fade away in the distance. Mascagni becomes slightly sentimental in the impressive church scene, and especially in the symphonic *Intermezzo*, which is the most famous piece in the opera.

Ruggiero Leoncavallo (1858–1919) had wanted to enter his opera *Pagliacci* for the Sonzogno competition in which Mascagni won first prize for his *Cavalleria Rusticana*, but as it was in two acts it was ineligible. Two years later, however, spurred on by Mascagni's success, he approached Sonzogno and submitted *I Pagliacci* to them. The opera had a tremendous success in Milan at its première there in 1892. The stylistic affinity between these two short operas led to their being joined together in a double bill, and this practice still continues. In fact they have come to be considered almost inseparable, and attempts to couple either of them with other pieces have seldom succeeded.

Leoncavallo pays open homage to musical naturalism and even says in the prologue (he was his own librettist): 'The poet of today boldly uses the terrible truths of life itself.' In fact the most dramatic text of *Pagliacci* is based on an incident that had occurred in Montalto, when an actor in a touring company murdered his wife after a performance. Leoncavallo's father was the judge at the murder trial.

PAGLIACCI (The strolling players). Drama in two acts by Ruggiero Leoncavallo. First performance: Milan, 1892.

Characters: Canio, the leader of a troupe of strolling players—tenor; Nedda, his wife—soprano; Tonio and Beppe, members of the troupe— baritone and tenor; Silvio, a villager—baritone. Villagers.

Place: Montalto, Calabria. *Time:* Feast of the Assumption, about 1865–70.

Prologue: Tonio comes in front of the curtain in his clown's costume and hints at the story of the drama, telling the audience that they are about to witness a real story about real people. He then announces that the performance is about to begin, and calls for the curtain to rise.

Act I. A troupe of strolling players enters the village square and is enthusiastically welcomed by the inhabitants. Canio has difficulty in making himself heard over the hubbub as he invites the people to the evening performance. Tonio tries to help Nedda down from the wagon, but the jealous Canio pushes him away with a box on the ear. The peasants laugh, but Canio cannot stand mockery; even strolling players have their honour, and if his wife should be unfaithful to him that would be the end of her. The peasants invite Canio to take a glass of wine at the local inn, and Beppe joins them. Nedda is left alone; Canio's words seemed to her like a threat, but she shakes off her fears. She wants to enjoy life and love; she listens to the birds, whose freedom she envies. Tonio comes up to her again, and when he becomes too insistent she strikes him across the face with a whip. He stumbles out, white with rage, thinking only of revenge. The young peasant Silvio, Nedda's lover, comes to see her. Nedda is frightened at his daring to come at that time, but he has seen Canio and Beppo drinking in the tavern and believes he is quite safe. He implores Nedda to leave her husband and her wandering life and to go away with him. Nedda finally yields to his passionate wooing and agrees to elope with him that very night. Tonio, who saw Silvio's arrival, has listened to this conversation. Now he fetches Canio, but Silvio escapes and Canio has to give up the pursuit. Threatening Nedda with a knife, he demands the name of her lover; Tonio and Beppe restrain him as his rage seems uncontrollable. In this state of extreme agitation and utter despair, he has to take part in the play that is about to start. 'Vesti la giubba' ('On with the motley'), he sings, and, tragically, 'Ridi, Pagliaccio' ('Laugh then, Pagliaccio').

Act II. People stream in from all sides to attend the performance. Benches have been set up in front of the little stage. Silvio is standing at the back among a group of villagers. Nedda goes among the audience, collecting money on a plate. When she comes to Silvio she warns him that Canio is plotting revenge. The performance at last begins. Columbine (Nedda) is waiting for her lover, Harlequin (Beppe). Her husband, Pagliaccio (Canio), is away and not expected back till morning. Instead of Harlequin, however, the foolish Taddeo (Tonio) enters and declares his love to Columbine who derisively rejects him. Harlequin's voice is heard serenading Columbine, who welcomes him joyfully; but a moment later he has to leave again, for Pagliaccio has returned unexpectedly. He overhears the end of Columbine's farewell to Harlequin—the same words that Nedda called after Silvio 'Tonight, love and forever I am thine'. The similarity makes Canio forget that he is Pagliaccio and he angrily demands from Nedda/Columbine the name of his rival. She remains steadfast, however, determined not to betray her lover. Canio takes a knife, and threatens her with death. The horrified peasants realize that the play has turned into stark reality. In terror Nedda cries out 'Soccorso . . . Silvio!' ('Help! Help!—Silvio!') and collapses, mortally wounded. Silvio rushes forward, and Canio rounds on him and kills him also. Men surround Canio; the knife falls from his hand, and he stands stupefied. To the excited audience Tonio cries 'La commedia è finita' ('The comedy is ended'). (It has become traditional for the Canio to utter the closing words, a habit probably started by Caruso.)

The score of *Pagliacci* is brilliantly constructed; the use of motifs points to Wagner's influence, the melodies are subtle and well-judged, the orchestra is used with elegance and the choruses are carefully polished.

The prologue is a stroke of genius, partly instrumental and partly vocal. The rhythmic *élan* of the main theme is immedi-

ately arresting; the curtain seems to be abruptly torn aside to carry the audience into the kaleidoscopic world of the strolling players. Agonizing sorrow pervades the second theme to which Canio sings his desperate words 'Ridi, Pagliaccio', and which in

a later variant becomes the theme of resentment, hate and

jealousy. A third, love-theme of voluptuous sweetness recurs

repeatedly in the course of the plot. The music of the Columbine play is completely self-contained, and is clearly set apart
from the rest of the score by its dance-like style. A capricious
minuet accompanies Columbine's preparations to receive her
lover, the serenade is a light-hearted waltz tune, and the
Taddeo-Columbine scene is a comic parody, though by the
use of the thematic accompaniment from the same scene in the
first act the underlying seriousness of the play is here suggested
for the first time. With Columbine's and Harlequin's love-
making we return to the tone of comedy accompanied by a

gavotte. At first Pagliaccio also tries to maintain the mood of
the play, but the dance-tune which accompanies this scene
gradually becomes sombre, until the unhappy man's passionate
desperation begins to break through. The dance-rhythms die
away, and the orchestra erupts in a savage outburst. Columbine
tries once more to keep the comedy going by reintroducing the

'VERISMO' OR REALISTIC OPERA

gavotte tune, but Canio takes this as mockery; he has finally lost all control of himself, and the play turns into reality.

While Mascagni and Leoncavallo have each only had lasting success with their one epoch-making short opera, the works of Giacomo Puccini, the third principal representative of *verismo*, have nearly all survived in the international repertory. Puccini's pre-eminence is entirely understandable, for he combines a unique talent for melody with an outstanding sense of instrumental texture, and his Italian musical temperament found its fulfilment in the rarefied emotions of French impressionism. Puccini developed an unfailingly effective dramatic style from Wagner's *leitmotiv* technique, and though he essentially based this style on 'Weltschmerz', or gentle melancholy, he was by no means afraid of violent outbursts in the *verismo* style. Puccini's style is entirely personal, and his flexible, intensely singable melodies are the most distinctive feature of his musical idiom. These melodies are always carefully polished and delicately harmonized, and always enchant the ear. The whole effect is quite remarkable. Puccini conjures up atmosphere in a way almost unprecedented at the time, and if this is occasionally at the expense of stronger dramatic effect, one is richly compensated by his magic lyricism. Puccini's style had a most stimulating effect on the music of his time and even the impressionists adopted many of his ideas. He left his mark particularly on light music and operetta—the later Lehár, for instance, is almost unthinkable without Puccini.

Puccini attracted general notice with his very first opera, *Le Villi* (*The Witches*) (1884), and interest in the young composer was increased by the appearance of *Manon Lescaut* (1893); but it was *La Bohème* (1896) which made him world-famous. This was followed by *Tosca* (1900) and *Madama Butterfly* (1904), two works which became extremely popular, although they were criticized as too sensational and sentimental. Puccini always insisted that his texts should be unfailingly effective, for he never forgot that he was writing for the theatre and felt he had to give it what it needed. His next work, *La Fanciulla del West*, was first performed in New York in 1910, with a story set in America, but in spite of its many beauties and sensational staging, this opera aroused much less enthusiasm than usual with Puccini premières. *La Rondine* (*The Swallow*), first performed at Monte Carlo in 1917, was virtually a complete failure; more successful were the three one-act operas, *Il Tabarro*, *Suor Angelica* and *Gianni Schicchi* (1918), intended as a triple bill entitled *Il Trittico*. In fact these three one-act operas are not often performed together today, as the very sentimental *Suor Angelica* has never been so effective or popular as the other two. Puccini's last opera *Turandot*, based on Gozzi's fanciful tale, was left uncompleted at his death.

The Abbé Prévost's novel, *Manon Lescaut*, attracted many other composers besides Puccini and Massenet (whose opera *Manon* has already been discussed in these pages), among them Auber, Balfe, Halévy and Hans Werner Henze. Massenet's and Puccini's works on this subject are however the two which still hold their own in the operatic repertory.

MANON LESCAUT. Opera in four acts by Giacomo Puccini. Text after Prévost by Giuseppe Giacosa, Luigi Illica, Giulio Ricordi, M. Praga and D. Oliva. First performance: Turin, 1893.

Characters: Manon Lescaut—soprano; Lescaut, her brother, sergeant of the King's Guards—baritone; the Chevalier des Grieux—tenor; Geronte di Ravoir, Treasurer-General—bass; Edmondo, a student—tenor; an innkeeper—bass; a music-master—tenor; a musician—mezzo-soprano; a lamplighter—tenor; a naval captain—bass; a sergeant—bass. Students, townsfolk, soldiers, girls, elderly, rich friends of Geronte's, singers, women convicts.

Place: Amiens, Paris, Havre, Louisiana. *Time:* second half of the eighteenth century.

Act I. An inn yard in Amiens. Students, townsfolk and soldiers are drinking, gaming and chattering as they wait for the coach from Arras to arrive. Edmondo, half-mocking, half-serious, soliloquizes on the sky, the breezes, the scents and the swallows. When the young des Grieux enters he is taunted for his lack of success in love and retorts with a mocking serenade to all the ladies present, 'Tra voi belle brune e bionde' '(Now among you dark and fair ones'). When the coach arrives, the young Manon, her brother Lescaut, and the elderly roué, Geronte, are among the travellers. As soon as des Grieux sets eyes on Manon he exclaims at her beauty and the moment she is left unattended goes up to her to ask her her name. They fall in love at first sight and in a few minutes he has persuaded her to meet him later that evening. Her brother calls to her from the inn where he has arranged their lodging for the night, and left alone des Grieux pours out his feelings in the aria 'Donna non vidi mai' ('Never did I behold so fair a maiden'). The students return to their gambling and Edmondo overhears a conversation between Lescaut and Geronte which makes it clear that the former, instead of taking Manon to a convent to complete her education, is quite willing to let the wealthy Geronte abduct her. Geronte orders a swift coach to be prepared within the hour, but Edmondo warns des Grieux of this plan. When Manon comes out to join him, she sings 'Vedete, io son fedele alla parola mia' ('Behold me! I have been faithful to my promise') and when des Grieux declares his great love for her she agrees to elope with him. Edmondo rushes in to tell the lovers that Geronte's coach is ready and lends des Grieux his cloak to hide his face. They enter the coach and are driven off to Paris. When Geronte in a fury tells Lescaut what has happened, the latter is quite unmoved (he has been drinking and gaming during the foregoing scene) and saying that a student's purse cannot last long assures Geronte that Manon will soon be back.

Act II. A sumptuous apartment in Geronte's house in Paris. Lescaut's prediction was correct and Manon has left the impoverished des Grieux for the luxuries of life with Geronte. However, as she tells her brother who enters and compliments her on her beauty, there is something in all this finery which chills her heart and she longs for the love she found with des Grieux—'In quelle trine morbide' ('In these soft silken curtains'). She asks for news of her former lover and hears that he has taken to gambling. Singers enter to entertain Manon with a madrigal, and this is followed by a dancing-lesson in which Geronte and some of his friends also take part. After the minuet a pastoral with chorus is sung and then Manon sings a gay gavotte. When Geronte and his friends have left, des Grieux enters, summoned by Lescaut to relieve his sister's boredom. First he reproaches her for her faithlessness, then makes ardent love to her, 'O tentatrice, tentatrice ('O fatal temptress, fatal temptress') he sings and the great love-duet begins—'Vieni! Colle tue braccia stringi Manon che t'ama' ('Oh, come love! In your arms enfold Manon who loves you'). They are interrupted by the sudden return of Geronte, whom Manon dismisses contemptuously, holding a mirror to his face and making fun of his age. Sarcastically he tells her he knows his duty and bids her farewell, saying 'We'll meet again'. Manon cannot bear to abandon all her newly-acquired riches and insists on gathering up her jewels before running away with des Grieux. 'Ah Manon, mi tradisce il tuo folle pensier' ('Ah Manon, the folly of your thoughts betrays me') cries des Grieux in an exciting outburst, reproaching her for the unhappiness she has caused them and will cause them in the future. Lescaut rushes in to tell them that Geronte has denounced Manon as an immoral woman, and that the police have already come to arrest her. She waits to gather up her jewels and the delay is fatal. The door opens to admit a grimly smiling Geronte and the police. Manon's cloak slips open, and the jewels fall to the floor. She is arrested, and when des Grieux tries to go to her aid Lescaut prevents him, saying that if he is arrested also there will be no one left to save her. 'O Manon, o mia Manon' ('Oh Manon, oh my sweet Manon') he cries after her in despair.

Act III. A square near the harbour at Havre. The act is preceded by an *intermezzo* suggesting the journey to Havre and the misfortunes which have befallen the two lovers since Manon's arrest—she has been sentenced to banishment to the French possession of Louisiana. It is dawn; in the prison the women are awaiting deportation and in the background loom the masts of the ship which is to take them to America. Lescaut and des Grieux enter, plotting to rescue Manon before she boards the ship. Lescaut speaks to the sentry and a few moments later Manon appears at a window of the prison. Des Grieux rushes to her and takes her hand through the iron grating. A lamplighter enters and sings a little song about Kathrine and the King. Lescaut re-enters to tell des Grieux that the plot has failed. The prison gates are thrown open and a squad of soldiers march out with the women in chains. The roll is called and the wretched prisoners cross the stage as their names are called out. Des Grieux refuses to leave Manon's side, then rushes to the ship to implore the captain to take him too, even as a deck-hand. The captain agrees.

Act IV. A vast plain near New Orleans. Manon and des Grieux have left New Orleans as a result of jealousy and intrigue. Manon is exhausted and des Grieux goes off to find help. Alone she sings of her despair 'Sola, perduta, abbandonata' ('Alone, lost and abandoned'), and reaches a climax with the words 'Non voglio morire—amore aiuta!' ('I do not want to die—beloved, oh help me!'). When des Grieux returns empty-handed she is already dying and he falls senseless and broken with grief across her lifeless body.

In addition to the many exquisite melodies that Puccini composed for this work, he made use of some of the themes almost as *leitmotivs*. In Act I the theme of des Grieux's great love-song 'Donna non vidi mai' is hinted at when he first speaks to her, and later comes to symbolize his great love and tenderness for her. It is heard in the cellos when Manon returns to keep her tryst with him, but is followed in the orchestra by the theme love-duet of the second act. The final dialogue between Lescaut and Geronte in Act I is accompanied by the chorus singing des Grieux's first, light-hearted serenade 'Tra voi belle'.

As Act II opens, Puccini cunningly suggests the complexity and frivolity of Manon's toilet with the use of triangle, flute, harp and celeste. Her aria 'In quelle trine morbide' is perhaps the best-known individual aria in the opera, though Manon's gavotte, 'L'ora o Tirsi, è vaga e bella' ('These are hours of joy's creating') is a brilliant show-piece for a soprano with a *pianissimo* top C.

The *intermezzo* before Act III contains a theme on the strings and harp to symbolize the miseries which attend the lovers, and it reappears in their love-duet in Act IV. The most moving piece of music in this act is des Grieux's impassioned plea to the captain 'Guardate, pazzo son' ('Behold me, I am mad').

When the captain has agreed to take on des Grieux, Act III closes to a thunderous E major rendering of the melody from the love-duet in the second act.

The last act is nothing more than a protracted final duet for the lovers. It opens and closes with the same savage chords, depicting the vast, pitiless, arid plain which is the scene of their final calamity.

LA BOHÈME (The Bohemians). Opera in four acts by Giacomo Puccini. Text after Henri Murger by Giuseppe Giacosa and Luigi Illica. First performance: Turin, 1896.

Characters: Rodolfo, a poet—tenor; Schaunard, a musician—baritone; Marcello, a painter—baritone; Colline, a philosopher—bass; Benoit, a landlord—bass; Mimi, a seamstress—soprano; Musetta, a grisette—soprano; Parpignol, a toy-vendor—tenor; Alcindoro, councillor and admirer of Musetta—bass; customs-house sergeant—bass; Students, working girls, citizens, shopkeepers, street vendors, soldiers, waiters, children.

Place: Paris. *Time:* about 1830.

Act I. A garret in the Latin Quarter. Marcello is working at a large oil-painting, while Rodolfo looks out of the window at the snow-covered city, absorbed in day dreams. But not for long, for it is too cold, and even their grim humour cannot make the two friends forget that they are cold and hungry. Rodolfo sacrifices the manuscript of his play, which is solemnly burned in the fire, act by act. Colline, the philosopher, enters, having tried in vain to pawn some books—all the pawnbrokers were closed, it being Christmas Eve. Schaunard, the musician, arrives with two errand-boys carrying wood and a huge basket full of delicious food and wine. He has earned a good fee for giving music lessons to an eccentric Englishman. He tries in vain to relate to his friends the strange events that happened, but they can only think of the food and the wine, and want to start on them at once. Schaunard is against this; he thinks they should all spend the evening in their usual haunt, the Café Momus, and only drink a bottle of wine beforehand. At this point, they are interrupted by the landlord, Benoit, who wants to collect the long overdue rent. The four friends ply him with wine and lead him on to make ribald remarks. They then pretend to be shocked and throw him out. Schaunard divides his remaining cash between his friends and they set off for the Café Momus in high spirits. Rodolfo remains behind to finish an article he is writing; he will join them later. Meanwhile it has grown quite dark. Rodolfo puts a candle on the table and tries to settle down to work. There is a knock at the door, and Mimi comes timidly in; her candle has gone out, and she wants to light it again. She is seized by an attack of coughing. Rodolfo is enchanted by her prettiness and delicacy. She goes out, but returns at once to get her key which she has left behind. Her candle is blown out in the draught, and so is Rodolfo's. They now look for the key in the dark, but when Rodolfo finds it he hides it quickly in his pocket. He comes close to Mimi and their hands meet. 'Che gelida manina' ('Your tiny hand is frozen'), he exclaims. He tells her that he is a poet, and then Mimi tells Rodolfo about herself. Hers is a poor life as she describes it, but she accepts it with pious resignation. The friends call to Rodolfo from the street, and he tells them to go on without him; he will follow them. Rodolfo turns from the window and sees Mimi before him, bathed in moonlight. Ecstatically, he exclaims 'O soave fanciulla' ('Lovely maid in the moonlight') and declares his love for her; they join in a passionate love-duet and leave the room together.

Act II. A small square in the Latin Quarter, with the Café Momus. It is Christmas Eve; all the shops are open and gaily lit; street vendors are crying their wares, and in front of the Café Momus people are sitting at small tables, while a merry crowd passes to and fro. Mimi arrives with Rodolfo. Schaunard is haggling over the price of a horn in one shop, while Colline buys an overcoat in another. In a milliner's, Rodolfo buys Mimi a pink bonnet which gives her great pleasure. The friends then contentedly sit down at a table outside the Café and Mimi is introduced to them. To a nearby table comes Musetta, very elegantly dressed, with her elderly follower Alcindoro. Musetta and Marcello were once lovers, but have since quarrelled and parted. They are, however, clearly not indifferent to each other's presence. Musetta tries to arouse Marcello's interest with a seductive waltz song and he cannot long resist. On a foolish pretext Musetta sends Alcindoro away and joyously falls into Marcello's arms. The guards march past; Marcello and Colline lift Musetta up and carry her away in triumph, while the others follow laughing. When Alcindoro returns, he finds that he has to pay the bills for both tables.

Act III. At one of the city gates of Paris stands a customs-house, in front of which is a small inn. It is winter and a snowy morning. Street workers and women with their shopping baskets arrive at the gate. Singing and noises are heard from inside the inn. Mimi comes to see Marcello, who is living in the inn with Musetta; he paints pictures on the walls and signboards for the innkeeper while she gives music-lessons. Mimi is distraught; she cannot understand why Rodolfo has abandoned her. When she sees him coming out of the inn, where he is staying with Marcello, she hides. Marcello reproaches Rodolfo with his behaviour, but Rodolfo tells him that he believes Mimi is dying and he cannot bear to see her so miserable in the cold attic. Mimi's coughing betrays her presence, and Rodolfo tenderly takes her in his arms. In a passionate duet the lovers are reunited; they decide to stay together until the spring comes. A quarrel which has just broken out between Marcello and Musetta contrasts strongly with these tender expressions of love. Musetta cannot and will not be faithful to Marcello, and again abandons her jealous lover.

Act IV. The garret, as in Act I. Rodolfo and Marcello, both abandoned by their mistresses, are finding it difficult to work. Rodolfo has no news of Mimi, but Marcello knows that Musetta is leading a luxurious life, kept by a rich lover. Schaunard and Colline come in for their scanty meal: bread and herrings. To forget their misery, the friends indulge in horse-play, dancing and fighting a mock duel. When their gaiety is at its height, Musetta rushes in to announce that Mimi is with her. She is dying, and has begged to be brought back again to the place where she was once so happy. The stairs have completely exhausted Mimi, and Rodolfo lays the helpless girl gently on his bed. Musetta gives Marcello her earrings to pawn to buy some medicine, and tells him to call a doctor; Colline takes off his coat and goes out to sell it for food, and Musetta runs off to buy a muff for Mimi's cold hands. Mimi relives in imagination her love for Rodolfo, from their first timid acquaintance to the height of their passion. Musetta comes back with a muff. While Musetta heats the medicine and Rodolfo tries to cover the window with a blanket, Marcello and Schaunard see that Mimi is dead. Colline returns, and all remain silent. Rodolfo asks why no one speaks—and then realizing what has happened throws himself weeping over her body.

Puccini was a past master at creating a situation, a mood or a milieu in a few strokes. The opera starts—there is no overture—with a spirited, powerfully rhythmic theme, which plunges us headlong into the middle of the action. This is the most important of the many themes characterizing the light-hearted bohemian atmosphere, which with their frequent recurrence establish one of the basic aspects of the work. This light-heartedness is then challenged by Rodolfo's dreamy tune, later

by Mimi's timid motif and by other, beautiful, melodies

expressing their tender love for each other, particularly the timorous and delicate love-song 'Che gelida manina' ('Your tiny hand is frozen').

The music for the second act is principally concerned with
the activities of the crowd; this act develops like a rainbow of
shimmering colours, in a completely naturalistic musical idiom.
Puccini's famous consecutive fifths shrill through the orchestra,

detached from the gay, secondary tunes around them, while
various sections of the chorus join in apparently haphazardly.
This merry kaleidoscope is only occasionally interrupted by
short lyrical interludes, for instance Mimi's delight with her
little bonnet. The climax of the act is Musetta's dramatic waltz-
song.

In sharp contrast to the colourful second act, the third act
takes on the pallidness of sombre everyday life, from the hollow
fifths at the beginning of the act, to the inconsolable monotony
of Rodolfo's description of Mimi's illness: 'Una terribil tosse
l'esil petto le scuote' ('By fierce incessant coughing her fragile
frame is shaken'). Even the soaring melody of the tender
ecstasy of love at the end of the act is tinged with sorrow. The
two levels of the music of *La Bohème*—naturalistic portrayal of
a situation and passionate lyricism—are most skilfully handled
and the transitions from one to the other effected with infinite
finesse.

In the final act the expressive love-tunes of the previous acts
return to accompany Mimi's pathetic reflections on her short

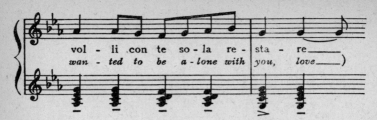

vol - li con te so - la re - sta - re____
wan - ted to be a - lone with you, love____)

life filled with a great love. A sombre theme is introduced, for
Mimi's heart is heavy with the foreboding of death, and with
it the opera comes to its implacable end.

The text of Puccini's next opera, *Tosca*, based on a thrilling
and very effective drama by Sardou, is more in the *verismo* style
than *La Bohème*, but throughout the composer softens the crude
outlines of the story with his music, always refraining from
extreme naturalism, and even making the horrifying torture
scene in the second act acceptable.

TOSCA. Opera in three acts by Giacomo Puccini. Text after Victorien
Sardou by Luigi Illica and Giuseppe Giacosa. First performance: Rome,
1900.

Characters: Floria Tosca, a famous singer—soprano; Mario Cavaradossi,
a painter—tenor; Baron Scarpia, chief of police—baritone; Angelotti, a
revolutionary—bass; the sacristan—bass-baritone; Spoletta, a police
agent—tenor; Sciarrone, a gendarme—bass; a jailor—bass; a shepherd-
boy—soprano. Choristers, townspeople, soldiers, guards, servants to
Scarpia.

Place: Rome. *Time:* 1800.

Act I. Inside the church of Sant'Andrea della Valle. The former Consu
of the Republic, Angelotti, enters the church furtively. He has escaped
from the Fortress of Sant'Angelo, and is hoping to find help in his flight.
His sister, the Marchesa Attavanti, has told him where to find the key
to the Attavantis' private chapel, where he hastily hides himself as footsteps approach. It is the sacristan, who is surprised to find the church still
empty, since he expected to see the painter Cavaradossi working on his
canvas. Cavaradossi enters to start work. He is painting a fair-haired
Magdalena who, to the sacristan, seems to resemble the beautiful unknown
woman whom he has often seen recently, praying in front of the chapel.
Cavaradossi admits that he has used her as a model, and the pious sacristan
is deeply shocked. Cavaradossi sings the *arioso* 'Recondita armonia di
bellezza diverse' ('Strange harmony of contrasts deliciously blending').
After the sacristan has gone, Angelotti comes out of his hiding-place.
Cavaradossi, a good friend of his, at first does not recognize him and

then offers to help him. The voice of Cavaradossi's mistress, Floria Tosca, is heard outside and he hurriedly pushes Angelotti back into the chapel, giving the exhausted man his basket of food, Tosca thinks she has heard voices in the chapel and is suspicious and jealous, assuming that there was another woman with Cavaradossi. He has great difficulty in dispelling her fears, which break out afresh when she sees a resemblance to the Marchesa Attavanti in his painting. Only a sincere display of his great love for her enables Cavaradossi to persuade her of his devotion. Tosca goes out, having arranged to meet her lover that night after the opera in which she is to sing. Cavaradossi now goes to Angelotti, and suggests he should hide in his near-by country house, but at that moment a cannon shot is heard from the fortress of Sant'Angelo, signifying that Angelotti's flight has been discovered. To make sure that Angelotti finds the country house, Cavaradossi decides to accompany his friend. Men and boys belonging to the choir enter the church and the sacristan tells them that Napoleon has been beaten at Marengo, and that they are to sing a cantata that same night at the victory celebrations, with Tosca singing the solo. Scarpia enters, with Spoletta. They have traced the fugitive to the church, and their swift interrogation of the sacristan casts suspicion of aiding Angelotti onto Cavaradossi. This suits Scarpia, who has desired Tosca for a long time, and knows of her relationship with Cavaradossi. He now hopes that by eliminating Cavaradossi he can win Tosca for himself. When Tosca returns to tell Cavaradossi that she has to sing that night after the opera as well, and therefore cannot meet him, Scarpia rekindles her jealousy by showing her a fan belonging to the Marchesa Attavanti which he claims to have found on Cavaradossi's easel. Tosca goes out in a rage to surprise her lover with the supposed rival. On Scarpia's order Spoletta follows her, while Scarpia savours the pleasure in store for him. The church has by now filled and a cardinal enters in a great procession. A *Te Deum* is sung, in which Scarpia joins with every appearance of devotion.

Act II. Scarpia's study in the Farnese Palace. Scarpia gives Sciarrone a note for Tosca, asking her to visit him after the concert, which is taking place on the first floor of the palace. Through the open window the orchestra can already be heard playing a gavotte. Spoletta enters to report that Angelotti could not be found at Cavaradossi's villa, but that they have arrested Cavaradossi for his contemptuous behaviour. Scarpia orders Cavaradossi to be brought in; through the window the festival cantata can be heard, with Tosca's unmistakable voice rising above the choir. Interrogated by Scarpia, Cavaradossi denies having helped Angelotti to escape. In a fury, Scarpia has the window closed, and the cantata music stops abruptly. Cavaradossi remains unshaken by Scarpia's threats. Tosca enters full of anxiety, and goes straight to her lover's arms. Before he is led away, he whispers to Tosca not to give away what she has seen. Mockingly Scarpia tells Tosca that Cavaradossi is about to be tortured in the adjoining room in order to extract a confession from him. If Tosca knows Angelotti's hiding-place, she could help her friend. From the adjoining room, Cavaradossi's groans are heard. Scarpia lets the torture continue, and finally orders the door to be opened so that they can hear

better. When an agonized cry breaks from Cavaradossi's lips, Tosca can
bear it no longer and quickly reveals Angelotti's hiding-place. The
torture is stopped, and Cavaradossi is dragged in semi-conscious; he asks
Tosca whether she has betrayed Angelotti's hiding-place while he was
being tortured. She assures him that she remained silent. At this Scarpia
orders Spoletta to return to Cavaradossi's villa and look in the well in the
garden. Cavaradossi rounds on Tosca for betraying him. At that moment
Sciarrone hurries into the room with the news that Napoleon has counter-
attacked at Marengo and the Austrian army is in flight. Cavaradossi is
transported with excitement and in his enthusiasm sings of the freedom
which this victory will bring. His words are enough to condemn him to
death for high treason, and he is dragged away. Tosca remains behind in
deep despair. Scarpia sits down to his supper and invites Tosca to join
him. When she asks the price of Cavaradossi's life, Scarpia laughs
cynically and says that she herself is his ransom. She indignantly rejects
his suggestion. Spoletta enters: Angelotti committed suicide when they
found him. Scarpia orders that his body be hung on the gallows, declaring
that the same fate awaits Cavaradossi. Tosca's spirit is now utterly broken,
and she gives Scarpia to understand that she will pay the price for her
lover's life. Scarpia cannot however simply release Cavaradossi: he must
appear to have been shot, and then he may escape abroad with Tosca.
Spoletta receives the command to arrange a mock execution 'as was the
case with Count Palmieri'. He understands his master only too well and
goes out. Tosca demands that Scarpia prepare a safe-conduct for herself
and Cavaradossi. While he is writing it, she sees a knife on the table, and
hides it behind her back. Sure now of his triumph, Scarpia tries to take
Tosca in his arms, but she drives the dagger into his breast, and he falls
to the floor, dying. Tosca is petrified; she wipes the blood from her hands,
takes the safe-conduct from the dead man's hand, puts two burning
candles on either side of the body and a crucifix on his breast, then leaves
the room, closing the door behind her.

Act III. On the ramparts of the Castel Sant'Angelo. It is a clear, starry
night. Cowbells and a shepherd-boy's song are heard in the distance,
and then the morning chimes of a church. Cavaradossi enters under guard.
He asks and receives permission to write a letter, then despairingly hides
his face in his hands. Tosca enters, shows him the safe-conduct and tells
him of Scarpia's death. Cavaradossi can hardly believe his eyes and ears.
She quickly explains about the mock execution that must be gone through,
and that he must do nothing to arouse suspicion. The firing squad marches
in and lines up. Calm and smiling, Cavaradossi stands facing them, the
shots ring out and he falls to the ground. Tosca has watched everything
without betraying her emotion and now waits impatiently for the soldiers
to go out. She runs to Cavaradossi, calls to him, lifts the cloth which has
been spread over him, and to her horror sees that he is indeed dead. Cries
which indicate the discovery of Scarpia's murder are heard coming
nearer and Spoletta enters to arrest Tosca. She leaps on to the ramparts,
and with the words 'Scarpia, we will meet before God', hurls herself to
her death.

Tosca begins with Scarpia's brutal theme, a particularly sinister and menacing sequence of chords, which threateningly announce Scarpia's first entrance, and end the first act with a display of

savage strength. Puccini lavished all his melodic wealth on Cavaradossi's and Tosca's music. Two themes dominate their great love-scene. The first belongs to Tosca and its final phrase

—which often appears on its own—typifies her capricious

nature. The second, broad, sweeping melody accompanies the end of the scene, when the two lovers express their happy

devotion. Both themes appear again frequently in various forms in the course of the drama.

Scarpia's character dominates the second act, and his two
great monologues show him as a man of power, completely
governed by his own desires. The characterizations of Cavaradossi and Tosca are intensified in this act and Cavaradossi attains
real greatness in his thrilling outburst of joy in the coming
liberation. Tosca, too, who is seen in the first act absorbed in
her whims and petty jealousies, touches deep emotion in her
prayer 'Vissi d'arte, vissi d'amore' ('Love and music, these have
I lived for'). The great love melody from the first act underlies
this act of humble resignation. Once again it is Scarpia's
demonic motif which has the last word, and dies away on a
note of menace.

A gloomy passage for horns and high woodwind in consecutive fifths conjures up an atmosphere of evil at the beginning of the final act. The sombre chord sequence of Scarpia's
theme rises out of the darkness like a heavy threat. When
Cavaradossi enters, the love-theme from the end of the first
act is heard delicately in the cellos and then gives way to a
sorrowful melody, on which is built Cavaradossi's aria 'E

lucevan le stelle' ('When the stars were brightly shining'),
evoking sad memories. With this mourning theme flaring into
passionate grandeur the opera closes.

Puccini wrote *Madama Butterfly* in 1904. After the fiasco of
the first night at La Scala, Milan, it was revised by the composer and produced three months later at Brescia with great
success. It was soon heard all over the world, and its success
was even greater than that of *La Bohème*. Musically *Madama
Butterfly* has virtually no connection with *verismo*. Puccini is
said to have listened to hundreds of oriental, especially Japanese,
melodies, before he started composing this opera, and doubtless
these studies were responsible for both the tunes and the very

subtle and exotic instrumentation of *Madama Butterfly*. The melodies, which often consist of a single line, are conceived pentatonically and only very occasionally harmonically developed.

MADAMA BUTTERFLY. Musical tragedy in two acts by Giacomo Puccini. Text by Giuseppe Giacosa and Luigi Illica. First performance: Milan, 1904.

Characters: Cio-Cio-San, called Butterfly—soprano; Suzuki, her maid —mezzo-soprano; Pinkerton, Lieutenant in the American navy—tenor; Sharpless, American Consul—baritone; Goro, a marriage-broker— tenor; Prince Yamadori—tenor; the Bonze, Cio-Cio-San's uncle—bass; Kate Pinkerton—soprano; the Imperial Commissioner—baritone. Butterfly's relatives and other wedding-guests.

Place: Nagasaki. *Time:* 1900.

Act I. A garden with a little Japanese house, on a hill near Nagasaki. The marriage-broker Goro shows Lieutenant Pinkerton the charming little house he has rented on his behalf for his honeymoon with the fifteen-year-old geisha Cio-Cio-San, called Butterfly, whom he is to marry 'for one hundred and ninety-nine years' in accordance with Japanese law, albeit on a monthly notice basis. The cook, the servant and the maid Suzuki come to greet their new master, and Pinkerton is very satisfied with all the arrangements. The first guest to arrive is the American consul, Sharpless, who comes to greet his young compatriot in his new home. He knows the ways of the country better than Pinkerton, and warns him against regarding his liaison with Butterfly too lightly, but Pinkerton waves aside these warnings and cheerfully drinks to his future marriage with a real American girl. From the valley are heard the voices of Butterfly's friends as they ascend the hill. She enters spellbound with her happiness, for she loves Pinkerton deeply and sees in him her ideal. Out of love for him she has just been to the Mission house to be baptized. The Imperial Commissioner who is to perform the marriage ceremony enters with the bride's relatives. The wedding is celebrated, and the Commissioner and Sharpless depart. The relatives and friends present their good wishes to the couple, and Pinkerton offers them *sake* wine. Threatening calls of 'Cio-Cio-San' float up the hillside and interrupt the celebrations. It is the Bonze, Butterfly's uncle and the head of the family, who has come to curse Butterfly because she has embraced an alien faith. Scandalized, everyone turns away from Butterfly and leaves. She weeps bitterly; she is now completely alone, and only her beloved Pinkerton is left to her. He draws her to him. Resisting at first, she then joyfully abandons herself to his embrace.

Act II, scene i. Inside Butterfly's house. Butterfly has been waiting in vain for three years for her husband to return. In the meantime she has given birth to a son, about whom Pinkerton as yet knows nothing. The faithful Suzuki is still with her mistress, although the small household is already burdened with serious money troubles. Butterfly is confident that Pinkerton will return. She sees, as in a vision, the day when a white warship will drop anchor in the harbour, and Pinkerton will hurry up the hill to her and to his house, and she sings 'Un bel dì vedremo' ('One fine day we'll notice'). Sharpless comes to visit her and she greets him cheerfully. He wants to prepare her for the news that Pinkerton is on his way to Nagasaki with his wife; he tries in vain to read Pinkerton's letter to her, for Butterfly is so overjoyed to have news of her husband at last that she refuses to listen. Prince Yamadori is announced by Goro. He has been courting Butterfly for a long time, but she smilingly refuses his flattering suit, since she feels herself already committed. Sharpless explains the position to her, and asks her what she would do if Pinkerton never returned. Butterfly does not understand how the consul can entertain such a horrifying possibility. Could he have forgotten her? She runs out and returns with her child, whose blue eyes and blond curls clearly show his parentage. Certainly Pinkerton could not forget this child! Deeply moved Sharpless withdraws. His words have wounded Butterfly. A cannon-shot from the harbour announces the arrival of a warship. Butterfly rushes out on to the terrace and recognizes the cruiser *Abraham Lincoln*, Pinkerton's ship. Beside herself with joy she and Suzuki go to gather flowers from the garden to decorate the house in welcome. Dusk slowly falls. Butterfly puts on her wedding-dress, adorns her hair with flowers, and decides to stay up all night to await Pinkerton. She pierces three holes in the paper walls for herself, the baby and Suzuki so that they can all keep watch. The quiet of night spreads over everything. Suzuki and the boy fall asleep on the cushions. Only Butterfly remains in her place, watching unceasingly.

Scene ii. Morning has come, and Butterfly still stands at the wall, watching out. The cries of the sailors are heard from the harbour. Suzuki awakes and persuades her mistress to rest for a while. Butterfly goes into the adjoining room with her child. Sharpless enters with Pinkerton, while Kate Pinkerton remains in the garden. Suzuki learns that Pinkerton has come to take his child away. He is deeply moved by the loving preparations for his arrival which he sees all round the house. Filled with remorse, he cannot face Butterfly and rushes out. Butterfly enters; she is horrified when she realizes from Sharpless's silence and Suzuki's crying that something terrible must have happened. At first she thinks Pinkerton is dead, but then she sees the strange lady in the garden and suddenly everything becomes clear to her. She agrees to give the child to Pinkerton, and says he may come to fetch him in half an hour. Left alone, Butterfly abandons herself to her sorrow and despair. She takes the knife with which her father had killed himself at the Mikado's order, and kisses the blade. The door opens, and Butterfly's child runs to his mother. She says goodbye to him, binds his eyes, and gives him an American flag to hold. She then goes behind the screen, and as the knife clatters on the floor, Pinkerton's voice is heard, calling 'Butterfly, Butterfly'. She drags herself to the door, and dies as Pinkerton enters.

The music of *Madama Butterfly* has extraordinary charm. Here the principal characteristic of Puccini's strong individuality and

highly personal style is more marked than in his previous
works: the soft, impressionistic, slightly sentimental yet always
dignified and lovely melodies. The short overture, a *fugato*, is

built on a busy theme which recurs whenever Japanese sub-
missiveness and diligence in the presence of the white man are
illustrated. The music of the two Americans' conversation at
the beginning of the first act is based on American folk song
and its carefree confidence, but when Butterfly enters the score
reveals its true character, and from then on it is dominated by
oriental-style melodies. A delicate motif stressing the magic

of the evening is heard here, and repeated until it bursts out
into Butterfly's great love-song. These themes of expectation

and love are taken up and blended together in the passionate
love-duet which brings the act to its splendid climax and close.
In the second act the lyrical moments are subordinated to
dramatic accent. Butterfly's profoundly emotional aria is of

course world-famous. The musical portrayal of nightfall at the end of the first scene of the second act is most delightful, with its distant humming chorus rising softly above the delicate orchestral rhythms.

After a relatively long pause Puccini had his next opera produced in New York in 1910. With this work, *La Fanciulla del West*, Puccini paid homage to North America, where since the appearance of *Madama Butterfly* his works had been unprecedentedly successful. Caruso's appearances as Rodolfo, Cavaradossi and Pinkerton at the Metropolitan Opera in New York were decisive landmarks in Puccini's ascent to fame. The subject of the new opera is taken from American life and history and musically Puccini treats it in his previous *verismo* style, with lyrical episodes which are secondary in importance to description of milieu.

LA FANCIULLA DEL WEST (The Girl of the Golden West). Opera in three acts by Giacomo Puccini. Text after David Belasco by Guelfo Civinini and Carlo Zangarini. First performance: New York, 1910.

Characters: Minnie, owner of The Polka—soprano; Jack Rance, the Sheriff—baritone; Dick Johnson (Ramerrez) a bandit—tenor; Nick, bartender at The Polka—tenor; José Castro, a bandit—bass; Ashby, agent of the Wells Fargo Transport Co.—bass; Billy Jackrabbit, a Red Indian—bass; Wowkle, his squaw—mezzo-soprano; Jake Wallace, a travelling minstrel—baritone; a courier—tenor; miners—three tenors, four baritones, one bass.

Place: A mining-camp in the Cloudy Mountains, California. *Time:* 1849–50.

Act I. Inside The Polka bar. Some of the miners are sitting at the tables, drinking, chatting and playing cards. The travelling minstrel, Jake Wallace, sings a nostalgic song about his homeland, in which everyone joins wistfully. One of the miners feels homesick, and his comrades start a collection to help him go home. Somebody cheats at cards and another mocks the sheriff, Rance, for his hopeless love for Minnie. There is a dramatic change of atmosphere with the arrival of Minnie, who, as the only woman among all these men, succeeds in being a good friend to each of them while preserving her innocence in the rough surroundings. She is highly respected by all the miners, to whom her word is as good as law. On her entry she stops a fight, tells them all off, and proceeds to hold her regular Bible-reading class. When the post arrives, Ashby receives a letter from a former girl friend of the bandit Ramerrez, telling him where to find him that night. Rance goes up to Minnie and starts to tell her how he loves her, but she interrupts him and when he bursts out into a passionate avowal she recalls her parents' love for each other and says she is waiting for love like that to enter her life. A stranger comes into the bar, and when the suspicious Rance demands to know his business, he replies that his name is Johnson and that he comes from Sacramento.

He and Minnie had met before, and she vouches for him. They clearly like each other, and when a waltz starts, hummed and sung by the men, Johnson invites Minnie to dance, to Rance's obvious annoyance. Meanwhile Castro is brought in, and says he will lead them to the bandit's camp. When Johnson enters, Castro manages to whisper to him that he will lead the miners on a false scent. Everyone goes out, leaving Minnie alone to look after the miners' treasure. Johnson stays with her. She is attracted by him, but thinks she is not good enough for him because of her lack of education. Johnson is fascinated by her childlike innocence. A whistle is heard outside; Johnson must rejoin his companions, but agrees to Minnie's suggestion that he should come to see her later; happy and yet afraid she will wait for him.

Act II. Minnie's hut. It is late at night. Minnie tells Wowkle to prepare supper for two and puts on what finery she has. When Johnson enters, they sit down to supper and she tells him how happy she is in her life here, with the mountains, the wild flowers and her school for the miners. Charmed by her, Johnson asks her for a kiss. She has never kissed a man before, and only after long hesitation does she give it to him. A storm has broken out in the meantime, and as Minnie does not want Johnson to go out in it she prepares herself a bed on the bearskin by the fireplace, while he is to sleep in her own bed. Rance, Nick, Ashby and one of the miners knock on the door and Minnie quickly hides Johnson behind the bed-curtains before she admits them. They have come to warn Minnie against Johnson, who they have discovered is the bandit Ramerrez. Minnie does not want to believe this, but when she is shown a photograph of the bandit she is no longer in doubt. As soon as the men have gone, she turns furiously on Johnson, and demands that he leave the house immediately. He admits that he came there to steal, but at the sight of her changed his mind. He tells her how he became a bandit, but now that he has met Minnie his only wish is to lead an honest life. As soon as he has gone, shots are heard. A body falls heavily against Minnie's door, and when she opens it, she finds Johnson, badly wounded. She hides him in the loft just as Rance enters. He searches the room, but without success, then tries to embrace Minnie who recoils from him. Drops of blood fall from the loft, and Rance calls to Johnson to descend. He comes down slowly and collapses at the foot of the ladder. As a last desperate resort Minnie suggests a game of poker, with herself and Johnson's life as the prizes if Rance wins; but if he loses, he must not betray Johnson. Rance cannot resist such a challenge, and Minnie wins by cheating, undetected by Rance, who leaves the house, while Minnie breaks out in sobs.

Act III. A clearing in the forest. The sheriff and his party are still searching for Ramerrez. After several false alarms he is captured and they prepare to hang him. He knows that he can expect no mercy, but makes an impassioned plea that Minnie should not know of his ignominious death. At the last moment Minnie dashes in on horseback. She has never before asked anything of the miners, but she now prays them to spare her the life of the man she loves, so that he can start a new life with her in some distant place. The miners agree that they cannot deny her such a favour, and she and Johnson go off into an unknown future.

Puccini was particularly fond of his music for *La Fanciulla del West*, perhaps just because in composing it he adopted such a different style from his previous works. The harsh naturalism which he strives for did not come easily to him and has therefore no immediate impact. The few lyrical episodes, as for instance Johnson's third-act *arioso*, are no adequate compensation.

Ch'el-la mi cre-da   li-be-ro e lon-ta-no,
(*Let her be-lieve me   far a-way in free - dom,*

so - vra u-na nuo-va vi - a di re-den-zio - ne
li - ving a life that leads____ to my re-demp-tion)

The music for the one-act opera *Il Tabarro* is very sombre and harsh, and of all Puccini's works this is without doubt the most in keeping with the spirit of *verismo*: in contrast with the consciously rough undertone of the music for *La Fanciulla del West*, however, it exudes all the magical Puccini sounds and some of his most inspired melodies. The other two one-act operas, *Suor Angelica* and *Gianni Schicchi*, which with *Il Tabarro* make up a 'trittico', or triple bill, are both masterpieces in their own way. In spite of this *Il Trittico* as such was not a lasting success.

IL TABARRO (The Cloak). Musical drama in one act by Giacomo Puccini. Text by Giuseppe Adami, after Didier Gold's *Houppelane*. First performance: New York, 1918.

Characters: Michele, a barge-owner, aged fifty—baritone; Giorgetta, his wife, aged twenty-five—soprano; Luigi, a stevedore—tenor; 'Tinca', a stevedore—tenor; 'Talpa', a stevedore—bass; Frugola, his wife—mezzo-soprano; a song-seller—tenor.

Place: Paris. *Time:* beginning of the nineteenth century.

A bank of the Seine, where Michele's barge is at anchor, with a view over Paris and Notre Dame. It is evening. Michele is gazing thoughtfully at the sunset. The stevedores are unloading the last sacks of cargo from the barge, and Giorgetta asks Michele to offer them a glass of wine when they finish work. Michele agrees, and comes up to Giorgetta to embrace her, but she draws back. The young stevedore Luigi tells the organ-grinder to play a waltz as Giorgetta wants to dance. The barrel-organ is horribly out of tune. Giorgetta first has to dance with the drunkard Tinca, but she then slips into Luigi's arms and happily abandons herself to the waltz. When Michele arrives, they stop at once. The song-seller sings a languorous *romanza* of the unhappy Mimi, and Mimi's theme from *La Bohème* is cleverly woven into the refrain. Frugola comes to fetch her husband, Talpa. They are both content with their modest life, and dream of the little house of their own in which they would like to spend their last years—a dream which will never be realized. Tinca and Luigi, however, can hardly bear their arduous existence any longer, which is the reason for Tinca's addiction to drink. Giorgetta is also sick of her life on the barge, and longs for the Paris suburb where she spent her youth and met Luigi. When everyone else goes off, Giorgetta holds Luigi back to arrange a rendezvous with him. Fearing that Michele might surprise them they dare not embrace, although they are both consumed with desire. They arrange that when Giorgetta lights a match that night it will mean that the coast is clear and Luigi can come quietly to her. He goes away, and as night falls Michele joins his wife. He reminds her of the good times they have spent together and of the child they lost, and implores her for a little love, a little tenderness; Giorgetta is unmoved, and pleading tiredness she goes to bed. 'You whore,' he mutters after her. He drapes his cloak round him and peers in through the cabin window to see Giorgetta still awake and apparently waiting. For whom? Who is her lover? In an agonized monologue Michele tries to guess his identity and swears a terrible revenge. He then relaxes on the deck and strikes a match to light his pipe, thereby unwittingly giving Luigi Giorgetta's signal. As the young man steals on to the barge, Michele jumps at him and seizes him by the throat. 'Confess that you love her,' he demands. Luigi can only choke 'Yes, I love her' before Michele strangles him. From the cabin, Giorgetta calls to ask Michele where he has been all this time, and then she comes up on deck. Michele hides the body under his cloak. Greatly frightened, Giorgetta asks him to warm her under the cloak, and Michele with a terrible cry opens it to reveal the body of Luigi.

The conflict between crude naturalism and melodic impressionism is completely solved in the score of *Il Tabarro*. In sparse, effective strokes the music defines the various characters and their contrasting temperaments: the contented elderly couple, Luigi and Giorgetta hungry for life and love, and between them the despairing philosopher, Tinca. A calm flowing melody portrays the action of the first scene and also returns later in the drama. The monotonous lapping of the water is expressed in

this theme, but it also contains a hint of impending disaster. The final scene is dominated by a sinister, creeping motif,

which builds up in excitement to the passionate climax of the final gruesome moments.

SUOR ANGELICA (Sister Angelica). Opera in one act by Giacomo Puccini. Text by Gioacchino Forzano. First performance: New York, 1918.

 Characters: Suor Angelica—soprano; the Princess, her aunt—contralto; the Abbess—mezzo-soprano. Nuns, novices, lay sisters.

 Place: Italy. *Time:* end of the seventeenth century.

 The opera, which takes place in the cloister of a convent, is divided into three parts. The first is concerned with a description of the life of the nuns, among them Sister Angelica, who is an authority on herbs. The second part contains the scene between Angelica and her aunt, the Princess. The Princess, who brought Angelica up in place of her mother, comes to visit her for the first time in seven years, and greets her without any show of affection. Angelica, who comes of a noble Florentine family, took the veil as penance for having given birth to an illegitimate child. The Princess asks her to renounce her dowry in favour of her younger sister, who is about to marry. Angelica agrees and humbly asks as her sole favour to be allowed to see her little son who has to live in the world without his mother. Coldly the Princess tells her that her child has been dead for two years. The contrast between the characters of these two women makes this an extremely powerful scene. The third and final part opens with the departure of the Princess. Overwhelmed with sorrow, Angelica is left alone and resolves to end her life. She prepares a potion of poisonous herbs, but as soon as she has drunk it she realizes that she has committed a deadly sin. She prays to the Virgin not to reject her, but to unite her with her beloved child. Her prayer is heard, and to the sound of angelic voices the Heavens open and the Blessed Virgin appears to the penitent, leading a little child by the hand. As the child slowly approaches Angelica to take her to the Virgin, she falls to the ground, dead.

It is the very sentimental text of *Suor Angelica* which, despite some beautiful musical passages, accounts for its lack of popularity. Only Angelica's lament 'Senza mamma' ('Without a mother') has enjoyed the fame which so many of Puccini's other arias have enjoyed. *Gianni Schicchi* is found much more often in operatic repertories; this is Puccini's only light opera, and is considered by many to be his best work.

GIANNI SCHICCHI. Comic opera in one act by Giacomo Puccini. Text by Gioacchino Forzano. First performance: New York, 1918.

Characters: Gianni Schicchi—baritone; Lauretta, his daughter—soprano; Buoso Donati's relatives: Zita, his elderly cousin—contralto; Rinuccio, her nephew—tenor; Gherardo, Buoso's nephew—tenor; Nella, Gherardo's wife—soprano; Gherardino, their son, aged seven—alto; Betto di Signa, Buoso's poor brother-in-law—bass; Simone, Buoso's old cousin—bass; Marco, his son—baritone; La Ciesca, Marco's wife—mezzo-soprano; Maestro Spinelloccio, a doctor—bass; Ser Amantio di Nicolao, a notary—baritone; Pinellino, a shoemaker—bass; Guccio, a painter—bass.

Place: Florence. *Time:* 1299.

The action takes place in the bedroom of the rich Buoso Donati, who has just died. His numerous relatives are kneeling round the bed, praying and lamenting. Betto has heard a rumour that Buoso has left his whole fortune to a religious order, and the other relatives in horror leave their devotions and can only talk of how to counter this if it be true. Old Simone says that they must first find out whether the will is in the house; if it is in the hands of a lawyer, there is nothing more to be done. A frantic search for the will begins. At last the young Rinuccio finds the all-important document. They all try to tear it out of his hand, but he first insists that they must consent to his marriage with Lauretta, Gianni Schicchi's daughter. For the sake of the will the relatives agree. Rinuccio sends little Gherardino to Gianni Schicchi's house to ask him to come at once with his daughter. Meanwhile the relatives have studied the will and found that in fact the whole large inheritance is to go to the religious house. They are all first furious, then deeply depressed, as they cannot see any solution. Rinuccio suggests that perhaps the cunning Gianni Schicchi might have an idea, but the relatives at first refuse to have anything to do with him. Rinuccio warmly defends his beloved Lauretta's father. Gianni arrives with Lauretta, and is astonished to learn that old Buoso has died and given his relatives such a terrible disappointment. Rinuccio begs him to think of a way out, but only when Lauretta joins all the relatives in imploring him to help does Gianni Schicchi look at the will. Once he has made sure that no one else knows of Buoso's death, he conceives a plan. He orders the men to take the body into an adjoining room, and the women to remake the bed. There is a knock at the door; it is the doctor, come to ask after the sick man's condition. On Schicchi's suggestion, the relatives tell the doctor that Buoso is better, and try to keep him out of the room. Buoso's voice is heard from the bed, where Schicchi is lying, imitating him. He assures the doctor that he is much better and only needs rest. The doctor, reassured goes away. The relatives now begin to understand Schicchi's plan. They all gather round him enthusiastically, each one asking him to give him or her a good share of the inheritance. A notary and two witnesses are sent for so that the new will can be drawn up at once, but Gianni Schicchi first warns the relatives of the terrible punishment which threatens them if this deceit were discovered: the loss of their right hands and banishment. They all join fearfully in the song 'Addio, Firenze'. The notary and witnesses arrive, and

Schicchi, in a plaintive voice, dictates his new will in which he declares all previous wills null and void. The money is to be divided equally among all the relatives, and each of them is also to receive a small country estate. The tension reaches its climax when he comes to the partition of the most valuable goods, the house in Florence, the mill at Signa and the mule, which they all dream of owning. To everybody's fury the sick man bequeaths these wonderful treasures to his dear friend, Gianni Schicchi. As soon as somebody dares to protest, Schicchi starts singing 'Addio, Firenze', which at once silences them. When the notary and witnesses have left, the relatives pour down curses on Schicchi and try to take away everything they can lay their hands on. Schicchi furiously chases them out, since the house now belongs to him. Rinuccio and Lauretta are engaged in a tender little love-scene and the sight of them calms the furious man. He then turns to the audience and asks whether the estate could have been better divided. Father Dante certainly would have sent him to hell for this roguish trick, but he thinks that the audience, which has been enjoying itself, will agree that there were extenuating circumstances.

In *Gianni Schicchi* Puccini reveals a subtle sense of humour, spiced with irony and even satire, but his delight in mockery is never malicious, and a mischievous grin always lurks behind it. The description of the relatives' hypocritical behaviour is delightfully expressed in a sighing theme, but when they forget

their feigned sorrow and start searching for the will, the sighs (now in double time) emphasize the abrupt change of mood. The threatening song, in which Schicchi describes the possible consequences if the trick is discovered, is quite delightful. The

Ad - di - o,   Fi - ren - ze,   ci-e-lo di - vi-no
(*Fare-well, dear   Flo - rence, dear   ci-ty of great charm*)

lovers' music provides a lyrical contrast to the main plot and its witty satire, and here, for instance in Lauretta's famous *arioso*

'O mio babbino caro' ('Oh my beloved daddy') Puccini's gift for melody really comes into its own.

Turandot, his last work, represents another amazing highlight in Puccini's creative work. In it he blends intense expressive power and pure magical language with perfect technical mastery. The first act and the beginning of the third act are among the most beautiful and moving passages Puccini ever composed; the second act however, in spite of great theatrical and dramatic display, has no such immediate impact. Puccini never completed the end of the opera; the last passage he composed was the really shattering music for the death of little Liù. His pupil Franco Alfano (1876–1954) completed the final scenes most sensitively in Puccini's style from drafts left behind by his master.

TURANDOT. Opera in three acts by Giacomo Puccini. Text by Giuseppe Adami and Renato Simoni. First performance: Milan, 1926.

Characters: Turandot, Princess of China—soprano; Altoum, Emperor of China—tenor; Timur, exiled King of Tartary—bass; Prince Calaf, his son—tenor; Liù, a slave girl—soprano; Ping, Grand Chancellor of China—baritone; Pang, Master of Provisions—tenor; Pong, Master of the Imperial Kitchen—tenor; a mandarin—baritone. People of Peking, guards and courtiers.

Place: Peking. *Time:* legendary.

Act I. Outside the walls of Peking. An excited crowd has gathered to watch a thrilling spectacle. One more claimant for the hand of the beautiful Turandot has failed the test (which consists of answering three riddles), and must pay the penalty—death. This time it is the Prince of Persia who will die by the executioner's axe. Among the crowd is the frail deposed King of Tartary, Timur, with his faithful slave Liù. In the jostling mob Timur falls, and when a young man comes to help him to his feet, Timur recognizes in him his own son Calaf, from whom he was separated when he was banished from his country. The Prince of Persia, followed by the executioner and his assistants, is brought in. Calaf feels great compassion for the unhappy youth, as do the people also, for they start calling on the Princess to pardon him. The scene is bathed in moonlight. Turandot appears on a balcony and with an imperious gesture orders the executioner to carry out the sentence. Calaf is overcome by her beauty and resolves to try and win her hand at once, expressing his readiness to submit to the same cruel conditions. In vain his father and Liù try to dissuade him, and three mandarins, Ping, Pong and Pang, join in the attempt. Calaf's resolve is unshaken, and he strikes the gong three times to indicate the presence of another candidate for the trial.

Act II, scene i. In a pavilion the three mandarins, Ping, Pong and Pang, lament the state of China and their own enforced participation in the commands of the cruel Turandot, while they only long for a quiet life. A drum-roll summons the ministers to the new trial.

Scene ii. The throne-room of the Imperial Palace. In the background rises a staircase at the head of which is the Imperial throne, where sits the old Emperor. The populace gathers round to attend the trial. Banners and standards of the Imperial court are carried in, and various dignitaries enter—the wise men who bring the solution of the riddles with them. The people kneel down before the Emperor, who calls on Calaf to withdraw from the contest, but he firmly answers that he wants to solve the riddles. Finally Turandot appears, splendidly attired, her face cold, as if carved in marble. In self-justification she tells the story of her ancestress, who thousands of years ago was dishonoured by a foreign conqueror and sent into exile, where she died of grief. Turandot has dedicated herself to avenging her. She poses the riddles to the young foreigner, who solves all three of them. They are these: 'What is the phantom that is born every night and dies every day ?'—the answer being 'Hope'; 'What is it that at times is like a fever, yet grows cold when you die, and blazes up at the thought of great deeds ?'—the answer being 'Blood'; and finally 'What is the ice that sets you on fire ?'—to which the answer is 'Turandot'. Turandot is horrified, and implores her father not to hand her over as a prize to the foreigner, but he reminds her of his oath. Calaf declares himself willing to renounce his right over her, since he does not want to win her by force. If she can discover his name before dawn, he will die for her.

Act III, scene i. The garden of the Imperial Palace. Heralds announce that no one shall sleep in Peking that night, until the stranger's name is known. Meanwhile Calaf dreams of his victory in the splendid aria, 'Nessun dorma' ('None shall sleep'). He is unmoved by the three man-darins' offers of riches and safety if he will disclose his name, so intent is he on winning Turandot. Timur and Liù, who were seen the day before speaking to the stranger, are dragged before Turandot. To protect old Timur, Liù says that she alone knows the stranger's name, but she will not reveal it. Turandot orders her to be tortured. When she can bear the pain no longer, Liù snatches a dagger from one of the guards and kills herself. Everyone is deeply moved, and even Turandot seems touched by this devotion. Her body is carried out, followed by the grieving Timur. Turandot and Calaf are left alone. He lifts the veil from her face and kisses her passionately. Her pride is broken, and she begs him to go and take his secret with him, but once again he puts himself at her mercy by telling her his name: Calaf, son of Timur.

Scene ii. The throne-room. Turandot, addressing the Emperor and his assembled court, says that she now knows the stranger's name—it is Love.

The oriental colour of the *Turandot* score is much harsher in style and expression than that of *Madama Butterfly*. The penta-tonic scale is more strictly adhered to, and the instrumentation is largely based on wind, percussion and *pizzicato* effects when-

ever the oriental atmosphere is evoked. The first act is dominated by the chorus, which throughout plays an important part
in the drama. There is a wonderful orchestral description of the
rising moon, in which Puccini reveals all the impressionist
magic of divided strings. The delicate children's chorus, which
also captures this atmosphere, introduces Turandot's theme for

the first time and then leads into the gruesome funeral march.
When Turandot appears her theme flares up in all the splendour
of the full orchestra. In the second part of this act the most
moving passage is the lyrical episode of Liù's supplication to the
Prince not to sacrifice himself, 'Signore, ascolta!', Calaf's sincerely emotional reply, 'Non piangere, Liù', and the splendid
sextet which follows. The music of the second act is most
effective, even if at times superficial. The introductory trio of
the three ministers sparkles with enchanting inventiveness but
lacks dramatic impact. In the final act the music again attains
the high expressive level of the first scene. Liù's song before
she dies, 'Tu, che di gel sei cinta' rises to great nobility, and the
music which mourns her death is built over the same theme and
is orchestrated for flute, solo violin and a distant chorus, which
dies away most movingly and delicately.

In 1896, the year which saw the first performance of *La
Bohème*, another very successful work appeared. This was
Andrea Chénier, the principal work of Umberto Giordano
(1867–1948) which is still a most popular repertory opera, at
least in Italy. It has never become really well established elsewhere however, in spite of its unquestioned musical beauties and
most rewarding roles.

ANDREA CHÉNIER. Opera in four acts by Umberto Giordano. Text
by Luigi Illica. First performance: Milan, 1896.
    Characters: Andrea Chénier, a poet—tenor; the Countess de Coigny—
mezzo-soprano; Madeleine, her daughter—soprano; Roucher, a friend
of Chénier's—bass; Bersi, a mulatto, Madeleine's maid—mezzo-soprano;
Charles Gérard, a servant at the Countess's castle—baritone; Fléville, a
cavalier—baritone; the Abbé—tenor; Mathieu, a waiter—baritone; a

Major-domo—baritone; Incredible, a spy—tenor; Madelon, an old woman—mezzo-soprano; Dumas, president of the tribunal—baritone; Fouquier-Tinville, attorney-general—baritone; Schmidt, a gaoler—baritone. Courtiers, citizens, soldiers, servants, peasants, members of the Revolutionary Tribunal, prisoners.

Place: Paris. *Time:* before and after the French Revolution.

Act I. The ballroom in the Countess de Coigny's château. Gérard is helping to arrange the room for a party, and comments mockingly and angrily on aristocratic wealth and luxury. The Countess and Madeleine enter, the one to check the detailed preparations for the party, the latter to discuss with her maid what she shall wear. Gérard comments on the beauty of Madeleine, whom he secretly loves. Among the guests who now arrive are Fléville, and the Abbé, who introduces Chénier to the Countess. He refuses her request to recite one of his poems, but consents to do so when Madeleine asks him. There follows the famous *Improvviso* 'Un dì, all'azzurro spazio' ('One day, in the azure heavens') in which he condemns the corrupt and selfish regime, to the annoyance of the other guests. Although the Countess tries to smooth over the embarrassment, Gérard introduces a band of beggars as 'His Lordship Misery' to emphasize Chénier's point.

Act II. The Café Hottot in Paris. The Revolution has started. Chénier and Bersi are sitting at different tables, and Incredible, the spy, is making notes on both of them. Roucher enters with a passport for Chénier, begging him to fly at once as he has powerful enemies, but Chénier will not hear of it. Robespierre and some other Revolutionary leaders, including Gérard, pass by, and in reply to his inquiries, Gérard gives Incredible a lyrical description of Madeleine, who is wanted by the authorities. Watched only by Incredible, Madeleine comes to meet Chénier, who at first does not recognize her. They agree to escape together, but by then Incredible has slipped out to fetch Gérard. Chénier draws his sword to defend Madeleine, and wounds Gérard in the ensuing fight, without either having recognized the other. On learning Chénier's name, Gérard warns him that he is wanted as a counter-revolutionary. When the police arrive, Gérard says he does not know the identity of his assailant.

Act III. The Revolutionary Tribunal. Gérard's eloquence stimulates the crowd to patriotic self-denial. When they have dispersed, Gérard learns from Incredible that Chénier has been arrested and that the spy assumes Madeleine will soon come in search of her lover. Gérard has to write out Chénier's indictment, but is haunted by his conscience. How can he denounce Chénier as 'an enemy of his country' ('Nemico della patria') ? Finally his love and desire for Madeleine sway his decision, and he signs the indictment. When Madeleine is brought in, Gérard freely explains his motives in having Chénier arrested, and Madeleine offers her love in return for her lover's release. Gérard promises to do what he can for Chénier. The Tribunal sits and in spite of Gérard's efforts Chénier is condemned to death.

Act IV. The courtyard of the St Lazare prison. Chénier, while awaiting the tumbril, is writing a poem. His friend Roucher asks him to read it aloud, then bids him farewell. Gérard brings in Madeleine, who will take the place of a woman condemned to death in order to die with Chénier. In an impassioned duet 'Vicino a te' ('By your dear side'), they rejoice that death will unite them.

Although Andrea Chénier was a historical character, a poet, dreamer and patriot who was first a participant in the Revolution and later its victim, Luigi Illica has woven a fictitious story about him. Into this opera Giordano poured a wealth of passion and lyricism, and it contains some wonderfully rewarding arias for Chénier, Gérard and Madeleine. The most impressive are perhaps Chénier's 'poem' in the last act—'Come un bel dì di maggio' ('Like some fair day that closes') and the final duet for Chénier and Madeleine 'Vicino a te'.

Giordano's other successful opera, Fedora, appeared two years later, and although it never achieved the success of Andrea Chénier, it is frequently performed in Italy. It is based on Sardou's most theatrical play of the same name, and tells of the tragic love of Count Loris Ipanov for the Princess Fedora. It is set in St Petersburg, Paris, and a Swiss mountain village at the period of the nihilist disturbances in Russia at the end of the last century. Some of its pages contain the composer's most lyric outpourings, and these together with the strong, dramatic situations, offer some wonderful opportunities to outstanding singing actors.

In Germany verismo had hardly any disciples. Certain features of this style can be traced here and there, as for instance in Kienzl's Evangelimann, but in few cases was naturalism taken up as a stylistic principle. The only naturalistic German opera of lasting fame is d'Albert's Tiefland. Eugen d'Albert (1864–1932), a world-famous pianist and pupil of Liszt, followed the Wagnerian style in his first operas. His light one-act opera Die Abreise (The Departure) (1898), built on flowing dialogue, seemed the start of a new and very acceptable style of comedy, but he unfortunately abandoned this line to join the ranks of verismo. Tiefland was, however, a world-wide success. D'Albert had a sure feeling for dramatic effect and so made a strong, if not very profound impression on a wide audience.

TIEFLAND (The Lowlands). Opera in a prologue and two acts by Eugen d'Albert. Text by Rudolph Lothar after Angel Guimerà. First performance: Prague, 1903.

Characters: Sebastiano, a rich landowner—baritone; Tommaso, the village elder (ninety years old)—bass; Moruccio, a mill employee—baritone; Marta—mezzo-soprano; Pepa—soprano; Antonia—soprano; Rosalia—contralto; Nuri, a little girl—soprano; Pedro and Nando, shepherds—tenors; the Priest—mime. Villagers.

Place: The Pyrenees and the Catalonian Lowlands. *Time:* beginning of the twentieth century.

Prologue. A rocky slope in the Pyrenees. Dawn is breaking as Pedro and Nando greet each other; Pedro mentions that he has not seen a soul for three months. He loves and enjoys this complete solitude in the midst of nature, but each evening he prays to God to fulfil his only wish and send him a wife. He tells Nando of a dream in which the Virgin appeared to him and promised him a wife and happiness. Nando laughs at him for thinking they are one and the same thing. Pedro shuts his eyes and turning around hurls a stone from his sling, saying it will mark the direction from which his wife will come to him. It nearly hits Sebastiano, who is coming up the mountain with Marta and Tommaso. When Nando tells Pedro who the visitors are, he retires into his hut. While Tommaso goes to fetch Pedro, and Nando to bring his master food, Sebastiano explains to Marta (who is his mistress) why he has brought her here. He reminds her how he took her and her father off the streets, and gave her father the mill, which she inherited when he died and for which she pays Sebastiano rent with herself. Now he has a command for her: he intends to marry her to Pedro, the handsome young shepherd who has just come into sight above them, so as to put an end to gossip. Marta is horrified and pleads with him not to do this. She refuses even to look at Pedro and flees down the mountain, while Pedro gazes after her in admiration at her beauty. Sebastiano tells him of the plan to make him his miller and to give him Marta in marriage. Pedro can hardly believe his good fortune for he has no idea that Marta is Sebastiano's mistress. Nando warns Pedro against life in the valley, but Pedro will not listen. An orchestral interlude leads straight into the first act.

Act I. Inside the mill. It is early evening. The women Pepa, Antonia and Rosalia try to induce Moruccio to tell them whether it is true that Marta is going to marry the shepherd Pedro, taunting him with wanting to marry her and be miller himself. Moruccio tells them nothing, but they learn of the planned wedding from the innocent young Nuri, Marta's confidante. She also relates a conversation she overheard between Sebastiano and Marta which clearly shows that this marriage will not mark the end of their relationship. The women are laughing about the prospective marriage when Marta enters and turns them out. Alone with Nuri she bewails her misery and loneliness, and disgust at the thought of marrying Pedro. She sends Nuri out and sings sorrowfully of her position as Sebastiano's property, her despair of ever breaking free from him, and her lack of courage to end her life. The villagers enter to announce Pedro's arrival. Moruccio finds that old Tommaso knows nothing of Marta's history and liaison with Sebastiano, and when Moruccio explains that the master has debts and wants to marry Marta off to stop gossip and enable him to make a rich marriage, the simple Tommaso dismisses the whole idea as malicious gossip. Pedro enters joyfully and is received with ironic salutations by the villagers, but in his innocence he does not notice their sarcasm. When Marta pleads again with Sebastiano he ignores her, but when everyone has gone to the church and Pedro is dressing for the wedding, he tells Marta that he has chosen Pedro, a clumsy lout who disgusts her, so that she will remain true to him, her master. He declares his love and abiding faithfulness to her, while they both make loveless marriages. She wants to break with him, but he says he will come to her room that very night. When she sees a light in her room, she will know that he is waiting there for her. Everything is ready for the wedding, and Marta and Pedro go to the church accompanied by the villagers. Moruccio refuses to go to the wedding and Sebastiano dismisses him. Tommaso holds Sebastiano back and taxes him with the rumours. When Moruccio swears on the soul of his mother than what he told Tommaso is true, and Sebastiano's denial is unconvincing, Tommaso wants to stop the wedding. But it is too late, and the wedding procession is already on its way back. Tommaso leaves with Moruccio for the mountains. Pedro and Marta enter. With shy sincerity and simplicity he tries to embrace her, but she is cold to him and asks him to leave her alone. Pedro tries to give her his dearest treasure, a *taler* given to him by the master when he had strangled with his bare hands a wolf which was robbing the flock. He tells her the whole story and she is touched by it. Marta finally realizes from his manner that he knows nothing of her past and has married her out of sincere love for her. A light appears in Marta's room. Pedro draws his knife and wants to investigate, but Marta holds him back, telling him that he is mistaken and must now rest. She is horrified at this new enormity of Sebastiano's and decides to spend the night in a chair. Pedro lies down at her feet and falls asleep.

Act II. The same as Act I. Dawn. Nuri is singing outside and wakes Marta, who gets up quietly and goes to her room. Nuri enters and wakes Pedro, who is full of mistrust and unhappiness. Nuri tries to soothe him, but when Marta returns and finds them talking together, she is jealous. She orders Nuri out of the house, but Pedro goes too, leaving Marta furious with jealousy and fear that Pedro will learn the truth. Tommaso enters and confronts her with her misdeeds. She confesses everything and appeals to his pity, telling him that she and Pedro really love each other. Tommaso tells her it is her duty to tell Pedro the truth. The women pester Nuri for the latest news of the newly-married couple, but she sings them a mocking ballad and escapes, as Pedro enters. He has heard something in the village, but still does not know the name of Marta's former lover. He tells Marta he is going back to the mountains. Marta implores him to pardon her and stay, but only by taunting him with not daring to punish her and by emphasizing her own guilt can she keep him from leaving her. In the end he throws himself on her and wounds her arm. He is horrified at his own deed, but she begs him to go on and kill her, that death may cleanse her of her sin. He replies by telling her of his love and his wish to take her to the mountains with him. She joins him in an ecstatic love-duet. As they are leaving the mill, Sebastiano meets them in the doorway. Ignoring Pedro he orders Marta to dance for him. Some villagers gather in the background and join in the chorus. Sebastiano sings and plays the guitar and Marta most unwillingly starts to dance. Pedro commands her to stop and come with him. Sebastiano first ignores, then mocks him when he finds Marta wants to go with Pedro. Then he strikes Pedro on the face. Marta cries to him that it is Sebastiano who is responsible for her shame and their misfortune, and who was in her room the night before. Beside himself with rage Pedro throws himself at Sebastiano, but the villagers seize him and drag him out, leaving Sebastiano gloating over the semi-conscious Marta. Tommaso enters and tells Sebastiano that he has told the whole story to his prospective bride's father, who has withdrawn his consent to the marriage. Sebastiano rushes out to try and put things right. Marta gradually recovers consciousness. As she rushes to the door in a panic to find Pedro, Sebastiano enters. All is lost to him except Marta and the mill; there he means to stay with her, ignoring all her pleas for freedom. He tries to kiss her despite her defiance and her announcement that she loves Pedro. She calls out Pedro's name in desperation, and at that moment he leaps into the room and forces Sebastiano to fight. After a short struggle Pedro strangles Sebastiano, as he had once strangled the wolf, and then he calls in the villagers to see how he has revenged himself. Nobody dares to hold him back, and with Marta at his side he leaves the Lowlands for ever to return to his mountains.

Even if a detailed study of the score reveals many borrowed passages in *Tiefland*, it has an overall unity of inspiration and deserves its success. The motif in fourths is certainly original,

and exactly catches the glacial atmosphere of the high mountains. The theme of longing is, to say the least, impressive and the harsh theme of the howling wolf is most distinctive. It is

extremely interesting to see how d'Albert works on these recurring themes. Marta's theme of bitter conflict is also used as a *leitmotiv*, but most of the other themes appear more episodically, supporting the individual scenes and very occasionally reappearing, as for instance the elegant and light-hearted dance-tune which accompanies the first conversation between Pedro

and Sebastiano, the maids' impudent mocking music or the strong rhythms of Pedro's arrival at the mill. These plastic, expressive ideas make a much greater impact than the surging drama of the great scenes between Marta and Sebastiano, and Marta and Pedro, which lack genuine high pathos.

Among d'Albert's numerous later operas only *Die toten Augen* (*The Dead Eyes*) (1916), enjoyed a substantial success. It is somewhat exaggerated in style, and the music changes from sugary sentimentality to tremendous sensuous power, with few gradations in between, which creates a strong atmosphere. The vocal parts are very impressive and the instrumentation is brilliant and effective, if somewhat crude.

Verismo opera found very little response in France, although naturalism had been introduced into French opera by Bizet in his brilliant *Carmen*. The most important French opera in the *verismo* style is *Louise* (1900) by Gustave Charpentier (1860–1956). This is a most original work of typically French charm, and is still among the most popular operas in France, though rarely performed elsewhere.

LOUISE. Musical romance in four acts. Music and text by Gustave Charpentier. First performance: Paris, 1900.

Characters: Louise—soprano; Julien, a young artist—tenor; Louise's father—bass; her mother—mezzo-soprano. Bohemians, ragmen, street-vendors, policemen, artists, artisans, grisettes, etc.

Place: Paris. *Time:* about 1900.

Act I. An attic room in a working-class tenement house. Through a large open window leading on to the balcony one can see the roofs of Paris, and in the foreground the terrace of a studio, from which Julien is serenading Louise, who comes out on to her balcony. The two young people are in love with each other, but Louise's mother, a simple, respectable woman, is against the match. In her opinion all artists are lazy good-for-nothings. Louise asks Julien to send a letter to her father asking for her hand, and if this should fail she promises to run away with

him. Her mother overhears part of this conversation and, pushing Louise
into the room, shuts the window. The father, a straightforward workman who is very fond of Louise, as she is of him, comes in for his supper.
When he has read Julien's letter, he is prepared to consider his proposal,
but the mother is strongly opposed to the whole idea and infuriates her
daughter by making disparaging remarks about Julien. The father asks
Louise to read the newspaper to him, but a reference to spring in Paris
causes her to dissolve in tears.

Act II, scene i. A street in Montmartre. It is early morning, and the
tramps and vagabonds of Paris are already abroad. Julien arrives to speak
to Louise as she comes to her work, but she is accompanied by her mother
and Julien hides. After the Mother has gone, Julien fetches Louise out of
the house, and hears from her the reaction of her parents to his letter.
He is furious at her submissive attitude, while she, tearing herself away
from her lover, hurries back to her work.

Scene ii. A workroom in a dressmaker's establishment. The girls, as
they work, remark on Louise's silence and laugh at her, suggesting that
she is in love. Music is heard from the street; it is Julien, serenading
Louise. His courting becomes more and more passionate until Louise can
stand it no longer, and on sudden impulse she leaves the workroom.
Through the window the girls excitedly watch her go off with Julien
down the street.

Act III. A house and a small garden in Montmartre, with a view over
Paris in the background. Louise and Julien are living happily together.
Dusk is falling, and Louise sings her famous romance 'Depuis le jour'
('E'er since the day'), declaring her great contentment in her love and
freedom. The lights of Paris begin to twinkle below. Bohemian friends
of Julien and local workmen come in a colourful procession to elect
Louise their queen and muse. When the gaiety is at its height, Louise's
mother, dressed in black, is seen standing apart, and everyone withdraws
apprehensively. The mother asks Louise to come home, since her father
is desperately ill and longing to see her again. Only when the mother
has solemnly promised that Louise may go back to Julien when she wishes,
does he consent to her leaving him.

Act IV. The attic room as in the first act. The father is happy to
have Louise back, and only sees in her his loving, devoted child, but
Louise speaks of her right to freedom and reminds her parents of the
promise given to Julien, that she might return to him. Her parents regard
her relation with Julien as a sin, and therefore do not consider their promise
binding. Through the window can be seen the lights of Paris going out,
while tempting voices are heard in the distance, and Louise abandons
herself to the thought of her love. Her father only thinks her depraved,
and in a wild turmoil of conflicting emotions he throws his daughter out
into the street. Louise flees, and her father is left alone in despair. Paris,
the great seducer, has taken his daughter away from him for ever.

A solemn fanfare introduces *Louise*, and the short overture is
built on this theme which recurs in varied form during the

course of the action. It is the theme of *joie de vivre*, a passionate exuberance which characterizes the style of the whole score. The first act has complete musical unity. The principal characters are clearly described both in the text and the music: Julien's impetuous high spirits, Louise's fearful hesitancy, the Father, portrayed as a most lovable character, with wonderful melodies. The frequent lyrical episodes never seem stylistically inconsistent with the naturalistic text.

The short orchestral prelude to the second act is called 'Paris s'éveille', and represents the gradual awakening of the great city. The Paris theme, at first only hinted at, then bursts out in

glowing colours. The charm of this scene lies in the brilliant portrayal of milieu; the most varied types of people, street-vendors, rag-collectors, night-birds, and all kinds of riffraff are introduced in colourful scenic and musical contrast.

Paris, the City of Light, is the real protagonist of Charpentier's musical romance, and he succeeds very well in reproducing the atmosphere of the city in his music. The idea of a seductive metropolis dominates every phase of the story and its pulsing life and activity is continuously present on the stage. In spite of this naturalistic setting the typical French love of beautiful melody continually finds expression, but unfortunately this rather sweet lyricism sounds faded and slightly dated in comparison with the original, realistic features in the score.

For the coronation of the Empress Anna Joannovna of Russia in 1730, August II of Saxony sent an Italian opera troupe to St Petersburg to show his special respect for the young sovereign. This troupe was to contribute to the celebrations with performances of some operas suitable to the occasion, and they did so with such success that shortly afterwards the Empress had her own troupe sent from Italy. This spread the dominance of Italian opera even to St Petersburg, where it lasted unchallenged until well into the nineteenth century. Among the many composers of the Neapolitan school who lived and worked for a while in St Petersburg the best known were Traetta, Paisiello, Galuppi and Cimarosa, while the most celebrated singers of the time appeared at the Imperial Opera with great success, and enthusiasm for Italianate singing became almost a mania in leading Russian circles.

Although at the end of the eighteenth century French *opéra comique* made its bow with some success in St Petersburg, it never established itself there, but contact with French comic operas (the material for which was mostly taken from simple country life) drew attention to the possibility of using episodes of Russian country life for the stage. This was the beginning of the first Russian *Singspiele*, which idealized Russian peasantry on the lines of French pastoral plays and drew their music from Russian folk songs, corrupted and sentimentalized.

Artistically these attempts to create a Russian opera should not be taken too seriously until Glinka's genius paved the way for a national style in Russian music, and his best-known work, *A Life for the Tsar* (1836), prepared the ground for a national Russian opera. Mikhail Ivanovich Glinka (1804–57) did not consciously write a 'reform' opera, but being a nationalist he quite naturally chose a text which would inspire his patriotic feelings. His instinctive appreciation of the value and essence of Russian folk music led him to recognize and exploit its great untapped possibilities as the basis for a national musical art. He gave full play to the often eccentric metres and changing rhythms, and disclosed those colourful harmonics which are as native to Russian folk song as to Slavonic hymns. These elements make up the great charm and originality of Russian music.

A LIFE FOR THE TSAR (Ivan Susanin). Opera in four acts and an epilogue by Mikhail Glinka. Text by Baron G. F. Rozen. First performance: St Petersburg, 1836.

Characters: Ivan Susanin, a peasant—bass; Antonida, his daughter—soprano; Sobinin, her bridegroom—tenor; Vanya, Susanin's foster-son—contralto; a Polish commander—baritone. Russian peasants, Polish officers and soldiers, citizens of Moscow, guards, etc.

Place: Domnin (a Russian village), Moscow and a Polish camp. *Time:* 1613.

Act I. The village street of Domnin. Sobinin is expected back from the wars. Susanin brings news that the Poles are marching on Moscow, but Sobinin, entering, assures everyone that the Poles have been routed. Susanin will not bless his marriage with Antonida until the times seem more settled and a new Tsar is nominated. Sobinin tells him that their landlord, the young Romanoff, has been elected Tsar and Susanin, happy at this news, gives his consent to the marriage.

Act II. The Polish headquarters. A magnificent ball is in progress. When the Poles learn of the election of Romanoff as Tsar, they decide to capture him at the nearby monastery where he is staying.

Act III. Susanin's house. Vanya and Susanin sing of the prosperity of Russia, and Vanja speaks of rumours of a Polish plot to capture the young Tsar. Peasants enter to congratulate Antonida and Sobinin on their wedding. Some Polish troops break in and try to force Susanin to guide them to the monastery where the Tsar is hiding. At first Susanin demurs, then pretends to accept their bribe and goes with them, having signalled to Vanya to ride ahead and warn the Tsar. When Sobinin hears what has happened, he gathers a band of peasants to follow and try to save Susanin.

Act IV, scene i. A forest at night. Sobinin cheers his cold and discouraged followers. (An alternative version of this scene composed by Glinka is set in the forest near the monastery. Vanya enters on foot, his horse having died from exhaustion, and manages to persuade the servants at the monastery of the danger to the Tsar.)

Scene ii. Another part of the forest. The Polish troops are bivouacking for the night, grumbling at Susanin for losing the way. Susanin resolves to give his life for the Tsar. When the soldiers wake at daybreak, Susanin tells them that he has deliberately led them into the remotest part of the forest so that the Tsar is now safely beyond their reach. They kill him.

Epilogue, scene i. A street in Moscow. A gaily dressed crowd is singing the Tsar's praises. They are joined by Antonida, Sobinin and Vanya. Susanin is mourned as a hero by everyone.

Scene ii. A square in front of the Kremlin. The Tsar's procession enters the capital.

The superb choral scenes in this work are truly Russian in character and represent the highest achievements of Glinka's score. The virile unison chorus of the boatmen in the first act is as impressive as the enchanting bridal chorus in $5/4$ time in the

third, while the final chorus in the coronation scene is tellingly
effective. The hero, old Susanin, is clearly and distinctively
characterized in very typically Russian music, and the orphan
Vanya is also very well portrayed in his rather sentimental songs.
The lovers are slightly pallid by comparison and musically
betray strong Italian influence. The second act contains brilliant
music based on national Polish tunes, including an elegant,
lilting mazurka of exceptional vivacity.

The success of this opera was extraordinary. As a Frenchman
remarked, 'This is more than an opera, it is a national epic'. It
was in fact an event of national importance, for with it the
history of Russian music really started. Naturally many people
considered the introduction of folk music into opera on such
a scale degrading to this form of art, but Glinka would not let
himself be dissuaded from his original aim, and in his second
opera, *Russlan and Ludmilla* (1842), the national Russian atmosphere is even stronger. Whereas *A Life for the Tsar* displayed
the more sentimental side of Russian folk music, *Russlan and
Ludmilla* introduced its powerful and sparkling dance-tunes
and rhythms but, in spite of splendid musical passages, it had
only a limited success.

Alexander Dargomizhsky (1813–69), whose opera *Russalka*
(1856) became very popular in Russia, can be considered a
direct successor to Glinka. Dargomizhsky also tried to contribute to a national Russian style, but he made many concessions
to contemporary taste, and did not possess sufficient talent to
continue Glinka's work effectively. Glinka's mantle really fell
on the group of five composers who went down to musical
history as 'The Five' or 'The mighty handful': Balakirev, César
Cui, Borodin, Mussorgsky and Rimsky-Korsakov, the founders
of the 'New Russian School'.

'The Five' set themselves to follow and develop the national
line traced by Glinka in Russian music and to purge it deliberately of any Western European influence. The 'Innovators', as
the five were usually called, also laid down their own rules for
opera, which was to shake off the foreign yoke of Italian
operatic formulae and adhere strictly to each dramatic situation
and the requirements of the text. These ideas might appear to be
influenced by Wagner's philosophy, but in fact there is no
doubt that they originated quite independently of him. In the

1860's Wagner was virtually unknown in Russia and his writings had been read by no one apart from his Russian apostle Serov, who had no influence on the Innovators. All five composers were at one time concerned with plans for operas and stimulated and encouraged one another. For Mussorgsky, however, who was without doubt the most talented of his circle, opera became the focal point of his creative activity.

Modest Mussorgsky (1839–81) is one of the most original figures in the whole history of music. He began his career as a guards officer but resigned his commission at the age of twenty-three in order to devote himself entirely to musical composition. Without taking up any organized course of studies, he wrote several works of varied scope, and his genius led him to explore musical possibilities which he would perhaps never have tried out if he had once submitted to the discipline of theoretical study. His first operas are mere experiments: *Salambô*, after Flaubert's novel, and *The Marriage*, a musical setting of the first act of Gogol's prose comedy of the same name. After these preliminary studies, Mussorgsky revealed his full musical talent in his main work, *Boris Godunov*. The flood-gates of his genius opened and out poured a uniquely powerful dramatic work.

BORIS GODUNOV. Musical drama in a prologue and four acts by Modest Mussorgsky. Text by the composer after Alexander Sergheievich Pushkin and Nikolai Mikhailovich Karamzin. First complete performance: St Petersburg, 1874.

Characters: Tsar Boris Godunov—bass-baritone; Feodor and Xenia, his children—mezzo-soprano and soprano; Xenia's nurse—contralto; Prince Shuisky—tenor; Pimen, a monk—bass; Andrei Shchelkalov, clerk of the Duma—baritone; the Pretender Dmitri, known as the monk Grigory—tenor; Marina Mnishek, a Polish princess, daughter of the Voivode of Sandomir—mezzo-soprano; Rangoni, a Jesuit—bass; Varlaam and Missail, vagabond monks—bass and tenor; the hostess of the inn—mezzo-soprano; the Simpleton—tenor; Nikitich, a constable—bass; two Jesuits—basses. People of Moscow, peasants, soldiers, guards, boyars, pilgrims, priests, Polish courtiers.

Place: Russia and Poland. *Time:* 1598–1605.

Prologue. Scene i. The courtyard of Novodevichy Monastery near Moscow. A crowd of people is gathered there, and commanded to persuade Boris by their prayers and pleas to accept the Tsar's crown. The peasants have no idea of what is happening, but they kneel and wail as they are ordered. As soon as the police officer's back is turned they stand up and chatter together. Tchelkalov enters and explains that Boris

Godunov is firm in his determination not to accept the crown. Some pilgrims pass through the crowd, distributing alms and relics on their way to the monastery, and they are greeted by the people with great demonstrations of reverence.

Scene ii. The courtyard of the Kremlin in Moscow, with the doorways of the two great cathedrals. Boris has finally given way to the pleas of the people, and a great crowd is assembled in the Kremlin for his coronation. The bells ring out festively, and the people sing the hymn of the Tsar again and again. Boris's short, meditative address rises gauntly above this jubilation, as he implores God's blessing on his reign and the people sense a feeling of impending doom. He ends by inviting everyone to eat as his guests on this day of celebration. The coronation procession goes into the cathedral amidst the cheers of the people.

Act I, scene i. A cell in the monastery of Chudov, five years later. Since Boris's coronation famine and plague have overtaken Russia, and for all this Boris, who has tried to rule wisely and well, is blamed. It is night and the old monk Pimen is working at his chronicle of the history of Russia, while the sound of chanting is heard in the distance. Grigory, who shares the cell with the old Pimen, suddenly awakens; he has just dreamed for the third time that he stood on a high tower looking down on the city of Moscow, derided by a crowd of people below him, and fell from the tower. Each time he awoke at that moment. He cannot bear monastic life and is attracted by the outside world. Pimen tries to persuade him to resign himself to the contemplative life, and tells him both of his own wild youth and of the many prominent figures in Russian history who ended their lives in prayer and meditation. Grigory asks about the Tsarevich Dmitri, who was murdered, and in wrathful tones Pimen tells him that Boris had the child killed, and that he would now be the same age as Grigory—nearly twenty. Grigory asks Pimen to bless him, while the chanting of the monks can be heard again. Pimen goes to matins, and Grigory is left alone; he is filled with excitement and swears to take revenge on Boris.

Scene ii. An inn on the Lithuanian frontier of Russia. Grigory has fled from the monastery and on his way has joined the two vagabond monks Varlaam and Missail, with whom he has reached the Lithuanian border. The monks order wine and begin to drink. Varlaam sings a rousing song about Ivan the Terrible's army at the siege of Kazan. Meanwhile Grigory asks the hostess the best way to the frontier. She tells him that the guards are out looking for a fugitive monk, but shows him a way to elude them. Varlaam is by now very drunk, but revives when the guards enter. They have received orders from Moscow to arrest a certain fugitive monk, Grigory Otrepiev. They suspect Varlaam, and question him closely, but they cannot read the description of the wanted man, and Grigory, when appealed to, pretends to read out a description of Varlaam. This is too much for the latter, who tears the paper from Grigory's hands and, spelling out the words with difficulty, plainly shows that it refers to Grigory, who jumps out of the window and flees.

Act II. The Tsar's apartments in the Kremlin. The Tsarevich Feodor is reading, while his sister, Xenia, is crying over the portrait of the dead

prince whom she was to have married. The nurse and the Tsarevich try
to comfort her by singing. Boris enters; he tries affectionately to console
his daughter and talks encouragingly to his son, who proudly shows him
the extent of the Russian empire on a globe of the world. Boris falls into
a reverie; it is true that he has absolute power, but happiness evades him,
and the people blame him for all their misfortunes. The thought of the
murdered Tsarevich, Dmitri, haunts Boris's tormented conscience.
Prince Shuisky is announced; he is an important boyar whom Boris
rightly does not trust. The prince does not deny Boris's accusations of
intrigue, then tells him that a claimant to the throne of Russia has appeared
in Poland; his name is Dmitri. The Tsar is deeply impressed, and tells
Shuisky to find out whether the body of the Tsarevich was identified
beyond doubt at the time of the murder. Shuisky goes into all the horrible
details, so as to torment the distraught Tsar. Boris controls himself
sufficiently to dismiss the prince calmly, but then he collapses into a chair,
feeling suffocated with remorse and panic. A chiming clock with moving
figures starts up, and in his hysteria Boris takes this as an apparition of the
murdered child. He falls to his knees and implores God to have mercy on
him.

Act III, scene i. The apartments of Marina Mnishek at Sandomir.
Marina is being dressed by her maids, who sing flattering songs praising
the beauty of their mistress, but Marina would rather hear songs of heroes
than songs of love and beauty. She dreams of winning Dmitri in order
to enter Moscow as Tsarina. The Jesuit Rangoni slips into her room; he
supports her ambitious plans, and tells her it is her duty to become
Tsarina so as to convert Russia to the true faith. He threateningly explains
to her that she must sacrifice everything, even her honour, to attain this
end.

Scene ii. The castle gardens. The false Dmitri is waiting for Marina,
whom he loves passionately. Rangoni assures him that Marina also loves
him. He asks to be allowed to follow Dmitri to Moscow, to support him
with his advice. Dmitri has to hide, since Mnishek's guests, and with them
Marina, are coming out of the house. They dance a polonaise, pay court
to Marina, and plan their campaign against Russia. (They are supporting
the cause of the Pretender as a pretext to make war on the Muscovite
Empire.) Soon Marina returns, and with stinging insults rouses the irresolute and hesitant Dmitri to commit himself to lead an army on Moscow.
Having once gained her purpose she can afford to respond to his protestations of love.

Act IV, scene i. The square in front of the Cathedral of St Basil the
Blessed, Moscow. Peasants are gathered before the Cathedral discussing
the claims of the Pretender. A group of urchins chase a Simpleton on to
the scene. They torment him, and steal his new kopek (coin). Boris and
his retinue emerge from the Cathedral, and the women and children beg
for alms. The Simpleton asks Boris to kill the urchins in the same way
as he once killed the infant Dmitri. When Shuisky gives order for the
Simpleton to be arrested, Boris bids him leave the man in peace, and asks
the Simpleton to pray for him. 'How can one pray for a Tsar Herod?'
asks the Simpleton; and left alone sings sadly of the fate of Russia.

Scene ii. The Granovitaya Palace in the Kremlin. The Duma (Council of the boyars) has met to discuss the threat to Moscow from the pretender and his advancing Polish army. Shuisky enters and relates how he has seen the Tsar talking deliriously as though to a spectre, which he was trying to drive away. Boris enters and the boyars are horrified to see that Shuisky was telling the truth and that the Tsar is out of his mind. Boris pulls himself together and Shuisky asks him to receive a holy monk. It is Pimen, who has come to tell of a miracle: a blind shepherd has regained his sight while praying at the tomb of the murdered Tsarevich. This is too much for Boris, who falls unconscious. When he recovers, and realizes he is dying, he asks for his son and for the 'skhima' or penitential robe in which a dying Tsar was by tradition received into the church as a monk. When, with deep emotion, he takes leave of his son, commending the Russian people and his sister Xenia to his care, he rises again to his full grandeur. He is terrified when he hears the passing bell tolling outside and monks chanting their prayers for the repose of his soul. The boyars enter in solemn procession and Boris, pointing to his son, cries 'Here is your Tsar' and falls dead to the ground.

Scene iii. A clearing in the forest of Kromy, near Moscow. As a result of Dmitri's invasion the country is in chaos. The mob which fills the stage drags in a supporter of Boris, binds him to a tree and torments him. Children tease a Simpleton, and steal his few pence. The vagabond monks Varlaam and Missail sing revolutionary songs and stir up popular feeling in support of 'Dmitri, the lawful Tsar', but when two Jesuits enter, singing the praises of the new Tsar Dmitri in Latin, they are attacked by the crowd and dragged off to be hanged. Dmitri rides in with his retinue and troops, releases the boyar and the Jesuits, and calls on everyone to follow him. The people enthusiastically acclaim him and join him and his supporters on the road to Moscow. The tocsin sounds, trumpets are heard and the glow of burning buildings is seen. The Simpleton is left alone, singing to himself 'Woe and sorrow always, lament, Russian folk, poor hungry folk'. As the curtain falls the music ends abruptly.

The originality of the music of *Boris Godunov* reveals itself in the very first notes of the score. The two scenes of the prologue depend almost exclusively on the chorus, and the short, related themes make a strong impression by their frequent repetition. This popular music, based on church idiom, is the essential foundation of the score and runs right through the work. The musical splendour of the coronation scene defies description. The continuous repetition of one musical idea, which is indicated in the first scene of the prologue, here becomes a ruling principle, so that the magnificent theme on the bells rises to an overwhelming clamour in the gradual *crescendo* of its rhythmical variations. The construction of this bell-theme can be regarded

as a prototype for all the splendid orgies of *ostinato* in modern
music, from Stravinsky and the impressionists to Orff. In contrast to the bell-theme and its orchestral *tutti* comes the simple,
solemn hymn to the Tsar, which mingles with it at the close of
the scene.

The first act, which deals mainly with the events concerning
Grigory, introduces the theme which serves both for him and

also for the murdered Dmitri, while placid *legato* music for the
strings accompanies Pimen's lines. The scene in the inn gives a
colourful description of peasant life; folk songs and folk
rhythms create the atmosphere of this scene, from the hostess's
delightful song of the drake and the whining, antiphonal chant
of the monks, to Varlaam's grandiose Tartar ballad which,
though it only consists of a very short musical statement and
much repetition, is made really breathtaking by the savagery
built up in the relentless accompaniment. Against this impressive background are set the dramatic events concerning
Grigory, whose theme is heard repeatedly in the orchestra.
Boris's great aria is the main feature of the second act, and is

dominated by an expressive theme, which stresses the grandeur

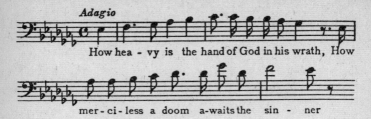

of the Tsar, in spite of all his spiritual turmoil. The powerful
beginnings dissolve, however, in a falling chromatic figure. The
final scene takes up the mood in which this aria ends. The
chimes of a great clock run through the music like the beat of
an anguished heart, to the weaving of a chromatic figure in the
strings, the strident clash of the woodwind and muted, threatening *tremolo* in the basses. The same orchestral colours return in
the scene of Boris's death, but more in the spirit of conciliation,
and not so implacably hard.

Obviously the Polish act has no part in Russian musical folk-
drama; the world described in it is quite different—a world of
glitter and vanity, and Western pseudo-culture, hostile to the
holy land of Russia—which Mussorgsky deliberately treated
with a smooth surface sometimes reminiscent of certain Italian
music. The cold, ambitious Marina has no *leitmotiv* of her own,
but instead a mazurka-rhythm accompanies her music. The
entrance of the Polish nobles is marked by a brilliant polonaise.
Musically the most powerfully defined figure is the Jesuit
Rangoni (an invention of the composer's). The only musical
feature which links this act with the others is the Grigory theme
from the first act which in varied forms accompanies the
entrance of the usurper.

Boris Godunov is generally performed today in the revised
version by Rimsky-Korsakov, a friend of Mussorgsky's and
executor of his estate, who thought that he could improve on
the latter's work by drastic revision, and certainly his orchestral
additions to what was technically a somewhat bald score contributed to its success. In any case it was this revised version which
was so enormously successful in all the important theatres

throughout the world. Recently, however, there have been highly successful productions in the original version which makes a stronger impression as a brilliant folk-drama, just because of its harshness. The most revolutionary change made by Rimsky-Korsakov was to transpose the order of the last two scenes; today this is generally considered a mistake, as the opera should end as it began with a scene concerning the people if it is to preserve its character as a popular drama with the Russian people as protagonist. However powerful Boris's death-scene may be, immeasurably more shattering and disturbing is the seemingly prophetic finale, with the Simpleton's song trailing away into nothingness. (This final scene was composed by Mussorgsky when he revised the score between April 1871 and June 1872, and it originally replaced the scene outside the Cathedral of St Basil. The Polish act also dates from this revision.)

With the exception of his early work, *Salambô*, *Boris Godunov* is the only opera Mussorgsky completed himself. Only sketches in notebooks for *The Marriage*, *Khovanshchina*, and *The Fair at Sorochinsk* were found at his death. *Khovanshchina* and *The Fair at Sorochinsk* are often performed outside Russia. *Khovanshchina* was completed and orchestrated by Rimsky-Korsakov.

KHOVANSHCHINA (The Khovansky Plot). Opera in five acts by Modest Mussorgsky. Text by the composer and V. V. Stassov. First performance: St Petersburg, 1886.

Characters: Prince Ivan Khovansky, leader of the Streltsy (Archers)—bass; Prince Andrey Khovansky, his son—tenor; Prince Vassily Golitsyn—tenor; the Boyar Shaklovity—baritone; Dosifey, leader of the Old Believers—bass; Princess Marfa, a young widow, an Old Believer—mezzo-soprano; the Scrivener, a public letter-writer—tenor; Emma, a young girl—soprano; Varsonofiev, an attendant upon Galitzin—baritone; Kuzka, a Streltsy—baritone; three Streltsy—one tenor, two basses; Streshniev—tenor; Susanna, an Old Believer—soprano. Streltsy, Old Believers, serving-girls and Persian slaves in the suite of Prince Ivan Khovansky, bodyguards of Peter the Great, populace.

Place: In and near Moscow; on Prince Khovansky's estate. *Time:* 1682–89.

The opera is set in Russia at the time of the accession of Peter the Great in 1682. His father, Tsar Alexei, had died in 1676, leaving the throne to his eldest son, Feodor, Peter's half-brother, who, dying in 1682, named Peter (then only ten years old) as his successor, to the exclusion of his own brother Ivan who was weak-minded. This step provoked an insurrection of the 'Streltsy' or armed militia, which was fomented by Ivan's sister, the grand-duchess Sophie, who in July 1682 secured the coronation of Ivan and Peter as joint rulers, with herself as Regent.

Prince Khovansky and his followers are engaged in political strife with Prince Golitsyn's party who support the Regent. The Old Believers, led by Dosifey, are the party who had refused to accept the reforms imposed as far back as the 1650's. In the end the new regime of Peter the Great was victorious over both the 'Streltsy' and the Old Believers.

Act I. The Red Square in Moscow. Kuzka and two other guards are discussing the situation in the usual way soldiers do. The Boyar Shaklovity appears and dictates a letter to the public letter-writer; it is a message to the Tsar informing him that Prince Ivan Khovansky is plotting against the throne and hoping to form a government from the ranks of the Old Believers, with his son Andrey as ruler of Russia. Groups of people pour into the square and begin to sing. They see an inscription posted up on the side of the pier, and ask the Scrivener to read it to them. At first he refuses, but then the crowd force him to read it. He tells them that the guards have killed and punished many notable people. Everyone seems alarmed and anxious. The crowd now prepares to greet Prince Ivan Khovansky and his son; they hail the former as the 'White Swan'. Khovansky tells the crowd that Russia and Moscow are in grave distress; he accuses the boyars of making trouble and invites the people and the guards to join him in the struggle for liberation. Emma, a young girl from the German quarter of Moscow, enters with Andrey, who is forcing his unwelcome attentions on her. The Princess Marfa, one of the Old Believers, with whom Andrey was formerly in love, intervenes; her taunts raise Andrey's wrath and he attacks her. Prince Ivan Khovansky returns to the square. He too is attracted by Emma, and orders the guards to bring her to him. Andrey defies his father and telling him that he can have Emma dead, he attempts to stab her. Dosifey, the leader of the Old Believers, entrusts Emma to the care of Martha and, kneeling down, prays for strength in the coming struggle. Prince Ivan Khovansky appoints his son colonel and orders his men to march against the Kremlin. Dosifey and his followers pray to be delivered from the 'temptations of antichrist'.

Act II. Prince Vassily Golitsyn's summer house in Moscow. Prince Golitsyn, a former sympathizer with Khovansky's movement, is reading a letter from the Regent Sophia. She is in love with him and longing to see him again; he wonders whether he can trust her. The Princess Marfa is announced. Galitzin has been consulting her as a fortune-teller. She forecasts the Prince's banishment and exile. At this, Golitsyn loses his temper and tells his servant Varsonofiev to drown her in the marshes. Left alone, Golitsyn muses on the present state of the country—he remembers how he defended the Poles and raised the prestige of Russia. Prince Ivan Khovansky enters unannounced, and reproaches Golitsyn for having betrayed the movement. Dosifey now arrives and tries to mediate between the two princes. Finally Shaklovity, as the Tsar's emissary, enters and announces that the Regent has ordered a proclamation to be posted in Ismailov stating that the Khovanskys are conspiring to overthrow the Empire. 'And what does Tsar Peter say?' asks Dosifey. 'He calls it the Khovansky plot (Khovanshchina) and orders their arrest,' replies Khovansky.

Act III. Army encampment near the Bielgorod quarter of Moscow. A group of Old Believers passes through the quarter singing of their 'victory' over the heretics. Marfa is left alone and sings of her rejected love. Dosifey suggests to her that she forget her quarrels with Andrey and concentrate her energies in helping her country. Shaklovity now enters and, anxious for Russia's destiny, prays for his country's prosperity. A group of drunken soldiers and their womenfolk arrive. Kuzka teases and mocks the assembled women. The Scrivener is heard crying for mercy, and enters screaming in terror. He tells the crowd that the Tsar's guards have burned down his house and killed women, children and relatives of the soldiers themselves. The crowd call on Prince Ivan Khovansky for help, but he tells them not to fight against Tsar Peter but to return to their homes. The people beg God to show them mercy.

Act IV, scene i. The banqueting hall of Prince Ivan Khovansky's house. The Prince is being entertained by his serving girls. Varsonofiev enters with a message from Golitsyn warning him to be careful as his life is in danger. The Prince tells him he is talking nonsense, and threatens to have him thrashed. He bids the girls send in his Persian slaves to dance for him. Shaklovity comes with a message from the Regent, convening a Grand Council. Prince Ivan bids his maids bring him his finest robes and jewelled cane. As he makes his way to the door he is stabbed by an assassin hired by Shaklovity. The latter looks at Ivan Khovansky's body and mockingly says, 'Glory to the White Swan'.

Scene ii. The square before the Church of St Basil, Moscow. The Tsar's guards conduct Prince Golitsyn into exile. Dosifey, who is looking on, is joined by Marfa; she tells him that the Tsar's army is approaching the forest where the Old Believers are hiding. Dosifey tells her to find Prince Andrey and bring him to the forest where he may find a martyr's death by fire. Prince Andrey enters, looking for Emma. He abuses Marfa, but she remains calm and tells him of his father's death and Prince Golitsyn's exile. She bids him accompany her as she will save him. The Prince's men are led in, on their way to execution; they are followed by their weeping wives begging for mercy. The Tsar's messenger arrives with the news that Tsar Peter has granted them pardon.

Act V. The Hermitage of the Old Believers in a pine wood near Moscow. With Dosifey at their head, the Old Believers have fled from the Tsar's guards. They have been joined by Prince Andrey and Marfa. Dositheus leads them all in a last prayer. In religious ecstasy they prepare for death—Andrey and Marfa's former love is reborn. Dosifey, Marfa and Andrey lead the Old Believers joyfully to their death by fire. Groups of people enter and, moved by what they see, pray for the salvation and prosperity of Russia.

The Fair at Sorochinsk has been skilfully revised and completed by Nikolai Tcherepnin (b. 1873) a pupil of Rimsky-Korsakov.

THE FAIR AT SOROCHINSK. Comic opera in three acts by Modest
Mussorgsky. Completed with instrumentation by Nikolai Tcherepnin.
Text after Gogol's story by the composer. First performance: St Peters-
burg, 1911. Revised version: Monte Carlo, 1923.

Characters: Tcherevik, an old peasant—bass; Gritzko, a young peasant
—tenor; Afanassi Ivanovich, the priest's son—tenor; a neighbour—bass-
baritone; the gipsy—bass; Parassia, Tcherevik's daughter—soprano;
Khivria, Tcherevik's wife—mezzo-soprano. Young men and women,
gipsies, merchants, Cossacks, Jews, etc.

Place: Sorochinsk, in the Ukraine. *Time:* nineteenth century.

Act I. A market scene. It is a hot summer's day and there is bustling
confusion everywhere. The peasant Tcherevik has come to the fair with
his wife and daughter. They have had an accident: on their arrival in
the village in their cart they become involved in a dispute with some
young people whom Khivria had annoyed with her scolding tongue.
To stop her talking, one of the young men had shut her mouth with a
well-directed handful of mud. This same young man, Gritzko, is in love
with the ravishing Parassia, who reciprocates his feelings. Tcherevik is
ready to consent to their engagement, especially since Gritzko proves
an extraordinarily good drinker, but Khivria is understandably prejudiced
against him. A gipsy tells the superstitious peasants that the devil often
visits the fair-ground at Sorochinsk in the shape of a pig, looking for the
red sleeve ribbons of a jacket he had once pawned. This gipsy now offers
to help Gritzko win round Parassia's parents in return for reducing the
price of some oxen he has for sale; Gritzko gladly agrees. Tcherevik and a
neighbour get very drunk at the fair. The neighbour starts a melancholy
song 'Over the steppe', but soon afterwards they sing a merry round, and
the act closes with a duet for Parassia and Gritzko.

Act II. A room in Tcherevik's house. Tcherevik is sleeping off his
drunkenness, while Khivria is cooking a meal. She is expecting her lover,
the priest's son, who cannot resist the delicacies she prepares for him. It
is only with great difficulty that Khivria gets rid of her husband, and soon
after the priest's son arrives, his pious words at variance with his obvious
intentions. As he is kissing her, they hear a noise outside, and Khivria
quickly hides him in a box over a hen-roost. Tcherevik, his neighbour and
some friends are coming back to the house, where they continue drinking
and singing, including the merry round 'Dumdu'. The neighbour is
relating the full legend of the devil and the red sleeve when suddenly the
window opens, and a pig's head appears. Horror and chaos ensue: the
priest's son, enveloped in one of Khivria's dresses, falls down from his
box; at first they all think he is the devil, until the gipsy, who has come
in with Gritzko and the young people of the village, unmasks him, to
Khivria's deep shame. Everyone starts the merry round again.

Act III. The village square. Tcherevik now has the upper hand and
nothing can stop him from giving Parassia's hand to Gritzko. Parassia
sings a charming *hopak*. Tcherevik enters, and the two young people
celebrate their future happiness in a delightful duet, 'Had the Tsar asked
me'. The villagers come to give their good wishes to the couple, and
a wild, fiery *hopak*, the Little Russian national dance, closes the opera.

The charm of Mussorgsky's music for *The Fair at Sorochinsk* rests on the tunes and rhythms of the Little Russian dance-song, and the rough, merry peasant scenes with the frequent return of the boisterous 'round' are most delightful and original.

Even the love-scenes are flavoured by folk songs, and possess a particularly delicate fervour, quite appropriate to the rich melodies of the lyrical songs of Little Russia.

My heart,—my poor—heart, what—makes you cry?

None of the works of the other 'Innovators' has had comparable success outside Russia. Every now and again an attempt is made to revive one or other of Rimsky-Korsakov's (1844–1908) many operas, but they remain mere attempts. In spite of being very colourful and melodious, they lack any great dramatic impetus. In Russia however, *Sadko*, with its famous Hindu song, *The Golden Cockerel*, with the well-known 'Hymn to the Sun', and the comic opera *The Snow Maiden* are often performed. *The Golden Cockerel* and *The Snow Maiden* have enjoyed considerable popularity in England and America. In his later works the composer was very much influenced by Wagner as exemplified in his *The Legend of the Invisible City of Kitesh*.

THE GOLDEN COCKEREL. Opera in three acts by Nikolai Andreievich Rimsky-Korsakov. Text by V. Bielsky after Alexander Sergheievich Pushkin. First performance: Moscow, 1909.

Characters: The Astrologer—high tenor; King Dodon—bass; Prince Guidon and Prince Afron, his sons—tenor and baritone; General Polkan —bass; Amelfa, the Royal housekeeper—contralto; the Queen of Shemakhan—soprano; the Golden Cockerel—soprano. Courtiers, attendants, soldiers, townspeople.

Place: In and near King Dodon's palace on the Steppes of Southern Russia and on a nearby mountain pass. *Time:* legendary.

Prologue. The Astrologer warns the audience to heed the moral of the story.

Act I. The council-chamber and courtyard of the palace. The country is in danger of attack and the King's sons suggest unorthodox ways of improving the defences. Not surprisingly, they meet with criticism from General Polkan, but the King supports his sons against the General. The Astrologer appears, and to help the King foretell the future offers him a Golden Cockerel, which by its crowing will predict either peace or disaster. The King is delighted, but dismisses the dissatisfied Astrologer with vague remarks about future payment. The King then settles to sleep and dreams of a lovely maiden. Twice the cockerel gives warning of danger and twice Polkan has to wake the King. The first time he sends his sons to war and imposes new taxes, the second time he heaves himself into his rusty armour to go to war himself, amid the cheers of his subjects.

Act II. A narrow mountain pass. It is night, and in the moonlight King Dodon finds the bodies, not only of many of his soldiers, but of his two sons, who have killed each other while carrying out the plan of campaign ordered by the King. The latter's mourning is quickly changed to alarm when dawn breaks and the mists disperse to reveal a silken tent which everyone at first assumes to belong to the enemy general. However when a ponderous piece of artillery has been mounted and fired at it, a beautiful young maiden steps out and sings the praises of the sun. The soldiers flee in terror, and the maiden then introduces herself as the Queen of Shemakhan, come to conquer Dodon by her beauty rather than by force of arms. The King is nervous of her at first, but once the bluff Polkan has been dismissed, at her request, she sets out to seduce Dodon, and after laughing at his grotesque attempts to sing and dance for her accepts his homage and the offer of his hand and throne. All depart in procession for Dodon's kingdom.

Act III. Outside King Dodon's palace. A crowd has assembled, speculating on the outcome of the war. Rumours of Dodon's young bride have already reached the capital. The procession finally enters but celebrations are interrupted by the Astrologer claiming no less a reward from the King than the Queen herself. After an angry altercation, King Dodon kills the old man with a blow from his sceptre. At once an ominous storm blows up, but the Queen takes all these events lightly. Suddenly the cockerel utters a piercing cry and pecks the King on the head. Instantly he falls down, dead, and when the darkened sky has cleared, Queen and cockerel have both disappeared.

In a brief Epilogue the Astrologer explains to the audience that it was just a fairy-tale, and that of all the characters in the story only he and the Queen were mortal.

The Golden Cockerel was Rimsky-Korsakov's fourteenth and last opera. The censor refused to sanction its performance during the composer's lifetime, as the resemblance between Dodon's court and that of Tsar Nicholas II, and the implied criticism of the inefficient conduct of the Russo-Japanese War were thought to be dangerous to the regime. The composer left elaborate instructions as to how the various roles in the opera should be acted, particularly Dodon and the Queen of Shemakhan, both of whom had complicated and strenuous dances to perform. When, however, the opera was performed in Petrograd it was thought too exhausting for the singers to dance as well, and so Fokine devised the idea of having them seated at the side of the stage in boxes. Rimsky-Korsakov's widow protested against this, but to no effect. It was in this version that the opera was first given in Paris and London by the Diaghilev Company.

Prince Igor, the only opera by Alexander Borodin (1833–87), is a powerful, and at times dramatic piece; like *Boris Godunov* and *Khovanshchina* it owes some of its international popularity to the revisions made by Rimsky-Korsakov.

PRINCE IGOR. Opera in a prologue and four acts by Alexander Borodin. Text after V. V. Stassov by the composer. First performance: St Petersburg, 1890.

Characters: Igor Sviatoslavich, Prince of Seversk—baritone; Yaroslavna, his second wife—soprano; Vladimir Igorevich, his son by his first marriage—tenor; Vladimir Jaroslavich, Prince Galitzky, brother of Princess Jaroslavna—bass; Konchak and Gzak, Polovtsian Khans—basses; Konchakovna, Konchak's daughter—mezzo-soprano; Ovlur, a baptized Polovtsian—tenor; Skula and Yeroshka, *gudok* players—bass and tenor; Yaroslavna's nurse—soprano; a young Polovtsian maiden—soprano. Russian aristocrats, boyars and their wives, old men, Russian warriors, young women, people, Polovtsian chiefs and soldiers, Konchakovna's women, slaves, Russian prisoners.

Place: The town of Putivl and the Polovtsian camp. *Time:* 1185.

Prologue. The market-place of Putivl. In spite of an eclipse of the sun, which the people regard as an evil omen, Prince Igor and his son Vladimir are going to war against the Polovtsians, who have invaded their country. Prince Igor leaves his country and his young wife in the care of her brother, Prince Galitzky.

Act I, scene i. The courtyard of Prince Galitzky's house. The Prince is betraying the confidence placed in him by leading an unruly life, drinking, oppressing the peasants and dishonouring their women. He is however spirited as well as irresponsible. The drunken *gudok* players, deserters from Igor's army, try to stir up the people in favour of Galitzky.

Scene ii. Jaroslavna's room, where in response to appeals from a party of girls rejected by Galitzky, the Princess compels her brother to give up a girl abducted by his henchmen. Terrible news arrives: the Russian army has been beaten and Prince Igor and his son have been taken prisoner.

Act II. The Polovtsian camp. It is evening. Young Polovtsian maidens sing and dance for their mistress, Konchakovna, who herself sings a

languorous nocturne. Prince Igor is treated with great consideration by
the Khan Konchak, but he still longs for freedom. Ovlur offers to give
Igor horses with which to flee, but Igor's honour prevents him accepting
the traitor's suggestion. His son Vladimir loves the beautiful Konchakovna, who passionately returns his love. Konchak is prepared to free Igor
if he promises never to go to war against the Polovtsians again, but Igor
cannot make this promise, and Konchak shows his appreciation of this
patriotic attitude. The act closes with a great banquet, during which
slaves and warriors perform the well-known Polovtsian dances.

Act III. The Polovtsians have won another victory over the Russians
and Putivl is to be completely destroyed. Igor can hesitate no longer,
and decides to accept Ovlur's proposal and flee the same night. The
circumstances are favourable, since after the celebration of the victory all
the Polovtsians get drunk. Konchakovna has learned about the plan and
implores Vladimir to take her with him, but when he refuses to do so
she raises the alarm. Igor escapes, but Vladimir is left behind. Again
Konchak treats Igor's flight with magnanimity and does not pursue him.
He then marries his daughter to Vladimir.

Act IV. Jaroslavna mourns for the destroyed city of Putivl. Two riders
are seen approaching; they are Igor and Ovlur. Husband and wife fall
into each other's arms and, summoned by the drunken *gudok* players, the
people run in to greet their prince.

Prince Igor is primarily a chorus opera. In their different styles
both the Russian and Polovtsian choruses are as powerfully
effective as the fascinating dances which enliven and characterize the first act. It was the Polovtsian dances which first attracted
interest in Borodin's work, since the Diaghilev Russian ballet,
successfully touring Western Europe at the beginning of the
century, made these dances one of the principal attractions in
their programmes. The music of the two Polovtsian acts is
markedly oriental in flavour, with fluent chromatics, three
semitone intervals and glittering harmonies contrasting with
the sacred, stately music of the Russian acts. The libretto,
written by Borodin himself, unfortunately offers little opportunity for dramatic development, but the composer did intro-

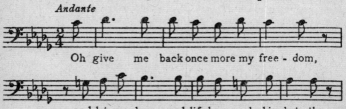

Andante

Oh give   me   back once more my free - dom,

and let my shame and life be quenched in bat - tle

duce a very strong dramatic impulse into his music. Igor's great aria, for instance, is very moving and impressive, with the three-fold return of the principal theme in mounting intensity, as is also the passionate third-act trio between Konchakovna, Vladimir and Igor. Unfortunately such effective dramatic outbursts are only isolated moments, and the final act, containing virtually no action, is something of an anticlimax.

Pyotr Ilich Tchaikovsky (1840–93), internationally recognized as a leading Russian composer, held aloof from the aspirations of the New Russian School, for which he had little sympathy. Mussorgsky's realism was positively distasteful to one whose aim was to create absolute beauty in his art, although he had to acknowledge Mussorgsky's genius. Tchaikovsky willingly absorbed all the influences of West European music, and succeeded in fusing them with his own fundamentally Russian musical heritage. The idiom of his music is the outcome both of the romantic era and of the truly Russian spirit and was immediately understood and admired all over the world.

Tchaikovsky's international fame is based on his symphonic works, while his operas are relatively little known. The most important of them, *Eugene Onegin* and *The Queen of Spades*, only gradually established themselves outside Russia, but the fact that these two works are being more and more often performed demonstrates a growing interest in Tchaikovsky's operas, despite unjust but widespread prejudice against them on the grounds that they lack dramatic force. In fact his music is full of an inner dramatic impulse which is only experienced by the hearer when he becomes deeply involved in the characters and their destinies. The protagonists of Tchaikovsky's two principal operas are very familiar to any Russian audience, since they are taken from the popular works of Pushkin, on which all Russians are brought up, and Tchaikovsky's music immediately arouses a strong response in any Russian heart.

EUGENE ONEGIN. Lyrical scenes in three acts by Pyotr Ilich Tchaikovsky. Text by the composer and K. S. Shilovsky after Alexander Sergeievich Pushkin. First performance: Moscow, 1879.

Characters: Madame Larina, a land-owner—mezzo-soprano; Olga and Tatiana, her daughters—mezzo-soprano and soprano; Filipevna, Tatiana's nurse—mezzo-soprano; Lensky, Olga's fiancé—tenor; Eugene Onegin, his friend—baritone; Prince Gremin, an old general—bass;

Zaretzki—bass; Monsieur Triquet, a French tutor—tenor; a Captain—
bass. Friends and neighbours of Madame Larina's, society ladies and
gentlemen of St Petersburg.

Place: On Madame Larina's country estate and in St Petersburg.
Time: early nineteenth century.

Act I, scene i. The garden of Madame Larina's house. Madame
Larina, who is sitting making jam with the nurse Filipevna, recalls her
romantic youth and its gradual disappearance in country affairs and
married life. Inside the house Olga and Tatiana are practising a duet. The
longings of youth and the renunciation of old age set in the calm of
separation from the world, create the atmosphere for this drama of four
young people. Some reapers enter and give their mistress a harvest-
wreath, and then, when somebody starts singing a merry tune, they dance.
The gay, light-hearted Olga wants to dance too, but for Tatiana the music
evokes dreams of distant lands. She is very serious-minded, and wholly
absorbed in the fate of the lovers in a novel she is reading. A neighbouring
landowner, Lensky, a young dreamer and poet who is engaged to Olga,
arrives with his friend Onegin, who has only recently settled in the
district. Onegin's superior and affected manner makes a great impression
on Tatiana. While Lensky and Olga talk of their love, Onegin tells
Tatiana about his life, and she listens to him ecstatically. Darkness falls
and they all go into the house.

Scene ii. Tatiana's bedroom. Tatiana, inwardly restless, sits in her
nightgown in front of the mirror, while Filipevna tells her to go to bed.
Tatiana does not listen to Filipevna's account of her own youth and her
marriage, but suddenly embraces her and confesses that she is passionately
in love. She begs Filipevna to leave her alone, because she wants to write
a letter. The nurse goes out. As soon as Tatiana is alone her violent
emotions break out. She has made up her mind to write to Onegin and
declare her love. He comes from another world like the hero of her
novel. Highly excited, she writes a letter in which she opens her heart to
him and puts herself completely at his mercy. Morning breaks, and a
shepherd's song is heard in the distance. Filipevna enters to wake her,
and Tatiana gives her the letter to carry to Onegin. Tatiana is left alone;
the die is cast.

Scene iii. The garden. Girls are picking berries and singing a folk
song. Tatiana runs in and falls exhausted on a bench. Onegin is
approaching; what will he say to her? Onegin follows her in. Calmly
and politely he tells her that he was very moved by her declaration of love,
but he cannot reciprocate it as love and marriage are not for him. Tatiana
is humiliated and wounded by his coldness. He gives her his arm and
leads her back into the house.

Act II, scene i. Madame Larina's house. A ball is being given in honour
of Tatiana's birthday. While the young people are dancing, their elders
look on and exchange reminiscences. Onegin is dancing with Tatiana,
and some of the guests, who do not like her, comment on this. Onegin
wonders why he allowed Lensky to persuade him to attend this provincial
ball. To provoke his friend, he openly flirts with Olga, who laughingly
humours him, but Lensky finds his behaviour very objectionable.

Monsieur Triquet, the old French tutor, has written a song in Tatiana's honour and now sings it with charming old-world grace. When the *cotillon* starts, Lensky offers Olga his arm, but Onegin reaches her first and says that she has promised the dance to him. Olga takes Onegin's arm, and Lensky, who becomes very angry, demands satisfaction from his friend. Everyone regrets this quarrel, but it has gone too far for any hope of reconciliation.

Scene ii. A winter landscape on the banks of a river. It is early morning. While his second impatiently paces up and down, Lensky sits on a tree trunk musing. He sings of his carefree youth and of his happy love for Olga. Onegin arrives, bringing the coachman as his second. Now that Onegin and Lensky confront each other as enemies, they recognize the folly of the situation, but neither of them feels able to take the first step towards a reconciliation. Onegin shoots first and kills Lensky.

Act III, scene i. The hall of an elegant house in St Petersburg. A ball is in progress, and guests are dancing to the strains of a sparkling polonaise. Onegin, who has spent several years abroad, has now returned home, and believes he recognizes one of the ladies present as Tatiana. He is not mistaken; she is now the wife of Prince Gremin, a kinsman of Onegin's. When the latter questions the Prince about the lady he has just brought in, the old man sings a moving aria describing his love for Tatiana. He presents Onegin to her, but she receives him coldly and shortly afterwards asks to be taken home. Onegin is for a moment speechless, then, in a passionate outburst, he declares that he loves Tatiana.

Scene ii. A room in Prince Gremin's house. Tatiana is waiting for Onegin, who has written to her to ask her to receive him. She is nervous at the thought of this meeting. Onegin enters and throws himself at her feet. She reminds him how cold and heartless he was once to her, and reproaches him, suggesting that he is only courting her now because she is prominent in society. Onegin implores her passionately to give herself to him, and she is convinced of his sincerity. In a moment of weakness she confesses that she still loves him, but then tells him clearly that she respects her husband and will remain faithful to him. Tatiana, summoning all her strength, leaves the room, and Onegin, in despair, recognizes that he has lost her.

Tchaikovsky took most of his libretto for *Eugene Onegin* direct from Pushkin, and gave his opera the sub-title *Lyrical Scenes*, to indicate the rather loose connection between the various incidents. He set the accent on the inner drama of the spiritual experiences of his hero and heroine, and dwelt with particular love and care on the delineation of Tatiana's character.

The short prelude is built on Tatiana's theme, a delicate, ardent melody which vividly depicts the exaggerated feelings of the shy young girl. The first scene is introductory in character, and the music is very restrained, with Tatiana's motif in the

foreground. Everything else is simply indicated, and only in
Lensky's *arioso* is a strong emotion fleetingly displayed. The
music gains in dramatic intensity in the letter-scene, the theme
of Tatiana's passion rising grandiosely in the orchestra. In an

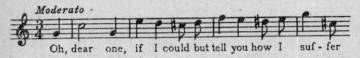

excited *allegro* passage Tatiana resolves to open her heart to

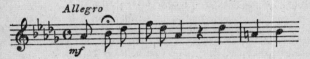

Onegin. To this emotional abandon is contrasted an intense
theme expressing Tatiana's trust and faith in Onegin. The calm

of this chorale-like theme is particularly effective after the
agitated passage that preceded it, and it is repeated with increased intensity at the close of this superbly constructed solo
scene.

The fourth scene, the ball in Madame Larina's house, is
equally successful. The action takes place exclusively within the
framework of the two dances, the swaying waltz and the fiery
mazurka, while such details as the old ladies' chatter, the gentry's
polite boredom and the flirtation between Onegin and Olga
are filled in by various subsidiary themes. A grimly threatening
mazurka theme describes the quarrel between the two former
friends. The dance stops, and the music rises sharply to the

dramatic climax of Lensky's furious challenge shouted to
Onegin, only to pass at once to the musical climax of the scene
in Lensky's melancholy recollection of the happy hours he had
spent in the home of his beloved Olga. On this melody is built

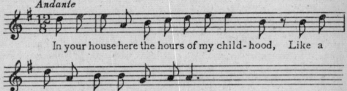

Andante

In your house here the hours of my child-hood,   Like a

won-der-ful song, flow'd a-way!

a transparently delicate ensemble—a haven of calm after all the
excitement. Lensky's aria before the duel 'How far, how far,
how far ye seem behind me, O day of youth, O joy of love!'
is profoundly moving, and is one of the most beautiful passages
in the whole score. Onegin's arias are not so important musically,
however impressive his short aria 'Can that be really the
Tatiana, To whom I once so close was brought?' in the final
act may be. (In Russia it is invariably encored.) It is based on
the same tune as that of the *allegro* passage in which Tatiana revealed her passion in the letter-scene.

The final scene overflows with musical beauties and dramatic
tension. Melancholy recollections alternate with passionate outbursts, and Tatiana's personality at this point assumes real
human grandeur. An inspired theme, as an expression of the
intensity of her feelings, crowns the magnificent final duet.

THE QUEEN OF SPADES. Opera in three acts by Pyotr Ilich Tchai-
kovsky. Text by Modest Tchaikovsky after Alexander Sergheievich
Pushkin. First performance: St Petersburg, 1890.
  Characters: Herman, a young officer—tenor; Count Tomsky—baritone;
Prince Yeletzky—baritone; Tchekalinsky and Sourin, officers—tenor and
bass; the Countess—mezzo-soprano; Lisa, her granddaughter—soprano;
Pauline, Lisa's friend—contralto; the governess—mezzo-soprano;
Masha, Lisa's maid—soprano; Master of Ceremonies—tenor; Tchaplitsky
and Narumov, gamblers—tenor and bass. The interlude: Chloë—
soprano; Daphnis (Pauline)—contralto; Plutus (Tomsky)—baritone.
People of St Petersburg, servants, guests, gamblers, children.
  Place: St Petersburg. *Time:* around 1800.
  Act I, scene i. The Summer Garden, St Petersburg. It is spring. Children
are playing, nurses sit chattering and people are walking up and down.

The officers Tchekalinsky and Sourin are discussing the odd behaviour of their friend Herman, who spends evening after evening at the gaming table, watching but never touching the cards. Herman enters with Count Tomsky, who asks his friend what has changed him so much lately. Herman confesses that he has fallen in love with a girl whose name he does not know, but who evidently belongs to a very distinguished family, so that he, a poor officer, will never be able to win her. Prince Yeletzky enters and announces happily that he has become engaged to be married that very morning. At that moment Lisa enters the park with her grandmother, and when Yeletzky points the girl out as his fiancée, Herman is amazed to recognize in her his secret love. Lisa and the Countess have noticed Herman and when Count Tomsky greets them they inquire who he is. When the ladies have left, Tomsky tells a wonderful story about the old Countess. As a girl she was considered a great beauty at the court of Louis XV, and all Paris was at her feet; but she was completely obsessed by her passion for gambling and was nicknamed 'The Queen of Spades'. One day she lost her whole fortune at the tables, and the Count St Germain, to whom people attributed magic powers, offered to tell her the secret of the 'three winning cards' in return for an assignation. As a result she had an amazing run of luck; it was rumoured that she passed on the secret to her husband, and years later to a young lover. Since then she had dreamt that if she were to reveal the secret to anyone else she would die. This story makes a great impression on Herman, who sees here a chance to acquire money and honour and to win his beloved. A storm breaks and, while everyone runs for shelter, Herman stands alone as if in a trance.

Scene ii. Lisa's room. It is evening; Lisa is seated at the harpsichord, playing for some friends. She and Pauline sing a dreamy duet, which Pauline follows with a moving romance. Such songs are to her mind not very apt for an engagement day, so she and some of the other girls start a merry Russian dance-song to try to cheer up the melancholy Lisa. The Governess enters, indignant at the noise, and Lisa's friends depart. Lisa is left alone and her thoughts go to the unknown young man whom she has seen several times. She compares him with her fiancé. Suddenly Herman appears at the window. Beside herself with fear, Lisa begs him to leave her at once, but he declares his love for her so fervently that she finds herself responding to him. The Countess is heard approaching and Herman hides. After she has gone, Lisa falls into Herman's arms in happy abandonment.

Act II, scene i. A reception room in an elegant house. A masked ball is taking place and Lisa, the old Countess, the Prince and Herman are there. Herman is obsessed by the thought of the three cards, and his distracted air draws everyone's attention to him. Yeletzky sings to Lisa most movingly of his love, and asks her to have confidence in him. Lisa, however, keeps silent. A pastoral play, *The Faithful Shepherdess*—the story of Daphnis, Chloë and Plutus, with music in the style of Mozart—is performed with great success. Lisa secretly gives Herman a key, telling him to enter the house through the Countess's room without being seen while the old lady is still playing cards. This key will open a secret door which leads to her own apartments. The curtain falls as everyone rises to welcome the Empress.

Scene ii. The Countess's bedroom with a portrait of her as a young woman, dressed as the Queen of Spades. Behind the portrait are the tapestried door and staircase leading to Lisa's room. It is night, and the room is only lit by the lamps before the icons. Herman slips in to go to Lisa, but he is arrested by the portrait of the Countess and, changing his mind, hides himself behind a curtain as the Countess enters with her maids, who prepare her for the night. The Countess compares present-day society gatherings unfavourably with the Paris of her youth, and sings an air from Grétry's *Richard Cœur de Lion* which she had once sung before Louis XV. She is angry to see that her maids are still standing curiously around her, and sends them all away. Half-asleep, and humming to herself, she suddenly finds Herman standing before her and gazing at her piercingly. She cannot utter a word. Herman urges her to tell him the secret of the three cards. When she does not answer, he becomes more pressing and even threatens her with a pistol. The Countess, who had only been staring at him in derision, stiffens and then falls dead of shock. Lisa enters and is horrified to see what has happened. Herman assures her of his innocence; he only wanted to get the secret of the three cards. Deeply disillusioned, she is sure that he only came to the house for this purpose and orders him to leave.

Act III, scene i. Herman's room in the barracks. It is late at night. Herman has received a letter from Lisa; she forgives him and accepts his explanation. She asks him to meet her again that very night on the banks of the Neva. Herman is haunted by his conscience; he hears funeral chants and sees the body of the Countess upon a bier before him. Suddenly the door opens, the draught blows out his candle, and in the doorway stands the ghost of the Countess, who tells him to marry Lisa, and then reveals to him the three winning cards: the three, the seven and the ace. The ghost disappears. Herman pulls himself together with difficulty and leaves the room.

Scene ii. The banks of the Neva. Lisa is anxiously awaiting her lover. Herman enters and they sing of their future together. He is however possessed with the thought of the three winning cards, and is irresistibly compelled to go to the gaming-house. In vain Lisa tries to hold him back; he pushes her aside and hurries out. In despair, Lisa throws herself into the river.

Scene ii. A large room in the gaming club. Prince Yeletzky enters with Herman. The latter announces that he intends to play today. He puts forty thousand on the three and wins; he then puts double the sum on the seven and wins again. Nobody now wants to play with him, except Prince Yeletzky. Herman puts all his money on the ace. When he draws the card, it is not the expected ace that turns up, but the Queen of Spades. At that moment he believes he sees the Countess's ghost at the table, staring at him derisively. Cursing the old woman, he kills himself, but, before he dies, implores the Prince to pardon him, and with Lisa's name on his lips, breathes his last.

Musically *The Queen of Spades* is far more dramatic than
Eugene Onegin. The opera opens with an idyllic scene of the
children playing in the park, while the townspeople stroll
up and down at leisure. Herman's entrance marks the onset of
excitement which mounts steadily in the music until it erupts
into the breaking storm. The accompaniment to the ballad of
the cards introduces the most important theme of the opera—
a sinister motif in fourths which recurs whenever Herman is

reminded of the Countess and her fatal secret. The second scene
repeats the transition from idyll to dramatic passion. From the
deeply moving *andante* of Herman's declaration of love emerges

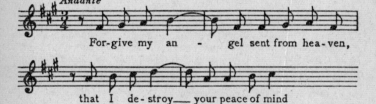

the stormy love music which is the second main theme of the

opera. These two themes form the content of the short orchestral overture which precedes the opera.

From the scene in the Countess's bedroom onwards, the
demonic elements dominate the stage. The Countess's great
scena can be immensely impressive, and strong dramatic talent
is more important in the interpreter of the role than sheer vocal
prowess. The spectral atmosphere of this scene and the scene
in the barracks is superbly evoked in the music, with the card
theme recurring like a dull threat in the orchestra. Lisa's aria

on the banks of the Neva is profoundly moving, and her cry of despair makes a truly shattering impact. An uneasy beating rhythm stresses the anguish of her heart, and the orchestra

harshly repeats this theme at the end of the scene when she takes her own life.

The third act is the climax of the opera, and the dramatic *crescendo* never relents for a moment. The few lyrical passages are exquisitely lovely, while the terrible tragedy of Herman's growing madness is vividly portrayed in the music. As he dies, the fervent love-theme appears again delicately in the orchestra, and brings the opera to a close on a note of forgiveness.

Czech music has also made an important contribution to the history of opera. Smetana and Dvořák were the founders of the national Czech operatic tradition which found its Slovak complement in Janáček, and a truly national continuation in Jaromir Weinberger's works. The development in Bohemia was very similar to that in Russia. The early compositions of Bedřich Smetana (1824–84) were very much in German romantic style. He first came into contact with folk music when the libretto of his light folk opera, *The Bartered Bride*, was submitted to him, and he at once recognized its tremendous unexploited resources as an art-form. *The Bartered Bride* therefore has the same importance in Czech national music as Glinka's *A Life for the Tsar* had in Russian music. Once the source of popular music had been uncovered, it poured unrestrained into musical compositions and soon dominated both symphonic and chamber music. The earthy vitality of Smetana's music made *The Bartered Bride* an immediate international success, whereas his other operas, *Dalibor*, *The Kiss*, *The Two Widows*, and *Libussa*, were comparatively unsuccessful abroad.

THE BARTERED BRIDE (Prodaná Nevěsta). Comic opera in three acts by Bedřich Smetana. Text by Karel Sabina. First performance: Prague, 1866.

Characters: Krušina, a peasant—baritone; Ludmila, his wife—mezzo-soprano; Mařenka, their daughter—soprano; Tobias Micha, a land-owner—bass; Hata, his wife—mezzo-soprano; Vašek, their son—tenor; Jeník, Micha's son by his first marriage—tenor; Kecal, a marriage-broker—bass; the Manager of a travelling circus—tenor; Esmeralda, a dancer—soprano; an Indian—bass. Villagers, circus artistes.

Place: A Bohemian village. *Time:* middle of the nineteenth century.

Act I. A village square with an inn. The peasants are gaily celebrating the consecration festival of their church. Mařenka does not join in the general merriment. Her parents are planning a rich marriage for her, though she is in love with Jeník, whose origin nobody knows. Jeník assures her that he comes of a good family but was driven out of his father's house by his unpleasant stepmother. He asks Mařenka to have confidence in him and she promises to remain faithful. Mařenka's father, the peasant Krušina, had promised years before that he would marry Mařenka to one of the sons of the rich landowner Micha. The marriage-broker Kecal does his best to arrange the match. According to him, Mařenka must marry Vašek, Micha's son by his second marriage, since the son of his first marriage has not been heard of for years. Mařenka says frankly that she does not want to marry anybody but her Jeník. The act closes with a polka.

Act II. In the inn. Jeník is drinking happily with the young men of the village, and they sing a chorus in praise of beer. Kecal enters and approaches him. Some of the womenfolk of the village enter and all join in dancing a *furiant*. Everybody then goes out, and the foolish, stuttering Vašek enters the inn in a state of great alarm at the prospect of having to court this girl his mother has chosen for him. Mařenka, realizing with horror that this must be the man her parents want her to marry, proceeds to warn him against the flighty Mařenka, who would lead him a terrible dance. She hints that a nicer, prettier girl is in love with him, and Vašek gratefully promises to renounce Mařenka. Kecal enters with Jeník, whom he hopes to buy off, and offers him a large sum of money to give up Mařenka. Jeník accepts this, but only on condition that Mařenka will marry the elder son of Tobias Micha. Kecal draws up the agreement at once, and Jeník signs before witnesses. He is the object of furious dis-approval for selling his fiancée so light-heartedly.

Act III. The village square as in Act I. A circus troupe enters, and the Ringmaster invites the villagers to attend the performance; his troupe gives a short demonstration of the delights in store for the audience. Vašek falls in love with the tight-rope dancer Esmeralda, and when the artist who should play the bear is found to be hopelessly drunk she easily persuades her new admirer to take his place. Meanwhile Mařenka has heard of Jeník's supposed betrayal and is in despair. When Vašek finds that she, the pretty girl with the good advice for whom he has been look-ing, is in fact Mařenka, he is overjoyed, but Mařenka asks for time to make up her mind. When Jeník enters, apparently in high spirits, treating the whole thing as a joke, she is furious and refuses to listen to him. Kecal joins them, and Jeník tries to persuade Mařenka to sign the contract, so that he can have his money. The villagers enter to congratulate Mařenka and Vašek; Micha and Hata also enter the square and, immediately recognize Jeník as the former's elder son; and since the contract reads 'the son of Tobias Micha', Mařenka makes her choice without difficulty. Kecal is furious at having been duped, and all make fun of him. Just then the bear shambles in, to everyone's terror, but it is only Vašek. Hata is deeply ashamed and leads the simple boy away. The opera closes with general rejoicing.

Though this work is full of the most attractive music, it was not appreciated at first, and only gradually did the Prague audiences come to like it. It was not performed abroad until eight years after Smetana's death. When it was produced in Vienna, in 1892, it was immediately successful, and it soon appeared in repertories all over the world.

The overture sets the mood of the opera; its lively, whirling theme storms enthusiastically through the strings, carrying all before it, and then a gay dance-tune takes us to Bohemia. These two contrasting themes alternate in an excellent introduction to the comedy that follows. Smetana's *Bartered Bride* is a folk opera in the most ideal sense of the term; the popular spirit appears in almost every bar, whether in fiery dances (lively polkas and *furiants*), in the melodious and slightly senti-

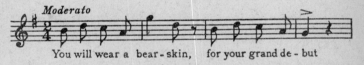

You will wear a bear - skin,   for your grand de - but

mental lyrical passages, or in the humorous sections. Through-

This girl I've found you, she will a-stound you, She's a real catch

out one hears the sounds and rhythms of Czech folk music, which gives this score its peculiar charm. The string of inventive melodies never flags, and each of them is filled with pulsating, dance-like rhythm.

Antonín Dvořák (1841–1904), the other Czech classical composer, wrote a series of operas which are hardly known outside his own country. A few attempts to mount *Russalka* or *The*

Jacobites elsewhere have not so far succeeded in establishing these
works in the repertory; it is a pity, for both works are beautiful,
and romantic in the best sense of the word.

An important event in the history of Czech opera was the
production in 1904 of *Jenůfa* by Leoš Janáček (1854–1928),
which in recent years has had great success outside Czechoslovakia. Janáček uses Slovak folk songs and dances in this
opera, but his music is rougher and more modern than that of
Smetana, and his attitude to peasant life and music is free from
any romantic gloss. One of the main characteristics of his
very personal style is the overriding declamatory manner
adapted to the original rhythms of Slovak folk music. Another distinctive feature is the uneasy flow of his melodies
or accompanying figures, which evokes a remarkably exciting
atmosphere. The few sustained sections in the score of *Jenůfa*
therefore emerge all the more strongly from this pulsating
background, and the dramatic tension is never relaxed. *Jenůfa*
was first performed in Brno in 1904. The first German-language
performance, in Max Brod's translation, took place in Vienna
in 1918, since when this powerful work has been taken up by
many theatres outside Czechoslovakia.

JENŮFA (Její Pastorkyňa—Her foster-daughter). Opera in three acts by
Leoš Janáček. Text after Gabriella Preissová by the composer. First
performance: Brno, 1904.
  Characters: Grandmother Buryja, owner of the mill—contralto; Laca
Klemeň and Števa Buryja, stepbrothers, her grandsons—tenors; Kostelnička (= the church elder's wife) Burya, a widow, her daughter-in-law—
soprano; Jenůfa, the Kostelnička's foster-daughter—soprano; the mill
foreman—baritone; the village magistrate—bass; his wife—mezzo-
soprano; Karolka, their daughter—mezzo-soprano; Barena, a servant at
the mill—soprano; Jano, a shepherd-boy—soprano; a maid—mezzo-
soprano; the aunt—contralto. Musicians, villagers.
  Place: A village in Moravia. *Time:* nineteenth century.
  Act I. In front of the mill. Jenůfa is anxiously waiting to hear whether
her beloved Števa has been conscripted. If he has to go into the army,
their marriage will be postponed and her sin will be public knowledge,
since it is becoming obvious that she is expecting a child. Laca, who is
near by, shaping a whip-handle with his knife, makes surly remarks to
the grandmother about her obvious preference for Števa, and is also bitter
in his remarks to Jenůfa about Števa. Jano, the shepherd-boy, comes in
rejoicing that he can now read, thanks to Jenůfa's teaching. Laca gives his
blunted knife to the foreman to grind, and comments harshly about
Jenůfa. The foreman is not deceived by his apparent dislike of her, and

tells Laca that Števa has not been conscripted and is coming home. Jenůfa overhears this news with delight and waits to greet Števa, who in his joy has got very drunk and enters singing with some recruits and a party of musicians. The Kostelnička is indignant at his rowdy and unpleasant behaviour and in her most authoritative tones tells him that he may only marry Jenůfa if he can lead a sober life for a whole year. The Grandmother tells Števa to go and sleep off his drunkenness, then tries to console Jenůfa. Jenůfa and Števa are left alone, and though Jenůfa pleads her love for him and her shameful secret, he is petulant and childish in his response. When Laca returns and finds Jenůfa alone, he speaks mockingly of Števa's discomfiture at the hands of the Kostelnička. This rouses Jenůfa to defend Števa, and Laca, torn with anger and jealousy, makes as though to embrace Jenůfa, but instead slashes her cheek with his knife to disfigure her. As she runs into the house he laments his cruel action, and though Barena tries to convince everyone that it was an accident, the foreman accuses Laca of having done it on purpose.

Act II. The living-room of the Kostelnička's house. Six months have passed, and Jenůfa's child has been born secretly, while everyone thinks she has been away in Vienna for several weeks. Jenůfa clearly shows her joy in the child, but her foster-mother's pride is hurt, and she is full of shame. She gives Jenůfa a drugged drink, and waits for Števa, whom she has sent for. Since her prayers for the child's death have remained un-answered, she has resigned herself to a marriage between Števa and Jenůfa. Števa enters. She tells him of the child's birth and implores him to marry Jenůfa, but Števa shrinks from seeing her and his son and explains that he cannot love her now her beauty has been spoiled. He will of course give her money for the child, but the whole affair must be kept secret, as he has promised to marry Karolka, the local magistrate's daughter. The Kostelnička reacts with horror and Števa runs out. Since Laca is still in love with Jenůfa and still hopes to win her, the Kostelnička sees in him the last chance to restore Jenůfa's respectability. She tells Laca about the child but when he recoils at the thought of taking him too she pretends that the baby is dead. Laca assures her that he still loves Jenůfa. Left alone, the Kostelnička realizes what she has started, and sees no other solution but to kill the child. She takes it out and drowns it in the mill-stream, which will be frozen for several months to come. When Jenůfa awakes and finds herself alone, she assumes the Kostelnička has taken the baby to show to Števa, and prays touchingly for the child's future. On her return, her foster-mother tells her she has been unconscious for two days and that the baby has died and been buried. She also breaks the news of Števa's attitude and coming marriage to Karolka. When Laca returns, Jenůfa agrees to marry him.

Act III. The same room. Two months have elapsed, and Jenůfa is preparing for her marriage to Laca. The Kostelnička seems haggard and agitated. The magistrate arrives with his wife to offer his congratulations, but his wife's comment on Jenůfa's refusal to wear the usual wedding garland distresses the girl. Laca is touching in his attentions and is obviously devoted to Jenůfa, at whose instigation he has made up his quarrel with Števa, who now enters with Karolka, a coquettish little minx. Barena

and some other girls arrive with flowers for Jenůfa, and the Grandmother
gives her and Laca her blessing. Suddenly shouts are heard from outside
and Jano enters, screaming that the body of a new-born baby has been
found in the mill-stream. The Kostelnička becomes hysterical, but just
then Jenůfa, who rushed out with everyone else, cries out that the body is
that of her baby. The suspicion of the inhabitants falls at first on her and
Števa, but Laca stands protectively in front of his bride. To save Jenůfa,
the Kostelnička now makes a full confession of her crime, and is ready
to take the consequences. With a great effort Jenůfa forgives her, and
she goes out with the magistrate. Jenůfa now offers Laca his freedom,
but he is determined to stand by her, and Jenůfa tells him happily that
through her sufferings her love for him has grown.

The tremendous success of *Jenůfa* resulted in repeated attempts
in recent years to revive Janáček's other operas, especially
Káťa Kabanová.

KÁŤA KABANOVÁ. Tragic opera in three acts by Leoš Janáček. Text
by Červinka after Ostrovsky's *The Storm*. First performance: Brno, 1921.
    Characters: Vanya Kudrjas, clerk to Dikoy—tenor; Feklusha and
Glasha, servants to the Kabanovs—mezzo-sopranos; Dikoy, a rich
merchant—bass; Boris Grigorievitch, his nephew—tenor; Marfa
Kabanová (Kabanicha) a rich merchant's widow—alto; Tichon Ivanitch
Kabanov, her son—tenor; Katerina (Katya) Kabanová, Tichon's wife—
soprano; Barbara, foster-child in the Kabanov household—soprano;
Kuligin, a friend of Vanya's—baritone. A woman in the crowd, a passer-
by, townspeople.
    Place: Kalinov, a small provincial town on the banks of the Volga.
Time: about 1860.
    Act I, scene i. A park by the river with the Kabanovs' house. It is
Sunday morning, and Vanya and Glasha are passing the time of day
until they see Dikoy approaching, when they retire to escape his angry
tongue. He enters, scolding his nephew Boris, whom he dislikes, for
laziness. When he has left again, Boris tells Vanya that he has to live with
his tiresome uncle and obey him, since this is the condition on which he
and his sister will come into an inheritance under his grandmother's will,
when they come of age. The Kabanovs are seen returning from church,
and Boris's sad voice betrays his love for Katya, a married woman, even
before he confesses this to Vanya. Kabanicha, a real family tyrant, commands Tichon to go to the market at Kazan, and although he agrees to
do so she reproaches him with lack of respect since his marriage. Tichon
tries to defend the gentle Katya against his mother's harsh tongue, but
when left alone with him Barbara abuses him for his weakness. It is clear
that she is devoted to Katya.
    Scene ii. The interior of the house. Katya is telling Barbara of her care
free early life and present unhappiness. She is beset with dreams which
tempt her to sin, to give in to another man's persuasions and go away

with him. Barbara tries to comfort her by making light of this. Tichon enters to take his leave, and Katya begs him not to leave her alone, or at least to make her swear not to speak to any man while he is away. He gently refuses to coerce her but in Kabanicha's presence mildly suggests she should not see other men in his absence.

Act II, scene i. The Kabanovs' living-room, It is later the same day and Kabanicha is nagging at Katya for not showing enough grief at her husband's departure. Barbara goes out, leaving Katya the key to the garden and saying she will tell 'him' to wait for her, Katya, by the gate. Katya is left a prey to conflicting emotions and it is clear that her love will prove too strong for her. Kabanicha enters with a rather drunk and maudlin Dikoy, who unburdens himself to her.

Scene ii. The garden. Vanya and Boris are waiting for Barbara and Katya respectively. The two couples sing of their contrasting feelings to music which exudes the magic of a summer night.

Act III, scene i. A derelict summer-house on a terrace by the river. Vanya and his friend Kuligin shelter there from a threatening storm. They are joined by Dikoy and Boris, but once the storm has passed only Boris and Vanya are left. Barbara comes in to tell Boris that Tichon is back and that Katya seems sick with worry. Just then the three Kabanovs enter and Boris hides. The storm breaks out again and Katya suddenly confesses her adultery and names her lover. Tichon is distraught with unhappiness, but Kabanicha congratulates herself on having predicted this misfortune.

Scene ii. The banks of the Volga. It is night and everyone is searching for Katya, who has fled. Tichon is torn between righteous condemnation of Katya and his continuing love for her. Barbara and Vanya decide to elope together to escape from Kabanicha. Katya enters, distraught and longing to see Boris again. He appears and tries to comfort her, but her mind is wandering. She speaks of returning to perpetual torment at the hands of Kabanicha, and they part sadly. She goes to the river-bank and throws herself in. Dikoy drags her body out of the water as Kabanicha and Tichon rush in. Kabanicha thanks her friends and neighbours for their kindness.

Janáček wrote strongly rhythmic music, scarcely less original than that of *Jenůfa*, to this passionate plot, but his next opera, *The Cunning Little Vixen* (1924) belongs to quite another genre —that of the fairy-tale opera. It is an exceedingly difficult work to stage, and this has largely prevented its popularity from spreading as far as it should. A number of successful productions in the last few years, especially that staged by Felsenstein at the Komische Oper, Berlin, and seen in Paris, Wiesbaden and elsewhere, have however clearly shown that in this work above all Janáček bewitched audiences with the fresh spontaneity of his music, grown from the roots of Moravian folk melodies.

THE CUNNING LITTLE VIXEN (Příhody Lišky Bystroušky). Fairy-tale opera in three acts by Leoš Janáček. Text after a short story by R. Těsnohlídek by the composer. First performance: Brno, 1924.

Characters: The Forester—baritone; his wife—contralto; the School-master—tenor; the Priest and the Badger—bass; Lapák, the Forester's dog—mezzo-soprano or tenor; Pepík, the Forester's son and Frantík, his friend—boy sopranos; Pásek, the innkeeper—tenor; his wife—soprano; Harašta, a poacher—bass; the Vixen Sharpears—soprano; Sharpears as a cub—child soprano; the Fox Goldenmane—soprano or tenor; the Rooster—soprano; the Hen—soprano; a cricket, a grasshopper, a mosquito, a frog—child sopranos; a screech-owl—contralto; a jay—soprano; a woodpecker—contralto. Children's ballet of animals. Peasants, hens, fox-cubs, forest birds and animals.

Place: A forest. *Time:* fairy-tale.

Act I, scene i. A forest. Summer afternoon. 'How they caught the vixen, Sharpears.' A badger smoking a long pipe sticks his head out of his hole, while small flies dance around him, and then a dragon-fly. All withdraw as the Forester enters, sweating and out of breath, but crickets and a grasshopper dance about while he settles himself for a sleep. Midges and a young frog join the dance. Sharpears runs in, and is caught by the Forester who wakens at that moment. He carries her away, re-marking that her eyes are like those of a certain gipsy-girl.

Scene ii. 'Sharpears in the yard of the Forester's lakeside cottage.' It is autumn. The Forester comes out of the house with his wife. Sharpears and the dog Lapák complain of their lonely and frustrated lives, knowing nothing themselves of love, though Sharpears tells a very human story of the marital and family life of some starlings she had known in the forest. The dog makes advances to her, which she repulses. The Forester's son and a friend come into the courtyard. The former torments Sharp-ears who bites him and tries to escape. The boy's friend recaptures her and the Forester ties her up. Darkness falls and Sharpears cries in her sleep, dreaming that she is a real human girl and free.

Scene iii. Morning breaks. 'Sharpears the politician; she runs away'. The cock and hens mock her plight, which is due to her uselessness—*she* lays no eggs. The vixen tries to incite the hens to rebellion, then pretends to be dead. When they and the cock creep nearer to investigate, she grabs him first, then starts eating the hens. The Forester's wife rushes out; appalled at what has happened she calls to her husband, whom she blames for everything, to shoot the vixen. He beats her, but she bites through the rope which holds her and runs off into the forest.

Act II, scene i. Forest scene as at the beginning of Act I. 'Sharpears the usurper of property.' Late afternoon. Sharpears peers in at the badger's lair and tempts him out with provocative remarks. She is joined by other small animals in taunting him, accusing him of hypocrisy when he criticizes her manners and morals. She approaches him seductively, then swiftly turns her tail into his face. He comes out of his lair in a rage, then, finding she has dispossessed him, he paces off with dignity, pipe in hand.

Scene ii. The village inn. Enter the Priest, very similar in appearance to the badger, also with a pipe. The Forester and the Schoolmaster are playing cards. The atmosphere is not gay: the Priest is to be transferred to another parish; the Forester is longing for his Terynka and bewailing his foolishness in bringing home the vixen. The Schoolmaster is contemplating marriage, but the other two are not encouraging. He goes out, and the unpopular Priest, warned by the innkeeper, escapes as an angry crowd of peasants comes out of the tap-room to find him. The Forester, alone with the innkeeper, laments his action in bringing Terynka to the village, to turn the Schoolmaster's head and be seduced by the Priest.

Scene iii. The wood. 'Sharpears' excursions.' It is night and moonlight. The Schoolmaster is trying to make his way through the wood, which he finds confusing. He sways about, watched now by Sharpears, and addresses a sunflower as his beloved Terynka. He stumbles over its stem, falls and lies still. Sharpears hides in the undergrowth as the Priest enters, muttering about Terynka and her bright eyes as the little fox's eyes gleam out of the bushes. The Forester enters and chases Sharpears across the stage. Shots are heard.

Scene iv. Sharpears' lair, bathed in summer moonlight. 'Sharpears' wooing and mating.' Goldenmane, a beautiful tawny dog-fox, enters, addresses her politely and offers himself as escort. Sharpears is very taken with him and tells him her story, to which he listens in wonder. She preens herself when he has left her, and he soon returns to lay a rabbit at her feet. There follows an enchanting scene of courtship, and they retire into Sharpears' lair. Morning breaks, and when Sharpears in some agitation has whispered a secret in Goldenmane's ear they seek out the woodpecker who marries them at once.

Act III, scene i. At the edge of the forest. 'How Sharpears came within range of Harašta's gun; her passing.' A fine spring day. Harašta enters singing, observed by the Forester, whom he tells that he is about to marry Terynka. The Forester sees Sharpears' pad-mark near the body of a hare, sets a trap and goes out with his gun to find her. Harašta goes off in the other direction and all the little foxes come out to play. Goldenmane and Sharpears are clearly still deeply in love with each other and delight in their large family. When Harašta returns with some stolen chickens Sharpears lures him away and the fox-cubs delightedly eat Harašta's spoil. When the enraged poacher comes back and fires into her family, Sharpears protects them with her body, and falls dead.

Scene ii. The village inn. The Forester is telling the Schoolmaster sadly of his unsuccessful search for Sharpears. In a neighbouring inn Terynka and Harašta are celebrating their wedding with music and dancing, and the Schoolmaster's attention wanders from the story. Apparently the poacher has given his bride a fox-muff, and the Forester is saddened to think of Sharpears being killed. He and the Schoolmaster are growing old, and springtime only emphasizes this.

Scene iii. The forest in spring. 'Baby Sharpears.' The forester nostalgically remembers the days of his courtship and early marriage in this very forest, many years ago. The reawakening of nature after her winter sleep comforts him for the passing years. He falls asleep, as in Act I, and in just the same way the forest comes to life and a baby frog—grandson of the previous one—awakens him. There among the animals is a vixen-cub, just like its mother. The story has come full circle.

Janáček's operas *The Makropulos Affair* (*Več Makropulos*) (1926) and *From the House of the Dead* (*Z Mrtvého Domů*) (1930) have never become established outside Czechoslovakia, but *The Excursions of Mr Brouček* (*Výlety Páně Broučkovy*) (1920), a fantasy opera depicting the adventures of a Czech *petit-bourgeois* on the moon and in the fifteenth century, has recently been performed in Germany. This strange subject also proved an inspiration to Janáček's powerful and earthy talent.

Schwanda the Bagpiper, by Jaromir Weinberger (born 1896), was in a sense a successor to *The Bartered Bride*. It is a light popular opera in which all the lasting elements of Czech folk music are colourfully interwoven.

SCHWANDA THE BAGPIPER (Švanda Dudák). Popular opera in two acts by Jaromir Weinberger. Text by Miloš Kares. First performance: Prague, 1927.

Characters: Schwanda—baritone; Dorotka, his wife—soprano; the bandit Babinsky—tenor; Queen Iceheart—mezzo-soprano; the Magician —bass; the Judge—tenor; the Executioner—tenor; the Devil—bass; the Devil's Familiar Spirit—tenor; the Captain of hell's guard—tenor; two forest rangers—tenor and bass. People of Queen Iceheart's city, servants of hell, peasants.

Place: Bohemia. *Time:* legendary.

Act I, scene i. Schwanda's cottage on the edge of the forest. The young peasant Schwanda, known everywhere as the best bagpiper of all, has just married the charming Dorotka, and is living happily with her. The bandit Babinsky, who is in hiding from the Rangers, takes a meal with them (they do not know who he is) and describes life out in the world in such seductive words that Schwanda decides to follow him, and does so in spite of Dorotka's protests.

Scene ii. The palace of Queen Iceheart. The Queen implores the magician to give her back her living heart which he has exchanged for a heart of ice, but the magician replies mockingly. Schwanda comes into the palace and enchants everyone with his music—even the Queen seems changed. She so falls in love with his music that she decides to marry the musician, and everything is prepared for the wedding. Just as Schwanda kisses the Queen, however, the magician brings in Dorotka who has followed Schwanda and accuses him of infidelity. He immediately returns to his senses, but when the Queen hears this she orders them both to appear before the judge.

Scene iii. A square near the city gates. The sentence of death is passed on Schwanda and Dorotka. Just as they are about to be executed, Babinsky exchanges the executioner's axe for a straw broom which falls

nd wins the game. Generously he gives the Devil back everything but
Schwanda's soul. Before leaving he plays a real devil's fugue, which
rouses the servants of hell to a state of incredible excitement.

Scene ii. Schwanda's cottage. Babinsky tells Schwanda he has been in
hell twenty years and that Dorotka is now old and will probably not
even know him, but Schwanda has learned his lesson and refuses to listen
to this kind of talk. He calls Dorotka, who comes out to him, young and
beautiful, and falls into his arms. Babinsky recognizes that he will have
no more luck here, and returns to the woods, to continue his merry life
as a bandit. Some neighbours passing by congratulate Schwanda on his
return home.

This Bohemian version of the old fairy-story of the magic
violin contains some charming passages, but in Weinberger's
work the individual dramatic episodes are perhaps rather too
long-drawn-out and therefore lose some of their effect. The
weakest part is the second scene in the Queen's palace, with its
recurring polonaise theme which characterizes the Queen and
her court, but the music is really refreshing when it stands on
its home ground of folk songs and rhythms. The many polka
tunes, the 'Odzernek' and the devil's fugue, have a dashing
vigour; they are as delightful as the various songs and duets
with which they are interspersed, and which are based on
popular rhythms with characteristically frequent changes of
tempo. Especially noteworthy is Dorotka's fervent song of her
homeland, which returns several times as a *leitmotiv*, and also
gives the opera its effective finale.

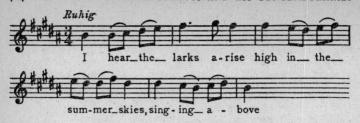

I hear the larks a-rise high in the sum-mer skies, sing-ing a-bove

In comparison with the great Russian and Czech contributions in the field of opera, those of the other Slav nations seem insignificant. There is a Polish national opera, *Halka*, by Stanislav Moniuszko (1819–72), while the lively Jugoslav opera *Ero, the Joker* (*Ero S Onoga Svijeta*) by Jakov Gotovac (born 1895) has from time to time been performed outside the composer's native land.

RICHARD STRAUSS AND HIS
CONTEMPORARIES

The romantic movement continued to dominate nineteenth-century music almost unchallenged until the end of the century. In French and Russian music romantic feeling then moved into impressionism, while in Italy reaction came in the form of *verismo*. In Germany, its birthplace, romanticism was too strongly rooted for any conclusive reaction to appear. The heritage of German romanticism, as exemplified in the works of Wagner, Brahms and Bruckner, was still very powerful and was bound to yield a further crop of descendants. The leading figure in this late romanticism was Richard Strauss (1864–1949), and thanks to him Germany retained its leadership through this final phase of musical romanticism—a phase which covered roughly the years between 1890 and the First World War, though its last signs can be traced right into the 1930's. One can therefore say that romanticism dominated music for a hundred years.

Strauss's first symphonic poems, *Don Juan* (1889), and *Tod und Verklärung* (*Death and Transfiguration*) (1890) gave a new

impulse to music. It is astonishing that Strauss, who developed
so bold and entirely original a style in his symphonic works,
should still have shown complete subservience to Wagner's
influence in his opera *Guntram*, composed shortly afterwards.
In fact Wagner's formal and idealistic world still dominated
opera to such an extent that even a genius like Richard Strauss
could not immediately shake off the master's influence.

His first operas, *Guntram* (Weimar, 1894) and *Feuersnot*
(*Beltane Fire*) (Dresden, 1901), seem in a way to make up a
tribute from Strauss to Wagner. If in *Guntram* Strauss appears
to be a follower, or even an imitator of Wagner, in *Feuersnot*
he has already gained his independence, though many Wagnerian features are still apparent in this work. Even in the text
Strauss acknowledged Wagner as his master, when his hero
Kunrad reproaches the people of Munich with having once
made the life of a certain Master Reichhart (Richard Wagner)
a hell on earth. The text of this rough, earthy one-act opera
was written by Ernst von Wolzogen, whereas Strauss wrote
his own libretto for *Guntram*. *Feuersnot* contains much more
that is genuine Strauss, from racy waltzes to enchanting love-
duets. Its enormous initial success did not, however, last, because
the text is full of topical allusions and comments which are
largely incomprehensible today.

In his search for a suitable operatic text Strauss chanced on
Oscar Wilde's *Salome* in Hedwig Lachmann's translation. In
the strangely glowing atmosphere of this one-act play Strauss
recognized a rare and inspiring basis for an opera, but the
poetic version prepared for him by the Viennese Anton
Lindtner did not appeal to him. He had already set to music the
first words—in fact the first scene—in his head, when he
realized that Hedwig Lachmann's wonderfully colourful and
flexible prose was ideally suited to his artistic plan, and he prepared the libretto with very little cutting or tightening of her
translation. He began composing the music in the summer of
1903 and completed it just two years later. The Dresden
première proved a real triumph.

SALOME. Opera in one act by Richard Strauss. Text after the German
translation by Hedwig Lachmann of Oscar Wilde's play of the same name.
First performance: Dresden, 1905.

Characters: Herod Antipas, Tetrarch of Judea—tenor; Herodias, his wife—mezzo-soprano; Salome, her daughter—soprano; Jokanaan (John the Baptist)—baritone; Naraboth, a young Syrian, captain of the guard—tenor; a page to Herodias—contralto; five Jews—four tenors, one bass; two Nazarenes—bass and tenor; two soldiers—basses; a Cappadocian—bass; a slave—soprano.

Place: Herod's palace at Tiberias Galilee, his capital. *Time:* about 30 AD.

On the open terrace of Herod's palace. Light and noise from the banqueting hall reach the dark terrace which is illumined only by the stars. 'How beautiful Princess Salome is tonight,' says Naraboth, the handsome young Syrian, his voice full of passionate desire. He and the soldiers of the guard are watching what is happening in the hall, where the Tetrarch Herod cannot take his eyes off Salome. Herodias's page warns Naraboth against the Princess. The quarrelling and shouting of the Jews is heard outside; the voice of the prophet Jokanaan rises from the cistern in the dark courtyard, filling them all with awe. Salome runs on to the terrace. She has been driven out of the room by the lust she saw in her stepfather's eyes. The atmosphere of gluttony and debauchery surrounding the Tetrarch and her mother repels the young princess, but she is already completely poisoned by its corruption and craves new experiences. Her curiosity is aroused by the voice of Jokanaan which is again heard from the cistern. When she hears that the prophet is still a young man, she longs to see him, and, although it is forbidden for Jokanaan to leave the cistern, Naraboth, who is in love with her, cannot resist her wiles and orders the prophet to be brought out. Everyone is seized by dread. The prophet, pale, emaciated and in rags, comes out of the cistern; raising his voice, he denounces the criminal pair who rule the kingdom and rages at Salome for her mother's sins. Salome is completely fascinated by him; she sinks into contemplation of his beauty and comes close to him with mounting desire. Finally she cries out her longing to kiss his mouth, but the prophet reacts to her advances by telling her to do penance. Naraboth, in despair at Salome's actions, kills himself with his own sword, unnoticed by Salome, who in a transport of excitement repeats her lustful wish. Jokanaan bids her seek out the only Man who can save her and then, cursing her again, descends into the cistern.

Herod leaves the banqueting hall and comes on to the terrace, followed by Herodias and his court. He is tormented by his conscience, but the cold Herodias is only concerned to restrain his sinful desire for Salome, which is increasing with his drunkenness. When Herod falls over the body of Naraboth and hears what has happened, he is filled with horror—horror at what could still occur. He turns with desire to Salome who, sunk in her own thoughts, seems cold and indifferent to his pleading; she refuses his invitation to drink and eat fruit with him and to sit on his throne. Jokanaan's voice interrupts their talk, but when Herodias commands the prophet to be silenced Herod will make no move against him, for he fears him and believes him to be a great prophet. This leads to a dispute among the five Jewish guests at the feast, for they claim their right to judge Jokanaan. Jokanaan's voice is again heard, and two

Nazarenes tell of the miracles of the man they believe to be the Messiah. This fills Herod with increasing forebodings of doom. Jokanaan's words infuriate Herodias while Salome becomes more and more excited by the sound of his voice. In order to distract himself and her, Herod asks her to dance, but Salome refuses. When he insists, she agrees on the condition that he will grant any wish she might express. She makes him seal this promise with an oath. Salome then performs the dance of the seven veils. Herod watches her, fascinated. When he bends over her as she lies exhausted on the ground, to ask her her wishes, she coldly demands Jokanaan's head. Herod is beside himself; he offers her all his most costly treasures if she will withdraw this demand, but Salome reminds him of his oath. Finally Herod gives in: Salome is to be granted her wish. Herodias, happy at being able to revenge herself on the prophet she detests, draws the death ring from Herod's finger. The executioner descends into the cistern, and Salome bends over the edge to watch. She cannot control her impatience and behaves as if she were inhuman. Finally a black arm appears from the cistern with the head of Jokanaan on a silver tray. Salome takes hold of it. Nothing can prevent her now from kissing the mouth she so madly desired, which was denied to her in life. In ecstasy she bends over the head and presses her lips to the dead mouth of the prophet. Even Herod is filled with disgust and finally breaks out 'Kill this woman'. The soldiers crush Salome beneath their shields.

There can be few operatic scores that possess such originality as *Salome*. The curtain rises at the first notes of the music, a dark run on the clarinets, the macabre, seductive Salome theme, a resplendent string *tremolo*. The sensual, sultry atmosphere is

clearly evoked in these very first notes, and as the first scene develops the essential conflicts in the drama are clearly revealed. A snake-like rising theme accompanies Salome's entrance, and a

shimmering, dance-like rhythm follows, wonderfully portraying

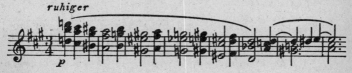

the atmosphere surrounding her. The Jews' characteristic theme appears several times in the orchestra, and then

follow the important themes of the prophet. Musically the figure of Jokanaan is pervaded with a calm grandeur; clear

harmonies underlie broad, simple, soaring tunes in vital contrast with Salome's colourful, opalescent music. A lambent theme which expresses her desire makes itself felt, and is followed by

the expansive lyrical theme of Salome's passionate love, until

she finally breaks out into her abandoned cry of desire.

Ich will dei-nen Mund   Küs - sen,   Jo-cha - na - an!
(*I want to kiss your   mouth,   Jo - ka - na - an!*)

The prophet curses her, and this theme rises in majestic grandeur against the savage passion of her music. This scene between Jokanaan and Salome is built up with tremendous dramatic power and tension in the orchestra which reaches an exceptional symphonic height as it develops and varies Jokanaan's and Salome's motifs in a steady flow, rising to its climax in a *fortissimo* presentation of Jokanaan's theme, and then moves into the great orchestral interlude.

With the entrance of Herod the music becomes even more colourful and opulent. The Jews' quintet is one of the boldest passages in the score, with extremely audacious weaving of the vocal parts, but unfortunately its performance often borders on caricature. The music for Salome's dance is written with real genius. It is based on two exotic, seductive dance-themes which are surrounded by all the Salome motifs in a voluptuous *crescendo* building up to the final moment of ecstasy.

The last scene is as repellent as it is musically superb. It is the symphonic climax of the opera in which all the themes flow together and are finally crowned by the splendid tune of Salome's passion. The power of this resplendent music makes one forget the ugliness and horror of the scene, because all one's emotions are perforce concentrated on the sweeping hypnotic music.

Strauss found the text for his next opera in a poem by Hugo von Hofmannsthal. The one-act tragedy, *Elektra*, made a deep impression on him at the first reading, and this was strengthened by a stage production by Max Reinhardt. The subject of *Elektra* is gloomy and bitter, and the background against which the events take place is more horrible than the atmosphere of *Salome*, for in line with the myths of heroic prehistory it is all of gigantic proportions.

ELEKTRA. Musical tragedy in one act by Richard Strauss. Text by Hugo von Hofmannsthal. First performance: Dresden, 1909.

Characters: Klytämnestra (Clytemnestra)—mezzo-soprano; Elektra (Electra) and Chrysothemis, her daughters—sopranos; Aegisth (Aegisthus)—tenor; Orest (Orestes)—baritone; Orest's tutor—bass; the confidante—soprano; the train-bearer—soprano; a young servant—tenor; an old servant—bass; the overseer—soprano; five maids—one contralto, two mezzo-sopranos, two sopranos. Slaves.

Place: Mycenae. *Time:* after the Trojan war.

After the death of their father, Agamemnon, Electra and Chrysothemis have led unhappy lives in their mother's palace. Electra lives like an animal, neglecting herself and behaving with unpredictable wariness, so that she arouses only antipathy and fear in others. She is obsessed with the idea of revenge against her mother Clytemnestra, and her mother's cowardly lover Aegisthus, for the murder of her father.

The scene represents the inner courtyard of the palace of Mycenae. The maids are chattering at the well, when Electra steals furtively past them. The maids only have unpleasant words for the princess who lets herself be beaten and eats with the dogs. Only the youngest girl stands up for her. The overseer sends them all into the palace, whence can be heard the cries of the youngest maid, whom the others are beating for her love for Electra. Electra comes out of the house. She relives the murder of her father, and intoxicates herself with the thought of avenging his death with the help of Chrysothemis and Orestes, who has not yet returned to Mycenae. She works herself into a frenzy of triumph, and dances as she will dance on the graves of her victims. When Chrysothemis enters and calls her sister's name, Electra starts as if waking from a dream. Chrysothemis warns her against their mother who wants to shut her in a dark tower. Chrysothemis can no longer stand the life she is leading with her sister; she cannot share Electra's brooding on revenge and wants to escape from the misery which is destroying them both. Younger than her sister, she is not so conscious of the horrible murder as Electra, and she is consumed with longing for a normal life.

Noises coming from the palace announce the arrival of Clytemnestra. Chrysothemis warns her sister once more against the Queen, and then rushes out to avoid meeting her. Electra is left alone to face her hated mother, who in turn hates and fears her. A fantastic retinue of servants and slaves passes before the windows which are lit by crude torches; animals for a sacrifice are brought in. Finally Clytemnestra appears in the doorway, bloated and disfigured by debauchery. She is haunted by hideous dreams, and demands that the wise Electra suggest a way in which the gods can be placated, so she may sleep. Electra declares she will be freed when a certain sacrifice, a woman, falls beneath the axe at the hand of a man of their kin. Clytemnestra does not understand the horrible insinuations, until Electra springs at her, crying that she herself must die. The confidante comes out and whispers in Clytemnestra's ear. Casting a triumphant glance at Electra, she goes in, supported by her servants.

Chrysothemis comes out, bringing the terrible news that Orestes has died under his horse's hoofs. Electra will not believe this, but if it should be true the duty of vengeance would fall on her and Chrysothemis alone. Chrysothemis is young and strong and must help her. The more Electra urges her on, the more Chrysothemis shrinks from her and finally rushes out in horror, followed by Electra's curses. Electra stands alone, and must accomplish the act of vengeance single-handed. She had previously hidden the axe with which Agamemnon was killed, and now goes to dig it up. At that moment she sees a stranger in the doorway; it is Orestes. They do not recognize each other, and at first he takes Electra for a maid; he says he has come to tell the Queen of Orestes's death.

Only when Electra tells him her name does he reveal his identity, and Electra's ferocity relaxes into tenderness and lyricism. They rejoice at the prospect of revenge. The confidante appears to take Orestes and his tutor before the Queen. Electra is alone, lamenting that she has not given him the axe of revenge. She hears shouts, and believes she hears Clytemnestra's voice crying out fearfully. 'Strike her again,' cries Electra. Chrysothemis and the maids enter the courtyard, drawn by the noises coming from the palace, and hurry in in terror. Aegisthus strolls into the courtyard, expecting to hear confirmation of the good news of Orestes's death. Electra, circling weirdly round him, offers to light his way with her torch in derisive zeal. Surprised by her unusual behaviour, Aegisthus hurries into the palace, only to reappear at a window calling for help, before he too suffers Clytemnestra's fate. Chrysothemis enters and joins in her sister's joy at Orestes's return. Electra's aim is fulfilled, and revenge has now been taken. Drunk with her triumph she begins to dance; no longer conscious of her surroundings, she whirls around like a maenad at ever more frenzied speed until she falls dead to the ground at the climax of her ecstasy. Chrysothemis rushes to the door of the palace and pounds on it, crying 'Orestes'.

Agamemnon's motif is the basis for the tragedy of *Elektra*. It appears at the beginning as the curtain rises, like a passionate accusation, and returns at the end, menacing and inflexible.

In between it recurs in Electra's monologues whenever she invokes her father's shade and sometimes it even moves splendidly to the major. This harsh, heroic theme is set against the main theme of the opera, a fervent, expansive melody, which points to Electra's strong attachment to her father, and the deep emotion which binds Agamemnon and his children. In con-

trast to the harshness of Electra's music, Chrysothemis's womanly feelings are rendered in glowing, beautiful melodies and rich harmonies, which never deteriorate into weakness but clearly declare the heroic origins of this daughter of Agamemnon. The fact that Electra is also capable of gentler emotions is revealed in the recognition scene with Orestes, where the wonderfully delicate orchestral tunes are also taken up by Electra. The musical and psychological climax of the opera comes in the scene with Clytemnestra. Her entrance is announced by savage, driving music, and a fearful excitement pervades her dialogue with Electra. The gruesome reality of the two women's emotions is revealed in the details of the music; suppressed evil grows during their quarrel to undisguised mutual hatred, and the expressive power of the orchestral accompaniment is as overwhelming here as in the rest of the score.

By comparison with the myriad glittering colours in the score of *Salome*, that of *Elektra* seems more bitter and more grandiose, but immeasurably more savage, which makes it harder to understand at first. In keeping with the harsh, angular idiom the musical phrases are mostly abrupt, but they blossom out into real *cantilena* wherever gentler feelings break through. The general effect of the music is shattering. The harmonies were in their day of unprecedented daring, interweaving and clashing regardless of dissonance, and the development of the various motifs is so complete that one can hardly take it all in at a first hearing. The orchestration is also very original, being written for one hundred and fifteen players—about the largest possible number for an opera orchestra.

These two gloomy tragedies of fate were directly followed by the glowing vitality and gaiety of *Der Rosenkavalier*, and one can scarcely imagine a more complete stylistic reversal. The first performance of this work also took place in Dresden, and provoked a greater sensation than anything which had gone before. Fifty performances in Dresden, all sold out well in advance, led to a series of successful performances in all major musical centres in Germany and elsewhere. These triumphs were largely due to Hofmannsthal's libretto, which formed a superb basis for the music with its colourful plot, its charm, gaiety, linguistic beauty and psychological insight.

DER ROSENKAVALIER (The Knight of the Rose). Opera in three acts by Richard Strauss. Text by Hugo von Hofmannsthal. First performance: Dresden, 1911.

Characters: The Feldmarschallin, Princess von Werdenberg—soprano; Baron Ochs von Lerchenau, her cousin—bass; Octavian Rofrano, nick-named Quinquin, a young nobleman—mezzo-soprano; Herr von Faninal, a wealthy *parvenu*—baritone; Sophie, his daughter—soprano; Marianne Leitmetzerin, her duenna—soprano; Valzacchi, an intriguer—tenor; Annina, his colleague—contralto; a commissar of police—bass; a notary—bass; an innkeeper—tenor; a singer—tenor; three noble orphans—soprano, mezzo-soprano and contralto; the Princess's major-domo—tenor; Faninal's major-domo—tenor; a dressmaker—soprano; a dog-breeder—tenor; servants of the Princess, of Baron Ochs, and of Faninal; four waiters; a little negro page; a flute-player; a hairdresser; a scholar; a noble widow.

Place: Vienna. *Time:* the reign of the Empress Maria Theresa (1740–80).

Act I. A bedroom in the Princess's palace. It is early morning, and birds are singing in the garden. The orchestral prelude suggests a scene of passionate love-making, and as the curtain rises Octavian, a youth of seventeen, is kneeling by the bed embracing the Princess who is lying on it. She is thirty-two, and fully aware that soon she will lose him to a younger woman. They exchange tender words, and the little negro page brings in the Princess's morning chocolate. The Princess in her negligée is served with elaborate, light-hearted courtesy by Octavian. A noise is heard in the antechamber, and at first the Princess fears it is her husband returning from his hunting expedition, but fortunately it is only her cousin, Ochs von Lerchenau, who forces his way in past the servants. Octavian, who has slipped into the clothes closet, now returns in a maid's dress and cap and tries to slip out, but the Baron catches the 'pretty maid' by the arm. Baron Ochs has come to announce to his cousin his betrothal to the only daughter of the extremely rich but middle-class Herr von Faninal. During his account of this satisfactory arrangement Ochs's eyes do not for a moment leave the charming 'Mariandl', and to the great amusement of the Princess 'she' encourages the Baron's advances. He asks his cousin to appoint a noble cavalier to present a silver rose on his behalf to his lady as a token of his suit, such being then the custom. Mischievously the Princess suggests the young Count Octavian Rofrano and shows Ochs a locket with his portrait. Lerchenau is at once struck by the singular likeness between the portrait and Mariandl, and then remarks with a grin that the old Count Rofrano must have sown some wild oats. It is now time for the Princess's levée, and a varied crowd of petitioners enter as Octavian slips out unnoticed. Three noble orphans, encouraged by their mother, make a diffident plea for help, a dressmaker and a dog-seller present their wares for the Princess to inspect, and a tenor-singer renders a languishing, tender aria in the style of the time. While this crowd mills to and fro, a hairdresser arranges the Princess's hair and she permits her chef to present the day's menu, while Ochs discusses his marriage contract with the notary. Valzacchi and Annina, a couple of

professional intriguers, offer Ochs their doubtful services. Ochs gives the
Princess a box containing the silver rose, asking her to pass it on to
Octavian. The Princess, looking at the result of the hairdresser's efforts in
the mirror, accuses him of turning her into an old woman. She dismisses
everyone, and left to her own thoughts she recalls her youth and falls a
prey to melancholy. Octavian, dressed in a riding habit, returns and invites her to ride with him. She is touched by his passionate wooing, but
knows that he will eventually forget her. Octavian denies this hotly and
reasserts his love, but she sends him away, and he leaves petulantly. No
sooner has he gone than the Princess remembers that she did not kiss him
farewell and she sends her servants to call him back, but he has already
left the house. She gives the box with the silver rose to her little negro
page to take to Octavian and looks again at her face in the mirror as the
curtain falls.

Act II. The reception room in Faninal's house. Faninal is happy and
proud to have found an aristocratic husband for his daughter. He goes to
fetch Baron Ochs, leaving Sophie to receive the Knight of the Rose.
Sophie is full of awed, suppressed excitement as she awaits the arrival of
the Rose-Cavalier. Shouts of 'Rofrano' are heard from the street; the
Knight of the Rose is approaching the palace with his retinue. Sophie's
duenna at the window reports every detail of his arrival. The door is
thrown open and there stands Octavian, all in white and silver, followed
by his servants in white and pale green; he enters, the silver rose in his
hand, and presents it to Sophie with great ceremony. After the servants
have withdrawn, Sophie, Octavian and the duenna seat themselves and
there begins a formal conversation during which Octavian and Sophie
move their chairs closer to each other. Ochs then appears accompanied
by Faninal and followed by his unkempt, disorderly servants. Sophie is
horrified by the manners of her future husband, who treats her without
respect. Ochs's eye falls on Octavian, and he is astonished at the resemblance to 'Mariandl' whom he believes to be Octavian's natural sister.
Octavian is unpleasantly surprised by Ochs's behaviour towards Sophie,
whom he fondles and slaps, ignoring her indignant, hurt innocence and
blithely assuming that she will quickly learn to respond to his love-
making. He woos her with a ravishing waltz-song. Faninal and his future
son-in-law go into the next room to sign the marriage contract, and the
duenna hurries out to still the turmoil caused by Ochs's servants molesting
Faninal's maids. Sophie and Octavian are thus left alone, and realizing
their love for each other they confess it in a delicate duet 'Mit ihren
Augen voll Tränen' ('With her eyes full of tears'). Valzacchi and Annina
have however been spying on them, and seizing them they summon
Ochs, who is quite unconcerned. However, when he tries to take Sophie
into the adjoining room to sign the contract, Octavian draws his sword.
For better or worse Ochs must draw too and Octavian wounds him
slightly in the arm. Everyone gathers round to help Ochs, while Sophie
tells her father that she can never marry him. Faninal is horrified at the
scandal. Octavian can do nothing but withdraw; but before he does so
he has a short interview with the two intriguers. Ochs recovers slowly
from his fright; he looks on Sophie's shrinking from him as a joke, and

is not at all worried. He merrily hums the waltz-tune, and is delighted when Annina returns with a letter from 'Mariandl' asking him to meet her the following night.

Act III. A private room in an inn outside Vienna. Octavian (disguised as Mariandl), Valzacchi, Annina and the innkeeper are making preparations for the amorous rendezvous with the Baron. Masked men are hidden behind curtains, under trap-doors and so on; Valzacchi shows Octavian a large bed in an alcove; the table is laid and candles are lit. Everyone disappears. Baron Ochs, one arm still in a sling, the other on Mariandl's arm, enters the room beaming with pleasure. Octavian most adroitly conveys the innocence and prudery of a young country-girl, and Ochs is thoroughly roused, although Mariandl's face continually reminds him of 'that damned young man'. Ochs relaxes, removes his coat and his wig, and is being heavily gallant when strange heads start appearing and disappearing all round the room. Ochs at first thinks they are ghosts, but the apparitions become more and more frequent until a heavily veiled lady in mourning appears at a window (Annina in disguise), claiming that Ochs is her husband; four children run in, crying 'Papa, papa'. The innkeeper and a waiter rush in, Ochs thinks he is in a madhouse, opens the window and calls for the police. The commissar, who arrives a moment later, takes it all very seriously. Faninal and Sophie arrive next, having received a message to come to the inn to meet Ochs, but of course sent for by Octavian. Faninal is most indignant at his future son-in-law's behaviour, all the more so when he learns that Ochs has tried to pass off Mariandl as Sophie. He is ready to collapse, and is hurriedly escorted into an adjoining room. Octavian now reveals his identity to the commissar and quickly changes his clothes. Meanwhile the Princess arrives, and satisfies the commissar by telling him it was all a jest. When Ochs realizes that Octavian and Mariandl are one and the same person, the Princess's relationship with Octavian dawns on him. She, however, reminds him of his rank and obligation to keep silent. She also requests him to leave Vienna, seeing that he has lost the game. Sophie tells him on her father's behalf that the engagement is finished, and there is nothing for Ochs to do but leave. As he does so, however, there is a great scene, with the innkeeper presenting the bill, Annina running in with the shouting children, and the waiter and the musician demanding tips. Calm returns to the stage. Octavian, quite at a loss, stands between the two women, not knowing what to do. The Princess leads Sophie up to him, and then withdraws and leaves them alone. The young couple fall happily into each other's arms. The Princess returns with Faninal whom she has invited to ride back to Vienna with her in her coach. As if spellbound the young couple stay behind for a few moments, and then they rush out; in doing so, Sophie drops her handkerchief. The stage is empty; then in comes the little negro page with a candle, searches for the handkerchief, finds it, and runs out again as the curtain falls.

The music for *Der Rosenkavalier* is the epitome of rococo art, and yet wholly original; in fact the work of a genius. It is as though Strauss had conjured up the spirit of Mozart and clothed it in a new and colourful garment. He ignored the traditional forms of rococo music and completely disregarded historical accuracy. One example is his choice of the waltz, and not the minuet, to express *joie de vivre* and exuberance.

The overture starts with the bright, swinging fanfare of the Rosenkavalier theme, and goes on to present the mutual love of young Octavian and the mature Princess in the prime of life,

in luscious colours and exquisite melodies. The expansive, deeply felt theme of the Marschallin introduces the first scene, which abounds in musical delights, such as the delicious little march when the negro page comes in, the elegant, minuet-like waltz which accompanies the gay breakfast conversation, and the over-solemn flourishes of the march which announces the entry of the coarse country nobleman Ochs, who is always trying to play the man of the world. The levée is a masterly piece of musical tapestry in which all the threads of interests, thoughts and feelings are woven together with consummate skill.

The entrance of the Rosenkavalier in the second act marks a glorious climax, as the harmonies become increasingly, brilliantly concentrated, and the Rosenkavalier theme rises to a radiant *fortissimo* and then dies away with infinite delicacy to give way to the enchanting theme of the silver rose, with its

strange, tinkling stream of harmonies in the flutes, solo strings and celeste. This silvery splendour also envelops the first tentative exchanges between the two young people, who seem to float on a cloud of blissful unreality. The second part of the act is dominated by Ochs's irresistible waltz-tune, which he keeps

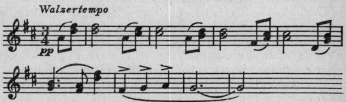

humming to himself, and which eventually brings the act to its sweeping close. Waltz themes also accompany the colourful events of the third act; the tunes blend elaborately with increasing grace and delicacy and the waltz which finally unfolds develops into a caricature of the gallant Baron when he makes his ignominious exit.

From the ensuing calm arises the glorious final ensemble. The three women's voices blend in a trio of unearthly beauty and their different feelings unite in an amazing unity. The trio starts with a sweeping melody for the Marschallin, in which

Sophie and Octavian join with delicate reserve. A simple tune then unites the two young lovers in a tender duet around which play the colourful, tinkling harmonies of the theme of the silver rose.

Strauss's first operatic 'period' ended with *Ariadne auf Naxos* (1912), an original masterpiece which developed somewhat unfortunately. Strauss originally planned this short opera to be performed after Molière's comedy *Le Bourgeois Gentilhomme*, but when he had finished the score it was found that the work ran for eighty minutes instead of twenty. This meant a shift of emphasis from play to opera, and the original idea of performing it in Max Reinhardt's Deutsches Theater in Berlin had to be abandoned. There was no question of using the huge stage of the Dresden Opera, where all previous Strauss premières had taken place, for this intimate little work, and the final choice fell on the small theatre in Stuttgart, which would make an ideal setting both for Molière and for *Ariadne*.

The idea of uniting play and opera was already seen to be a failure at the première itself. The comedy, though compressed into two acts and accompanied by some enchanting music, was too long and too exhausting for the audience to give its full attention to the somewhat complicated opera which followed. Even extensive cuts could not correct this fault, and Strauss and Hofmannsthal therefore resolved on a radical solution; they abandoned Molière altogether and wrote a prologue to explain the strange origins of the opera itself. *Ariadne* was first performed in this version in Vienna in 1917, and even if this new form was not completely satisfactory, at least it achieved the essential point by concentrating attention on the opera, which perhaps contains some of the most beautiful passages Strauss had yet written.

ARIADNE AUF NAXOS (Ariadne on Naxos). Opera in one act and a prologue by Richard Strauss. Text by Hugo von Hofmannsthal. First performance of the new version: Vienna, 1917.

Characters in the Prologue: the major-domo—speaking role; the composer—soprano; the music-master—baritone; the dancing-master —tenor; the prima donna (later Ariadne)—soprano; the tenor (later Bacchus)—tenor; Zerbinetta—soprano; Harlequin—baritone; Scaramuccio—tenor; Truffaldino—bass; Brighella—tenor; an officer—tenor; the wig-maker—bass; a lackey—bass.

Characters in the Opera: Ariadne—soprano; Bacchus—tenor; Naiad—soprano; Dryad—contralto; Echo—soprano; Zerbinetta—soprano; Harlequin—baritone; Scaramuccio—tenor; Truffaldino—bass; Brighella —tenor.

Place: Vienna and the island of Naxos. *Time:* middle of the eighteenth century and classical antiquity.

Prologue. The town house of a *nouveau riche* Viennese. A grand party is about to take place, for which the host has commissioned the opera *Ariadne auf Naxos*, but feeling that his guests might be bored by such a serious work he decides to follow it with a light intermezzo *Zerbinetta and her lovers*. The young composer of the opera is in despair when he learns this, but worse is in store: shortly before the beginning of the performance it is announced that the two entertainments are to take place simultaneously, with interludes of singing and dancing punctuating the opera.

The composer is determined not to be associated with this ludicrous idea, which would bring him so much humiliation, but the charming *soubrette* Zerbinetta succeeds in convincing him that the performance can be so arranged by cutting the opera here and there and shortening the play a little. She and her companions are accustomed to improvise and they guarantee that all will go smoothly. The composer agrees to everything. Only when they give the signal for the beginning of the performance does he come out of his trance and realize too late that he should never have allowed his opera to be so abused.

Opera. The scene represents a deserted island with a cave in the background where Ariadne lives. When the curtain rises Ariadne is lying asleep in front of her cave, watched over by three nymphs who lament her sad fate. A deep sigh indicates that Ariadne is awake, but she only slowly regains consciousness. She recalls the memory of Theseus in beautiful melodies, but she has no further desire to contemplate earthly joys, her only wish being to enter the realms of death, whose messenger, Hermes, will receive and welcome her. Zerbinetta and her companions try repeatedly to interrupt Ariadne's outbursts of despair and console her in her anguish, but all is in vain, and Ariadne pays no attention to this gay quintet. Zerbinetta cannot understand such persistent sorrow and asks her companions to distract the Princess with merry songs and dances. Finally Zerbinetta abandons her mask of cheerfulness and turns to Ariadne as woman to woman, to persuade her to a happier view of love; all men are faithless, and no lost love is worth weeping over, since love and faith are subject to perpetual change. Ariadne retires into her cave. Harlequin, who sees in Zerbinetta an excellent partner for a game of love, openly declares himself to her. She does not seem unwilling, and the other three join in, each trying to win Zerbinetta himself. Only Harlequin stands aside, sure that the final victory will be his. In the end he and Zerbinetta fall into each other's arms and the others, neglected and depressed, stop their dance.

The nymphs rush in, full of excitement, to announce the arrival of Bacchus and to tell how this demigod has fled from the enchantress Circe, who tried to change him into an animal. In the distance the voice of Bacchus is heard, still singing of the charms of Circe. Ariadne comes out of the cave, drawn by his voice as if by a spell. The nymphs sing in trio 'Töne, töne, süsse Stimme' ('Sing on, sing on, gentle singer'). When Bacchus approaches Ariadne, she believes he is the longed-for messenger of death, and sinks on to his breast. Ariadne feels that the messenger of the gods has wrought a subtle change in her, and Bacchus too realizes that he has altered under the power of love. The cave of sorrow is to become that of pleasure for them, and a canopy slowly descends on the two lovers as they embrace passionately. As in a dream the trio of nymphs is once again heard in the distance. Zerbinetta peeps out from behind the scenery, delighted at the happy outcome of Ariadne's fate.

The prologue merely serves to establish the curious mixture of *opera seria* and *opera buffa* which we are to experience in the opera in such disconcerting form, and introduces the two protagonists as private people in ordinary clothes, so that we may laugh at the vanity and affectations of the prima donna and the tenor, as well as at the frivolous superficiality of the *buffo* characters. Strauss has drawn the character of his composer with great affection. His fiery, youthful theme in various forms

dominates the whole prologue, and his role is portrayed in a sweeping, melodious vocal line, in contrast to the lightly bustling recitative in which the gay, innocuous proceedings are conducted.

The opera proper starts with a short, very characteristic overture describing Ariadne's sorrow and anguish of spirit, and the same themes return in her monologue. From amongst a plenitude of beautiful musical passages the radiant theme of the messenger of death (which later returns significantly at Bacchus's

entrance) is outstanding. A grand, passionate theme wells up to the highest pitch of ecstasy in this final scene. The music

glows with increasing warmth as the death theme rises to
fortissimo and gives way to the theme of love, which bursts out
at first in magnificent splendour and then with infinite delicacy
dies away.

The dainty microcosm of the *opera buffa* is contrasted with
this sublime operatic pathos and the two worlds at times even
intermingle. The first ensemble in which Zerbinetta asks her
companions to cheer Ariadne by dancing and singing is among
the most ravishing ensembles ever written for *buffo* opera; a
rather leisurely theme, which was frequently heard in the

etwas behäbig

Es gilt, ob Tan-zen, ob Sin-gen tau-ge, von
(*Can song or dance some new ma-gic bor-row to*

Trä-nen zu trock-nen ein schö-nes Au-ge
ba-nish the tears of a mai-den's sor-row)

prologue, provides its basis and round it the other voices gather
with gay flourishes, through which the main theme surges up
again and again, drawing everything along with it. The second
quintet, which culminates in a dashing waltz, is also quite
charming in its exuberance, but it cannot match the soaring,
carefree lightness of the first ensemble. The show piece of the
opera is Zerbinetta's great aria, which in daring coloratura,
chains of trills and decoration of every kind exceeds all the demands of classical Italian music. These vocal acrobatics, however, are blended with wit and high spirits as an apt expression
of Zerbinetta's capricious and charming personality. The
abundance of exquisite musical inspiration in this score is unrivalled, and makes *Ariadne auf Naxos* the undisputed crown of
Strauss's creative work. If this strange opera is not properly
appreciated as yet, this is due, as often happens, to the over-
literary text. Hofmannsthal—Strauss's favourite librettist—was
not nearly so successful with *Ariadne* as he was with *Der
Rosenkavalier*.

The next collaboration of Strauss and Hofmannsthal was even
less fortunate. *Die Frau ohne Schatten*, in spite of impressive,

beautiful and clear music, failed to make any real impression. The strange, symbolic story—an attempt to write a modern version of *Die Zauberflöte*—actually impeded the success of the music. This opera, finished in 1917, was first performed in Vienna in 1919.

DIE FRAU OHNE SCHATTEN (The Woman without a Shadow). Opera in three acts by Richard Strauss. Text by Hugo von Hofmannsthal. First performance: Vienna, 1919.

Characters: the Emperor of the South Eastern Islands—tenor; the Empress—soprano; the nurse—mezzo-soprano; a spirit-messenger—baritone; the voice of the falcon—soprano; the voice from above—contralto; the keeper of the gates of the temple—soprano or falsetto tenor; apparition of a youth—tenor; Barak, the dyer—bass-baritone; his wife—soprano; the One-eyed, the One-armed and the Hunchback, Barak's brothers—two basses and a tenor. Six children's voices—three sopranos and three contraltos; voices of the nightwatchmen—three basses. Servants of the Emperor, children, spirits.

Place: legendary. *Time:* legendary.

Act I. The Imperial Gardens. The young Empress, a supernatural being, daughter of Keikobad, king of the spirits, has been married for a year without bearing a child, and therefore without acquiring a shadow—the shadow being the symbol of fertility. Assured that this is the case, the spirit-messenger tells the nurse, who is crouching on the flat roof above the garden, that in three days' time the Empress must return to her father, while the Emperor will be turned into stone. The Emperor enters and tells how he found his wife; she stepped out of a white gazelle he shot while out hunting. Since that day he has not seen his favourite falcon. He tells the nurse that he is going hunting for three days. The Empress enters and hears the falcon's voice relating the fate in store for her and her husband. To avoid this she decides on the nurse's advice to buy a shadow from a mortal. An orchestral interlude marks their descent to earth, and the scene changes to the poor hut of the dyer Barak, where the dyer's three deformed brothers are fighting. The good-natured dyer is contrasted with his nagging wife in the scene which follows. His only reproach to her is that she has not borne him a child in the nine months of their marriage. He goes out to market, and the Empress and the nurse enter, dressed as servants. The nurse works on the vanity and greed of the dyer's wife until she agrees to sell her hopes of motherhood. The visitors leave, promising to return. When Barak comes home he finds his bed separated from that of his wife, but assumes that this is only a temporary measure.

Act II, scene i. Barak's hut. The nurse tempts the dyer's wife with the apparition of a handsome youth, but the woman cannot quite bring herself to deceive her husband.

Scene ii. The forest. The Emperor has found his falcon again. He finds the Empress and feels sure that she has been in contact with earthly things in his absence.

Scene iii. Barak's hut. The nurse and the dyer's wife go out together; left alone with Barak, the Empress feels the first stirrings of pity for him and guilt at what she is doing.

Scene iv. The Empress's bedroom in the falcon-house, where she and the nurse are sleeping. She dreams of the falcon's words in the first scene, but now thinks of Barak's distress as well.

Scene v. Barak's hut. A storm is gathering, and Barak's three brothers are howling in animal fear. The dyer's wife tells her husband what she has done, and by lighting a fire it is proved that she throws no shadow. When he threatens to kill her she is overwhelmed with remorse, and says that she only *wanted* to sell her shadow. The Empress and the nurse leave and the earth swallows up the hut and its occupants.

Act III. A subterranean vault, with a wall down the middle. Barak and his wife, one on either side, are unaware of the other's presence. The vault vanishes and the Empress and the nurse enter. The Empress is summoned to appear before her father, Keikobad, which she is ready to do, knowing her husband is being judged there also. The nurse is afraid and wants her to return to earth to find herself a shadow. Called on to drink the water of life, the Empress refuses, since this will be the undoing of Barak and his wife. She resists the temptation, even when she sees her husband turned to stone, his eyes pleading with her for life. As soon as she cries 'I will not', her renunciation brings her husband back to life and causes her to cast a shadow. They are happily reunited, as are also Barak and his wife, to the sound of the voices of their unborn children.

Strauss wrote his own libretto for his next opera, *Intermezzo*, which belongs, together with the symphonic poems *Ein Heldenleben* and *Sinfonia domestica*, to his autobiographical works. In the twelve scenes of this bourgeois comedy with symphonic interludes Strauss relates an episode from his own married life. As he explains in the foreword, he put the maximum of dramatic declamation and lively *tempi* into the musical dialogue, which became thereby a distinctive characteristic of this work. His achievements in *Ariadne auf Naxos* are excelled in *Intermezzo*, where the orchestra does not drown the dialogue but expresses in the symphonic interludes all that could not be said in the accompaniments, which have the most varied emotions to depict.

INTERMEZZO. A bourgeois comedy with symphonic interludes in two acts by Richard Strauss. Text by the composer. First performance: Dresden, 1924.

Characters: Christine—soprano; little Franz, her son, aged eight—speaking role; Hofkapellmeister Robert Storch, her husband—baritone; Anna, her maid—soprano; Baron Lummer—tenor; the notary—baritone;

his wife—soprano; Stroh, a conductor—tenor; a commercial councillor
—bass; a councillor of justice—baritone; a distinguished singer—bass.

Place: Grundlsee and Vienna. *Time:* beginning of the twentieth century.

Act I, scene i. The dressing-room of Storch's house. The Kapellmeister
(conductor) and his wife are packing for his forthcoming tour. She is very
short-tempered with him and with the servants, and after her husband
has left she goes tobogganing with a friend.

Scene ii. The toboggan tracks. Christine collides with a young man on
skis; she abuses him roundly for the accident but when she finds out he is
Baron Lummer her manner changes, she is all over him and invites him
to her house.

Scene iii. An inn at Grundlsee. Christine and the Baron are dancing,
in a lively, light-hearted atmosphere.

Scene iv. The Storch's dining-room. Christine is writing to her husband
about her new young cavalier. The Baron enters, and discusses his future
studies with Frau Storch, who promises him her husband's patronage on
his return.

Scene v. The Baron's lodgings. The Baron, impatient at having to
dance attendance on Frau Storch, writes to ask her for a thousand
marks.

Scene vi. The Storch's dining-room. Christine is highly indignant at
his letter, and when he enters asks him not to spoil their pleasant relationship in this way, but to wait for her husband's return. The maid brings in
a note for Herr Storch, which Christine opens. She reads with horror a
tender request for opera-tickets and a rendezvous 'as usual'. Horrified,
she wires her husband to say that she knows of this liaison and is leaving
him for good.

Scene vii. The child's bedroom. In spite of her melodramatic abuse of
his father, the child accuses her of causing all the unpleasantness.

Act II, scene i. A comfortable sitting-room in the commercial
councillor's house in Vienna. A 'skat' game is in progress; the guests are
discussing Storch's amiability and his wife's unpleasantness when Storch
enters and tells them of Christine's letter and her new escort, the Baron.
He will not listen to criticism of her, and says she is very stimulating and
has a heart of gold. The telegram arrives and fills Storch with consternation. His colleague Stroh, reading it, is astonished to learn that Storch
also knows the lady—one Mieze Meier—who wrote to him, but Storch
is too distraught to take in his remark and leaves quickly, while his friends
comment in surprise on this new aspect of Storch's character.

Scene ii. The notary's office. The notary learns with surprise that
Frau Storch wants a divorce, not on account of the Baron but because of
evidence against her husband.

Scene iii. The Prater in Vienna. A storm is raging. Stroh tells the distracted Storch that Mieze Meier's note was probably meant for him, and
Storch insists that his colleague put the misunderstanding right at once.

Scene iv. Christine's dressing-room. Christine is packing, and scolding
the servants. She is beginning to think that there may have been a misunderstanding, and to regret having sent the Baron off to interview
Mieze Meier, when Stroh is announced.

Scene v. The dining-room. Storch rushes in, to be greeted coldly by Christine. He rounds on her, tells her off severely for her bad temper, and stalks out of the room. Returning, he pretends to be jealous of the Baron, but soon they are laughing together about the whole incident, and their reunion and reconciliation is complete.

Although in portraying her capricious and quarrelsome char-acter Strauss does not spare his heroine in any way, he clearly shows that she is a splendid woman, and that he would not have her any different. The dialogue is full of references which may be incomprehensible to an outsider, but the exchanges, often completely irrelevant, are always lively and amusing. This is of course due to the sparkling music which illustrates the innocuous events most delightfully. It is light-hearted, carefree music, alternating swiftly between light fluent conversation and splendid interludes, which take up the atmosphere and ideas and develop them further. In the few lyrical moments, as for example Christine's longing for her husband in the fifth scene, or the reconciliation at the end of the work, Strauss's great gift for melody is revealed, and supported by rich, glow-ing tones in the orchestra.

The first performance of *Intermezzo* took place in Dresden, in the smaller, drama theatre and not in the Opera House, in keeping with the intimate character of the work.

Die Aegyptische Helena, which was produced in Dresden in 1928, suffers like *Die Frau ohne Schatten* from a confused plot; transferring these classical heroes into a magic fairy-tale has only served to lessen one's interest in them.

DIE AEGYPTISCHE HELENA (The Egyptian Helen). Opera in two acts by Richard Strauss. Text by Hugo von Hofmannsthal. First perform-ance: Dresden, 1928.

Characters: Helena—soprano; Menelaus—tenor; Hermione, their child —soprano; Aithra, daughter of the King of Egypt, a sorceress—soprano; Altair—baritone; Da-Ud, his son—tenor; the Omniscient Sea-shell— contralto.

Place: A small island off the coast of Egypt, and at the foot of the Atlas Mountains. *Time:* after the end of the Trojan War.

Act I. On the island of Aithra. The Omniscient Sea-shell tells Aithra that Menelaus, who is on his way back from Troy, intends to kill his wife, Helen, whom he has just recovered. Aithra raises a storm which wrecks Menelaus's ship. Menelaus carries Helen to the shore of the island and so comes to Aithra. Aithra gives Menelaus a magic potion which makes him

believe that Helen spent the ten years of the Trojan War in Egypt, longing for him, while the Helen stolen by Paris was only a phantom. He and
Helen are reunited in blissful realization of their love.

Act II. A tent in a grove, at the foot of the Atlas Mountains. At
Helen's wish Aithra has brought the lovers here, where no one knows
anything about her. Altair approaches with his son Da-Ud at the head
of a troop of riders. Menelaus, in a fit of blind jealousy, kills Da-Ud.
Helen does not want to live in a dream any longer and gives Menelaus a
potion to restore his memory. His first impulse is to kill Helen, but Aithra
arrives in time and also saves Menelaus from the fury of Altair. Reconciled, the couple return to Sparta.

The music is splendid, particularly the great love-scene in the
first act and the arrival of Altair in the second, the vocal melodies are more glowing than ever, and the orchestration brilliant,
though very restrained when accompanying the singers. All
this musical beauty is, however, not enough to make the work
dramatically effective, because one is too little moved by the
events on the stage. The opera was revised by the composer for
the 1933 Salzburg Festival, and again by Clemens Krauss and
Rudolf Hartmann for Munich in 1940.

Hofmannsthal's last libretto for Strauss, *Arabella*, was another
most successful one, which gave the composer a real source of
inspiration in spite of some psychological exaggeration.

ARABELLA. Lyrical comedy in three acts by Richard Strauss. Text by
Hugo von Hofmannsthal. First performance: Dresden, 1933.

Characters: Count Waldner—bass; Adelaide, his wife—mezzo-
soprano; Arabella and Zdenka, their daughters—sopranos; Mandryka, a
landowner from Walachei—baritone; Matteo, an officer—tenor; Count
Elemer, Count Dominik and Count Lamoral, Arabella's suitors—tenor,
baritone and bass; the 'Fiakermilli'—coloratura soprano; a fortune-
teller—soprano. Servants, Arabella's duenna, three card-players, a doctor,
a groom.

Place: Vienna. *Time:* 1860.

Act I. The salon of a Viennese hotel. Count Waldner is very anxious
to marry his beautiful daughter Arabella to a rich man. He has large
gambling debts and his credit at the hotel is now exhausted; the only
hope seems to be a rich son-in-law. Arabella's younger sister Zdenka is
being brought up as a boy, since Count Waldner cannot afford to have
two daughters coming out at the same time. Zdenka loves an officer
Matteo, who for his part is passionately in love with Arabella, who takes
no notice of him. To console Matteo, Zdenka writes him letters and lets
him think they are from Arabella, who dare not show her love openly.
Arabella has many suitors, but she cannot decide on any one of them and

is still waiting for the right man on whom to bestow her love. Count Waldner has written for financial help to a rich and eccentric former army comrade of his, enclosing a portrait of Arabella. As soon as Mandryka, the nephew and heir of the rich friend, sees the portrait he falls in love with Arabella and comes to Vienna to ask for her hand. He is very successful with the Count, who is fascinated by his bulging wallet. With the words 'Teschek, bedien' dich' (Please, help yourself') he offers Waldner the wallet, and Waldner helps himself. Mandryka seems very pleasant and sincere, and Waldner wants to introduce him to his wife and daughters at once, but Mandryka refuses. He will stay at the hotel and wait until he is called. That afternoon Arabella had met a strange gentleman who made a great impression on her, and she is now longing to see him again. It is the Shrove Tuesday Carnival; Arabella is in an odd mood; she is to go to a masked ball, the 'Fiakerball' (a 'Fiaker' is a two-horse cab) that night, and she feels that something exciting is going to happen.

Act II. A ballroom. Here Mandryka meets Arabella, who seems to him to be even more beautiful than in the picture. Arabella recognizes him as the man she saw that afternoon. Mandryka is astonished that her father has not told Arabella of his request for her hand, and discloses to Arabella his love for her. She also thinks that he is the right man for her. If, Mandryka says, she were a girl from Slavonia, his country, she would go that evening to the fountain for a glass of pure water and bring it to him as a sign of their betrothal. Arabella asks Mandryka to give her another hour in which to take leave of her girlhood. Mandryka orders a magnificent champagne supper for all his well-wishers, while Arabella goes into the ballroom where she is welcomed as the queen of the ball. Zdenka gives Matteo a letter which is supposed to come from Arabella. There is a key in it, which, Zdenka murmurs to him, will open Arabella's room. He must go to the hotel at once, and Arabella will follow in a quarter of an hour. Mandryka overhears this dialogue and believes he is being betrayed since Arabella has in fact left the ball. He pretends to be merry, and flirts with the Fiakermilli, a pretty girl, extravagantly dolled up for the occasion. Waldner reproaches him for such behaviour, unbecoming in a fiancé, and asks him to accompany him to the hotel to clear up the misunderstanding.

Act III. The hall of the hotel. Arabella returns from the ball in a happy mood. Matteo, coming downstairs, is astonished to meet her in the hall, and cannot understand her coldness, since he has just been embracing her in her room. His mounting ardour and excitement only serve to bewilder Arabella. Waldner, the Countess and Mandryka arrive, and the latter, recognizing Matteo as the man who had the key to Arabella's room, is furious, ignores his fiancée's protestations and is about to challenge Matteo to a duel, when Zdenka, in a negligée, comes down the stairs and confesses that it was *she* who wrote the note to Matteo, and that the key opened *her* room. It was dark, and Matteo could not have known. Arabella sweetly comforts and supports her sister, and Mandryka asks for Zdenka's hand in Matteo's name. Their happiness assured, everyone retires, leaving the contrite Mandryka with Arabella. She asks a servant to get a glass of water from the fountain in the courtyard and bring it to her room. She goes upstairs, and Mandryka is left alone in despair. Then Arabella reappears at the head of the staircase; she is carrying a glass of water on a tray and solemnly approaches Mandryka, to give him the symbolic drink. Mandryka drinks it in one gulp and Arabella falls into his arms.

Strauss clothed his *Arabella* in music of magical redolence and noble mastery. The characterization of the many and varied personalities is exceptionally lucid and the vocal line is consistently lush and melodious. Lyrical episodes of elegant delicacy are freely interspersed into the light dialogues, as for instance the sisters' duet in the first act, in which Arabella

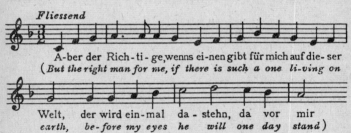

Fliessend

A-ber der Rich-ti-ge, wenns ei-nen gibt für mich auf die-ser
(*But the right man for me, if there is such a one li-ving on*

Welt, der wird ein-mal da-stehn, da vor mir
earth, be-fore my eyes he will one day stand)

declares that she must wait for the right man. Here Strauss uses a Jugoslav folk tune and fills the simple melody with all Arabella's girlish sweetness and awkwardness. The duet between Arabella and Mandryka in the second act is also based on

Andante mosso

Und du wirst mein Ge-bie-ter sein, und ich dir un-ter-tan —
(*And you shall give the orders, sir, and I shall do your will*)

a Jugoslav folk song, and their strong, uncomplicated devotion is ideally rendered in this simple duet. Mandryka's music has throughout a popular flavour which matches his forthright manner. The unsophisticated tunes, the gay orchestral colours,

Presto

Kom-men mei - ne Ver-wal-ter: was ists mit unserm Herrn?
(*Come then my — masters, what is the mat-ter with our lord?*)

the simple harmonies and the Viennese waltzes in the score all express gaiety and happiness and create that carefree atmosphere which is the charm of the music of *Arabella*.

Die Schweigsame Frau, first performed in Dresden in 1935, is another comic opera. Stefan Zweig's amusing libretto, based on a comedy by Ben Jonson, takes up the popular comic theme of the duped uncle, which Donizetti had also exploited in his *Don Pasquale*.

DIE SCHWEIGSAME FRAU (The Silent Woman). Opera in three acts by Richard Strauss. Text by Stefan Zweig after Ben Jonson's comedy *Epicoene, or the Silent Woman*. First performance: Dresden, 1935.

Characters: Sir Morosus, a retired admiral—bass; his housekeeper—contralto; Schneidebart, a barber—baritone; Henry, Sir Morosus's nephew, an actor—tenor; Aminta, his wife, an actress—coloratura soprano; Isotta and Carlotta, actresses—coloratura soprano and mezzo-soprano; Morbio, Vanuzzi and Farfallo, actors—baritone and two basses. Other actors, neighbours, etc.

Place: Sir Morosus's house in a London suburb. *Time:* about 1780.

Act I. A room in Morosus's house. The room is untidy and shows that Sir Morosus is a retired sailor. The housekeeper tries to enlist the barber's help in persuading her master that he should marry her, but the barber does not think much of the idea. Sir Morosus enters, complaining bitterly about the noise people are always making around him, and bemoaning his lonely bachelor state. The barber, challenged by Morosus, undertakes to find him a young and silent wife. His nephew Henry, whom he had thought dead, enters, and he greets him with real delight, which however turns to anger when he hears Henry has become an actor and brought his troupe along with him. The old man refuses to acknowledge Aminta as his niece, disinherits Henry and orders the barber to find him a wife at once. As soon as he has left the room, barber and actors rack their brains for a way to pay out the old man and retain the inheritance for Henry. The barber suggests that Aminta, Isotta and Carlotta should be dressed up and produced as likely candidates for Morosus's hand. Aminta is a kind-hearted girl and at first does not want to be party to this trick, but in the end she agrees.

Act II. The same afternoon. Sir Morosus is putting on his best clothes to receive the three girls found by the barber, and ignores his house-keeper's warnings of a trick. The three actresses have cast and dressed themselves as three contrasting girls, and it is on Aminta (who calls her-self Timida) that the old man's choice falls. He apologizes touchingly for the discrepancy in their ages. A mock marriage takes place with two of the actors playing the parts of priest and notary, and then some more actors enter, claiming old acquaintanceship with Morosus and trying noisily to celebrate his marriage until he manages to drive them out. Left alone together, Morosus finds his Timida changed into a wilful, bad-tempered shrew, who makes a series of noisy scenes until Henry turns her out of the room and consoles his uncle. A short final scene between Henry and Aminta shows the latter's good heart, and the fact that she could only bring herself to behave like this for her husband's sake.

Act III. The room is being completely redecorated on Aminta's orders. The sound of hammering is heard, and to increase the turmoil Henry, in disguise, is giving Aminta a singing lesson. Sir Morosus is in despair when the Chief Justice of England is announced, and they discuss possible grounds for divorce. The legal gentleman finally gives judgment that no divorce is possible, and Henry and Aminta put poor Morosus out of his misery by disclosing the whole plot. After some initial anger he laughs heartily at his own expense and relaxes into happy contentment in his peaceful, bachelor life.

The rather coarse jokes in this comedy are decked out by Strauss with delightful music, but unfortunately there are no great lyrical outbursts such as one might expect.

Friedenstag (1938) is a heroic opera about an episode during the Thirty Years War.

FRIEDENSTAG (The Day of Peace). Opera in one act by Richard Strauss. Text by Josef Gregor. First performance: Munich, 1938.

Characters: The Commandant of the besieged town—baritone; Maria, his wife—soprano; a Piedmontese—tenor; the Holsteiner, commander of the besieging army—bass; the Burgomaster—tenor; the Bishop—baritone; officers and men of the garrison—one tenor, three baritones, three basses; a townswoman—soprano. Soldiers of both armies, elders, women of a deputation, townspeople.

Place: citadel of a besieged city during the Thirty Years War. *Time:* 24 October 1648.

A circular room with arrow-slits and staircases going up and down. Soldiers are singing, but a deputation of hungry townsfolk, led by the Burgomaster and the Bishop, contrasts with their mood. They plead in vain with the Commandant to surrender. An officer enters to tell the Commandant that all the ammunition is spent, but the latter refuses to allow the secret supply to be fetched from the cellars. He finally gives in to the deputation's urgent pleas, and says he will give a great sign at midday to announce the surrender. After they have gone, the Commandant's plan is made clear. He intends to blow up the citadel with himself and the garrison as the enemy enters. His wife, younger than himself, refuses to leave the citadel and resolves to die at his side. Just as the fuse is about to be lit, the city bells are heard ringing out as in times of peace, and the Burgomaster rushes in to announce that the enemy troops are entering the citadel to make peace. The Commandant at first refuses to greet the Holstein commander, but is at last persuaded to do so by his wife, and the opera ends with a hymn in praise of peace.

Strauss wrote his opera *Daphne* almost simultaneously with *Der Friedenstag*. The librettist was once again Josef Gregor, who described this work as a bucolic tragedy. It is pure idyll, almost bereft of dramatic action and very difficult to understand, since the highly poetic libretto is so full of vague symbolism that one cannot always follow the thread of the plot. Yet the text has a strange magic, which explains why Strauss was so deeply moved by it. This was, it will be remembered, the subject of the very first opera ever written.

DAPHNE. Bucolic tragedy in one act by Richard Strauss. Text by Josef Gregor. First performance: Dresden, 1938.

Characters: Peneios, a fisherman—bass; Gaea, his wife—contralto; Daphne, their daughter—soprano; Leukippos, a shepherd—tenor; Apollo—tenor. Shepherds, maids, masks of the Bacchic procession.

Place: Greece, outside Peneios's hut near Mount Olympus. *Time:* mythical antiquity.

A classical landscape on the banks of a river. The four shepherds are returning home with their flocks and discussing the feast which is about to be held in honour of Dionysus—traditionally an occasion for mating. Daphne, daughter of the fisherman Peneios, enters, and in a monologue tells how she feels identified with the trees, the flowers and the river; she loves the day and the sun, because she feels the tie with nature more strongly in light and warmth; the night robs her of her sisters and brothers, the trees and the flowers. The young shepherd Leukippos loves Daphne, but she does not respond to his wooing. He asks her to dance with him in the evening, but she refuses because the festivity gives her no pleasure. Her mother Gaea comes with two servants to dress Daphne for the feast, but she refuses to adorn herself and rushes away. The servants are astonished; they hear Leukippos lamenting his lot, and persuade him to wear Daphne's festive garments. Daphne's father enters and calls the shepherds to the feast, declaring his belief that Apollo will come among them. Just then Apollo enters dressed as a herdsman, and tells how he has been rounding up his cattle, which had run wild. Peneios sends for Daphne to take care of the guest. Shepherds and shepherdesses retire, leaving Apollo and Daphne alone. Apollo calls her his sister, which moves her, for she feels a strange affinity with him, but his words are otherwise incomprehensible to her. When he tries to embrace her with desire, she breaks free from him. It has become completely dark. The shepherds enter again, and sing the Dionysiac chorus. The feast begins, girls dance as *bacchantes* and shepherds, disguised as *aries*, pursue them. Leukippos, disguised as a girl, asks Daphne to dance. She does not recognize him and does so. Apollo, indignant that an impostor should desecrate the celebration, brings on a storm; the shepherds hurry away to protect their flocks, and Daphne and Leukippos are left alone. Leukippos throws off his woman's clothes and asks Apollo to reveal his identity. Apollo says that he is the sun. He draws his bow to strike Leukippos with an arrow, but Daphne throws herself between them. Apollo asks her to follow him, but she refuses. Leukippos curses Apollo and is mortally wounded by his arrow. Daphne is horrified to find that she has lost Leukippos, and at last realizes that her lover is a god. Apollo asks Zeus to give him this unapproachable virgin, who feels so close to nature, in the form of one of the trees she loves so well, so that he may honour her. Apollo disappears, and night falls. Daphne stands as if bound· to the earth, and gradually changes into a laurel tree, from which at first her voice rises in a marvellous melody, then dies away and becomes a part of nature itself.

Strauss turned to opera relatively late in life and remained faithful to it until his old age. As a result of their many conversations, his supreme interpreter, the conductor Clemens Krauss, wrote him a libretto entitled *Capriccio*, which was exactly suited to his genius. Krauss described it as a musical conversation piece, for it discusses the question of whether words or music are the more important, an argument which raged in Paris in Gluck's day and drew all lovers of the arts into this controversy.

CAPRICCIO. Opera in one act by Richard Strauss. Text by Clemens Krauss. First performance: Munich, 1942.
　　Characters: the Countess—soprano; the Count, her brother—baritone; Clairon, an actress—contralto; Flamand, a musician—tenor; Olivier, a poet—baritone; La Roche, a theatre director—bass; Monsieur Taupe, a prompter—tenor; two Italian singers—soprano and tenor; the major-domo—bass; eight servants—four tenors, four basses. A young dancer, three musicians (instrumentalists).
　　Place: a castle near Paris. *Time:* about 1775.
　　In the Countess's house a group of people are discussing the question of the pre-eminence of music or words in opera. Flamand and Olivier, representing opposite viewpoints, are also contestants for the Countess's affections, while her brother is principally concerned with his feelings for Clairon, and La Roche takes a more professional view. Each character finds a parallel between his attitude to the Countess and the other guests on the one hand, and to the problem under discussion on the other.

At the first performance of *Capriccio* a select audience willing to follow this strange opera was most appreciative of the charm of both text and music. (It lasts nearly two and a half hours without an interval.) It remained open to doubt, however, whether the general public would understand this esoteric work, because for some time *Capriccio* was only performed at festivals. Not until 1956, when it was revived at the Städtische

Oper in West Berlin—admittedly in a superb production—did *Capriccio* prove its power to enchant the ordinary public, and this was confirmed by subsequent performances elsewhere, including Paris.

Die Liebe der Danae, completed in 1940, brought Strauss back to the realm which had always inspired him strongly—ancient mythology—but unfortunately Josef Gregor's libretto is not entirely satisfactory. The figure of Jupiter is reminiscent of Wotan, and the language, too, frequently recalls Wagner, while the burlesque episode with the quartet of Jupiter's loves seems very affected. However, the lyrical passages make a wonderful basis for the kind of Strauss melody which one finds in his most splendid works, *Die Frau ohne Schatten* and *Ariadne*.

DIE LIEBE DER DANAE (The Love of Danae). Opera in three acts by Richard Strauss. Text by Josef Gregor. First public performance: Salzburg, 1952.

Characters: Jupiter—baritone; Mercury—tenor; Pollux, King of Eos— tenor; Danae, his daughter—soprano; Xanthe, her servant—soprano; Midas, King of Lydia—tenor; four kings, nephews to Pollux—two tenors, two basses; four queens, Semele, Europa, Alcmene and Leda— two sopranos, one mezzo-soprano, one contralto; four watchmen— basses. Creditors, servants and followers of Pollux and Danae, populace.

Place: Eos. *Time:* mythical antiquity.

Act I, scene i. The throne-room of King Pollux. The room is shabby and part of the golden throne is gone. Creditors besiege the King for payment of his debts, but he asks them to wait, as he hopes that King Midas of the golden touch will make an offer for the hand of his daughter Danae.

Scene ii. Danae's bed-chamber. Danae has dreamt of a rain of gold which showered down all over her. When Xanthe announces a new suitor for her hand, she declares that she will only accept the man who can bring her the gold.

Scene iii. A pillared hall in the palace overlooking the sea. It is announced that the new suitor, who is approaching in a golden ship, is indeed Midas; he sends in advance a golden garland to Danae. She resolves to accept him as her husband. Midas enters, simply dressed and calling himself Chrysopher, a friend of Midas, sent ahead to bring Danae to the King. She is very much attracted to him, and he indicates his reluctance to take her to Midas.

Scene iv. The harbour. Everyone gathers to welcome Midas, whose place had been taken by Jupiter, in whom Danae recognizes the object of her golden dreams.

Act II. A splendidly furnished bedchamber. The four queens are adorning the bridal bed when the supposed bridegroom enters. In various forms he (Jupiter) has been the lover of each of them, and they are all jealous of Danae, for whom Jupiter has retained the shape of a man. He explains his love for her and his fear of Juno's jealousy which has prompted his impersonation of Midas. The four queens agree to keep his secret, but each wants to claim him as her lover again. Midas enters and puts on the golden robes Jupiter had been wearing. The latter reminds him that only by absolute obedience can he retain the golden gift and therefore his wealth. The god commands Midas not to take away Danae's love, and then disappears. Danae enters and Midas tries to explain the position to her. When he turns objects in the room to gold Danae realizes who he is, but as she falls into his arms she at once becomes a golden statue. Jupiter enters, and he and Midas offer the statue all that lies in their gift—Jupiter offers dreams and temples, Midas human love and poverty—for she must decide which she loves. Her voice is heard calling Midas's name.

Act III, scene i. Danae and Midas awake by a roadside. He has once again become a humble donkey-driver for love of her and she accepts her lot.

Scene ii. A mountain forest. Mercury tells Jupiter the consequences of this incident. The four queens enter and try to win Jupiter back, but he is proof against their pleading. Pollux, his nephews and creditors, enter and accuse Jupiter of playing a trick on them. He rains money from the skies, and they go out satisfied. Prompted by Mercury, Jupiter decides to try once more to win Danae's love.

Scene iii. Midas's hut. Jupiter enters and tries to discover whether Danae is contented with her lot. He is finally convinced of her fidelity to Midas and leaves, full of respect for her greatness, while Danae goes out to meet her husband.

The music of *Die Liebe der Danae* is wonderfully luminous. All the splendour of Strauss's gift for orchestration is revealed in the 'rain of gold' in the first interlude. Danae's own music is very beautiful and melodious, and this work also contains

tunes which are moving in their simple sentiments, as for instance Midas's theme after the spell has left him. The ageing

Ruhig

composer showed an astonishing wealth of creative imagination
in this work, but certain lengthy passages, especially in Jupiter's
scenes, could be improved by skilful cutting.

Die Liebe der Danae was to have been performed at the
Salzburg Festival in 1944, but the whole Festival was cancelled
because of military developments, and this carefully prepared
première could not take place in public. Instead a general rehearsal was held before an invited audience. The exceptional
nature of this occasion, a performance in the presence of the old
master of what was probably his last opera, was at once a pain
and a pleasure for everyone there. The first public performance
did not take place until 1952 at Salzburg.

Among Richard Strauss's contemporaries the most important
opera-composer is probably Hans Pfitzner (1869–1949). All his
life Pfitzner was overshadowed by Strauss, and hailed by his
own supporters as Strauss's greatest rival, which has continually
led to misunderstanding. Pfitzner is in fact a completely independent musician. While Strauss's works created the musical
language of the time which was more or less accepted by almost
all his contemporaries, Pfitzner's speculative nature strove for
an original, personal style, which attained its loftiest form of
expression in his main works, the opera *Palestrina* and the
cantata *Von deutscher Seele* (*Of the German soul*). Pfitzner's quest
for intense introspection was utterly foreign to Strauss's open
receptiveness to all new ideas. While Strauss was conquering
the world, Pfitzner's works were known only to a small but
devoted circle of supporters. He composed four operas, spread
over four decades. He was at first a disciple of Wagner, and
James Grun, the librettist of his first opera, was also so bound
up in Wagner's sphere of ideas and expression that his text,
which strongly appealed to Pfitzner, drew the composer to
write very much in the Wagnerian idiom. Yet Pfitzner, who
was twenty-four years old when he wrote *Der arme Heinrich*
(*Poor Henry*) in 1895, showed in this work more independence

from Wagner's influence than did Strauss at the age of twenty-nine in his first opera, *Guntram*.

Though Wagner's influence is very apparent in the music of *Der arme Heinrich*, it contains indications of the original style Pfitzner later developed. The austere melodies and restrained harmonies in the style of church music and the delicate orchestral colourings all command the listener's attention, while the grandiose succession of narration and dialogue continually prove the considerable ability and astonishing maturity of the young composer. His weakness lies in his lack of passionate, vitalizing dramatic spirit, and this he never managed to acquire.

Pfitzner's second opera, *Die Rose vom Liebesgarten* (*The Rose from the Garden of Love*) (1901), was also written very much under Wagner's influence, and its score overflows with musical beauties. The spring festival represented in the overture contains one wonderful inspiration after another, as exquisitely lovely tunes pour out, but after all this splendour the greyly shrouded central acts can seem rather wearisome, in spite of their numerous musical highlights. The raindrop theme in the prelude to the second act and the shattering funeral march are both particularly impressive, but all this musical greatness cannot conceal the undoubted weakness of the libretto with its exaggerated, almost incomprehensible and tedious symbolism.

The first performance of the musical legend *Palestrina* took place in Munich in 1917. Although this was an unfortunate moment, right in the middle of the First World War, this unusual work was very well received and immediately acknowledged as something very much out of the ordinary. It is not really suitable for repertory performances, and it is chiefly Munich that has continued to cultivate this work, especially during the annual summer festivals.

Pfitzner's *Palestrina* can almost be termed a 'mystery play'. It is the mystery of creation, the eternal secret surrounding the involuntary creative urge, which Pfitzner here fashions into a poetic and musical experience. Pfitzner himself wrote the superbly poetic libretto, a revelation of his most personal feelings, which with the music forms a unified work. He relied entirely on his own gifts when writing *Palestrina* and the austerity of style indicated in his earlier works here comes to fruition. The often harsh linear clarity of sixteenth-century church music on which he consciously based his style is nothing new for Pfitzner, but in *Palestrina* he blends it with romantic, emotional melodies to form this convincingly original style.

PALESTRINA. Musical legend in three acts by Hans Pfitzner. First performance: Munich, 1917.

Characters: Pope Pius IV—bass; Morone and Novagerio, Papal Legates—baritone and tenor; Carlo Borromeo, a Roman Cardinal—baritone; Madruscht, Prince-Bishop of Trent—bass; Giovanni Pierluigi Palestrina—tenor; Ighino, his son—soprano; Silla, his pupil—mezzo-soprano. Members of the Council of Trent, choir-singers, various apparitions.

Place: Rome and Trent. *Time:* 1563.

Act I. A room in Palestrina's house. Silla, Palestrina's pupil, is trying out a secular song. He inclines towards the new monodic music which has just begun to take root in Florence and breaks all the rules of polyphony. Knowing that in so doing he is betraying his master Palestrina, he is nevertheless determined to pack his belongings and go to Florence. His young friend Ighino, Palestrina's son, is very worried about his father who, ever since the death of his mother, has lost interest in life and cannot bring himself to compose again. He has no sympathy with Silla's enthusiasm for innovations, particularly the new musical style, which he only sees as a threat to his beloved father's greatness. Silla does however persuade him to listen to his *canzone*. The text 'Schönste, ungnädige Dame, Nymphe mit den Sternenaugen' ('Beautiful, cruel lady, nymph with starlike eyes'), is set to music no less secular in mood. Cardinal Borromeo, who enters the house at this moment with Palestrina, is shocked by these profane sounds. Palestrina has more understanding of young people and has long been aware of Silla's leaning towards the new music. The boys leave the room, and Borromeo tells Palestrina that he has come to offer him a very important commission: the old church music, hallowed by tradition, had been showing undoubted signs of decline, and was in danger of disintegration. Palestrina is commissioned to write a great mass as witness that the old figured music is still alive, and thus resolve the dispute which has broken out in the Council of Trent. Palestrina does not however feel equal to this task; he replies that his creative power is broken and he must refuse. Disappointed and offended the Cardinal leaves him. Palestrina feels more alone than ever, now that Borromeo, his last friend, is gone. Dusk falls. From the dark recesses of the room emerge the shades of nine great composers of the past to speak to Palestrina in his despair. They tell him that his earthly task is not yet fulfilled, and urge him to add the last link to the chain of his creations. The words of these revered masters move Palestrina deeply, as their figures slowly fade back into the darkness. Palestrina seizes his pen; the heavens seem to open above him and the voices of angels are heard, singing the *Kyrie* of his mass. With flying pen he writes down what he believes he has heard and new and powerful inspiration seizes him. While his room dissolves around him into a universe, he writes his

Gloria, borne to him by rejoicing angel voices through the air. Palestrina completes the score in a state of intense excitement, the angelic forms vanish, the pen drops from his hand and he falls, exhausted, into a deep sleep. He is found by Silla and Ighino who enter the room at dawn and see the floor covered with the sheets of music. Ighino gathers the pages together and realizes that during the night his father has written a great mass.

Act II. The council chamber at Trent. The Papal Legate Novagerio announces the Pope's command that the Council should be terminated as soon as possible, and that the question of church music must be finally solved. Novagerio learns from Borromeo that the great new mass is not yet available, but soon will be, as he has had the obstinate Palestrina thrown into prison to compel him to write it. The Council continues its deliberations with intense disagreement, as it seems impossible to reconcile the differences between the Italians, the French, the Spaniards and the Germans. Finally the haughty Spanish legates succeed in disrupting the conference entirely. Everyone leaps up in anger, and the President of the Council, the Papal Legate Morone, has difficulty in persuading those present to take part in a final session the same afternoon. After all the dignitaries have left the room, the servants of the Italians, Germans and Spaniards start quarrelling and fighting, and are only stopped by the Prince-Bishop Madruscht's ruthless action in ordering his bodyguard to fire on the combatants.

Act III. In Palestrina's house. Ighino has taken the music of the new mass to the Cardinal, and after weeks of harsh imprisonment, which have seriously affected the health of the ageing composer, Palestrina has at last been released. This very day the new mass has been performed for the first time in the Sistine chapel, in the presence of the Pope. The choristers enter to tell Palestrina of the immense impression the performance has made. The highest honour awaits Palestrina: the Pope is carried in his chair to Palestrina's house. He enters, blesses him and names him director of the Sistine Chapel. Borromeo has followed the Pope and, greatly moved, he falls at Palestrina's feet. The whole town joins in the rejoicing, and repeated cries of 'Evviva' resound in Palestrina's quiet room. The last to leave is Ighino, who goes out to join the gay crowds in the street. Palestrina is left alone: he is scarcely moved by the honours, his new office and the great popular enthusiasm. He sits quietly at the organ, touching the keys with an unassuming and dedicated air, while the sounds of rejoicing die away in the distance.

The prelude to *Palestrina* is full of that same mystery which fills the preludes to *Tristan* and *Lohengrin*. From the infinite realm of sound notes materialize and group together into harmonies which in turn develop into sound-pictures of great spiritual power. The medieval chanting which forms the principal theme evokes a deep, religious feeling, as though one had been transported into the spaciousness of a gothic cathedral where this

miracle of music becomes experience. Into this isolation is set the figure of Palestrina, whose dedication to his destiny is expressed in the fervent theme of resignation, which returns at

significant moments in the course of the drama and brings the work to its moving close.

The scene of Palestrina's heaven-sent inspiration is among the great pieces of music in twentieth-century opera. The first phrases for solo angelic voices convey a sense of release and joy after the awe-inspiring, weighty ensemble of the nine masters. One feels with Palestrina the lifting of a burden from his heart, the return of his creative power, the rush of inspiration and the touch of divine grace in the splendid *Gloria* which breaks over him in a myriad of angelic voices. One is still so completely absorbed by the splendour and delight of this musical revelation that the short final scene with its return to mundane reality, passes almost unnoticed.

The second act unfolds a very realistic picture of the outside world from which Palestrina has retired because he feels it has rejected him. This act is conceived with brilliant poetic and musical verve and conducted in finely polished dialogue spiced with wit. Although it is in its way a most talented piece of writing, it represents only a description of milieu and does nothing to further the dramatic action. It can therefore be somewhat tedious, particularly if one can only understand isolated passages of the dialogue.

The entry of the Pope marks a particularly impressive climax; his words are full of nobility and dignity and the musical line of his *arioso* recitative is especially lovely, while the medieval cadences give his oration a very personal expression.

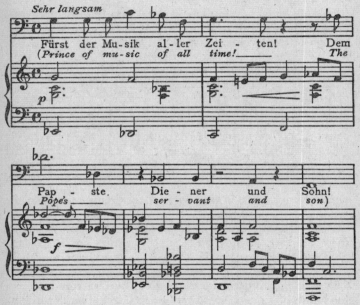

Fürst der Mu-sik al-ler Zei-ten! Dem
(*Prince of mu-sic of all time!___ The*

Pap - ste. Die - ner und Sohn!
Pope's ___ ser - vant and son)

Pfitzner had little success with his last opera, *Das Herz* (*The Heart*), which had a double première in Munich and Berlin in 1931. Neither musicians nor public showed much interest in it, and it soon disappeared from the repertoires.

In 1906 Pfitzner also wrote some stage-music for *Das Christ-Elflein* (*The Little Elf of Christ*), a Christmas fairy-tale by Ilse von Stach, and in 1917 he revised the work as a short light opera.

Of the numerous operas by Emil Nikolaus von Rezniček (1860–1945) only *Donna Diana*, a gay opera of lasting quality,

is occasionally performed in Germany and has greatly benefited
by the revision made by Julius Kapp in 1933. One is immediately
struck by the grace and elegance of the music which relies
largely on the short forms of popular songs and dance-tunes.
The *élan* of Spanish folk-themes and rhythms cannot however
conceal the fact that Rezniček's music is of Viennese origin and
that its charm is the spontaneous charm of Vienna.

In his early works, such as *Ingwelde* (1894) Max von Schillings
(1868–1933) was greatly influenced by Wagner, and even his
very charming light opera *Der Pfeifertag* (*The Parliament of
Pipers*) (1899), contains many pieces of imitation, especially of
Die Meistersinger. In *Moloch* (1906) Schillings follows his own
line and passionate impulse drives his glowing, colourful music
to great effect. Real success came to him finally with *Mona Lisa*
(1915), partly because of its excellent dramatic text, which inspired Schillings to a full revelation of his musical and dramatic
talents, while in spite of some important advantages over
Mona Lisa, *Moloch* was never wholly successful.

MONA LISA. Opera in two acts, a prologue and an epilogue by Max
von Schillings. Text by Beatrice Dovsky. First performance: Stuttgart,
1915.

Characters: Francesco del Giocondo (in the Prologue and Epilogue, the
stranger)—baritone; Mona Lisa, his wife, (in the Prologue and Epilogue,
the stranger's wife)—soprano; Giovanni de Salviati (in the Prologue and
Epilogue, a lay-brother)—tenor; Dianora, Francesco's little daughter by
his first marriage—soprano. Guests of Francesco and others.

Place: Florence. *Time:* in the Prologue and Epilogue, the present; in
Acts I and II, end of the fifteenth century.

Prologue. A stranger on honeymoon in Florence with his much
younger wife visits the palace which now serves as the home of the
Carthusian monks but centuries earlier belonged to the rich merchant
Francesco del Giocondo. A young lay-brother acts as guide to the
strangers and tells them the story of Francesco's third wife, Mona Lisa,
whose portrait was painted by Leonardo da Vinci with such mystic
beauty.

Act I. A room in Francesco del Giocondo's house. It is Carnival-time
and the sound of the revels in the streets reaches the palace where Francesco is happily dining with his friends. Mona Lisa returns from confession
with a garland of white iris in her hand. Francesco tries to embrace her,
but she will not let him. Francesco complains to his friend Pietro about
his wife's coldness and her enigmatic personality, which Leonardo so
well conveyed in his portrait but which he himself cannot penetrate. The
young Giovanni comes to see Francesco on a mission from the Pope, to

buy from him a particularly beautiful pearl. Francesco is a well-known
collector of pearls, the most precious and beautiful of which he keeps in
an exquisite cupboard in the wall, while the key he always carries on his
person. Giovanni was Mona Lisa's first love, and at this meeting their
passion flares up again. After everyone has left the palace, Giovanni
comes back stealthily to see his beloved once more, but their meeting is
observed by Francesco. Giovanni hides in the wall-cupboard and
Francesco swiftly shuts its doors thus condemning the unfortunate man
to death by suffocation. In vain does Mona Lisa plead for mercy for her
beloved; triumphant and contemptuous, Francesco throws the key out of
the window into the Arno.

Act II. The next morning, Ash-Wednesday. Mona Lisa remembers
her horrible experience of the preceding night. There is no movement in
the cupboard; Giovanni must have suffocated long before. Her stepdaughter Dianora enters in all innocence with the key which she has
found in her boat, anchored below the windows of the palace. When
Francesco sees the key in his wife's hands, he tears it from her and opens
the cupboard. Mona Lisa has just strength enough to push him inside and
close the doors behind him, before she collapses fainting.

Epilogue. The same room, which looks very bleak without its splendid
furnishings, carpets and tapestries. The strangers and the lay-brother are
sitting together. He has just finished his story. The woman, very moved,
gives him some money to say a mass for the unhappy Mona Lisa, and in
doing so she drops a bunch of white iris which she was wearing at her
waist. She then follows her husband out.

Schillings wrote savage and passionate music to this highly
dramatic text. The very first notes with their bold, rising Mona
Lisa theme enchant the listener and hold him spellbound until
the end. The musical climax comes with Mona Lisa's mad-scene
in the second act.

Though Strauss, Pfitzner and Schillings all freed themselves
eventually from the Wagnerian influence which overshadowed
their early works, it was Strauss who assumed the leadership
and set the style for his contemporaries. It was he who coined
the type of musical expression adopted to a greater or lesser
extent by all composers in the first decades of this century.
Admittedly certain composers of outstanding talent such as
Busoni or Schreker did in the end evolve their own style and
Paul von Klenau experimented with dodecaphony, but even
they are unmistakably marked with the stamp of Strauss's
musical idiom, as for example his exceptionally glowing
melodies, colourful harmonic progressions or brilliant orchestral texture with horn pedal-point. Such typical Strauss char-

acteristics are even discernible in composers twenty or thirty years younger than he, and unite such disparate musicians as Graener and Gerster, Bittner and Schoeck, Respighi and Pizzetti. All the operas of these late romantics contain an essential unity of style.

Paul Graener (1872–1944) unloosed his considerable talents on the writing of a great number of operas, with undoubted dramatic impulse and tension. His methods are traditional and he explores no new paths. His music exemplifies the language of the period, being highly cultivated in form and phrase as well as in the invariably elegant orchestration. Graener's first opera, *Don Juans letztes Abenteuer* (*Don Juan's Last Adventure*) (Leipzig, 1914), was very successful, but there followed several failures until he wrote *Friedemann Bach* in 1931, which with its effective and slightly sentimental text by Rudolf Lothar was also a success. Graener wove some well-known *lieder* by F. Bach most skilfully into the music of this work, and built up on one of them a most effective ensemble. Throughout, Graener shows his skill in blending the style of his time with that of the eighteenth century.

In Graener's operatic creations the emphasis always lay in the field of tragic opera, but he did write a little masterpiece of a light opera, *Schirin und Gertraude* (*Schirin and Gertrude*) (Dresden, 1920), which reveals his considerable talent for delicate humour and robust comedy, as clearly as do his popular morning-star songs. The text of *Schirin und Gertraude*, by Ernst Hardt, is a version of the old story of Count von Gleichen and his two wives, who get on so well together that in the end the poor Count finds himself the dupe. It is a matter for regret that this charming work has never been revived on the German stage.

In 1912 Hermann Wolfgang von Waltershausen (1882–1954) scored a remarkable success with his opera *Oberst Chabert* (*Colonel Chabert*). Both textually and musically this work is a product of its times, for it clearly shows the influence of Wagner, Strauss, and of *verismo*, but the stamp of a personality of compelling stature is discernible on both language and music. Waltershausen himself wrote the libretto after a story by Balzac about the predicament of the man, supposed dead, who on his return home finds his wife happily married to someone else.

The *Enoch Arden* problem is psychologically intensified and presented in a splendidly effective dramatic manner. Waltershausen could not repeat the success of *Oberst Chabert* in his subsequent operas, *Richardis* (1915) and *Die Rauensteiner Hochzeit* (*The Rauenstein Marriage*) (1919), and his last opera, *Die Gräfin von Tolosa*, has never been performed.

Another exceptional composer, an artist whose sphere of emotion and expression was well ahead of his time, was Rudi Stephan (1887–1915). By generation he was one of Strauss's successors, but in fact he only belongs among them to a very limited degree. He completed his only opera, *Die Ersten Menschen* (*The First Men*) in 1914. He fell on the Russian front in 1915, and a great hope died with him. Judging by this one work, which was produced in 1920, he appears to have been closely bound to the traditions created by Richard Strauss, but it contains frequent indications that he was striving towards an independent musical language. His audacity in piling chords one on top of the other and his insistence on contrast between the musical lines are typical of his time, but the individual variations he introduces already foreshadow the young Hindemith.

The operas of the Viennese composer Erich Wolfgang Korngold (1897–1957) belong to the *verismo* tradition, and at a first hearing his music seems like a synthesis of Richard Strauss and Puccini. Korngold was famous as an infant prodigy for his pantomime *Der Schneemann* (*The Snowman*), and his one-act operas *Der Ring des Polycrates* (*The Ring of Polycrates*) (1916), and *Vera Violanta* (1916), both aroused interest in the young composer. *Die tote Stadt* (*The Dead City*) came out in 1920 and firmly established his reputation for an outstanding feeling for sound, especially when depicting the horrific or the supernatural. Korngold's last opera, *Das Wunder der Heliane* (*The Miracle of Heliane*) (1927), was not a success.

In the group of opera composers connected with Richard Strauss, Franz Schreker (1878–1934) is one of the strongest and most original personalities. He was greatly overrated in his day and has now been completely forgotten. His first opera *Der Ferne Klang* (*The distant Sound*) (1912), attracted great attention with its exciting, sensuous sounds, original type of melodies and charmingly syncopated rhythms. In the opera *Die Gezeich-*

neten (The Stigmata) (1918), this new world of sound seemed intensified, or perhaps already exaggerated considering that it required an orchestra of over one hundred players. In spite of their brilliant scores, most theatrical libretti (all of which he wrote himself) and great initial success supported by enthusiastic reviews, these early works, and even the later ones like *Der Schatzgräber (The Treasure-Seeker)* (1920) never really appealed to popular taste.

The significance of the opera *Notre Dame* (1914) by the Viennese composer Franz Schmidt (1874–1939) should not be overlooked. From the point of view of sheer sound the score ranks with those of Richard Strauss or Schreker, and is besides rich in melodic inspiration and original use of harmonies. It has scarcely ever been performed, however, because the plot, based on Victor Hugo's novel, holds no interest for modern audiences.

The many operas by the Swiss composer Othmar Schoeck (1886–1957) are all really experiments, because he was constantly trying out new forms and new ways of expression. For his most important work, *Penthesilea*, after Kleist's drama, he uses in part rhythmical speech accompanied by dramatic music in an attempt at the ancient classical style which Orff later adopted in his *Antigonae*. Schoeck did not however carry this to its logical conclusion, for *Penthesilea* also contains great melodic lines of delightful austerity. His songs show him to be a composer of particularly sensitive originality and even in his operas he cannot reject his environment, which is the world of Richard Strauss.

Though born in Denmark, Paul von Klenau (1883–1946) belongs entirely to the German cultural sphere, even writing his librettos in German. Once he had paid homage to Wagner and Strauss with his first opera *Gudrun auf Island (Gudrun in Iceland)* (1918), he sought and found new channels for his subsequent works. Klenau tried to find a synthesis of dodecaphonic technique and tonal principles, which gives his music a certain rigidity. His most interesting operatic attempt was *Michael Kohlhaas* (1933) in which he intersperses the music with spoken dialogue, gives the chorus an important role to play and introduces chorales and popular songs. *Rembrandt van Rijn* (Berlin, 1937) made a stronger impression with its impressive account of the fate of a genius misprized by the world. Klenau achieved no lasting success either with this work or with his last opera, *Elisabeth von England* (1939).

The operas of Robert Heger (b. 1886) are more bound to Strauss's example than are those of Klenau, but his talent is more dignified and less studied. *Der Bettler Namenlos* (*The Nameless Beggar*) (Munich, 1932), is the story of Odysseus's return to Ithaca, and the music is colourful and powerfully dramatic. These qualities are more evident still in Heger's second opera *Der Verlorene Sohn* (*The Lost Son*) (Dresden, 1936), a coloured phantasmagoria which gives the composer an opportunity to use a rich scale of expression, from crude sensuousness to high religious fervour. Heger's last opera *Lady Hamilton* made a strong impression when it was first performed in Nuremberg in 1950.

Ottmar Gerster (b. 1897) wrote a very successful opera, *Enoch Arden* (1936), with music of immediate impact and a most impressive text. The striking theme of the gull's cry with which

the overture begins, pervades the music of the whole work, and Gerster captures the sounds of the stormy sea with hollow fifths, chords in fourths, whistling *tremolos* and the shrill use of piccolo or trumpet. Relaxed sailors' dances and the placid *legato* 'Ich brauch ein stilles, festes Haus' ('I need a quiet, steady home') provide necessary contrast which Gerster uses to strong dramatic effect. His other operas, *Madame Lieselotte* (Essen, 1933) and *Die Hexe von Passau* (*The Witch of Passau*) (1941), were not nearly so successful. *Enoch Arden* is a true folk-opera, whereas *Madame Lieselotte*, his earlier attempt in this genre, is in fact more like an operetta. The same happened to Georg Vollerthun (1876–1946) with his successful opera *Der Freikorporal* (*The Volunteer Corporal*) (1931). The various dances and marches are the most enjoyable features of his music, which, though it consciously strives for popular effect, deteriorates into a morass of sentimental pathos.

Joseph Haas (b. 1879) has given the German theatre one of the most beautiful of popular operas, *Tobias Wunderlich*.

TOBIAS WUNDERLICH. Opera in three acts by Joseph Haas. Text by Hermann Heinz Ortner and Ludwig Andersen. First performance: Cassel, 1937.

Characters: Tobias Wunderlich, maker of wooden shoes—baritone; Barbara—soprano; Barbara, a gipsy—mezzo-soprano; the mayor—bass; Fink and Wurm, village councillors—tenor and bass buffo; Mr Brown and Rosenzweig, art-dealers—bass and tenor.

Place: in the German Alps. *Time:* the present.

The parish council of a mountain village wants to auction the wooden gothic figure of Barbara from their church, but Wunderlich protests indignantly. When he is left alone in the Church, the saint comes down from her pedestal and promises to be his servant. The whole village is roused to indignation by Tobias and his new maid and accuses them of an immoral relationship, which goads Tobias into telling everyone who in fact his maid is. By so doing, however, he forfeits his right to her. In front of everyone the saint returns as a wooden figure to her niche in the church. The news of this miracle soon spreads abroad and the little church becomes a place of pilgrimage. Tobias secretly carves a new wooden figure for himself. He thinks of his former happiness when the saint lived in his house, and falls asleep. His Barbara descends from her niche, lays the table, wakes Tobias, signs to him to be silent and then says grace. A tender, pious and simple duet brings them together.

The music for *Tobias Wunderlich* is a combination of sophisticated yet popular high-spirits, sincere warmth of feeling and genuine piety. The best scene from the dramatic point of view is the pilgrimage scene outside the church, which forms a link between the two different spheres, very much in the manner of Bruckner.

Haas's comic folk-opera *Die Hochzeit des Jobs* (*The Marriage of Job*) (1944), harks back to the tradition of the old German *Singspiel*. Ludwig Andersen's most appealing text allowed the composer to give rein to his natural feeling for sincere and naïve humour.

The operas of the Viennese composer Julius Bittner (1874–1939) are also popular operas in the best sense, with typical Viennese music based on song and dance, and a strong feeling for drama. Bittner wrote his own libretti, mostly based on episodes from Austrian village life, and set them to appropriately rustic music. One of the most lastingly successful of his works is *Höllisch Gold* (*Infernal Gold*) (Darmstadt, 1916), a

Singspiel, but his other works, among them the tragedy *Bergsee* (*Mountain-lake*) (Vienna, 1911), which was perhaps his best opera, were unfortunately very soon forgotten.

There is only a relatively small crop of light opera to set beside the splendid serious operas written by Strauss's immediate successors and to continue the great tradition of *opera buffa* into the beginning of this century. One such work is the one-act opera *Versiegelt* (*Sealed*) (1908), by Leo Blech (1871–1958). The sparkling, witty and charming music continuously holds the attention of the listener, but the *biedermeier* text, on which such elegant music is wasted, is too simple to arouse any lasting interest.

Shortly before the outbreak of war in 1914, the comic opera *Herr Dandolo* by Rudolf Siegel (1878–1948) was first produced in Essen, and was immensely successful. Its fame however never spread, because of the unfortunate moment of its first appearance, but it is without doubt one of the best German comic operas.

A special place in this list of light operas belongs to *Die Schneider von Schonau* (*The Tailors of Schonau*) (Dresden, 1916), by the Dutchman Jan Brandts-Buys (1868–1933). The music of this innocuous romp set in the milieu of craftsmen intentionally aims at parallels with *Die Meistersinger*, but with such charm and skill that one completely forgets the hint of subtle mockery and willingly accepts the exuberance of this music which moves between the grand style and caricature.

Walter Braunfels (1882–1954) wrote a minor masterpiece, his lyrical, fantastic opera *Die Vogel* (*The Birds*) (Munich, 1920). The text, freely adapted by the composer from Aristophanes, tells of the eternal longing of men for the unattainable. The two men in the story, Ratefreund and Hoffegut, wander in the realm of the birds, but have no understanding of the essence and meaning of this strange world. Ratefreund returns to his fellow-creatures, disappointed, while there lingers in Hoffegut an inexplicable longing aroused in him by his love for the nightingale. A rare enchantment emanates from the music composed for this highly unrealistic subject, mostly due to its strange quality of sound, produced by a lavish use of half-tones. The melodies are sweet, yet noble in line and wonderfully singable. It is possible that the short-lived popularity of *Die*

Vogel and of Braunfels' other operas, *Prinzessin Brambilla* (1909) and *Don Gil von den grünen Hosen* (*Don Gil of the Green Stockings*) (1924), is due to the over-delicate grace of the music which never rises to compelling stature.

Another very gifted composer of light opera is Mark Lothar (b. 1902) whose opera *Schneider Wibbel* (*Tailor Wibbel*) (Berlin, 1938), is one of the best comic operas of its day. The text, after the well-known comedy by Hans Müller-Schlösser, tells of the fate of the poor little tailor who has to go to prison because he has offended Napoleon. His partner goes to prison in his place, and dies there as Wibbel, while the real tailor leads a miserable life in the dark cellar of his house. The music for this gay farce is always inventive and consists partly of merry caricature—the solemn, grotesque burial of the false Wibbel is wonderful—and partly of lyrical sentiment, as for instance in the fervent, simple love-duets.

Mark Lothar's *Rappelkopf* (Munich, 1958) was also immensely successful. The libretto is a free adaptation of Raimund's well-known magic opera *Alpenkönig und Menschenfeind* (*Mountain-king and Misanthrope*) and gives the composer a wonderful opportunity to let loose his talent for illustrative music. The lyrical episodes are set to rich melodies, the comic scenes are dramatically most effective and the orchestral interludes are grandiosely conceived, particularly the skilfully constructed Storm Fugue.

A very lovable and really notable exponent of comic opera is Ermanno Wolf-Ferrari (1876–1948). He was half German, half Italian, and as such his musical talent combines the melo-diousness and the charm of a Rossini or Donizetti with German thoroughness in musical construction and the use of motifs. His comic operas continue the best Italian *buffo* tradition, in the virtuoso use of light *parlando* and the forthright delineation of the characters, which are mostly drawn from the *commedia dell'arte*. His greatest successes were *Le donne curiose* (*The Inquisitive Women*) (Munich, 1903), and *I Quatro Rusteghi* (*Four Boors*—known in England as *The School for Fathers*) (1906), both with charming texts in the style of Goldoni, whose original plays were cleverly adapted by L. Sugano and Pizzolato. The composer evidently felt particularly happy in this milieu, since he returned several times to the world of the *commedia dell'arte* with great success, in *Gli Amanti Sposi* (*The Married Lovers*) (Venice, 1925), *La Vedova Scaltra* (*The Wily Widow*) (Rome, 1931) and *Il Campiello* (Milan, 1936).

I QUATRO RUSTEGHI (The Four Curmudgeons, or The School for Fathers). Comic opera in three acts by Ermanno Wolf-Ferrari. Text by Giuseppe Pizzolato. First performance: Munich, 1906.

Characters: Lunardo, a Venetian antique dealer—bass; Margarita, his second wife—mezzo-soprano; Lucieta, Lunardo's daughter—soprano; Maurizio, a merchant—bass; Filipeto, his son—tenor; Marina, Filipeto's aunt—soprano; Simon, a merchant, her husband—baritone; Canciano, a wealthy burgher—bass; Felice, his wife—soprano; Count Riccardo Arcolai—tenor.

Place: Venice. *Time:* about 1800.

Act I, scene i. A room in Lunardo's house. Margarita and Lucieta are knitting and embroidering, their thoughts—it being carnival-time—on the gaieties of others. Margarita remembers merrier days before her marriage to Lunardo and Lucieta looks forward to marriage and freedom. (Lunardo is one of the 'rusteghi' of the title, domestic tyrants who insist on their womenfolk leading completely housebound lives, and who disapprove of anything which might distract them.) Lunardo enters and tells Margarita that he and Maurizio have decided that Lucieta and Maurizio's son Filipeto should marry one another. The young people have never met, but Lunardo brushes aside Margarita's objections, and insists on his orders being obeyed. Maurizio and Lunardo now discuss the marriage contract, showing their narrow-minded, ungenerous attitude to feminine foibles.

Scene ii. The house of Marina and Simon. Filipeto comes to ask his aunt if she knows any more about his prospective marriage than his father's brusque announcement. He is determined not to marry a girl he does not like. Simon enters, and shortly after Felice with her husband and her admirer Count Riccardo. The two women discuss ways and means of thwarting the unreasonable fathers of the young people.

Act II. Lunardo's house. Lucieta has borrowed a few trinkets from Margarita, but her father makes her take them off again. Marina and Simon enter, and for a while the men are left together, lamenting the frivolity of their women-folk. Felice enters, the two men go out, and the women tell Lucieta that they plan to smuggle Filipeto in, disguised as a girl and masked, it being carnival-time. He enters, and he and Lucieta are very much attracted to one another. The men return unexpectedly and Filipeto and Riccardo (who escorted him to the house) are quickly hidden. Maurizio brings the news that Filipeto, whom he went to fetch for the betrothal, has gone out with Riccardo and cannot be found. When Canciano rails against Riccardo, the latter, incensed, comes out of hiding and challenges him. Filipeto is then discovered, and Lunardo angrily orders them both out of the house, declaring that Lucieta shall not marry.

Act III. The men grumble about the 'wickedness' of their wives, and wonder how to punish them without causing themselves undue inconvenience. Felice enters and gradually brings them round to a more reasonable attitude. Lunardo eventually relents and agrees to Lucieta and Filipeto's marriage.

For this innocuous plot Wolf-Ferrari wrote enchanting music with arias, duets, trios, large ensembles and delightful flowing recitatives. At first one might even think one were listening to Rossini, an impression which is strengthened by the chamber-music orchestration, until one detects the spirit of the twentieth century in many little harmonic, rhythmic and instrumental usages. Wolf-Ferrari created his personal style by just this blending of two musical eras into real unity, even if the style as such as not dazzlingly original.

Il Segreto di Susanna (Susanna's Secret) by the same composer has often been performed. The story—Susanna's secret is in fact that she surreptitiously smokes cigarettes—seems nowadays so terribly childish that even the captivating music cannot make this little curtain-raiser acceptable.

Perhaps Wolf-Ferrari's most important work, musically, is the opera *Sly* (Milan, 1927), based on the Prologue to Shakespeare's *The Taming of the Shrew*, a work with more serious undertones which penetrate its superficial gaiety without destroying the sense of unified construction. He had by then left behind him the light Rossini style of his early works and developed more maturity and stature, but yet this important work has had no lasting success. His only tragic work, *I Gioielli della Madonna (The Jewels of the Madonna)* (Berlin, 1911), shows close affinity with *verismo*, and an abandonment of his own, lovable style, but even this score is studded with brilliant detail which contributed towards the great, if short-lived, success of a very effective work.

In the attempt to escape from the influence of *verismo* or of Puccini, other Italian opera composers of the next generation, such as Ottorino Respighi, Riccardo Zandonai, Franco Alfano, and Ildebrando Pizzetti, consciously adopted the style of Richard Strauss, thereby sacrificing the Italianate nature of their music. The operas by these composers have not stood the test of time. Their best-known works are listed below:

Ottorino Respighi (1879–1936): *Belfagor* (Milan, 1923); *La Fiamma* (Rome, 1934).

Riccardo Zandonai (1883–1944): *Francesca da Rimini* (Turin, 1914); *Giulietta e Romeo* (Rome, 1922); *I Cavalieri di Ekebù* (Milan, 1925); *La Farsa Amorosa* (Rome, 1933).

Franco Alfano (1878–1954): *Risurrezione* (Turin, 1904); *Cyrano de Bergerac* (Rome, 1936).

Ildebrando Pizzetti (b. 1880): *Fedra* (Milan, 1915); *Debora e Jaële* (Milan, 1922); *Fra Gherardo* (Milan, 1928); *Vanna Lupa* (Florence, 1949); *Ifigenia* (Radio opera, 1950); *La Figlia di Jorio* (Naples, 1954); *Assassinio nella Cattedrale* (1958).

Ferruccio Busoni (1866–1924) belongs more to the generation of Richard Strauss and Puccini and was therefore older than the Italian composers just mentioned. He was however far bolder and more modern both in feeling and expression. Like Wolf-Ferrari, he was of German-Italian origin, and while he belonged more to the German cultural tradition in his thought and studies, in his creative work he never turned his back on his Italian heritage. He was a great innovator in all branches of music, and his strivings towards a new classicism naturally resulted in the use of classical forms which, though misunderstood in his time, are today much better appreciated. In many ways Busoni can be regarded as a connecting link between the old and the new.

In his operas *Turandot* and *Arlecchino (Harlequin)*, presented as a double bill in Zurich in 1917, Busoni tried to realize his ideal of *opera buffa* which consisted of song and dance, aria and ensemble, linked by short passages of dialogue. In *Arlecchino* these short forms are grouped into four larger sections, rather like a light suite. The story is a lively charade in the style of the *commedia dell' arte*, in which the well-known figures of Harlequin and Colombine, the Doctor, the Abbot and above all the Tailor Matteo play out their merry tricks in a whirl of gaiety. The music tries to capture the charm and grace of eighteenth-century *buffo* music and to give it a modern look, but it does not always attain the necessary lightness.

From the purely musical point of view *Turandot* is the more effective work. The merry, grotesque episodes take second place to the lyrical and dramatic events. Though both elements are enchanting in atmosphere, each mood is only lightly touched on, without any real development of the drama or any great attempt to create an oriental setting. Busoni's strong sense of style is still recognizable within these limitations, but the result

of his restraint in developing any of his dramatic effects was
to rob the work of the success it deserved. When Puccini's
Turandot appeared in all its glory, Busoni's was completely forgotten. His greatest operatic work, *Doktor Faust*, was completed
after his death by his pupil Philipp Jarnach. Busoni himself wrote
the libretto, as for his other operas, and took for his source the
old puppet-play.

DOKTOR FAUST. Opera in two prologues, one interlude and three
scenes by Ferruccio Busoni. Text by the composer. First performance:
Dresden, 1925.

Characters: Doktor Faust—baritone; Wagner, his familiar—baritone;
Mephistopheles (in various disguises)—tenor; The Duke of Parma—
tenor; The Duchess—soprano; the major-domo—bass; the girl's
brother, a soldier—baritone; a lieutenant—tenor; three Polish students—
one tenor, two basses; a theologian—bass; a jurist—bass; a doctor of
natural history—baritone; four students from Wittenberg—tenors; five
spirit voices—two tenors, one baritone, two basses; another spirit voice
(Mephistopheles)—tenor. Churchgoers, soldiers, courtiers, hunters,
Catholic and Lutheran students, country-folk.

Place: Wittenberg and Parma. *Time:* fifteenth century.

First prologue. Faust's study in Wittenberg. Three mysterious
students from Cracow enter and give him a magic book, together with
its key and his credentials as its owner.

Second prologue. The same. Faust uses the magic book to invoke a
servant of the devil, but the first five voices which speak out of tongues of
flame do not satisfy his requirements. The sixth, however (Mephistopheles) claims to have the speed of human thought. When Mephistopheles
appears, Faust demands of him all possible human experience, but
Mephisto will only serve him in this way if Faust will thereafter serve
him for ever. Reminded of his creditors, and the young soldier who wants
to kill him for seducing his sister, Faust reluctantly agrees and signs the
pact.

Interlude. In a chapel of a cathedral, where the young soldier is praying
for revenge. Mephisto conjures up some of his fellow-soldiers, who kill
him for supposedly murdering their captain.

Scene i. At the court of the Duke of Parma. Elaborate celebrations of
the Duke's marriage are in progress. The famous Faust is announced, and
conjures up visions to amuse the Duchess. Each couple which appears
resembles Faust and the Duchess. This the Duke notices with alarm. Faust
and Mephisto decline the Duke's invitation to the banquet, and leave,
while the Duchess sings dreamily of her love for Faust. Daylight breaks
and the Duke's chaplain (really Mephistopheles) tells the Duke that the
Duchess has eloped with Faust.

Scene ii. An inn in Wittenberg. Faust is talking with some students,
who quarrel among themselves, some being Catholic and some Protestant.
Prompted, he tells them of the most beautiful woman he ever loved, a

Duchess, on her wedding-day a year before. Mephistopheles enters as a messenger, to tell Faust that the Duchess of Parma has just died, and sent Faust a memento of herself. He presents Faust with the dead body of a new-born baby and cynically recounts Faust's amorous adventure to the students. He then sets fire to the corpse—which turns out to be nothing but a bundle of straw—and conjures up Helen of Troy from the smoke. Faust, left alone, is about to seize the vision when it vanishes, and three dark figures from the shadows are heard demanding back the book, the key and the letter. Faust dismisses them contemptuously and welcomes the thought of death.

Scene iii. A street in Wittenberg on a snowy night. Wagner has just been made Rector of the University and Faust recognizes Wagner's house as the one which had once been his. He gives some money to a beggar woman with a child, who turns out to be the Duchess. She gives Faust the child, who is dead, and disappears. Faust tries to go into the church to pray, but the dead soldier blocks his path until Faust spirits him away. He can find no words of prayer, and is horror-struck to see the body of Helen of Troy on the crucifix. He then lays the dead child on the ground, surrounds it with his girdle and from within this magic circle prays that his spirit may enter the child and that it may atone for his faults and shortcomings. He dies, and as midnight strikes a naked youth rises from his body and walks away. The watchman bends over Faust's dead body, wondering how he died.

Busoni wrote music of overwhelming strength and grandeur for this rather confused scenario. The greatest climaxes come in the choral scenes: the off-stage *Credo* chorus, while Faust signs his pact with the devil, and the *Gloria* which follows, as well as the impressive quarrel-chorus of the Catholic and Protestant students, in which the fanatical Protestants sing their Lutheran hymn against the *Te Deum laudamus* of the Catholics. There is also great sombre power in the appearance of the 'Cracow students' with their wierdly inflexible rhythms, or the desperate invocation in the final scene. In crude contrast to these exciting descriptive passages, the scenes at the ducal court are mostly built on lively dance rhythms.

In treating such a romantic subject Busoni made greater use of contemporary methods of musical expression than in his other works. In his comic operas he had deliberately turned away from romanticism in favour of a neo-classical style, which opened the way to the operatic works of the 'New Music'.

The tremendous tensions which affected all spheres of spiritual and artistic life after the First World War caused a particularly marked crisis in musical style. Although this crisis had been threatening for a long time, it had a completely revolutionary effect when it was suddenly sparked off by the circumstances of the time. At first general opinion ranged itself against the new movement, which having once clearly established the path it was to follow did not allow itself to be diverted or restricted.

Whether the various movements grouped together under the term 'New Music' were atonal or polytonal, neo-classical or neo-baroque, based on a twelve-note ground-row or some exotic scale, they had one thing in common—a decisive repudiation of romanticism, and a natural reaction against the excesses of the late romantics.

At first 'New Music' showed little interest in opera. This was wholly in keeping with the nature of the movement, for the external trappings which inevitably belong to opera—splendid stage settings, great vocal displays by soloists and massive choruses and orchestra—were quite incompatible with the aims and ideals held by the leaders of 'New Music'. While the struggle for these aims was carried on in the field of chamber music where Hindemith was the key-figure, Strauss and Schreker were as before the focus of operatic interest. But opera was not by-passed by the new movement for long. As soon as the forms and formulae for absolute music were established, some of the leaders of this 'Sturm und Drang' era turned to opera—Hindemith and Křenek in Germany, and Milhaud and Honegger in France. Not only did they have to reject the means of expression of the preceding epoch, but the *forms* of romantic opera as well, since if they were to draw opera into their orbit, it was also necessary to adapt it to their fundamental ideas of form. The first operatic attempts were hampered by unsolved problems, but already showed signs of a fundamentally healthy vitality. The will to break with tradition and blaze new trails opened up hitherto unsuspected possibilities and completely new perspectives, thus introducing a new era for opera.

The nineteenth-century operatic ideals of music-drama and Italian singers' opera were deposed; the theatrically effective dramatic text was thrown out and preference given to one-act works. In some cases there was a reversion to Renaissance opera, in others to oratorio; the spoken word was heard again, and then the dance took its place. Fairy-tales, legends and grotesque stories were favourite material, and around folk song and folk dance revolved the plot which was no plot, but only hinted at or frozen into sculpted formality. The quantity of forms was at first confusing, but they were fairly quickly sorted and grouped until valid shapes emerged in the spirit of the new music which could provide suitable vehicles for the musical content.

A review of Igor Stravinsky's (b. 1882) stage works gives a unique yet satisfactory resumé of this process—unique, because Stravinsky's early works exhibit in principle all the formal experiments of the new composers in the 1920's and 30's; satisfactory, because in his probably quite unconscious and un-intentional harmony the broad, unified lines of a new conception of music took on convincing shape and lasting validity.

Opera takes second place to ballet in Stravinsky's stage compositions; in fact, his only operas in the traditional sense are Le Rossignol (The Nightingale) (Paris, 1914), and The Rake's Progress (Venice, 1951). His many other stage works of varying length cannot be called ballets; yet they are not operas either, but rather operatic sketches—inspired studies of the problems of opera. Stravinsky never bothered about the effectiveness of his works and scarcely acknowledged basic dramatic concepts. His only concern was to make music, and he was completely indifferent to the possibility of popular success. He said himself that it was of no interest to him to write music to words and to a plot at the same time, and this repudiation of the basic pre-requisite for opera explains his unique experimentation with its problems. From his abundant supply of inspired creative energy, Stravinsky poured out a prodigal quantity of ideas which were seized on from all sides, tested and developed into multifarious independent forms.

The first drafts for Le Rossignol go back to 1907, and in 1908 Stravinsky finished the music for the first act and then set it on one side. Five years later he took it up again, but meanwhile he had produced his wonderful ballet music for Petrushka (1911), and Le Sacre du Printemps (The Rite of Spring) (1913), in which all the forces of his creative nature burst out in their full power. In the spring of 1914 the score of *Le Rossignol* was completed, and the first performance took place in Paris during one of the Diaghilev seasons. Naturally the music of the second and third acts was fundamentally different from that of the first act. Stravinsky was himself conscious of this divergence, but left the music as it was, for his early style, bound as it was to lyrical impressionism, seemed to him well suited to the delicate, poetic atmosphere of the first act.

LE ROSSIGNOL (The Nightingale). Fairy-tale opera in three acts by Igor Stravinsky. Text after Hans Andersen by the composer and S. Mitusov. First performance: Paris, 1914.

Characters: The nightingale—soprano; the cook—mezzo-soprano; the fisherman—tenor; the Emperor of China—baritone; the chamberlain—bass; the bonze—bass; Death—contralto; three Japanese envoys—two tenors, one baritone. Courtiers; ghosts.

Place: China. *Time:* fairy-tale time.

Act I. A forest by the sea. It is night and the fisherman in his boat is throwing out his net, while to his delight the nightingale is singing. Led by the cook, the chamberlain and the bonze come with some courtiers to admire the miracle of the nightingale's song. The cook has told the Emperor about the bird, whom she now invites in her master's name to sing at the palace. The nightingale agrees and goes on the cook's hand, while the fisherman continues to sing its praises.

Entr'acte. The courtiers question the cook, who tells them about the nightingale.

Act II. The Emperor's palace. The royal procession enters with the nightingale, who sings so charmingly that the Emperor forgets his melancholy. Envoys of the Emperor of Japan enter, bringing as a gift a golden mechanical nightingale. When it starts singing, the real nightingale quietly flies away. The Emperor is so indignant that he banishes the faithless bird from his lands for ever. The fisherman's voice is heard as the curtain falls.

Act III. The Emperor's bedroom. The Emperor is very ill, and Death is sitting at the foot of his bed, wearing his royal regalia, while ghosts crowd round him. When he calls for music, the nightingale enters and with its lovely songs drives Death and the ghosts away. When the courtiers arrive, expecting to find the Emperor dead, the room is flooded with light and their ruler rises to greet them. The fisherman calls on everyone to acknowledge that the nightingale has conquered disease and death.

In addition to various song-cycles, two very original works resulted from Stravinsky's study of Russian folk songs—*Renard* (*The Fox*) and *Les Noces* (*The Marriage*). These pieces are neither opera nor ballet, they are both highly problematic in form but very stimulating in their boldly stated stage requirements. *Renard* is almost a pantomime: four dancers present the legend in front of the curtain, while two tenors and two basses sing from the orchestra-pit. The text comes from Russian folk-lore: the fox, the cock, the cat and the billy-goat are the *dramatis personae* and there is no question of dramatic effect, because words and story are simply a pretext for the music. The music is however written in delightful popular manner with impudent touches of burlesque, and is undeniably funny throughout. In style it is full of free improvisation with changing metres, endless rhythmic subtleties and bold digressions from tonality which is then re-established by *ostinato* passages. This is most satisfyingly carefree music, unshackled by convention and subject only to its own laws which it most convincingly displays.

The music for *Les Noces* is also improvisation. Here the effect rests mostly with the chorus, while the four solo voices are sometimes absorbed by it, and sometimes come forward to represent an individual character. The accompaniment consists of four pianos and a complex percussion section—an aggressively revolutionary orchestration which aroused much comment and disapproval. The music pulses with primitive vitality, but does also contain certain mystical features. The bells which ring out repeatedly from voice and accompaniment embody in their lively tones the duality of this fascinating music.

Stravinsky calls this work 'Choreographic Scenes'. The visual aspect is concerned with rustic wedding customs, while a plot is only briefly indicated. Chorus and soloists sing from the orchestra-pit (as do the soloists in *Renard*), unseen by the audience, while the dancers mime the action on the stage.

Stravinsky knew that he could not expect these two works, written during his wartime exile in Switzerland, to be performed at the time they were written, because of the excessive technical demands of both scores. In fact *Renard* was first produced in 1922, and *Les Noces* in 1923, both in Paris.

It was natural that Stravinsky's next idea for a stage-composition was a work which could be mounted, without musical or scenic conventions, on an improvised stage with a handful of performers and musicians. Together with his friend, the poet Ramuz, he conceived and wrote *L'Histoire du Soldat* which, though its nature was determined by practical considerations, was immediately regarded as revolutionary, and only much later fully acknowledged and appreciated in its full significance as an inspired example.

L'HISTOIRE DU SOLDAT (The Soldier's Tale). Drama to be read, acted and danced in two parts, by Igor Stravinsky. Text by Charles Ferdinand Ramuz. First performance: Lausanne, 1918.

Characters: the narrator; the soldier; the devil; the princess.

Part I. The soldier, on his way home for a fortnight's leave, stops to rest beside a stream. He takes his kit, including a violin, out of his knapsack. The devil, disguised as an old man, tries to buy his violin or to exchange it for a magic book. The soldier agrees to the exchange, and to spending three days with the old man, to teach him to play the violin in exchange for being taught the secrets of the magic book. The three days turn out to be three years, and when the soldier reaches his village nobody recognizes him. The devil, now disguised as a cattle-merchant, reminds him of his magic book, which can make him rich very quickly, but riches do not make the soldier happy and he longs for his violin. Disguised as an old woman, the devil shows him the violin, but when the soldier snatches it back, he cannot get a sound out of it. In a fury he throws the violin away, tears up the magic-book and finds himself a poor soldier again.

Part II. The king's daughter is ill, and whoever can cure her may marry her. In the castle the soldier meets the devil, masquerading as a violinist. The soldier makes the devil drunk, gets hold of the violin and cures the princess with his playing. The devil threatens to destroy him, but the soldier seizes the violin again and makes the devil dance to his tune until he falls exhausted. Although the devil warned the soldier not to go back to his village, where he would fall into his power, the soldier cannot resist his longing for his home, and sets out on the road, accompanied by the princess. As the soldier reaches the village boundary the devil throws himself on him and seizes the violin. To the sound of an unearthly triumphal march played by the devil, the soldier is compelled to follow him down to hell.

L'Histoire du Soldat was originally intended for performance at fairs, in the open air, or in barns, and this primitive setting and atmosphere must therefore be deliberately recreated in the theatre. On one side of the stage sits the narrator at a small table with a bottle of wine and a glass. On the other side sits the orchestra, which consists of violin, double bass, clarinet, bassoon, cornet, trombone and percussion. Changes of scene are just indicated by moving a few 'props' about. This work has little to do with the conception of opera, all the basic elements of which have been simplified in the extreme until there are no externals to interfere with the stage action or distract concentration from the music, which is of immediate and compelling fascination.

At first one is struck by the insistent, asymmetric, inflexible rhythm, then by the *ostinato* principle, the constant recurrence of the accompanying figures in often crude variations, until the strangely harsh melodies begin to take hold of one and the whole style exerts a peculiar fascination. Often the most widely varied elements are superimposed on each other with extremely complex results, especially in the metres and rhythms, but these alternate with simple, impressive passages, like the soldier's

march at the beginning, or the tune from the 'little concert',

which recurs later in the princess's tango. Each of the seven orchestral instruments is handled according to its individual character and technique. The percussion, with emphasis on the drum, plays an important part, and the narrator's rhythmical speech is strongly effective. It is astonishing that this work should have had such an influence on the development of opera, with the essence of which it has nothing in common.

Stravinsky's next work for the theatre was the one-act comic opera *Mavra*, which he wrote as a tribute to the Russo-Italian opera, in memory of the deep impression made on him in his childhood by the operas of Glinka, Dargomizhsky and Tchaikovsky.

MAVRA. Comic opera in one act by Igor Stravinsky. Text after Pushkin by Kochno. First performance: Paris, 1922.

Characters: Parasha—soprano; the neighbour—mezzo-soprano; the mother—contralto; the hussar—tenor.

Place: a small Russian provincial town. *Time:* about 1800.

Parasha is busily working when her lover, the hussar Basil, comes to the window. They are both unhappy because they cannot be together. The old cook has died, and Parasha's mother cannot find a new servant. Parasha brings her hussar into the house disguised as a cook, and for a while the lovers are happy. Unfortunately the mother enters while the hussar is shaving, and faints. While the neighbour shouts for help the hussar escapes through the window, leaving Parasha calling after him.

The music of *Mavra* is derived from Russian folk songs, with harmonies which are in part primitive, in part exaggeratedly bizarre, and enlivened by constant changes of rhythm. The *buffo* tradition is revived in its arias and ensembles, which frequently border on parody.

In 1925 Stravinsky decided to set an ancient classical drama to music, with a text in Latin to underline the monumentalism and eternal validity of the subject. His choice fell on Sophocles's *Oedipus Rex*, the plot of which he intensified to the highest possible degree in collaboration with the French poet Jean Cocteau. To make the work more comprehensible to the audience they introduced a narrator, who comes down to the footlights in modern dress, and in the language of the country relates, at stated points throughout the drama, what is about to happen.

OEDIPUS REX. Opera-oratorio in two acts by Igor Stravinsky. Text after Sophocles by Jean Cocteau. Latin version by J. Daniélou. First performance (as an oratorio): Paris, 1927. First stage performance: Vienna, 1928.

Characters: Oedipus, King of Thebes—tenor; Jocasta, his wife—mezzo-soprano; Creon, Jocasta's brother—bass-baritone; Tiresias, a soothsayer —bass; a shepherd—tenor; the messenger—bass-baritone; men of Thebes—tenors and basses.

Place: Thebes. *Time:* mythical.

Act I. The plague is raging throughout Thebes. King Oedipus, who rescued the city from the Sphinx, is called on to help his people again. Creon returns from Delphi where he has consulted the oracle, and reports that the murderer of the previous king, Laius, is still living in Thebes. Until he is discovered and punished, the city cannot be freed. Oedipus promises to find the murderer and avenge Laius's death. The blind soothsayer Tiresias announces that the murderer of the king is a king himself. Oedipus is furious at the implication of these words. The act ends with a chorus of praise to Queen Jocasta.

Act II. Jocasta enters, drawn by the sounds of anger, and declares that she does not believe in the oracle. An oracle predicted that her former husband Laius would be killed by his son, whereas he was killed by robbers at the cross-roads outside the city. Her story impresses Oedipus deeply, for he remembers that twelve years before, on his way from Corinth to Thebes, he had killed a stranger at that cross-roads. A messenger enters to announce the death of King Polybus of Corinth, Oedipus's supposed father, and to inform Oedipus that he was only Polybus's *adopted* child. A shepherd tells how he rescued Oedipus in the mountains where he had been abandoned as a child. Jocasta guesses the truth and withdraws horror-struck. Oedipus too now understands his horrible crime; he is the son of Laius and Jocasta, and was abandoned by them in order to confound the terrible prophecy of the oracle that Laius would fall at the hand of his own son. The oracle has come true; he has murdered his father and married his mother. Jocasta kills herself, and Oedipus puts out his own eyes with Jocasta's golden pin. Deeply moved, the men of Thebes sing to him a last farewell, before he leaves the city.

Stravinsky's deviation from the type of material used in his earlier works was quite deliberate, and with it his musical style changed, as though automatically, from atonality to a stricter, neo-classical form of monumental simplicity, interspersed however with hints of the most varied stylistic tendencies. The coloratura in Oedipus's first arias is reminiscent of Handel, Jocasta's aria reminds one of Verdi, and the messenger's song of Mussorgsky, but these occasional digressions are quite unimportant in relation to the magnificent overall concept, and the elemental grandeur to which Stravinsky here attains.

While the plot is carried by the soloists, the chorus (of male voices only) comments on the events. Its sympathies lie with Oedipus, but it also bears the message of fate. The pitilessly monotonous hammering rhythm of the first chorus, which also accompanies the appeal to the gods, and then returns in the final chorus to complete the circle, embodies the idea of inexorable fate. Piano, kettledrums and harps accompany the throbbing double basses.

Oedipus's self-assurance and complacency are characterized by lively coloratura against the marble hardness of Creon's

words and Tiresias's stiff recitative. Jocasta's music is gentler in
melody and characterized by the use of chromatics. The tonal
simplicity of church music, reminiscent of Gregorian chant, is
heard in the messenger's tale, while the shepherd's story is set
in ⁶/₈ time to convey pastoral simplicity. The characters are
clearly defined with a few strokes in varied style, and yet the
overall effect is one of complete unity, principally because of
the choruses which underline or at least frame each scene and
leave the most abiding impression. The final scene, the shattering climax of the opera, is almost completely borne by the
chorus: a fanfare of trumpets announces this epilogue, and then
sounds the voice of the messenger announcing the death of
Jocasta. This theme is repeated three times more, alternating

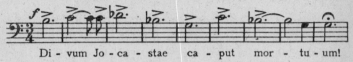

Di - vum Jo - ca - stae   ca - put   mor - tu - um!

with powerful choral passages. At the end the chorus takes up
again the melancholy theme from the introduction, the orchestra
reiterates the triplet theme of destiny and the people take leave
of their blind King. The inexorable blows of fate die away in
unearthly grandeur, pitiless and yet propitiatory in their stern
inevitability.

Oedipus Rex was first performed in Paris in 1927 as a concert
oratorio and was met with complete amazement. The stage
première followed in Vienna in 1928, in a static, masked production wholly appropriate to the nature of the work, and
captivated its audience. It has subsequently been revived in a
similar mode of presentation with great success.

Between *Oedipus Rex* and *The Rake's Progress* (Stravinsky's
last opera) there was an interval of almost a quarter of a century,
during which his stage works were confined to ballets and
pantomimes. *The Rake's Progress* is a full-length work, in which
Stravinsky comes to terms with the problems of opera and
subscribes to traditional forms. From the well-known series of
pictures by the eighteenth-century English painter Hogarth,
the English poet W. H. Auden and the American Chester
Kallman drew their inspiration for a colourful libretto which
tries to unite surrealistic elements with baroque reality.

THE RAKE'S PROGRESS. Opera in three acts by Igor Stravinsky. Text by W. H. Auden and Chester Kallman. First performance: Venice, 1951.

Characters: Trulove—bass; Anne, his daughter—soprano; Tom Rakewell, her sweetheart—tenor; Nick Shadow—baritone; Mother Goose, a brothel-keeper—mezzo-soprano; Baba the Turk, the bearded lady of a circus—mezzo-soprano; Sellem, an auctioneer—tenor; Keeper of the Madhouse—bass. Servants, whores, citizens, madmen.

Place: England. *Time:* eighteenth century.

Act I, scene i. The garden of Trulove's house in the country. Tom is engaged to Anne, but will not conform to Trulove's ideas for a respectable son-in-law, and refuses his offer of an office job, because he has grander ideas for himself. He sighs 'I wish I had money', whereupon Nick Shadow suddenly enters with the news that Tom has come into a huge inheritance, and in order to take possession of it Tom goes off with him to London, agreeing to pay Nick the value of his services a year and a day hence.

Scene ii. Mother Goose's brothel in London. Nick introduces Tom as a novice. The scene is uproariously gay and Mother Goose herself claims Tom for the night.

Scene iii. Trulove's garden. Anne has had no news from Tom since he left and decides to follow him to London.

Act II, scene i. The morning room in Tom's house in London. Tom is sick of his life of low debauchery and thinks nostalgically of Anne. Nick persuades him to marry Baba the Turk, a bearded lady who appears at fairs. The foolishness of the proposal persuades Tom to accept it.

Scene ii. The street outside Tom's house. Anne has reached London, and is waiting here for him. Tom enters in a sedan-chair and getting out tries to persuade Anne to go home again. At that moment Baba pokes her head out of the chair with exclamations of impatience, and Tom confesses to Anne that Baba is his wife. Anne goes out, and Baba and Tom enter the house, acclaimed by a crowd, whom Baba rewards with a sight of her beard.

Scene iii. The morning room. Baba the Turk has filled the house with a fantastic collection of possessions, picked up all over the world. Tom is disgusted and does not conceal this from her. When she loses her temper and begins to shout, Tom covers her face with his wig. Tom's only resort is sleep and he dreams of inventing a machine which makes bread out of stones, thereby relieving the sufferings of mankind. When he awakens, there is Nick beside him, demonstrating just such a machine, and persuading Tom that it will make his fortune.

Act III, scene i. The same room in Tom's house. Baba the Turk is still sitting in her chair without having moved, the wig over her face; and everything in the room is covered in dust and cobwebs. The whole contents of Tom's house are to be sold by auction, since Tom has disappeared, leaving large debts behind him. Citizens examine the goods for sale, but when Anne enters, searching for Tom, no one seems to know his whereabouts. Sellem, the auctioneer, enters, and starts to sell the goods, but when he comes to Baba and takes the wig off her face she comes to life and finishes the phrase she had been singing when Tom suddenly silenced her. Tom and Nick can be heard singing outside. Baba suggests that Anne should find Tom, who still loves her, and look after him. As for herself, she has decided to go back to her career.

Scene ii. A churchyard. Nick tells Tom that his time is up, and that he requires his soul, rather than his money. However, if Tom can beat him at a game of cards he may save himself from hell. Tom wins, but Nick, enraged, condemns him to madness, then sinks from sight into a grave. At dawn Tom is found sitting on a tombstone, weaving grass into his hair and singing childishly to himself.

Scene iii. Bedlam. Tom, surrounded by madmen, tells everyone that he is Adonis, and that Venus will soon come to visit him. The gaoler enters with Anne, whom Tom greets as his Venus. They sing a love-duet, and then Anne rocks him to sleep with a lullaby. He wakes after she has gone, raves of his Venus, and sinks back, dead.

Epilogue. Anne, Baba, Nick, Tom and Trulove come in front of the curtain to point the moral of the story: 'For idle hands and hearts and minds the devil finds a work to do'.

This rather distasteful story is decked out in the forms of classical opera—arias, recitatives, duets, trios and choruses— while the finale is built up into a grand ensemble. Stravinsky has composed it all with subtle simplicity which often conceals a note of parody, as in Anne's virtuoso *cabaletta* in the classical style:

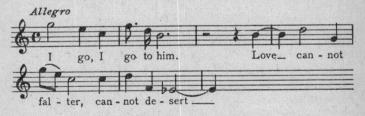

Arias and duets are traditional in form and remind one of Handel and Mozart both in expression and content. We find coloratura, cadenzas, and an effective use of *stretta* in the style of Verdi. The music is tonal, harmonically clear and extremely singable, while rhythmical and metric oddities, only to be expected from Stravinsky, continually enliven the transparent scoring, and occasional false relationships, capricious bass phrases and bitonal passages give a piquant charm to the harmonic background. The work is scored for a classical orchestra, without trombones, and a harpsichord is even included for the recitatives. In spite of these limitations the orchestration is always colourful and interesting.

Of all Stravinsky's works for the stage only *Le Rossignol* and *The Rake's Progress* can be called true operas, while the others have virtually nothing in common with opera in the accepted sense of the term. They have their own, very original laws of form which were conceived by Stravinsky more or less playfully but were to have a stimulating influence later on and be raised to the status of principles, from which derived the most vital forms of modern opera. Honegger and Prokofiev, Orff, Egk and Reutter, Britten and Frank Martin, and in part also Křenek and Hindemith, were inspired by Stravinsky's formal innovations and also followed his choice of subject—legendary, classical, popular and topical. In their works the chorus plays an increasingly important part in the plot, pantomime is used a great deal, a narrator is often introduced, and the scenic oratorio or static choral opera acquires the greatest importance. The unique development of opera during the last thirty years is of course not attributable to Stravinsky's influence alone, for many strong personalities have had a part in it. The line leading from Stravinsky to the most important representatives of modern opera does, however, establish the convincing uniformity of musical style today in spite of all its contradictory elements.

Arnold Schönberg (1874–1951), the second great representative of 'New Music', has not had such a decisive influence as Stravinsky on the development of operatic form. Schönberg was only marginally interested in opera, whereas the influence of his compositions and his teaching on the 'New Music' cannot be disregarded today. The champions of his theories, the representatives of twelve-tone music, form only one small section of those who consciously or unconsciously depend on him. Not until Schönberg smashed the laws of harmonics were barriers really raised to reveal the potentialities which have led to the invasion of tonality and thence to the decisive policies of the 'New Music'.

Schönberg's first stage-work *Erwartung* (*Expectation*) was written in 1909. It is a half-hour monodrama for soprano and full orchestra. The text by Marie Pappenheim tells of the horrifying experience of a woman searching for her lover in the dark forest and finally stumbling on his lifeless body. Schönberg's music plumbs the deepest spiritual emotions of fear, horror, passion and despair, revealing infinitely subtle gradations of feeling. The vocal line is extremely expressive, faintly reminiscent of the music for Kundry in *Parsifal*, or for Electra in Strauss's opera. The first production was at Prague in 1924.

Schönberg himself wrote the text for his next stage work, *Die Glückliche Hand*, which also provides for only one singing voice, while the presence of various mute characters turns the stage-action into a sort of pantomime.

DIE GLÜCKLICHE HAND (The Lucky Hand). Drama with music by Arnold Schönberg. Text by the composer. First performance: Vienna, 1924.

Characters: A man—baritone. A woman and a man—silent roles. Chorus of six female and six male voices.

At first the stage is dark. A man is lying on the floor, with a fabulous cat-like creature crouching on his back. Through gaps in the back-drop one can see the feebly illumined faces of the chorus who, partly singing, partly murmuring tonelessly, pity the man who longs for the unattainable. The chorus and the fabulous creature vanish. In a series of tableaux the man experiences desire for the woman, disappointment and despair. The final scene shows him again lying on the floor, with the animal on him, digging its teeth into his neck. In severely accusing tones the chorus asks, 'Did you have to go through it again?' Finally there comes a sympathetic whisper, 'Poor thing'.

It is the nightmare atmosphere of late Strindberg which Schönberg conjures up in this opera, and intensifies through the music. Words and mimed action are of secondary importance compared with his colour symbolism, which constantly changes like a kaleidoscope, each new image being taken up and emphasized by the music. The resulting effect is wholly unrealistic and persistently goes beyond the limits of comprehension. The content of the work is revolutionary, and the indications of a new style which falls so completely outside the customary framework are almost shocking.

In 1929 Schönberg wrote his one-act *Von Heute auf Morgen* (*From One Day to the Next*) to a text by Max Blonda which, like that of Hindemith's *Neues vom Tage*, is conceived as a topical satire. A married couple, each slightly tired of the other, are finally reconciled after brief digressions. 'Everything changes from day to day' is the final moral, and the whole plot is as tenuous as that. It was first performed in Frankfurt in 1930, but without success, since even the complex and continually interesting twelve-tone music could not compensate for the dullness of the text.

Schönberg never completed his great operatic work *Moses und Aron*, though he turned to it repeatedly and intensively in his later years.

MOSES UND ARON. Opera in three acts by Arnold Schönberg. Text from the third chapter of Exodus by the composer. First stage performance: Zurich, 1957.

Characters: Moses—bass; Aaron—tenor; a girl—soprano; a sick woman —mezzo-soprano; a youth—tenor; a boy—tenor; a man—baritone; an Ephraimite—baritone; a priest—bass. Voice from the Burning Bush, beggars, old people, elders, leaders of the Tribes, people of Israel.

Place: Egypt and the Wilderness. *Time:* fourteenth century BC.

Act I. Egypt. God speaks to Moses out of the Burning Bush, naming him leader of his people. Moses demurs, for he has not the gift of eloquence, but God tells him his brother Aaron will be his spokesman. The scene changes to the desert, where the brothers meet. Aaron believes God to be a product of man's highest imagination and cannot understand Moses' more personal concept. Aaron has a deep love for his people and wants to make them an image so that they can visualize God. He hopes for their deliverance from bondage, whereas Moses knows that his and his brother's thoughts can project themselves into action. The scene changes back to Egypt, where the people go about their daily tasks. Some young people tell how Aaron was led to Moses in the wilderness by a pillar of fire. In the next scene the people are arguing about the nature of the new God and the leadership of Moses, who despairs of rallying them. With Moses' staff Aaron performs miracles which fill the people with fear, and conviction of the power of their God. This and their longing for freedom unite them in accepting Moses' leadership. In an interlude we see the people a prey to fear and doubt, since Moses has disappeared up the slopes of Mount Horeb to receive God's commandments.

Act II. At the foot of the mountain. The people are all uneasy, and Aaron cannot dispel their mistrust. In the second scene open revolt has broken out and Aaron's only recourse is to offer the people back their old forms of worship. Their mood soon changes to one of rejoicing, and they worship the Golden Calf. In the third scene Aaron turns his back on God by fostering the cult of idolatry in the people and turning their thoughts to themselves. They offer sacrifices and indulge in orgiastic revels. The only person—a young man—who still believes in the one God is killed by an Ephraimite. In scene iv Moses descends the mountain with the tablets containing the Ten Commandments, orders the destruction of the Golden Calf and calls Aaron to account. The latter pleads his love of the people and his desire to lead them by ways they can understand, for Moses' invisible God is too hard for them to grasp. In his despair Moses destroys the tablets and Aaron, full of confidence, rallies the people to the pillars of fire and cloud and leads them away towards the Promised Land. Moses, bewildered and cast down by his lack of eloquence and power over the Israelites, seeks strength through prayer.

Act III. Moses has had Aaron bound and accuses him again of seducing the people from the true God to follow after idols. Aaron tries to justify his God. When a warrior asks if he should be killed, Moses tells them to free him, since God will show whether he is to live. As soon as his chains are loosened, Aaron falls dead, and Moses reassures the people of their future destiny in communion with God.

Schönberg had already finished composing the second act in 1931, but he could never bring himself to complete the whole, although another twenty years of creative activity remained to him. In any case he believed that this biblical mystery-play was virtually impossible to perform, and therefore all the more credit must go to the Stadttheater at Zurich for mounting it for the first time in 1957. The impression it made was extraordinary and when it was revived at the Berlin Festival in 1959 in an excellent production by the Städtische Oper its significance and theatrical impact were firmly established. The Berlin version included the third act, for which Schönberg never wrote the music: whether it is suitable, or even justified, to accompany the dialogue between Moses and Aaron in this act with music taken from Act I is an open question. In the Zurich performance, which finished with Act II, the fact that it was only a fragment in no way detracted from its effect; on the contrary, being left at the end in agonized doubt as to where the truth lay, was a most thrilling experience. Schönberg's music is extraordinarily effective in intensifying the diversity of happenings on the stage, from the fascinating choral effect of the Voice from the Burning Bush to the savage orchestral ecstasy of the dance round the Golden Calf. The demands made on chorus and orchestra are as unusual as those Schönberg made on stage technique; like Stravinsky, when writing an opera he completely ignored its limitations and strove exclusively for the realization of an ideal, which makes his works very difficult to mount. His use of form and his musical stature, however, have been a considerable source of inspiration and a force to be reckoned with since the 1920's.

Among Schönberg's pupils, Egon Wellesz and Alban Berg turned to the problems of opera. Wellesz (b. 1885) tried in his *Alkestis* to revive baroque opera, and Alban Berg (1885-1935) tried to use the strictest principles of form in his operas. He pursued the same course of ideas as Busoni, whose effect as champion of the new operatic idea cannot be overestimated. Berg was more fortunate than Busoni or Wellesz in realizing his ideas, and his opera *Wozzeck*, which was at first greeted with enthusiasm by a small circle of admirers and rejected by everyone else, has since overcome all opposition. Performances all over the world have repeatedly testified to the profoundly evocative quality of Berg's musical idiom.

WOZZECK. Opera in three acts by Alban Berg. Text after Georg Büchner's drama by the composer. First performance: Berlin, 1925.

Characters: Wozzeck, a soldier—baritone; The drum-major—tenor; Andreas—tenor; the captain—tenor; the doctor—bass; two workmen—baritone and bass; a fool—tenor; Marie—soprano; Margret—contralto; Marie's child—child soprano. Soldiers, maids, children, servants.

Place: A German provincial town. *Time:* beginning of the nineteenth century.

Act I, scene i. The captain's room. The captain is being shaved by Wozzeck, his batman. The captain, in a continuous flow of chatter, criticizes Wozzeck for always being in a hurry, and goes on to comment on the fact that he has an illegitimate child, to which Wozzeck replies that poor people like himself cannot afford conventional morality.

Scene ii. A field near the town. Andreas and Wozzeck are cutting sticks. The latter's mind is slightly unhinged and he babbles a lot of nonsense out of his overwrought, fearful imagination.

Scene iii. Marie's room. Marie is watching the band go by and singing with it. The drum-major waves to her, and her neighbour Margret comments slyly on her interest in soldiers. She leaves the window and sings a lullaby to her child. Wozzeck knocks at the window, too hurried to come in or even greet his child, and full of confused talk which frightens her.

Scene iv. The doctor's study. The doctor accuses Wozzeck, on whom he is trying out some diet experiments, of not doing as he is told. Wozzeck gets more worried and frightened, so that the doctor suspects he may be going mad.

Scene v. The street outside Marie's house. The drum-major makes advances to her until with a shrug of resignation she lets him in.

Act II, scene i. Marie's room. When Wozzeck enters, Marie tries to hide her new earrings, then tells him she had found them. He gives her the money he has earned from the captain and the doctor, and leaves her sadly thinking about her unfaithfulness.

Scene ii. The street. The doctor is taunting his friend the captain with the possibility that he may soon die of apoplexy when Wozzeck comes lurching past. They stop him to tease him with hints about Marie and the drum-major and are horrified at his violent reaction.

Scene iii. The street outside Marie's house. Wozzeck insinuates that he knows her secret. She goes into the house, leaving him dazed outside.

Scene iv. A beer-garden. A band is playing; Wozzeck finds Marie dancing with the drum-major and is filled with jealousy. Soldiers and drunken workmen sing, and the scene ends with the fool coming over to Wozzeck and talking about blood, the thought of which is beginning to obsess Wozzeck.

Scene v. The barrack-room. Wozzeck cannot sleep for thinking of Marie and the drum-major. The latter enters, very drunk, and boasting of his conquest. He and Wozzeck have a brief fight, and Wozzeck is knocked down. When Andreas says that he is bleeding Wozzeck once again starts muttering about blood.

Act III, scene i. Marie's room. It is night; Marie is reading the story of Mary Magdalen and prays for forgiveness for her own, similar, sin.

Scene ii. Near a pool in the wood. Wozzeck and Marie are out walking. Wozzeck refuses to let her go home when she wants to, draws his knife and cuts her throat.

Scene iii. An inn. Wozzeck is dancing with Margret. When she sees blood on his hand and others crowd round him, he rushes out.

Scene iv. The wood. Wozzeck returns to look for the knife, which he throws into the water. He looks at Marie's body and then begins raving about blood, as though it were everywhere around him, and staining his hands and clothes. He walks into the pool to wash himself and goes on walking until the waters close over his head.

Scene v. The street outside Marie's house. A group of children are playing; they discuss the news that Marie has been found dead. Her child, however, cannot understand what is being said, and while the rest run off to see Marie's body, he goes on playing by himself on his hobby-horse.

The music of *Wozzeck* stresses both the physical events and all the shades of emotion in the story which, told in fifteen short scenes, has a direct and powerful impact. At moments of intensity Berg is not afraid of resorting to painfully harsh passages where the music seems to deteriorate into mere noise. Berg's orchestral language can be defined as musical *pointillism* for it is full of dotted notes and splashes of musical colour, the inevitable outcome of his expressive musical painting. Above this orchestration, which faithfully reflects all the horror of the story, are heard the solo voices, sometimes in lyrical, rhythmic *cantilena*, sometimes in a musical speech which only hints at

Ich bin stolz ——— vor al - len Wei - bern!
(I am proud ——— a-bove all wo - men)

pitch. The music is deliberately atonal, and one frequently
comes across twelve-tone rows. To the strange theatricality of
Büchner's play Berg's music contributes the ultimate in spiritual
depth. Some individual scenes acquire a truly terrible grandeur:
the Bible scene, when Marie is filled with fearful foreboding, the
horror of the murder by the pool in the wood, and the crude,
gay colours of the scene in the beer-garden. This last scene
clearly shows that the illustrative details like the dance-music
and the bawling singing of the girls and boys are only the background which throws into relief the spiritual events; in this case
the emotions whirling about in poor, humiliated Wozzeck's
confused mind. The dance-music is blurred in outline, and the
song of the hunter from the Pfalz suffers horrible distortion

Ein   Jä-ger aus der Pfalz   ritt   einst durch ei - nen grü-nen
(A   hunter from the south   was   ri-ding through a   sha-dy

Wald!   Hal - li,   Hal - lo!
grove!   Hal - li,   Hal - lo!)

through the confusion of its chords. This is expressionism, in
spite of all the realism of the drama—an expressionism which
carries tremendous tension and lasting vitality.

The dramatic and musical construction of *Wozzeck* is extremely concise; each act is divided into five scenes, and each
scene is built on certain types of form used in absolute music,
such as fugue, passacaglia, fantasy, rondo and scherzo. The five
movements then join together in the second act into a symphony, and in the last act into a series of six inventions. At a

first hearing one only grasps isolated instances of this construction, such as the fugue passages, the march, the lullaby or the eerie fantasy over an organ pedal-point in the murder scene. The astonishing concentration of musical ideas which emerge through these forms must strike a receptive listener, however unconsciously, but the form is only the basis on which Berg built up his wonderfully evocative and expressive tone-pictures.

Berg never quite finished his second opera, *Lulu*, based on Wedekind's *Erdgeist, oder die Büchse des Pandoras*, but left part of the third act in draft-form. The first two acts were first performed in Zurich in 1937 with great success, in spite of the work being incomplete.

LULU. Opera in a prologue and three acts by Alban Berg. Text by the composer after Wedekind. First performance: Zurich, 1937.

Characters: Lulu—soprano; Countess Geschwitz—mezzo-soprano; a wardrobe-mistress in Act I and a young student in Act II—contralto; the doctor—speaking role; the painter—tenor; Dr Schön, an editor—baritone; Alwa, his son, a writer—tenor; an animal-tamer in the Prologue and Rodrig, an athlete, in Act II—bass; Schigolch, an old man—bass; the prince, a traveller in Africa—tenor: the theatre director—bass-buffo. Casti Piani, a white-slaver, Lulu's clients in the final scene.

Place: A German provincial town, Paris and London. *Time:* end of nineteenth century.

Prologue. An animal-tamer introduces his circus-troupe to the audience. Among them is Lulu, dressed as Pierrot.

Act I, scene i. The painter's studio. Lulu, in pierrot costume, is having her picture painted, while Dr Schön looks on. Dr Schön's son, Alwa, arrives to take him to a dress-rehearsal of a work he has written. The painter makes advances to Lulu, who evades him, but when her husband bursts in, the shock of finding her in apparently compromising circumstances causes him to collapse, and Lulu gradually realizes that he is dead. She does not seem unduly upset, and in a duet with the painter shows that she is a simple, spontaneous woman without any depth of intellect.

Scene ii. A well-furnished room. The portrait of Lulu dressed as Pierrot is hanging on the wall—the painter is now her husband. Lulu reads with surprise that Dr Schön is to marry again. An old beggar comes in, and turns out to be Schigolch, whom Lulu believes to be her father. No sooner has he left than Schön enters to tell Lulu he must stop seeing her, but she claims that she belongs to him, since he rescued her from begging as a child. Her husband, she says, seems not to notice anything she does. In a scene with the painter, Schön tells him something of Lulu's feckless love-life, whereupon the painter goes out and commits suicide. Alwa enters with the news of revolution in Paris. Schön is worried about the possible effect of the painter's suicide on his plans, and Lulu expresses her confidence that Schön will finally marry her.

Scene iii. Lulu's dressing-room in the theatre. Alwa and Lulu comment on Schön's desire to be rid of her. A prince, a suitor for her hand, enters and sings her praises most fulsomely, just as she is carried in in a fainting condition, brought on (she says) by having to dance in front of Schön's fiancée. Left alone with Schön, Lulu shows her power over him by forcing him to break off his engagement.

Act II, scene i. The palatial hall of the house where Lulu is living with Schön, now her husband. Countess Geschwitz, mannishly dressed, calls on Lulu, who goes out with her. Schön is almost insane with jealousy, but Lulu soon returns and they go out together. Geschwitz comes back and hides herself. Schigolch, an athlete and a young student enter. The boy is in love with Lulu and their meeting has been arranged by Schigolch. Soon after Lulu's arrival, Alwa comes in, and everyone else hides. Alwa is also in love with Lulu, but she tells him that she was responsible for his mother's death. Schön overhears this, chases the athlete from his hiding-place, leads his unhappy son away, and suggests to Lulu that she kill herself; but when he presses her she fires at him, wounding him mortally. She is full of remorse, for he was the only man she had ever really loved. Schön dies, calling on his son to avenge him, and in spite of Lulu's pleas Alwa calls the police.

Scene ii. The same room in a slovenly condition. Geschwitz, Alwa and the athlete are planning to rescue Lulu, who is in the prison hospital, suffering from cholera. Geschwitz is to take her place, and she and Schigolch go out together, the latter soon returning with Lulu. Her sickly appearance causes the athlete to change his mind about marrying her and he goes out, while Schigolch fetches the tickets for Paris and Alwa and Lulu leave together.

Act III, scene i. An elegant house in Paris. Casti Piani threatens to give Lulu up to the police unless she enters a brothel. She refuses, dresses as a boy and escapes.

Scene ii. A room in a London slum. Lulu is keeping Alwa and Schigolch on her earnings as a prostitute. Geschwitz enters, to the alarm of one of Lulu's clients. Finally Lulu brings in Jack the Ripper, who murders her, and then kills Geschwitz when she tries to help Lulu.

The principle of fitting each individual scene to the forms of absolute music is applied here as in *Wozzeck*, and the melodies are built up on the twelve-tone row system much more consistently. The strong delineation of mood, which gives the *Wozzeck* music its colourful background, is missing from the score of *Lulu*, but instead modern dance-rhythms are introduced where appropriate to the given situation, and give a slight effect of parody. The dramatic crescendos are intensively built up, and climaxes like the final duet of each act are made compelling by inexorable insistence on the thematic material. This style has nothing in common with the usual *ostinato* technique; it is contrapuntalism, which attains great dramatic tension through an increasingly concentrated density of melodic line.

Béla Bártók (1881–1945) only wrote three stage works—two ballets and one one-act opera—none of which were very successful (nor indeed performed), until several years after they were written. *Duke Bluebeard's Castle*, written in 1911, first appeared on the stage in 1918 and then vanished again for nearly fifteen years. Nowadays its musical significance is generally acknowledged and each new production confirms the compelling dramatic power of the music. The somewhat nebulous text is the only obstacle to its even wider popularity.

DUKE BLUEBEARD'S CASTLE (A kékszakállú Herceg Vára). Opera in one act by Béla Bártók. Text by B. Balázs. First performance: Budapest, 1918.

Characters: Duke Bluebeard—bass; Judith, his wife—mezzo-soprano. His three former wives—silent roles.

Time: legendary. *Place:* legendary.

Scene: A large gothic-style room, without windows, with a staircase and seven large doors. Bluebeard and Judith enter, she still diffident and nervous of him. She wants to open all the doors to let in light and he gives her the keys. Through each of the first five doors she sees blood—blood on the walls of the torture-chamber, on the weapons in the armoury, on the jewels in the treasury (from which she takes a jewelled robe and a crown), on the flowers in the garden, in the cloud hanging over Bluebeard's Kingdom. Behind the sixth door is water—the water of tears, Bluebeard tells her; and when she opens the last door out step three exquisitely lovely and beautifully dressed women—his former wives, who represent to him the earlier stages of his cycle of life. He assures Judith that she is his last love, and goes to fetch the cloak and crown for her. One by one the doors have closed, and after pleading with him Judith in her regalia goes out through the seventh door, leaving him alone again.

Paul Hindemith (1895–1963) is the most important key-figure of the 'New Music' after Stravinsky and Schönberg. He had already made vital contributions to the new musical style in his instrumental works, when in 1926 he decisively entered the field of opera with *Cardillac*. The one-act pieces which had drawn attention to him as an opera composer before that can be regarded as important stages in the development of his solving of the problems of opera. *Mörder, Hoffnung der Frauen* (*Murder, Hope of Women*) (1921), after a poem by Kokoschka, is still wholly music-drama, and the influence of Wagner is quite obvious even in its melodies. *Das Nusch-Nuschi*, which was given in the same programme, is a play 'for Burmese puppets' by Franz Blei; in it Hindemith noticeably abandons the nature and form of music-drama in favour of the concise forms of *opera buffa*. He also clearly attempted musical stylization in his third one-act work, *Sancta Susanna* (1922), in which the music is developed from a single central theme according to the purely instrumental technique of variations.

In *Cardillac* (Dresden, 1926) he most successfully fulfilled the urge for stylization and a return to stricter form in opera which was postulated by Busoni (and in his own strange way fulfilled by Berg in *Wozzeck*) in order to restore the predominance of the music, even in music-drama. For Hindemith, too, opera was only a pretext to compose music, and the libretto merely the necessary foundation on which to base his music. The need for absolute form was to him the first consideration, even if this meant sacrificing dramatic effect or ignoring the text altogether. In its formal rigidity the first version of *Cardillac* is a perfect example of the ideal anti-romantic opera as envisaged by musicians in the 1920's.

In 1952 Hindemith revised this early work, and in reshaping the text he intensified the psychological impact of the action and also made it much more dramatically effective. The musical changes are no less important, for the rigid formalism of the first version has been weakened in favour of flowing, dramatic orchestral language. Effective recitatives alternating with melodic passages of glowing splendour now mingle with the arias and ensembles of the first version, which have been modified and smoothed out in keeping with the new trend. In the new version *Cardillac* may have lost its *avant-garde* significance, but it has undeniably gained in theatrical effect.

CARDILLAC. Opera in four acts by Paul Hindemith. Text by the composer after a play by Ferdinand Lion, itself based on a story by E. T. A. Hoffmann. First performance: Dresden, 1926. (New version: Zurich, 1952.)

Characters: Cardillac, a well-known goldsmith—baritone; his daughter —soprano; his partner—tenor; the prima donna at the opera—soprano;

an officer—bass; a young cavalier—tenor; the contralto, the tenor, the bass, choristers and dancers in the opera *Phaeton*; the Marquis—silent role. People, guards, theatre staff.

Place: Paris. *Time:* the last decade of the seventeenth century.

Act I, scene i. A city square. There has been another murder, and as on all the previous occasions a valuable piece of jewellery was stolen from the victim. The people are very disturbed by these events, and even the cavalier discusses them with the opera singer to whom he is paying court. He buys a gold belt from Cardillac in order to win her favour.

Scene ii. The singer's bedroom. The cavalier gives his mistress the precious gold belt, but while they are embracing a masked figure climbs in through the window, stabs him, snatches the belt and escapes.

Act II. Cardillac's room. The master and his partner are at work. The latter asks Cardillac for the hand of his daughter in marriage, but is refused. The officer enters to arrest the partner whom he suspects of the recent murders. The prima donna comes in with her patron, a rich Marquis, to choose a jewel which the Marquis wants to give her as a present. Cardillac's daughter sells the Marquis the belt which had caused the death of the cavalier, and the prima donna recognizes it.

Act III. Lully's opera *Phaeton* is being performed at the Académie Royale, and the set for this act includes an oblique view of the Académie stage with part of the wings. During the performance, in which the prima donna is singing, Cardillac's partner, who has escaped from prison, comes on to the stage to warn her that her life may be in danger, for she is wearing the fatal piece of jewellery. When the opera is over stage-hands move the scenery and find Cardillac hiding behind the set. The prima donna believes she knows the reason for Cardillac's strange behaviour; he must commit murder, so as to regain possession of the works of art he has created. The officer also guesses this, and takes the belt to prepare a trap for Cardillac.

Act IV. The square outside the Opéra. Cardillac seizes hold of the officer at the stage entrance. The partner throws himself between them and Cardillac escapes without being recognized. The crowd thinks that the partner, who is holding both dagger and belt in his hand, is the murderer. Cardillac is called on to testify for his partner. He enters with his daughter, who is wearing the belt which the prima donna had given her. The sight of it drives Cardillac mad, and he confesses the horrible secret of his crimes. The people throw themselves on him and kill him.

(In the revised version there are only four scenes, the equivalent of Act I, scenes i and ii, Act II and Act IV, and the whole of the Lully opera episode is eliminated.)

The tendency towards rigid musical stylization is still apparent in the new version, but without loss of dramatic impetus. The means Hindemith uses to attain his dramatic climaxes are very varied, and often differ radically from the usual operatic forms of expression. For instance, when Cardillac steals in in the first act, and when the cavalier is stabbed, the music suddenly stops. And these are moments of the greatest dramatic suspense! The great flute duet which precedes this scene has always been the most misunderstood part of the opera, for the idea of accompanying a love scene with the hollow sound of two flutes seems incomprehensible. It is understandable that Hindemith should not write a traditional love-scene with string *tremolo* and horn, but go to the other extreme in his choice of instrument. The result, however, is astonishing, because the break in the music is all the more effective after the idyllic flute nocturne.

It is principally the rhythm that carries the dramatic impetus in Hindemith's music. This is particularly marked when the rhythmic idea is expressed in dense, firm chords beneath the polyphonic texture which includes the singing voice. The corner-stones of the opera are the two great, contrasted choral scenes: the wildly agitated introductory choruses and the tranquil, expressive finale—further evidence of the composer's strict ideas of shape and form.

Hindemith's next opera, *Neues vom Tage*, is a comic work, with a text by the revue writer Marcellus Schiffer. The choice of this text can only be understood in the context of the Berlin atmosphere at the time, when anything, however cheap, was worth a laugh. Hindemith had always enjoyed poking fun at the middle-classes, but here he was on less familiar ground. In *Cardillac* he had occasionally deliberately ignored his libretto, but in *Neues vom Tage* Schiffer's foolish text has hardly anything in common with his invariably distinguished music.

NEUES VOM TAGE (News of the Day). Comic opera in three parts by Paul Hindemith. Text by Marcellus Schiffer. First performance: Berlin, 1929.

Characters: Laura—soprano; Eduard—baritone; the handsome Herr Hermann—tenor; Herr M.—tenor; Frau M.—mezzo-soprano; the hotel manager—bass; the registrar—bass; the tourist guide—bass; the nurse—soprano; the head-waiter—tenor; six managers—tenors and basses.

Place: Berlin. *Time:* the late 1920's.

After a serious quarrel the young couple Eduard and Laura decide to separate. Friends of theirs, Herr and Frau M., who have just returned from their honeymoon, call on them to try and reconcile them, but in so doing they start quarrelling themselves and decide to divorce. The M's are soon happily divorced thanks to the Office for Family Affairs which provided the handsome Herr Hermann as co-respondent. Laura too contacts the handsome Hermann and meets him in the museum where they are surprised by Eduard, who is so angry that he breaks a famous statue of Venus and is sent to prison. Laura for her part goes to meet the handsome Hermann at the Savoy Hotel. While she is taking a bath there, the jealous Frau M. rushes in and rouses the whole hotel, creating such a scandal round Laura and Eduard that they receive offers to appear on the stage, in films and variety shows. They become famous, earn a lot of money and would like to resume married life together. This however is no longer possible, since they are branded in the minds of the public as a couple who are about to be divorced.

Marcellus Schiffer also wrote the text for Hindemith's sketch *Hin und Zurück* (*There and Back*) (1927). However unfortunate this collaboration seemed in *Neues vom Tage*, Schiffer was undoubtedly more adept at the shortest kind of opera. The point in *Hin und Zurück* is that the steeply rising dramatic crescendo of a series of scenes will, through the intervention of a 'higher power from the supernatural sphere', run backwards from its climax until it finishes at the starting point. Hindemith clothed this amusing idea in charming, lively music, appropriate to each situation. The basic structure is of course determined by the character of the piece, but Hindemith elaborates on it freely with his music, avoiding exact inversions which must have seemed very tempting to such a skilled contrapuntalist. To accentuate the humour of this splendid joke, Hindemith restricts his orchestra to six wind instruments and two pianos.

Mathis, der Maler was written in 1934. The libretto (by the composer) is a true literary work, imbued with the deep artistic urge for expression in both language and ideas. It tells the story of the painter Matthias Grünewald and describes the creation of one of the most beautiful masterpieces of Western culture, the altarpiece in the church at Isenheim. Little is known about Grünewald's life, but Hindemith identifies the painter of the Isenheim altarpiece with an artist from Aschaffenburg, Mathis Neidhardt, who was artistic adviser to the Archbishop of Mainz from the year 1511. It is from this mixture of history and legend that the evocative and impressive libretto springs.

MATHIS, DER MALER (Mathis, the Painter). Opera in seven scenes by Paul Hindemith. Text by the composer. First performance: Zurich, 1938.

Characters: Albrecht von Brandenburg, Cardinal Archbishop of Mainz—tenor; Mathis, a painter in his employ—baritone; Lorenz von

Pommersfelden, Dean of Mainz—bass; Wolfgang Capito, counsellor to
the Cardinal—tenor; Riedinger, a rich citizen of Mainz and a Lutheran—
bass; Hans Schwalb, leader of the peasants' army—tenor; Truchsess von
Waldburg, leader of the confederate army—bass; Sylvester von Schaumberg, one of his officers—tenor; Graf von Helfenstein—silent role; his
wife—contralto; Ursula, Riedinger's daughter—soprano; Regina,
Schwalb's daughter—soprano.

Place: In and near Mainz. *Time:* the Peasants' War, about 1525.

Scene i. The courtyard of St Anthony's monastery at Mainz. Mathis
is painting a fresco in the cloister; he stops work to admire the beauty of
nature on this splendid spring day. He is torn by doubt as to whether he
is worthily fulfilling his mission as a painter. Hans Schwalb, leader of the
peasant army, rushes into the cloister with his daughter Regina, seeking
sanctuary. The monks tend Schwalb's wounds while Mathis talks with
Regina, whose purity impresses him. He gives her a ribbon for her hair.
Schwalb's pursuers come into sight, and Mathis lends Schwalb his horse.
Mathis frankly tells Sylvester von Schaumberg that it was he who helped
Schwalb to escape.

Scene ii. The hall in the Martinsburg (the Archbishop's palace).
Citizens of Mainz, Catholic and Protestant, have gathered to welcome
back the Archbishop from a journey and they are arguing among themselves. Mathis arrives after a year of absence. Ursula, the daughter of the
rich Protestant citizen Riedinger, is very happy to see Mathis, with whom
she is in love. Some Lutheran books are to be burnt in the market-place
and though the Archbishop is at first opposed to this he has to give in
when Pommersfelden points out that the edict comes from Rome. After
a dispute about Mathis's paintings, Schaumberg enters and accuses Mathis
before the Archbishop of helping Schwalb to escape. Mathis admits his
deed and implores the Archbishop to give more freedom to the peasants
and to support their cause. When the Archbishop answers that he has no
freedom of choice in this matter, and that Mathis would do better to
mind his own business and not worry about things he does not understand, Mathis asks and receives permission to withdraw from the Archbishop's service.

Scene iii. A hall in Riedinger's house. In the market-place outside the
heretical writings are to be burnt. Capito, counsellor to the Archbishop,
hopes to persuade his master to join the cause of the Protestants by
abandoning his celibacy and marrying the daughter of a rich Protestant—
perhaps Ursula Riedinger—so as to be able to pay his debts at last.
Riedinger hints at this to Ursula, before going out. Mathis enters to bid
Ursula farewell. They are in love with each other, and she is ready to
share everything with him, but he feels he must leave her to fight in the
cause of freedom. He goes out leaving Ursula in despair. She assures her
father of her unswerving allegiance to her faith.

Scene iv. The peasants have seized the village of Königshofen and killed
Count Helfenstein before his wife's eyes. Mathis, who in the meantime
has joined the peasants' cause, defends the Countess and is ill-treated for
his pains. Schwalb arrives with Regina and announces the approach of
the confederate army. The peasants are utterly defeated, and Schwalb

also falls. Mathis is captured and is about to be executed, but is saved by the intervention of the Countess. Mathis is completely crushed by his failure as a man of action. He sees Regina weeping over her father's body and takes her away with him.

Scene v. The Archbishop's study. Capito tries to persuade his master to abjure his faith and to marry, but the Archbishop resents his interference. Capito brings in Ursula, who tells him she is only prepared to marry him for the sake of her faith. He is deeply impressed; her words show him the way to tolerance and a renewal of his own faith. He dismisses Capito, resolving to lead a simpler life, declares religious tolerance in his diocese, and gives Ursula his blessing.

Scene vi. In the Odenwald. Mathis and Regina pause in their flight; she is still tormented by thoughts of her father, but Mathis calms her by telling her of his vision of the Concert of Angels, and she goes to sleep. Mathis's meditation changes to a vision, in which he sees the pictures he must paint for the altar of Isenheim, which is to be the great work of his life. He himself assumes the shape of St Anthony and undergoes the Saint's temptation. The Countess of Helfenstein appears as the symbol of luxury, Pommersfelden as wealth, Ursula as a beggar, a courtesan and then a martyr; Capito as scholarship and Schwalb as a knight in armour. Mathis withstands all the trials, even the demons of doubt sent to torment him. The picture changes and a quiet landscape appears. The Archbishop in the shape of the Apostle Paul comes to comfort him and to tell him to return to his art, as only thus can he find himself and fulfil his mission and duty to the people.

Scene vii. Mathis's studio in Mainz. Mathis is asleep and Ursula is watching over the dying Regina, reflecting on the meaning of life and on Mathis's amazing new inspiration. Regina wakes and asks Ursula to return to Mathis the ribbon he gave her when they first met, and Ursula recognizes it as one she had given him. She awakens Mathis, who goes to Regina and holds her hand as she dies.

After an orchestral interlude, the studio is seen again, almost empty. The Archbishop comes to say farewell to Mathis, whose work is finished, and who now wants to look for a quiet place where he can die. Even the Archbishop cannot dissuade him from this plan. Left alone, Mathis opens a chest into which he puts a few books, his tools for drawing and painting, a golden chain and Regina's ribbon—all the symbols of what had once been his life.

In *Mathis, der Maler* Hindemith's style takes on an exceptional lucidity. Even if each note is clearly written in his earlier hand-writing, the polyphonic vocal line, the harmonies, and the texture of rhythm and sound are all simplified into a calm, expressive form. The complex polyphonic shapes are now joined by harmonic chord passages, and the melodic language is austere but impressive. Medieval German tunes and baroque-type melodies are blended with Gregorian chants into a concise

unity. This clarified style is already apparent in the prelude—the
Concert of Angels—and continues through the richly variegated
series of scenes to the spiritual and musical climax of the opera,
the miraculous comforting of St Anthony by St Paul. In this
scene Hindemith's gift for artistic construction reaches the
epitome of spiritual concentration until the music has the
quality of a mystery and his musical expression attains a simplicity exceptional even in this score. A delicately sculptured
theme, introduced in the vocal line and taken up by the orchestra

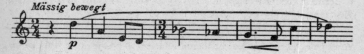

in unison, is repeated several times significantly before it gives
way to the surging power of a hymn. This ecstatic duet is
smoothed away by the tranquil final scene which follows,
centred around the deeply moving burial interlude in the
orchestra. The final passages die away in quiet resignation,
leaving the listener in the grip of deep emotion.

The first performance of this important work took place in
Zurich in 1938, several years after its completion, because it was
banned in Germany under the Third Reich and did not appear
there until 1946 (Stuttgart) when it made a lasting impression
throughout the country. Now that he had an adequate libretto,
drawn from his own emotional world, Hindemith's limpid,
clearly constructed music was generally appreciated. The long-
drawn-out ensemble passages are a little tedious, but the
colourful, dramatic events in the individual scenes and the
powerful tension of the recitatives are ample compensation.
The general effect is that of a significant work of art.

Hindemith chose another historical subject for his last opera,
Die Harmonie der Welt, for which he again wrote the libretto.
The story revolves around the great astronomer Kepler, whose
vision of the harmony of the spheres, which finds its parallel in
the harmony of music, Hindemith adopted as his own. The
grandiose final apotheosis, which ends in a passacaglia in the
brilliant key of E major, is unquestionably the musical climax
of the work. The splendid characteristics of Hindemith's style
of composition appear here at their most effective: the clear

formal construction, the assured execution of large ensembles, the noble pathos of polyphonic texture, the splendid baroque, and yet quite modern, orchestral sound. It was first performed at Munich in 1957.

Ernst Křenek (b. 1900) like Hindemith first started the creation of an original style in his instrumental works, and his exuberant talents conquered all other fields of music before he turned to opera. His first stage works then followed each other in quick succession: in 1922 the scenic cantata *Die Zwingburg* after a poem by Franz Werfel (not staged until 1924) and in 1923 *Der Sprung über den Schatten* (*The Leap over the Shadow*) to a text of his own. In subject and music these two works are vastly different, although they both deal with problems of the time, and indeed carry topical theatre on to the opera-stage. While *Die Zwingburg* anticipates Stravinsky's and Honegger's much later opera-oratorios, *Der Sprung über den Schatten* is a bold step in the direction of atonal operetta, with contemporary dance-rhythms and jazz music. Both these fundamentally dissimilar types of work suited Křenek's talents, for he was receptive to any new idea, were it atonal polyphony or jazz, and his astonishing versatility and great technical skill enabled him to tackle new problems one after the other without appearing to suffer from stylistic inconsistency. The same contrasts between these first two operas also appear in his next works, the rigidly formal *Orpheus* (1926) and the jazz-opera *Jonny spielt auf* (1927), and are then resolved into a measure of unity in *Das Leben des Orest* (*The Life of Orestes*) (1930). From then on Křenek concentrated on opera, for his years of practical work at the Staatstheater in Cassel had strengthened his ties with the theatre and his delight in its colourful atmosphere. He continued to write sincere, unaffected works, full of life and drama, which for a time at least won him the leadership over his contemporaries in the field of opera.

Křenek's best music is probably that of *Orpheus und Eurydike*. Although he was only twenty-three when he wrote it, his very personal style is already fully developed, the score is clearly constructed, the melodic lines appear at first to be tonally determined, though they often break into atonality, a strong impetus drives every scene and the solemnity of the musical language goes far towards glossing over the many puzzling passages of dialogue. Kokoschka's very confused libretto is probably still the reason why this significant work is not revived.

With *Jonny spielt auf*, however, the text of which he wrote himself, Křenek won international acclaim, and in the first two years after the Leipzig première it was performed in more than a hundred theatres. It was greeted with praise, amazement and some dislike, and became the operatic sensation of the 1920's.

JONNY SPIELT AUF (Jonny strikes up). Opera in two parts by Ernst Křenek. Text by the composer. First performance: Leipzig, 1927.

Characters: the composer, Max—tenor; the singer, Anita—soprano; the negro, Jonny, jazz-band violinist—baritone; the violin virtuoso, Daniello—baritone; the chambermaid Yvonne—soprano; the manager—bass; the hotel manager—tenor; a railway official—tenor; three policemen—tenor, baritone and bass. Hotel guests and employees; travellers; people.

Place: A large Central European town; the Alps; Paris. *Time:* the present.

The singer Anita loves the composer Max, but during a concert-tour in Paris she also falls in love with the violin virtuoso Daniello. Daniello and Anita are staying in the same hotel where the negro Jonny leads the jazz-band. He is passionately eager to own Daniello's wonderful old violin. He even manages to steal the precious instrument, but then does not dare to keep it, and hides it first in Anita's room, then in Max's, so that Anita is accused of the theft. The last scenes take place at the railway station, where everyone is taking the train to Amsterdam. Daniello falls under the incoming train, Max is arrested but then freed by Jonny and brought to the station at the last minute when he jumps on the moving train to rejoin Anita. Jonny climbs on a railway signal, triumphantly waving the violin. The station clock changes into a globe on which Jonny stands. Everything whirls around him, as 'Jonny strikes up'; the New World conquers the old Europe with a dance.

As may be gathered from the story, *Jonny spielt auf* is a jazz-opera. In so far as the jazz elements are used to characterize the world of the negro violinist, they undoubtedly enrich the music with rhythmic variations and new orchestral colours. Unfortunately the jazz style spills over into the serious parts of the opera, and the whole work deteriorates into operetta-like banality. There are also passages of luscious romanticism which are equally embarrassing. It is of course in keeping with Křenek's original musical gifts that the whole opera is constructed with great skill and strong dramatic impetus, and that it contains many ravishing episodes and some hints of parody.

This successful idea of revitalizing the forms of expression of 'New Music' by the introduction of jazz was followed up by Křenek in his three one-act operas (1928): a naturalistic drama, *Der Diktator*, and the operetta *Das Schwergewicht* (*The Heavyweight*) in which the idolized champion boxer is shown up as a helpless idiot, both of which deal with topical subjects. Between these two strongly satirical pieces Křenek inserted *Das geheime Königreich* (*The Secret Kingdom*), a romantic fairy-tale.

Křenek next tried to blend all these elements—romanticism and contemporary theatre, musical drama and jazz—into a 'grand opera', *Das Leben des Orest*, which represents both a synthesis of his previous operatic creations and their temporary cessation.

This bold attempt to cover the whole fateful tragedy of the Oresteia in one evening was only partially successful. It does contain individual scenes of strongly expressive power, such as the fair scene, but others are ruined by the need for extreme compression. A very successful device is the introduction of realistic moments which give the mythological events timelessness and affinity with our own feelings and experience. This also explains the introduction of jazz-like elements into the music. The rhythmic throbbing of the double basses forms an exciting background to the dramatic action, and fox-trot rhythms give the dances a popular note. Little of the bold atonal technique which characterized Křenek's earlier works is to be found in *Orest*, where the dominant means of expression is a simple tonality, sometimes provocatively primitive, so that one suspects a tendency towards parody. It is the strong dramatic impulse which must be admired in *Orest*, in particular in the third act, which is constructed with real dramatic and musical mastery. There is especial charm in the idyll of Orestes's return to his homeland, sandwiched between the two bloody and horrible scenes of the murders of Agamemnon and Clytemnestra.

The different means of expression which Křenek had used in his operas with varying success are partly exhausted and partly carried *ad absurdum* in *Das Leben des Orest*, so that no further development along these lines seemed possible, and in fact his next opera, *Karl V* (1933, not produced until 1938) represented a completely new departure. In this work Křenek returns to twelve-tone music, partly in a very free form peculiar to himself, and partly seeking new effects within the strict disciplines of this technique. He handles his material quite differently from Berg, and *Karl V* still bears the unmistakable imprint of Křenek's pen, even though the subject also represents a complete break with his previous habits. Though this opera contains many indications of oratorio style, they are outweighed by its dramatic elements in the style of grand opera. *Karl V* is epic music-drama in its most committed form. The old Emperor has abdicated and retired from the world. In the peace of the monastery he tells his confessor the story of his life, of which the most important moments are shown on the stage; these include visions of Luther, Francis I of France, Charles's sister Eleonora, whom he married to his greatly admired rival Francis, and his wife Isabella. Wars and Councils pass in review before us, seen through the eyes of a man disappointed in himself and his uncompleted mission in life. The work is great and noble in conception, but this cannot conceal its lack of dramatic concision or climaxes.

The same serious sense of mission characterizes Křenek's next stage work *Pallas Athene Weint* (*Pallas Athene Weeps*) (1956). The passionate dramatic text describes the fall of Athens, the frivolities of General Alcybiades and his sudden downfall, and the death of Socrates. The opera opens with Pallas Athene's heart-rending lament over the ruin of Athens, the city she herself founded, and closes with a moving cry from the women's chorus—'Pallas Athene weeps'. Between these two musical climaxes is compressed a tense, dramatic story with moments of staggering brutality, set to exciting music characteristic of Křenek, who remains faithful to twelve-tone technique in this last work, though with bold and interesting variations and strong dramatic impulse.

The sensational success of Křenek's *Jonny spielt auf* was surpassed in 1928 by Weill's *Die Dreigroschenoper*. If Křenek made contact with popular taste when he adopted the style of operetta, Kurt Weill (1900–50), a highly cultured musician and a pupil of Busoni's, who started by writing chamber music, went a step farther. He even dropped the external form of opera, strung together his short songs in dance-rhythms with spoken dialogue, and wrote such easy, catchy tunes that they could be performed

by actors with little or no musical training. Since this enabled
every small theatre to perform the work, the number of productions soon rose to an unprecedented level, such as one only
connected with immensely successful operettas. The deter-
mining factor was Bertold Brecht's text, which was exactly in
tune with the mentality of the time, and therefore could not
fail. Subsequent revivals have shown that however amusing
this work may be in itself, the text at least is too topical for a
repetition of its initial success.

DIE DREIGROSCHENOPER (The Threepenny Opera). Musica
drama in a prologue and three acts by Kurt Weill. Text by Bertold Brech
after John Gay's *Beggar's Opera*. First performance: Berlin, 1928.
  Characters: J. J. Peachum, a fence; Mrs Peachum; Polly, their daughter;
Macheath (Mack the Knife), a crook; Tiger Brown, commissioner of
police; Lucy, his daughter; Pirate Jenny, a prostitute; a clergyman;
Smith, a constable. Beggars, whores, constables, street boys.
  Place: Soho, London. *Time:* beginning of the twentieth century.
  Polly, the daughter of Peachum the king of the London beggars, is
celebrating in a stable her marriage to the well-known Macheath, who
is going under the name of Mack the Knife. The Police Commissioner,
Brown, who had been a war comrade of Macheath's, attends the celebration. When Peachum hears of the wedding, he swears that he will hand
over Mack to the police at the first opportunity, and Polly begs her
beloved to lie low. He goes to a brothel in Tonbridge, where his former
love, Pirate Jenny, denounces him to the police. Polly goes to see her
husband in prison and there meets Lucy, the daughter of the police chief,
who is also in love with Macheath. In a scrap between the two women
Polly gets the worst of it and Lucy helps Mack to escape. Peachum plans
to create a great disturbance with his beggars at the coronation celebrations for Edward VII. Hearing of this, Brown cautions Peachum, who
takes advantage of his meeting with Brown to incite him against Macheath. Brown is obliged to have his old friend arrested again and Mack is
condemned to be hanged. With his head in the noose he is waiting for
the sentence to be carried out, when a king's messenger rides up, gives
him a pardon and announces his elevation to the peerage.

Die Dreigroschenoper is of course modelled on the old *Beggar's
Opera* by Gay and Pepusch which was first performed in 1728—
exactly two hundred years before—as a satire on Handel's
work. Weill's opera has few traces of parody, but relies for its
success on its ballads, which have distinctly vulgar words and
barrel-organ tunes, skilfully spiced with jazz. However much
one may dislike the spirit behind it, the infectious zest of the
impudent music is hard to escape.

In spite of all his success, Weill made no impression on the further development of modern opera, but had a great influence on *Kabarett*, films and operetta. *Die Dreigroschenoper* stood out as an exception in the sphere of opera, though Weill tried—and failed—to repeat its success in 1929 with *Aufstieg und Fall der Stadt Mahagonny* (*Rise and Fall of the City of Mahagonny*), in which he tried a more truly operatic form by writing continuous music, introducing large ensembles, and using a symphony orchestra instead of the jazz-band from *Die Dreigroschenoper*. But the spirit remained the same, as did the milieu of rogues and whores that Brecht depicts here in a bright, harsh sequence of scenes. In spite of all its operatic trappings, *Mahagonny* also revolves round its songs, which perhaps have an even more aggressive effect as a result of their harshly formalized words and the mechanical monotony of their accompaniments.

Mahagonny can be recorded as the most extreme operatic example of the so-called topical theatre, in the sense of social criticism, to which Hindemith contributed with *Neues vom Tage*, Křenek with *Jonny spielt auf* and Schönberg with *Von Heute auf Morgen*. It also marked the temporary abandonment of this rather unsuccessful type of opera. Together with Brecht, Weill then wrote in 1930 an opera for educational radio, *Der Lindberghflug* (*The Flight of Lindberg*) and a school-opera *Der Jasager* (*The Man Who Said Yes*). This latter work is a particularly good example of Weill's very personal style with its trenchant effects achieved through persistent monotony. Unfortunately very few other composers took up Weill's and Brecht's idea of writing school-operas to arouse the interest of young people in 'New Music' and the new operatic ideals.

In 1932 Weill wrote *Die Bürgschaft* (*Hostage*) to a libretto by Caspar Neher. This is an opera-oratorio like Stravinsky's *Oedipus Rex* in which the chorus plays a decisive role, reporting or commenting on every event, and sometimes even taking part in the action. It deals with the question of right and wrong in parable form, and comes to the inexorable conclusion that money can be correlated with power, and power with right. The same inflexibility is also found in Weill's music, which scrupulously avoids any expression of emotion. Here the song plays a secondary role, only appearing in the trios of the rogues, who in the course of the action embody the negative principle of evil, as creditors, robbers, blackmailers and so on. There is a bitter pathos about the grand dramatic scenes, which are rendered relentlessly rigid by their hard and hammering rhythms. In his later stage works, Weill returned to lighter subjects, and a mixed operetta-form in such works as *Down in the Valley* and *Lost in the Stars* which were very successful in New York.

Measured by the quantity and variety of music written in Germany in the 1920's, the French contribution to the development of 'New Music', and particularly new opera, seems relatively small, but the importance of the two leading personalities of the post-war generation in France, Honegger and Milhaud, cannot be overestimated, for they both won international fame in a very short time, due to the brilliance of their compositions and their influence on the younger generation.

Both Honegger and Milhaud belong to 'Les Six', the group which represented the musical *avant-garde* in Paris after 1920. Their aim was to bring about a renaissance of French music by turning away from romanticism, and therefore also from impressionism, which had dominated French music until then. They hoped to achieve this aim by simplifying all musical media and by strongly stressing clarity of form, a principle which has always been very close to the Latin artistic temperament. Seen from this viewpoint the problem of opera was naturally tackled in the first place from the formal side.

Le Roi David (*King David*) was the first great success of Arthur Honegger (1892–1955). It was originally conceived as an opera and first performed as such at Mézières in 1921, but soon after won world-wide fame as an oratorio. Honegger remained faithful to the opera-oratorio form, following *Le Roi David* with another biblical subject, *Judith*, which was first performed in a non-operatic version, that is to say as a play with incidental music, at Mézières in 1925, and then staged at Monte Carlo the following year. *Antigone*, a version by Jean Cocteau of Sophocles's tragedy, followed at Brussels in 1927. One cannot help comparing this work with Stravinsky's *Oedipus Rex*, written in the same year, also to a text by Cocteau. These two opera-oratorios are very similar in form, but differ basically in their development. Stravinsky starts from opera and ends in oratorio, while Honegger does the reverse, for *Antigone* was written as an oratorio which he then tried to transplant onto the stage. The form and expression of the sung roles therefore belong to oratorio; even the dramatic recitatives seem stylized while the score rests firmly on the choruses. Though it is stylistically more unified and concise than *Oedipus Rex*, *Antigone* is not nearly as dramatically effective.

In 1935 Honegger began to set to music Paul Claudel's poem *Jeanne d'Arc au Bûcher*. It was first performed as an *oratorio dramatique* at Basle in 1938 and was also heard in Orléans, Paris and Brussels, but it was not until after the war, when it was successfully revived with Ingrid Bergman as Saint Joan and produced by Roberto Rossellini, that it became a success. As in Stravinsky, and in Honegger's earlier works, a narrator is introduced to relate the story, on which the chorus comments, while solo singers, actors and dancers portray the dramatic action.

JEANNE D'ARC AU BÛCHER (Joan of Arc at the stake). Opera in eleven scenes by Arthur Honegger. Text by Paul Claudel. First performance: Zurich, 1942.

Characters: Joan of Arc—speaking role; Brother Dominic—speaking role; Le grand Heurtebise—speaking role; Madame Botti—speaking role; the Virgin—soprano; St Margaret—soprano; St Catherine—contralto; Cochon—tenor; two heralds—tenor and bass; a soprano voice; a baritone voice; a bass voice; a boy's voice. Heralds, priests, nobles, populace.

Place: Rouen. *Time:* 1431.

Scene i. The Voices of Heaven. The chorus is singing of the sad plight of the land of France when a heavenly voice rings out with the name of Joan.

Scene ii. The Book. The market-place at Rouen. Joan is standing chained to a pole on the pyre. Brother Dominic approaches her, holding a heavenly Book in which her life is recorded.

Scene iii. The Voices of Earth. He starts to read to her from it, and when she recoils in horror at the accusations, he tells her her judges were wolves.

Scene iv. Joan given up to the beasts. She sees a vision of the Court which tried her, presided over by a pig, supported by sheep and an ass for Chancellor. The pig tells her she must confess the diabolical origins of her inspiration and then the flames can purify her from her sin. She protests that this is not true, but is nevertheless condemned to death.

Scene v. Joan at the stake. Dominic points out that to this court the angels seem nothing but foolishness, and only the devil is real.

Scene vi. The Kings or the Invention of the Game of Cards. Joan asks how all this has come about, and Dominic explains by illustrating it with a game of cards. The game includes four kings, four queens and four knaves. This is a ballet sequence in which the King of France is accompanied by Her Majesty the Lady Folly, the King of England by Lady Presumption, the Duke of Burgundy by Greed and King Death by Lust, but it is the Knaves, the Duke of Bedford, Prince John of Luxembourg, Regnault de Chartres and Guillaume de Flavy, who decide the game, and in the end Guillaume de Flavy gives her over to the Court.

Scene vii. Catherine and Margaret. Bells are heard pealing in the darkness, and through them Joan hears the voices of St Margaret and St Catherine, her patrons.

Scene viii. The King who goes to Rheims. Joan remembers how these voices awoke her to her sacred mission, how she was led to free her country and restore her King to his throne. The giant Heurtebise, disguised as a windmill, enters with his wife Madame Botti, and a procession of rustics carrying bread and wine. Their grotesque dancing and revelry is interrupted by the pealing of bells, and the procession of the King and his court to Rheims for his coronation.

Scene ix. Joan's sword. Jeanne relives this climax of her life and, cries out in exultation and joy. St Margaret's voice is heard encouraging her. Brother Dominic asks her about her miraculous sword, but she tells him that to understand it he must be a little child in Lorraine once more.

Scene x. May song. Children's voices are heard and Joan feels around her all the beauty and freshness of spring in the forest. She remembers how she leapt on her horse and all France followed her and her sword of love. Hope and Faith are on her side, even if Rouen burns her.

Scene xi. The burning of Joan of Arc. The flames of the pyre begin to blaze up, some of the crowd bless Joan and some curse her. Brother Dominic has disappeared, and Joan is alone and afraid, waiting for death. The Virgin tells her she is not alone. The devil approaches her disguised as a priest, trying to make her sign a recantation, but she refuses, saying that even if her hands were not chained, the chains of Love would prevent her putting her name to a lie. The voice of the Virgin is heard giving her hope (is she not herself a fire which will kindle all France ?) and courage to abandon herself to the purifying and liberating flames of the pyre and enter God's grace. The crowd join in praise to the martyr, and the sacrifice is completed.

Claudel's most poetic and dramatic text is matched by the quality of Honegger's music, to which he gives a meticulous period flavour by the use of simply harmonized folk songs, a monotonous antiphonal Gregorian plain-chant and touches of seventeenth-century dance-music, all of which serves to capture the feeling of medieval music. Honegger typically combines this with the freest treatment of vocal and instrumental lines, including bold discords and equally bold harmonic construction. These wholly unrelated stylistic elements do however blend effortlessly into a united whole. The overall conception, and particularly the treatment of the strangely penetrating recitative melodrama passages, is one of deep religious feeling, while there is a truly noble grandeur in the final chorus.

Darius Milhaud (b. 1892) is in all ways more restless, more colourful and more varied in his work. His delight in trying out new ideas can be seen in his favourite musical sphere, that of opera. His first operatic success was the one-act piece *Le Pauvre Matelot*, for which Jean Cocteau wrote him a realistic text.

LE PAUVRE MATELOT (The Poor Sailor). 'Lamentation' ('Complainte') in three acts by Darius Milhaud. Text by Jean Cocteau. First performance: Paris, 1927.

Characters: the poor sailor—tenor; his wife—soprano; his father-in-law—bass; his friend—baritone.

Place: a French port. *Time:* beginning of the twentieth century.

The scene shows a bar kept by the wife, the street and the friend's wine shop. There are no intervals and the whole lasts only about thirty-five minutes.

Act I. For fifteen years the sailor's wife has waited faithfully for her husband's return, and his friend admires her constancy. Her father wants her to remarry, but she firmly believes her husband will come back. The sailor enters, but decides first to visit his friend, from whom he learns of his wife's fidelity. He swears the friend to secrecy, as the following day he wants to enjoy a last adventure—that of presenting himself to his wife as a stranger.

Act II. The sailor tells his wife that he is a friend of her husband, who will come to her after dark, for fear of his creditors. She tells him they have no money, either, but rejoices at the news of her husband's return. The supposed shipmate shows her a pearl necklace he was given in reward for being the lover of a barbarian queen—a reward her husband rejected. He asks to stay the night, and when he is asleep the wife is struck by his likeness to her husband.

Act III. The wife kills him with a hammer while he sleeps, for the sake of the pearls, and enlists her father's help to dispose of the body. The friend knocks at the door, but since everything is quiet in the house he goes away again. Father and daughter drag away the body of the supposed stranger, while the woman sings ecstatically of her husband's imminent return.

Milhaud sets this gloomy ballad to music in the style of a dirge. The first notes which introduce the principal theme of the

Tempo di Java

opera catch the street ballad-singer's manner, which recurs throughout the opera. Milhaud is very sparing in his musical characterization and portrays a situation with just a few strokes, with the hint of a motif or simply with an accompanying figure. He uses very simple means of expression, but occasional bitonal chords in which two keys clash give his music charm and bite.

With his *Opéras Minutes* (1927) Milhaud tried to establish a short form of opera not lasting longer than ten minutes, and comprising only a few singers and a chamber orchestra. The three tiny operas are based on classical stories. *L'enlèvement d'Europe* (*The Rape of Europa*) is in eight scenes, which tell the story of Europa, Jupiter and Europa's rejected suitor, Pergamon. The chorus of six soloists gives the framework for the principal characters' short scenes. The construction is straightforward and the music, which passes freely from tonal to atonal, contains some very charming passages. This was first performed at Baden-Baden in 1927, and the other two operas, *L'Abandon d'Ariane* and *La Délivrance de Thésée*, were given, together with the first, at Wiesbaden in the same year.

Milhaud's most important opera is certainly *Christophe Colombe* (*Christopher Columbus*), a large-scale work in twenty-seven scenes, first performed in 1930 at the Berlin State Opera, which recounts the life of the great explorer.

This is the first opera to include a film in its scenario. The protagonist of the plot is the chorus, which takes on the role of interpreter. Paul Claudel wrote the libretto, which in its Catholic symbolism resembles the medieval mystery plays. The diversity of happenings on different levels of consciousness can be slightly confusing, but the music is very clearly constructed. Milhaud's preference for a bitonal line is here developed to a point where polytonality becomes a stylistic principle. The sharp conflicts resulting from this are mostly left unresolved and the tension unrelieved. Even the rhythm is subjected to the formal concept, and rhythmical figures are persistently repeated—a practice more often employed by Milhaud than melodically determined *ostinato*.

Christophe Colombe contains endless intimations of a *Gesamt-kunstwerk* in the sense of 'New Opera': rhythmical speech from soloists and chorus, sophisticated percussion accompaniment to the narrator's voice, choral singing on a single vowel, the assemblage of all types of performance by simultaneous action on several stages by speakers and singers (sometimes in tableaux, sometimes in movement), the introduction of pantomime, ballet and film, the mingling of reality and dream, allegory and Christian symbolism, flashbacks and breaks in consciousness. This infinite variety is oppressive, and the complete absence of dramatic development paralyses the work.

Much the same criticism can be levelled against Milhaud's next opera, the colossal five-act *David* (Milan, 1955), which demands the services of no less than forty-three singers, two full choruses, dancers and augmented orchestra. This epic musical theatre in the grand style poses a variety of problems which were to be solved in part by composers such as Orff, Egk, Blacher, Frank Martin and Britten.

Luigi Dallapiccola (b. 1904) has made a unique contribution to modern opera. In his one-act opera *Volo di Notte* (*Night Flight*) (1940) after the novel *Vol de Nuit* by Saint-Exupéry, he tackles a topical problem, postulating that those responsible cannot shrink from demanding great sacrifices if they believe in the supreme importance of an aerial operation. Dallapiccola's music in parts gives this very dramatic material a staggering banality, and in parts elevates it to a much loftier plane, and this contrast of levels is immensely effective.

For the opera *Il Prigioniero* (*The Prisoner*) (1944, produced 1950), Dallapiccola drew his text from *La Torture par l'Espérance* by Comte Villiers de l'Isle Adam, and from Charles de Coster's *La Légende d'Eulenspiegel et de Lamme Goedzac*. The story deals with the seventeenth-century rule of the Spanish Inquisition in the Netherlands. Does true freedom exist in a world of tyranny? is the question posed in a gruelling series of scenes. It appears that the prisoner has escaped: he emerges from the dungeons into the open, under a starry sky, but then is finally annihilated.

The music, in which the chorus plays a decisive part, is as shattering as the story, but in spite of its hard orchestration, harsh harmonies and rhythms and the prevalence of twelve-tone row technique in its melodies, they do exude Italianate mellifluousness.

After the First World War Stravinsky did not return to his home country and so cannot be reckoned as a Soviet musician. The greatest of the post-Revolution Russian composers are Serge Prokofiev (1891–1953) and Dimitri Shostakovich (b. 1906), whose stage works are only just becoming familiar outside Russia. Little information, however, reaches the outside world about the apparently rich fund of other operatic works within the Soviet Union.

Prokofiev's serious operas, *The Gambler* (1929) after Dostoevsky, and *War and Peace* (1946) after Tolstoy, have not won much recognition in Western Europe, whereas his lighter works, *The Love for Three Oranges* (Chicago, 1921), and *The Betrothal in a Monastery* (1946), have been much more successful. *The Love for Three Oranges*, based on a fairy-tale by Gozzi, is a colourful, fantastic piece, but the libretto is weak. The amusing, inventive and exuberant music is however well qualified to dominate the text and make one forget its inadequacies.

The Betrothal in a Monastery is a *buffo* opera based on Sheridan's comedy of errors called *The Duenna*. It uses old comic tricks most skilfully and is wrapped in a score of infinite charm, both in the lyrical and grotesque passages.

The Fiery (or Flaming) Angel, after a story by Valery Bryusov, was completed in 1925. It was first heard in Paris in a concert performance in 1954 and the next year was produced at the Venice Festival, since when it has enjoyed a fair success in Europe. It is a variation on the Faust legend, and considered by many people, including the composer himself, to be his best opera.

Shostakovich's *Lady Macbeth of the Mtsensk District* became world-famous as a result of the storm it unleashed in the Soviet Press. At its first performance in Leningrad in 1934 it was enthusiastically acclaimed by the Press and public, but two years later it was banned in the campaign against so-called formalism and did not appear again in Russia until 1963. Productions in England, Italy, Yugoslavia and the United States soon followed.

LADY MACBETH OF THE MTSENSK DISTRICT (Katarina Ismailova). Opera in four acts by Dimitri Shostakovich. Text by the composer and A. Preis after a short story by Nikolai Leskov. First performance: Leningrad, 1934. (Revised version: Moscow, 1963.)

Characters: Boris Timofeyevich Ismailov, a merchant—baritone; Zinovy Borisovich Ismailov, his son—tenor; Katarina Lvovna Ismailova, his wife—soprano; Sergei, a workman—tenor; the idiot—tenor; Aksynya—soprano; the priest—bass; a police sergeant—baritone; a constable—bass; a junior officer—baritone; a guard—bass; Sonyetka, a convict—soprano; an old lag—bass. Workmen, wedding-guests, guards, convicts.

Place: Russia. *Time:* middle of the nineteenth century.

Act I. Katarina is unsatisfied and unhappy in her marriage to the weakling Zinovy, but she does not dare lift a finger against her husband for fear of her father-in-law, the tyrannical old Boris. Zinovy has to go off to inspect a distant mill, and while he is away the rough Sergei arouses in Katarina a violent passion. She throws all caution to the winds and abandons herself completely to him.

Act II. Boris catches Sergei climbing out of Katarina's window early one morning, and calls the other servants to hold him fast, so that he can thrash him. In revenge Katarina kills the old man with rat-poison. While she is enjoying her love with Sergei, the ghost of the murdered man returns to haunt her. Zinovy comes home, accuses his wife of dishonourable behaviour, and ends by striking her. She calls on Sergei to help her, and together they kill Zinovy and bury his body hastily in the cellar.

Act III. Katarina and Sergei are about to marry and have invited the whole village to the wedding-breakfast. By chance the body is found in the cellar and Katarina and Sergei are arrested.

Act IV. A transit camp for convicts. Katarina creeps up to Sergei at night, consumed with desire for him, but he will have nothing more to do with her and makes advances to the young convict Sonyetka. Sonyetka promises to give him what he wants if he will get Katarina's warm stockings for her. When asked to by her beloved, Katarina willingly takes off her stockings, but when Sonyetka boasts of her new stockings Katarina realizes what has happened and, throwing herself on her rival, jumps with her over the ruined parapet into the river. The two women are drowned, and the other convicts form into a column and set off for Siberia.

The reason for the original lack of success in Western Europe of Shostakovich's *Lady Macbeth of Mtsensk* lies in the crudity of the text which is stressed by the realistic music. The savage, adulterous passion and the brutal beating of Sergei seem to have inspired Shostakovich to write powerfully descriptive music, though by an indiscriminate use of material: Russian dance-rhythms for local colour, operatic lyricism which borders on banality, and brutal outbursts in the style of the young

Stravinsky. The result is a lack of stylistic unity, but the vitality which pulses through the music is undeniable and most effective. The revision by the composer is mostly of the text, the crude eroticism of certain passages being modified, though there is a new orchestral interlude in the third act.

MODERN GERMAN AND SWISS OPERA

By comparison with the *avant-gardistes* of the previous decade, the operatic composers of the 1930's appear mature and balanced. At this point two figures emerged to take the lead in the development of German opera: Egk and Orff, both stimulating influences, and both South Germans, which comes out clearly in their music. They both started working in Munich, where they founded a Society for New Music. Egk, who is a few years younger than Orff, was the first to establish himself, and soon assumed the leadership of the German operatic world.

Werner Egk (b. 1901) may well be the first composer of international importance to emerge via the radio. The works he wrote between 1925 and 1932 were exclusively composed for this newly developing medium in Germany. He was always open to new ideas and immediately recognized the importance and the potentiality of the new technical achievement. He also showed a sure instinct in complying with the peculiar conditions and requirements of radio, thus playing an important part in the formulation of a radio style. His works for radio, such as *Ein Cello singt in Daventry (A Cello sings in Daventry)* or *Trebitsch Lincoln*, for all of which he wrote his own texts, were full of dramatic drive. Then came the oratorio *Furchtlosigkeit und Wohlwollen (Fearlessness and Good-will)* and *Columbus* (1933), after which he moved on naturally to opera, his first being *Die Zaubergeige* (1935), which was the last in this series of radio works and therefore had none of the characteristics of a first opera, but was a mature and well-balanced work from every point of view.

DIE ZAUBERGEIGE (The Magic Violin). Opera in three acts by Werner Egk. Text by Ludwig Andersen and the composer after Pocci. First performance: Frankfurt, 1935.
    Characters: Kaspar—baritone; Gretl—soprano; the farmer—bass; Ninabella—soprano; Amandus—tenor; Guldensack—bass; Amalie—

contralto; Cuperus—bass; Fangauf—tenor; Schnapper—bass; the mayor
—tenor. Lackeys, court officials, elemental spirits, populace.

Place: a fairy-tale land. *Time:* legendary.

Act I. Kaspar and Gretl are employed as manservant and maid, but
Kaspar is attracted by the wide world and wants to leave the rich farmer,
their employer. The farmer, however, does not want to let Kaspar go,
because according to his reckoning Kaspar still owes him money. Gretl
says she will stay on to pay off Kaspar's debts, and when he leaves she
gives him three farthings to bring him good luck. At the crossroads in
the wood Kaspar meets a beggar who asks him for alms, and although
Kaspar is hungry himself he gives him his three farthings. The landscape
changes to the spirit world, where Kaspar finds himself standing before
the beggar who is in fact Cuperus, the king of the spirits. As a reward for
his good deed Kaspar may have one wish, and he wishes for a magic
violin with which to enchant everyone. His wish is fulfilled on condition
that he renounces love. He is standing again at the crossroads in the wood
when the wealthy racketeer Guldensack comes by. Kaspar decides to try
out his fiddle on him and as he plays Guldensack is compelled to dance
until he falls to the ground unconscious. Kaspar goes away, and the
snoring Guldensack is stripped of everything down to his shirt by the
bandits Fangauf and Schnapper. When Guldensack recovers consciousness, he swears revenge on Kaspar, the devil's musician.

Act II, scene i. Ninabella's castle. Guldensack is working here as
steward and Gretl as maid to the beautiful chatelaine. There is to be a
party that evening, at which a troupe of actors is expected, but their visit
is cancelled. Ninabella tells Guldensack to engage the violinist Spagatini
who has just arrived in the town. Gretl is also sent to Spagatini with a
note from Ninabella, who hopes for a private rendezvous with the
famous virtuoso.

Scene ii. An elegant hotel room. The great violinist (none other than
Kaspar) has taken lodgings here, and is enjoying himself eating and drinking. Guldensack enters to carry out his commission, and, recognizing the
devil's fiddler, decides to do everything he can to ruin him. Gretl also
comes in and is delighted to find her Kaspar again, but he coldly turns
away from her without being able to explain to her why. Gretl goes out,
sobbing, and in his despair Kaspar gets drunk. The mayor enters with a
delegation from the town to give their famous guest a chair of honour
and an enthusiastic ovation.

Act III, scene i. The castle garden. Ninabella is enraptured by Kaspar's
playing, and he is also very attracted to her. He cannot resist her seductive
advances, but as he embraces her Guldensack arrives with the guard to
have him arrested. Kaspar seizes his violin, but it will not play for him
because he has broken his promise to renounce love. Kaspar is led away
in chains and Cuperus takes back his fiddle.

Scene ii. The place of execution outside the town. Kaspar has been
condemned to death as a thief, and is about to be hanged. Among the
crowd are the bandits Fangauf and Schnapper. Kaspar insists that he is
innocent, and Gretl joins her pleas to his, but all in vain. Kaspar must die.
At the last moment Cuperus appears and gives Kaspar his fiddle. Gulden-

sack tries to stop Kaspar playing, but the crowd insists. When Kaspar begins to play, the executioners leave him, and at Cuperus's command the two bandits dance before the people and confess that it was they who robbed Guldensack. Kaspar is now free again, but Cuperus tells him that he cannot rescue him another time if he does not keep his word. Kaspar gives him back the fiddle, saying he will gladly forgo wealth and honours, but he will not leave his Gretl again.

This work is a genuine popular opera, full of touching folk tunes, a robust humour in the best tradition of *opera buffa*, especially in the robbers' scenes, and some nice romantic touches. The music is made even more charming by the slight undertone of sophisticated irony. The *ländler* and polka rhythms

of Bavarian folk music with their fluctuating double time-signature, constantly recur, and the frequent changes of rhythm contribute an irresistible verve, while the bitonal parallel melodic lines, which occasionally appear in this otherwise strictly tonal music, give it a peculiar charm.

The overwhelming success of *Die Zaubergeige* brought Egk a commission from the Berlin State Opera, for which he chose the story of Ibsen's *Peer Gynt*, adapting it freely into a libretto himself. The first performance took place in 1938 in Berlin with unquestioned success, for this work brilliantly demonstrated Egk's ability and originality, and the varied story kindled his musical imagination quite exceptionally. He conveys with equal success the three utterly different spheres in which this drama unfolds: Peer's and Solveig's homeland in the Norwegian mountains, the subterranean kingdom of the Trolls and the Spanish-American scenes. In spite of the sharp characterization of each realm and its inmates, *Peer Gynt* is pervaded by a unity of style which is Egk's alone, full of varied rhythms and bold harmonic effects.

Egk's next work, *Columbus*, a revision of his 1933 radio oratorio, was first performed in Frankfurt in 1942. When adapted for the stage, however, it lost none of its forceful originality, and in fact some passages became more effective than they had been over the radio. Its conception as a scenic oratorio, drawing on ideas from Stravinsky and Honegger, proved a particularly happy one, and it demonstrates the theatrical validity of this highly disputed form. Egk gave his work the sub-title 'Report and image'. The report is made by two narrators who also comment on their contributions, while the events they describe appear before us in grandiose musical tableaux. Egk's libretto is marvellously bold in its treatment of the historical material, and powerfully evocative in its language. The original conception for broadcasting is unmistakable, but it proves particularly adaptable and effective on the stage.

COLUMBUS. Report and image. In three parts (nine scenes) by Werner Egk. Text by the composer. First performance: Frankfurt, 1942.

Characters: Columbus—baritone; King Ferdinand—tenor; Queen Isabella—soprano; three counsellors—one baritone, two basses; a monk—bass; a herald—baritone; a singer—tenor. Two narrators, soldiers, emigrants, sailors, counsellors, priests, Indians, people.

Place: Spain and America. *Time:* 1484–1506.

Part I. King Ferdinand has no sympathy with Columbus's fantastic plans, which he dismisses as folly, and he sends the suppliant away. Queen Isabella, on the instigation of her confessor, receives Columbus and promises to help him. She summons a council meeting, and again Columbus's request is rejected, but after his victory over the Moors the King has three ships equipped for him. Since no one volunteers to join the expedition, the crews are made up by convicts. Columbus spends the night before his departure in prayer, and weighs anchor full of confidence.

Part II. After forty days at sea Columbus finally reaches the New World and formally takes possession of the country in the name of Spain. The Indians, who take these strange white people for gods, worship Columbus and bring him presents made of gold. Columbus decides to go in search of the source of this gold.

Part III. All Spain is rejoicing and thanksgiving services are held in the churches; Ferdinand and Isabella give praise to the Creator, who has lavished such riches on them. Soon however complaints against Columbus and the abuses of his administration reach them. Columbus is brought to Spain in chains. He is able to justify his actions but, deprived of his offices, he is soon forgotten and dies in poverty.

The choruses are the most important element in the music of *Columbus*. The introductory chorus, which returns at the end of the first part and again at the end of the opera, has a grandeur and power which sets the character of the work. Harsh declama-

tion, austere melodies, mixed chords in the accompaniment and a calm, steady flow of movement paint these alfresco pictures in broad, sweeping strokes, even when describing the individual characters. Columbus's music soars in great thrusting arches,

while Isabella's is narrowly concentrated around a basic theme.

Isabella's dreamy ecstasy is thus as clearly expressed as Columbus's stubborn masculine conviction. The strongest musical effects occur in the final scene of the first part, 'Farewell and Departure', and in the grandiose church scene, but dramatic moments are less important in *Columbus* than epic presentation, which is strengthened through the meditative choruses.

After the sensational success of his ballet-pantomimes, *Joan von Zarissa* and *Abraxas*, in which Egk portrays the figures of Don Juan and of Faust in compelling personal interpretations, he turned to lighter opera, and wrote *Circe* (1948) to his own libretto, based on Calderon's famous work.

Festivals, fights, enchantments and pantomimes make the splendid setting for this subtly and penetratingly handled love-story. A burlesque sub-plot deals with the adventures of Klarin and Leporell, two of Ulysses's servants. Klarin is changed by Circe into a monkey, which Leporell tries to tame without suspecting its real identity, and so on. Although these comic scenes provide splendid scope for Egk's pronounced feeling for forthright humour, they occupy rather too much space. The large ensembles and the ballet-scenes are well conceived and handled, but the strongest effect derives from the lyrical passages, where the musical draughtsmanship is particularly subtle and Egk's typical harmonies seem more transparent and balanced than in his earlier works, in spite of harsh dissonances and bold blending of chords. The music of *Circe* is on the whole particularly clear and fine in its design, which matches the lightness and gaiety of the subject.

Egk took the subject of his next big opera, *Irische Legende*, from a play by the Irish poet W. B. Yeats, and again wrote the libretto himself, developing the very modern subject to high poetic grandeur.

IRISCHE LEGENDE (Irish Legend). Opera in five scenes by Werner Egk. Text by the composer after W. B. Yeats's *The Countess Cathleen*. First performance: Salzburg, 1955.

Characters: Cathleen—soprano; Aleel, a poet—baritone; the tiger—baritone; the vulture—tenor; two owls—soprano and contralto; two hyenas/two merchants—tenor and baritone; two shepherds—tenor and bass; an apparition of the damned Faust—bass; Oona, a nurse—contralto; the administrator—baritone; the serpent—dancer. Chorus of angels.

Place: Ireland. *Time:* the future.

The world of the demons, embodied in such beasts of prey as tigers, vultures, hyenas and owls will henceforth dominate mankind, and driven by hunger and fear men will be forced to sell their souls to the devil. Even the beautiful Countess Cathleen is pursued by the demons with hunger and fear; her flocks die, her crops wither, her treasures are stolen and Aleel, the poet she loves, is seduced by the demons and abandons her. Cathleen is ready to sell the only thing she has left, her soul, so as to save her land and her people from destruction. She accepts death voluntarily, but there can be no pact between damnation and salvation, and Cathleen's soul belongs to the angels. Aleel, who has now recognized his sin, comes back to help, but too late. In a vision he sees the demons plunging down to Hell and Cathleen's ascent to the kingdom of the angels.

Egk's musical imagination deals superbly with the clear contrast between the world of the demons and that of Cathleen, and within his own typical style he creates scenes of tremendous power, such as the weird opening, or the tumultuous scene of the sale of souls, in which the shrill fairground music grotesquely underlines the horrid events, and finally the great angelic vision with the intense harmonies of the choruses. Without being dramatic in the theatrical sense, both action and music are effective and impressive.

Egk took the subject for his next opera from a literary classic. Gogol's comedy *The Government Inspector*, which had proved very effective on the stage, made a reliable libretto well suited to Egk's exuberance.

DER REVISOR (The Government Inspector). Comic opera in five acts by Werner Egk. Text by the composer after Nikolai Gogol. First performance: Schwetzingen, 1957.

Characters: Clestakov—tenor; Ossip, his servant—bass; captain of the town militia—bass-baritone; Anna, his wife—contralto; Maria, his daughter—soprano; Misha, his servant—tenor; the postmaster—tenor; the curator—bass; the judge—bass; Bobshinsky—tenor; Dobshinsky—baritone; a young widow—soprano; the wife of the locksmith—mezzo-soprano; a waiter—silent role.

Place: A small Russian town. *Time:* middle of the nineteenth century.

The captain of the militia tells the town notables that a Government Inspector from St Petersburg will very shortly be visiting the town. Two gentlemen, Dobshinsky and Bobshinsky, tell of a mysterious stranger who has been staying at the inn for several weeks without paying his bill. Everyone is sure that he must be the feared Government Inspector, lurking there incognito, and will by now have noted all the by no means innocent goings-on in the town. The captain decides to invite the supposed Government Inspector to stay with him, and so the cunning

Clestakov, quick to assume his new-found dignity, moves from the dirty inn to the captain's house, where he turns the situation to his own advantage, fleecing the various officials, courting the captain's wife, and even getting engaged to the captain's daughter, so that the delighted father-in-law lends him considerable sums of money, believing him to be very rich. At last the time comes for Clestakov to disappear, and he fondly takes leave of his fiancée and future mother-in-law, promising to return soon. The captain and his ladies wallow in their dreams for the future, and receive the congratulations of their friends with dignity. But they are all torn from their illusions by a letter, which the postmaster has opened and read as usual, in which Clestakov relates the whole comedy to a friend and mercilessly pillories corrupt provincial society. Everyone is furious at having fallen so hopelessly for the trick, but their confusion is interrupted by an official announcement that the real Government Inspector has just arrived from St Petersburg and wishes to see all the town officials. The curtain falls with everyone paralysed with fright.

If one is tempted to ask how such a dazzling comedy of words can be adequately set to music, Egk's unfailingly entertaining score provides the answer. The colourful scenes dance past in brilliant (but very taxing) *parlando* frequently interrupted by effective ensembles, but infrequently by arioso passages. The dashing tempo and truly comic and inventive *élan* rule out any question of tedium.

In 1937 the scenic cantata *Carmina Burana* by Carl Orff (b. 1895) attracted widespread attention when it was first performed at the Frankfurt Festival. It was the greatest operatic success in Germany for years, although it is difficult to call this work an opera. It is in fact a cantata, originally written for the concert hall, and consistently effective in concert performance, but it gains substantially from stage presentation. The *Carmina Burana* are derived from a *Benedictbeuern* manuscript of the thirteenth century; they are songs of travelling minstrels, partly in Latin and partly in Middle High German. There is no action, and in a stage performance the main chorus stands to right and left of the stage, while dancers and a small chorus mime the meaning of the songs.

CARMINA BURANA. Secular songs for soloists and chorus with instrumental and scenic accompaniment by Carl Orff. First performance: Frankfurt, 1937.

The Prologue is a grand introductory chorus in praise of Fortuna, whose whims govern everything on earth. The first part comprises praise to the spring, to nature and to the joy of life. The second part, entitled 'In the inn', is made up of the grotesque solo songs of the 'roasted swan' and of the 'Abbot of Cucanien', and of an impassioned choral hymn to earthly pleasures. The third part tells of love and its many and varied guises. The Fortuna chorus returns as the Epilogue.

From the very first chorus, the music of *Carmina Burana* is immediately fascinating. Orff launches into bold, primitive radicalism, repeating simple little tunes in common time, and adhering to the key of D minor without any modulations, but he does build up climaxes of immense intensity by progressive rhythmic variations and tonal subtleties. The complete novelty of the sound is immediately striking, with its special emphasis on percussion, particularly xylophone and piano, and its sudden dynamic changes between *forte* and *piano*. This music is restless and intensely vital, and it is quite unimportant that Orff achieved this effect by the subtle use of amazingly primitive musical devices. The point is that he had found his style.

Orff's next work, *Der Mond*, after the fairy-tale by the Brothers Grimm, is set to his own very skilful and dramatic libretto. Both here and in *Carmina Burana* it is clear that Orff's main source of inspiration was Stravinsky, whose influence is recognizable in many musical details, such as in the 'Fortuna' chorus in *Carmina Burana*, or the peasant dances in *Der Mond*, and scenically in the static treatment of the chorus on stage and the use of mime in *Carmina Burana*, or the role of the narrator in *Der Mond*. Orff has however a surer dramatic touch, and where Stravinsky just indicated, he has often established a form.

DER MOND (The Moon). A fairy-tale opera by Carl Orff. Text by the composer after the Brothers Grimm. First performance: Munich, 1939.

Characters: The narrator—high tenor; four lads who steal the moon—two baritones, one tenor and one bass; an old man called Petrus who keeps heaven in order—bass. An innkeeper, a mayor, peasants, corpses.

The stage is divided horizontally into two parts—the earth and the Underworld. The narrator's desk divides the earth into two exactly similar sections, each with its oak-tree and its inn. There are stars and clouds in the sky.

The narrator reads from a book about a land where the moon has never shone. Four boys from that land enter and see the luminous disc hanging on the tree and throwing out a circle of light. The boys decide to steal the moon and take it back to their country. They are joyfully

welcomed when they return with the moon, which now gives light at
night in their land too. The narrator tells how the boys have now grown
old and grey, and are demanding a quarter of the moon each, to take
into their graves. This last wish is granted, and when they are all dead,
darkness descends on all the earth. In the Underworld the boys stick the
pieces of the moon together again and hang it up as a lamp. The unaccustomed light wakes up all the dead, who start moving about and
making a noise as though they were on earth. The tumult is heard in
heaven and Petrus decides to go and see what is happening in the Underworld. He is fascinated by the moon and at first joins in the merriment,
but he soon realizes that world order must not be disrupted. He therefore
takes the moon away, tells the dead to go back to sleep and returns to
heaven, where he hangs the moon high up on a star. Ever since the
moon has given light to the whole earth.

The music is conceived on the same lines as *Carmina Burana*,
with the same primitive melodies and harmonies, and the same
⁴/₄ time with frequent repetitions. The light comic tone sometimes borders on farce, and there is a certain sentimentality,
very charmingly expressed in the text, which does not always
come out so well in the music. The orchestral colours, more
varied than in *Carmina Burana*, yet equally characteristic of
Orff's style, are quite outstanding, and beautifully suited to the
fairy-tale atmosphere.

DIE KLUGE, the story of the King and the clever woman, by Carl Orff.
Text by the composer after a story by the Brothers Grimm. First performance: Frankfurt, 1943.
    Characters: The King—baritone; the peasant—bass; his daughter—
soprano; the gaoler—bass; the man with the donkey—tenor; the man
with the mule—baritone; three vagabonds—tenor, baritone and bass.
    The peasant has been thrown into prison. While ploughing his field
he had found a gold mortar and taken it to the King. His daughter warned
him that if he did so he would only be suspected of having kept the
pestle, and this is in fact what happened. Now he is in prison, moaning
'Had I only listened to my daughter!' The King hears his cries and has him
brought into his presence. The peasant tells him of his daughter's wise
advice, whereupon the King insists on meeting her. When she arrives,
he tells her that if she can solve three riddles he will desist from punishing
her father any further. The daughter easily guesses the answers and the
King makes her his wife.
    The man with the donkey and the man with the mule, followed by
three vagabonds, come before the King while he is playing chess with
his young wife, and ask him to judge their case. The donkey and the
mule were stabled together at the inn; during the night the donkey bore
a foal, but since the foal lay nearer the mule the man with the mule insists

that the foal belongs to him, although this is against the laws of nature. The King gives judgment for the man with the mule, who goes happily away with the vagabonds. The Queen consoles the donkey-man, telling him that if he follows her advice everything will be put right. The following day the King meets him dragging a large fish-net backwards and forwards along the ground. He answers the King's query by saying that if a mule can bear a foal, he may catch fish on dry land. The King angrily suspects that his wife is behind this impertinence, which the trembling donkey-man confirms. The King sends his wife away, but tells her she may fill one chest with such of his treasures as she likes best. The following morning he wakes up in the chest, where his wife had put him after giving him a strong sleeping-draught, and she tells him he was the most treasured thing she wanted to take with her. 'You are the cleverest woman,' shouts the King full of admiration, but she says it was only pretence, because no one on earth can be clever and love at the same time. As the King takes her in his arms, the peasant comes past, and comments 'She found the pestle after all!'

Theatrically *Die Kluge* is Orff's most successful work. Music, text and dramatic construction combine most happily, and both conception and execution are so clear and natural that even a routine performance will be found amusing. Musically the style is that of the earlier works: lively declamation, bright orchestral colours, rhythmic *élan*, and a continuous, urgent flow of music. Orff's typical pure declamation yields to some extent to lyricism, particularly in the 'Clever Woman's' role, which contains some lovely melodic passages. The harmonic basis remains unchanged, and a single key, or even a single chord, can act as foundation for an entire scene, and yet, far from being boring, the music is magnificently entertaining. The innumerable, persistent repetitions at the beginning 'Had I only listened to my daughter' are downright funny and the sharply orchestrated *ritornellos* in the scene when the King and the clever woman first meet are really fascinating.

Orff's next work was *Catulli Carmina*, like *Carmina Burana* a scenic cantata, in which the text is sung by the chorus while dancers mime the action.

CATULLI CARMINA. Scenic cantata by Carl Orff. Text by the composer after verses by Catullus. First performance: Leipzig, 1943.
   Characters: Catullus; Lesbia, his mistress; Caelus, his friend; Ipsitilla and Amiana, rivals. Girls, youths, old people.
   The stage is raised, leaving the front section, where the secondary action takes place, at its usual level. Here girls and boys express their

mutual affections while their elders try to interrupt their love-making by reminding the young people of the fate of the poet Catullus, who died of love. His fate—Catulli Carmina, Catullus's songs—is now portrayed as a warning to them.

In the three scenes which follow, Catullus's love for the beautiful Lesbia is mimed on the main stage, while a chorus in the orchestra-pit sings some of Catullus's loveliest verses. Lesbia betrays him with his friend, Caelus; he seeks a fleeting consolation in Ipsitilla's arms; Lesbia wants to return to him, but he rejects her though he still loves her. This tale in no way frightens the young people, but on the contrary to the horror of their elders, they return to their passionate cries: 'For ever, for ever I am yours.'

The outer scenes are accompanied by an orchestra of four pianos, kettledrums and extensive percussion, to which the choruses of youths, girls and old people sing and act on the front part of the stage. The music for the principal action however is built on a mixed *a cappella* chorus placed in the orchestra-pit. The work pulses with the same vitality as *Carmina Burana*, but the naïve directness of the earlier work is lacking. In *Catulli Carmina* everything is more studied and sophisticated, though Orff's original, highly distinctive style is here developed with sureness and clarity. The chorus 'Miser Catulle' has an *ostinato*

bass of fourths over sevenths, with the upper voices in fifths and fourths, showing in this strong geometric technique a convincing example of the power of modern *a cappella* art.

Orff carries his style to its furthest limits in *Antigonae*, for which he used Hölderlin's paraphrase of Sophocles's drama.

ANTIGONAE (Antigone). Tragic opera by Carl Orff. Text by Friedrich Hölderlin after Sophocles's tragedy. First performance: Salzburg, 1949.

Characters: Antigone—soprano; Ismene—soprano; Creon—baritone; a watchman—tenor; Hämon, Creon's son—tenor; Tiresias—tenor; a messenger—bass; Eurydice, Creon's wife—soprano. Chorus of the elders of Thebes.

Place: Thebes. *Time:* mythical.

During the siege of Thebes the two brothers, Eteocles and Polynices, who were fighting on opposite sides, have both been killed. King Creon decrees that the body of Polynices, who had fought with the enemy, should not be buried. Antigone, Polynices' sister, defies this command, but while trying to bury her brother she is caught by the watchman and condemned to death. Creon is determined to let the sentence be carried out, in spite of the attempts of his son Haemon, Antigone's betrothed, to save her. Only the prophecy of old Tiresias, that if Creon perseveres in forbidding the burial of Polynices, great misfortunes will fall on his house, makes Creon waver. But it is too late; Antigone has killed herself, Haemon has followed her, and Eurydice, Creon's wife, has also committed suicide. Creon is left, alone and mourning.

Orff first introduces the singing voices in quiet rhythmic speech on one note, and only gradually frees them from this monotonous chanting to launch into melodic expressions of feeling. This monotone chanting remains in the background throughout, even underlying the rich melodic passages, such as the ecstasies of the blind Tiresias, or Creon's cries of despair. The orchestra, whose unique sound is determined by the use of pianos, harps, kettledrums, xylophone and drums, plays a purely secondary role to the recitatives and its simplicity is carried to the extreme, for a single chord or figure is sustained or repeated throughout an entire scene. Orff reaches his dramatic climaxes through sudden dynamic changes between *piano* and *forte* and through occasional acceleration of tempo. The strongest musical and dramatic effect comes in Antigone's great solo scene at the end of the third part, where her voice rises in a passionately expressive *crescendo* over the rigid ground bass. The melodic line is slight, and the accompaniment repetitive, and yet the effect is positively elemental. It is natural for monotony to be tedious in the long run, but when it is carried to such extremes it does emanate an extraordinary fascination.

Ten years after the first performance of *Antigonae*, Orff brought out another work based on Hölderlin's version of a Sophocles tragedy, *Oedipus der Tyran* (*Oedipus the Tyrant*), which was first performed in Stuttgart in 1959. Here we find the ascetic style of *Antigonae* in even more marked form, with lofty declamation on a limited number of notes suddenly breaking into wild coloratura. Speech and recitative alternate, accompanied by a weird orchestra of pianos, harps, double basses, six flutes, six oboes, six bassoons and a variety of percussion. The structure is based on sustained organ pedal-points, deliberately concentrated repetitions of themes and fanatical *ostinati*. This broadly maintained monotony has an extraordinarily evocative effect.

In 1953 Orff wrote the scenic cantata, *Trionfo di Afrodite*, and joined it to *Carmina Burana* and *Catulli Carmina* to make a full-length triple bill under the title *Trionfi* (*Triumphs*).

TRIONFO DI AFRODITE (The Triumph of Aphrodite). Scenic cantata by Carl Orff. Text by the composer after verses by Catullus, Sappho and Euripides. First performance: Milan, 1953.

Characters: the bride—soprano; the bridegroom—tenor. Chorus of virgins, youths, old people, relatives and friends.

The youths and girls are waiting for the young couple to arrive for their wedding celebration. They are taken in solemn procession to the wedding tent where they submit themselves to the laws of Aphrodite. The goddess appears, and everyone breaks into jubilant song.

The events in *Trionfo di Afrodite* can hardly be called an opera plot, but are intended more as the ritual observance of a cult. The chant-like recitative of *Antigonae* also dominates this work, which reaches its greatest musical climaxes in the young couple's ecstatic songs. Again, as in *Antigonae*, one finds the persistent repetition of a chord or motif and the same elemental effect through the subtle use of this simple material.

Orff wrote other dramatic works which belong more to the legitimate than the musical theatre, even where the music occasionally plays an important part. The best of them are the drama *Die Bernauerin* (1948), the grotesque *Astutuli* (1954), and the Easter-play *Comoedia de Christi Resurrectione* (1955). All these plays are written in an old Bavarian dialect which Orff imbued with extraordinary linguistic colour and power.

Hermann Reutter (b. 1900), also from South Germany and of the same generation as Orff and Egk, approaches the problems of opera with great caution and careful preparation. Each opera is for him a new dramatic complex and at the same time a new challenge in musical style. The spontaneity which is so striking in both Orff and Egk is missing in his works, and he even lacks a uniform personal style, for which he searches.

Reutter has much in common with the great Swiss *lieder* composer, Othmar Schoek, for Reutter is also a *lieder* writer and has had much success in the field of oratorio, but he has never really succeeded in opera, despite many and varied attempts. His first dramatic work, the one-act *Saul* (1928), belongs musically to the 'Sturm und Drang' period of the 1920's, being full of unselfconsciously bold dissonances and chord formations. The text, after the play by Alexander Lernet-Holenia, deals with Saul's meeting with the witch of Endor, and gives Reutter marvellous opportunities for impressive dramatic climaxes. His greatest success was *Dr Johannes Faust* (Frankfurt, 1936), derived from the old puppet-play. With deliberate simplicity he tries to create a folk-opera as Egk did with *Die Zaubergeige*, but he cannot match the latter's vitality and originality.

In his second full-scale opera, *Odysseus* (1942), Reutter pays homage to the principle of the opera-oratorio in Stravinsky's style, just as Egk and Orff did at about the same time. The chorus, standing on both sides of the stage, explains Odysseus's adventures: his departure from Troy, Circe's island, Nausicaa, Calypso, the return to Ithaca, the fight with the suitors and the reunion with Penelope. Except for the great dramatic climax at the end, these scenes are lyrical in character and handled with wonderful perception. He expresses himself with particularly glowing effect in the farewell to Nausicaa, in spite of his use of delicate half-tones. The orchestra is more prominent than in *Faust*, but still the main impetus comes from the vocal lines, which are kept very much in character. Reutter's musical differentiation between the various female characters is truly masterly.

Reutter's *Don Juan und Faust*, after Christian Dietrich Grabbe, was produced at Stuttgart in 1950. In it he returns to the style of *Saul*, with the same strength and audacity though with more maturity in the structure and generally more clarity and reflection. The themes, which are sometimes related to motifs from *Dr Johannes Faust*, are mostly written in broad sweeping lines, while the recitatives, largely unaccompanied, are freely and characteristically improvised. This is certainly Reutter's most important opera, but the fact that it has never got beyond Stuttgart is probably due to its unsatisfactory text, which has many parallels with Mozart's *Don Giovanni* and introduces the ageing Faust as an unsympathetic rival.

Rudolf Wagner-Régeny (b. 1903), has a very personal style; his first full-scale opera, *Der Günstling*, which has been justly appreciated, is compelling, both in its music and in the consistent execution of its declared formal pattern.

DER GÜNSTLING (The Favourite). Opera in three acts by Rudolf Wagner-Régeny. Text by Caspar Neher. First performance: Dresden, 1935.

Characters: Queen Mary Tudor of England—soprano; Fabiano Fabiani, an adventurer and a favourite of the Queen—tenor; Gil, a man of the people—baritone; Jane, an orphan, Gil's foster daughter and betrothed—soprano; Simon Renard, a minister—bass; Erasmus, an old man from Naples—speaking role.

Place: London. *Time:* about 1550.

Act I. The maladministration of Fabiani, the Queen's favourite, arouses general indignation, and the minister Renard hopes to prove Fabiani's treachery to the Queen so as to ruin him. In secret Fabiani visits Jane, the foster daughter and betrothed wife of a workman, Gil. Erasmus, whose wife and daughter Fabiani has seduced, threatens him with exposure, whereupon Fabiani kills Erasmus and makes Gil help him to sink the body in the water. With a mocking laugh Fabiani tells Gil that Jane is his mistress. Gil broods on revenge, and Renard promises to help him.

Act II. The Queen promises Fabiani that she will make him her husband, if he will be faithful to her for ever. Renard brings Gil into her presence, as witness of Fabiani's faithlessness. They fake an attempt on the Queen's life and Gil denounces Fabiani as the chief conspirator.

Act III. Fabiani is condemned to death, and also Gil, who appeared to have taken part in the conspiracy. The Queen wants to pardon Fabiani, since she still loves him. She asks Renard to save Fabiani, but Renard is immovable and Fabiani is executed. Gil however is set free and marries his Jane.

The violence of this dramatic story leads one to expect realistic music, but in fact the exact contrary is the case. Wagner-Régeny aims at strict objectivity, avoids any suggestion of dramatization, keeps his orchestra in subdued, sober colours, alternates arias and duets with reflective choruses, and gives the work a formal symmetry reminiscent of pre-classical style. In spite of the deliberately non-dramatic attitude, this rigid and wholly contemporary music is effective.

Wagner-Régeny's next opera, *Die Bürger von Calais* (*The Burghers of Calais* (Berlin, 1939), was less successful, although Caspar Neher tried to adapt the text to his temperament and style by stressing its oratorio aspect, which produced a certain uniformity of text and music. The opera *Johanna Balk* (Vienna, 1941), in which again Wagner-Régeny's peacefully flowing music accompanies an exciting dramatic story, did not have much luck either, but his *Prometheus* (Cassel, 1959) was more successful. The text, adapted freely from Aeschylus, is in a static oratorio style, and the music is hard and angular. Once a rhythm has been introduced, the composer adheres to it obstinately, while a calm but steady impetus keeps the music flowing. Prometheus's *arioso* outbursts form strong dramatic climaxes, while the female choruses play a decisive part in the musical and stage happenings. His *Das Bergwerk zu Falun* (*The Mine at Falun*) (Salzburg, 1961) was a failure.

Boris Blacher (b. 1903) has a distinctive musical personality and has made substantial contributions in the field of opera. Everything he touches he immediately stamps with his imaginative originality, and at first his music seems spontaneous, fresh and nonchalant, until one realizes how skilful and ingenious is this apparently natural style. Imagination and intelligence are well balanced in his music. Blacher oscillates between fantasy and fact, and consciously or unconsciously he has made considerable contributions towards the solution of many operatic problems. The libretto of his first opera, *Fürstin Tarakanowa* (*Princess Tarakanova*) (Wuppertal, 1941), is orthodox in construction, but the music goes far beyond the limits of the text. Most of the music for this work is written in a clear bitonal manner, which however is very freely handled and frequently goes beyond the limits of tonality. Blacher is not afraid of harsh dissonance, and yet the music always seems elegant and flexible. Each scene is a self-contained entity, attained by Blacher through the use of one short motif, which then dominates the whole scene. Sometimes it is just a rhythmic motif, which comes out in many melodic forms and is occasionally employed in strict *ostinato*. The light *parlando* of the vocal line sometimes breaks into *arioso*, and the flow of music is only interrupted by the great climactic scenes between Orloff and the Princess.

In 1945 Blacher wrote the chamber opera *Romeo und Julia* (*Romeo and Juliet*), which was originally intended for concert performance. It was produced on the stage at Salzburg in 1950. In this work he is even more consistent and effective in his use of individual scene motifs. *Die Flut* is also a chamber opera, orchestrated for five wind instruments in addition to a string quintet. It was originally composed for the radio, and was first heard on Radio Berlin in 1946, but is also very effective when performed on the stage, as it was at Dresden in the following year.

DIE FLUT (The Tide). Chamber opera in one act by Boris Blacher. Text by Heinz von Cramer. First performance: Dresden, 1947.

Characters: The fisherman—baritone; the girl—soprano; the old banker—bass; the young man—tenor. Chorus.

Place: The wreck of an old sailing ship stranded on a sandbank. *Time:* today or yesterday.

A party of travellers, consisting of an old banker with his mistress and a young man, have been brought by a boatman to see a wreck embedded in a sandbank. During their visit the tide suddenly rises, and they are cut off from the shore. The tide rises higher until it covers parts of the deck. The girl, bored with city life, flirts with the brawny fisherman, and in the face of certain death they both dream of love. The banker offers the young man all the money he carries on him—a considerable sum—if he will swim to shore and fetch help. The young man contemptuously refuses the money which in the present situation is worthless.

The tide slowly starts to recede and they are all saved. Now that the danger is past, the young man begins to crave for the money. When the banker refuses to give it to him, he brutally stabs him. The girl parts from the fisherman, promising that she will go to him that same night. The young man approaches her and shows her how much money he now has. She is horrified when she realizes what he has done, but is willing to go with him. They hurry out, while the fisherman sings happily in anticipation of the girl he will never see again.

Die Flut is sparse and incisive in its musical form and expression, and the scene-motif principle seems even clearer and more convincing in a single-act work. The structure is broken by the choral passages which describe the action and were originally inserted for the benefit of a radio audience. However, they fit easily into the stage presentation. There is a duality of rhythm and metre in Blacher's music which gives it a particular charm without ever clouding the clear simplicity of the structure.

Preussisches Märchen (Prussian Fairy-tale) (1952), is a comic opera, with a text by Heinz von Cramer which gives an original slant to the story of the Captain of Koepenick. To this impudent, light-hearted story Blacher wrote witty and subtly pointed music, always original and deliberately novel, even though it derives from *opera buffa* in the best sense. The large ensembles and the powerfully austere instrumentation reveal the hand of a skilled and thoughtful master of his art, but the charm of this ballet opera derives from its vivacious, dance-like rhythms.

With *Abstrakte Oper nr I (Abstract Opera No. 1)* (1953), Blacher boldly launches into experimentation. The idea and the text of this problematic work derive from Werner Egk, who had the idea of taking a series of typical contemporary situations and arranging them in abstract form (that is without any connecting plot) and with the help of an abstract text, the words of which are chosen for their musical and phonetic values and powers of association in the mind of the listener. The first scene 'Fear', for instance, is based on the vowel sounds 'ah' and 'oo', and the text of the scene 'Negotiation' on childish English and Russian syllables. 'Fear' is followed by a duet 'Love I' then by portrayal of 'Pain'; 'Negotiation' is followed by 'Panic', and after 'Love II' comes 'Fear' again, which closes the circle as symptomatic of modern times.

This bold excursion into unknown country is scored for three soloists, chorus, wind, piano and percussion, while dancers mime the action on stage. As always with Blacher, the music is amusing, original and austere, with straightforward instrumental effects and fascinating rhythmic versatility. In view of the boldness of this experiment, it was only to be expected that the first performance (in the Mannheim National Theatre in 1953) would cause a scandal, but when the work was revived at the 1957 Berlin Festival under Hermann Scherchen it was well received, as it has been on all subsequent occasions.

For the 1960 Berlin Festival Blacher wrote *Rosamunde Floris* to a strange, free text based on a play by Georg Kaiser which gave him an opportunity to write a completely new kind of opera. All the musical expression is left to the vocal line and the orchestra is given a very secondary part to play, with only occasional dramatic or lyrical passages, but it is important in its outstanding clarification of the text. The musical dialogues are often very dramatic, but the greatest climax comes in Rosamunde's self-accusation and acknowledgment of guilt, the effect of which is emphasized by a few notes on the brass.

Among the other composers in Blacher's circle, Gottfried von Einem (b. 1918) is one of the strongest personalities. His first opera, *Dantons Tod*, was well received when first performed at the 1947 Salzburg Festival.

DANTONS TOD (The Death of Danton). Opera in two parts by Gottfried von Einem. Text by the composer after Georg Büchner. First performance: Salzburg, 1947.

Characters: Georges Danton—baritone; Camille Desmoulins—tenor; Hérault de Séchelles—tenor; Robespierre—tenor; St Just—bass; Hermann, President of the Revolutionary Tribunal—baritone; Simon, a prompter—bass; a young man—tenor; two executioners—tenor and bass; Julie, Danton's wife—mezzo-soprano; Lucille, Camille's wife—soprano. Populace.

Place: Paris. *Time:* 1794.

Part I. Camille tells his friends Danton and Hérault that two more innocent victims have gone to the guillotine and that it is time to combat the Reign of Terror. Danton counsels caution. A riot breaks out in a nearby alley where a young man is in danger of being strung up to the nearest lamp-post by the mob, just because he owns a handkerchief. Robespierre enters and promises the people a further blood-bath. Danton cannot help reproaching Robespierre, who ignores his remarks. Danton goes away. St Just advises Robespierre to have Danton and his friends arrested and condemned, since they oppose him. Robespierre decides to follow this advice even though it means losing his best friend, Camille. Danton is warned that he is about to be arrested, but refuses to hide. Lucille fears for Camille, too, but he counts on Robespierre's friendship to protect him.

Part II. In front of the prison the crowd is arguing about the rights and wrongs of Danton's arrest. Danton and Camille appear at the windows of the prison. Camille is desperate at the prospect of death, and Danton tries in vain to calm him. Lucille comes in, half mad with fear. When he is accused before the Revolutionary Tribunal of having dealings with the enemies of the Revolution, Danton asks for a commission of inquiry. Some of the mob take his side and the prisoners have to be removed by force from the ensuing disorder. The crowd are dancing and singing the Carmagnole in the Square of the Revolution. Danton, Camille and their friends sing the Marseillaise from the steps of the guillotine, but are shouted down by the mob. Camille, Hérault and finally Danton are beheaded, and the crowd disperses. Lucille, who has gone mad, sits down on the steps of the guillotine and sings through her tears 'Es ist ein Schnitter, der heisst Tod' ('There is a reaper whose name is death').

The music of this 'revolutionary' opera is built on strong rhythmic impulses, such as the quick march in the introduction to the second part. The individual scenes are self-contained and convincingly dramatic, but most impressive of all are the big chorus scenes in the Tribunal and around the guillotine at the end, when the Carmagnole and the Marseillaise are interwoven.

For his second opera, *Der Prozess*, von Einem attempted to set Kafka's well-known novel to music, which he did most skilfully and with a sure theatrical instinct.

DER PROZESS (The Trial). Opera in two acts and nine scenes by Gottfried von Einem. Text by Boris Blacher and Heinz von Cramer after the novel by Franz Kafka. First performance: Salzburg, 1953.

Characters: Josef K.—tenor; a supervisor, a passer-by, a manufacturer, a priest—baritone; Fräulein Bürstner, wife of the court-usher, Leni—soprano; the examining magistrate—baritone; the lawyer—baritone; Albert K.—bass; the student—tenor; the court-usher—bass; Titorelli—tenor; Frau Grubach—mezzo-soprano.

Time: 1919.

Act I, scene i. The confidential bank-clerk Josef K. is told one morning that he has been arrested, but for the moment can move about freely.

Scene ii. Josef K. tells the occupant of the next-door room, Fräulein Bürstner, of this unusual form of arrest.

Scene iii. A passer-by in the street gives Josef K. the summons to appear before the court.

Scene iv. Before the examining magistrate Josef K. realizes how ridiculous the proceedings taken against him are, but his truculent manner deprives him of the privilege of being cross-examined. The court-scene is interrupted by the episode of the usher's wife which, together with the scene with Fräulein Bürstner, shows Josef K's coarse attitude to sex.

Scene v. Josef K. watches the two men who had brought him the summons being flogged, and so perceives again the folly and corruption of the whole juridical system.

Scene vi. Josef K. is introduced by his uncle to an old lawyer, but by making love to Leni, the lawyer's servant, he destroys his chances in this quarter.

Scene vii. The manufacturer, a bank client of Josef K.'s, advises him to go to the painter Titorelli, who has very important connections.

Scene viii. During his interview with the boastful Titorelli, Josef K. becomes convinced that there can be no justice for him.

Scene ix. The prison chaplain tells Josef K. that his case has gone against him. Two men step out of the darkness and lead him away to a quarry where he is to be executed.

The nine episodes of this opera are musically almost too formal, clear-cut and self-sufficient, being based on scene-motifs mostly determined by chords. The uneasy flow of the music is given a certain rigidity by *ostinato* rhythms appropriate to the inexorable severity of the text. Even the vocal melodies are intentionally restricted to a monotone, but the declamation is always very natural and clear. This is robust stage music: the crashing, blaring trumpets in the court-scene remain in one's memory as firmly as the tremendous organ pedal-point in the final scene, where the fearful horror of the events is mainly conveyed through the use of subtle orchestral colours.

Wolfgang Fortner (b. 1907) came to opera relatively late in life, when at the age of fifty he was already an established composer. His success was immediate. His first opera was *Die Bluthochzeit* after the drama by Federico Garcia Lorca, for which he had written some incidental music in 1950. He then set to music the most important scene in the play, the wood scene, which verges on the unrealistic, and finally decided to compose a full-length opera, using for his libretto the complete German translation by Enrique Beck.

DIE BLUTHOCHZEIT (Blood Wedding). Opera in two acts by Wolfgang Fortner. Text by Enrique Beck after the drama by Federico Garcia Lorca. First performance: Cologne, 1957.

Characters: the mother—dramatic soprano; the bridegroom, her son—speaking role; the bride—soprano; the bride's father—speaking role; Leonardo—baritone; Leonardo's wife—contralto; her mother—contralto; the maid—mezzo-soprano; the child—soprano; Death in the guise of a beggar-woman—*chanson* role; the moon—tenor; three woodcutters—speaking roles. Girls, youths, guests, women neighbours.

Place: Spain. *Time:* beginning of the twentieth century.

Act I. The mother, whose husband and elder son were murdered some years previously, clings passionately to her younger son, the only one left to her, and only grudgingly agrees to his engagement, especially as her son's fiancée had previously been engaged to Leonardo, who comes of the family responsible for the murder of her husband and elder son. Leonardo has since married a relative of the girl's, but she is not happy, and at night he haunts the street under his former fiancée's window. She is also uneasy, but hopes to forget her previous lover in the arms of her future husband.

Act II. The whole village, including Leonardo and his wife, attends the wedding. When the time comes for the wedding dance, the bride is nowhere to be found. She has fled with Leonardo into the wood, but they are soon followed there. The bride begs Leonardo to leave her and save himself, but he faces the pursuers and in the ensuing duel both rivals, Leonardo and the bridegroom, are killed. In the final scene the two widows are brought together. Leonardo's wife abandons herself to her sorrow, while the bride is ready to pay the price for her action, but the mother does not bring any accusation against her, since she acknowledges the hand of fate in the bloody events which have overtaken them all.

Recognizing all the significance of Lorca's work, Fortner does not attempt to reshape it into an opera. The dramatic substance of the plot and the poetic beauty of the language have such strong and immediate effect that Fortner often lets the text speak for itself without musical assistance, and only breaks in wherever action and words cry out for music. This means mixing singers and actors, which in its turn creates great stylistic difficulties for the producer, since many secondary characters and even the bridegroom himself have spoken roles. Musically Fortner uses many folk-lore elements, interspersing his score with typical Spanish folk-melodies, the electrifying rhythms of Spanish folk-dances, and the characteristic Spanish sound of mandolines, castanets, tambourines and guitars. For the most part, however, the music consists of a free, often twelve-tone, melodic line, supported by dissonant chord sequences and bitonal passages. The most powerful music comes in the scene in the wood. The wild, exciting flight interlude is followed by the infinite peace of the woodland scene, expressed in a twelve-tone canon on two solo violins, softly accompanied by sounds from the percussion, until the moon spreads its light over everything to the gradual *crescendo* of the whole orchestra. Fortner's music is not dramatic in the usual sense, since he leaves the dramatic action to make its own effect without additional musical emphasis, and this economy makes his musical passages all the more impressive.

Fortner was again drawn to Lorca for his *In seinem Garten liebt Don Perlimplin Belisa* (Schwetzingen, 1962), and again he left the play almost untouched, just providing it with a musical frame. The score is strictly organized as a musical whole and is highly sophisticated.

The Swiss composer Heinrich Sutermeister (b. 1910) attracted considerable and justified attention with his first opera *Romeo und Julia* (Dresden, 1940) which has frequently been performed. The main strength of his considerable talent lies in his direct dramatic perception, which gives his operas great drive and compensates for the eclecticism of his music.

The libretto, written by the composer himself, concentrates on the love-story in Shakespeare's play, which makes the scenario amazingly concise. When the brilliant fanfares of Capulet's party give way to the delicate notes of the solo violin which accompanies the lovers' first shy conversation, a lyrical atmosphere is created which, because it is truly operatic in conception, is also strongly dramatic. The same applies to the poetic, ecstatic garden duet and to the final scene. Though the use of distant choruses is very effective, the result is of only just bearable sweetness. The vocal melodies, which are Sutermeister's strong point, also represent a pitfall for him, but it is the wonderful feeling for sound governing his exploitation of all impressionistic musical devices that holds the balance in his favour.

Die Zauberinsel (*The Magic Island*) followed in 1942, another adaptation of Shakespeare (this time of *The Tempest*), and again with a première in Dresden, but it did not even approach the success of *Romeo und Julia*. This work also overflows with melodic ideas, and comic scenes successfully complement the lyrical climaxes, but it is all perhaps a little too polished to have a really deep effect. Sutermeister's third opera *Raskolnikoff* was much more impressive, and nearly equalled the success of *Romeo und Julia*.

RASKOLNIKOFF (Crime and Punishment). Opera in two acts (six scenes) by Heinrich Sutermeister. Text by Peter Sutermeister after Dostoevsky. First performance: Stockholm, 1948.

Characters: Raskolnikoff, a poor student—tenor; his *alter ego*—baritone; his mother—contralto; Rasumichin, his friend—speaking role; Marmeladoff, a former government official—bass; Mme Marmeladoff, his consumptive wife—soprano; Sonia, their daughter, a prostitute—soprano; Lena and Polechka, Sonia's younger sisters—speaking roles; a woman money-lender—speaking role; a bear-owner—baritone; a policeman—baritone. Populace, stall-holders.

Place: St Petersburg. *Time:* middle of the nineteenth century.

Act I, scene i. Raskolnikoff's room. In the brooding midday heat Raskolnikoff is lying on his divan doing nothing. Rasumichin brings him a letter announcing the arrival of his mother. He tries to cheer his friend up and finally calls the landlady, Mme Marmeladoff. The Marmeladoffs are in a very bad way: he has drunk away all their money, she has consumption, and their daughter Sonia has had to become a prostitute in order to keep her family. Raskolnikoff loathes this poverty in which he lives. He wants to be strong and the master of his fate. His *alter ego* frees itself from him and whispers to him seductively: the strong kills the weak!

Scene ii. The hay market. The money-lender has opened her pawnbroker's stall in front of her house. A bear-owner demonstrates his art, and everyone but the money-lender gives him something. Sonia asks the old woman for a loan, but is disdainfully turned away with a recommendation to find herself a client who pays well. Raskolnikoff comes to pawn his watch, for which, to his indignation, the woman only gives him two roubles. His *alter ego* points out to him the injustice that both Sonia and he have to tolerate, and rouses in him murderous thoughts. He seizes an axe and breaks into the old woman's house. Soon after, the lights in the house go out, a cry is heard, and Raskolnikoff rushes out into the street and runs away.

Scene iii. Raskolnikoff's room. Old Marmeladoff has had an accident while he was drunk and is carried, seriously hurt, into Raskolnikoff's room. When his wife and Sonia come in he asks their forgiveness and dies. The neighbours take the body away. Raskolnikoff holds Sonia back and asks her what will happen to her mother and her little sisters. Sonia replies that she believes and trusts in God. Raskolnikoff is left alone, deeply shaken. Murder has shut him out from human society, and in his despair he breaks down and prays to God for pardon.

Act II, scene i. Raskolnikoff's room. His mother has come to town and cannot understand her son's changed and unstable behaviour. He tells her that he must leave her and asks for her blessing.

Scene ii. A graveyard. In the chapel Marmeladoff's funeral is in progress, but Sonia does not dare to take part in the service. Raskolnikoff goes up to her, feeling as cut off as she does. He tells her that he knows who murdered the money-lender; she guesses the truth and feels drawn to him. To be of some help to him she tries to give him the cross from round her neck. Raskolnikoff recoils in fear and runs away.

Scene iii. A solitary place on the banks of the Neva. Mme Marmeladoff has gone mad and is wandering about the streets with her little children, exhorting them to dance before an imaginary audience. Raskolnikoff is haunted by his *alter ego*, who is leading him to commit suicide, telling him there is no other way out. Raskolnikoff refuses to accept this; he challenges his *alter ego* to look him in the eyes and to understand him. When his *alter ego* slowly drops its eyes, Raskolnikoff goes up to his double, and embraces it in forgiving compassion. The *alter ego*, the demon of his split personality, returns into Raskolnikoff, giving him the strength to admit his crime. When Sonia comes to him he can now ask her for the cross and with her tread the path of penitence.

Peter Sutermeister, the composer's brother, was astonishingly successful in turning the spiritual experiences of Dostoevsky's hero into an operatic text. The division of Raskolnikoff into his true self and his *alter ego* offers unusual possibilities for musical exploitation which Sutermeister was able to develop most interestingly. Stylistically *Raskolnikoff* differs widely from Sutermeister's previous operas, for in it he turns to neo-naturalism, sketching a situation or evoking an atmosphere in a few strokes, with invariably compelling effect. Through the first scenes steals a creeping, groping unison theme to describe

Raskolnikoff's spiritual confusion. The chorus, usually off-stage, plays an important part and is often made responsible for increasing dramatic tension, as for instance in the first scene, where the whisper of the *alter ego*, 'Denn der Starke tötet den Schwachen', is taken up and intensified to the utmost by the chorus. Perhaps even more impressive is the choral entry in the second scene, where the physical and spiritual spheres clash, and realistic

Denn der Star - ke tö-tet den Schwa-chen
(*For the strong one de-stroys the weak - ling*)

music and expressionist evocation of the soul are exquisitely
fused. Unfortunately the two last scenes of the opera are something of an anticlimax, largely on account of the nature of the
plot, but they still contain powerful climaxes in the scenes of the
mad Mme Marmeladoff and Raskolnikoff's last struggle with
his *alter ego*. The great duets with Sonia are pallid by comparison.

In 1958 the successful première of Sutermeister's burlesque
opera, *Titus Feuerfuchs*, took place at Basle. Nestroy's farce *Der
Talisman*, on which the story is based, afforded the composer
many opportunities for musical finesse. He employed all kinds
of dance-rhythms and his delightfully varied couplets were as
successful as his grandiose parody of opera. All in all, this is a
charming comic opera and invariably a success, at least in
German-speaking countries.

An interesting personality from Western Switzerland is the
composer Frank Martin (b. 1890). In fact he is more important
in the field of oratorio than opera, and his main work, *Le Vin
Herbé* (*The Love-potion*) (1941), should be regarded as an oratorio,
though it was staged in Salzburg in 1948. The text deals in
broad epic form with three episodes from the Tristram legend
in the version by Charles Bédier. The cast consists of twelve
singers, sometimes used as a chorus, and sometimes as soloists,
when one of the protagonists speaks, and the orchestra consists
of seven strings and piano. The work is completely undramatic
in conception and execution and the uniformity of the orchestral score has a very pallid effect in the long run, but still this
original work has its fascination. The very personal style of
composition is mainly based on chord sequences which seem

to be unattached to any tonal system, and this is strictly maintained throughout with compelling consistency.

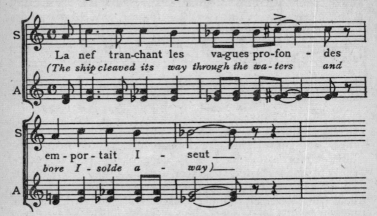

La nef tran-chant les va-gues pro-fon — des
(The ship cleaved its way through the wa-ters and

em-por-tait I — seut
bore I-solde a — way)

Frank Martin's opera *Der Sturm* (*The Tempest*), first performed in Vienna in 1956, is based on Shakespeare's *The Tempest* in Schlegel's translation with only a few cuts, and is consequently somewhat long-winded. Frank Martin's personal style, however, strikes one with its superb declamation, masterly handling of the orchestra, skilful introduction of jazz elements to portray court society, and the use of an off-stage chorus to sing Ariel's songs, while his role is taken by a dancer. It is sad to record that this delicate, temperamental music lacks any strong dramatic impetus. *Le Mystère de la Nativité*, a scenic-oratorio demanding an enormous cast, was first given at the 1960 Salzburg Festival with little success.

Rolf Liebermann (b. 1910), who comes from Zurich, created with his *Leonore 40/45* (1952), a genuine opera which gracefully and undemonstratively tells the story of a German soldier's love for a Parisian girl against the background of war, occupation, catastrophe, and the reconciliation of their two nations. The analogy with Beethoven's *Fidelio* suggested by the title is a little too strong, but this ceases to matter when one looks closely at the charming, inventive libretto, which affords excellent opportunities for musical effects—opportunities which Liebermann seizes upon admirably. He uses twelve-tone technique, but very freely. He is particularly successful with his clever parodies (of anyone from the classical composers to Stravinsky) and with his blending of the serious and the comic in the manner of *opera semiseria*.

Liebermann's *Penelope*, first performed at the 1954 Salzburg Festival, is very cleverly conceived from every point of view and was well received.

PENELOPE. *Opera semiseria* in two parts by Rolf Liebermann. Text by Heinrich Strobel. First performance: Salzburg, 1954.

Characters: Penelope—soprano; Telemachus—soprano; Penelope's three suitors—baritone, bass and tenor; Ercole—tenor; Achilles—baritone; the mayor—tenor; Odysseus—baritone.

Time: afternoon and evening of the 3,649th day after the end of the Trojan War.

The two levels of the opera—antiquity and modern times—intermingle. The classical plot is in *buffo* style: three grotesque military types woo Penelope, who is awaiting Odysseus's return from the Trojan War. To frighten her suitors, Penelope conjures up a vision of the future, an episode of modern times. Today's Penelope has not waited for her husband but has married again, and is living very happily with the Marchese Ercole. Penelope is shocked to learn that Odysseus, whom she had thought dead, has been delayed with some companions, and is now on his way home, but when she goes to greet the newcomers in the market-place she learns that her husband has died of a heart-attack due to the rigours of the journey. Relieved, she hurries home, only to find that her husband Ercole has hanged himself.

In an apotheosis Odysseus appears, restored to Penelope through the marvellous power of poetry. The classical and modern world now merge again, as art bestows new life. 'Only when suffused by the world of art is life worth living.'

In exploring such different spheres of style, Liebermann shows the light touch of a musician who is at home everywhere. Light songs are mixed with highly dramatic arias, and heroic pathos is as accurately depicted as the dances. The tunes are very appealing although mostly in twelve-tone, and the concise harmonic structure is nearly always tonal, so that in its general effect the music is readily understandable even to the layman.

Liebermann chose an entirely comic subject for his next opera, *Die Schule der Frauen* (*The School for Wives*) (1955), the libretto of which was written by Heinrich Strobel after Molière's well-known comedy, *L'Ecole des Femmes*, and wrote light and amusing twentieth-century music in piquant contrast to this charming baroque comedy. Liebermann's style is assured and personal, and his tunes range freely between keys, which are indicated in the accompanying chords or figures. His vocal line is always interesting, whether it is light *parlando*, dramatic recitative or lyrical *arioso*, and the voices are never drowned by the light, virtuoso touch of the orchestra. A particular feature of the score is the quantity of ensembles such as the duet about the Greek alphabet, the quartet which includes the two lovers, or the *fugato* sextet which points the final moral.

BRITISH AND AMERICAN OPERA

The English composer, Benjamin Britten (b. 1913), had an immediate international success with his first opera *Peter Grimes*. (His earlier *Paul Bunyan* (1941) has been withdrawn.) English opera until then had not had much influence abroad, and even leading composers like Frederick Delius (1862-1934) and Ralph Vaughan Williams (1872-1958) scarcely made an impression in the international operatic field, but *Peter Grimes* was soon performed in the most important theatres of the world, although it is truly and unmistakably English in its text, music and feeling.

PETER GRIMES. Opera in a prologue, an epilogue and three acts by Benjamin Britten. Text by Montague Slater after a poem by George Crabbe. First performance: London, 1945.

Characters: Peter Grimes, a fisherman—tenor; John, his apprentice—silent role; Ellen Orford, a widow, the village schoolmistress—soprano; Balstrode, a retired merchant captain—baritone; Auntie, landlady of The Boar—contralto; her two 'nieces'—sopranos; Bob Boles, fisherman and Methodist preacher—tenor; Swallow, a lawyer—bass; Mrs Sedley, a widow—contralto; the Rev. Horace Adams, the rector—tenor; Ned Keene, apothecary and quack—baritone; Hobson, carrier—bass. Townspeople, fishermen.

Place: The Borough, a small fishing-town in East Anglia. *Time:* around 1830.

Prologue. The moot hall, where the inquest on Peter Grimes's apprentice is being held. He died at sea, and the townspeople suspect Grimes of causing his death. Grimes tells how they were driven off their course when out fishing and how the boy died of exposure. The verdict is accidental death, but suspicion remains in the minds of everyone except Ellen Orford and Balstrode, and the former quietly reasserts her faith in Grimes.

Act I, scene i. The beach. The Borough comes to life; the fishermen repair their nets, Auntie opens up The Boar for the day, and the Rector and Mrs Sedley exchange pleasantries. Grimes's voice is heard calling for help with his boat, but the villagers refuse to help him. Keene and Balstrode lend him a hand. Keene then tells him that he has found him a new apprentice, but Hobson is reluctant to fetch the child from the workhouse until Ellen, standing out firmly but gently against malicious gossip, offers to go with Hobson and take care of the boy on the way home. A storm blows up and as everyone goes home Grimes tells the sympathetic Balstrode about the terrible ordeal of the boy's death and about his future ambitions. Balstrode begs him to marry Ellen now, but he refuses to do so until he has made enough money from his fishing to gain respectability in the eyes of the town.

Scene ii. The Boar. The storm is raging outside. Mrs Sedley, a surprise customer, comes in to wait for Ned Keene, who is bringing her laudanum. Bob Boles gets drunk and has to be prevented from molesting the nieces, while Auntie and Balstrode try to keep the peace. Grimes arrives and, oblivious of his surroundings, sings of the stars and of man's fate. The

general embarrassment caused by this is dispelled in the 'round'—'Old Joe has gone fishing'—which follows. Hobson and Ellen come in, soaked in the storm, with the new apprentice, whom Grimes takes home with him at once.

Act II, scene i. The beach. It is Sunday morning and everyone is at church. The scene between Ellen and John, the new apprentice, takes place against the background of the church service. Ellen finds signs of ill-treatment on the boy's body, and when Grimes comes in she accuses him outright. There is a quarrel, because Grimes wants to take the boy off fishing, in spite of its being Sunday, and Ellen cries out in despair that they have failed to solve Grimes's problems. He strikes her, and goes out.

Auntie, Keene and Boles have overheard something of the quarrel, and
as the congregation comes out it is clear that some of them, especially
Mrs Sedley, are indignant but only half understand what is going on.
Ellen is called on to explain, but when she tries to, it is clear that everyone
connects her irrevocably with Grimes's bad behaviour. The men of the
town, headed by the Rector and Swallow and called together by Hobson's
drum, go off to Grimes's hut to see what is going on. Ellen, Auntie and
the nieces are left meditating gently on the ways of men.

Scene ii. An interlude leads to the interior of Grimes's hut, an upturned
boat. Grimes sings of his hopes for the future with Ellen, and gives a
feverish description of his terrible experience when his first apprentice
died. He hears the procession approaching and bundles John out to descend the cliff and so elude them. As he starts to follow, a scream is heard
which tells that the boy has fallen to his death. When the townsfolk
enter they feel rather foolish in the face of this tidy, empty hut, and
retire. Only Balstrode, looking out of the door which leads down the
cliff, sees something which startles him, and goes out that way.

Act III. The beach at night. A dance is being held in the moot hall, and
there is much coming and going between the hall and The Boar. Ned
Keene and Swallow pursue the nieces with wholly dishonourable intentions. Mrs Sedley tries to persuade Swallow that Grimes—whom no
one has seen for days—is a murderer, but Swallow is in no mood to
listen. Mrs Sedley overhears a conversation between Balstrode, who has
seen Grimes's boat, and Ellen, who is horrified to recognize the sweater
Balstrode has found washed up on the beach as one she had made for the
apprentice. Ellen sings the 'Embroidery aria', a most touching musical

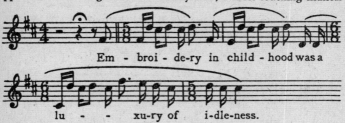

passage. Mrs Sedley goes off to fetch the reluctant Swallow who, hearing
Grimes is back, tells Hobson to take some men and find him. They gather
in an ugly and menacing witch-hunting mood and rush off. An interlude,
leading us from the mob to Grimes, introduces the next scene, some hours
afterwards. Grimes enters, and to the persistent off-stage calls of his name
and the sound of the fog-horn, raves and babbles of his tragic past, with
snatches of reminiscent music. Ellen and Balstrode find him. Balstrode,
lapsing into speech, tells him to take his boat out to sea and sink it. They
go out together to launch it, then Balstrode returns to take Ellen away.
The day breaks, the fishermen come down to the beach to take up their
daily tasks exactly as in the first act, and to the same music. Swallow looks
through his glasses to see if he can see the boat which the coastguard

reports is sinking far out at sea. No one is really interested: the people of The Borough have already forgotten Grimes.

The dominant element in *Peter Grimes* is the sea: the sea during a storm, the sea glittering in the sun, the sea in fog. In every scene it is present and gives the music its essential impulse, beat and character, while in the interludes this concept of nature in music rises to grand, symphonic proportions. The second interlude conjures up a picture of a storm at sea, and is based on a wild, sweeping theme which recurs during the inn-scene whenever somebody opens the door and lets in the wind. The third interlude, by contrast, represents the splendour of the sun on the sea, which glitters and twinkles in the calm thirds on the woodwind. A convincing effect is obtained here by simple means. Britten knows how to convey with maximum clarity the essentials of a situation, and the principal feature of his music is the evocation of atmosphere in each scene. He has a sure instinct for using the right means of musical expression, whether simple harmonic progressions or abrupt bitonal chords, and is as imaginative and original in his artfully constructed ensembles as in his fishing-songs in stanza form. The grand choral ensembles are perhaps the most effective. The monotone choruses of the fishermen mending their nets exactly catch the grey atmosphere of the village community, the treatment of the chorus in the lively inn-scene is magnificent, but perhaps most impressive are the distant cries which eerily punctuate Grimes's unaccompanied monologue, come nearer and nearer and finally break into a *fortissimo*, apparently quite close and only concealed by the fog. This is novel, exciting and the work of a genius.

Britten's next opera *The Rape of Lucretia* is infinitely bolder and more original in conception, and even deviates in its form from the usual operatic layout. It is a chamber opera, scored for twelve orchestral players and three male and three female soloists, supplemented by a Male Chorus and a Female Chorus. It is very stylized, and strictly balanced between drama and music.

THE RAPE OF LUCRETIA. Opera in two acts by Benjamin Britten. Text after André Obey by Ronald Duncan. First performance: Glyndebourne, 1946.

Characters: Tarquinius, Prince of Rome—baritone; Junius, a Roman general—baritone; Collatinus—bass; Lucretia, his wife—contralto; Lucia, her attendant—soprano; Bianca, her nurse—contralto; Female Chorus—soprano; Male Chorus—tenor.

Place: in and near Rome. *Time:* 510 BC.

The Female Chorus and Male Chorus are seated on thrones on either side of the stage and describe the tragedy. They also sketch in the historical background: the Tarquins are in power in Rome, which suffers severely from their oppression, and there is war with Greece.

Act I, scene i. The generals' tent in the camp beyond the Tiber, Junius and Prince Tarquinius are drinking together and discussing their bet of the night before, when the generals rode home unannounced to surprise their wives. Among all these women only Collatinus's wife, the beautiful Lucretia, was virtuously at home. Tarquinius taunts Junius with being a cuckold, and they quarrel, but Collatinus makes the peace. Junius is furiously jealous of Lucretia's chastity, but finally goes off, leaving Tarquinius to brood on the thought of putting her to the test. Finally Tarquinius decides to go to Rome that very night, and the Male Chorus describes his journey during the orchestral interlude.

Scene ii. The hall in Lucretia's house, the same evening. Lucretia and her attendants, Bianca and Lucia, are quietly spinning and commenting on the peace when there are no men about. They prepare to retire to bed, when a loud knocking announces Tarquinius's arrival. They are surprised by his request for hospitality, but Lucretia does not dare to turn the Prince of Rome away. She has a room prepared for him and bids him good night.

Act II. The two Choruses tell us that the Romans are preparing for insurrection in secret and are only waiting for a sign to rise against the Tarquins.

Scene i. Lucretia's bedroom. Tarquinius silently enters the room and sings an aria describing his emotions. He bends over the sleeping Lucretia and wakes her with a kiss. She is horrified and tries to persuade him to leave her room, while he attempts to convince her that her resistance is weakening. Finally he threatens her with his sword. Lucretia in desperation tries to defend herself, but he tears the covers from the bed and puts out the candle. In an interlude the two Choruses comment on this scene ' in Christian terms.

Scene ii. The hall in Lucretia's house. It is early morning and the room is flooded with sunlight. Bianca and Lucia are adorning the hall with flowers. Lucretia, full of foreboding and on the edge of hysteria, enters the room and orders a messenger to be sent to the camp at once to summon Collatinus. But it is no longer necessary; Collatinus and Junius have already arrived, since the absence of Tarquinius had made them fear the worst. Lucretia slowly enters the room, dressed in purple mourning. Collatinus guesses the reason for her sorrow and tries to console her affectionately, but Lucretia cannot bear the dishonour; she stabs herself and dies in her husband's arms. Appalled, they all gather round the body; Lucretia's sacrifice must be the signal to rise against the oppressors—the beacon for Rome's liberation. The chorus reminds us of Christ who bears our sin and does not fall.

The Rape of Lucretia is a pioneering work, novel and original from every point of view, particularly in the treatment of the vocal line. From the expressive phrase, typically Britten, with which Tarquinius lustfully reiterates Lucretia's name in the first

scene, is derived Lucretia's own theme which from then on often appears merely as an accompanying figure in the orchestra. The Choruses sing in recitatives of nobility and austerity— qualities which characterize the whole opera. Occasionally the two Choruses join in a grand *cantilena*, which often recurs as a *leitmotiv* in the course of the action.

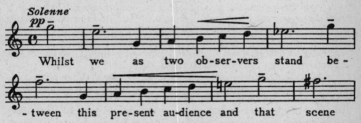

The good-night quartet which forms the finale of the first act is perhaps the best of the exquisite ensembles in this opera. Graceful, yet mysterious, the various parts unfold over Tarquinius's majestic but pliable theme, and each of the four characters is revealed in his or her most appropriate idiom, while the threat of misfortune hovers over them all. The finale of the second act is built on an *ostinato* figure which, like a

funeral march, rises to solemn grandeur. At the end the two Choruses take up the noble unison theme from the beginning, and the *ostinato* figure which represented the end of all things fades gently away in the orchestra.

The opera *Albert Herring*, which Britten completed in 1947, was doubtless conceived as an antithesis to *The Rape of Lucretia*. It is also written for chamber orchestra, but is a comedy, in contrast to the tragic story of Lucretia.

ALBERT HERRING. Comic opera in three acts by Benjamin Britten. Text adapted from Guy de Maupassant's *Le Rosier de Madame Husson* by Eric Crozier. First performance: Glyndebourne, 1947.

Characters: Lady Billows—soprano; Florence Pike, her housekeeper—contralto; Miss Wordsworth, teacher at the church school—soprano; Mr Gedge, the vicar—baritone; Mr Upfold, the mayor—tenor; Superintendent Budd—bass; Sid, a butcher's assistant—baritone; Nancy, from the bakery—mezzo-soprano; Albert Herring, from the greengrocer's—tenor; Mrs Herring, his mother—mezzo-soprano; Emmie and Cis, village children—sopranos; Harry—treble.

Place: Loxford, a market town in Suffolk. *Time:* April and May, 1900.

Act I, scene i. The breakfast room in Lady Billows's house. Florence admits Miss Wordsworth, the vicar, the mayor and the superintendent, who form the committee to elect a May Queen. Lady Billows enters, graciously greets the committee and broods aloud on the sad state of the town's morals, from which she hopes the May Festival may rescue it. All nominees are vetoed swiftly, and it is therefore decided to elect instead a May King. Albert Herring, a paragon of virtue, is chosen, in spite of the suggestion that he is perhaps a little backward.

Scene ii. Mrs Herring's greengrocer's shop. The children steal some apples, which Sid, happening by at that moment, removes from them, keeping one for himself. He tries to tempt the innocent Albert, firmly tied to his mother's apron-strings, with thoughts of poaching and other forbidden pleasures. Albert then hears him making a date with Nancy for a moonlight walk, and really begins to wonder whether obeying his strict mother is worth while. The committee, under the chairmanship of Lady Billows, comes to the shop and announces to Mrs Herring and her son the high honour which is to fall on Albert, including prize-money of £25. Albert is not very happy at the thought of having to wear the white clothes for the Festival, in his capacity as May King, but when he objects his mother sends him upstairs like a small child to repent at leisure.

Act II, scene i. The tea-tent set up in the vicarage garden for the May celebrations. Miss Wordsworth rehearses the children in their anthem in honour of the May King. Everyone gathers for the Festival, the anthem is sung, flowers are presented, speeches made and toasts drunk. Of course there is only lemonade to drink, but Sid has added a good measure of rum to Albert's glass, and Albert becomes very merry under the effect of the unaccustomed spirits. During the orchestral interlude the atmosphere changes from the festival to a may night.

Scene ii. Mrs Herring's shop. Albert returns home, not unnaturally in a merry and noisy mood. He sees and hears Sid and Nancy kissing and setting off on their rendezvous, and with sudden resolve sets out to find out what he has been missing.

Act III. The greengrocer's shop. Albert has been absent for a whole day and everyone is convinced that he has had an accident. Every search is in vain and Lady Billows is already determined to call in Scotland Yard. Finally Albert arrives, unperturbed but dishevelled, and amid the clamour of rebuke tells of his adventures, mostly by innuendo. He innocently thanks the committee for providing him with the money to taste life, and blames his present outbreak on his over-coddled past. Realizing they can no longer patronize their May King, everyone retires in indignation. Only Nancy, Sid and the children stay with him. Albert seizes his orange-blossom crown and cheerfully throws it into the audience.

Britten's music gives this more than innocuous story a very spicy flavour. Whether he is writing in childlike vein or mordant caricature he is always amusing and original. Countless inventive little ideas enliven the score, jokes of instrumentation (Sid, for example, 'doctors' Albert's drink to the *Tristan* motif), comic twists of style and so on. His recitatives, which are accompanied by solo piano, bring a completely new note into comic opera; the recitative-like ensembles are admirable and have an air of free improvisation, only coming together or breaking out in different directions again at certain set moments. A good example is the end of the May Day scene, when ensemble is lost in a complete confusion of the voices.

Britten's children's opera, *Let's Make an Opera* (1949), again shows his skill, wit and charm. The audience is drawn into this work when the children's opera *The Little Sweep* is performed. The extracts learned during the rehearsal in the first act are then performed in the second as a complete whole. This is a charming idea, made even more enjoyable by the music, which is both easy to join in with, yet wholly modern in idiom.

With *Billy Budd* Britten returns to the same kind of subject as in *Peter Grimes*. This work also deals with the sea, but contains no love-story, and in fact no female characters at all. The music is exceptionally concise in style, and the frequent recurrence of sea-shanties lend it the atmosphere essential to an understanding of the plot.

BILLY BUDD. Opera in four acts by Benjamin Britten. Text after Hermann Melville by E. M. Forster and Eric Crozier. First performance: London, 1951.

Characters: Edward Fairfax Vere, Captain of HMS *Indomitable*—tenor; Billy Budd—baritone; John Claggart, master-at-arms—bass; Mr Redburn, First Lieutenant—baritone; Mr Flint, Sailing Master—baritone;

Lieutenant Ratcliffe—bass; Red Whiskers—tenor; Donald—baritone; Dansker, an old seaman—bass; a novice—tenor; Squeak, ship's corporal —tenor; Bosun—bass-baritone; Seamen, midshipmen, officers, powder monkeys, drummers, marines.

Place: on board HMS *Indomitable*, a seventy-four. *Time:* 1797.

Act I. Captain Vere as an old man meditates on his career and its lessons, the mysteries of Providence, and his own doubts about man's ability to judge right and wrong. As his mind dwells on the events on board the *Indomitable* in 1797, the stage is revealed as the deck of that ship, which seamen are scrubbing, and the atmosphere is set by a few incidents which show the tight hold being kept on the seamen for fear of mutiny. (The action takes place just after the Nore and Spithead mutinies, which have been kept secret from the sailors.) Three new recruits come on board, pressganged from a merchantman, the *Rights o' Man*, among them Billy Budd, a lively young boy with one defect: when he is excited he loses his power of speech and just stammers. For fear that his cry 'Farewell, *Rights o' Man!*' has some political significance, Claggart is told to keep a special watch on Billy, and in turn tells off Squeak to spy on him and provoke him. In an incident over the flogging of the novice, Claggart is shown as cynical and sadistic. The whole ship's company is called on deck, and Captain Vere tells them simply and in tones which inspire confidence about the imminent battle. Billy leads a chorus of praise to the captain.

Act II, scene i. The Captain's cabin. A week has passed. Vere is reading, and prays that he and his ship's company may emulate the virtues and courage of people of ancient times. Redburn and Flint come in to drink with him at his invitation. Mutiny overshadows their thoughts, but the sound of the crew singing sea-shanties allays their fears a little. Enemy land is sighted, and the officers go to their stations.

Scene ii. The berth-deck. Billy, Donald and Red Whiskers are singing sea-songs. Billy goes to get Dansker some tobacco from his kit-bag and surprises Squeak. A fight starts, which Billy soon wins, and when Claggart enters and is told how it all started he has Squeak arrested. He praises Billy, but later, in a soliloquy, broods on Billy's goodness with loathing. He sends for the novice and with threats of further flogging forces him to get evidence against Billy by inciting him to mutiny. When he realizes what the novice is getting at, Billy loses his temper and stammers. The novice runs off. Old Dansker warns Billy against Claggart and his methods, but Billy cannot believe that Claggart does not like him.

Act III, scene i. The deck, as in Act I. Through the rising mist can be seen a French warship. Claggart approaches Vere and starts a long, vague story about mutiny, but has to break off while everything is prepared for battle; however the wind fails, the mist comes down again and the pursuit of the enemy ship has to be given up. Claggart resumes his story and accuses Billy of leading a mutiny. The Captain is frankly incredulous and sends Claggart and Billy to his cabin, where Claggart is to confront Billy with the accusation.

Scene ii. The Captain's cabin. Claggart repeats his charge. Called on by Vere to reply, Billy can find no words, and suddenly in his frustration strikes Claggart on the forehead. It is soon clear that Claggart is dead, and against their inclinations the officers of the quickly assembled court-martial have to find Billy guilty of murder and condemn him to death. Vere refuses their appeal for guidance.

Act IV, scene i. A bay of the gun-deck. It is shortly before dawn. Billy, in irons, sings a slow, resigned song of farewell. Dansker joins him and

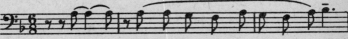

Look!— Through the port comes the moonshine a-stray!

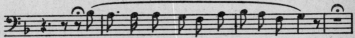

It tips the guard's cutlass and sil-vers this nook

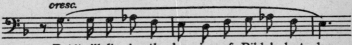

But 'twill die in the dawn-ing of Bil-ly's last day.

speaks of a movement among the crew to free him, but Billy is so appalled at the thought of his fate provoking mutiny that he gains new courage and firmly rejects any such suggestion.

Scene ii. The main-deck and quarter-deck just after dawn. The whole crew gathers to attend the execution. Billy's last words are 'Starry Vere, God bless you', before he marches smartly out to mount the mast. There is danger of a mutiny, but the men's growling changes to the noises associated with the routine ship's work, which seem to carry a message of confidence in justice.

Captain Vere is once again standing alone on the stage as an old man, murmuring in distress that he could have saved Billy. He finally takes comfort from Billy's last words and the knowledge that he understood that the Captain had no alternative.

In 1961 Britten revised the score and arranged the opera in two acts, the old Acts I and II becoming Act I, and Acts III and IV becoming the new Act II. There are also a few cuts, the most important of which is that of the Captain's muster at the end of the old Act I. This revised version was first heard in a broadcast on the BBC in January 1961, and three years later, almost to a day, it was seen on the stage at Covent Garden.

This is possibly Britten's most powerful and masterly score, and, as in *Peter Grimes*, the influence of the sea is the dominating factor. Bugles, fanfares and sea-shanties establish the atmosphere of the man-o'-war, and the big ensemble of the sea battle that is never joined shows Britten's mastery of the operatic medium. There is much moving music in the soliloquies of Vere and especially in Billy's touching scene when he lies in irons awaiting execution—'Billy in the Darbies'. As the late Erwin Stein wrote:

'It was indeed Britten's chamber operas that prepared the ground for *Billy Budd*. The part which they played can hardly be overrated. He took them as seriously as grand opera and studied their special problems. Yet the flexibility of operatic form and texture which he established is not only to the advantage of small-scale opera; *Billy Budd* has proved that grand opera also can gain from it.'

For the coronation of Queen Elizabeth II in 1953, Britten wrote a new opera for Covent Garden, *Gloriana*. For this opera about Elizabeth I, Britten chose certain episodes from Lytton Strachey's *Elizabeth and Essex* which were fashioned into a libretto by William Plomer. The opera, which was composed with the full knowledge and permission of the Queen, received its première at the Coronation Gala at Covent Garden on 8 June. At the time all thought this a wonderful idea and a tribute to England's greatest living composer but, in retrospect the choice of the Coronation Gala for the première seems not so wise. The musical tastes of most of the audience that assembled for the occasion were hardly likely to include Britten, and the opera failed to please. In the popular Press the philistines ran riot, and after ten performances, and three more the following autumn, the work vanished from the repertory.

A revival of the work in concert version for the composer's fiftieth birthday at the Royal Festival Hall, London, in November 1963, brought about some serious rethinking concerning the musical merits of the opera. The composer's skill in the handling of dramatic incidents is again in evidence; the choral writing outstanding; and the purely melodic inspiration possibly the composer's most striking.

The Turn of the Screw (Venice, 1956) marks another climax in Britten's musical achievements. It is a most original work, written for the English Opera Group and scored for seven singers and a chamber orchestra of twelve players, like *The Rape of Lucretia* and *Albert Herring*.

THE TURN OF THE SCREW. Opera in two acts by Benjamin Britten.
Text by Myfanwy Piper after the story by Henry James. First performance: Venice, 1954.

Characters: The Prologue—tenor; the governess—soprano; Miles
and Flora, children in her charge—boy soprano and soprano; Mrs Grose,
the housekeeper—soprano; Quint, a former manservant—tenor; Miss
Jessel, a former governess—soprano.

The opera is based on the famous story of the same name by Henry
James. It tells of two children, Miles and Flora, living in a lonely country
house; they have been corrupted by the valet, Peter Quint, and the
governess Miss Jessel, both now dead. The ghosts of these two evil people
materialize in the struggle for the souls of the children. The new governess, and the housekeeper Mrs Grose, try to combat the evil spirits and
save the children's souls, but to no avail. At the end of the opera, Flora is
taken away by Mrs Grose, and the governess forces Miles to confess that
he stole a letter she had written to the children's guardian. With the
words 'Peter Quint, you Devil! on his lips, Miles dies in the governess's
arms.

The Turn of the Screw is written in two acts and eight scenes,
connected by interludes in the form of variations on the short
theme which opens the opera, immediately after the sung pro-

Very slow

(Timp.trem.) (Hn.sust.) (Harp.trem.)

logue. This scheme gives the musical structure of the work
great strength and unity. The eerie, oppressive atmosphere of
the supernatural world is most grippingly portrayed in the
music, which is throughout powerfully dramatic and intensely
sensitive.

Britten's eighth work for the opera stage in fifteen years,
A Midsummer Night's Dream, is a setting by himself and Peter
Pears of the Shakespeare play. The libretto has been fashioned
from Shakespeare's play by the composer and Peter Pears,
skilfully tailored to the needs of a three-act opera. About half
the original text has been omitted but the librettists have been
completely faithful to the text. They have added one line—
'Compelling thee to parry with Demetrius'—spoken by
Lysander early in the opera, in the passage beginning:

A good persuasion, therefore hear me, Hermia,
I have a widow aunt, a dowager, *etc.*

As Britten has explained, the sung word takes much longer than the spoken word, and had he set the complete text of the play, the result would have been an opera as long as the *Ring*!

A MIDSUMMER NIGHT'S DREAM. Opera in three acts by Benjamin Britten. Text by the composer and Peter Pears after the play by Shakespeare. First performance: Aldeburgh, 1960.

Characters: Oberon, King of the fairies—counter-tenor; Tytania, Queen of the fairies—soprano; Puck—speaking role; Peaseblossom, Cobweb, Mustard-seed, Moth and fairies—young boys' voices; Theseus, Duke of Athens—bass; Hippolyta, Queen of the Amazons, betrothed to Theseus —mezzo-soprano; Lysander, in love with Hermia—tenor; Demetrius, also in love with Hermia—baritone; Hermia, in love with Lysander but betrothed in law to Demetrius—mezzo-soprano; Helena, in love with Demetrius—soprano; Bottom, a weaver—baritone; Quince, a carpenter —bass; Flute, a bellows-mender—tenor; Snug, a joiner—bass; Snout, a tinker—tenor; Starveling, a tailor—tenor.

Place: Athens and its vicinity

Act I. It is evening and the two groups of fairies enter the woods, soon to be joined by Puck, whom they challenge. Oberon and his consort Tytania appear and quarrel about the changeling boy whom Tytania has taken for her page and of whom Oberon has grown jealous. Tytania refuses to yield the boy to Oberon and leaves her with her attendant fairies. Oberon plans his revenge—he will drop the juice of a magic herb in the eyes of Tytania while she is sleeping, so that she will fall in love with the first living creature she sees. He sends Puck to find the herb.

Lysander and Hermia, the first of the mortals, now appear. Hermia is fleeing from her home and Demetrius, who loves her to no avail. No sooner have they left than Oberon returns, and being invisible to mortals, overhears the conversation between the love-lorn Helena and Demetrius who will have none of her. Oberon swears that before Demetrius leaves the wood, he will seek Helena's love. Puck, returning with the magic herb, is bidden by Oberon to seek out Demetrius and anoint his eyes with its juice, thus making him love Helena.

The rustics, led by Peter Quince, come in to discuss the play they are to present at Duke Theseus's wedding festivities. After they have gone Lysander and Hermia reappear and lie down to sleep. Puck, mistaking Lysander for Demetrius, squeezes the magic juice into his eyes, so that when he is awakened by the distraught Helena, who is still vainly pursuing Demetrius, he immediately falls in love with her. Helena is offended and rushes off with Lysander in pursuit. Hermia awakens and finding herself alone goes to find Lysander.

Tytania now returns with her fairies, who sing her to sleep, while Oberon waits close at hand to bewitch her with the magic herb.

Act II. Later that night the rustics meet in the wood for their first rehearsal, near the sleeping Tytania. Puck enters and decides to change Bottom's features into those of an ass. This so frightens the rest of the rustics that they run off, leaving Bottom alone. He begins to sing, which awakens Tytania, who immediately falls in love with him. She instructs her fairies to attend him; and then she and Bottom fall asleep.

Oberon and Puck reappear, shortly followed by Hermia and Demetrius. Overhearing their conversation Oberon realizes that Puck has placed the magic juice in the wrong eyes, and when Demetrius lies down to sleep, Oberon tries to make amends by anointing Demetrius's eyes with the herb. This only makes for more confusion, for Lysander and Helena enter, and Demetrius, awakening and seeing Helena, immediately falls in love with her. There is a fierce quarrel.

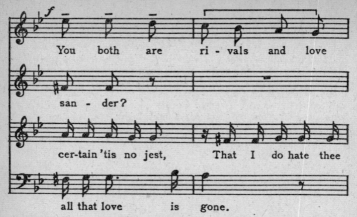

Oberon, more furious than ever, scolds Puck, who by imitating Demetrius's voice, draws away Lysander, and then by pretending to be Lysander makes sure that the men do not meet face to face. The four lovers, all exhausted, fall asleep in the wood. Prompted by the fairies Puck squeezes the magic juice into Lysander's eyes.

Act III. Early next morning Oberon, moved by Tytania's infatuation for Bottom, removes the spell from her and they are reconciled.

The four lovers now awaken, and happily and correctly paired off at last, depart for Athens. Bottom wakes up and rejoins his friends. They learn that their play is to be acted before the Duke.

The scene changes to Theseus's palace. The Duke and his newly-wed Hippolyta pardon the four lovers, and all are entertained by Peter Quince's company, who present 'The Most Lamentable Comedy and most Cruel Death of Pyramus and Thisbe'. The mortals retire to bed. The fairies enter, and Oberon and Tytania bid them bless the three happy couples while Puck, left alone, recites the epilogue.

The play and opera take place on three planes; the world of the fairies, the world of the lovers, and the world of the rustics. Britten has provided each with characteristic music. The mysterious string *glissandi*, the brilliant use of harp and celesta, and harmonies that sound almost supernatural for the fairies; a more natural, warmer and moving music for the lovers – sometimes highly nervous as so often in Britten – culminating in the Quarrel quartet, perhaps the most operatic music Britten has ever written, and certainly the most fluent and dramatic pages in this opera; for the rustics, earthy, lumbering rhythms, and a march tune that sticks in the head.

Lennox Berkeley (b. 1903) studied for six years with Nadia Boulanger. He did not, however, take up opera until he was fifty, and his first stage work, the three-act *Nelson*, produced in London at Sadler'sWells, was not a success. His comic opera, *A Dinner Engagement* (1954) with a libretto by Paul Dehn, and his one-act opera, *Ruth* (1956), with a libretto by Eric Crozier were increasingly successful. But as a whole, Berkeley has not really come to terms with the problems of opera.

Michael Tippett (b. 1905), on the other hand, has shown both in *The Midsummer Marriage* (1955) and *King Priam* (1962) that he is deeply concerned with the whole concept of music drama. The first opera, despite its deeply-felt and often beautiful music, failed because of its complicated allegorical libretto (by the composer) – a kind of twentieth-century *Magic Flute*. *King Priam*, however, is, to quote Tippett's own words, 'Monumental in quite a different way from *The Midsummer Marriage*. It is taut, sparse and condensed in the way classical Greek tragedy is condensed . . . It is concerned with the problem of moral choice. It is constructed to drive forward inevitably to the tragic end – Priam's death at the altar as Troy burns. The musical style, and the forms of the musical patterns, all combine to effect this, and as inevitably as the drama demands.'

Gian-Carlo Menotti (b. 1911) is Italian by birth, but generally regarded as an American composer, since he emigrated to the United States as a young man before any of his operatic successes. There is something very American about his librettos, which he writes himself with an assured theatrical instinct, and also about his fresh and uninhibited music, but Menotti can never deny his Italian origin, for Puccini's example shines through everywhere. His first works included the one-act comic operas *Amelia Goes to the Ball* (1936), *The Old Maid and the Thief* (1937), *The Medium* (1946) and *The Telephone* (1947). International success came to him with his full-length opera *The Consul* (1950).

THE CONSUL. Opera in three acts by Gian-Carlo Menotti. Text by the composer. First performance: Philadelphia, 1950.

Characters: John Sorel—baritone; Magda Sorel, his wife—soprano; the mother—contralto; Secret Police Agent—bass; the Secretary—mezzo-soprano; Mr Kofner—baritone; the foreign woman—soprano; Anna Gomez—soprano; Vera Boronel—contralto; a magician, Nika Magadoff—tenor; Assan—baritone; recorded voice—soprano; two plain-clothes men—silent roles.

Place: somewhere in Europe. *Time:* after the Second World War.

Act I, scene i. John Sorel's house. John Sorel, a member of a secret movement, has been wounded while fleeing from the police and staggers home. His wife and mother bind up his wound and he hides. The Secret Police Agent who enters soon after does not find him, but utters veiled threats to Magda. After he has gone John says that he must hide in the mountains, while Magda gets the necessary papers to leave the country. When their window is broken by a stone, they must send for Assan, the glass-cutter, who will have a message from him. John takes his leave and goes.

Scene ii. The waiting-room at a foreign consulate. The Secretary sits checking papers, distributing questionnaires and forms to be filled in, and officiously keeping everyone waiting. Among the applicants is a Mr Kofner who proudly presents all the necessary papers for a visa, only to be told that the photos are the wrong size. A foreign woman, for whom Kofner acts as interpreter, tells a pathetic story of her sick daughter, but is just given forms to fill in and told she may be able to visit her in about two months' time. Magda enters and asks to see the Consul, but is coldly rebuffed with talk of numbers and forms. The magician tries to impress the Secretary with some conjuring tricks, but soon gives up and joins in the hopeless ensemble of those who wait each day at the Consulate.

Act II, scene i. Sorel's house a month later. The mother tries to cheer up the baby, while Magda, asleep, has a terrible nightmare about her husband and the Secretary. A stone shatters a window-pane and she summons Assan by telephone. The Secret Agent enters and asks her for the names of her husband's friends, in return for permission to join him; she screams at him to get out. Assan arrives to tell her that John is still in the mountains at the frontier and determined to come back if she should not be able to join him. She instructs Assan to tell John that all her preparations are complete, then turns to the mother, only to realize from her face that her under-nourished baby has just died peacefully in his sleep.

Scene ii. The consulate. The same people are still waiting. The magician shows off his powers of conjuring and hypnotism, puts everyone to sleep, then makes them all dance. The Secretary is merely put out, and when all is normal again Magadoff leaves the room. Magda is allowed to jump the queue, and implores the Secretary to let her see the Consul. She is again put off and breaks into a passionate tirade against the cold business methods of bureaucracy. Finally the Secretary tells her that she can see the Consul when his important visitor leaves. As she goes to the door, the Secret Agent walks out, and Magda faints.

Act III, scene i. The consulate. Magda is waiting to see the Consul, although the office is about to shut. Vera Boronel comes in and receives her papers. Assan hurries in to tell Magda that having heard of the death of their child and of his mother, John now wants to come back to fetch her. Magda gives Assan a note which she says will stop John coming back. She leaves the consulate. The Secretary is about to close the office when John Sorel comes in search of Magda. He cannot leave again to catch up with her, because the police are at his heels. The Secret Agent enters with two plain-clothes men and John's gun is knocked out of his hand. The Secretary protests, but the Secret Agent says John will go with them of his own free will. There will be no arrest in the consulate. The Secretary goes to the telephone to ring Magda.

Scene ii. The Sorels' house. The telephone is ringing, but it stops before Magda enters. She prepares to commit suicide, turns on the gas, and then the walls dissolve and through her confused thoughts appear the figures of her husband, her mother, the Secretary, and all the people from the consulate. They seem to be calling her, and the magician repeats, hypnotizing her, the words: 'You are tired, you want to sleep.' The scenes become more and more unreal. Suddenly the telephone rings, but Magda has no longer the strength to lift the receiver. She falls dead to the floor while the bell is ringing.

The music is as strongly dramatic as this unusually theatrical text, for Menotti is first and foremost a dramatist with an outstanding feeling for stage effect. His musical language is not very original, being derived from Puccini's idiom, interlarded with contemporary harmonic and rhythmic passages, but his composition technique is always masterly, particularly his way of presenting and building up each scene through steady *crescendo* to its climax, and the effects he thus creates are truly gripping. The most impressive moment of all is the entry of the magician in the fourth scene, the hypnotic puppet-like dance and Magda's genuinely passionate outburst. This is thrilling musical theatre.

His next opera, *The Saint of Bleecker Street*, is even more naturalistic, for the music captures the everyday street noises as well as the choral splendour of the stigmata vision. The result is a very effective modern folk-opera.

THE SAINT OF BLEECKER STREET. Musical drama in three acts (five scenes) by Gian-Carlo Menotti. Text by the composer. First performance: New York, 1954.

Characters: Annina—soprano; Michele, her brother—tenor; Desideria —mezzo-soprano; Don Marco, a priest—bass; Carmela—soprano; Salvatore, her fiancé—baritone; Assunta—contralto; Maria Corona, a newspaper-seller—soprano. Neighbours, children, wedding-guests, passers-by, policemen, etc.

Place: the Italian quarter of New York. *Time:* the present.

Act I, scene i. Annina's room. Neighbours, some out of curiosity and some out of piety, have come to see the miracle which happens to Annina every Good Friday: she receives a vision of the Crucifixion, and the stigmata appear on her hands. The people are wild with excitement when it happens, but Annina's brother, Michele, enters and roughly sends everyone out, even the priest.

Scene ii. A backyard. Michele has forbidden Annina to take part in a local procession, but the neighbours throw themselves on Michele, tie him up and take Annina, their saint, away in the procession. Michele is freed by his fiancée Desideria.

Act II. Annina's friend Carmela is celebrating her wedding in a restaurant and Michele and Annina are among the guests. Desideria wants to go to the party, too, but she is not invited, because she is a prostitute. She persuades Michele to take her in with him, but Don Marco tries to stop her. During the quarrel which follows Desideria jealously accuses Michele of being in love not with her, but with his saintly sister Annina. In a fury, Michele throws himself on Desideria and stabs her, then flees.

Act III, scene i. A subway station. Annina meets her brother in secret and begs him to go to the police. Michele tries again to persuade her to go away with him, but Annina tells him that she wants to enter a convent.

Scene ii. Annina's room. Annina is ill in bed. She is to take the veil in front of her friends and supporters. When the ceremony has started Michele rushes into the room and pleads with Annina to give up her intention. Seeing that it is too late, he collapses. Annina, at the end of her strength, dies.

Maria Golovin (1958) has not become established in the same way in spite of its initial success. Though the libretto is very dramatic the music is largely conventional. Menotti has to be regarded as an exceptional case, for the means of musical expression which he uses so skilfully are not original enough to establish neo-naturalism as a new operatic style.

Of much greater importance from the musical point of view is *Porgy and Bess* by George Gershwin (1898–1937), the famous champion of symphonic jazz.

PORGY AND BESS. Opera in three acts by George Gershwin. Text by du Bose Heyward and Ira Gershwin. First performance: New York, 1935.

Characters: Porgy, a cripple—baritone; Crown, a stevedore—bass; Bess, his girl—soprano; Robbins, a neighbour—tenor; Serena, his wife—soprano; Peter, the honey man—tenor; Jake, a fisherman—baritone; Clara, his wife—soprano; Sporting Life, a dope-pedlar—tenor; Maria, keeper of the cook-shop—contralto; Mingo—tenor; Frazier, a negro 'lawyer'—baritone; Annie—mezzo-soprano; Lily, Peter's wife, strawberry-woman—mezzo-soprano; Jim, a cotton-picker—baritone; Nelson —tenor. A crab-man, an undertaker, a coroner, a detective, a policeman; men, women and children of Catfish Row.

Place: Charleston, South Carolina. *Time:* end of the nineteenth century.

Act I. In Catfish Row, a negro tenement. The cripple Porgy, whom everyone likes, is being teased about his love for the beautiful Bess, who comes in with Crown. Crown is drunk, but insists on joining the crap game. When he loses to Robbins he is furious, throws him down and kills him, to everyone's horror. Bess gives him money and tells him to go away quickly before the police arrive. He says he will come back. The debauched Sporting Life tries to console Bess with cocaine and to persuade her to go to New York with him, but Bess wants to stay in Charleston. Nobody in Catfish Row wants her, but Porgy opens his door to her just as the police arrive.

Scene ii. Serena's room. The neighbours are mourning over Robbins's body. The detective gets someone to say that Crown did the murder, and the scene ends with mourning spirituals.

Act II, scene i. The same, a month later. Although a storm is gathering the fishermen are preparing to put to sea. Porgy, a happier man since Bess came to live with him, sings from his window. Sporting Life returns and Maria gives him a piece of her mind; he then tries to tempt Bess away, again unsuccessfully. Porgy hurts his wrist with his strong grip, and warns him to keep away from Bess. Everyone gets ready for the picnic, and Bess is persuaded to join the party, although Porgy cannot go.

Scene ii. Kittiwah Island, the same evening. They all have a merry time, but when Bess lingers behind the others Crown appears, and in spite of Bess's pleas to be left in peace with Porgy he exerts his old fascination over her and she stays with him on the island after the boat has gone.

Scene iii. Catfish Row. Bess is in Porgy's room, delirious after being lost for two days on the island. She calls for Porgy, who knows she was with Crown and says it makes no difference to his love. She begs him to stop Crown taking her away with him.

Scene iv. Serena's room. The storm is raging outside, and in the crowded room all are singing and praying for the fishermen. Crown enters

imperiously. Clara rushes out to find Jake, whose boat she has seen
floating upside down. Crown is the only one who dares to follow her.

Act III, scene i. In the courtyard. Everyone is mourning for Clara,
Jake and Crown, all of whom they believe lost in the storm. Sporting
Life hints that Crown is not dead and wonders what will happen between
him and Porgy when he comes back for Bess. Everyone has gone to bed,
when Crown steals into the empty courtyard. As he creeps up to Porgy's
door a hand with a knife flashes out of the window and stabs him. Then
Porgy slowly throttles him in a grip of iron.

Scene ii. The courtyard, the following day. The police come to
enquire into Crown's death. Porgy is taken away reluctantly to identify
the body, and in his absence Sporting Life tempts Bess with 'happy dust',
this time successfully.

Scene iii. A week later. Porgy returns from a week in prison for refusing
to identify Crown's corpse, with presents for everyone, bought out of
his crap winnings. But Bess is missing, and when he hears she has gone
to New York with Sporting Life he sets out on his little cart to find her,
full of hope.

The lively main plot takes place in a rich setting of local colour,
splendidly captured by Gershwin in his music. He is a superb
writer of tunes, of which the most magical in this work are
perhaps the ravishing lullaby 'Summertime' and the enchanting
love-duet.

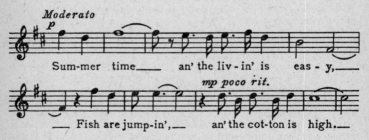

For his friend Samuel Barber (b. 1910) Menotti wrote the
libretto to his opera *Vanessa* (New York, 1958) but here he seems
to have lost his dramatic touch, while Barber's music is also of
little interest. The City Center in New York, where special
seasons of new American operas have been staged in recent
years, has mounted the premières of Marc Blitzstein's *Regina*
(1949), Aaron Copland's *The Tender Land* (1954), Carlyle
Floyd's *Susannah* (1958), Douglas Moore's *The Wings of the
Dove* (1961), and Robert Ward's *The Crucible* (1961).

Floyd followed his *Susannah* with *Wuthering Heights* (1958) and *The Passion of Jonathan Wade* (1962); these, together with Douglas Moore's *The Devil and Daniel Webster* (1938) and *The Ballad of Baby Doe* (1956) are mostly written in American folk-idiom, and have had regular and successful performances in the United States.

RECENT EUROPEAN OPERA

Those German operas written during the last few years which are worthy of general attention are much more advanced in idiom and more experimental in form than some of the works by Britten and most of those by Menotti mentioned above. It is the uncompromising nature of these German operas which is particularly noticeable and also convinces one of their significance, even if they have not so far been very widely accepted.

In 1948, the chamber opera *Des Simplicius Simplicissimus Jugend* (*The Youth of Simplicius Simplicissimus*) by Karl Amadeus Hartmann (1905–63) appeared. Hartmann describes his work as 'scenes from the development of German destiny' and it deals in three scenes with the horrors of the Thirty Years War. When one thinks that this work was completed in 1936, three years before the Second World War, one is profoundly struck by the moral which is drawn—that essential humanity must be preserved in spite of any horror; it was not produced, however, until 1949. In form this is a chamber opera, resembling Stravinsky's *L'Histoire du Soldat*, but musically Hartmann goes entirely his own way. Chorale-like passages, dance forms and seventeenth-century-style tunes lend his music an archaic sound, but the harmonies are sharply dissonant, and a perpetual rhythmic movement supported by a quantity of percussion underlines the incisiveness and impetus of the musical flow. All externals are discarded and much in both text and music is merely indicated, but the effect is all the more intensified. Although this work is principally epic in character, the effect of its music remains compellingly dramatic.

Even more uncompromising in manner is Paul Dessau (b. 1894) in his opera *Das Verhör des Lucullus* (*The Trial of Lucullus*) (Berlin, 1951), to a libretto by Bertold Brecht. The text of *Lucullus* is very impressive in its originality: the great general Lucullus, highly honoured by everyone, is brought after his death before a court where his victories and triumphs are of no consequence, and only the destruction he caused during his wars is held against him. He is therefore condemned and damned. Dessau's music is fragmentary and is limited to short flourishes which are strangely effective in their wild extravagance. There is something oppressive about this effect from which the listener cannot escape, just as the weird beating rhythm of the music pursues one relentlessly.

Winfried Zillig (b. 1905) tries to extract the whole musical structure of his opera *Troilus und Cressida* (Berlin, 1951) from a few motifs, which underline the individual events in continually changing variations. Zillig sometimes uses the twelve-tone method, which is in itself a technique of variations, but tonal passages occur frequently throughout. The decisive effect is given by the choruses which frame the individual scenes, entering into the events and intensifying their significance. Zillig himself wrote the text after Shakespeare's play and may well have taken the oratorio form of Stravinsky's *Oedipus Rex* as an example.

Much more experimental than Zillig and more consistent in his observance of the twelve-tone technique is Hans Werner Henze (b. 1926). Henze's music for the lyrical drama *Boulevard Solitude* (Hanover, 1952) cannot however be explained, or his style classified, as simply as this. Grete Weill's very original libretto treats the story of Manon Lescaut (already used by Massenet and Puccini) in a modern setting. The dance element, with its interplay of dream and reality, has great dramatic importance, and jazz-rhythms form the main thread of the music, which is over-subtle and often hardly comprehensible. Henze's music sometimes repels, sometimes convinces, is sometimes conceived with genius, and sometimes cheap in effect, but it is always interesting.

Henze's *König Hirsch* (*King Stag*) (Berlin, 1956) is a work of some importance. The poetic text by Heinz von Cramer after Gozzi's *De Cervo* tells the old fairy-story of the nobleman who voluntarily turned into an animal; here it is a king who turns into a stag. The realization that such an attempt to escape from life can offer no solution leads the king back to an awareness of man's responsibility towards the life he has been given. This symbolic main plot is set in a richly varied fairy-tale world. Henze's music for *König Hirsch* is much more compact and vital than that of *Boulevard Solitude* which often lost itself in nothingness. Here there is dramatic impulse allied with delicate lyrical feeling and the voices unfold in lush *cantilena* set in an orchestral accompaniment of the subtlest rhythms. In this work Henze renounced the severity of twelve-tone technique in favour of freer, rhythmic melodies, thick layers of chords alternate with simple triads, and everything is united in an impressive and very personal style. This work was also performed in Darmstadt and Bielefeld, but its inordinate length proved a handicap and Henze withdrew it. It reappeared, considerably revised, under the title *Il Re Cervo oder Die Irrfahrten der Wahrheit*, at Cassel in 1963. Henze made cuts totalling a quarter of the original length of the work, simplified the harmony and altered the orchestration.

Henze's next opera, *Der Prinz von Homburg* (Hamburg, 1960), is even more personal in musical expression, and more concentrated than *König Hirsch*, with its lush colours, while the orchestration is much more transparent and economical, without any loss in exact characterization of each mood and situation. Henze's range of musical expression spreads from the restraint of a dream to the outburst of ardent passion, and his exceptional dramatic gifts are again in evidence in this work. Ingeborg Bachmann adapted Kleist's play most skilfully, but it is Henze's music, with its effortless flow of arias and duets, fugues and passacaglias, which really turns it into operatic material.

Henze's next opera, *Elegy for Young Lovers* (1961), was written to an English text by W. H. Auden and Chester Kallman. Henze, with his perfect knowledge of English and of Auden's works, said that his aim in this work was to 'Penetrate fully into the world and imagination of Auden and thereby achieve the greatest possible harmony between libretto and score . . . I have rarely composed to any text with so much enjoyment, emotion, excitement and pure pleasure'.

The opera is about the souls of five people and about a sixth who does not possess one, the poet Gregor Mittenhofer, a recreation of the late-romantic egocentric genius, reminiscent of Wagner, Debussy or D'Annunzio. Mittenhofer lives in a hotel, the Schwarzer Adler, in the Swiss Alps, with his rich young muse, the beautiful Elisabeth Zimmer and his aristocratic, secretary and patroness, Carolina Kirchstetten. Also in the ménage are Dr Wilhelm Rieschmann, Mittenhofer's personal physician, his son Toni, who falls in love with Elisabeth, and an old widow, Hilda Mack, who has been waiting forty years for the return of her bridegroom, who vanished in the mountains during their honeymoon. Hilda Mack's visions over the years have proved a source of inspiration to the poet, and when she has a vision in which she sees the young lovers, Elisabeth and Toni, dying in the snow, Mittenhofer seizes on this as a theme for his new poem, an 'Elegy for Young Lovers', dedicated to the memory of Elisabeth and her new lover. The opera ends with the poet reading his new work to a society audience in Vienna.

Henze has built his opera on a single twelve-note series, and has given his characters real melodies to sing. There are solos, concerted numbers, recitative passages; and Hilda Mack's mad-like scenes with their coloratura and flute accompaniment are of course in the true tradition of nineteenth-century Italian opera! The orchestra is basically of chamber size, with eight wind-players and an enormous percussion section, including tambourines, tomtoms, bongos and triangles.

Giselher Klebe (b. 1925), after Henze the most respected exponent of extreme modernity in recent years, chose Schiller's *Die Räuber* (*The Robbers*) for his first opera, written in 1957. He himself undertook the adaptation, discarded all secondary matter and built the drama exclusively on the conflict between the brothers Franz and Karl Moor, thereby stressing their relationship with Amalia, who thus becomes a more important character than in the original play. Musically Klebe is a disciple of Alban Berg, but melodically he is more consistent in his use of twelve-tone technique and harmonically even more radical than his predecessor. The effective declamatory recitatives dominate the flow of the music, which only seldom breaks into *arioso*. The choral scenes are much more exciting, but the musical and dramatic climax comes in the scene in the third act where on one side of the divided stage Karl quarrels with the priest and on the other side Franz courts Amalia. At the end of this scene Amalia and Karl ecstatically embrace as they sing a duet with a broad, sweeping melody.

In 1959 Klebe completed two more operas, again choosing his material from world literature and adapting it himself. One was *Die tödlichen Wünsche*, from Balzac's novel *La Peau de Chagrin*, and the other a one-act work, *Die Ermordung des Cäsar* (*The Murder of Caesar*), based on Schlegel's translation of the third act of Shakespeare's play.

DIE TÖDLICHEN WÜNSCHE (The Fatal Wishes). Opera in three acts (fifteen scenes) by Giselher Klebe. Text by the composer after Balzac's novel *La Peau de Chagrin*. First performance: Düsseldorf, 1959.

Characters: Raphael von Valentin—tenor; Pauline, a young girl—soprano; the Croupier, the owner of the curiosity shop, the lawyer Cardot and Raphael's servant Jonathan (one singer)—baritone. Courtesans, playboys, gamblers, idlers, etc.

Place: Paris and an unnamed watering-place. *Time:* middle of the nineteenth century.

After losing all his money at the casino Raphael determines to commit suicide. In the street he meets Pauline, who secretly loves him, and bids her farewell. In the curiosity shop he tries to take his own life, but the owner shows him the mysterious pelt which can fulfil any wish. One must however calculate one's wishes carefully, because with each one the pelt shrinks and the owner's life becomes shorter. Raphael eagerly seizes the pelt, declaring that he will now live life to the full, and enjoy everything it has to offer. With every wish he expresses, in order to create new pleasures for himself, the pelt shrinks. He meets Pauline, and when he wishes to be loved by her the pelt does not change shape. Joyfully deciding he is now free from the spell, he throws the pelt out of the window, not realizing that his wish was already fulfilled in Pauline's unselfish and unspoken love. When the talisman comes back to him, fished out of the well under his window, he realizes that there is no more hope of escape, and dies in Pauline's arms.

The music is exceptionally subtly constructed and more varied in tonal colour than that of *Die Räuber*. It is uneasy, nervous music, full of tensions which are released in harsh dramatic emphasis. The orchestration is very transparent so that the voices rise effortlessly above it. The music exudes a quite original and attractive atmosphere, but does not always avoid the danger of monotony because of the twelve-tone technique used consistently throughout the melodies.

Three months after the Düsseldorf première of *Die tödlichen Wünsche*, *Die Ermordung des Cäsar* (*The Murder of Caesar*) was first staged in Essen. The action opens with Caesar's murder by Brutus, Cassius and the other conspirators, and goes on to Mark Antony's moving speech over Caesar's corpse, in which he completely reverses the mood of the crowd which had just been acclaiming Brutus as their deliverer from tyranny. Brutus and his supporters are forced to flee, the mob throws lighted torches into their houses and calls for an uprising against Caesar's murderers. If he showed courage in choosing such a subject, Klebe showed even more in the way he set about turning it into an opera. He abandons the splendour of strings and builds his orchestra on quantities of brass, saxophones and percussion, with amplified tape-recordings. The results are often very strident and shrill, but still effective, and his harsh, powerful accentuation makes for great dramatic effect.

Heimo Erbse (b. 1924) shows great gifts, particularly for musical humour, in his opera *Julietta* (Salzburg, 1959). Unfortunately the libretto, adapted by the composer from Kleist's short story *Die Marquise von O*, is poor and forms a considerable obstacle to the success of the amusing, inventive music.

The burning desire to find something new, even if it inevitably involves stylistic eclecticism, is a distinguishing feature of the most recent German operas.

The Swedish composer Karl-Birger Blomdahl (b. 1916) broke completely new ground in the subject-matter of his opera *Aniara* (1959), which deals with life on board a space-ship, escaping from an earth saturated with radiation. Due to a technical fault the ship leaves its course and finds itself in orbit round the earth with no hope of reaching its objective, the planet Mars. The passengers are condemned to eternal wandering, from which only death can release them. The cramped conditions on board the *Aniara* set the scene for the plot of the opera, which was first performed in Stockholm in 1959. The Press acclaimed it as a work of unique artistic audacity and power. The mixture of electronic and concrete music on tape seems natural and convincing. Blomdahl's music is inspired and very personal in style, and varies from simple songs to passionate *expressivo*.

When considering the development of opera during the last decade there seems at first no simple, unified trend to record. In the light of the different forms introduced by Stravinsky it was not difficult to postulate a formula for modern opera, and the immediate possibilities of such formulae have frequently been referred to. However, any attempt at classification is bound to result in narrowing the issue, whereas the extraordinary attraction of opera today lies in its very versatility.

There are, however, two clearly distinct basic trends: in form, there is the tendency towards simplification apparent in all types of opera over the last ten years, and especially in the opera-oratorio: in music, the definite aim of introducing into opera modern musical language in all its variations. This healthy, forward-looking trend in new operas gives one confidence in the future of this much admired and much despised form of art, which is now over three hundred and fifty years old.

INDEX OF MUSICAL TERMS

INDEX OF NAMES AND WORKS

Concert Guide

Gerhart Von Westerman

Dr Gerhart von Westerman, for many years director of the
Berlin Philharmonic Orchestra, intends his *Concert Guide*
primarily for the layman who has little or no musical
knowledge, but it will also be invaluable as a reference book to
the more experienced concert-goer, record-collector, or indeed,
amateur musician.

The *Guide* combines the history of the concert itself with
simple technical explanation and appreciation of all the
important music of the last two and a half centuries that is
likely to be heard in concert halls, or on records, today. The
story begins with the origins of the well-known forms—
symphonies, oratorios, concertos—and follows their
development and perfection in the hands of Bach and Handel,
Haydn, Mozart and Beethoven, the Italian composers of the
seventeenth century (many of whom have only recently been
'rediscovered'), the Romantics, the Moderns, such as
Hindemith, Webern and Schönberg, and our own
twentieth-century composers, Elgar, Benjamin Britten, Tippett.
A chapter on Contemporary Music by the translator and
editor, Cornelius Cardew, himself a composer, brings the book
unusually up to date. His absorbing account of the most recent
developments, of Nono, Boulez and Stockhausen, for instance,
and experiments in electronic music, will be a revelation to the
less conservative concert-goer, who wishes to venture on to the
contemporary scene.

There are, too, chapters on the development and composition
of the orchestra and its instruments; the rudiments of musical
theory and harmony are laid out briefly and clearly,
although the author stresses the fact that the non-musician has a
natural feeling for the basic principles of musical form even
before he acquires more detailed knowledge. The text is
supplemented by musical examples of the main themes of
many of the works described.

Concise Encyclopaedia of Antiques

The Connoisseur's Concise Encyclopaedia of Antiques,
complete in 2 volumes, surveys over 500 years of skilled
craftsmanship in the creation of Antiques. Illustrated with 32
pages of full colour and 64 pages of black and white
photographs, it is not only a superb record of a vanishing
tradition but also an invaluable work of reference for the
collector.
*The central chapters of Volume Two are those on Pottery,
Porcelain and Silver. The remaining chapters include Pewter, Tea
Chests, Objects of Vertu, Victoriana and Wine Labels.*